MEDIEVAL PIETY
FROM RELICS TO THE EUCHARIST
A PROCESS OF MUTUAL INTERACTION

STUDIES IN THE HISTORY

OF

CHRISTIAN THOUGHT

EDITED BY

HEIKO A. OBERMAN, Tucson, Arizona

IN COOPERATION WITH

HENRY CHADWICK, Cambridge
JAROSLAV PELIKAN, New Haven, Connecticut
BRIAN TIERNEY, Ithaka, New York
ARJO VANDERJAGT, Groningen

VOLUME LXIII

G.J.C. SNOEK

MEDIEVAL PIETY
FROM RELICS TO THE EUCHARIST

TUTA SUB AEGIDE PALLAS
· 1683 ·

MEDIEVAL PIETY FROM RELICS TO THE EUCHARIST

A PROCESS OF MUTUAL INTERACTION

BY

G.J.C. SNOEK

E.J. BRILL
LEIDEN · NEW YORK · KÖLN
1995

The paper in this book meets the guidelines for permanence and durability of the Committee on Production Guidelines for Book Longevity of the Council on Library Resources.

Library of Congress Cataloging-in-Publication Data

Snoek, G. J. C. (Godefridus J. C.), 1934-
  [Eucharistie- en reliekverering in de Middeleeuwen. English]
  Medieval piety from relics to the Eucharist : a process of mutual interaction / by G.J.C. Snoek
      p.   cm. — (Studies in the history of Christian Thought, ISSN 0081-8607 ; v. 63)
  Includes bibliographical references and index.
  ISBN 9004102639 (alk. paper)
    1. Lord's Supper—History—Middle Ages, 600-1500.   2. Lord's Supper—Miracles.   3. Christian saints—Europe—Cult.   4. Relics.
  I. Title.   II. Series.
  BV823.S513   1995
  265'.9—dc20   94-44924
                                                                                  CIP

Die Deutsche Bibliothek - CIP-Einheitsaufnahme

Snoek, Godefridus J. C.:
Medieval piety from relics to the eucharist : a process of mutual interaction / by G. J. C. Snoek. – Leiden ; New York ; Köln : Brill, 1995
  (Studies in the history of Christian thought ; Vol. 63)
  Einheitssacht.: Eucharistie <dt.>
  ISBN 90–04–10263–9
NE: GT

ISSN   0081-8607
ISBN   90 04 10263 9

PRINTED IN THE NETHERLANDS

To Jet

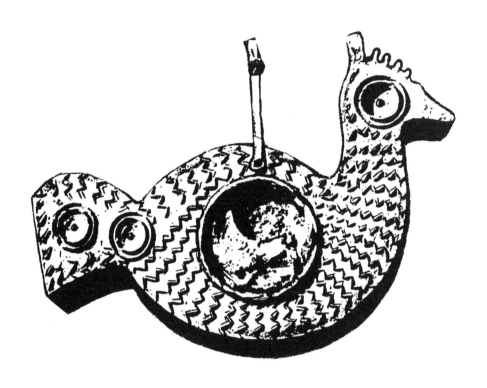

The illustration above is a stylised drawing based on a photograph that Fr. P. Michel Defrennes of St. Anne of Jerusalem was kind enaugh to send us. The object dates from the 4th-5th century in a grave at Oumm-Thouba, near Bethlehem. It is 23,5 cm long, 16 cm high and 1 cm thick. The opening in the centre, which is 5,5 in diameter, originally has a glass cover and was probably used to hold the reliquiae of the Eucharistic bread (see p. 125).

CONTENTS

ACKNOWLEDGMENTS

I have had the benefit of the generous assistance and advice of many during the preparation of the publication of the revised study *Eucharistie-en reliekverering in de Middeleeuwen*, Amsterdam, November, 1989.

I would like to thank Prof. A.H. Bredero for writing the preface of this version of my book.

I would like to express my gratitude to Prof. Dr. H.A. Oberman for including my book in: *Studies in the History of Christian Thought*.

I have enjoyed the kind and effective service of Drs. J.L. Wenneker, who checked the Latin texts closely.

In the Library of the University of Leiden I appreciated the quiet help of the librarians and assistants. Their efforts are remembered.

I am grateful to the Mr. Paul de Gruyter foundation for their financial support.

Last but not least I owe special thanks to Mrs. Heidi Kartawidjaja. Unselfishly she gave me her support putting in practise her knowledge of computer systems and programmes for hours on end.

PREFACE

Since the Reformation a great deal of attention has been paid to the way the Eucharist was venerated in the Middle Ages, on the one hand by way of a plea to maintain the then current forms of devotion in an unchanged form and, on the other, to expose such forms as deviants from the essential nature of the sacrament. Parallel to the theological debate concerning transubstantiation there was also a polemic concerned with matters that should rather be described as the effects of the ritual 'independence' of the Eucharist. This notion refers to "the gradual separation, in the forms of devotion, of the bread and wine from their sacramental and liturgical context".[*]

There have been many controversial writings about the devotions which sprang up, many of the works repeating previous statements, but in later times authors were more interested in writing descriptively on the nature of the devotional forms related to the Eucharist and the accompanying prayer formulae which gave substance to the derived Eucharistic belief. Among such writings is the work of Adolf Franz at the beginning of this century and the works of Peter Browe published between the wars.

However with very few exceptions these descriptions have thus far paid little if any attention to the mutual relationship in the Middle Ages between reverence for the Eucharist and devotion to the relics of the saints. Occasionally incidental cases were given a casual glance and the link was referred to, but writers on the subject never pushed their research any further into that particular field.

This book performs the service of setting out an analysis of the relationships in question. Which means that henceforth any study focusing merely on Eucharistic and reliquary devotion seen as separate from one another will be sadly out of date. The author's analyses demonstrate the relative, epoch-bound value of medieval forms of Eucharistic devotion in such a penetrating manner that the present English-language edition will fulfil a need felt by many. The devotional forms at issue turn out to be largely unauthentic, being derived from forms of devotion shown to the relics of the saints- forms which in their turn would seem to be partially pre-Christian and fetishist. The author also shows that the Eucharistic devotion current in the Middle Ages was mainly experienced as tangible,

---

[*]definition of the author

something one would expect of a society in which the ability to think abstractly was a relatively rare commodity. And this is an element which will need to be taken into account at the present time on a worldly level in the efforts to achieve an aggiorniamento, an updating of Christianity.

Another service performed by this book lies in its contribution to a breakthrough in the impasse in the dialogue between Rome and Reformation, which is still a reality with regard to the Christian sacrament par excellence, the Eucharist. This study implicitly illustrates the extent to which fundamentalist thinking in both camps has been applied to derived forms of devotion to the Eucharist, which in many ways now appear to be mainly products of their own specific time and society.

Adriaan H.Bredero
(Free University of Amsterdam)

INTRODUCTION

It is only in the last decade that the literature has begun to pay anything more than minimum attention to the central question dealt with in this study: *to what extent has there been a relationship in the past between Eucharistic devotion and the devotion paid to relics?* Writings dealing with the Eucharist appeared to ignore the existence of relics, while works concerned with the cult of relics gave no sign of the existence of the Eucharist. By way of illustration the following is revealing: the 35-page bibliography accompanying the collective work *Studia Eucharistica* published in 1946[1] contains not a single title dealing with our subject and even in the 1975 dissertation by D.S. Devlin, *Corpus Christi: a study in medieval eucharistic theory, devotion and practice*, the only nod in the direction of the cult of relics is constituted by two isolated references[2]. The reverse side of the coin is demonstrated by the two-volume work by S. Beissel on medieval devotion to the saints and their relics in Germany[3] which gives no sign of a relationship between Eucharist and relics, the same applying to E.A. Stückelberg's history of relics in Switzerland[4]. This is the usual pattern in works on relics by such authors as Delehaye, Kötting, Fichtenau, Boussel or Heinzelmann.

Two authors have, however, made the link in articles: P. Browe in 1931 and A. Andrieu in 1951. The former, whose work has represented an important source of information, wrote an illuminating statement on: "Der Segen mit Reliquien, der Patene und Eucharistie". Just as a blessing was given using the relics during a procession, so too the passage was made to giving a blessing with the Holy of Holiest during or following the procession on the feast of Corpus Christi[5]. Andrieu studied the relationship between certain reliquaries, the *ostensoria*, and the Eucharistic monstrances, underpinning his study with - among other

---

[1]Bussum-Antwerpen, 1946.

[2]Devlin (1975), 238, 240.

[3]Beissel (1976), I, II.

[4]Stückelberg (1902).

[5]Browe (1931a), 383: "Wohl in Nachahmung dieses Brauches hat man ihn am Fronleichnamsfeste während oder nach dem feierlichen Umgang mit dem Sanctissimum erteilt".

sources - the substantial works of J. Braun[6]. Using photographic material he had collected he was able to demonstrate that the *reliquaria* were 'reconstructed' in order to contain the host. He concluded his article on the origins of the cult of the Sacrament with the observation "celui-ci n'aurait sans doute pas exactement revêtu les formes extérieures que nous voyons, si la piété chrétienne n'eût trouvé d'immédiates inspirations dans les pratiques depuis longtemps imaginées en l'honneur des reliques"[7].

More recent literature has shown a greater degree of awareness of the relationship between the two forms of devotion, but the odd remarks on the subject are not supported by further evidence nor are the underpinned by systematic research. In his 1977 work, *Miracles and Pilgrims*, R.C. Finucane agreed with Andrieu when he remarked in passing that "old attitudes towards relics, which were kept in reliquaries, carried in processions and occasionally exhibited to the public in a kind of formal 'viewing', have re-emerged in the midst of later medieval Eucharistic devotion. The same may be said of the Eucharistic miracle-stories, which treat the Host like any 'traditional' Saint's relic"[8].

Four years later, N. Mitchell stated the following in his study of the Eucharist outside the confines of the Mass: "The cultic and devotional attitudes which in an earlier era were directed towards objects such as relics, altars, and the gospels were ritually transferred to the Eucharistic species, especially the host"[9]. Regarding the similarities with the role played by relics in miracles Benedicta Ward wrote: "the host was separated from its context to become a focus of power like the relic of a saint"[10]. And in 1988 Charles Zika noted regarding the effect of this that in the 15th century hosts were regarded as analogous to relics because "they possess miraculous power, confer benefit, deal out punishment when removed or tampered with, mediate power at specific locations and times or when exposed"[11]. Finally in 1991 Meri Rubin wrote: "Whether it induced benefit or harm, the people insisted on treating the eucharist as a relic"[12].

---

[6]Braun (1932), (1940).

[7]Andrieu (1950), 418.

[8]Finucane (1977), 198.

[9]Mitchell (1982), 185.

[10]Ward (1982), 18.

[11]Zika (1988), 47.

[12]Rubin (1991), 341-342.

The two articles mentioned above and the related statements in the subsequent literature led us to undertake further study of the link referred to, a link which we call: *Transposition of forms of reverence*, a relationship which we define thus: *the bringing up to date of forms of reverence towards the Eucharist which had already occurred at an earlier date with regard to relics.*

The link, mentioned in passing by Finucane, Ward and Zika, between relics and the host in their involvement with miracles, had already attracted Browe's attention when he classified the Eucharistic miracles in 1938, for some of his classifications were illustrated by similar miracles recorded in connection with relics. In his treatment of miracles involving light he wrote: "Wie man sich von jeher im Folklore aller Völker das Götliche und gottgeweihte Dinge und Reliquien als durchleuchtet vorstellte, so sah man auch die Hostie, unter deren Hülle ja Christus, die Sonne und das Licht der Welt zugegen war, als Trägerin wunderbaren Glanzes an"[13].

We checked to see if further information, gathered particularly in the field of the history of relics, could prove this suggested link and whether this would lead to more information concerning the position and regard accorded to the Eucharist and relics. The name to be given to any such link was obvious: *similarity in miraculous power*, by which we mean: *similar miraculous traits in the presentation of phenomena.*

Finally we distinguished a third link, outside the area of miracles and of much earlier date. Oaths were taken both on relics and on the Eucharist, and solemn communion - as a demonstration of innocence - is a clerical variant of oath-taking. In the pre- and early medieval period both relics and Eucharist were retained in private dwellings and accompanied a corpse to the grave as a means of protection. Within the same context, relics and the Eucharist were carried in an amulet worn by travellers. This third dimension demonstrating the link between relics and Eucharist we have typified as: *parallel application in concrete use.* This is meant when we are considering *relics and the bread of the Eucharist used for a particular end in a similar manner, either together, distinct from one another or as replacements one of the other.* Such uses occurred in early Christianity and the early Middle Ages. This category includes the daily use against dangers and two ecclesiastical forms: 'cementing in an altar stone' and 'prayer of supplication'. Attention was drawn to the former

---

[13]Browe (1938), 18.

phenomenon, after J. Corblet[14] at the end of the 19th century and J. Braun[15] in 1924, by Nicole Hermann-Mascard[16] in 1975. From the 8th to the 13th century this practice, carried out during the consecration of an altar, consisted of cementing three particles of a consecrated Host - together or instead of relics - in the altar stone or *sepulcrum*. 'Prayer of supplication' was a cry for help addressed to the saint, whose relics were placed on the ground - the *humiliatio* - but also a cry for help to the Lord in his sacrament at the *clamor* in the course of the Mass.

The three linked forms that we have distinguished would seem globally to have come into being in phases: *parallel application in concrete use* began to appear in early Christianity and the early Middle Ages and continued till the 13th century, the *transposition of forms of reverence* was evident from the 13th to the 14th century and the *similarity in miraculous power* principally from the 11th and 12th centuries. This can be explained by a development that can be roughly described as the *process of independence* of the Eucharist. By this we mean: *the gradual loosening of the ties, in devotional forms, between the bread and wine and their sacramental and liturgical context, the communal meal.* From being an 'action' the Eucharist became an 'object'[17].

This process was already under way in apostolic times, when the celebration of the communal meal became limited to a ritual taking of the bread and wine. During the 9th century the Eucharist as such became the object of a theological debate regarding the relationship between the historical Jesus and the Eucharistic body of the Lord. A more essential factor in the process of 'independence' was, however, the alienation of the congregation with regard to the Eucharistic liturgy: the people simply no longer understood the language.

The second controversy surrounding the Eucharistic meal, in the 11th century, once again concerning the presence in the Eucharist, resulted in the *praesentia realis*, the Real Presence of Christ in the Eucharist after the Consecration, being emphasised in theological statements and the many miracle stories. This led, in the 13th century, to a physico-realistic conception of the Real Presence and, around the 13th

---

[14]Corblet (1185-86), II, 79: "Du 8e au 14e siècle, dans quelques églises d'Occident on a cru pouvoir substituer aux reliques qui faisaient défaut, trois parcelles d'une hostie consacrée ou un morceau du corporal sur lequel on avait célébré".

[15]Braun (1924),I, 623-629.

[16]Hermann-Mascard (1975), 159-161.

[17]Mitchell (1982), 4: "how did the eucharistic *action* become a eucharistic *object* ?"

and 14th century, ended in new forms of reverence outside the context of the Mass being called for: visits to the tabernacle, the procession of the Blessed Sacrament, the exposition of the consecrated Host and the use of the Host in blessings, following which - in the 14th-15th century - the evening service of praise to the Sacrament (Benediction) came into being.

This gives a elucidation of the *transposition of forms of reverence* in the 13th-14th centuries. At the same time, the 'process of independence' goes some way to demonstrating that the gap existing between relics and Eucharist within the Church must have widened gradually. In his 1978 study of 'holy thefts' of relics, P.J. Geary pointed out that the enclosure of the consecrated Host in the altar stone was still regarded in the 9th century as "a physical relic of Christ, the host, which was to be treated like other relics (...) True, it was the most worthy because it was the body of Christ, but it functioned just as did many other relics (...) Moreover, relics, like the eucharist, might be placed on the altar"[18].

He indicates an area of tension, that took form in the 10th century, and in which the Host gradually occupied the superior position, until in the 13th century it was accorded a unique position in the recently developed Christocentric form of reverence made visible in the 'elevatio'. The custom of placing particles of a consecrated Host in the altar stone gradually disappeared, since the practice no longer corresponded to the reverence required to be shown towards the Host and the goal of the Host as perceived at the time: food for the soul. Geary rendered valuable service in coupling the disappearance of this type of use to the change in the perceived relationship between relics and Host, a process brought about by the increasing 'independence' of and reverence accorded to the Eucharist. His study shows that around the 13th century not only was the practice of enclosing particles of the Host in the altar stone disappearing but the age of the apparently unchallenged *parallel application in concrete use* had passed its apogee.

It can be said that as far as official forms of reverence were concerned, sacramental piety exclusively concentrated on the consecrated Host caused a growth in the gap between relics and the Host. But as far as the ordinary people were concerned, a number of Eucharistic miracles decreased the gap between the Host and relics since the Host, deprived of its liturgical context, was perceived 'as a relic', with a corresponding power to bring about miracles.

---

[18]Geary (1978), 28.

This type of relationship could, indeed, only make its appearance when the Eucharistic miracles were, from the 11th-12th century increasingly brought to public attention. In this parallelism the *virtus* of the relic was mirrored by the miraculous power of the privatised, independent Host and, to a lesser extent, that of the wondrous blood.

Our subject begins in ancient Christian times and covers the whole of the medieval period. This circumstance means that the study of the sources is based on the very extensive literature. For both Eucharistic devotion and reverence of relics there is an extremely large amount of literature, but the two subjects are always treated independently of one another. Thus it was not our primary task to draw attention to new material but rather to search through the sources and the literature to discover the information spread here and there which would be relevant to the types of relationship we have distinguished. The source material, in its turn, proved to be in plentiful supply but again it consists almost exclusively of incidental reports, unrelated to one another, and well reported in the literature. We have verified the information in so far as which was possible. Wherever this working method led to a deviant or richer result the sources naturally come more independently into play than where our research merely confirmed what is reported in the literature. Because of the wide diversity of the sources consequent on the diachronic nature of the research, it was not always possible to provide further confirmation of their historical value. However the fact that the information often points in the same direction was considered sufficient reason to regard this as symptomatic for our hypothesis regarding the link, despite the sometimes legendary context in which the information was situated.

Though the East is not left entirely out of consideration, the main emphasis of this study is on the West. It was not always possible to avoid combining information obtained from places widely separated geographically in order to illustrate a specific aspect. When demonstrating the types of relationship we were occasionally confronted with literature concerning the Eucharist or relics which contained more information than we could do justice to. Such cases are indicated by an asterisk (*). Moreover it was essential to place certain limits whenever the treatment of an aspect thus discovered threatened to turn into a complete study in its own right.

The distinction made between the three types of relationship contains the danger of artificiality, since they sometimes overlap. However the distinction offered a framework permitting an orderly arrangement of great quantities of unstructured data and determined the sections dividing up this work, which describes the mutual interaction between medieval Eucharistic devotion and the reverence paid to relics. This is why the two introductory chapters, which are summary in nature and mainly based on the literature, deal with these two aspects separately. The first chapter deals with the subject - in so far as it is relevant - entitled 'from martyr's grave to cult of relics'. The second describes the 'process of independence of the Eucharist', since the nature of the relationships is reflected in the extent to which the Eucharist became more independent. Various concepts which return in other contexts at a later stage are given a place in these chapters. Both chapters begin in early Christian times, whence developed the earliest type of relationship to appear: 'parallel application in concrete use', the title of the third and most extensive chapter. The Eucharistic gifts and relics then functioned to some extent parallel to one another, at first in the private domain and later more in relationship to oaths, prayers of intercession and the consecration of altars or churches. Then we take a look at the 'transposition of forms of reverence', which developed at the same rate as the 'process of independence of the Eucharist', and finally the 'similarity in miraculous power'. This, however, still leaves an intriguing question unanswered: to what extent was the Eucharist always distinguished from the relics within the three types of relationship and to what extent was that distinction reflected in the types of reverence? The chapter entitled 'the unique relic?' deals with this question, to the extent that this study provides an answer.

A diachronic study such as this is something of a reconnaissance and thus deviates from the dominant tendency in historical studies to be more specific, tied to time and place. Once we had started down this road, the experiences gained in this far too distant and long voyage of discovery soon made us realise that a search confined to a city or region could perhaps have led to a more subtle and better underpinned result. The result thus obtained could then perhaps have made a greater contribution to the still current debate on 'culture folklorique' and 'culture ecclésiastique' than has turned out to be the case. For it is a fact that many detailed studies of the Middle Ages, concerned with 'popular culture' - despite the fact that this concept is far from unambiguous and is difficult to use - are needed in order to reach any further generalisations there may be and to take a critical look at the existing ones[19]. However, that culture mentioned is not the subject of this study, although some aspects of it are dealt with, explicitly as well as implicitly. But this study aims in the first place at answering a core question regarding the historical relationship between devotion to the Eucharist and that given to relics, and the development of this relationship.

The remaining pros and cons of the diachronic approach adopted we leave to the creative imaginings of the reader, apart from one final remark. This study is merely descriptive and not of a theological nature, but it does possibly contain material conducive to further theological elaboration. It can neither claim to be exhaustive nor do adequate justice to the essential and local differences which came into being in these forms of devotion in the Middle Ages. The temptation to make facile generalisations was sometimes almost irresistible, but we hope that we have avoided this pitfall. The image whose outlines we have wished to sketch with this preliminary reconnaissance will most certainly require filling in and adjusting with detailed studies in which greater attention can be given to regional and time-related differences and based on limited amounts of source material.

---

[19]Lauwers (1987), 258; the works of Goerjewitsch (or Goerjewitsj, Gurevich) are a particularly important source of information but unfortunately they are not all (yet) translated from the Russian; see Goerjewitsj (1992), 4 n. 2: *Medieval culture and society in the judgement of contempories: the exempla of the 13th century*, Moscow, 1989 (in the Russian); *The medieval world: the culture of the silent majority*, Moscow, 1990 (in the Russian).

CHAPTER ONE

FROM MARTYR'S GRAVE TO CULT OF RELICS[*]

In the ecclesiastical context relics are sacred objects which have been in contact with Christ or with his saints.[1] Those which aroused the greatest interest were the relics of the True Cross which have been spread around Christendom since approximately the 5th century.[2]

Of much earlier date was the reverence accorded to the bones that had once belonged to a martyr, a form of reverence which is principally to engage our attention. This type of cult goes back to the 2nd century or even earlier[3], having originated in cemeteries or catacombs.[4] The first Christian communities regarded the date of death of a martyr as the date of his birth to eternal life. He was already in Paradise with God, while the rest of the dead had to wait for the last trumpet to sound. Appeals for his intercession would create the movement leading to the flowering of his reliquary cult.[5]

At its outset this type of cult was fairly modest. The cult of a martyr was best expressed when the Christians celebrated the Eucharist close to his final resting place and took care to commemorate the anniversary of his death. In the pre-Constantinian era such a celebration was probably performed without too much show, with a small number of believers congregating around an unremarkable grave in the midst of other burial sites. For it was a fact that the society of the day regarded the martyr as a criminal condemned under Roman Law. Honour paid to such a person was nothing less than an act of provocation. Hence the need for discretion. Moreover personal memories, such as a parent, a brother, a sister or friend might have of the one so brutally slain required a degree

---

[*]A list for further reading can be found in: Heinzelmann (1979) to which is referred for short; see also Jounel (1987) and Legner (1989).

[1]DACL XIII, 2, 2313.

[2]Marrou (1964), 205, 267, Frolow (1961a).

[3]DACL III, 2, 2319, based on the *Martyrium Ignatii*, Bishop of Antioch († approximately early 2nd century) and the *Martyrium Polycarpi* († c. 156), Bishop of Smyrna: "il est à conclure que c'était là une pratique, remontant à l'âge subapostolique" (P. Séjourné); ed. Dehandschutter (1979), 219.

[4]Klauser (1974a), 222: "Der Märtyrkult ist an das Märtyrgrab gebunden".

[5]Angenendt (1982), 210, 227-228; Daniélou (1963), 142; Deichmann (1983), 54.

of piety and assured discretion in the world of the 2nd and 3rd centuries.[6]

The Edict of Milan was proclaimed in 313. By granting freedom of religion it changed the situation: reverence could now be openly displayed and appeared as a kind of revision of what had gone before. The martyr's grave was promoted from hiding place to memorial, the group of private persons visiting the grave turned into a massive stream of pilgrims. Small buildings - known as *martyria* - rose up close to and over the graves of those who had been the first to bear witness in their own blood. The *martyria* were hung around with lamps and people expressed a wish to be buried in the vicinity. All this was followed by the building of commemorative churches.[7]

The temporary altars, originally set up temporarily by the faithful for the Eucharistic meal to commemorate the anniversary of the deceased, were gradually replaced by permanent constructions more and more closely allied to the martyr's grave. This transformation, from Christian altar to tomb altar, was probably encouraged by the bishops in order to minimise the pagan character of the meal of the dead with generous sacrificial offerings, once the increase in the numbers of believers consequent on the proclamation of religious freedom began to lead to an increase in pagan influence among the faithful.[8]

Ambrose († 397) stated the theological reasoning behind the inner bond between Christ and his blood witnesses gathered around the altar, for it was there that was celebrated the sacrifice of Him who had suffered to bring salvation from sin. Under the altar were the bodies of those who had given their lives for Him[9]. Against this background a similar 'grave space' was provided in other churches, which were reserved exclusively for the celebration of the Eucharist, space under or close to the altar in which relics were placed. Paulinus of Nola († 431) regarded relics as occupying so central a place within the church building that he qualified them as "the holy of holiest sanctified by the altar".[10]

However it was not always a simple matter for local churches in the West, especially those in Rome and the surrounding areas, to obtain corporeal remains. In fact until the middle of the 7th century the papacy

---

[6]ibid. 55, 59; Hermann-Mascard (1975), 25.

[7]Deichmann (1983), 60.

[8]Wieland (1912), 145-163; Heinzelmann (1979), 26, n. 40; Wegman (1991), 107-108.

[9]Dassmann (1975), 55; Angenendt (1989), 10 with illustr.

[10]CSEL 29, 286-287, ep. 32, c. 11.

obeyed the Roman law in which the peace of the dead was protected and which forbade the opening or re-siting of a definitive grave.[11] Relief came with the extension of the meaning of 'relic', which also accompanied a growth in the interest in relics shown by private individuals.

The rapid growth of the numbers of faithful after the declaration of religious freedom led to efforts to find tangible symbols to support a belief that was not always of the strongest. The various relics gave concrete form to the sacral and were signs of the mediation in heaven exercised by the saint in question in times of personal earthly trouble, a typical Christian belief and theology. There are early signs of a certain 'added value' accorded to relics in the writings of Cyril of Jerusalem († 386) and of Gregory of Nazianze († c. 390), both of whom credited relics with a special power or *virtus*. The former quoted the example of the healing power of the handkerchief and belt of the apostle Paul, concluding that the bodies of the saints too possessed a comparable power of healing.[12] The latter regarded the *virtus* to be present when the relics were touched or venerated. He quoted in this regard the ashes of St. Cyprian († 258) which expelled demons, cured the sick and foretold the future.[13] At a later date Chrysostom († 407) stated that the martyrs' shrines could exercise as great a power as the bones contained therein.[14] When Saragossa was besieged by the Merovingian Childebert († 558), the inhabitants clad in penitential garments carried the tunic of the martyr Vincent († 304) along the city walls and begged God for mercy, according to the account given by Gregory of Tours.[15]

Once the persecutions had ended, the relics of ascetics, virgins and bishops were added to those of the martyrs. According to his biographer Sulpicius Severus († 420), threads from the garments of St. Martin of Tours († 397), a bishop venerated in innumerable churches, possessed the power of healing.[16] The French monarch kept the cloak or *cappella* of this patron of France as if it were a precious jewel[17]. His bed was also

---

[11]Hermann-Mascard (1975), 26 sqq.

[12]PG 33, 1038, *Catech.* XVIII, 16; Hermann-Mascard (1975), 28; Lane Fox (1986), 98-167; Taylor (1993), 316, 323.

[13]PG 35, 589, *Contra Iulianum* I, 59; 1192, *Oratio in laude s. Cypriani*, 18.

[14]PG 50, 640, *De ss. Bernice et Prosdoce* 7; 576.

[15]MGH SRM I, 133-134, *Hist. Franc.* III, 29.

[16]PL 20, 170, *Vita b. Martini*, 18.

[17]Delehaye (1930), 45-46.

preserved for posterity,[18] just like that on which St. Nicetius († c. 560) had slept,[19] the bed of Pope Gregory († 604) and those of many other saints.[20]

The treasure-house of relics included other types of objects in the examples quoted. Everything that had come into contact with the saint during his life and with his corpse or tomb after his death was eventually included. These indirect or secondary relics were also called contact, symbolic or representative relics. They are mentioned in the sources as *reliquiae, sanctuaria, pignora, patrocinia, merita, beneficia* or *vocabula*.[21] Of all these objects, pride of place was given to clothing worn by the saint, utensils, the torture instruments used in his last hours, but also oil from the lamps by his tomb or filings from the fence surrounding it. From the earliest days of Christianity these types of relic - and occasionally corporeal relics - were, like the Eucharistic bread, kept at home to provide protection, were worn round the neck as a substitute for the pagan amulet and taken into the grave in the hopes of resurrection with the martyr in question.

The indirect relics also included the *brandea* or *palliola*[22] frequently referred to. These were linen cloths which had touched the saint's dead body, his bones or his grave. Pope Leo I is said to have celebrated Mass on or near the tomb of the apostle or martyr whose relics had been requested. He divided into pieces the corporal[23] which had been in contact with the Eucharistic species and with the tomb and distributed them to the interested parties as relics of the saint in whose honour the Mass had been celebrated.[24] According to the biography

---

[18]MGH SRM I, 605, Greg. v. Tours, *De virtutibus s. Mart.* lib. I, c. 35.

[19]ibid. I, 698, *Vitae patrum,* c. 8 n. 8.

[20]AASS OSB, t. I, 415, *Vita s. Gregorii auct. Iohan. Diac.*, lib. II, c. 6: "ubi usque hodie lectus eius, in quo recubans modulabatur, et flagellum eius ipsius quo pueris minabatur, veneratione congrua cum autentico Antiphonario reservatur"; Vieillard-Troiekouroff (1976), 387.

[21]LW II, 2375. This could also indicate corporal relics. The explicit words used for these are *ossa* or *corpus*: Heinzelmann (1979), 23.

[22]LW I, 316.

[23]That is, "the small piece of linen on which the Eucharistic offerings are placed during the Mass. Originally it would have covered the whole of the altar" (LW I, 478).

[24]MGH SS VI, 308, *Sigiberti Chronica,* a. 441: "Hic quoties rogabatur ab aliquibus, ut eis aliquorum apostolorum vel martirum reliquias daret, consuefecit ad corpora vel memorias apostolorum vel martirum, quorum reliquiae petebantur, missas celebrare in honore ipsorum, et sic brandeum altaris, quo consecratum corpus Domini involverat, particulatim dividebat et pro reliquiis apostolorum vel martyrum dabat. Unde si ab aliquibus dubitabatur, cultello pannos illos pungens, sanguinem eliciebat; sic palam cunctis faciens, quod in consecratione mysteriorum Christi, sanguis apostolorum vel martyrum, qui pro illo effusus est, intret per

written by Paulus Diaconus († c. 799) the same was done by Pope Gregory I. He distributed the pieces of cloth in small boxes or *buxeda* which carried his personal seal.[25]

His contemporary namesake, Gregory of Tours, gives a detailed description of what went on at the tomb of St. Peter under the saint's altar: the petitioner addressing prayers to the prince of the apostles put his head through a small window or *fenestella* above the tomb. If he wished to take a relic of St. Peter back home with him he placed a carefully weighed piece of linen on the tomb then prayed fervently for intercession. If he had shown sufficient faith he would note that his *brandeum* had increased in weight.[26] The author states that the proof of weight gain was a normal procedure in Rome. He also knew of a similar practice in Tours, where the same test had been applied at the tomb of St. Martin. Leaving aside the question of the historicity or otherwise of this practice of weighing, the story says even more about the ambivalent spiritual 'weight' that was given to the *brandea*, scraps of which have been found in archaeological digs in Roman churches.[27] Did they still enjoy complete acceptance as precious relics representing the saint himself[28] or does the story contain some note of doubt held in the West at the time with regard to contact relics?

Against this background we can also spot the attempts made by Gregory I to demonstrate the equal value of contact and corporeal relics. In his *Dialogues* he asks the question how it can be that the martyrs can perform powerful works and wondrous miracles not so much through their bodies as through their relics - or *brandea*. And he answers: "It cannot be doubted that the holy martyrs can produce many signs there where their bodies are at rest".[29] However, he adds that they have to perform even greater wonders there where their bodies are not resting in order to convince the doubters.

In a letter to the empress Constantina of Byzantium this pontiff once again came to the defence of the *brandea*, writing that when Pope Leo made a cut in the contact relic, blood of the apostles or martyrs

---

divinam   virtutem in pannos illos; et ideo merito illos dari pro   reliquiis sanctorum, in quorum honore consecrati sunt".

[25]PL 75, 53-55, *S. Gregorii magni vita auctore Paulo Diacono*, c. 24.

[26]MGH SRM I, 504, *In gloria martyrum*, lib. I, c. 27.

[27]Hermann-Mascard (1975), 47.

[28]Delehaye (1933), 118.

[29]*Greg. M. dial.* II, 38.

immediately flowed out, thereby convincing certain Greeks who had doubted the value of relics of this type. Gregory derived benefit from this 'proof' of the saint's presence in that it somewhat softened his refusal to give the empress the head of St. Paul, which she had requested in order to place it in a new basilica to the saint's honour in her palace. The efforts made by the papacy to retain the privileged position of the bishop of Rome by placing a ring of martyrs' graves around the city will most probably also have had a part to play in this incident.[30] But it is equally imaginable that the pope was having to resist the growing demand for corporeal relics in the West. Whatever the case, the changes made in the story are symptomatic when, within a century following Gregory's death, it re-appears in *The Earliest Life of Gregory the Great*, written by an anonymous English monk. The disappointed people are no longer from the East but from the West and it was not Pope Leo who caused the blood to appear but Pope Gregory himself. Pope Boniface V († 625) was to attempt at a later date to make the *brandea* somewhat more exclusive by deciding that only priests were allowed to take them from the tomb. This measure illustrates yet another proof of the increasing scepticism regarding the contact relics made available by Rome.[31] Whatever the true facts of the story may have been, Constantina had to make do with secondary relics. Gregory allowed her to have filings from the chains in which the apostle had been bound. In so doing he held steadfastly to the current tradition in Rome and based his refusal on the fact that "the Romans were not accustomed to touching the bodies of the saints themselves when giving relics".[32]

In the East, on the contrary, there were no objections to the *translatio* or re-housing of mortal remains nor to *dismembratio*: taking the remains to pieces and distributing them to several churches and sometimes to several individuals. Thus in 365 the emperor Constantius attempted to bring 'the new Rome' up to the standard of the relic-rich old Rome. He ordered the

---

[30]MGH Ep I, 265, *Gregorii I registri, indictio* XII, ep. IV,30: "praedictus pontifex hoc ipsum brandeum allatis forficibus incidit, et ex ipsa incisione sanguis effluxit"; Fichtenau (1952), 84; McCulloh (1980), 322.

[31]ed. Colgrave (1968), 110, c. 21: "Cum autem esset oratum ab omnibus, tulit ipse cultellum quem sibi iussit donare et unum e pannis pungendo secavit, ex quo confestim sanguis secto cucurrit"; McCulloh (1980), 315-318.

[32]MGH Ep. I, 264-265, *indictio* XII, ep. IV, 30: "quia Romanis consuetudo non est, quando sanctorum reliquias dant, ut quicquam tangere praesumant de corpore. Sed tantummodo in buxide brandeum mittitur atque ad sacratissima corpora sanctorum ponitur"; CC SL 140, 249.

relics of Timothy to be brought and, a year later, those of the apostle Andrew, "the first-called" (Jn. 1:40-41) and of Luke. These translations, which were organised with a great deal of pomp and circumstance, were merely the beginning of a great number that were to follow in the 4th and 5th centuries.[33]

The dividing and spreading of corporeal relics can be seen from information contained in the 'Forty Martyrs of Sebaste' († 320). Basil († 379) reports that their bodies were incinerated and the remains housed with honour at various places.[34] Gregory of Nyssa († 394) states that he has such a relic in his possession[35] and in Caesarea Gaudentius of Brescia met two of Basil's nieces who turned out to be the happy owners - thanks to their uncle - of these relics.[36] More than half a century later Theodoretus of Cyrus († 460) informs us that the countless basilicas regarded as possessing the body of a saint in fact contained no more than part of the body and sometimes merely a fragment.[37] This did not, however, lead to any objections as regards the miraculous workings of the relic, the *virtus* of the saint being regarded as residing just as much in the partial relics as in the intact corpse.[38]

Dismembratio, which led to these particles ending up in the various churches of the East, was formally forbidden in the West (as was *translatio*) but this does not mean that it did not happen at all until the mid-7th century. Though it is true that the principle of never undertaking *dismembratio* was seldom broken, the fragments of saints from the East, such as blood, ashes, hair or teeth,[39] were enthusiastically accepted. The relics of the first martyr, Stephen, from Caphegamala in Palestine, found their way to the West at the beginning of the 5th century, to which the many churches dedicated to St-Étienne still bear witness in France.[40] The hairs of John the Baptist were sent to Reccared, king of the West Goths,

---

[33]PG 67, 1078, Sozomenos, *Hist. Eccl.* lib. II, c. 14; 1439-1442, lib. VII, c. 10; PL 21, 536-537, Rufinus, *Hist. Eccl.* II, c. 28; DACL XIII, 2, 2333-2334; Delehaye (1933), 53-57.

[34]PG 31, 521, s. Basilii Magni, *Homilia in sanctos XL martyres,* 8.

[35]PG 46, 784; see p. 113, n. 59.

[36]PL 20, 965, Gaudentius Brixiensis Sermo XVII. In early 5th-century Constantinople a certain Eusebia possessed relics of this kind; see p. 112.

[37]PG 83, 1347, ep. 130; Delehaye (1933), 62.

[38]Heinzelmann (1979), 20-21.

[39]Hermann-Mascard (1975), 39; Heinzelmann (1979), 21 n. 22, 23 and 24; Beissel (1976), I, 17-18, 22, 71-72.

[40]Meer v.d. (1962), 45; Marrou (1963), 204-206; Kötting (1950), 259 sqq.; Saxer (1980), 245 sqq.

by Pope Gregory the Great in the 6th century. Thedolinde, queen of the Lombards, received from him relics including the ashes of martyrs and linen drenched with their blood.[41]

There was even "a substantial number" of translations - substantial when we consider the fact that the practice was forbidden. They constituted the exception to the rule, allowed if the martyr had died in exile or if there was a risk of profanation of the tomb. A third justification was the desire to grant the saint - sometimes one previously unidentified and recently discovered thanks to a 'divine revelation'[42] - a more worthy grave.[43] At the end of the 4th century St. Martin had his predecessor Saint Gratianus, who died in 250, transferred from a cemetery outside the city to a basilica.[44] It was stated of Milan that the city took its example from the East by its famous translations ascribed to Ambrose.[45] The translation was, of course, preceded by the discovery, or *inventio*, of the bones and then their removal from the ground (*elevatio*). This practice of exhumation in order to provide a more honourable resting place, either under or - more usually - behind a refurbished altar increased from the 6th century onwards. The development brought about a change in custom which even penetrated as far as Rome: from the 7th century the popes gradually began to permit the transfer of mortal remains from outside the city to the Roman basilicas.

Political circumstances hastened the definitive setting aside of the already weakened ban on translation. The Lombards, keen on conquest and threatening Rome under Aistulf and finally halted in 756 by the king of the Franks, Pippin III, had transformed into ruins the already neglected burial sites outside the city. The mortal remains were so much the worse for wear and in some cases scattered "in stables and sheep pens"[46] that Pope Paul I († 767) decided to open the graves and move the relics. The remains of more than 100 saints were involved, which were subsequently distributed among churches and monasteries. Half a century later these

---

[41]MGH Ep II, 224-225, *indictio* II, ep. IX, 228.

[42]Delehaye (1933), 70; Marrou (1963), 111; Hermann-Mascard (1975), 39-40.

[43]ibid. 35-39.

[44]MGH SRM I, 443, Gregorius of Tours, *Hist. Franc.* X, 31.

[45]Delehaye (1933), 65.

[46]Mansi XII, 645-650, ep. XII *Pauli papae I ad Ioannem abbatem;* McCulloh (1980), 323.

numbers were vastly exceeded by the '2300 saints'[47] which Pope Paschal I († 824) had removed to Rome from the ruined catacombs. The crowds that gathered gave witness to their approval and sang psalms during the translations, which were implemented by the popes during the 8th and 9th centuries. The cemeteries were henceforth deserted; the pilgrims had no reason to go there; only a few went looking for forgotten remains.[48] Whereas the early Christians had taken their churches to the tombs of the saints, from the early Middle Ages onwards the Christians of the time carried their saints to the churches.[49]

The political situation not only encouraged the transfer of relics from the periphery of Rome to the city but it also opened the way to the translation of mortal remains to the Frankish empire beyond the Alps. Once agreements had been reached between Rome and the Carolingians the popes could no longer refuse to grant - to a limited degree - requests for corporeal relics.[50] Princes, bishops and abbots wished to acquire relics, especially in Gaul and Germania, made greedy, one could say, by the countless relics that had been removed from the opened graves. The journey northwards and the reception of the relics at their destination was accompanied by celebrations recalling the kind of rejoicing following an historic victory in battle or the exuberance seen on the occasion of a consecration or coronation.[51] These events caused the West to experience an early 'Eastern Renaissance'.

The need felt for relics, particularly corporeal, was brought about in the Frankish empire by various historical causes. In the Merovingian period many local churches were painfully aware of the scarcity of relics of martyrs from the early years of Christianity, a fact which was

---

[47]Stückelberg (1902), 5.

[48]Hermann-Mascard (1975), 53; Riché (1976), 211.

[49]McCulloh (1980), 313.

[50]Prinz (1967); Hermann-Mascard (1975), 58-60.

[51]ibid. 58; see also Martin (1987), n. 28, for details (illustrated with maps) of translations of relics that occurred between 600 and 1200; the situation in Britanny (approx. 850-1250) was different: in her detailed study (1990, p. 336) Julia M. Smith states that in the Breton hagiography a lack of importance is attached to corporal relics. Secondary relics were sufficient. There is no record of the subdivision of any Breton saint's body before the tenth century nor of huge relic collections assembled by Frankish churches. "Nor is there any hint that the Breton churches studed here were interested in acquiring foreign relics" before the arrival of the mendicants; various symptoms during the translation (e.g. a majestic procession, bishops carrying the shrine, torches, hundreds of people being jubilant and touching the shrine) are still up to date as appears from the translation of the relics of San Ponziano († c. 170) southwards (Utrecht-Spoleto) in August 1994; see Vliet v. (1994), 224-226.

emphasised when Pepin the Short and Charlemagne introduced the Roman liturgy.[52] The expansion of the Carolingian realm went hand in hand with missionary activities and led to the foundation of new churches and monasteries, which were anxious to acquire relics from their very inception. The presence of saints in the shape of their mortal remains were believed to give the sanctuaries on foreign soil a gloss that would outshine the pagan gods.[53]

Trading, cheating and - a factor to keep in mind - theft[54] cooperated in encouraging the thirst for relics. Alleged discoveries or purchases were often subject to a twisting of the truth, giving rise to dubious local cults, a phenomenon which was the subject at an early stage of a complaint voiced by Gregory of Tours.[55] In his *Admonitio Generalis* of 789, which quoted the Council of Carthage in 401, Charlemagne warned the clergy not to be taken in by "uncertain saints", whose saintliness had not been established by the ecclesiastical authorities.[56] He did, however, have a high regard for relics, which the author of the *Libri Carolini* - written in the same spirit - considered superior to the icons which had come to be revered in the East, since the relics would participate in the general resurrection on the last day whereas the icons would not.[57] He granted official legal status to the custom, in use since the 5th century, of taking oaths on relics.[58] In 803 he laid down that all oaths had to be sworn in a church or on the relics.[59] He further emphasised the presence of the relics in the *sepulcrum* of the altar,[60] where they had been placed at the consecration of the church.

Such church consecrations were not decisive in maintaining the Frankish interest in martyrs' relics from Italy and Spain (which was largely occupied by the Moors). Even as early as the time of Gregory of

---

[52]Klauser (1974), 139-151; Hermann-Mascard (1975), 57; Heinzelmann (1979), 95.

[53]Hermann-Mascard (1975), 58; Angenendt (1990), 339-342.

[54]Kraus (1972), 1-6; Geary (1978).

[55]MGH SRM I, 522, *In gloria martyrum,* c. 50; Beissel (1976), I, 128 sqq.

[56]MGH Conc II, 170; Hermann-Mascard (1975), 84; Beissel (1976), I, 129; Bredero (1994³), 160.

[57]Beissel (1976), I, 49 sqq.

[58]The taking of the monastic vow in Benedict's rule, for instance, resembled an oath on the relics.

[59]MGH Cap I, 118, 47: "Omne sacramentum in ecclesia aut supra reliquias iuretur (...) sic illum Deus adiuvet et sancti quorum istae reliquiae sunt ut veritatem dicat"; Geary (1978), 44.

[60]MGH Cap I, 170; MGH Conc I, 270; Geary (1978), 42-43.

Tours it was felt that something was lacking if no relics were entombed in the altar.[61] The scarcity of relics in the Carolingian period could have influenced the introduction, around the 8th century, of the use of consecrated particles of the Host as a substitute for relics. This custom was gradually to disappear after the 13th century as the Eucharist detached from its liturgical context gradually acquired its unique position in Christian devotional practice.[62]

On the occasion of the consecration (*dedicatio*) of a church, in which the celebration of the Eucharist was indeed central, the relics destined for the *sepulcrum* were placed in a nearby church on the eve of the consecration. The following morning the congregation processed to the church to be consecrated where the arrival, or *adventus*, was accompanied by the singing of a litany. After the bishop had ceremonially opened the doors, the faithful entered the church in solemn procession. Then followed the *depositio*, the placing of the relics in the *sepulcrum* of the altar.[63]

The high points described can be recognised in reports of other translations, whether these originated elsewhere or were carried out on the spot, in the latter case the bones being transferred to a more beautiful tomb under or behind the altar. In translations of this sort the saint became the *dominus* and *patronus* of the local community. His triumphal *adventus* recalled the arrival of a prince, celebrated since ancient times, but represented particularly the regal entry of Jesus into Jerusalem on Palm Sunday and His return on the Day of Judgement. The *adventus* took place at the entrance to the city or on the border of the diocese or limits of the monastic lands and proclaimed the start of the saint's spiritual protection, guaranteed by his *virtus* and miracles. On the occasion of the imminent arrival of the relics of St. Nazarius at the Benedictine abbey of Lorsch around 760 a whole group went out to the edge of the Vosges mountains to greet the saint.[64]

And here we come up against another reason for the extent of the desire for relics north of the Alps: the people were looking for

---

[61]MGH SRM I,2, 56, *In gloria martyrum*, 30; 250, *Liber vitae patrum* VIII, 11; Heinzelmann (1979), 28, n. 51.

[62]Geary (1978), 28; Nussbaum (1979), 187, n. 89.

[63]Heinzelmann (1979), 48-49.

[64]MGH SS XXI, 343, *Chronicon Laureshamense*: "In cuius occursum tota simul provincia, plebs utriusque sexus, iuvenes et virgines, senes cum iunioribus, usque ad saltum qui Vogesus dicitur, catervatim ruunt. Comitesque nobilissimi (...) thesaurum beati corporis (...) excipiunt, et cum ymnis canticisque spiritalibus, prosequente infinita populi multitudine, usque ad locum celitus provisum deferunt".

supernatural protection against violence and danger. In Merovingian times there had arisen a custom within the Frankish empire of proclaiming a saint patron of a city or region in which the relics were housed. The custom became so widespread in the Carolingian period that any such relics were simply known as *patrocinia*.[65]

The concepts of *patronus*, *intercessor* (mediator) and *defensor* (protector) already used by Ambrose[66], had passed into general use in the feudal-vassal relationships.[67] For the local community they gained an almost exclusive meaning when central power disintegrated and the local holder of power acquired virtual independence. People had to rely on this 'seigneur' in the violence which the process of feudalism brought with it. The people had to fall back on his protection against attacks by Saracens, Hungarians or Vikings, all of whom preyed on the decayed empire. But in addition to the earthly protector there was the representative of the unearthly powers: the holy *patronus*. His intercession with God would not only look after sun, wind and rain, grass and cattle, but he would also come to the aid of those threatened with plunder and other horrors of war. Bishops, monks and lay people knelt by his relics and pleaded for his intercession in all kinds of need. It was assumed that miracles could not be discounted if it was a question of proving the saint's powers. The abbot Paschasius Radbertus († 859) of the Corbie monastery, a man who was not averse to miracles, stated that since the beginning of time never had there been greater things done anywhere in the world than in his time, a time in which the saints cooperated in performing miracles as cocks react to one of their number crowing.[68]

Attachment to the patron saint was indeed very great. When the Vikings threatened Paris in 845 and the population believed they had no time left during the evacuation of the city to take the bones of Saint Germanus with them, the Parisians both young and old preferred to die than to allow this to happen.[69] After they had nonetheless succeeded in taking flight with the relics, the plunderers were given a free hand. In contrast, during the siege of 885-886 they followed a different strategy: they bore the relics of both St. Germanus and St. Genoveva to where the

---

[65]Beissel (1976), I, 34; Head (1990), 135-201: *"The posthumous patronage of the Saints"*.

[66]PL 16, 251, *De viduis* IX,55; 1022, *Ep.* 22,10; Heinzelmann (1979), 32.

[67]Guth (1970), 131; other synonyms for the saint who is *potens* as mediator: *suffragator* and *advocatus*, see: Beaujard (1991), 180.

[68]PL 120, 1608; Geary (1978), 20.

[69]Heinzelmann (1979), 73.

greatest threats were posed and they had success. In 913 the canons of Tours seized the opportunity of taking the body of St. Martin to the city gate which the Vikings had almost forced and putting the invaders to flight, after which they were set upon and cut down by the besieged citizens.[70]

The saint present in his relics worked in such an inspiring manner that the people would on occasions leave a threatened area with their patron to go to the abbey, something which happened at Corbie. In 1074 Robert of Flanders wanted to take repossession of the goods which the monks had received from his distant ancestor, St. Adalardus († 826). Carrying the bones of their former abbot the Benedictines set out towards the count and put the fear of God into him as he was engaged in laying siege to a small town in the neighbourhood of Doornik. As soon as he heard of their approach, he went towards them barefoot, took the shrine of his holy opponent on his shoulders and carried it to the nearest church where with all speed he returned to the monks that which he had taken from them. In the same way the 'Noodkist' (emergency casket) in Maastricht repeated protection from danger.[71]

Monks were obliged to have recourse to such strategies since they could not threaten formally with excommunication or interdict, such being reserved to princes of the church, although excommunications were, in fact, sometimes pronounced by religious.[72] This was usually linked to a 'cursing', *clamor* or *humiliatio*, three further types of defence available to the monks, which generally involved them in refusing henceforth to pray for the usurper.

When a cursing was to be performed, the Mass was interrupted after the Gospel or *Credo*. At the altar the priest pronounced the curse before God and in the presence of the relics of the saint. The text was taken from psalms[73] or adapted from the book of Deuteronomy, where Moses pronounces a series of curses on lawbreakers.[74] Cursing became popular from the post-Carolingian era up to the 12th century.[75]

---

[70]Hermann-Mascard (1975), 218-219.

[71]MGH SS XV, *Miracula s. Adalhardi*, 862-865; AOB V, 82; Bock (1873), 122; Beissel (1976), II, 4; Hermann-Mascard (1975), 228-231; Jong de (1982).

[72]Du Cange (1883-87), VII, 555: *spinis circumdare cruces et imagines signum excommunicationis et interdicti*; Little (1979), 51-53.

[73]Ps. 20, 34, 51, 68 and 82; Little (1975), 381; (1979), 44-45.

[74]Dt. 27 and 28.

[75]Little (1975), (1979).

Another weapon was the *clamor*, an urgent prayer for succour at the end of Mass, while the congregation's attention was still on the consecrated bread. The *clamor* was often combined with the *humiliatio*. The shrine containing the relics was placed on the ground and covered with thorns in order to beg the saint for intercession and face him with the hard need felt so that he would lend his aid. In addition to the prayer of intercession for mediation, the *humiliatio* contained an element of intimidation trait. It acquired the character of a reprisal measure, comparable to the termination of vassal fidelity, since the holy protector had failed to live up to his duty of protection.[76] Candles no longer burned near his humiliated shrine, no hymns were sung and the doors of his sanctuary remained locked.

This type of rebuff to the relics makes one thing clear: "the relics *were* the saint".[77] He could deal a fatal blow to anyone committing perjury on his grave or in another circumstance, as the *vitae* stated vividly to the faithful.[78] In Nijvel the arm of St. Gertrude emerged from the shrine to receive offerings, while in Ghent Saint Bertulf caused knocking sounds to come from his shrine to bring the passers-by to repentance.[79] Bishop Gerard of Cambray dedicated the cathedral to the Virgin Mary around 1030. For the occasion he caused relics to be brought from the entire diocese and grouped them hierarchically around the altar. The relics of his predecessor, St. Gaugerik, who had died five centuries before, were placed on the bishop's throne. Thus the saint took possession of his episcopal throne for one more day and was considered to be presiding at the consecration.[80]

The shrines such as those used during the *humiliatio* or those brought to Cambray, contained partial relics. The increasingly frequent translations had long since contributed in the West to the disappearance of the original ban on *dismembratio*. The ban can be found expressed - though in a somewhat 'wrapped-up' fashion, since the story does not deal directly with the subject - in a tale told by Gregory of Tours concerning a woman from St. Jean-de-Maurienne, who was reputed to have brought back from the Middle East a finger of John the Baptist, which she had acquired in some miraculous fashion. Three Gallic bishops each wished to

---

[76]Heinzelmann (1979), 41; Geary (1985), 136.

[77]Geary (1978), 39; Graus (1965), 178-179.

[78]Sigal (1976).

[79]AASS 17 mart. II, 598; Kroos (1985), 38-39.

[80]Boeren (1962), 174.

have part of the finger, but it proved impossible to split the bone, even
after a night spent in prayer. At a second attempt St. John began to take a
personal interest and blood emerged from the relic and fell on a cloth. In
the end it was the cloth that was divided up as a '*brandeum*'.[81]
Elsewhere in Gregory's work a saint is reported as having shown
recalcitrance when attempts were made to divide up his corporeal relics
even further.[82] The aversion to *dismembratio* continued into the 7th
century. When the bishop of Toledo, St. Hildefonsus († 667), made an
attempt to take some part of the remains of the patron saint of Toledo,
St. Leocadia († 304), at her *elevatio*, the latter is reported to have drawn
back violently while the people is said to have wept and wailed in protest.
And St. Audoin of Rouen († 684) was given a divine revelation to desist
from removing the head of St. Markulf († c. 558) from the saint's
body.[83]

The more often graves were opened and the more frequent became
the translations, the easier it was to ignore the objections against the
dividing up of a skeleton, all the more so since all the practical
circumstances seemed to point towards division. It was, first and
foremost, a pragmatic solution to the demand for relics. This existing
need was increased further by the desire on the part of some to start
collections of relics, prime examples in ecclesiastical circles being
Theodoric of Metz († 984) and Bruno of Cologne († 965).[84] The latter,
as brother of emperor Otto I and as prince of Lorraine was able to fall
back on "the custom of kings" which had existed since the time of the
Merovingians - that of taking relics and building up a collection.[85]

---

[81]MGH SRM I,2, 47 sqq. *In gloria martyrum* c. 13: "tres episcopi (...) voluerunt partem
de hoc pignore elicere (...) dum partem auferre conantur, una ex eo gutta sanguinis cecidit
super lenteum (...) Deinde prostrati coram sancto altare, dum supplicant (...) duae iterum ex
eo fluxerunt guttae"; Beissel (1976), I, 17 and 22.

[82]MGH SRM I,1, 350-351, *Hist. Franc.*, lib. VII, c. 31.

[83]AASS OSB, II, 517-518, *Vita s. Hildefonsi episc. Toletani,* c. 4: "Clamabat inter
voces populi velut mugiens, ut aliquod incisorium deferrent, unde quod manibus tenebat
praecideret: et nemo illi accurrebat, quia populus vastis ictibus rictibusque frendebat. Nam et
sancta Virgo quae voluntatem submiserat, ut desideria crescerent, violenter retrahebat"; I,
133, *Vita s. Marculfi,* c. 21: "Cum autem apud se caput tractaret auferre, chartula
huiusmodi verbis exarata manui eius coelitus immissa insedit: Ceterorum membrorum
Beatissimi Marculfi quod voles sumito, caput autem eius nullatenus tangere praesumas";
Hermann-Mascard (1975), 41.

[84]MGH SS IV, 473 sqq. *Vita Deoderici* I; MGH SS, N. S. 10, ed. Irene Ott (1958), 31,
Ruotgeri Vita Brunonis, c. 31: "Sanctorum corpora atque reliquias et quelibet monimenta, ut
suis patrocinia cumularet et per multos populos ultra citraque hac celebritate gloriam Domini
propagaret undecumque collegit"; Fichtenau (1952), 85-88.

[85]MGH SRM III, 651, *Vita Betharii*: "et pignora multa sanctorum quae secum deferebat
(Clotharius II) ut mos est regum".

Contained in reliquaries of many shapes and sizes, relics were part of the princely equipment and thus served to confirm the monarch's status and leadership. They were donated to churches, functioned as gifts in diplomatic negotiations and were regarded as guarantees of success in military campaigns.[86] And how much easier it was to carry relics which had been divided up into smaller portions when it was necessary to take to one's heels pursued by Viking or Saracen. The possibility had now been created of bearing the shrines in processions and pilgrimages or bringing the relics to the truce of God councils, of which that held in Charroux in 989 is an early example.[87] The population attended in great numbers in order to "share in the protective power of the saints in all its varied expressions".[88] The oath "to observe an inviolable peace" and to leave the defenceless in possession of their "ox, cow, pig, sheep, lamb, goat or ass" was taken on the relics.[89] Placed in reliquaries behind or even on the altar table, the relics were more easily approachable for the faithful, who were no longer constrained to descend into awkward crypts with narrow entrances, dating from the Merovingian period.[90]

The further dividing up of the corporeal relics led to a rise in the quantity available. The flood of relics from the East since the period of the Crusades and the new canonizations, immediately after which *dismembratio* was performed, further reinforced the effect.[91] Consequently the contact relics which, as already suggested, had begun to be the object of scepticism at the time of Gregory the Great, continued to decline in popularity. From the 9th century, according to the sources, ecclesiastical authorities seldom opted for *brandea* or other objects which had merely been in contact with the saint after his death. From the 12th century the same authorities even lost interest in acquiring as new relics objects from the saint's daily life. The 'ablution water', wine or water that had been poured over the mortal remains of the saint after *elevatio* or at some other moment, remained 'popular' - i.e. held in regard by the

---

[86]Heinzelmann (1979), 38-39; Albert (1990), 309-311; Vroom (1992), 8 and passim.

[87]Raoul Glaber, ed. Prou (1886), 104-105, lib. IV, c. 5,16; AASS OSB, IV,1, 434: Letaldus of Micy, *Delatio corporis s. Juniani ad synodum Karoffensem,* c. 2; Fichtenau (1952), 69; Hermann-Mascard (1975), 223-225; Head (1990), 175-177.

[88]Bredero (1994³), 122.

[89]Duby (1976), 51; (1981), 36.

[90]Hubert (1977a), 414.

[91]Cauteren v. (1985), 18; Vauchez (1981), 504.

'*populus*', the common folk: this fluid had been endowed with the saint's power and was used as medicine for the sick or the possessed.

Also the relics which had been in contact with Jesus himself and other secondary relics from the early days of Christianity continued to hold great appeal for the imagination since they were reminders of the Holy Land and Jerusalem - Mary's belt or cloak, John the Baptist's shirt[92] or St. Peter's tunic[93]: they were exhibited to the crowds in public showings, and even today the shrine of the Three Magi still adorns Cologne cathedral. As regards the latter, a 12th-century legend would have it that the relics of the Magi reached Milan via Constantinople in the 6th century. In 1164 they were translated to Cologne by Frederick Barbarossa's chancellor, Rainald of Dassel.[94] The city became more attractive as a place of pilgrimage, with all the concomitant economic advantages.[95]

Pilgrims seeking cures represented an important source of income for many churches and monasteries. The crowds pouring in brought with them livestock, food, candles, gold and silver jewellery and - of course - coinage.[96]

Coinage was used increasingly after the birth of the money economy in the 11th century. The population increased, clearances satisfied the need for land, agricultural methods improved and the desire for profit stimulated production. The central authorities, on their way to the nation state, were able to exercise their authority more efficiently in the centuries that followed. All these changes meant that the enclosed nature of local communities was to some extent split open and the situation of independence with reference to the *patronus*, present in the relics, was changed. The local saint lost his function as principal protector both in both political and economic terms.

His influence also changed because of the reverence accorded to saints with a greater 'worldwide' appeal. For instance, from the 12th century the Cistercians, later followed by the mendicant orders, preached devotion to the Virgin Mary, patron of all their monasteries.[97] Another figure that towered above local communities was that of St. Nicholas,

---

[92]Bredero (1994[3]), 79-104.

[93]Hermann-Mascard (1975), 68-69.

[94]Fichtenau (1952), 72.

[95]Aalberts (1985), 48-49.

[96]Fichtenau (1952), 75.

[97]Brown (1982a), 329 sqq.; Geary (1978), 27.

revered as the patron of sailors from Scandinavia to the southern Italian town of Bari, to where his relics were translated from Myra in 1087.[98]

Moreover, in the early Middle Ages the relics of the apostles and early martyrs, no longer tied to their original place of burial but contained in "series of reliquaries made in specialised workshops"[99], were regarded as "representatives for the whole world".[100] As has already been mentioned, the West was flooded with these and other relics, some of them of doubtful origin, during the period of the Crusades. In this regard, the aberrant Fourth Crusade (1202-1204), in the course of which the Crusaders conquered and put to fire the Christian city of Constantinople, made itself a name. Since the 5th century Constantinople had been home to a huge collection of relics, some of which had reached the West prior to the Fourth Crusade.[101] The relics of the Passion attracted the greatest interest since they were reminders of the suffering of Jesus. In 1222 Philip II Augustus purchased from Baldwin, the first emperor of the Holy Roman Empire, a relic of the True Cross that was "a foot long",[102] and Louis IX obtained from the last emperor to reign there, Baldwin II, the Crown of Thorns which, in 1239, this unbelievably happy man carried into Paris on his shoulders with the help of his brother. To house the relic he caused to be built the delicate structure known as the Sainte Chapelle, a 'shrine' of stained glass. In 1247 other relics were bought and placed there, including the blood of Christ, a particle of the True Cross, the sponge which was reputed to have been used to quench Jesus' thirst, the purple cloak, the swaddling clothes from the crib and a portion of His shroud.[103]

This summary is symptomatic for the new spirituality that was popularised in the 12th-13th centuries, centred on following Christ, the *imitatio Christi*. The Crusades, the pilgrimages and commercial contacts had brought the Holy Land closer to home and had caused people to discover the historical Jesus once again. Connected with the reverence paid to the Holy Sepulchre, to the alleged relics of the Passion and to the objects that had been brought back from the holy places, the people's

---

[98]ibid. 115-127.

[99]Cauteren v. (1985), 19.

[100]Geary (1978), 27.

[101]Bredero (1994³), 91.

[102]Lefeuvre (1932), 133.

[103]ibid. 136; Boussel (1971), 55-56; the Crown of Thorns is at present in the treasury of Notre Dame, where it is exposed and reverenced on Good Friday.

attention was once more directed to the human condition of Jesus, to His human suffering and to His compassionate mother. This caused the saint's responsibilities to take a different direction: henceforth the saint was to direct the faithful towards God[104] and, something that could hardly be dispensed with, to intercede between the local community and God in His heaven. Of course, there was also the direct route in addition to this indirect approach: piety was, in fact, centred on the person of Jesus Himself: piety consisted in honour shown directly to Jesus in the form of reverence paid to His five wounds, to the instruments of His torture and to His pierced side, all of which became 'popular' in the image of the *Pie Pellicane* in the penultimate verse of the 14th-century composition *Adoro te*.[105]

This rhyming hymn addressed to the 'living bread' raises the Host literally and metaphorically above the relics contained in or behind the altar. The 'living bread' is the adored and physically present Jesus Himself.[106] Indirectly it is possible to note here that various forms of 'parallel application in concrete use', such as the cementing of particles of the Host in the *sepulcrum* of the altar, took a back seat since such practices no longer concurred with the Eucharistic devotion referred to.

Driven from the role of principal protector of a local community, the saint was experienced in a more subjective manner from the 11th-12th centuries, a change which was expressed in the privatisation of reverence. Some saints were appealed to in particular circumstances - to provide aid against a particular illness, for instance - and it goes without saying that appeal to the relics was regarded as an effective act to accompany this type of prayer.[107] St. Lawrence († 258), for example, of whom tradition relates that he died roasted on a grill, became the patron saint of those suffering from burns and back complaints. His legendary contemporary. St. Apollonia, whose martyrdom included the violent extraction of her teeth before she was burnt at the stake, was appealed to by those suffering from toothache.[108]

---

[104]Bredero (1994³), 94, 338.

[105]Dumoutet (1932), 115; *Adoro te* (I adore Thee), is "a hymn in honour of the Blessed Sacrament, which was probably composed in the 14th century and is ascribed to Thomas Aquinas" (LW I, 51).

[106]Duval (1946), 382.

[107]Boussel (1971), 209; Heinzelmann (1979), 24.

[108]Beek (1974), 185-189; Bredero (1994³), 341; Pernoud (1984), 329-334.

Requests for private help began to make their appearance in the official prayer formulae of the Church, in which certain special saints are named for particular illnesses and complaints. A good dozen of the blessed were addressed by the Church when the tortured human cry of "Lord, that I may see" (Lk. 18:41) was heard.[109]

Even the corporal was accorded powers of healing. During a bout of serious illness St. Clare († 1253), called on as patron of the blind because of her name (clara: i.e. clear), wove fifty corporals of the finest linen for the churches in the plains and mountains around Assisi. This work was, of course, seen as separate from her 'speciality', but bears witness to her own and contemporary devotion to the Eucharist, which often figures in pictorial representations of this saint. It is reported that she used the Eucharist in 1240 to chase off the Saracens.[110] This event inevitably recalls to mind the happenings in Paris in 885, already referred to, and the happenings in Tours in 913 when the Vikings were driven off by the canons thanks to the body of St. Martin. The agreement in the use of relic and Eucharist was inspired by the belief in the protective nature of both.

In a somewhat embarrassing episode, according to the report, Hugh of Lincoln († 1200) made a practical comparison between receiving the Eucharist and dealing with a relic. In the late 12th century he was visiting the monastery of Fécamp where, to the utter amazement of the abbot and congregation, he bit off a few particles from the arm bone which was reputed to have belonged to Mary Magdalene. Hugh reassured the witnesses to this event by saying: "Why should I not try to take a few morsels of the bones of the saint for my protection since I have just taken between my unworthy fingers the most holy body of the holiest of holiest, have eaten of it and touched it with my teeth and my lips?".[111]

Another exceptional example would seem to be the way in which the stole belonging to St. Hubert († 727), patron saint of rabies victims, was handled. The translation of his relics from Liège to the abbey of Andange in the Ardennes occurred in 825. During the transfer of the relics a stole had been taken from the saint's shrine, a stole which from

---

[109]Franz (1909), II, 484-498.

[110]ed. Grau (1960), 53, *Leben und Schriften der heiligen Klara*, Buch I, c. 21 en 22; II, c. 28.

[111]ed. Douie (1985), 2, 170: "Si, inquit, ipsius sancti sanctorum paulo ante corpus sanctissimum digitis licet indignis contractavimus, dentibus quoque vel labiis attrectatum ad interiora nostra transmisimus, quare non etiam sanctorum eius membra ad nostri munimen et ipsorum venerationem atque memoriam nobis impensius conciliandam, fiducialiter attrectamus et debito cum honore servanda, nobis cum facultas datur adquirimus".

about the 11th century had been laid upon on the bite suffered by the victim. Reports would have it, however, that operations had been performed in which two priests inserted a particle of the stole under the skin of the victim's forehead who, once cured, became a living, ambulant reliquary.[112]

A further well-known example is that of St. Hubert's bread, blessed on 3rd November, the day of the *elevatio* of his relics in 743. The bread was eaten as a medicine to protect people against the dreaded affliction of rabies.[113]   Bread   of   this   type   was   often   designated   as   a 'sacramental'.[114] It derived its power from the saint and was of a different order from the bread of the Eucharist: it served only as protection for health threatened by sickness. It was not a food for the soul, as was the consecrated bread, and did not merit adoration. St. Blaise's bread was regarded as useful for the health of man and animal alike. On 15th February, the feast of this saint in the West, it was blessed together with water, which was used to sprinkle on the animals. The relics of this Eastern saint († 316) are said to have arrived in Reichenau in the 9th century, and his cult spread from there throughout Western Europe in the 12th century. He was the patron saint of throat afflictions, since tradition relates that he saved the life of a boy who had swallowed a fish bone. A third example is the bread blessed on 10th September, feast day of Tolentino († 1305), an Augustinian hermit who, in death as in life, was regarded as a comforter and healer of the sick.[115]

Bread blessed in honour of a saint became a fashion when the *eulogia*, which can be compared with it, lost their significance in the West. These were pieces of blessed bread distributed to the faithful on Sundays and feast days after Mass. The custom still exists in the Byzantine rite as a symbol of unity. As far as the West is concerned, Gregory of Tours repeatedly mentioned the practice. The time at which the bread was distributed is not clear from his writings but Hincmar of

---

[112]AASS 3 nov. I, 828, *Liber secundus miraculorum*, n. 26: "Qui (...) quasi ad exitum in dies declinaret, nocte quadam personam venusti vultus, cum stola pontificali vidit in somnis sibi assistere (...)"; ibid. 829: "ruptaque cicatrice praeteritae incisionis, particulam auri de stola sancti pontificis, in pectine invenit. Diu multumque miratus, tandem: *Ecce*, ait, *XXX anni sunt hodie, ex quo hanc ferebam in fronte; reponatur ergo, donec quid inde fieri debeat, inveniam in consilio*"; Beek (1974), 67-69, 210, n. 87.

[113]Franz (1909), I, 95, 215-216, 274; LW I, 1010-1011.

[114]"Sacred signs which, in a manner somewhat analogous to that associated with the sacraments, symbolised principally spiritual values, acquired through the Church's invocation" (LW II, 2485).

[115]Franz (1909), 202-206, 267, 271, 274, 458-459; Schreiber (1959), 74-79.

Rheims († 882) specifies that it took place at the end of the Mass. From the 12th century the difference between the Eucharistic bread and the *eulogia* was emphasised, not only in the form in which they were presented but also in the manner. This became necessary because the practice of *eulogia* was causing the people to tend towards an underestimation of the value of the Eucharist. From this period, interest in the *eulogia* declined and they disappeared from the Sunday liturgy in the West.[116]

In addition to the 'sacramentals' mentioned above, there was also unblessed miracle bread. This bread falls into the category of contact relics and issued from churches or monasteries where the mortal remains of famous saints rested. Thus the monastery of Fleury gained a reputation because it housed the relics of St. Benedict. It was recognised that both bread and wine from such places had special powers. It is somewhat confusing that in this context the term *eulogia* is used - which also applies to water from the Jordan, holy ground, oil and other contact relics used as talismans.[117]

The picture of the late Middle Ages populated by a colourful collection of saints, relics, reliquaries and 'sacramentals' differs enormously from the picture provided by the martyr's grave, where the simplest form of reverence towards relics came into existence. In a comparable manner the Eucharist detached itself from its origins - the community meal of the Lord.

---

[116]Franz (1909), 229-264; sources 245-248; LW I, 329, 717-719.

[117]Kötting (1950), 118-120; 403-413; Grabar (1958), esp. 63-67; (1972), II, 343; Engemann (1972), 11-12; (1975), 40; LW I, 717.

CHAPTER TWO

THE PROCESS OF INDEPENDENCE OF THE EUCHARIST[*]

In the early Christian church the celebration of the Eucharist implied a meal, an obvious activity since Jesus had instituted the Eucharist within the context of a Jewish Passover meal. In his first letter to the Corinthians (I Cor. 11:17-34) written in 55 AD, the apostle Paul assumes this tradition and, with his disciple Luke, gives the most ancient description of the Eucharistic meal. Central to it was the command given by Jesus: "Do this in memory of *Me*" (Lk. 22:19; I Cor. 24:25) or the pronouncement of the Eucharistic blessing, transforming the bread and wine into signs of Christ and His saving act, followed by the eating of the bread and the drinking of the wine. This act of eating and drinking was an 'active' form of participation, an "entry into the paschal mystery of the Lord"[1].

Over the centuries attention shifted increasingly from the *activities surrounding* the bread and wine within the Lord's supper to *reverence for* the bread and the wine themselves. Up to the 10th century this was still within the context of the Mass but subsequently was placed more and more outside its liturgical setting. This gradual uncoupling of the Eucharistic gifts from their sacramental and liturgical context, the community celebration of the meal, is sometimes referred to as the process in which the Eucharist became "independent" or 'disengaged'.[2]

The seeds of this 'process of independence' can be found in the early shift from community meal or '*agape*' to the ritual consumption of His body and blood alone. It was practically an automatic process whereby the emphasis came to be placed more on Christ's presence as food for the soul and less on His eschatological presence in the community nature of the ritual, which was centred on praise of God, repentance and forgiveness. Within this process of limitation, from real to merely sacramental meal - a phenomenon already apparent in apostolic times - the taking of the Eucharist to those prevented from being present

---

[*]A list for further reading and sources can be found in: O. Nussbaum (1979), N. Mitchel (1982) and in Rubin (1979) to which brief reference is made in the notes.

[1]Verheul (1974), 13, 70, 77-82; Dix (1945), 743-744.

[2]Mitchell (1982), 4: "How did the eucharistic action (...) give way to a pattern of devotion quite independent?"; ibid. 20-29.

at the ritual was a logical step. In this way they too were enabled to share
in Jesus by receiving the food over which the community prayer of
thanksgiving had been uttered. Justinus Martyr mentions this custom in
his *Apologia* written around 150 AD[3].

Following logically from this development, and helped partly by the
persecutions, it became the custom to preserve and receive the Eucharistic
at home during the week. Home communion as celebrated in early
Christian times persisted until the 7th century, although it was less
common from the 4th century onwards. Despite this tendency towards
privatisation, the church remained attached to the link with the community
celebration, something clearly seen in the practice of the *fermentum*, a
piece of the Eucharistic bread which, around the year 400, the pope
caused to be sent to the other titular churches[4] of Rome as a symbol of
unity with his celebration.

The customs of the *fermentum* and home communion during ancient
Christian times show that the presence of Christ in the Eucharistic bread
was not a source of awe at the time. The Eucharistic was seen primarily
as the *anamnesis* - remembrance - which made actual Christ's work of
salvation. It was about the real and continuing memorial of Christ in His
salvific acts. The emphasis was not so much on the awe-inspiring and
cultic reverence of the actual body and blood of Christ.[5] But it should be
noted that as early as the 3rd century a protecting and magical power was
attributed to the Eucharist preserved at home, similar to the powers to
affect everyday life believed to be exercised by house relics in the then
still heathen structures. Hence the practice of taking the Eucharistic bread
on a journey or having it buried along with a corpse. The way to this
magical interpretation lay open once the emphasis was shifted from the
Eucharist as community meal to the Eucharist as individual ritual food,
designed to create communication between the communicant and Christ
and His church. It became possible to regard the Eucharist as an

---

[3]ed. Quasten (1936), 17, *Apologia* I, c. 65; 20 c.67; BKV XII, 80, 82; ed. Bartelink
(1986), 82, 83; ed. Wartelle (1987), 193, *Apologie*, 67,5; ["puis on fait à chacun la
distribution et le partage de la nourriture eucharistique, et l'on envoie leur part aux absents,
par le ministre des diacres"

[4]i.e. in early Christian practice these would have been private places of worship denoted
by the name of the individual owner (*titulum*); later the term was applied to a basilica or to
one of the Roman parish churches (LW II, 2678); Wegman (1991), 58: small regional
churches in the city where the presbyters celebrated the liturgy in the pope's name.

[5]Browe (1938), 147: with reference to the sacrificial meal Browe remarks: "Dafür sagte
man: das unblutig Opfer, das Fleish und Blut Christi empfangen; der Ausdruck: Christus
empfangen, gebrauchte man nur gelegentlich einmal, d. h. man sah die Sache, die Speise,
nicht die Person, die sich darbot"; Betz (1955); Mitchell (1982), 15.

individual guarantee of protection both at home and when travelling or as a means of confounding sinners, especially when it was kept within easy reach. Hippolytus († 235) speaks of the apotropaic or protecting force of the Eucharist in circumstances of mortal danger and in an exemplary anecdote Cyprian († 258) portrayed the Eucharist as unapproachable by sinners: it would seem that a certain woman had been made aware of her sins and, on arriving home, saw flames coming from the *arca*, or small box, where she kept the Eucharist.[6]

Trust in the somatic healing powers of the Eucharist through communion can be seen in the advice given by Cyril of Jerusalem († 386) who recommended that after drinking from the chalice the communicant should touch his wet lips with his hand and then his eyes, his forehead and other senses. Cyril is also the origin of the following recommendation for communion - once more practised in the Catholic church since Vatican II[7]: "Make of your left hand a throne for your right hand in order to receive the King in the latter; take care that your palm is hollow and there receive the body of Christ, saying: Amen".[8] This devout reverence shown at communion is reported by more authors from the 4th-5th century onwards. The Eucharistic gifts were not only consecrated and blessed but also treated with reverence. Thus Augustine († 430) underpinned the showing of reverence towards the Eucharist - provided that it was interpreted as 'sacramental' - using the words of the psalm: "Exalt ye the Lord our God, and worship at his footstool; for he is holy" (Ps. 99:5).[9] Another sign of reverence was the solemn showing of the Eucharist just before the communion.[10] Nonetheless, up to Carolingian times, the 9th century approximately, similar modest expressions of reverence remained within the context of the liturgical celebration.

---

[6]CSEL 3,1, 256; SC 11 bis, 118.

[7]Second Vatican Council, 11th Oct. 1962 - 8th Dec. 1965.

[8]PG 33, 1126, *Catech.* XXIII, c. 22: ["Tum vero post communionem corporis Christi accede et ad sanguinis poculum: non extendens manus, sed pronus, et adorationis ac venerationis in modum, dicens, *Amen*, sanctificeris, ex sanguine Christi quoque sumens. Et cum adhuc labiis tuis adhaeret ex eo mador, manibus attingens et oculos et frontem et reliquos sensus sanctifica"]; ibid. 1123-1124, XXIII, c. 21: ["sed sinistram velut thronum subiiciens dexterae, utpote Regem suscepturae: et concava manu suscipe corpus Christi, respondens: *Amen*"].

[9]CC SL 39, 1384-1385, *Enarrationes in Psalmis*, XCVIII, 8,9: "Exaltate Dominum nostrum. Et adorate scabellum pedum eius, quoniam sanctus est"; "Nemo autem illam carnem manducat, nisi prius adoraverit".

[10]Mitchell (1982), 47-49.

The accompanying increase in Eucharistic ceremonial lent itself to allegorical interpretation. An early indication of this can be found in the Greek church writer Theodore of Mopsuestia († 428). He saw the Eucharistic liturgy as a ritual allegory designed to reactivate Christ's suffering, death, burial and resurrection. When the deacon spreads the altar cloths on the altar, this is no longer the preparation of the community table for the Lord's supper but is seen rather as the dressing of a bier or tomb, on which the bread is laid as the risen body of Christ.[11] In the West an early symptom of the passion for allegory can be found in the *Expositio Antiquae Gallicanae* ascribed to Germanus of Paris († 576) where the tower-shaped container used to hold the Eucharistic is seen as an analogy of Christ's tower-shaped rock tomb.[12]

The tendency towards allegorical explanations won a great deal of ground in Carolingian times. Amalarius of Metz († c. 852) regarded the Mass as the life of Jesus, as a passion play whose interpretative cloak enfolded even the most ordinary gestures and actions. He regarded the Introit prayer as the prophets announcing the coming of the Messiah, and the Gloria was the song of the angels. The subdeacon reading the Epistle was given the significance of John the Baptist, which was why the subdeacon stood one step lower than the reader of the Gospel, since the preaching of the 'Precursor' was subordinate to that of the Messiah. In the same spirit he explained the ritual surrounding the *Sancta*, the bread remaining from the previous celebration which was placed in the chalice as a sign of the unity of the Eucharistic continuity within the local church. It had the same significance as the *fermentum* which came into use later when, in Rome, the Mass was celebrated simultaneously in more than one church. This originally simple action involving the *Sancta* grew into a rich ceremonial, described in the *Ordo Romanus Primus*, dating from the 7th-8th century. The bishop, accompanied by other priests and acolytes bearing censers and candles, carried it solemnly into the church.[13] Unfortunately Amalarius ignored the original significance since he failed to see the mingling of the bread and wine as the continuity with the

---

[11]ed. Tonneau (1966), 331-332, IIe homilie *sur le baptême,* par. 6; 485, Ve homilie *sur la messe,* par. 15; 505, par 26: ["Et quand ils l'ont apportée, c'est sur le saint autel qu'ils la placent pour le parfait achèvement de la passion. Ainsi croyons-nous à son sujet que c'est désormais dans une sorte de tombeau qu'il (le Christ) est placé sur l'autel et que déja il a subi la passion. C'est pourquoi certains des diacres qui étendent des nappes sur l'autel, présentent par cela la similitude des linges de l'ensevelissement"]; ed. Mingana (1933), VI, 21, 79, 86.

[12]PL 72, 93.

[13]Andrieu (1931-61), II, 82; Mitchell (1982), 56-59; Wegman (1991), 230.

previous celebration, regarding it as symbolic for the return of Christ's soul into His body.[14]

Up to the time of Amalarius such allegorical interpretation had been incidental. Following him the allegorical bent continued right through the Middle Ages[15], supported from the time of the Crusades by the devotion to the sufferings of Christ. According to Bernold of Konstanz († 1100) the priest with outstretched arms symbolised the shape of the Cross.[16] The more than twenty signs of the cross made over the Eucharistic offerings during the prayer of the Canon were seen by Rupert of Deutz († 1135) to symbolise such things as the journey of Jesus to the Mount of Olives, the betrayal by Judas, the witness of the centurion and the piercing of Christ's side.[17] Although while still a cardinal the future Pope Innocent III († 1216) did something to put a stop to the allegorical interpretations which occasionally showed great powers of imagination, his own explanation of the Canon proves an exception to his efforts by presenting an even more refined numerological symbolism than his predecessors had been capable of.[18] The canonist, William Durandus († 1296), was to take Innocent's vision as his model.

To the extent that these pious and pseudo-historical meanderings of the ecclesiastical mind affected the bread and wine, they did so by - at a very early stage - removing the community and sacramental significance of these symbols. As far as the sacramental significance is concerned, Christian antiquity always showed a more differentiated approach, depending on the metabolism of Ambrose († 397) or the symbolism of Augustine († 430).[19] Ambrose's basic assumption was the transformation of the nature of the bread and wine by the words of consecration, while Augustine emphasised the visible symbol - the sacramental character of the Eucharistic gifts - as an expression of the invisible: the Christ whom we were to meet. In addition Augustine distinguished between the sacrament itself and its power or *virtus*, which brings piety, unity and

---

[14]ed. Hanssens (1948-50), I, 275, *Codex Expositionis*, II, XIV: "Quoniam et in alio loco evangelii confessus est non se esse Christum, stat in inferiori gradu qui verba horum qui incipes Iohannis adnuntiat"; ibid. 320, *Ordinis missae expositio* II, 15: "Quid enim est panem in vinum mittere? Animam Christi ad eius corpus redire".

[15]LW I, 95-98; II, 1627-1634.

[16]PL 151, 987, *Micrologus de ecclesiasticis observationibus*, c. 16.

[17]CC SL 7, 32-61, *De divinis officiis*, lib. II; Meyer (1965), 238.

[18]PL 217, 773-916, *De sacro altaris mysterio*; Jungmann (1962), I, 147 sqq.

[19]TRE I, 89.

love into being.[20] This *virtus* unavoidably calls to mind the special power
or *virtus* emanating from a relic which, however, was no symbol but a
tangible remnant of the saint.

The tensions surrounding the question of the *praesentia realis*
increased in the early Middle Ages. The sacred act, the Eucharistic
celebration within the community, the *anamnesis* of Christ's sacrifice in
which He is made present - all this lost its dynamism in the manner in
which the Eucharist was experienced. This symbolic realism was replaced
by a reality regarded as exclusively historically tangible, whereby the way
was closed off from an understanding of the Eucharist that would indicate
the sacramental. The approach adopted meant that the symbol was no
longer an independent and dynamic reality: there was room only for a
remembrance in allegorical form.[21] This caused the bread and wine to be
released from the community liturgical context and to start to play a role
in the allegorical representation of Christ's suffering and death during the
Mass. Even that symbol - the table - which called out for active
community participation in praise and thanksgiving to the Father for our
salvation lost its community significance and was transformed into an
allegorical tomb. The community aspect of the Eucharist lost in
significance and the 'process of independence' increased.[22]

Meanwhile the intriguing question regarding the relationship
between the sign and the sacramental reality kept minds busy and, in the
9th century, gave rise to the Eucharistic controversy between Paschasius
Radbertus († 859), recorded in the previous chapter, and his pupil
Ratramnus, who was also a monk of Corbie in northern France. This was
a controversy that can be regarded as an early aspect of the 'process of
independence' since both authors concentrated on the Eucharist as object,
which meant that it became, in their arguments, isolated from the
invisible reality of God's mercy and from the Eucharistic activity around
the table.[23] They were concerned with the nature of the change wrought
in the bread and wine and the manner of Christ's presence, which each
described in two separate books with the same title: *De corpore et
sanguine Domini.*

Pachasius insisted on strict Eucharistic realism. He maintained
complete identity between the sacramental body of Christ, present in a

---

[20]Gerken (1973), 94-95.

[21]TRE I, 90.

[22]Gerken (1973), 65-74.

[23]Mitchell (1982), 35, 54.

mystical, non-measurable and non-material way, under the appearances of bread and wine, and Christ's historical body, born of the Virgin Mary, crucified and risen.[24] The Eucharistic gifts are, he stated, spiritual food and after consecration they hold within themselves a miraculous physical reality, a belief he regarded as supported by the realistic miracle legends of Christian antiquity.

Of these there were two classic examples taken from the *Vitae Patrum*, which were constantly re-copied, re-told and added to throughout the Middle Ages. The first concerned St. Basil of Caesarea († 397). It tells of a Jew who pretended to be a Christian in order to get at the truth behind the Mass and communion. He saw how the Christ-child was slaughtered in the saint's hands, and when he went to communion with the rest of the faithful he ate real flesh and drank real blood from a full chalice.[25] The second tale tells of a miracle said to have been experienced by the desert father St. Arsenius († 450). This authority related how a particular old man was incapable of believing in the real presence until he saw with his own eyes an angel slaughter the infant Jesus during celebration of the Mass and the blood being caught in the chalice. To his amazement, when the old man went to receive communion he was given flesh soaked in blood to eat, and it only became bread and wine again when his faith in the real presence had been restored.[26]

Hrabanus Maurus († 856), John Scotus († ca. 877) and - particularly - Ratramnus († ca. 868) opposed the excessively realistic Capharnaistic notions (Jn. 6:52) exemplified in these stories. Ratramnus dealt with the question at the request of the emperor Charles the Bald († 877). He emphasised the real and the sacramental presence as distinct from a real and literal presence, the latter stating that a small-sized Christ was as it were contained in the Eucharist. His approach left no room for blood-soaked images, since the bread and wine were not literal but sacramental signs of Christ's body and blood. For the believer the bread and wine were changed in a spiritual manner, *in figura*, but this did not

---

[24]CC SL 16, 27, c. 3; 30, c. 4: "Vera utique caro Christi quae crucifixa est et sepulta, vere illius carnis sacramentum quod per sacerdotem super altare in verbo Christi per Spiritum Sanctum divinitus consacratur. Unde ipse Dominus clamat: *Hoc est corpus meum*"; Ratramnus: ed. Bakhuizen van den Brink (1954).

[25]PG 29, CCCII, *Vita apocrypha*, c. 2; Paschasius, CC SL 16, 87-88, *De corpore et sanguine Domini*, XIV.

[26]PL 73, 301-302, *De vitis patrum*, lib. I; 979, lib. V; PL 72, 94, *s. Germani exp. brevis ep.* 1; CC SL 16, 88-89.

mean that this spiritual food was identical to the flesh that was crucified and the blood that was shed on Calvary.[27]

The 9th-century Eucharistic controversy did not, however, place a strong enough emphasis on the presence of Christ in the Eucharist to prevent the rise of the veneration of the Eucharist outside the liturgical context. The theological debate largely went over the heads of the parish clergy or it was neglected. In a document such as the 9th-century catechism, known as the *Disputatio Puerorum*, a pastoral guide for the laity, the question is ignored.[28] The progress of the conflict only became truly evident in the second Eucharistic debate from the middle of the 11th century and in general devotion at the beginning of the 13th century, when the official church finally decided in favour of Radbertus' previous opinion.

However there was a gradual growth in the split between priest and people relative to the Eucharist, partly because the people no longer understood Latin - which had already been the case for some time in the non-Romance countries. The Mass thus became exclusively a clerical ritual in which the people could scarcely share. The problems stemming from the use of Latin can be deduced from an instruction issued by the Council of Tours in 813, requesting that bishops should preach in (old) French (*rustica romana lingua*) or in German so that the people could at least understand.[29]

The granting of special status to the priest was partly encouraged by the anointing of the ordinand's hands, a ritual by which he was thought to gain the unique power to change the bread and wine into the body and blood of Christ - which, according to the followers of Radbertus, were the real, physically present body and blood of Jesus. The *Missale Francorum*, a Gallic sacramentary dating from the 8th century, contains two texts used at the anointing of the hands[30] and in a mid-9th-century sacramentary of St. Denis we read: "O Lord, bless and consecrate these hands of your priest, so that they can consecrate the sacrificial gifts

---

[27]Neunheuser (1963), 18.

[28]PL 101, 1099-1144; Mitchell (1982), 100-101.

[29]MGH Conc II, 288 can. XVII: "Et ut easdem omelias quisque aperte transferre studeat in rusticam Romanam linguam aut Thiosticam, quo facilius cuncti possint intellegere quae dicuntur"; Mitchell (1982), 69; Gy (1987), 533-539; Lauwers (1987), 228: literature dealing with the knowledge of Latin in the Middle Ages.

[30]ed. Mohlberg (1957), 10, n. 33 en 34.

offered for the sins and omissions of your people".[31] At a later date, in the midst of the delicate questions surrounding the Investiture Controversy, Pope Urban II († 1099) is reported to have said that the priest's hands had the power "to create the Creator of all things and offer him to God for the salvation and healing of the world". Indeed, people kissed the priest's hands because they had touched the Divine Majesty, surrounded by angels.[32]

From Carolingian times, therefore, only the priest could understand the sacred texts and the Eucharist was increasingly regarded as belonging to the spiritual domain of the celebrant, who consecrated the bread and wine. Because of this unique relationship with God the priest was alone given the right to touch the Eucharistic offerings. This was the reason for the changeover in the 9th century from communion received in the hand to communion received in the mouth, though the fear of desecration also played a part here.[33] In addition to other 9th-century declarations issuing from Italy, Spain and France, a council held in Rouen made matters crystal clear: "Do not place the Eucharist in the hand of a lay person, neither man nor woman, but only in the mouth".[34]

The laity was also gradually denied the right to handle the chalice. From the 7th century a custom came about in Rome whereby some of the consecrated wine was mixed with ordinary wine in a chalice and given to the faithful to drink. In the same period outside Rome a reed, or *fistula*,[35] was used to suck up the wine in order to prevent spillage. The third way of administering communion with the wine, and for long the most popular method, was the *intinctio*, where the Host was dipped in the consecrated wine and handed to the communicant. The opponents of *intinctio* considered that this too closely resembled the gesture employed by Jesus during the Last Supper to identify Judas as the one who was to betray him.[36] This was, in fact, the argument used by Innocent III to put

---

[31]ed. Assemanus (1749-66), t. VIII, 128: "Benedic Domine, et sanctifica has manus sacerdotis tui ad consecrandas hostias, quae pro delictis atque negligentiis populi offeruntur"; Angenendt (1982), 194; Mitchell (1982), 89.

[32]Southern (1975), 128; Delaruelle (1975), 71.

[33]Mitchell (1982), 90;Browe (1932a), 601; Nussbaum (1969), 27-28.

[34]Hardouin, VI, p. 1, 205, c. 2: "nulli autem laico aut feminae eucharistiam in manibus ponat, sed tantum in os eius (...) ponat" (anno ca. 878); Mitchell (1982), 597-598.

[35]The *fistula, pugillaris* or *calamus* was not made of natural material but of gold or silver (LW I, 754).

[36]LW II, 1466; Nussbaum (1969), 28-29, 48; Freestone (1917), 152-165.

an end to the custom at the beginning of the 13th century.[37] In the meantime the theologians had advanced the opinion that Jesus was entirely present under each separate species, so that *intinctio* was superfluous. Depriving the laity of communion from the chalice contributed in no small way to Eucharistic piety being directed almost exclusively towards the Host. Outside the Mass Eucharistic devotion became, in fact, devotion to the Host.[38]

A practical reason for abolishing *intinctio* was the fear of spillage. The presence of Christ required extreme care that not a drop should be lost. This almost scrupulous piety was also applied to the Host. Around the year 800 came the first prescriptions calling for the use of unleavened bread. This type of bread, which does not produce crumbs, came into general use from the 11th century. The introduction of separate Hosts did away with the breaking of the bread.[39] The Hosts were prepared with the utmost care: the monks of Cluny washed themselves and combed their hair beforehand and picked out the wheat grains one by one and washed them. Even the millstone was cleansed. The monks were careful that neither their saliva nor their breath came into contact with the Hosts.[40]

Once consecrated, the bread belonged in sacred vessels. In Carolingian times the custom arose of consecrating such vessels, a gesture again exclusively reserved to the priest. The first sacred formulae for this type of ritual are to be found in the Gallic sacramentaries. The *Missale Francorum*, for instance, contains prayers for the consecration of the paten,[41] the chalice and the chrismale, the latter called allegorically by the *Missale* "a new tomb for the body of Christ".[42]

Not only the manner but also the time at which the believers received communion served to lay increasing emphasis on the separation between priest and laity. A first indication is contained in *Institutio* of Angilbert († 814), who had gone from the court of Charlemagne to take up residence in the Centula-Saint Ricquier monastery in the diocese of

---

[37]PL 217, 866, *De sacro altaris mysterii*, VI, 13.

[38]Devlin (1975), 189-190; Mitchell (1982), 159-163; LW I, 1078.

[39]Nussbaum (1979), 107; LW I, 328.

[40]d'Achery, I, 694, *Antiquiores consuetudines Cluniacensis monasterii, collectore s. Udalrico*, lib. III, c.13; PL 149, 757-758, *De hostiis quomodo fiant*; Pijper (1907), 65; Jungmann (1962), II, 44-45.

[41]This was originally a large tray used for distributing the leavened bread. When unleavened bread was introduced in the 8th-9th century and small Hosts became more common, the tray lost its original shape and turned into a small, flat dish on which the celebrant's Host was placed. (LW II, 2170).

[42]ed. Mohlberg (1957), 19.

Amiens. He became abbot and prescribed that at Christmas and Easter communion should be distributed to the children and lay adults had not yet received it only after the clergy had left. We have to imagine the following scenario: the celebrant gave communion to the monks while another priest did the same for the laity, assisted by a deacon and subdeacon. Once the celebrant was finished, distribution of communion was halted and the celebrant continued with the Mass in order not to make the service too long. Leaving aside a few indications dating from the 9th and 10th centuries, reports of communion after Mass date from the 12th century and later. By the end of the 13th century the custom had become general on major feast days.[43]

The increasing liturgical independence of the priest relative to the laity in Carolingian times was further emphasised by his private prayers during Mass at the time of communion or at the *Sanctus*. The people meanwhile were kept occupied with singing. In a manuscript written at the time in Sarum (Salisbury), in which Radbertus's influence can be clearly felt, the priest prays: "God, Father (...) by your mercy your only Son came down to this earth for our sakes. According to your will he took on the flesh which I now hold in my hands". And leaning forward he then addresses the Host: "I adore you, I glorify you, from the depth of my heart I praise you (...)" The humble words spoken by the centurion: "Lord, I am not worthy" (Lk. 7:6) were part of these private prayers until the 13th century, after which they were said out loud, by priest and congregation together, just before the communion.[44] A similar personal prayer can also be found in the late 9th-century sacramentary of Amiens, the prayer being said while the people sang the *Sanctus*. Sometimes the priest even began the Canon on his own, a practice opposed by archbishop Heraldus of Tours. The celebrant, he stated, would do better to sing with the people.[45]

The communal aspect of the celebration of the Eucharist probably lost most ground by the increase in the practice of private Masses, which Theodulph of Orleans vainly tried to oppose with his statement that "a

---

[43]Hallinger, I, 295-296; Heitz (1963), 27; Nussbaum (1979), 44-47; Mitchell (1982), 226-227.

[44]Martène (1788), I, 241; Browe (1935), 31-32; Dijk v.(1960), 49-51; Jungmann (1962), II, 428-430.

[45]PL 121, *Capitula Heraldi*, XVI: "Et ut secreta presbyteri non inchoent antequam *sanctus* finiatur, sed cum populo *sanctus* cantent"; Leroquais (1927), 442.

priest should never celebrate the Mass alone".[46] The private Mass was
no longer a novelty in his time. The question as to how it came into being
has not yet been given a satisfactory answer.[47] The source must lie in the
6th-century monasteries, where more and more monks were ordained
priests. At the time of Gregory the Great the monks were going out on
mission and it was desirable that they should be priests. The priest-monks
felt the need within the monasteries to celebrate Mass more frequently
than would have been the case simply by taking turns to be celebrant for
the whole community. Moreover ground was being gained by the idea
that a greater share in the church's treasury of mercy was obtained not
only as regards personal sanctity but also for the dead if the Mass was
celebrated more often. The desire to honour the relics contained in the
many altars was also of some significance.[48]

A further factor was that the Masses - sometimes great numbers of
them - came to be regarded as 're-payment' of the penances handed out in
private confession, a practice originating in Ireland and which spread
rapidly in the 7th century. The penitent was granted forgiveness or
absolution immediately following the confession of his sins and then had
to do some form of penance. This could consist of having Masses said,
involving payment of a gift or *stipendium*. Usually the penitent did not
attend the *missa specialis*, which was celebrated in complete privacy.[49]

In the 8th century the daily private Mass was a familiar
phenomenon in monasteries, an example followed by the secular clergy in
the 9th century[50] despite theological objections. Walahfrid Strabo († 849)
criticised the opinion that the mercy of the Mass could be directed
towards one single person, and Peter Damian († 1072) remarked:
"Whereas the Lord on His cross suffered for the salvation of the whole
world (...) now the sacrifice of salvation is offered for the benefit of one

---

[46]Mansi XIII, 996, capitulare Theodulfi, VII: "Sacerdos missam solus nequaquam
celebret: quia sicut illa celebrari non potest sine salutatione sacerdotis, responsione
nihilominus plebis, ita nimirum nequaquam ab uno debet celebrari. Esse enim debent qui ei
circumstent quos ille salutet, a quibus ei respondeatur: et ad memoriam illi reducendum est
illud dominicum: *Ubicumque fuerint vel tres in nomine meo congregati, et ego in medio
eorum* ".

[47]Häussling (1973), 357; Vogel (1980), 232: "Les raisons (...) nous échappent encore, en
grande partie"; Angenendt (1983), 153.

[48]Nussbaum (1961), 136 sqq.; Klauser (1969), 103; Häussling (1973), 219, 223-225, 232
sqq.; Jungmann (1974).

[49]Angenendt (1982), 183-185; Mitchell (1982), 109-112.

[50]Dijk v. (1960), 45 sqq.; up to the end of the 8th century the demarcation between
regulars and seculars was not so sharply drawn: Stemmler (1980), 78-111.

son of man".[51] This echoed the warning given by St. Ignatius of Antioch
(† ca. 118): "Be sure to celebrate one supper of the Lord, for there is
only one body of Our Lord Jesus Christ and only one chalice of unity in
His blood; that is why there is only 'one altar' and one bishop together
with his priests and deacons".[52]

Around the year 600 this principle had thus been laid aside in the
monasteries. The Masses celebrated at the side altars, placed against the
wall of the monastery church, implied that the priest stood with his back
to any congregation present. The situation in which the priest stood
between the altar and the faithful was already a fact in the East, in small
churches in Syria in the 4th century and in Greece and Egypt
in the 5th century. From the 7th century onwards it happened regularly
in Palestine and Asia Minor.[53] In the West it was only North Africa that
followed the example of the Eastern church, but in the parish churches
the celebrant's position was, until the 7th or 8th century, *versus populum*,
facing the congregation.

The origin of the change in the position adopted by the priest can
be traced back to the 4th century. The edict of tolerance of 313 meant
that Christian worship could be carried out in public. The liturgy became
more and more ornate, borrowing elements from court ceremonial. The
majestic portrayal of the teaching Christ, great and imposing among his
disciples arranged round him like 'courtiers', can still be seen in the
mosaic in the apse of the 4th-century church of Santa Pudentiana in Rome
or in the 6th-century mosaics of the churches of San Vitale and the San
Apollinare Nuovo in Ravenna.[54]

Heaven and earth, the visible and invisible, were joined together;
angels and archangels crowded round the altar wreathed in incense. The
sacred was withdrawn from view; participation by the faithful began to
take a back seat; choir and clergy took over their task. Less and less
notice was taken of the congregation, so that it was almost a logical step

---

[51]PL 145, 501: "Sed cum passus sit Dominus in cruce pro salute mundi, nunc mactatur in altari pro unius commodo et facultate presbyteri. Tunc crucifixus est pro totius populi multitudine, nunc quasi pro unius homuncionis utilitate salutaris hostia videtur offerri"; Angenendt (1983), 180.

[52]SC 10, 1969, 123, Philad. 4: ["Ayez donc soin de ne participer qu'à une seule eucharistie, car il n'y a qu'une seule chair de notre Seigneur Jésus-Christ, et un seul calice pour nous unir en son sang, un seul autel, comme un seul évêque avec le presbytérium et les diacres]; Klauser (1969), 106.

[53]Nussbaum (1965), 408-421: *"Die Abwendung des Liturgen von der Gemeinde"*.

[54]ibid. 415, n. 261: lit.; Hauser (1975), 92, illustr. 36-39.

for the celebrant to place himself between the people and the altar.[55] In the West the *missa sine populo*, or private Mass, encouraged this development. The growing number of side altars in cathedrals monastery churches were used exclusively for private Masses, the high altar being reserved for High Mass celebrated for the monastery or parish. There too, around the year 1000, the celebrant stood between the people and the altar. Soon there was no objection to the altar being placed against the wall of the apse. It was to remain there until the Second Vatican Council. The back of the altar table provided plenty of space for the relics on rich retables.

The situation thus came about that the priest celebrated Mass no longer with the faithful present but in their name. The Canon, recited out loud by the celebrant in the Roman church up to about the 8th century, was now whispered inaudibly.[56] After the change undergone by the Eucharist in early Christian times from liturgy to individual ritual food had detracted from the communal character of a meal, and subsequently the allegorical interpretation had deprived the symbols of their communal significance - the table became a tomb - the intensification of the priestly relationship to the Eucharist isolated the people even more from the liturgy of the Mass. The alienation was revealed in the descriptions given of how communion should be received, the failure any longer to understand the liturgical language, the private Mass and the priest's private prayers uttered with his back to the people.

These symptoms, contributing to the 'process of independence of the Eucharist', were up to this point manifested within the Eucharistic liturgy. But in the 10th century we see the first signs of a cultic reverence outside the Mass itself, in the practice of communion for the sick. This custom had existed as long ago as in the 2nd century, as can be seen in the allusion made by Justinus Martyr. There was at the time no fixed ritual. No-one objected to lay people giving one another communion at home.[57] From about 800, however, the pastoral aspect was clarified and normally speaking the practice of *viaticum* was reserved to the clergy.[58] According to Theodulph of Orleans († 821) the sick person was brought

---

[55]Nussbaum (1965), 419.

[56]Klauser (1969), 97-101; Jungmann (1941), 88.

[57]See above n. 3.

[58]Hincmar of Rheims († 882): PL 125, 779, *Capit. synod.* II, c.10: "Si ipse presbyter visitet infirmos et inungat oleo s. et communicet per se et non per quemlibet, et ille ipse communicet populum nec tradat communionem cuiquam laico ad deferendum in domum suam causa cuiuslibet infirmi"; Rush (1974), 31; Mitchell (1982), 113.

to the church[59] while St. Dunstan celebrated Mass in the home of a sick woman.[60] Around the year 970 Dunstan's disciple, bishop Ethelwold of Winchester, addressed to the English monasteries his *Regularis Concordia*, in which he describes a third form of communion of the sick, a form which was most usual and was accompanied by a certain degree of ceremonial: after the Mass the priest went with the Eucharist to the sick person's home, preceded by praying and psalm-singing acolytes and servers bearing incense and candles.[61]

Round about the same time the Eucharist began to take on a role in the Good Friday solemnities. At the end of the 10th century Gerard, the cathedral provost of Augsburg, described in his *Vita* of bishop Ulrich († 973) that after the faithful had received communion it was the prelate's 'normal custom' to carry the remaining Eucharistic bread to the church of St. Ambrose and there bury it symbolically by laying a stone on it. On Easter morning Ulrich celebrated Mass there, took out the Eucharist and carried bot it and the book of the Gospels, surrounded by candles and incense, to the church of John the Baptist in order to sing Terce, the second Office of the day. Then the procession continued on to the cathedral for the Easter Mass.[62]

This *depositio* and *elevatio* can also be found in Ethelwold's document, but he states that it was the Cross and not the Eucharist that was placed in a grave next to the altar. This is probably the oldest form of the ritual. From about 1100 both Cross and Eucharist were placed simultaneously in the holy sepulchre.[63]

---

[59]PL 137, 427.

[60]PL 105, 220.

[61]Hallinger VII-3, 141, c. XIV, 98: "sacerdos casula exutus cum reliquis ministris illius missae eucharistiam ferentibus praecedentibus cereis et turibulo cum omni congregatione eant ad visitandum infirmum canentes psalmos penitentiales consequente laetania et orationibus"; PL 137, 500 c. 12; Nussbaum (1979), 96.

[62]MGH SS IV, 392-393, *Gerhardi vita s. Oudalrici ep.* c. 4 (21, 23): "Et sacro Dei ministerio perpetrato populoque sacro Christi corpore saginato, et consuetudinario more quod remanserat sepulto (...) Desiderantissimo atque sanctissimo paschali die adveniente, post primam intravit aecclesiam sancti Ambrosii, ubi die parasceve corpus Christi superposito lapide collocavit, ibique cum paucis clericis missam de sancte Trinitate explevit. Expleta autem missa, clerum interim congregatum in scena iuxta eandem aecclesiam sitam solemnibus vestibus indutum antecessit, secum portato corpore Christi et evangelio et cereis et incenso, et cum congrua salutatione versuum, a pueris decantata, per atrium perrexit ad aecclesiam sancti Iohannis baptistae, ibique tertiam decantavit"; Young (1920), 17; Nussbaum (1979), 190.

[63]Hallinger VII-3, 118, c. VI, 74: "Depositaque cruce, ac si domini nostri Ihesu Christi corpore sepulto, dicant antiphonam"; PL 173, 493, c. 6; Gschwend 1965, esp. 59, 161 sqq.; Nussbaum (1979), 191-197.

There are approximately 200 documents witnessing to these three manners of ritual burial on Good Friday. In most cases only the Cross was buried, in fewer cases both Cross and Eucharist and relatively infrequently only the Eucharist. The three variants show, in the incidence with which they are reported, similarities to the custom which increased in frequency from the 8th century during the consecration of a church: the *depositio* of three particles of the Host in the *sepulcrum* of the altar, either instead of or together with the relics. The oldest form, as we saw in the previous chapter, consisted of the placing of relics alone in the altar. From Carolingian times particles of the Host were used, possibly - as stated - because of a lack of relics. In this way the altar was turned not only allegorically but also practically into tomb, a tomb for the 'relics' of Christ as well as for those of His saints.[64] However, wherever the sources mention the placing of the Eucharist in the altar, they usually state that this was done together with relics.

The Good Friday solemnities described in the life of St. Ulrich and in the *Regularis Concordia* represented an extension of the veneration of the Cross that had existed in the West since the 7th century. The *depositio* and *elevatio* were a dramatisation of the burial and resurrection of Jesus. Host, Cross and book of the Gospels represent Christ, who was also represented in the late Middle Ages by a life-size statue with a cavity in the chest designed to contain the Eucharist. As far as the faithful were concerned this holy sepulchre contained Christ himself in His 'unique relic',[65] just as since the 10th century the images and shrines had contained the relics of the saints behind little doors or windows.

The desire was to approach reality. In Ulrich's *vita* the solemnities of Palm Sunday are described: a wooden donkey with a statue of Christ[66] mounted upon it, arms held out in blessing, was led through the streets in procession, and in the *Roman-German Pontificale* dating from approximately 950 the processional Cross was the focus of attention.[67] In

---

[64] Young (1920); Brooks (1921); Browe (1931d), 100-107; Corbin (1960); Gschwend (1965).

[65] Brooks (1921), 38; Browe (1931d), 107; Beck (1978), 161-167, illustr. 17-27; Nussbaum (1979), 190, 199: "die kostbarste und wirkmächtigste Reliquie des Herrn".

[66] MGH SS IV, 391, *Gerhardi Vita s. Oudalrici Ep.*, c. 4: "evangelioque et crucibus et fanonibus, et cum effigie sedentis Domini super asinum, cum clericis et multitudine populi ramos palmarum in manibus portantis, et cum cantationibus ad honorem eiusdem diei compositis"; Nussbaum (1979), 199.

[67] ed. Vogel (1963), II, 40-51, *Ordo de die palmarum*, 47: "Ut autem pervenerint cum palmis ubi statio est sanctae crucis, clerus populusque reverenter stant per turmas in ordine suo cum baiolis et reliquo ornatu".

the 11th century the *decreta* of Lanfranc († 1089) reveals a transposition
of this form of reverence: the new focus of the Palm Sunday procession is
now a shrine containing the Eucharist, surrounded by candles and incense
and reverently greeted with genuflections.[68]

Lanfranc, who was later made archbishop of Canterbury thanks to
William the Conqueror's influence, had entered into a controversy by
correspondence with archdeacon Berengarius of Tours († 1088), whose
theology was once more centred on the presence of Christ in the
sacrament.

Berengarius was continuing the Augustinian line taken by
Ratramnus. He characterised Radbertus and his followers as 'carnal
illiterates' and characterised some of the miracles quoted by Radbertus as
'fables' and 'foolishness'. In his opinion, bread remained bread after
consecration and wine remained wine, precisely in order to be a sign of
the holy one, of the mercy, a *sacramentum* of the body and blood of
Christ, the risen one, the one who was present, the unassailable Lord.
After consecration the Eucharistic gifts were on a higher level of reality.
They had become signs (*sacramenta*) of the invisible spiritual body of
Christ. This *res sacramenti* had an enormous spiritual effect on the soul
of the faithful receiving communion "as if it were the real body of
Christ".[69]

The 'Ambrosian', Lanfranc, differed by making a distinction
between the form or appearance of bread and wine after consecration (the
visible reality) and the essence that it concealed (the invisible reality),
namely the body and blood of the Lord.[70] He and his disciple Guitmund
were the principal opponents of Berengarius, and the latter lost the
argument. In 1059 the synod of Rome obliged him to recognise that after

---

[68]Hallinger, III/IV, 23: "Praecedant famuli cum vexilis sequatur conversus ferens situlam
cum aqua benedicta; alii duo portantes duas cruces, item duo cum duobus candelabris,
accensis desuper cereis, alii duo ferentes duo thuribula igne et thure referta"; 24: "Cantore
autem incipiente antiphonam *Occurrunt turbae* exeant duo sacerdotes albis induti, qui portent
feretrum, quod parum ante diem ab eisdem sacerdotibus illuc esse debet delatum, in quo et
corpus Christi esse debet reconditum. Ad quod feretrum praecedant statim qui vexilla
portant, et cruces, et caetera qui superius dicta sunt (...) Pueri vero accedentes stabunt versis
vultibus ad ipsas reliquias (...) Finita antiphona *Occurrunt turbae*, incipiant pueri (...)
Osanna filio David, flectentes genua (...) Quibus transeuntibus flectant genua, non simul
omnes sed cinguli hinc et inde, sicut feretrum transibit ante eos (...) Cum venerint ad portas
civitatis stationem faciant separatis ad invicem prout locus patietur utriusque lateribus.
Feretrum vero ante introitum portarum sic ponatur super mensam pallio coopertam"; see p.
260, n. 51; Stemmler (1970), 195; Mitchell (1982), 130-131; 137-150.

[69]Browe (1938), 182; Beekenkamp (1940); Engels (1965), 375; Montclos (1971), 143;
Devlin (1975), 42-43, 53.

[70]PL 150, 430, *Liber de corpore et sanguine Domini*.

consecration the body and blood of Christ were really, physically and not just sacramentally present on the altar and that this body of Christ was touched and bitten by the teeth of the believer.[71]

He recanted this declaration in his book *Regarding the sacred meal (De sacra coena)*,[72] but in 1079 he was again called to order. The future lay with realism and with a sensual interpretation of that realism. Long after his death Berengarius continued to make life difficult for his doctrinal opponents with the philosophical question as to whether, as seen from the realistic point of view of the Eucharist, the body and blood of Christ was subject to decay or burning and whether it could be consumed by animals. The question: "What does the mouse eat?" kept the theologians occupied for many subsequent centuries.[73]

The supporters of substantial change and the real presence had difficulty in providing further formulation and description of these concepts. The process of theological reflection resulted in the doctrine of change of essence or transubstantiation, a distinction being made between *accidentia* and *substantia*, for which Lanfranc had laid the foundations. The doctrine was formulated at the Fourth Lateran Council in 1215. By formulating this dogma the church took a stand against the heresy of the Albigenses, who regarded the Eucharistic bread as mere bread, indistinguishable from other types of bread.[74]

After the victory over Berengarius, transubstantiation was given due emphasis by miracles involving blood and Hosts, all of which served as confirming evidence at synods, in scholastic works and in sermons. The miracle stories retailed by Radbertus and dating from the time of Gregory the Great - or even earlier - supported the doctrine, but even more so did the growing number of miracles of change reported after the end of the 11th century. Almost all of them referred to the mystery of the consecration, convincing doubters or rewarding believers.

---

[71]DS 690; Mitchell (1982), 137.

[72]ed. Beekenkamp (1941).

[73]Guitmund: PL 149, 1418, *De corporis et sanguinis Domini veritate,* lib. II: "Mihi equidem sacramenta haec nequaquam a muribus vel aliquibus brutis animalibus videntur posse corrodi"; Peter Lombardus († 1160): ed. *Bibliotheca franciscana scholastica* (1951-57), IV, 204, *Sent.* IV, 8: "Quaestio est propter, quod si corpus Christi ibi est, non sumitur a brutis animalibus"; Inn. III († 1216): PL 217, 863, "*De sacro altaris mysterio,* IV, c. 11: "si vero quaeratur quid a mure comeditur, cum sacramentum corroditur, vel quid incineratur cum sacramentum crematur"; TW III, 4593-4599, esp. n. 4.

[74]TRE 1, 92-93; Nussbaum (1979), 128.

Not infrequently miraculous Hosts were conserved as objects of reverence, a phenomenon unknown in ancient times and the early Middle Ages. Browe provides a list of Eucharistic miracles which caused a place of pilgrimage to spring up: eight in the 11th century, nineteen in the 12th, fifty in the 13th, sixty-five in the 14th, forty in the 15th, five in the 16th and one in the 17th. The end of the 13th century and the whole of the 14th century were the high points. Desecrations of the Host, blamed on the Jews, were also reported in the same period. The desecrated Hosts all began to bleed.[75]

St. Thomas Aquinas († 1274) says of all of this: "Whatever that blood may be, one thing is sure: it is not the blood of Christ". For he rejected vigorously the bilocation or multilocation of Christ in His own appearance. The risen Lord was present in his bodily form in one place only, and that was Heaven. Moreover Thomas regarded the preservation of His so-called "flesh and blood" behind glass objectionable and unbecoming. And not only that: one could no longer speak of His sacramental presence once the *accidentia* or appearances - the smell and taste of bread and wine - had disappeared. Nor could he agree with the realistic view of things that made Christ a prisoner in His tabernacle where, he states, only consecrated Hosts are to be found, or sacramental forms, which realise the bodily presence of Christ in a sacramental manner. Albertus Magnus († 1280) and Bonaventure († 1274) supported his critical views regarding the excessive formula of 1059 which Berengarius had had to subscribe to. This 13th-century university reaction to the sensualist opinion failed, however, to win general approval and passed over the heads of the faithful. The collective consciousness remained captive to the realistic notion of the Eucharist.[76]

Within the liturgy the Host was accorded a dominant position and, in the mind of the people, even became a source of power with the same kinds of miraculous effect that the relics had been believed to produce. Parallel to this, there was a move towards using the Host for private ends such as during sickness or when fire broke out, or when the Host was carried about to afford protection against natural disasters or to ensure a good harvest. Sometimes such activities descended to the level of magic. It was not unknown for women to keep the Host in their mouth until after

---

[75]Browe (1927); (1929e); (1938), 2, 128-146, 182-183.

[76]Browe (1929d), 312 sqq.; Schillebeeckx (1967), 8 n. 2; *Summa Theol.* III, q. 76, art. 8,2 and 2: "Sed caro aut sanguis miraculose apparens non sunt consecrata, nec conversa in verum corpus et sanguinem Christi. Non ergo sub his speciebus est corpus vel sanguis Christi"; ed. Blacfriars, vol. LVIII.

the end of the service in order to win the love of a partner with a kiss, as recounted by Peter Damian († 1071) and Caesarius of Heisterbach († ca. 1240). According to Herbert of Clairvaux († ca. 1180) the Host was scattered over the fields to increase fertility or sewn into garments to ensure the acquisition of money and goods.[77] This sort of behaviour was one of the reasons why the Fourth Lateran Council required the Host to be preserved behind locked doors. Safety precautions were taken with regard to relics at the same time.[78]

Within the context of the 'process of independence of the Eucharist' there is another important decision taken by the same council. The Fathers felt constrained to fix the frequency of communion at a minimum of once per year, at Easter or thereabouts. The Council thus took account of the actual situation: people received communion very infrequently. This is significant for the extent to which the Eucharistic forms were perceived as separated from what they were intended for as bread and wine: to be eaten and drunk.[79]

This attitude had been gaining greater acceptance from as early as the 4th century, in marked contrast to early Christianity when the faithful were accustomed to bring bread and wine every week as a sacrificial meal and to consume them together with the priest. The synods of Elvira in 306 and Sardika in 343 felt obliged to prescribe punishment for those who failed to fulfil this duty for more than three weeks.[80] Ambrose († 397) in the West[81] and John Chrysostom († 407) in the East[82] voiced

---

[77]PL 185, 1374, *De miraculis,* c. 3, 29: "Quidam rusticanus atque pauperculus homo, a nescio quo impostore maligno audierat quia si Dominicum Corpus secum assidue circumferret, in modico tempore divitiis abundaret. Accipiens itaque die Pascha sacrosanctum Domini Corpus, integrum ore retinuit. Quod protinus assuens in margine cappae, multo secum tempore tulit, nec ei tamen aliquando paupertas et miseria defuit"; PL 145, 173, *Opusc.* 34; ed. Strange (1851), II, 171, *Dial.* IX, c. 6; Browe (1930), 135, 138; Trexler (1980), 56.

[78]Nussbaum (1979), 106-107; 369-370.

[79]Mansi XXIII, 197, c. 21 : "Omnis utriusque sexus fidelis, postquam ad annos discretionis pervenerit, omnia sua solus peccata confiteatur fideliter, saltem semel in anno, proprio sacerdoti et iniunctam sibi poenitentiam studeat pro viribus adimplere, suscipiens reverenter ad minus in pascha eucharistiae sacramentum, nisi forte de consilio proprii sacerdotis ob aliquam rationabilem causam ad tempus ab eius perceptione duxerit abstinendum; alioquin et vivens ab ingressu ecclesiae arceatur et moriens christiana careat sepultura. Unde hoc salutare statutum frequenter in ecclesiis publicetur, ne quisquam ignorantiae caecitate velamen excusationis assumat"; Browe (1940), 43, 44 n. 101; Nussbaum (1979), 125.

[80]Browe (1938a), 1-10; (1940), 31.

[81]PL 16, 452; Browe (1938a), 9.

[82]PG 62, 29, *Eph. hom.* 3, 4.

complaints about the lack of participation in the Lord's meal. A prescription formulated by the provincial synod of Agde in 506 was repeatedly quoted until the high point of the Middle Ages, so that it almost took on the force of a general law: it uncoupled the duty to attend Mass on Sunday from the duty to receive communion, which had to be received at least at Christmas, Easter and Pentecost.[83]

The former monk of Lérins who presided over the synod, Bishop Caesarius of Arles, spoke with contempt of all the members of the congregation who left the church at the moment of communion.[84] In order to prevent this happening, in subsequent centuries measures were taken including, as already mentioned, having communion after Mass on busy feast days. And though it was not the intention,[85] a regulation of this sort had the effect of seeming to reduce the all-important communal component, the receiving of the Eucharistic gifts by the faithful, to a kind of appendage of the Mass.

Despite the prescription issued by Agde and renewed pressure in the Carolingian era for people to receive communion regularly, something strongly emphasised by Jonas of Orleans († 844) in his *Manual for the Laity*, the reductionist tendency could not be held back. People even took little notice of the new minimum, laid down in 1215. Almost everywhere complaints could be heard about the situation in the 13th and 14th centuries.[86]

There were many causes for what happened. It is not unjustified to assume that after its recognition in 313, the Christian faith drew more and more newcomers who became Christians in name but not in deed. And the influence of the Germanic peoples, who had not gone through a maturing process in their approach to Christianity, must have contributed to the growing number of fashion-followers and indifferent believers.[87] It is also remarkable that in the early Middle Ages the rot set in at its strongest in those regions where Arianism had to be combated: in the Grecian East and in the part of the West covered by the Gallic liturgy. In the struggle against these phenomena the deity of Christ was emphasised because it was precisely that which the Arians denied. In consequence the

---

[83]Mansi VIII, 327, can. 18: "Saeculares qui natale Domini, pascha et pentecostem non communicaverint, catholici non credantur, nec inter catholicos habeantur".

[84]CC SL 103, 307, sermo 73, 2.

[85]Browe (1931b), 760; Nussbaum (1979), 46.

[86]PL 106, 202-204: *De institutione laicali*; Browe (1929), 18.

[87]Browe (1932a), 5; (1938a), 133.

Eucharist was characterised as the 'awesome mystery' which, in the Gallic liturgy, created a gulf between the laity and the divine Eucharistic gifts, a gulf that could only be bridged by piety.[88]

The purification prescriptions involving both soul and body only served to increase this pious fear. Jerome († ca. 420) required the faithful to abstain from sexual intercourse for several days before receiving communion.[89] Caesarius of Arles († 542)[90] and the Bavarian synod of Riesback-Friesingen in 799 were no less demanding.[91] The synod of Chalons-sur-Saône in 813 required of the communicant extreme discretion, citing the biblical text: "For he that eateth and drinketh unworthily, eateth and drinketh damnation to himself" (I Cor.11:29). Purity of body and soul was a sine qua non, just as the priest Achimelech refused to give the hallowed bread to David unless his servants had not had any contact with women (1 Sam.21:4-5). The synod of Ingelheim in 826 also required three days of abstinence from sexual intercourse before communion.[92]

The awareness of impurity and its incompatibility with liturgical activities can be found in all cultures and is of pre-Christian origin. It is not unimaginable that some remnants of this were still to be found in the 'culture folklorique' when the Irish monks brought the Judaic way of thinking to continental Europe. Various prescriptions contained in the book of Leviticus, whether reinforced or watered down, had been implanted in Christianity and remained in force certainly until the 13th century.[93] Even involuntary ejaculation and menstruation were included under the same heading of bodily impurity.[94] The same applied particularly to masturbation, following which the offender was not even allowed to touch a reliquary. Alcuin († 804) puts the question, in a *speculum*, a checlist of questions drawn up for clerics and monks in

---

[88]Jungmann (1962), II, 450; Nussbaum (1969), 29-31.

[89]CSEL 54, 377, ep. 49, 15.

[90]CC SL 103, 195-200, sermo 44.

[91]MGH Conc. II, 52, c. 6; Mansi XIII, 1027: "Ut sanctum sacrificium sumere non tardent, sed ante aliquantos se dies ad hoc praeparare conentur, abstinentes a fornicatione nec non et licentia coniugali, ut dignos se exhibeant"; Nickl (1930), 58; Browe (1932b), 376.

[92]MGH Conc II, 283; 552; Browe (1938a), 19.

[93]Jungmann (1962), II, 451, n. 23; Vauchez (1975), 12; the rules laid down in the penitentials from the 6th to the 11th century have been quantified by Flandrin (1983), 32; Guyon (1985), 75-77.

[94]Martène (1788), III, c. 19 n. 11: "Infantibus vero et his quibus tale quid in nocte contigerit, minime dantur"; Browe (1934), 95-96; (1940), 89.

preparation for confession, as to whether the penitent may not have touched the sacred vessels, books or relics after a defilement.[95]

It is understandable that the fear of receiving communion unworthily had a grip on many.[96] In this connection it should be noted that the requirement to receive communion in a state of sobriety was strictly applied throughout the Middle Ages, so that the taverns refused to serve food or drink until after High Mass.[97]

Spiritual preparation before the 8th century consisted mainly of penance, alms and prayer. Advent and Lent in some measure guaranteed that this would be so. Confession was neither obligatory nor customary. Later the church began to insist on confession, especially by way of preparation for Easter communion, a requirement which - all unwittingly - threw up another barrier. Regino († 915), abbot of Prüm, and Burchard († 1025), bishop of Worms, insisted on confession during Lent.[98] In the Lateran prescription of 1215, previously alluded to, the Easter confession and communion were mentioned in one breath, failure to fulfil the prescription leaving the perpetrator liable to exclusion from church and church burial.[99] In the day-to-day practice of the faith, communion and confession rather than consecration and communion came to form a unity. Both sacraments had to be received in the parish church, a monopoly that the mendical orders were, as a general rule, unable to break. The penitent was given a little instruction in the faith, accompanied by warnings, during the confession.[100]

Parishes were, however, too large and understaffed, which led to superficiality in the care of souls. This problem was made worse in the late Middle Ages by the 'altarists',[101] who were mentally insufficiently equipped and, because of their poverty, socially inadequate for the care of

---

[95]PL 101, 499 ; "reliquias et s. codices et s. vasa indignus et sordide atque negligenter contrectavi?" ; this *speculum* was a checlist (used by the confessor), drawn up in question form of the sins committed most frequently and designed to help the penintent in his examination of conscience.

[96]Browe (1938a), 19; Leclercq (1962), 303.

[97]Browe (1931c), 281; Jungmann (1962), II, 454-455; Nussbaum (1979), 103: "wie bereits die Juden das Paschamahl als heilige Speise nicht vollem Magen geniessen durften".

[98]Browe (1932b), 375-397; (1940), 9; Devlin (1975), 144-146.

[99]See above, n. 79.

[100]Browe (1929b), 484 sqq.; 503 sqq.; (1932b), 394; Meyer (1965), 349; Michaud-Quantin (1971), 168-170: at the beginning of the confession the *proprius sacerdos* made sure that the penitent knew the Our Father, the Hail Mary and the Creed.

[101]This is the name given to priests, operating mainly in the towns, whose task was to celebrate the Mass and recite the Office daily. (LW I, 125-126).

souls. A further material circumstance working against frequent communion was that of the offerings brought to church. When unleavened bread replaced leavened, the offerings served only to maintain the poor and the priests. To the extent that they were obligatory, they constituted an obstacle to no few of the faithful. The reverence for Christ's sufferings, the flood of relics from the East following the Crusades, the cult surrounding them and the innumerable sacramentals also took on the character of replacements for the Eucharist and clouded men's view of communion. From the 11th-12th century the new forms of Eucharistic devotion - to be discussed later - were just as harmful to the practice of communion since they tended rather to replace it. Moreover individual devotion to the person of Christ required a personal encounter with the Saviour, whose coming demanded an ascetic preparation. Excessive communion could only be harmful.[102] In the later Middle Ages Gerard Zerbolt of Zutphen († 1398), member of the movement of reform, *Devotio Moderna*, reckoned that thousands of years of preparation and all the aid of the saints would still not be sufficient for a worthy preparation.[103]

The clericalisation of the celebration of the Eucharist constituted an obstacle to participation on the part of the people. The priest functioned in the name of the people and also received communion in the name of the people.[104] The celebration of the Mass had become a *mysterium depopulatum* and the Eucharist itself a *mysterium tremendum*.[105] The people were outwardly forced into the role of passive spectators of the awesome happening and found an answer to this new situation in the

---

[102]Browe (1938a), 134-138; 141-144; 148; 154, 157.

[103]ed. Woude v.d (1951), *Over de hervorming van de krachten der ziel*, 67: "Bedenk, indien gij u gedurende duizenden jaren tot dit sacrament hadt voorbereid door reine gebeden en allerheiligste meditaties, dit nog niets zou betekenen voor een waardig ontvangen. Ook als gij alle verdiensten van de heiligen zoudt bezitten" (Reflect on this: that had you prepared yourself for thousands of years with pure prayers and the holiest of meditations for the reception of this sacrament, all of that would mean nothing for a worthy reception. Even if you had performed all the services of the saints).

[104]Brandt (1924), 233; Jungmann (1962), II, 452-453; Kidd (1958), 40; Meyer (1965), 304.

[105]Mayer (1926), 93; Nussbaum (1979), 120. This transformation, based only on observable facts, seems too absolute and too negative. See: Lukken (1990), 30: "Maintenant il est possible de discuter cette transformation non seulement d'une façon négative, à savoir que le peuple n'est plus sujet de faire, mais aussi d'une façon positive: le peuple devient destinataire ou destinateur/destinataire ou actant observateur, selon le point de vue que l'on adopte. Bien qu'il n'y ait pas d'unanimité dans ce domaine d'études, il faut dire que la sémiotique peut nuancer le parler quelque peu simpliste dans la littérature liturgique courante".

adoration of the Host, really transformed into the body of Christ during the consecration of the offerings.

In the explanation of the Mass of Isidore of Seville († 636) the consecration was taken to include the whole of the Canon,[106] but from the 9th to the 11th century it gradually came to be limited to one moment, the uttering of the words of consecration.[107] This change occurred under the influence of the theological dispute regarding Christ's presence and its resolution by the adoption of a mainly realistic approach.

The emphasis laid on Christ's actual presence caused a new 'elevatio' to come into being in the course of the 12th century in addition to the existing raising up of the bread and chalice at the doxology that closes the Canon. This 'elevatio' - raising the Host and, later, the chalice - with both hands during the Consecration went back to the Jewish table ritual, where the bread and wine are taken up in a solemn gesture. In the liturgy the gesture took on a new significance, the underlining of Christ's words, "Who, the day before he suffered, took bread into his sacred hands".[108] In the East the gesture is reported as having this significance from the 4th century and in the West intermittently from the 9th century. In the 12th century the Host was raised increasingly higher and for an ever-longer period as a symbol of Christ raised on the cross.[109] Moreover the generally increasing desire on the part of the people to see the sacred species was a further cause. The awareness of Christ's presence was intensified by the solemn upward gaze directed at the Host, a precursor of the end of a Christian life: to see God himself.[110] It was also a form of protest against the doctrines of Berengarius and the Albigensian heresy. Some reports, including that of Hildebert, archbishop of Tours († 1134), show that the words that wrought the change[111] were sometimes pronounced during the 'elevatio'.[112]

The synodal statutes of Paris (1205-1208) drawn up by bishop Eudes of Sully († 1208) set the time of the 'elevatio' precisely in order to

---

[106]PL 83, 752, *De eccles. offic.* 1, 15.

[107]Geiselmann (1933), 87-118 and passim; Jungmann (1941), 120 sqq.; (1962) II, 127 sqq.

[108]Browe (1933), 46-48; Jungmann (1943).

[109]Meyer (1963), 162-163; Nussbaum (1979), 127.

[110]Dumoutet (1924); Macquarrie (1972), 97.

[111]*hoc est enim corpus meum, hic est enim calix sanguinis mei.*

[112]PL 171, 1186, *Carmen de officio missae*: "Panis in hoc verbo, sed adhuc communis ab ara sumitur et sumptum tollit utraque manu. Nec prius in mensam demittit quam tua, Christe, verba repraesentans explicet ista super"; Browe (1933), 30, n. 22.

ensure that those present did not adore an unconsecrated Host. The 'elevatio' was not permitted until the words of consecration had been pronounced over the bread. In laying down this prescription the synod implicitly took sides in a new debate that had broken out after the second Eucharistic dispute: was Christ only present after consecration of both bread and wine or immediately after the words "This is my body"?[113] The synod opted for the latter opinion: the 'elevatio' of the Host was the explicit sign that the consecration had taken place and the adoration was indeed directed towards the body of Christ. The synod further instructed the priest to raise the Host sufficiently high that the faithful - to whom the priest's back was turned - could see the Host clearly.[114]

The instruction fulfilled a need. Fifteen years later the 'elevatio' had become the indispensable high point of the Mass, characteristic of the desire to practise Eucharistic devotion, which had come to occupy a special place in the spirituality of the Cistercians and Franciscans.[115] The speed at which the devotion spread is comparable to the rate at which altars were turned around in Catholic churches following the Second Vatican Council.[116] The many forms of devotion centred on the Host and which came into being around 1200 remain typical of the reverence accorded to the Eucharist until *the end of conventional Christianity*.[117]

Whereas up to the 12th century the obeisances made by the priest had been mainly directed towards the altar and its relics, from the turn of the 13th century he bowed before the consecrated bread before raising it for all to see. In the 14th century genuflection was added before and after the 'elevatio'. The faithful in the body of the church had long before been instructed to show this sign of reverence. They sank to their knees at the ringing of the bell, which was usually attached to the wall of the sanctuary.[118] When the Host was only raised chest high the bell served to focus the attention of those present on the happening which, for them,

---

[113]Kennedy (1944); Quirin (1952); Nussbaum (1979), 131; Mitchell (1982), 151-163.

[114]ed. Pontal (1971), 82: "Precipitur presbyteris ut, cum in canone misse inciperint *Qui pridie*, tenentes hostiam, ne elevent eam statim nimis alte, ita quod possit videri a populo, sed quasi ante pectus detineant donec dixerint *Hoc est corpus meum*, et tunc elevent eam ita quod possit ab omnibus videri"; Mansi XXII, 682; Rubin (1991), 55 n. 251; Caspers (1992), 22.

[115]Browe (1933), 28, 37; Nussbaum (1979), 122.

[116]Smits (1965), 86, n. 18.

[117]Pol v.d (1967), *Het einde van het conventionele Christendom*, 332.

[118]Browe (1929c), 43-50; Meyer (1963), 167, 169; Jungmann (1962), II, 262, n. 51; the altar bell dates from the 15th/16th century; Nussbaum (1979), 132.

was invisible.[119] From the 13th century it was a signal calling the people to adoration, including those in the surrounding neighbourhood. In the second half of the 13th century the bell in the church tower was sounded for their benefit. They could then bow their heads or genuflect during their work and share in thought the sacred moment or even make their way to the church. This was the reason for the ringing of the bell at the *Sanctus*. In mid-15th-century Koblenz the sexton announced the approaching Consecration at an even earlier moment - at the Gospel.[120]

The *Sanctus* candle had the same warning effect as the bell, even though it was originally a practical measure. In the early morning darkness the altar server provided light for the celebrant so that the Host could at least be seen.[121] Both the number and the duration grew: the single candle became a whole 'row of wax', burning around the altar from *Sanctus* to Communion. In the later Middle Ages the polyphonic singing of the *Sanctus* prepared the Consecration and 'elevatio', while the *Benedictus* closed the Canon, its words thereby taking on the power of reality: "Blessed is he that cometh in the name of the Lord".[122]

The efforts made to ensure that the Host was as visible as possible led to excesses. The priest was tempted to hold the Host on high for a time and turn to right and to left. When genuflecting after the 'elevatio', a gesture that began to become fashionable here and there at the end of the 14th century, he deliberately gave those present the opportunity of seeing the Host three times. The 'small elevatio' during the doxology of the Canon sometimes literally got on top of the celebrant[123] and the Dominicans held on high the two halves of the broken Host above the chalice for the faithful to adore from the *Agnus Dei* to the Communion, an example copied by the secular clergy of the Rhineland at the end of the 14th century.[124]

---

[119]Quirin (1952), 15, 22.

[120]Browe (1929c), 39; Meyer (1963), 167, 175, 264.

[121]DACL III, 1057; Jungmann (1962), II, 261, n. 45, 176, n. 14; Meyer (1963), 167-168.

[122]Browe (1929c), 40-43; Meyer (1963), 171, 185, n. 64; Jungmann (1962), II, 164, 172, 269; Nussbaum (1979), 133.

[123]Franz (1902), 104, 176; Browe (1929c), 49; (1933), 63-64; Meyer (1963), 170, 190; Nussbaum (1979), 133.

[124]Marténe (1788), I, c. 4. a. 9 n. 4: "Datum est ordini nostro, ut in missa post *Agnus Dei* ante communionem tenerent fratres hostiam elevatam super calicem, ut sic adoretur ab universo populo (...) et ne deponeretur usque ad communionem"; Quirin (1952), 124.

Attempts to put a stop to such practices met with varied success. They were symptomatic of the Eucharistic desire and 'revival'.[125] Indeed, from the 13th century in various dioceses 'elevatio' indulgences were granted. In a 14th-century letter of indulgence for an unnamed Dutch convent of nuns the ejaculation: "Jesus, Son of the living God, protect me" was granted 40 days indulgence.[126]

At the end of the 13th century, in order not to obstruct the congregation's view of the Host, a start was made on pulling back the side curtains of the altar, which had been intended to ensure that the Canon should proceed without being disturbed by extraneous noise. The Carthusians and the Celestines even opened the choir screens. In 1312 the Carmelites instructed the incense-bearers to ensure that the Host did not disappear behind the sweet-scented clouds of smoke. At the beginning of the 16th century in Spain, England and France it became the custom to hang a black or purple curtain behind the altar so that the white Host would stand out more sharply.[127]

All these provisions were inspired by the desire to see the Host, to which end every opportunity was seized. During her illness Oringa of Tuscany († 1310) had herself carried to the chapel for that very purpose. After the 'elevatio' the Viennese beguine, Agnes Blambeckin († 1315), sought a place in the church from where she could still see the Host. Geert Grote († 1384) prayed at the Friars Minor church in Deventer before a small window through which he could see the 'elevatio' in the adjacent church without being disturbed and Dorothy of Montau († 1394) could not have satisfied her desire to see the Host if she had managed to do so a hundred times a day.[128]

In the personal eye contact with the Host and through the inner ejaculatory prayers the people were expressing their deepest faith in Christ as Majesty, but also as Christ made flesh, the crucified God. Such prayers as the *Ave verum corpus Christi*, the *Ave salve caro Dei* and the *Ave sacer Christi sanguis* were very popular in the church books and missals of the later Middle Ages. Believers who did not know these prayers were recommended to say the Lord's Prayer and the Hail Mary five times each, in commemoration of the five wounds of Christ. The

[125]Mens (1946), 157.

[126]i.e. as much from punishment for sin as if 40 days of penance had been performed; Verdam (1902), 120 ; Browe (1933), 170; Quirin (1952), 73-75; Nussbaum (1979), 134.

[127]Browe (1933), 56; Quirin (1952), 87-88; Jungmann (1962), II, 260, n. 44; Meyer (1963), 176-177; Nussbaum (179), 133-135.

[128]Meyer (1963), 190 sqq.

faithful also joined in with singing: the *Ave verum*, the *Adoro te* or the *O salutaris Hostia* were among the hymns sung between *Sanctus* and *Benedictus*.[129] "Many prayers were heard at the sight of the body of the Lord and rich treasures of mercy were granted", wrote William of Auxerre († 1231) around 1200. Alexander of Hales († 1245) thought along the same lines.[130] The adoration of the Host was thus a personal encounter with Jesus in his sacrament and over the years ended up by almost completely replacing sacramental communion. The theological tracts, other writings and sermons emphatically encouraged the faithful of the late medieval period to practise the *manducatio spiritualis* or spiritual communion. The awe of the "Holy of Holies" already referred to, as well as the many limiting prescriptions regarding sobriety and abstention, combined with the preaching, must have created the situation in which this *manducatio* gained, in Eucharistic piety, the 'status' of a form of communion 'equal in value'. The dying no longer able to receive communion sacramentally were shown the Host as a final consolation so that they could now unite themselves with Christ.[131]

Hosts, it was said, gave out light or changed into the child Jesus. These miracles were a response the divine gift of the Eucharist, particularly in the circles of Cistercians and Beguines, where such visions were repeatedly witnessed in the 13th and 14th centuries.[132]

Sometimes the elevated Host was seen as an real *ex opere operato*, event[133] described in the *Instructions for parish priests* written by John Mirk towards the end of the 14th century. The sight of the Host was not only credited with spiritual benefits but also with physical good. Someone who had been present at the 'elevatio' could be sure that they were guarded for the rest of the day against fire, blindness, infectious disease or sudden death,[134] which parallels the insurance said to be offered by such objects as relics or an image of St. Christopher.[135]

In the late medieval period the tendency arose to regard the 'elevatio' as a substitute for the whole of the Mass. People would slip into

---

[129]Browe (1929c), 55; Meyer (1963), 178-187; (1965), 272.

[130]ed. Pigouchet (1964), 261: "Multorum petitiones exaudiuntur in ipsa visione Corporis Christi: unde multis infunditur gratia"; Nussbaum (1979), 130.

[131]Browe (1933), 58; Caspers (1992), esp. 213-230, 267.

[132]Browe (1938), 104-111; Rode (1957).

[133]Browe (1929c), 59.

[134]ed. Kristensson (1974), 85; Nussbaum (1979), 137.

[135]Oakley (1979), 119.

church when they heard the bell ringing and only to walk out again
immediately after the 'elevatio'. It is not without reason that there were
complaints about townsfolk going from church to church in order to see
the 'elevatio' again and again.[136] People under interdict were not above
drilling a hole in the church door in order to be able to witness the
'elevatio'. Even the animals were not allowed the miss the event: in
Gaishofen on the Danube and in the surrounding district the horses were
allowed to participate in the feast of the popular St. Leonard by sticking
their heads through a round hole in the outer wall, or else the horses were
ridden into the church through doors specially designed to accommodate
them.[137]

The 'process of independence' of the elevated Host within the context of
the Mass was given shape around 1300 in various new and long-lasting
forms of reverence outside the Mass, forms which lasted until the 1960s:
visits to the Blessed Sacrament, procession of the Blessed Sacrament,
exposition of and blessing with the 'Holy of Holies'.

    Visits to the Blessed Sacrament, kept on or close to the altar, were
adopted on a wide scale from the 14th century by the secular clergy and
the religious orders. To the extent that locked church doors made this sort
of devotion impossible for the laity, they indulged in the practice only
sporadically from the 15th century onwards until it became generalised
towards the end of the Middle Ages.[138] The lamps which used to burn
at the martyr's graveside and which were lit in honour of the saints and
the deceased were now transformed into the sanctuary lamp, burning in a
sacred silence. Its use was sparse in the 11th century, more frequent after
that and practically general in the monastery and collegiate churches after
the 14th century. The reverence paid to the altar, directed towards the
saints and their relics, now turned into reverence paid to the tabernacle,
concentrating on the sacred Host, which had pushed the relics into the
background.[139]

    The main driving force behind this new piety originated in the
desire to show reverence at the 'elevatio' and to give due credence to the
miracles. But a further factor which cannot be ignored is the introduction,
in 1246 by Robert of Turotte, bishop of Liège, of the feast of Corpus

---

[136]Browe (1929c), 65; Meyer (1963), 192; Nussbaum (1979), 137.

[137]Nussbaum (1979), l.c.; Rothkrug (1979),30; (1980), 65-66.

[138]Browe (1933), 23; Delaruelle (1975), 405.

[139]Mitchell (1982), 170; Geary (1978), 29.

Christi. It was brought in at the instigation of Juliana van Cornillon († 1258), representative of a group of pious women, who did not keep her reverence "under a bushel".[140] The feast was intended as a special mark of reverence towards the institution of the Eucharist, which received too little attention on Maunday Thursday. In 1264 the former cardinal-legate of Liège, Pope Urban IV, placed the feast officially in the church's calendar.[141] It was slow in gaining popularity because of the tensions between supporters and opponents, or "between the more common-sense and the more emotional approach to faith". Moreover the mainly secular opponents were perhaps suspicious of the major influence of the laity, and certainly of that of women, whose mystical tendencies were regarded as too "fanatical and too populist".[142] The feast was first introduced in the former German Empire and it was not until the second decade of the 14th century that it began to gain ground rapidly in England, Scandinavia and the Romance countries.[143]

At the same time the procession of the Blessed Sacrament, originally not part of the feast day itself, began to achieve greater popularity. The lengthy hesitation in adopting the practice would seem to be related to the shockingly high costs involved. So it was that the procession did not reach full glory until some time around the 16th century, not only on the feast day of Corpus Christi but also on its octave and on other days of prayer, penance and thanksgiving. In addition to the problem of money, the resistance encountered by introduction of the feast also played a role - as did the objection to carrying the exposed Host around for so long. Besides one was afraid of blunting of veneration by the people seeing the Host too frequently.[144] On the other hand, people were used to major feasts and saints' days thanks to the centuries-old practice of carrying the reliquaries in procession, housed since the 13th century in *ostensoria*. In line with this tradition the procession of the Blessed Sacrament was introduced on the feast day - and in addition there were several long-standing precedents: the solemn procession of the

---

[140]Wegman (1986), 45.

[141]Browe (1933), 70; Stemmler (1970), 174-175; LW II, 2494.

[142]Wegman (1986), 46.

[143]Browe (1928a), 130, 137, 143; Stemmler (1970), 172-173; Caspers (1992), 42-44; 62-66.

[144]Schannat Hartzheim, V, 408 (Council of Mainz in 1451): "Propter reverentiam Divinissimo Eucharistie exhibendam et ne populi fidelis devotio ex frequenti eius visione tepescat"; Nussbaum (1979), 158-159; Browe (1933), 91 sqq.; Martimort (1984), 267-268.

Sacrament to the sick or dying, the Palm Sunday procession and its transfer to the holy sepulchre in Holy Week.

The introduction of the procession on the feast of Corpus Christi led to 'exposition', a kind of static 'elevatio', consisting of placing the Eucharistic bread on or above the altar, either invisible in a *ciborium* covered with a *velum* or visible in a re-built reliquary-ostensory (the forerunner of the monstrance), for the purposes of adoration and meditation. After the procession a Mass was celebrated during which the *ciborium* or *ostensorium* was left standing on the altar. The practice was later recalled in the 'Mass with exposition', celebrated on major feast days at the high altar and usually on Thursdays at a side altar with the celebration of a votive Mass.[145] Such Masses, with the exposed Sacrament torn free from its liturgical context, were introduced in the north of Germany and in Hungary from the 14th century and in other places from the 15th century.[146]

Exposition of this kind could also take place completely separate from the Mass, a form which developed from the feast of Corpus Christi. In churches where the divine Office was sung, the 'bread of angels' was placed on the high altar at the beginning of the morning Office in honour of this feast and it was left there the whole day during the singing of the Office. In order to meet the demands of the people with regard to the reverencing of the Host, the separate hours of the Office were extended to honorific sacramental feasts. The faithful sang hymns to the Blessed Sacrament - such as *Ecce panis angelorum* - antiphons[147] and responsories[148] that they were accustomed to sing before and after the Mass with exposition celebrated on Thursdays. It was not long before the practice was extended to cover the entire octave, a development which started in Germany in the 14th century and became general from the 15th.

Subsequently such services in honour of the Blessed Sacrament were introduced outside the octave of the feast. This happened in the 14th century, again at first in the Germanic lands. A century later the evening services in honour of the Blessed Sacrament were a familiar phenomenon.

---

[145]i.e. a Mass celebrated outside the context of the ecclesiastical calendar for the intentions of the donor of the *stipendium* (LW II, 2878).

[146]Browe (1933), 141-147; Nussbaum (1979), 162.

[147]i.e. a versicle with its own melody following a psalm; it expresses an essential idea (LW I, 169).

[148]i.e. part of the Divine Office that matches up with the readings and the capitula (LW II, 2398).

In other countries development was slower and did not come to full flower until during the Counter-reformation.[149]

In 1435 the Premonstratensians demonstrated the enormous value attached to exposition of the Eucharist. From the archbishop of Trier they obtained the privilege of introducing the practice on days when the Mass was not celebrated. The 'perpetual adoration' or year-long exposition was the crown on the increased 'process of independance of the Eucharist'. And of course this gave further impetus to the practice of visits to the Blessed Sacrament.[150]

The custom known as Quarant'Ore - forty continuous hours of exposition of the Blessed Sacrament for reverence and prayer - came into being not in the Middle Ages but in the 16th century. It fitted well with the medieval tradition of forty hours of wake at the holy sepulchre, which had been on the increase since the 10th century as a dramatisation of the events of Holy Week. In a sermon preached in the Church of the Holy Sepulchre in Milan in 1527, Gian Antonio Belotti encouraged his listeners to spend forty hours in prayer before the Blessed Sacrament at the end of Lent. He established a fraternity in order to repeat this four times annually. In 1529 the cathedral of Milan adopted the practice and in 1537 it became the custom for all the city's churches to take turns so that the adoration would be perpetual. Subsequently the 'Forty Hours' devotion was spread throughout Italy by the Capuchins and throughout Germany by the Jesuits, following which it became general practice throughout Europe around 1600.[151]

A fourth type of the 'process of independence of the Eucharist' outside the Mass has been mentioned: blessing with the Holy of Holies. This too grew out of the procession of the Blessed Sacrament and was first reported in the 14th century during a procession in Hildesheim, after which it appears more frequently in 15th-century sources. In all likelihood the practice was already being followed occasionally in the course of the 15th century during the evening services dedicated to the Virgin Mary. This latter type of service had come into being in Italy in the 13th century and under the name of *Hail* or *Salve* - the first word of the hymn to Mary entitled *Salve Regina* - spread throughout Europe.[152] At the beginning of

---

[149]Nussbaum (1979), 162-163.

[150]ibid. 163.

[151]Jungmann (1952); Nussbaum (1979), 164-166; Mitchell (1982), 311-318.

[152]Mitchell (1982), 182.

the 15th century, in the presence of the Corpus Christi fraternity,[153] the Dominicans of Hamburg gave an undertaking that they would not practice the blessing with the Holy of Holies during the Salve. They agreed that every Sunday evening during the procession after Compline[154] they would place the statue of Mary, donated by the fraternity, on the altar and, after singing the *Salve Regina*, would bless the faithful while the bell rang three times.[155]

However nothing is mentioned about blessing with the Blessed Sacrament during this service dedicated to Mary, although exposition had been practised during the *Salve* since the 14th century. Once the blessing had become a fixed component of the procession of the Blessed Sacrament, it eventually became an integral part of the *Salve*, later to be known as 'Benediction' or blessing.

---

[153]Dossat (1976).

[154]i.e. the Church's evening prayer (TW I, 443).

[155]Browe (1933), 158.

CHAPTER THREE

PARALLEL APPLICATIONS IN CONCRETE USE

Before the presence of Christ under the Eucharistic appearances had been emphasised by the clericalisation of the liturgy in Carolingian times, a tendency expressed in such phenomena as the secret recitation of the Canon, the gulf between Eucharistic bread and relics was less wide in spiritual acceptance. Both bread and relics were, as it were, 'applied in parallel'. They were both used to provide protection in this vulnerable existence: at home, on journeys and even in the grave. And when the gulf widened, they both still continued to be used for the same ends. However the Eucharist would seem to have gained some 'weight' and, when the two were used together, would appear to have been intended to reinforce the power of the relics, as during the *clamor* and in the placing in the *sepulcrum* of the altar. In the latter case the Eucharist could even replace the relics, just as in the communion test, which was applied to priests in place of the oath on the relics.

We characterise this similarity of use as 'parallel application'. This applies here when both the Eucharistic gifts and the relics are used in a similar manner for the same end, simultaneously or separately, or when they can replace one another.

In ancient Christian times and during the early Middle Ages the attitude shown towards both Eucharistic forms, bread and wine, was simple, almost sober. An illustration of the simplicity of the attitude towards the Eucharistic bread is the practice of the *fermentum*, mentioned at the beginning of the previous chapter. The pope had these particles of bread carried by acolytes to the priests of the titular churches in Rome as a sign of unity with his celebration. The acolytes were present during the Mass he celebrated and when the bread was broken after the consecration they took part of it on the corporal.[1]

The first reports of this usage date from as early as the 2nd century. However a really clear description was not given until a later date, to be found in a letter written in 416 by Innocent I to bishop Decentius of Gubbio, where the pope counsels Decentius not to send the *fermentum* to members of the community outside the city, since this

---

[1]Jungmann (1952a); Nussbaum (1979), 179-185.

would mean that the Eucharist would have to be borne over an excessive distance.[2] A few years previous to this the Council of Laodicea had put an end to the sending of Eucharistic bread from bishop to bishop, a usage that had become common in the East and, again because of the distances involved, was not considered suitable for the Sacrament.[3] From that date, the Eucharistic bread was usually replaced by *eulogia*.[4] In Rome itself the *fermentum* was still used as a common sign of *communio* or "community" in the 6th century. Later the practice became steadily more limited to the major feasts, to end finally with it being confined to the Easter vigil. The *Ordo of Saint-Amand* reports that on that evening every parish priest sent his *mansionarius* to the basilica of St. John Lateran to receive a particle of the Eucharistic bread. He brought it straight back to the celebrant who placed it in the chalice to the accompaniment of a prayer for peace.[5] The practice of distributing the *fermentum*, which also occurred in other Italian towns, continued in Rome until the 9th century.[6]

In the mid-8th century this expression of unity was added to the episcopal ordination ceremony. The pope gave the newly-ordained bishop a large consecrated Host, which the latter was required to consume over a forty-day period together with bread he himself had consecrated. The custom spread throughout the West, though not on a large scale, from the 10th century, only to disappear in the 13th century when concelebration became the norm at the Mass of ordination.[7]

At the end of the 8th century the ritual would appear to have been introduced into the ceremony of priestly ordination, according to the *Ordo of Saint-Amand*, and not just in Rome. In the Frankish empire the sending of the *fermentum* from the principal church to the other parish churches had scarcely any or no sense at all because of the smallness of the towns and their scarcity. And yet the practice was regarded as very desirable, more because of the sacramental, individual power with which it was

---

[2]PL 20, 556 sqq., ep. 25, 5; Häussling (1973), 186, n. 51.

[3]Mansi II, 566, can. 14.

[4]Nussbaum (1979), 179 sqq.

[5]Andrieu (1931-61), III, 474, ordo 30 B, 65: "Et transmittit unusquisque presbiter mansionarium de titulo suo ad ecclesiam Salvatoris et expectant ibi usquedum frangitur Sancta, habentes secum corporales. Et venit oblationarius subdiaconus et dat eis Sancta, quod pontifex consecravit, et recipiunt ea in corporales et revertitur unusquisque ad titulum suum et tradit Sancta presbitero. Et de ipsa facit crucem super calicem et ponit in eo et dicit: *Dominus vobiscum*. Et communicant omnes".

[6]Corblet (1886), I, 525-526; Häussling (1973), 185-186. Nussbaum (1979), 180-182.

[7]Nussbaum (1979), 183; concelebration is a Mass celebrated by two or more priests simultaneously.

endowed than because of a bond of unity with the consecrator. However the number of days on which the priests were allowed to reserve consecrated bread at home as 'power-giving bread'[8] was slowly reduced. Around the year 900 it was reduced to eight. Bishop Fulbert of Chartres († 1018) regarded two days as more than sufficient, in order to avoid negligence. For him it had totally lost its symbolism of unity, since he made an allegorical comparison between the former forty days with the forty days that Christ remained on earth after His resurrection.[9] The 13th century thus brought to a close this way of treating the consecrated bread.

Analogous to the episcopal and priestly ordination, the *fermentum* was introduced into the ceremony of consecration of virgins, the first witness to this being the 9th-century *Pontificale of Angers*.[10] In this consecration too the *fermentum* was emphasised as extra sacramental strength in accepting the new style of life. It was used in this significance particularly in France, and very frequently from the 10th to the 13th century, and even sporadically until the 15th.[11]

A further symptom of this easy relationship with the Host was the mixing of ink with the sacred Blood when signing an official document. At the tomb of St. Peter, Pope Theodore I († 649), for instance, signed the excommunication of Pyrrhus and his followers, after the patriarch's return to monotheletism[12], using a pen which was dipped into ink to which a few drops of consecrated wine had been added.[13] The condemnation of patriarch Photius and his disciples at the Council of Constantinople in 870 was, according to the biographer of St. Athanasius, signed in the same way: "The bishops signed his dismissal after dipping their pen not only in ordinary ink but also in the blood of the Saviour

---

[8]ibid. 184 and 290: *firmata oblata*.

[9]PL 141, 194, ep. 3: "Haec ergo occasione accepta quaerendum ab episcopo aestimavi, si videretur sibi salva ordinis religione sanctificatum panem primo aut secundo sanctificationis die posse totum simul percipere, quem videbat non sine periculo posse tanto tractu temporis minutatim sumere".

[10]Leroquais (1937), 30: "Iterum accipiens caeras et stans inclinata usquedum finiatur missa, et communicet et reservet de ipsa communione unde in diem octavum communicet".

[11]Nussbaum (1979), 185; King (1965), 15.

[12]i.e. the doctrine that states that there was only one will in Christ, namely the will of the Logos (TW 2513, 3346-3348).

[13]ed. Boor de (1883-85), *Theophanis Chronographia* , I, 331; II, 207: "quo papa comperto Theodorus, plenitudine convocata ecclesiae, ad sepulcrum verticis apostolorum accessit et divino calice postulato ex vivico sanguine atramento stillavit et ita propria manu depositionem Pyrrhi et ei communicantium"; ed. Goar-Combefis (1665), 275: ["Theodorus papa (...) ad Coryphaei apostolorum sepulchrum astans, calice afferri iusso, ex vivifico Christi sanguine stillam in atramentum immiscens, Pyrrhi (...) condemnationem propria manu exaravit"].

himself".[14] In both examples the use of the consecrated wine imparted to the signature the nature of an oath, something that will also be seen in the taking of oaths.

A familiar treatment of the Eucharist such as this made it suitable for private usages, such as 'reservation at home', 'taking it on a journey' and 'succour at death and burial'. Relics were treated in a similar way, so that we can speak of 'parallel application'. After these three subjects, we turn to the matter of oaths, always taken on *res sacrae*, sacred objects. After the oath we will deal with the calling on God and the saints for their intercession during the *humiliatio* and the *clamor*. Then follows the closing up in the altar stone of relics and particles of the Host, a subject already alluded to in the two previous chapters. This cementing up in the altar on the occasion of the consecration of a church was no longer in the private sphere, just like oath-taking and the cry for intercession, but in the community involved. The close correlation between relics and Eucharist on and around the altar table closes this chapter, a correlation expressed in the similarity of nomenclature of relic holders and sacred vessels and in the fact that relics and Eucharist were safeguarded in the same place, something that encouraged the transposition of forms of reverence.

The use of the Eucharist in a manner analogous to the way relics were retreated was not without its opponents, though not all usages were objected to simultaneously. The earliest forms were the first to be criticised. Around the 5th century opposition arose to the reservation of the Eucharist in people's homes, since after cessation of the persecutions the practice was no longer necessary and the Eucharist was kept for ends other than consumption. About the same time the placing of the Eucharist in a grave was also subjected to criticism, encouraged by the fact that it was not even possible for the dead to consume the Eucharist.

It was only later that opposition arose to the taking of oaths on the Eucharist and the cementing up of particles of the Host in the altar. The former practice began to be criticised around the 11th century and the latter from the 12th. Both practices were regarded as being out of tune with the significance of the sacrament. The 13th-century criticism of the customs surrounding the calling for God's intercession arose not from the way the Eucharist was treated but from the *humiliatio* of the relics. This disappeared, while the *clamor* was maintained.

---

[14]Mansi XVI, Constantinopolitanum IV, 263: "Subscripsere (episcopi) depositioni, calamis, non nudo atramento, sed, in quo penitus contremiscas (ut eos qui rem norant asservantes audivi), ipso Salvatoris sanguine tinctis".

Around the 13th century - a period when Eucharistic devotion, even outside the Mass, blossomed as never before - 'parallel application' of relics and Eucharist had largely disappeared. To the extent it was maintained after this period it almost exclusively concerned the relics. A 'new' form of usage came into being in the 11th-12th centuries, when the Eucharist was endowed with a 'similar miraculous power', previously credited almost exclusively to the saints and their relics. The application of this miraculous power continued into the later Middle Ages and is discussed in chapter V.

1   RESERVATION IN THE HOME

Both Eucharist and relics were kept in people's homes in Christian antiquity and in the Early Middle Ages. There they were in the immediate and day-to-day environment of the inhabitants.

We have already seen how, in the *Apologia* of Justinus Martyr[15], the Eucharist is reported as being taken to those not present at the celebration. Such a report does not necessarily imply the practice of communion in the home. Because of the familiarity of various authors with this practice at the beginning of the 3rd century, it can safely be concluded that it was rule rather than exception in the last quarter of the 2nd century.[16]

Various reasons were behind the birth of this custom. In the first place, it accorded with an existing non-Christian custom of taking home the remains of a sacrificial meal.[17] Moreover communion at home made it possible for the faithful to receive the Eucharist on days when there was no celebration of the Last Supper. An additional important factor was the strengthening powers which people derived from the Eucharist in times of persecution or more general types of mortal danger.[18] Hippolytus († 235) even regarded these powers as apotropaic.[19] It was partly because of this that the Eucharist was kept at home. It was customary to

---

[15]See p. 32 and p. 44.

[16]Nussbaum (1979), 275-276.

[17]Dölger (1929-50), V, 242-247.

[18]Nussbaum (1979), 276-277.

[19]SC 11 bis, 118, *Traditio Apostolica*, 36: "Si enim ex fide percipit, etiamsi mortale quodcumque datum illi fuerit, post hoc non potest eum nocere"; Dölger (1922), II, 569-571.

reserve the Eucharist in the sleeping area where the relics, too, were given a place of honour.

When the growing number of smaller communities provided greater opportunity to receive communion on the one hand and, on the other, the frequency of communion fell, this put a stop to communion in the home. And yet this was not the only reason: from the 5th century onwards there were voices increasingly raised against carelessness, lack of reverence and magical usage. From that time communion in the home for lay people gradually fell into disuse. Until the 9th century priests continued to reserve the Eucharist in their domiciles as *viaticum*[20] and as *firmata oblata* after the Mass of consecration discussed above.[21]

Home relics or private relics were hardly discussed in the West until the 10th century. In the 11th century the 'Gregorian movement' forced back the worldly influence within the church, which was beginning to centralise, and thus began to question the legitimacy of possession of relics by lay persons, a phenomenon that only increased in the 11th and 12th centuries because of the Crusades.[22] When the discussion first arose, it did not put an end to gifts and legacies by private individuals but it did raise some questions. It began to be realised that relics really belong in church.

This slight change in opinion grew in strength in the theological works of the 13th century and the papal prescriptions of the 14th century. Geoffrey of Trani († 1245)[23] and the well-known glosser of Bologna, Accursius († 1263)[24] excluded lay people from possession of relics. The latter regarded churches and consecrated places as alone worthy to contain relics. The same opinion was expressed by the canonist, Nicolo de

---

[20] i.e. communion administered to someone in danger of death (LW II, 2810).

[21] Nussbaum (1979), 277-282, 288-291.

[22] Sigal (1985), 42; Hermann-Mascard (1975), 315 e.v.: "La propriété des reliques et ses limitations"; the objections raised from the 11th century onwards were nothing new; on p. 321 she quotes two early texts against the private possession of relics: one from an Arabic collection of canons from Nicaea (325) and a letter written by Pope Leo I († 474). The first was unknown in the West before the 16th century and cannot have had any influence, she notes. The same applies to the second since it was never published. However they do indicate some early resistance. She could also have mentioned the Canones Epaonenses of 517 in which the same objections (raised in vain) are voiced. According to c. 25 the relics may not be placed in the *oratoria* of the villae if there are no priests in the immediate vicinity to pray the psalms on a regular basis. MGH AA VI-2, 171, *Aviti appendix*, XXV: "Sanctorum reliquiae in oratoriis villaribus non ponantur, nisi forsitan clericos cuiuscumque parrociae vicinos esse contingat, qui sacris cineribus psallendi frequentia famulentur. Quodsi illi defuerint, non ante proprie ordinentur, quam eis conpetens victus et vestitus substantia deputetur"; Mansi VIII, 562.

[23] Goffredus Tranensis, *Summa*, fo. 158 sqq.; Hermann-Mascard (1975), 325-327.

[24] Accursius, *Codices sacratissimi*, 32, 60, 90.

Tudeschi († 1445) or Panormitanus.[25] But most authors continued to agree with the point of view expressed by Thomas Aquinas († 1274) that it was a pious and legitimate custom to wear relics with reverence.[26] This implicitly stated that private possession of relics was permissible and the custom continued throughout the Middle Ages, despite a few limitations placed on the practice in the 14th century. In 1311, for instance, pope Clement V permitted Roger of Sicily to keep relics at home. However he granted this permission only on condition that Roger placed them in a portable altar on which, with permission of the Holy See, Mass could be celebrated.[27] In 1317 John XXII laid down the requirement of 'at least a consecrated place'[28] and the provincial Council of Béziers in 1368 strictly forbade the keeping of relics in dwelling places.[29] Practice once again proved stronger than the teaching.

1.1 Home relics

The sources speak frequently of the use of private relics as if it were quite usual.[30] At an early date there was custom in Egypt whereby the mortal remains of highly-placed persons, and especially martyrs, were reverenced at home. The hermit, Anthony († 356), voiced his objections to the practice. Shortly before his death he issued instructions to his disciples in order to prevent this being done with his corpse.[31] After all,

---

[25]Panormitanus, *Commentaria*, t. V, 84.

[26]*Summa theol.*, II,II,4, (1897), 335, q. 96, art. 4,3: "Sed reliquias sanctorum licet homini collo suspendere vel qualitercumque portare, ad suam protectionem"; 4,4: "Quia si portentur ex fiducia Dei et sanctorum, quorum sunt reliquiae, non erit illicitum"; ed. Blacfriars, vol. XL.

[27]Clemens V, *Regestum*, t. V, 254, n. 7156, 28 iun. 1311: "Eidem indulget, ut sanctorum reliquias in domo sua habere valeat, praesertim cum ex apostolicae sedis indulgentia habeat altare portatile, in quo sibi facit per proprium capellanum temporibus congruis divina officia celebrari".

[28]ed. Mollat (1904-47), *Joannis Papae XXII (1316-1334), Litterae Communes I*, 355, n. 3884: "indulget, ut reliquias sanctorum quas in vasis pretiosis venerabiliter recondidit ac in aliquo loco sacro deposuit, possit ad alium sacrum locum reverenter transferre".

[29]Martène (1717), IV, 638, c. 70: "Item monemus omnes et singulos operarios ecclesiarum civitatis et dioecesis Bitterensis, ne reliquias sanctorum, vel vasa pro tenendis ipsis reliquiis facta, calices, corporalia (...) in domibus laicorum teneant: sed in armario vel archa in tutiori parte ecclesiae aut domibus sacerdotalibus".

[30]CSEL 30, 129, S. Paulini Nolani episcopi, *Carmen*, XVIII; Heinzelmann(1979), 20; see e.g. p. 15.

[31]CC SG 91, 42-43; PG 26, 971, s. Athanasii opp. I, *Vita s. Antonii*, c. 91: ["et si qua mei vobis cura sit, et mei tanquam patris, recordamini, corpus meum in Aegyptum transferri patiamini, ne in domibus deponant"].

he had earlier proclaimed the patriarchs, the prophets and the Lord himself were placed in a normal grave.[32] In the West private relics of this kind were mainly of secondary nature in early Christian times and the early Middle Ages,[33] with a few exceptions.

Despite the fact that Eucharist and relics were often kept in the same house, only one case is known where consumption of the Eucharist was related to the reverence paid to the relics. In order to prepare for communion, the widow Lucilla of Carthage kissed a small bone belonging to an unknown saint, which she wore for protection, before receiving communion. For this she was reprimanded by archdeacon Caecillianus in 311. The condemnation, which caused great offence to the lady, was pronounced because of the dubious origin of the relic and not because of the expression of piety as such.[34]

There are repeated explicit reports of relics being kept at home in the sleeping area for protection and veneration. Far away from home the twelve-year-old Peter the Iberian remained faithful to this custom when a Hostage at the court of the emperor Theodosius II († 450). He possessed particles of bone belonging to Persian martyrs and he placed them in a shrine in his bed chamber and paid them nightly reverence with prayer, candles and incense. We do not know if he also reserved the Eucharist there.[35] The poet Prudentius, singing the praises of the martyr St. Vincent at the beginning of the 5th century saying the many Christians had soaked their clothing in the blood of the martyr and subsequently kept them at home as protection for themselves and their descendants.[36] The same type of power that was believed to protect the owner from all types of evil at home was also accredited by tribune Hesperinus to sacred soil which, sealed in a *capsa*, was brought from Jerusalem. He hung this relic

---

[32]ibid. c. 90.

[33]See p. 12 sqq.

[34]CSEL 26, 18-19, *Optati Milevitani*, lib. I: "Quae ante spiritalem cibum et potum os nescio cuius martyris, si tamen martyris, libare dicebatur, et cum praeponeret calici salutari os nescio cuius hominis mortui, et si maryris sed necdum vindicati, correpta cum confusione irata discessit".

[35]ed. Raabe (1895), 25, Vita, 17: ["Er hatte nämlich Gebeine heiliger Märtyrer (...) Diese hatte er mit allen Ehren in eben dem Gemach (cubiculum, conclave), in welchem er seine frommen Übungen anstellte, in einen Schrein gelegt. Und dort schlief er vor ihnen auf der Erde und vollbrachte die göttlichen Dienste mit Lichtern und Wohlgerüchen und mit Hymnen und Gebeten"]; Nussbaum (1979), 271; Saxer (1980), 233.

[36]CC SL 126, 306, *Peristefanon* V, 341-344: "Plerique vestem linteam stillante tingunt sanguine, tutamen ut sacrum suis domi reservunt posteris"; CSEL 61, 346.

close to the place where he slept, according to Augustine.[37] In a similar spirit Jerome († c. 420) expressed himself not only in one of his letters[38] but also implicitly in his work *Contra Vigilantium*.[39] There he attacks with his characteristic vigour this Aquitanian priest who dared to criticise the long-established custom of venerating collected relics. And even bishop Theodoretus of Cyrus († 460), a person of some note in the Greek church in his capacity as early Christian theologian, hung close to his bed a small bottle containing 'holy oil of martyrs' for protection.[40]

The story told by Gregory of Tours about a certain Eufronius of Bordeaux is also worth mentioning. This trader possessed a finger joint of the holy martyr Sergius, which he had placed in a small chest high up against the wall close to the house altar. The finger joint had saved his house on an earlier occasion when the town had gone up in flames.[41] There was even a rumour that it was capable of putting a whole army to flight as had been proved in the East. The Merovingian Gundovald desired this relic at a time when he was involved in a civil war and he sent his ally, Mummolus, together with bishop Bertram, to the trader who was deeply shocked and tried to use money and pleading to save his relic. Mummolus refused to budge and had the chest taken down from the wall. He made holes in each side of the joint with his knife in an attempt to break it. But it burst into pieces, which flew all over the place, a phenomenon interpreted as a sign of anger on the part of the saint. They began to pray furiously and the pieces were all recovered. Mummolus took one of them, but it did Gundovald no good: he died a violent death.

Gregory of Tours reports not only on others' reverence for relics[42] but also about his own attachment to them. At home he had set up a small

---

[37]CSEL 40, *De civitate Dei,* lib. XXII, c. 8, 602: "Acceperat autem ab amico suo terram sanctam de Hierosolymis adlatam, ubi sepultus Christus die tertio resurrexit, eamque suspenderat in cubiculo suo, ne quid mali etiam ipse pateretur".

[38]CSEL 54, 165, ep. 22. 17, *ad Eustochium,* 165: "martyres tibi quaerantur in cubiculo tuo".

[39]PL 23, 339-352: this pamphlet and the correspondence of Jerom is the only source for the position of Vigilantius; see Beaujard (1991), 183.

[40]PG 82, 1442, *Hist. Religiosa,* 21: ["Intellexi ergo, martyrum chorum ab eo dici lecythum olei martyrum, qui collectam a multis martyribus benedictionem continens ad lectum meum suspensus erat"]; SC 257, 96-97, 21, c.6.

[41]MGH SRM I,1, 350-351, *Hist. Franc.* lib. VII, c. 31: "Nam cum tempore quodam Burdegalensis civitas maximo flagraretur incendio, haec domus circumdata flammis nullatenus est adusta"; "(reliquiae) erant enim in sublime parietes contra altarium in capsola reconditae".

[42]MGH SRM I, 2, 43, *In gloria martyrum,* c. 8; 58, c. 33.

place for prayer with the relics of St. Martin and others under the altar.[43] Pope Gregory the Great († 604) also had such a place , as described in one of his *vitae*.[44] It is likewise known that St. Eligius († 660) kept his relics in his sleeping area so that he could reverence them in the night hours.[45]

At the Council of Paris in 829 it was taken for granted that lay people too kept relics at home[46] and, as already stated, in the subsequent centuries the reverencing of relics in the home came up in the church at regular intervals. The objections raised by the church had little effect since private relics simply did not disappear. In the late Middle Ages they even increased.[47] The saint was physically close to the daily lives of people.[48] Individuals made serious efforts to become owners of his relics, as was seen after the death of Elizabeth of Thüringen in 1231. During her life she had won respect for her real love for the poor and the sick, for whom she had had a modest hospital built. Her popularity at the time is still widely expressed by the many hospitals dedicated to "St. Elizabeth". While she was laid out after death people cut pieces from the wrappings around her corpse and cut off the nails from her fingers and toes. Not even her extremities and breasts were spared.[49]

A highly-placed functionary like Jacob of Vitry († 1240), bishop of Akko and cardinal of Tusculum, was proud to be able to wear a finger of

---

[43]MGH SRM I, 2, 309, *In gloria confessorum*, c. 20: "De oratorio autem nostro, in quo reliquiae sancti Saturnini martyris ac Martini antestitis cum Illidio confessore vel reliquorum sanctorum collocatae sunt"; 220, *Vitae patrum*, c. 2, 3.

[44]AASS OSB I, 453, *Vita s. Gregorii Magni*, lib. III, c. 58: "Nam (...) quae in Oratorio domus meae in suburra positae per eas (reliquias) Deus omnipotens fecerit, non celabo"; PL 75, 168.

[45]PL 87, 485, *Vita s. Eligii episcopi Noviomensis*, lib. I, c. 8: "Habebat itaque in cubiculo, ubi assidue cubitare solitus erat, multorum pignora sanctorum in supremis dependentia sub quorum sacro velamine reclinato in cilicio capite orare consueverat nocte".

[46]Mansi XIV, 592, lib. II, can. 13: "Sicut sunt nonnulli, qui orandi gratia ecclesiae limina frequentare negligunt, ita e contrario existunt plerique, qui pro eo quod basilicas adire nequeunt et reliquias sanctorum praesto non habent, idcirco vota precum suarum ad Dominum, ut oportet, supplici devotione non fundunt (...)"; Hefele (1907-42), V, 60.

[47]Vauchez (1981), 503; Kiechefer (1984), 168; Kroos (1985), 25-30; see p. 26.

[48]Huizinga (1921²), 286-287; (1990), 161.

[49]ed. Huyskens (1908), 50, Vita of Elisabeth by Caesarius of Heisterbach: "Cumque idem corpus sanctissimum tunica grisea involutum faciem habens pannis circumligatam iaceret in feretro, plurimi ex hiis, qui presentes aderant, corporis sanctitatem non ignorantes devocione accensi particulas pannorum eius incidebant, alii rumpebant, nonnulli ungues manuum sive pedum eius decurtabant. Quidam eciam summitatem mamillarum eius et digitum unum de manu eius precidebant pro reliquiis ea servantes"; ed. Hilka (1937), 379-380, c. 30.

St. Mary of Oignies around his neck. He had been her spiritual director.[50] Thomas of Cantimpré, who reports this fact, had himself set his heart on obtaining a hand or the head of his friend, the cistercian nun, Lutgarde of Tongeren, after her death. When her sisters had informed her of this not exactly modest wish, she smiled at him and asked if he could not be satisfied with her little finger. And after her death in 1246, that is what the Flemish Dominican had to content himself with.[51]

Private relics and their reverencing in the home were extensions of one another and were thus accepted.[52] They were also taken from the house on journeys, sometimes for the last journey of all.

1.2 Home communion

In early Christian times from about the middle of the 2nd century[53] and in the early Middle Ages the Eucharist too was kept in people's homes in the sleeping quarters or in the area set aside for prayer. After the Sunday celebration the faithful took the Eucharistic bread home[54] in a linen cloth (*dominica*), a basket or a box specially made for the purpose (*arca*).[55] This was usually placed in the sleeping area so that the inhabitants could receive communion in the morning before taking any other food. Tertullian († c. 220) mentions the receiving and the reservation of the Eucharistic in one breath[56] and both he[57] and Hippolytus report the receiving of communion before eating.[58]

---

[50]AASS 23 iun. IV, 673, A, *Supplem. ad vitam s. Mariae Oigniac., c. III,16*: "Tunc Acconensis Episcopus ipse roganti exultabundus arridens; Est, inquit, digitus eius argenteo locello reconditus, assidue mihi suspensus ad collum, qui me utique in diversis periculis et inter marina discrimina semper tutavit illaesum"; ed. Huygens (1960), 1, 72.

[51]AASS 16 iun. III, 261, E, *Vita s. Lutgardis v. cist., c. III,18*: "ut secundum promissum piae Lutgardis eius digitum obtinerem".

[52]Hermann-Mascard (1975), 327: "Bien des auteurs admettent qu'on vénère privatim des reliques, laissant entendre ainsi qu'on peut en avoir dans sa demeure".

[53]Nussbaum (1979), 276.

[54]CSEL 3.3, 8, Novatianus, *De Spectaculis*, c. 5: "qui festinans ad spectaculum dimissus e dominico et adhuc gerens secum ut assolet eucharistiam".

[55]Nussbaum (1979), 277.

[56]CC SL 1, 268, *De oratione*, 19, 4 : "Accepto corpore domini et reservato (...)".

[57]CC SL 1, 389-390, *Ad uxorem* II, 5: "Non sciet maritus, quid secreto ante omnem cibum gustes?".

[58]SC 11 bis, 118, *Traditio Apostolica*, 36: "Omnis autem fidelis festinet, antequam aliquid aliud gustet, eucharistiam percipere".

The daily celebration of Mass was unknown at the time and the community had not had to deal with a measure of abuse that would cause home communion to become a suspect practice. The practice was even recommended. Basil the Great († 379) of Caesarea placed the reservation of the Eucharist in the home against the backdrop of daily communion, which he named "something beautiful and useful". He did not regard the taking of the Eucharist and the reception of communion at one's own hand during the persecutions as reprehensible since it was the usual practice in Alexandria, and elsewhere in Egypt as far as he was aware.[59] Jerome stated that the custom also existed in Rome. He expressed no opinion regarding the reservation of the Eucharist in a private dwelling, but he did have something to say about its reception, namely that it should be done in an appropriate manner as in church. For this reason people were recommended not to receive communion after sexual intercourse.[60]

People reserved the Eucharist at home in the first place in order to receive communion whenever this was not possible in the context of a community celebration. In addition from the beginning there was a close link made between the Eucharist and the threat of death.[61] The Eucharist also gave extra strength in times of persecution. It is reported, for instance, that St. Eudoxia was suspected of having the Eucharistic bread on her person when danger was acute. When the henchmen of prefect Diogenes under the emperor Trajan (98-117) came to arrest her she asked - according to the account in her legendary *vita* - for a moment's respite. She went into her "blessed chamber" where the *arcula* was which contained the "divine gift of the remaining holy body of Christ. After she had hidden the particle in her bosom she went with the soldiers". Some time later the Eucharistic bread emitted aggressive flames aimed at her torturers when they attempted to take hold of her.[62] According to a

---

[59]PG 32, 483, ep. 93: ["ac participem esse sancti corporis et sanguinis Christi, bonum est et perutile"]; 486: ["Alexandriae autem et in Aepypto unusquisque etiam de plebe ut plurimum habet domi communionem, et quando vult, per se ipse fit illius particeps"].

[60]CSEL 54, 377, ep. 49, 15: "Scio Romae hanc esse consuetudinem, ut fideles semper Christi corpus accipiant, quod nec reprehendo nec probo (...) sed ipsorum conscientiam convenio, qui eodem die post coitum communicant (...) Quod in ecclesia non licet, nec domi licet".

[61]Nussbaum (1979), 74 sqq.

[62]AASS 1 mart. I, 19, *Vita s. Eudociae mart.*, c. *XII,44*: "Verum antequam traderet ultro se lupis agna Christi, brevi mora impetrata prodeundi, accurrit in sacram aedem, reserataque illic arcula, in qua divinum donum reliquiarum sancti corporis Christi servabatur, inde particulam acceptam sinu recondidit; et sic statim cum militibus abiit"; 21, c. XIII,49: "Hanc e terra sublatam, nescientes quid esset, diaboli ministri deferunt ad praesidem, qui cum manum extenderet ad capiendum quod offerebatur, repente sacrum pignus, in ignem

source dating from around the year 1000, Saints Indes and Domna acted in the same way as Eudoxia during the persecution of Diocletian in 301. It is also said that they were able to take the Eucharist with them secretly when they were arrested. In this way they were able to benefit for a long time from the "living bread" while they were imprisoned.[63]

The Eucharist represented a safe haven not only in time of danger during the persecutions but also under normal circumstances at home and when travelling. People expected from the Eucharist the same protection they believed was given by relics. Both Eucharist and relics were sometimes kept at home in the same manner. The Eucharistic bread was sewn into a cloth as an amulet and placed in the bed, hidden in the wall or carried round the neck as a protection, especially during sea journeys.[64] The priest Addai Philoponus asked of the versatile scholar Jacob of Edessa († 708) whether it was right to give everyone a piece of the Eucharistic bread to take home since the practices surrounding the custom reeked of superstition. The answer Jacob gave amounted to: the Eucharist should not be worn around the neck, placed in the bed or the wall or buried in vineyards and other types of garden together with a crucifix or with the bones of a saint or with other consecrated objects as a means of protection. Those following customs of this nature had lost sight of the fact that this holy Sacrament was given as food for the soul and not as a source of physical protection. Practices of this type placed the sacrament of the body and blood of Christ on the same level as any other object worthy of reverence. If priests should succumb to such practices they should be dismissed from office, be excluded from the Eucharistic celebration for three years and join the group of penitents. In the case of lay people he recommended a period of four years.[65]

---

conversum, dilatantibus se per gyrum flammis, apparitores praesidis incendit, ipsius quoque laevum humerum corripuit".

[63] Surius XII, 28 dec. 515, Simeon Metaphrastes (ca.1000), *Martyrium*: "et lignea arcula, in qua reposuerant sacram oblationem, cuius fiebant participes (...) His sic inclusis longo tempore, solus panis vivus erat nutrimentum".

[64] Dekkers (1950), 144.

[65] ed. Kayser (1886), 13-14, 9: [Addai: "Ob es recht ist, dass Jedem, der ein Stück der Sakramente mit nach Hause nehmen will, dasselbe ohne Prüfung gegeben werde (...) Da sich nämlich Leute finden, die Theilchen von Sakramenten nehmen und dieselben sogar als eine Art Zauberbändern zusammennähen und in einen Beutel binden oder sich als Amulete anhängen oder in ihre Betten legen und in die Mauren ihrer Häuser"; Jakob: "Die aber, welche jenen Frevel begehen in Betreff der anbetungswürdigen Sakramente des Leibes und Blutes Christgottes, dass sie dieselben nur wie irgend welch andre gewöhnliche und den Christen ehrwürdige Dinge ansehen, dass sie dieselben auch mit dem Kreuz oder mit Knochen der Heiligen und geweihten Gegenständen, um den Halz sich hängen oder wie zum Schutz in ihre Betten oder in die Mauren ihrer Häuser legen, oder in Weinberge oder Gärten oder Parks oder überhaupt zum Schutz von etwas Körperlichem (verwenden) und nicht

But here we are going too far ahead in history. As early as at the beginning of the 3rd century we find a magical view of the Eucharist in the statement made by Hippolytus that even deadly poison could not prevail against someone who had received the Eucharist at home with the appropriate intentions.[66] The bishop was not alone in his belief. Dölger, who lists a large number of examples, assumes that there was a link between the pagan religious custom of taking some part of the sacrificial meal home in order to gain protection and the practice of the reservation of the Host at home, the Host worn as an amulet or used as protection against sickness and poisoning.[67]

In the grey area between pre-Christian and Christian customs, the practice of home communion could also lead to difficulties. Tertullian foresaw them in the case of a mixed marriage. The husband will want to know what is going on, he assumed, when he sees his wife eating this bread before having broken her fast.[68] Zeno of Verona († c. 372) had even greater worries: he was afraid of home communion being mingled with the sacrifices brought home from the celebration of heathen cults. This could happen by accident and lead to a blasphemous situation and unsavoury scenes in the house.[69]

In addition to this practice there were the first signs of yet another development which was not to be reached its maturity until after the year 1000: the miraculous power, expressed in healing and wondrous light. Within the context of communion in the home we provide just one example from ancient Christian times and the early Middle Ages. The miraculous powers ascribed to the Eucharist will be further detailed in chapter V.

Gregory of Nazianze († c. 390) reports the following concerning his sister Gorgonia. She had sustained ugly abrasions in falling from a cart. Tortured by the persistent pain, she mixed the remains of the Eucharistic bread from the altar with her tears and laid the mixture on her

---

bedenken, dass diese heiligen Sakramente allein Seelenspeise derer sind (...) die sollen, wenn es Kleriker sind, durchaus abgesetzt und 3 Jahre lang von der Abendmahlsgemeinschaft ausgeschlossen werden"]; ed. Hindo (1943), 300-301; ed. Ricciotti (1931), 75-76: Codex Iuris Canonici, *De custodia et cultu s.s. Eucharistiae*, can. 1265-1275: "Illi qui partem sanctificatorum (i.e. 'Eucharistiae') in amuletis consuunt, aut simul cum cruce ad collum suum appendunt, aut simul cum ossibus martyrum, aut in grabatis suis vel parietibus vel vineis vel hortis suis quasi ad custodiam ponunt, prohibeantur hoc facere; secus, excommunicentur"; Bar-Hebraeus († 1286), IV, 4 (ex Iacobo Edess.).

[66]See above n. 19.

[67]Dölger (1922), II, 529, 570; (1974²), I, 8; V, 242-244.

[68]See above n. 57.

[69]PL 11, 309 lib. I, *Tractatus* V, 8.

wounds, with a favourable result. The healing power of the Eucharistic reserved at home is also illustrated in a story told by a certain Acatius to Augustine. The man had been born with sealed eyelids. His mother did not wish to call on a healer so she made a poultice of consecrated bread and laid that on his eyes, following which he was cured.[70] We have already reported the miraculous light with its preventive powers mentioned by Cyprian († 258): the fire sprang from the *arca* when a woman with unclean hands tried to open it.[71] Even more miraculous is the light told of by John Moschus († 619). A heretic found his wife absent from home. She had gone to visit a neighbour to receive communion there. He followed her in order to prevent the deed but arrived too late. In anger he grabbed her by the throat so that she vomited out the sacred bread. He knocked it aside into the mud and immediately a flash of light appeared and swallowed up the consecrated bread on the spot.[72]

Resistance to these abuses and the fact that community celebration of the Eucharist was possible with far less danger and more frequently than previously contributed to a diminution of the practice of communion at home from the 5th century onwards.

The Councils of Saragossa in 380 and Toledo in 400 required Christians in the West to receive the Eucharist immediately after its distribution.[73] The aim of this prescription was, however to make believers suspected of heresy[74] show their true colours and was not directly aimed at suppressing communion at home, although it is possible

---

[70]PG 35, 810-811, *Oratio*, VIII, c. 18: ["Cum caput suum pari cum clamore lacrimisque (...) altari admovisset (...) ac deinde hoc suo pharmaco corpus totum perfudisset; et si quid uspiam antityporum pretiosi corporis aut sanguinis manus recondiderat, id lacrimis admiscuisset (...) statim liberatam se morbo sensit"]; PL 45, 1315, *Opus imperf. contra Iulianum* III, 162: "imposito ex eucharistia cataplasmate".

[71]CSEL III, 1, 256, *De lapsis*, 26: "et cum quaedam arcam suam, in qua Domini Sanctum fuit manibus inmundis temptasset aperire, igne inde surgente deterrita est ne auderet adtingere".

[72]PG 87, 2878, *Pratum spirituale*, c. 30: ["Mox autem vidi coruscationem in eodem loco sanctam assumpsisse communionem"]; SC 12, 70-71.

[73]Harduin I, 806, Saragossa, c. 3: "Eucharistiae gratiam si quis probatur acceptam in ecclesia non sumpsisse, anathema sit in perpetuum"; Mansi III, 1000, Toledo, can. 14: "Si quis autem acceptam a sacerdote eucharistiam non sumpserit velut sacrilegus propellatur"; Hefele (1907-42), I,2, 987.

[74]viz. followers of Priscillianus (385), an enthusiastic Spaniard dedicated to an ascetic movement in which Gnostic and Manichaean elements were mingled. His enemies were able to have him condemned on the grounds that he used magic.

that it did place limitations on the practice.[75] In the East, Hesychius of Jerusalem proclaimed in the middle of the 5th century that the body of the Lord could only be received in church at the altar[76] and abbot Schenute of Atripe († 466) reserved some caustic remarks for communion in the home.[77] Canon 24 of the collection of canons attributed to the Armenian metropolitan, Sahak († 440), forbade priests to take the Eucharist to lay people in their homes unless they were sick.[78]

By way of contrast it is known that Dorotheus, a disciple of Eutyches[79], had Eucharistic bread distributed in baskets so that people could take it home when, in 519, a persecution was at hand.[80] Around the same time Syrian Christians ensured a supply of Eucharistic bread at home in order not to be dependent on - in their eyes - unworthy clergy. Severus of Antioch noted his opposition to this practice.[81] Corblet assumes that communion at home was everywhere as good as obsolete by the beginning of the 6th century.[82] Yet a legend of John Moschus states that it was in this century that the custom still existed of taking the Eucharistic bread home on Maunday Thursday. In Seleucia someone placed the bread in a cupboard at home on this day and gave the key to his master, a righteous man who was, nonetheless, a follower of monophysitism. The servant subsequently went away on a trading trip. When, a year later, he had not returned, the master decided to burn the bread. He could not carry out his resolve because, to his amazement, the

---

[75]Nussbaum (1979), 279.

[76]PG 93, 886, *Comment. in Lev.* verse 31-36, lib. II, 8 : "quod intus oportet in ecclesia, in loco sancto, id est altare coqui et comedi: alibi vero nequaquam".

[77]ed. Leipoldt (1903), 184.

[78]ed. Mai (1838), 280: "Presbyteri extra ecclesiam non audeant eucharistiam ad laicorum domos deferre, ibique illis sacrum panem impertiri, excepto infirmitatis casu".

[79]i.e. an archimandrite who proclaimed that there was only one nature - the divine - in Christ (monphysitism).

[80]CSEL 35, 2, 643, *Collectio Avellana*, ep. 186, 4: "si haeretici non sunt, quomodo tanta sacramenta confecerunt, ut canistra plena omnibus erogarent, ne imminente, sicut dicebant, persecutione communicare non possint?".

[81]ed. Brooks (1904), II,2, 231-249, Select Letters III,1-III,4; 237, ep. III,3; ["it is a very superfluous and hurtful thing that the holy communion beyond the boundaries should be sent to you by my feebleness"]; 246, ep. III,4: ["In the case of the religious deacon Misael also, as well as the Christ-loving brothers Ammian and Epagatheus, who about two years ago sent me a box and asked to have it filled full for them with the communion or holy oblation, I did not fall in with the impiety or holy oblation"].

[82]Corblet (1886), I, 524; Nussbaum (1969), 20; (1979), 266-274.

bread had grown stalks bearing ears of corn.[83] Around the year 600 the Council of Auxerre saw itself obliged to speak out against the privatisation of the Eucharist at home[84], while Bede († 735) mentions another example from the 7th century. In this passage the Eucharist occupies centre stage in the dying hour.[85]

***

The above information justifies the conclusion that the 'legal' form of communion at home for lay people gradually disappeared. From the 8th century no further examples appear. The situation in which both relics and Eucharistic bread were reserved at home for separate or joint use lent itself with ease to separate or joint use in the taking of an oath, at death or burial or during travels.

2   USE ON JOURNEYS

Following the Edict of Milan in 313 the Christian religion gradually became the dominant and recognised religion. The Christians came out into the open and their numbers grew rapidly.[1] This enabled heathen customs to slip in more easily than before, requiring an appropriate reaction.[2]

The amulet is an example of this. In the Christian religion it was replaced by a Cross, a Gospel text[3] or relics, enclosed in what were known as *capsellae* or *pendulae*, hung around the neck. These tiny relic holders, also known as *encolpia*, *chrismaria* or *fylacteria* were usually made of gold, silver or crystal. A close relative of the *fylacterium* -

---

[83]PG 87, 2935-2938, *Pratum spirituale*, c. 79: ["dimissa (...) sancta communione in armario (...) apertoque (...) vidit omnes sanctas particulas culmos et spicas germinasse"]; SC 12, 125.

[84]MGH Conc I, 179, III: "Non licet conpensus in domibus propriis nec pervigilius in festivitates sanctorum facere"; Du Cange (1883-87), II, 464, "compensus".

[85]ed. Colgrave (1979), 420, *Historia Ecclesiastica*,IV, c. 24: "et iam mediae noctis tempus esset transcensum, interrogavit [frater quidam] si eucharistiam intus haberent. Respondebant: 'Quid opus est eucharistia? neque enim mori adhuc habes, qui tam hilariter nobiscum velut sospes loqueris'. Rursus ille: 'Et tamen', ait, 'afferte mihi eucharistiam'".

[1]See p. 10 and 51.

[2]Marquès-Rivière (1950), 141-175; Nussbaum (1964), 12 sqq.

[3]e.g. Mtt. 4:24; Jn. 19:36.

'means of protection'[4] - is the *Agnus Dei*, still worn today in some places
as an object designed to confer blessings.[5] The *fylacteria* - of which a
substantial number are still in existence - described by Braun it can be
deduced that these purse-shaped reliquaries must have been spread far and
wide. They were particularly popular in Merovingian, Carolingian and
Ottonian times.[6] A legend attached to a reliquary of this type in the
cathedral at Hildesheim is illustrative. Louis the Pious, lost while out
hunting, hung this *fylacterium* on a rose bush in bloom. He prayed before
it and, as a reward, re-found his companions. He is reported to have built
a church on the site, dedicated to the Virgin Mary, of which the present
cathedral is an extension, with the bush in question in 'Unser leven
Ffrouwen Hyligthum'.[7]

In a similar manner - or perhaps even more so - the Eucharistic
bread was credited with a protective power, so that it was carried on the
person in a (usually cross-shaped) *encolpion,* keeping off evils.[8] The
Syrian poet Cyrillonas used unusually metaphorical terms when writing of
Christ around the year 400: "He bound the mysteries as it were into a
string of pearls and hung them round the neck; he laid the parables on his
breast like precious beryl".[9] Whether these rich images are a poetic
reflection of day-to-day reality is an open question. The facts agree.
People carried the Eucharist with them on journeys, something proved by
the dialogue between Jacob of Edessa and Addai Philoponus that has
come down to us.[10] In the same period abbot Anastasius of the Mt. Sinai
monastery defended the practice of taking the Eucharist on journeys using
the argument that Christ himself travelled around on the earth. This
reasoning was also probably an 'oratio pro domo', since Anastasius
Sinaita himself was a great traveller.[11] While it is true to say that the

---

[4]Dölger (1929-50), III, 84 sqq.

[5]i.e. "a round or oval disc, decorated on one side with a representation of the Lamb of
God and, on the other, with the representation of one or more saints and stamped with a
papal stamp" (LW I, 81); Bock (1989), 155-157.

[6]Braun (1940), 200.

[7]Tschan (1942-52), I, 8; Beissel (1976), II, 91.

[8]Dölger (1929-50), V, 242: "Die hohe Wertung der Eucharistie führte dazu, dass man
auch sie in einem ähnlichen Sinne verwenden sollte".

[9]BKV 6, 31: "Unser Herr opferte Seinen Leib zuerst selbst und erst nachher opferten ihn
die Menschen (...) Er verband die Geheimnisse wie zu einer Perlenschnur und hing sie sich
um den Hals; er legte die Gleichnisse auf seine Brust wie kostbare Berylle".

[10]See p. 77.

[11]PG 89, 765, quaestio 113: ["Sanctissimum Christi corpus nulla iniuria afficitur ex hoc
quod circumfertur; nam ipse Christus olim ad omnes circuibat et circumferebatur"].

document entitled *De remediis peccatorum* pointed out the responsibility incumbent on all believers to rescue the unbaptised from the devil before their death, monks in particular were called on to administer Baptism in an appropriate fashion and to carry the Eucharist with them on their journeyings.[12] This prescription is a prelude to the new application of the Eucharistic bread on journeys, namely that of serving as *viaticum* in times of mortal danger, an element often brought to the fore not only in this but also in other writings. The protection factor often shows through here. It would also appear that administering the *viaticum* was developing into a clerical activity. To the extent that the Eucharist was carried by lay people on journeys, something of which there are very few reports, the practice must have come to an end in the West at the same rate as the practice of communion at home gradually disappeared in the course of the 5th and 6th centuries. On the basis of the data we can conclude that the practice continued in the East until the end of the 7th century.[13]

The wearing of the *fylacterium* containing the relics is also concealed behind the daily pattern of life - seldom described - in early medieval times. Reports which are largely to be found in the hagiographies place clerics centre stage, although it cannot be said that lay people are entirely ignored. The *fylacteriun* in fact was part of the 'equipment' belonging to every household in the early Middle Ages - and may even have usually been part of an individual's personal possessions.[14] Otherwise the sources often speak of the relics as 'travelling companion' but not so frequently of the Eucharist. The extent to which lay people carried relics or Eucharist with them could be reflected in such references. There is, however, only one explicit mention off the two combined - in far from usual circumstances: during a sea-journey undertaken by St. Louis.

---

[12]Martène (1733), VII, 39, *De remediis peccatorum*, c.9: "sed et omnibus licet fidelibus ubi forte morituros invenerint non baptizatos, immo praeceptum est animas eripere diabolo per baptisma, id est benedicta simpliciter aqua in nomine Domini, baptizare illos in nomine Patris et Filii et Spiritus Sancti, intinctos aut superfusos aqua: unde oportet eos qui possunt fideles, monachos maxime et scientiam habere baptizandi et si longius alicubi exierint, eucharistiam semper secum habere".

[13]Nussbaum (1979), 85.

[14]Angenendt (1990), 187.

2.1   Relics as travelling companions

The first reports of people carrying relics as a form of protection date from the second half of the fourth century. In the *vita* of St. Makrina († 379), the sister of Gregory of Nyssa († c. 394), there is talk of a particle of the True Cross that this lady carried around her neck.[15] John Chrysostom († 407) reports that both men and women valued this type of adornment[16] and Augustine, writing around 425, spoke favourably of a widow and her daughter "who wore the relics of the most holy and glorious Stephen".[17]

Judging from the relics which St. Amator († 418) wore in a *pendula* around his neck, the inhabitants of the area through which he was travelling concluded that he must be a man of God. They therefore cleared the way of thorns and thistles, as his *vita* reports.[18] His successor, St. Herman of Auxerre († 448), "filled with the Holy Ghost", took the *capsula* from around his neck in full view of all, prayed to the Trinity and laid the relics on the eyes of a blind girl, who recovered her sight in a miraculous fashion.[19]

According to Johannes Diaconus, Gregory of Tours wore a silver relic cross or *fylacterium*[20] and he sent to Dynamius, governor in Gaul, a small cross containing filings from the chains of St. Peter and the grill of St. Laurence, so that these could be worn around his neck.[21] This type of practice with regard to relics can be found in various places in the

---

[15]ed. Jaeger (1953), 404, *Vita Macrinae*; SC 178 (1971), 239-243, c. 30.

[16]PG 48, 826, *Contra Judaeos et Gentiles*, c. 10: ["cur particulam eius multi sumentes auro inclusam, tum viri tum mulieres a collo suspendunt ad ornatum"].

[17]PL 33, 965, *Epistolarum classis* III, ep. 212: "Portant sane secum reliquias beatissimi et gloriosissimi Stephani".

[18]AASS 1 mai, t. I, 57, *Stephani Africani Vita s. Amatoris episc.* n. 25: "et cum eis esset ignotus, pulchritudine vultus et capsellari honore quo reliquias inclusas pendulas collo gestabat, cognoverunt Dei esse famulum ac cultorem".

[19]MGH SRM VII, 262, *Vita Germani episcopi Autissiodorensis*, c. 15: "Ac deinde Germanus plenus Spiritu sancto invocat Trinitatem et protinus adhaerentem lateri suo capsulam cum sanctorum reliquiis collo avulsam manibus conprehendit eamque in conspectu omnium puellae oculis adplicavit; quos statim evacuatos tenebris lumine veritatis implevit"; see also: 281, c. 43; 253, c. 4.

[20]PL 75, 228, Joannes Diaconus, *Vita s. Gregorii,* IV, 80: "Quod autem reliquiarum phylacteria tenui argento fabricata, vilique pallio, de collo suspensa fuisse videntur, habitus eius mediocritate demonstratur".

[21]MGH Ep I, 192, lib. III, ind. XI, ep. 33: "Transmisimus autem beati Petri Apostoli benedictionem, crucem parvulam, cui de catenis eius beneficia sunt inserta. Quae illius quidem ad tempus ligaverunt, sed vestra colla in perpetuum a peccatis solvant. Per quattuor vero in circuitu partes, de beati Laurentii craticula, in qua perustus est, beneficia continentur".

writings of Gregory of Tours. St. Perpetuus († 491), bishop of the town a century before Gregory, offered his brother Eufronius a silver relic-holder "which it was his custom to wear".[22] King Chilperik took relics with him in his journeys in order to turn evil into good. When, in 567, he entered Paris in breach of the treaty he had drawn up with his brothers, he sent before him the relics of a great number of saints, hoping in this way to escape the consequences of his bad faith.[23]

In Gregory's *vita* of the holy abbot St. Aredius († 591), bishop of Limoges, the *chrismarium* that "the saint was accustomed to carry on his person"[24] repeatedly plays a role. He filled it with sand from the site where the martyr Julian had been killed.[25] An ampulla filled with oil, that functioned as a *chrismarium*, overflowed when he added a tiny drop of the oil of St. Martin.[26] His own *chrismarium* provided protection against storms[27] and caused a dead person's eyes to open again the moment it was hung round his neck.[28] Elsewhere in this document Aredius is mentioned in connection with a confidential message passed on from deacon Vulfolaic to Gregory. In the company of the abbott the deacon had visited Martin of Tours' church. When they were preparing to leave again, the saint placed a little of the dust from the grave in a small box, which he hung round his neck. When they arrived back at the abbey in Limoges they witnessed how the contents suddenly multiplied at such a rate that it forced its way through the container.[29]

The protective power of a *chrismarium* filled in this way, according to Gregory, caused the wind to change at a critical moment in Poitiers, so that the fire raging in a house next to the church did not cross the gap to

---

[22]PL 71, 1151, Appendix ad opera s. Gregorii Turonensis,   *Testamentum Perpetui Toronensis episcopi*: "Tibi fratri et consacerdoti dilectissimo Eufronio thecam ex argento de reliquiis sanctorum do, lego. Illam intelligo quam deferre solebam".

[23]MGH SRM I, 295, *Hist. Franc.*, lib. VI, 27: "reliquias (reliquiis) sanctorum multorum praecedentibus, urbem ingressus est".

[24]PL 71, 1140, *Vita s. Aridii abbatis*, c. 35: "chrismarium quod vir beatissimus Aridius gestare consueverat".

[25]ibid. 1125, c. 7.

[26]ibid. 1128, c. 20; AASS 25 aug. IV, 179, n. 9.

[27]ibid. 1134, c. 29.

[28]ibid. 1141, c. 36.

[29]MGH SRM I, 381, *Hist. Franc.*, lib. VIII, c. 15: "Revertensque cum eo, ille parumper pulveris beati sepulchri pro benedictione sustulit, quod in capsulam positum ad collum meum dependit. Devectique ad monasterium eius Limovicino in termino, accepta capsula, ut eam in oratorio suo locaret, in tantum pulvis adcrevit, ut non solum totam capsam repleret, verum etiam foris inter iuncturas, ubi aditum repperire potuit, scatiret".

the church building.[30] While journeying at sea he was able to use the
chrismarium to still a storm and was convinced that he was saved from
danger while in Koblenz thanks to the protection afforded by the relics of
Martin and of other saints "which he carried on him". While he was
attempting to cross the Rhine in a rowing boat, so many people climbed
aboard the vessel that it filled with water up to the gunwales. Thanks to
the protection afforded by the saints, the boat did not sink during the
speedy crossing of the river, and all reached the far side safely.[31]
Gregory's *chrismarium* was inherited: his father had for a long time been
inseparable from it when he undertook long journeys, the same applying
to his mother after the death of her husband. She, in her turn, gave it to
Gregory as a gift.[32]

In various *vitae* dating from the Merovingian and Carolingian
periods the limelight is miraculously turned on to the protective power of
the *fylacterium*. By way of an example: it is related of Saint Gallus
(† 635) how he took a hazel twig, made a cross of it and planted it in the
earth. He then hung on it the *capsella* which he wore around his neck,
containing relics of the Mother of God and the martyrs Maurice and
Desiderius.[33] Stretched out on the ground in prayer during the night, he
used his construction to restrain a wild animal. His companion pretended
to be sleeping and was thus witness to the entire occurrence. In
bewilderment he threw himself at Gallus's feet and uttered the words
taken from the Bible: "Now I know that you are a man of God (I Cor.
17:24) for even the beasts of the desert submit to you". However, Gallus

---

[30]MGH SRM I, 2, 208, *De virtutibus s. Martini*, lib. IV, c. 32, De incendio urbis
Pictavae: " Sed ille de pulvere beati sepulchri secum habens, elevatum chrysmarium contra
ignem, exortus subito ventus vento illi contrarius, flammas a tecto ecclesiastico defendens,
alia pepulit in parte, et sic domus ecclesiae liberata est".

[31]MGH SRM I, 380, *Hist. Franc.*, lib. VIII, c. 14: "Ascendentibusque nobis, inruit turba
hominum diversorum, impletaque est navis tam hominibus quam aquis. Sed virtus Domini
adfuit non sine grande miraculo, ut, cum usque labium impleta fuisset, mergi non possit.
Habebamus enim nobiscum beati Martini reliquias cum aliorum sanctorum, quorum virtutem
nos credimus fuisse salvatos"; see also PL 71, 120, *Vita s. Gregorii Turonensis*, c. 9; 123,
c. 16.

[32]MGH SRM I,2, 94, *In gloria martyrum*, c. 83: "pater meus (...) voluit se sanctorum
reliquiis communiri petivitque a quodam sacerdote, ut ei aliquid de hisdem indulgeret, quo
scilicet in viam longinquam abiens tali praesidio tutaretur (...)"; 95: "Post multos vero
annos has reliquias a genetrice suscepi; cumque iter de Burgundia ad Avernum ageremus,
oritur contra nos magna tempestas (...) Tunc extractas a sinu beatas reliquias, manu elevo
contra nubem; quae protinus divisa in duabus partibus (...) neque nobis neque ulli deinceps
nocuit".

[33]PL 114, 987, *Walfradi vita Galli, abbatis*, lib. I, c. 11: "Habebat autem pendentem
collo capsellam, in qua continebantur reliquiae beatae Dei genetricis Mariae et sanctorum
martyrum Mauricii et Desiderii (...) Sed vir sanctus (...) surgens prostravit se in figuram
crucis ante capsellam, et preces Domino devotas effudit".

replied with the words spoken by Jesus on Mount Tabor: "See that you tell non-one of this until you see the glory of God", a command that was quite obviously not heeded.

St. Theodardus († c. 670), bishop of Tongeren and Maastricht, drove thieves away by showing the relics he carried with him.[34] The *capsa* also figures[35] in the lives of St. Willibrord († 739) and St. Boniface († 754) as also in that of St. Willehad, who was rescued from certain death when his *chrismarium* turned aside the sword of an attacking heathen.[36] Such stories appear equally in lives written after the year 1000. Richard of St. Vannes († 1046) carried around his neck relics which he is reported to have been given by the bishop of Jerusalem.[37] And bishop Walo of Paris carried on his visit to St. Anselm († 1109) the relics that had been handed to him in Rome.[38] The 'insatiable collector'[39], Hugh of Lincoln (†1200), had set in his ring a tooth of St. Benedict which had been presented to him by the monks of Fleury.[40] In this way he experienced the closeness of him whose 'Rule' became a book of law just as Jacob of Vitry felt the proximity of St. Mary of Oignies by wearing her finger round his neck.[41]

The wearing of the *capsella* was not only reserved to clerics since private possession left the practice open to lay people, the parents of

---

[34]AASS OSB IV, 2, 179, *Translatio s. Mauri*: "Abba (Theodoratus) vero capsula reliquiarum, quam in pectore suo detulerat, eum in fronte percussit, atque insuper haec protulit: Deus omnipotens per merita s. Mauri aliorumque sanctorum quorum reliquiae in hac capsula reconditae venerantur poenas, et vindictam de suis et servorum suorum reposcet contemptoribus maximeque de te, qui rapinae malo inserviens, ducatum talibus praebes praedonibus. Et post haec de Monasterio eos proturbari iubet"; AASS 10 sept. III, 580-592.

[35]PL 101, 709, B.F.Albini seu Alcuini operum, pars V, *Hagiographia, Vita s. Willibrordi*, lib. I, c. 27: "Quidam etiam officio diaconus, et non merito, in ecclesia sancti viri crucem auream, quam vir sanctus secum in itinere portare solebat, cum aliis denariis ecclesiae, infelicissimo non horruit abstrahere furto"; AASS 5 iun. I, 471: "Sed et thecas, quibus multa inerant librorum volumina et reliquiarum capsas abstulit"; see also MGH AA IV, 2, 67-73, *Vita s. Medardi* (560); MGH SRM VI, 199- 200, *Vita s. Wilfridi* (709); ed. Stubbs (1965), *Vita s. Dunstani* (988), 190 ; AASS SOB VI,1, *Vita b. Richardi Abbatis* (1046), 528; see also ed. Rock (1905), II, part. I, cah. VI, 145-149: "the reliquary worn around the neck by all English bishops whenever they sang high mass".

[36]AASS 8 nov. III, 843, *Vita s. Willehadi*; MGH SS II, 381, *Anscharii vita s. Willehadi*.

[37]AASS 10 iun. II, 998, *Vita ven. Richardi ab. Verdun.*, c. IX,79: "Post haec reliquias, quas Hierosolymitanus patriarcha ei dederat, sibi afferri praecepit: et salutatis eis atque deosculatis cum multa reverentia, eas quas collo ferre consueverat exposuit et ante se reverenter sisti praecepit".

[38]PL 158, 111, *Vita s. Anselmi*, lib. II, c. 6.

[39]Sumption (1974), 25.

[40]ed. Douie (1961-1962), II, 168.

[41]See p. 74; Hermann-Mascard (1975), 316-317.

Gregory of Tours being prime examples.[42] But in the sources it is primarily prominent people who are related to have thus been privileged. The *vita* of Betharius, bishop of Chartres, written at the beginning of the 9th century, states that this was a "common practice of kings".[43] Agobard of Lyon († 840) set himself against the practice by giving a wide-ranging exposé of the superstitious background.[44]

Relics as companions on a journey served not only to protect the traveller but also on occasions to offer solace and healing to the sick, which recalls the sacrament of the sick and dying or '*viaticum*'. In his chronicle dating from around 1114 Ortlieb of Zwiefalten abbey describes the rich reliquary contents of bishops' crosses. He lists a large number of relics in the abbey's possession and adds the following comment: "It was the abbot's custom to carry these with him on a journey for the benefit of the sick".[45]

The pendants containing the relics - like the healing stones people ear today - could be very beautiful. Around 1230 the treasures of Lüneburg had an onyx designed to be worn around the neck and containing relics.[46]

The wearing of a relic, Gospel text or cross carried the risk of the wearer according it the same value as that given to the pagan amulet. This was not an imaginary danger, since people tended to transfer to the relic the power held by the saint from whom it originated. In such a case the

---

[42]Dölger (1929-50), III, 90 (with reference to a great number of reliquary crosses, originating praticularly in Syrna, Asia Minor, and Palestine which are to be found in the Kaiser Friedrich Museum in Berlin): "Die Reliquienkreuze waren ehedem nicht eine besondere Auszeichnung der Bischöfe, sie waren ebenso in der Volksfrömmigkeit im Gebrauch".

[43]MGH SRM III, 615, *Vita Betharii episcopi Carnoteni*, 5: "Lotharius rex secundus, filius Chilperici regis, cum regina Fredegunde nomine regnabat (...) audiens famam beatissimi viri, suum constituit archicapellanum et pignora multa sanctorum, quae secum deferebat, ut mos est regum, ditioni illius constituit".

[44]PL 104, 221, *Liber de imaginibus sanctorum*, c. 26: "Sic consimile quid beatus Hieronymus loquitur, cum verba Domini illa tractaret, quae ita se habent: 'Dilatant enim phylacteria sua, et magnificant fimbrias'. Pittaciola, inquit, illa decalogi phylacteria vocabant: quod quicunque habuisset ea, quasi ob custodiam et munimentum sui haberet; non intelligentibus pharisaeis, quod haec in corde portandi sint, non in corpore"; see also PL 87, 528-529, *Vita s. Eligii*: "Nulla mulier praesumat succinos ad collum dependere, nec in tela vel in tinctura (...) Praeterea quoties aliqua infirmitas supervenerit, non quaerantur praecantatores, non divini, non sortilegi, non caragi, nec per fontes aut arbores, vel bivios diabolica phylacteria exerceantur; sed qui aegrotat in sola Dei misericordia confidat, et eucharistiam corporis et sanguinis Christi cum fide ac devotione accipiat"; DACL VI,1, 432-433 "Gallicane (église)".

[45]MGH SS X, 89-90, 90: "Istae reliquae in cristallo altero sunt inclusae quem domnus abbas propter infirmos solet secum in itinere ferre".

[46]MGH SS XXIII, 399: "Sub onichino lapide, qui portatur in collo, iste continentur reliquie: de sancta cruce, s. Philippi apostoli".

direct apotropaic power was accorded to the *fylacterium* itself rather than to the indirect protection afforded by divine providence.[47] As early as in the second half of the 4th century the Council of Laodicea[48] pronounced on abuses of this kind, as did John Chrysostom († 407)[49], Epiphanius of Salamis († 403) and Jerome († 420)[50], who compared the gaudiness of the *encolpia* with the broad prayer belts and large tassels affected by the Pharisees (Mtt. 23:5).[51] Agobardus of Lyon appealed to these writers when he set down his suspicions - alluded to above - in connection with the superstitious use of the *fylacteria*.

A further problem was that of self-glorification. The Spanish provincial Council of Braga in 675 exposed several bishops who had had themselves carried into church on the feast of certain martyrs - whose relics they wore around their necks - "as iff they themselves were reliquaries".[52]

Pope Nicholas I († 867) approved of the kissing and wearing of relic-crosses, provided that those so doing were pure in body and mind. He quotes Isaiah 52:11: "(...) be ye clean, that bear the vessels of the Lord". By this he meant both the Cross of Jesus and the relics of the saints "whose bodies are temples and vessels of the Lord".[53] This

---

[47]Engemann (1975), 40 sqq.; Hillgarth (1986), 20.

[48]Mansi, II, 570, canon 36: "Quod non oportet eos qui sacrati, vel clerici, esse magos, vel incantatores, vel mathematicos, vel astrologos, vel facere ea quae dicuntur amuleta, quae quidem sunt ipsarum animarum vincula: eos autem qui ferunt, eiici ex ecclesia iussimus".

[49]PG 57-58, 669, *In Matthaeum Homilia*, 72, 2: ["Dilatant enim phylacteria sua, inquit et magnificant fimbrias vestimentorum suorum. Phylacteria quid essent (...) Quae phylacteria, quasi dices conservatoria, vocabantur ut multae nunc mulieres evangelia ex collo pendentia habent (...)"]; PG 49-50, 194, *Ad populum Antiochenum Homilia*, 19, 4: ["Non cernis ut mulieres et parvi pueri pro magna custodia collo evangelia suspendunt et ubique circumferunt quocumque abierint.."]; PG 59, 561 (Pseudo-Chrysostomus), *Sermo de pseudo-prophetis*, 7: ["Quot Christiani Judeorum gentiliumque fabulis incumbunt, genealogiis, vaticiniis, auguriis, veneficiis, phylacteriis"].

[50]PG 41, 245-246, *Adversus Haereses*, lib. I,1, c. 15.

[51]PL 26, 174-175, *Commentarium in evangelium Matthaei*, lib. IV, c. 23.

[52]Mansi XI, 157, c. 6: "agnovimus quosdam de episcopis quod in solennitatibus martyrum ab (ad) ecclesiam progressuri, reliquias collo suo imponant et ut maioris fastus apud homines gloria intumescat (quasi ipsi sint reliquiarum arca). Laevitae albis induti in sellulis eos deportant".

[53]MGH Ep VI (Karolini Aevi), 572-573, ep. 99, c. VII: "Sciscitamini praeterea, si liceat crucem Domini cum reliquiis mundo sive immundo hanc habenti osculari vel portare. Quod ei, qui mundus est, omnino licet"; "cum summa reverentia et corpore et corde mundissimo (...) ut et 'per abstinentiam carnem' semper afficiatis et per compassionem necessitatem proximorum vestram putetis"; "Immundum autem hanc portare nullo pacto permittimus; scriptum autem est: 'Mundamini, qui fertis vasa Domini'. Nullum vero Domini vas sacratius est cruce dominica, quae ipsum portare Dominum meruit"; "De reliquiis vero sanctorum eadem dicimus, quorum corpora templa et vasa fuere suntque Dei quibusque ad omnia bona opera tamquam organis sanctus usus est, quando voluit, spiritus".

attitude of pope Nicholas recalls the rules for purification in Alcuin's *speculum* for the confession with reference to contact with relics as also the strict prescriptions designed to ensure worthy reception of communion, which were emphasised in the church from the time of Jerome up to the 13th century.[54] A 'sacred vessel' could serve to hold the Eucharist just as well as to contain relics.[55]

We noted that Thomas Aquinas stated that the wearing of relics must be founded on a trust in God and his saints.[56] This formulation is adopted by Anthony of Florence († 1459) in his *Summa*.[57] Since this subject appears to be still relevant in the 15th century, we can assume that the custom of carrying a *fylacterium* while travelling, a custom repeatedly alluded to in the sources, continued to be practised until the end of the Middle Ages. But in all likelihood the emphasis placed by the church on a worthy reservation of relics and the encouragement to place them at the disposal of the church will no doubt have had a braking effect on the devotional practice.

2.2   The Eucharist as travelling companion

Just like relics, the Eucharist was taken, enclosed in a *bursa* or *pendula* as a means of protection not only on journeys overland but - and especially - when travellers ventured onto the whimsical sea. The risk entailed in such a voyage is recounted by the apostle Paul, who "suffered shipwreck three times and once spent a whole day in the water" (2 Cor. 11:25). When the ship in which he was travelling had wallowed for fourteen days in a savage storm and finally land was sighted, a landfall that turned out to be the island of Malta, "he took bread, thanked God in the presence of all, broke it and began to eat" (Acts 27:35).

These words, chosen for their correspondence with the words spoken at the last supper, reflect the Eucharistic act. During ancient Christian times and the early Middle Ages the Eucharistic bread was eaten on board ship as a *viaticum* in times of danger, but it also served - a

---

[54]See p. 52 .

[55]See further: 206 sqq.

[56]See p. 71.

[57]Antonius Pierozzi, *Summa Theologica*, 541, t. III, tit. XII, c. 8: "Item portare reliquias sanctorum ad collum, si hoc fiat ex devotione et fiducia ad Deum et sanctos quorum sunt, licitum est secundum Thomam".

fylacterium, as it were - as a replacement for the amulet. This can be seen in the panegyric preached by Ambrose at the burial of his older brother, Satyrus, where the bishop of Milan revealed, in 378, what the deceased had gone through during his sea voyage. His ship went into a cliff and although not yet baptised Satyrus asked his Christian fellow-passengers if he might partake of the Eucharistic bread, which they always had with them 'from home',[58] for times of emergency. Following the example of his companions, Satyrus wrapped the Eucharist up in a linen cloth, or *orarium*, wound it round his neck and cast himself into the foaming sea. Even when floating on a loose spar he showed no sign of care, regarding the Eucharist as his only salvation[59] and he came safely to land. This occurrence was at least four years before his death, since he was baptised in 374.[60] This is the only example found in the West in ancient times or during the early Middle Ages of the Eucharist serving 'as a travelling companion' for lay people. The examples below all refer to clerics.

Use of the Eucharistic bread as *apotropaeon* and as *viaticum* for journeys appeared at the same time in the East. Hilary of Poitiers († 367) reports on riots caused by supporters of Arianism in Ancyra when one of the most powerful opponents of this doctrine, bishop Marcellus, returned there from Rome. Priests who sided with this prince of the church were dragged naked to the market square and the consecrated bread which they "wore around their necks" was destroyed in the tumult.[61]

An anti-Arian attitude can also be detected in a fragment taken from the *vita* of Porphyrius († 420) who, in his capacity of bishop of Gaza, had visited the anchorite Procopius on the island of Rhodes. On the return journey a fierce storm came up and shipwreck seemed imminent. Procopius appeared to him in a dream and predicted a safe journey if the Arian captain renounced his heresy. The man was only too pleased to oblige and received the Eucharistic bread from the bishop's hand.[62]

---

[58]Dölger (1929-50), V, 235-236.

[59]CSEL 73, 233.

[60]Dölger (1929-50), V, 232.

[61]Ancyra or Ankara; CSEL 65, 55, *Collectanea Antiariana Parisina* (fragm. hist.), 4,9: "et in Anquira provinciae Galatiae post reditum Marcelli haeretici domorum incendia et genera diversa bellorum. Nudi ab ipso ad forum trahebantur presbyteri et, quod cum lacrimis luctuque dicendum est, consecratum domini corpus ad sacerdotum colla suspensum palam publiceque profanabat".

[62]*An. Boll.* 59, 171-172: ["eum cruce Dominica signarunt sacrisque mysteriis communicarunt. Tunc, uno temporis puncto, compescuit Deus ventum illum vehementem"]; PG 65, 1237, *Marci Diaconi vita s. Porphyrii episcopi Gazenensis*, c. 57; ed. Grégoire (1930), 56-59; DACL XIV, 1479-1504.

Porphyrius must have been carrying the Eucharistic as *fylacterium* and *viaticum*, since it is hardly likely that in such circumstances a Eucharistic celebration could have been held.[63]

A Maronite nomocanon, translated in mid-11th century from Syriac into Arabic, grants permission to priests to take the Eucharistic with them on journeys lasting more than a day. However they were allowed to eat and drink only at the end of each stage of the journey.[64] In the 13th century the usage seems to have disappeared in the East since it was from there that the Latin church was accused of allowing people to carry the Eucharist in a pouch around the neck. Constantine Stilbes, who was bishop of Cyzicus under the name of Cyril, includes this practice in a list of grievances against the Latins which he drew up at the beginning of the 13th century.[65]

In a letter to a Gallic monk, Rusticus, Jerome praises the bishop of Toulouse for always carrying on his person the body of the Lord in a small basket and the blood of the Lord in a vial.[66] In the West the clerical custom of carrying the Eucharist on journeys was widespread.[67] The Roman region may have been an exception to this at the beginning of the 5th century because of the objections made by Innocent I to the sending of the *fermentum* over long distances.[68]

The Eucharistic gifts functioned on journeys not only as *viaticum* but also as *fylacterium* in times of mortal danger. Saint Gregory was visited in Constantinople by the Roman abbot Maximianus († 594). The pope relates the following concerning the abbot's return journey home: when crossing the Adriatic the situation became so critical that "the ship

---

[63]Nussbaum (1979), 87.

[64]Maronites: a Christian grouping from the 8th century onwards, named after St. Maron († c. 410), who supported the doctrine of monotheletism (see p. 67, n. 12); nomocanon: from the 6th century onwards a collection of canons (ecclesiastical prescritions) and nomoi (imperial edicts regarding church matters); Kitab al'Hudâ, see Khoury (1966), 258: ["Le prêtre ne doit pas porter le Corps pur ni le 'Myron' saint d'un pays à un autre sans être à jeun; et s'il peut le faire à pieds, cela est meilleur et préférable. Si le lieu vers lequel il se rend est plus (éloigné) qu'une étape, et si le prêtre s'est arrêté à l'arrivée de l'étape, il le déposera dans l'endroit le plus ûr posible; puis il récite la louange de la foi et mangera; et lorsqu'il reprendra son voyage, il portera de nouveau à jeun, jusqu'à ce qu'il arrive au lieu où il va"].

[65]Darrouzès (1963), 75, grievance 54: ["Ce qu'ils considèrent le corps du Christ, l'azyme' lorsqu'ils partent en voyage, ils le portent comme une provision quelconque dans des bourses qui pendent le long des cuisses et sur le postérieur"].

[66]CSEL 56, 141, ep. 125, 20: "Nihil illo ditius, qui corpus domini canistro vimineo, sanguinem portat vitro, qui avaritiam proiecit e templo".

[67]Nussbaum (1979), 87.

[68]See p. 65.

seemed to be less in the waves than the waves in the ship". Maximianus
gave the Lord's body and blood as *viaticum* to his brethren, but the
Eucharist also manifested itself as a protection. The storm died down and
the vessel arrived in a safe harbour. As soon as the abbot had left the
boat, the last to do so, it sank like a stone [69].

An account of how the Eucharist could function merely as
apotropaeon can be found in the statutes of the Abbey of Bangor where
they speak of the founder, St. Comgallus († 602). Just as Theodardus put
thieves to flight by showing his relics,[70]so too this famous Irishman and
disciple of St. Columbanus kept plundering Scots at bay with the
Eucharist. While he was working on the land they threatened him. They
were already leading away the inhabitants of a settlement they had
attacked, with their cattle, to the ships lying at anchor. But when they
caught sight of the 'chrismale', which the saint was wearing
demonstratively on his mantle, they did not dare touch him, convinced
that this was the God of Comgallus.[71] The story does not say whether
Comgallus was really wearing a 'chrismale' containing the Eucharist, as
was the habit among the Irish monks, or whether the robbers were
mistaken and that the 'chrismale' is referred to here in its original
meaning and contained only the holy oil or chrism.[72] The latter seems
less likely since the underlying theme of the story is the protective force
of the Eucharist.

The monk Berinus, of St. Andrew's monastery in Rome, was very
deeply attached to it. Around the year 630 he was sent by pope Honorius
to England to proclaim the Gospel in those regions where no missionary
activity had as yet been undertaken. Once on board the ship that was to
take him there he noticed that he had left behind the corporal (*palla*)
given to him personally by Honorius. He immediately jumped into the
water, waded to the shore and went to get it in order thenceforth to carry
the Eucharist around his neck. The 11th-century author of the life of

---

[69]SC 260, 408-410, *Greg. Dial.* III, 36, : "ita ut non tam navis inter undas quam undae
iam intra navem esse viderentur"; "omnes (...) corpus et sanguinem Redemptoris
acceperunt"; PL 77, 304-305.

[70]See p. 87.

[71]AASS 10 maii II, 584-585, *Alia vita s. Comgalli ab. Benchor.*, lib. II, c. 21: "Cum
ergo venissent gentiles ad s. Comgallum foris operantem et chrismale suum super cappam
suam vidissent, putaverunt chrismale illud Deum s. Comgalli esse et non ausi sunt eum
tangere latrunculi causa timoris Dei sui"; Plummer (1968), II, 11.

[72]Freestone (1917), 206.

Berinus reports that his clothing remained dry, which made such a deep impression on his fellow passengers that they became his first converts.[73]

It was a practice characteristic of the early medieval Irish and Anglo-Saxon missionaries that they carried the 'chrismale' everywhere with them to serve mainly as *viaticum*. The practice is referred to once or twice in the *vitae*[74] and repeatedly in the penitentials as *perula* or Host-holder for use in the home, during work or while travelling.[75] A certain measure of discipline was required to avoid careless handling. Columbanus' rule († 615) sets the penance for dropping the 'chrismale' accidentally or leaving it behind at a year on bread and water.[76] The confessional books of Saint Gildas († 570),[77] Cummianus († c. 661),[78], Theodore of Canterbury († 690)[79] and Egbert († 729)[80] also specified the penance to be performed for losing the Eucharist while travelling. Similar prescriptions can also be found in the *De remediis peccatorum* of the pseudo-Bede already alluded to.[81] The requirement this contains, that the traveller should always carry the Eucharistic when on a journey in order to be able to offer it as *viaticum* in times of need, was not infrequently placed on priests and monks, even on the Continent. The regulations issued by Boniface in 745 as bishop of Mainz contained the prescription: "Priests may not travel without carrying with them the holy *chrisma*, the blessed oil and the saving Eucharist, in order to be able to

---

[73]Surius XII, 3 dec. 68; Martène (1788), I, 253, lib. I, c. V, art. 4.

[74]AASS 13 mart. II, 284, *Vita s. Mochoemi seu Pulcherii*, c. III,25; Plummer (1968), II, 173: "sed tamen anima eius coram praesentiam Dei in caelo est; et ideo resurrectio eius debet esse inter monachos, baculus meus et crismale cum isto interim in extremo loco sepelientur", see below p. 127, n. 140; aug. III, 658-659, *Vita Daygaei*; Plummer, ibid. 223, *Vita s. Moluae;* DACL III,1, 1478.

[75]Braun (1932), 287-288; ibid. (1940), 27-28; King (1965), 24-25; PL 71, 1003-1004, b.

[76]ed. Walker (1957), 162, c. 15: "Quicumque sacrificium perdiderit et nescit ubi sit, annum paeniteat"; 148, c. IV: "Qui oblitus fuerit chrismal pergens procul ad opus aliquod, quinis quinqueis percussionibus; si super terram in agro dimiserit et invenerit statim, denis quinqueis percussionibus"; PL 80, 217, 219; King (1965), 24.

[77]ed. Hadden-Stubbs, I, 114, Praef. Gild. de Poen. 9: "Si casu negligens quis sacrificium aliquod perdat, per III. XL mas peniteat, relinquens illud feris et alitibus devorandum".

[78]ed. Bieler (1963), 130, *Paenitentiali Cummeani* (11) 12, de quaestionibus sacrificii, 3: "Qui autem perdiderit suum crismale aut solum sacrificium in regione qualibet et non inveniatur, tres XL mas vel annum"; PL 87, 996.

[79]ed. Hadden-Stubbs, III, 187, *Poen. Theodori*, c. 12, 8: "Qui sacrificium perdit feris vel avibus devorandum, si casu, ebdomadas ieiunet, si negligens, III. XL mas".

[80]ibid. 427-428, *Poenit*, c. 12, 6: "Qui autem in plebe suum crismal perdiderit, et non invenit..poeniteat".

[81]See p. 83; PL 94, 574; see also PL 78, *In s. Gregorii librum sacramentorum notae, Hugonis Menardi Praefatio*, c. 10; PL 105, 701, *Halitgarii (831) episcopi Cameracensis liber poen.*.

fulfil their office everywhere and at all times".[82] Bishop Adalbertus of
Prague († 997) carried the Eucharist "as *viaticum*" in snow-white linen on
his journeys to Hungary, Poland and Prussia, where he died a martyr's
death.[83]

Receiving the Eucharist at sea is mentioned in a story, shot through
with sagas, in which Duke Ernst of Bavaria figures in the time of
emperor Otto I († 973). In a raging storm with the prospect of a certain
death the passengers prayed for deliverance. They begged for spiritual
salvation if physical safety could no longer be granted. The clerics on
board then distributed communion under both species to the duke and his
men.[84] The ship ran onto a cliff and broke in two. Most off those on
board were drowned. Only Ernst himself and a few others survived the
disaster in a spectacular manner: they were able to deceive griffons that
had come to feed on the corpses and, clad in skins, persuaded the birds to
give them a lift to the coast. Less dramatic circumstances are reported in
the *vita* of St. Aderaldus, when pirates attacked the ship in which the saint
was travelling as a pilgrim to Jerusalem at the beginning of the 11th
century. The passengers received the Eucharist as they awaited their end,
and the saint's prayers brought them deliverance.[85]

In the *vita* of archbishop Laurence of Dublin († 1180) it is stated
quite literally that the protective function of the Eucharistic while on a
journey is closely bound up with its function as *viaticum*. Four priests
were set upon by robbers who desecrated the Host, which the priests were
carrying "as *viaticum* and as safe guide on the journey, as was then the
custom".[86] Thomas à Becket, renowned for his violent murder in the

---

[82]d'Achery , I, 508, *Statuta quaedam s. Bonifatii*, IV: "Ut presbyteri sine sacro
chrismate et oleo benedicto et salubri eucharistia alicubi non proficiscantur. Sed ubicumque
vel fortuitu requisiti fuerint, ad officium suum statim inveniantur parati in reddendo debito";
Mansi XII, 385; this prescription was repeated in the mid-9th century by Benedict Levita III,
c. 186, PL 97, 769; also by Bishop Heraldus of Tours around 858, PL 121, 768, *Capitula*,
56: "Ut presbyteri chrisma, oleum et eucharistiam semper habeant, ut parati inveniantur".

[83]AASS 23 apr. III, 186 C, *Vita s. Adalberti ep. mart.*, c. VI,27: "Ibi missarum
solennia celebrans Patri immolat Christum, cui non post multos dies illos, seipsum pro hostia
fuerat oblaturus. Quidquid vero de eo superfluit, quod ipse et novi baptizati
communicaverunt, colligere iubet et in mundissimo panno involutum servabit sibi pro viatico
deportandum"; MGH SS IV, 583.

[84]Haupt (1849), 222, 32-35: "haec eiulans eiulantibus ait et tam ipse quam comes
Wezilo, quin et omnis exercitus participati sunt vivificum corpus et sanguinem Christi per
mysteria sacerdotum, quos etiam in societate illa interfuisse dubium non est".

[85]AASS 10 oct. VIII, 992-993, *Vita s. Aderaldi*, c. 12: "Eucharistia sumpta, iam capiendi
ab illis, mortem deflebant et proximam sentiebant".

[86]Surius XI, 14 nov. 478: "mox quattuor sacerdotes (...) qui eucharistiam, sicut tunc
moris erat pluribus, secum pro tuto viatico ac securo duce itineris publice deferebant"; An.
Boll. 33, 134.

cathedral, also hoped for protection from the Eucharist. Before the confrontation between this archbishop of Canterbury and Henry II in Northampton in October 1164, a meeting described by Knowles as "one of the most dramatic and revealing encouters in medieval history",[87] he celebrated Mass on the advice of his confessor. He mounted his horse "with the stole still under his cloak, while he carried the sacred Host with him as *viaticum*", as relates the eye-witness and biographer Fitz-Stephen.[88] The trial of strength resulted in his fleeing to banishment in continental Europe. The following popes are also known to have been accustomed to carrying "the bread of strength" - *panis fortium* - around the neck: Stephen III († 772), Stephen V († 891), Gregory VII († 1085), Urban II († 1099), Paschal II († 1118), Gelasius II († 1119) and Alexander III († 1181).[89] The power of the Eucharistic to turn aside evil also figures in a metamorphosis of two Irishman, recounted by Gerard of Wales. It is said that a man and a woman were turned into wolves in 1182 or 1183. They were restored to human form when a priest pulled out the *pendula* containing the Eucharist from under his garments and held it before them, after which they received communion.[90] This legend ascribes to the Host a kind of miraculous power which was to be relied on in 1212 at the taking of a Saracen stronghold in Spain. The chronicler, Albricus of Trois-Fontaines, tells that a priest was required to walk in front carrying the Eucharist towards the fortress amid the projectiles launched by the enemy.[91] The same atmosphere is evoked in the story of a Franciscan, John of Winterthur. Around 1340, it is told, a friar minor took a consecrated Host with him when a schoolmaster in Brandenburg invited him to come and view the Holy Trinity. They landed in a company of heretics, where three members in shining robes were in the process of deceiving those present. The mendicant monk took out the Eucharist and the three deceivers disappeared immediately from the scene,

---

[87]Knowles (1971), 94.

[88]MB III, 57.

[89]Martène (1788), I, 253, lib. I, c. V, art. IV: "Praetereo summos pontifices..de quibus vide quae scripsit Angelus Rocca in singulari libello de Sacro Christi Corpore Romanis Pontificibus iter conficientibus praeferendo"; Thiers (1677), 8.

[90]RS 21,5, ed. Dimock (1867), 102, *Topographia Hibernica*, 2, 19: "ostendens ei perulam, librum manualem et aliquot hostias consecratas continentem; quae more patriae presbyter itinerans (sub indumento) a collo suspensa deferebat".

[91]MGH SS XXIII, 894, *Chronica Albrici monachi trium fontium.*: "Franci quidem castrum istud ceperunt, et ita miraculose fregerunt, quod presbiter quidam primus omnium cum corpore Domini intravit et plus quam 60 sagittas excepit in alba, qua indutus erat, nec tamen fuit laesus".

leaving a diabolical stench behind them.[92] In the Florentine Sacchetti's *Il Trecentonovelle* († 1400) some lay people were saved from a raging stream by a priest holding the Host high above the waters.[93]

However the Eucharist carried on journeys required reverence in consequence of its increasing 'process of independence'. As early as 1030 Robert the Pious of France liked having the Host in close proximity in order to be able to praise the Lord. Wherever he went - as he is portrayed by the monk and biographer Helgaud de Fleury condemning the "neglect of bishops and abbots" - he always had with him a cart bearing a tent in which the "divine *ministerium*" or the 'chrismale' was kept.[94] At every resting place the Sacrament was praised with the psalmist's words: "The earth is the Lord's, and the fullness thereof; the world and they that dwell therein" (Ps. 24).[95] For his return journey from Syria the crusader Saint Louis († 1270) was granted by the papal legate the privilege of carrying the Eucharist with him. he requested this permission because of those travelling with him, because they had never experienced such a thing on board ship and needed to become accustomed to it. The king had a costly chapel tent, made of silk sewn with gold, set up on the after-deck. There the Eucharist could be venerated and received, with special attention being paid to the sick crusaders. And yet the protective element too, both of the Eucharist and of the relics, was present for during a storm the monarch prayed to almighty God to grant help "before the sacred body of Christ and the holy relics".[96] The latter will have been placed on or near

---

[92]MGH SS, NS, vol. III, 151, *Chronica*: "quidam rector puerorum..dicens ei: Venite mecum et ego ostendam vobis sanctam aperte trinitatem (...) frater corpus Christi de brachiali, in quo absconditum tulit, extrahens et in altum porrigens subintulit (...) Ad cuius aspectum demones, qui in specie trinitatis homines diu deluserant et dementaverant, cum fetore pessimo, quem post se relinquebant, disparuerunt"; Browe (1938), 87-92.

[93]Sachetti, 241-243, Novella LXXXIX; Trexler (1980), 56.

[94]DACL III,1, 1480: "Le chrismal est aussi appelé ministerium, c'est-à-dire vase".

[95]ed. Bautier (1965), 100-102: "Quocumque illi erat eundum, preparabatur vehiculum quod deportaret divini ministerii tentorium; quo in terram fixo, deponebantur ibi sancta ut, quia secundum psalmistam: "Domini est terra et plenitudo eius orbis terrarum et universi qui habitant in eo', proderet se devotum famulum quovis in loco Deo devotas persolvere" laudes".

[96]RHF XX, 388: "Ex devotione enim sua fecit poni in navi corpus Domini Jesu Christi pro communicandis infirmis, ac pro seipso et suis, quando sibi expediens videretur. Et quia alii peregrini quantumcunque magni hoc facere non solebant, obtinuit super hoc a legato licentiam specialem"; "et coram sacro corpore Christi ac sanctis reliquiis devote prostratus, humiliter exorabat ut omnipotens Deus praesente periculo subveniret".

the altar, in front of which Louis prayed thankfully after they were saved.[97]

***

The aim of taking the Eucharistic bread on journeys reflects the changing appreciation of the Eucharist in the course of the centuries. When attitudes to the Eucharist while travelling had still not been affected by the realisation of the *praesentia realis* in the spirit of Pachasius Radbertus, it was considered as both *apotropaeon* and *viaticum*. Slowly but surely the protective function which the Eucharist shared with the relic phylactery faded into the background while a new aspect began to claim attention: the reverence and adoration of the Sacrament. The sources already quoted would seem to place the change in the 12th-13th century: Robert the Pious - an early herald of change - is quoted by his biographer as having praised the "divine ministerium" with psalms while on his travels, but in the *vita* of Laurence of Dublin the Eucharist is still regarded 'true to tradition' as *viaticum* and guarantee of a safe journey. Both these functions would seem to have been present in the use made of the Eucharist by Thomas à Becket and the popes quoted. In the tale of the sea journey undertaken by Saint Louis we see signs of the heights attained by the Eucharist in the 13th-14th centuries with the introduction of the 'elevatio' and the forms of adoration outside the Mass. The body of Christ revered would end up pushing the relics into second place. However in addition the Host was endowed with miraculous power in the legendary reports as if it were a miraculous relic. In the accounts of Albricus, John of Winterthur and Sachetti the Eucharist is presented a if it were a *fylacterium*, as used by Gallus against a wild animal, by Theodardus against robbers or by Willehad against a sword. This parallel will be looked at further in chapter V.

In consequence of the development first mentioned, that of the adoration, the question arose as to whether 'the Eucharist as travelling companion' accorded with the reverence required. The express permission given by the papal legate to Louis is an indication, and Caesarius of Heisterbach († c. 1240) provides two examples of objections of this type. A certain brother Henry accompanied a respectable number of priests on board ship at Damiate. Once it had left the island of Cyprus, all the

---

[97]ibid. "Mane facto, rex fidei plenus reversus est secreto ante altare prostratus devotus gratias super tanto et tam mirabili beneficio sibi et suis exhibito reddidit omnium salvatori"; see also RHF XXIII, 162.

elements seemed to turn on them and everyone thought they were doomed. Then Henry saw a Venetian priest taking the Eucharist to someone who was sick. The situation was immediately clear to him: "It is right", he told the venetian, "that God should punish us so, for it is not allowed to have the Eucharist on board ship. Moreover it is not respectful to keep the Host in an *arca* so that the sailors as it were walk over it and play dice above it". The priest thus accused made reply, whereupon the rest of the clerics became involved. The agreed unanimously with Henry's point of view and brought further reasoning to bear on the question. The Eucharist would become the food of fish if someone were to become seasick or if a passenger were to die and be buried at sea after receiving communion.[98] In another example the objections were made even more clear. During a military expedition the Eucharist was taken on board ship despite a very emphatic ban. The vessel in question refused to obey, the passengers were washed overboard and the pyx fell into the sea. The drowning people were rescued from the waves by ships that came to their aid, but the pyx saved itself: it remained floating and sailed towards the ships. When it had been taken on board and opened it was noted that not a drop of water had entered. "For the earth itself recognizes her Creator in this sacrament", concludes Caesarius.[99]

After the 13th century this custom - which had, in any case, declined considerably - of taking the Eucharist on journeys as *viaticum*,[100] although it did occur a few times up to the 17th century - and even later during the French revolution.[101]

There would seem to be on exception to this general conclusion: from the 14th to the 18th century the tradition was maintained of bearing the Sacrament in papal processions on a white horse.[102] Wherever this papal tradition is referred to no mention is made of its former function of *apotropaeon* and *viaticum* for which purpose the popes themselves had carried the Eucharist around the neck. Browe believes that this festive papal tradition cannot be explained on the basis of the old custom.[103] The fact that William Durandus († 1296) makes no mention of the

---

[98]*Mirac.* ed. Hilka (1937), 32-34, lib. I, c. 12.

[99]*Dial.* ed. Strange (1851), II, 176, lib. IX, c. 13: "Terra etiam in hoc sacramento suum recognoscit auctorem".

[100]Corblet (1886), I, 529.

[101]Nussbaum (1979), 90-91.

[102]ibid. 89-90; Zika (1988), 46-47, n. 68.

[103]Browe (1933), 139-140.

Eucharist when writing of the papal procession can be used as evidence that this was not originally done. However he does mention the altar and the relics required for it. To this end a hinny walked behind the processional cross in the pontificate of Boniface VIII (1294-1303).[104] In the course of the 14th century interest began to grow in the procession of the Blessed Sacrament. The papal procession drew inspiration from this and took on the same character: the Sacrament carried by the horse, a baldachin the lamp and candle bearers.[105] The love of pomp and splendour in the Renaissance - even the pope was carried on the shoulders of bearers under a baldachin - will have made this practice familiar.

A spontaneous link is made between the 'chrismale', or Eucharist holder, and the *chrismarium* or relic-holder. Can the term *chrismarium* be directly related to the root word *chrisma* or is it merely a deformation of *chrismale*?[106] In practice the two terms became intertwined. There is one text in which the *chrismarium* is used as a variant on the 'chrismale'. It is a cryptic poem on the Eucharist written by bishop Aldhelm of Sherborne († 709) and is entitled: *On the 'chrismale' or the chrismarium*.[107]

From the same century Braun gives two examples of *chrismaria* which first served as 'chrismale'.[108] The first refers to a *chrismarium* with a saddle-shaped cover in the parish church of Mortain (Manche) which, according to the runic characters, was originally not a relic-holder but a Eucharistic 'chrismale'.[109] It came from Northumbria and is probably the only 'chrismale' which has come down to us from the Irish monks, in whose *vitae* the 'Host holder' is often mentioned under this name, as we have already noted. The second example is a small bursa-shaped relic-holder, found in the reliquary treasure of St. Valeria in Sitten. It is 10.7 cm long and 9 cm high and dates from the Merovingian

[104]Durandus, *Rationale,* divin. offic. c. 41 n. 50: "Mula etiam capellam Domini Papae squillam fert ob reverentiam reliquiarum quas portat"; Browe (1933), 138.

[105]Corblet (1886), I. illustr. p. 531, 533; Nussbaum (1979), 90, illustr. 2 and 3.

[106]Braun (1940), 28.

[107]ed. Giles (1844), 262, ep. ad Acircium: *"de Chrismale sive Chrismaro";* PL 89, 194.

[108]Braun (1940), 199.

[109]Cahen (1930), 7: "Ce petit meuble, destiné à être suspendu au cou, a dû, au moins dans le principe, servir de *chrismatorium* bien que il ait été converti après coup en reliquaire"; Blouet (1953).

era. The inscription "Amalrich" must have been the name of the original owner.[110]

With the gradual disappearance of the practice of taking the Eucharist on journeys the 'chrismale' was probably put to another use, that of containing relics. Braun mentions two *ciborium*-like containers from a later period which underwent the same fate. They served as relic-holders while the name '*viaticum*' still recalled the period when they contained the Eucharist.[111]

If the assumption made is correct, a development occurred in the early Middle Ages contrary to that which took place in the late Middle Ages, when the reliquaries were transformed into Eucharistic *ostensoria*, to be dealt with in the fourth chapter. In the first case, the increase in piety was an obstacle to the continuation of the practice of using the Eucharistic as a travelling companion, so that the now superfluous 'chrismale' was made into a container for relics. In the second, it was precisely the desire to see and adore the Eucharist that encouraged the transformation of the reliquary into a Eucharistic monstrance. The carrying of relics outstripped the carrying of relics, while the desire to see the Eucharist put the desire to see the relics in the shade. The 'chrismale' that became a *chrismarium* emphasised by the interchangeability of the terms the 'parallel application' for the same end: the guarantee of safety while travelling. The passage from relic-ostensorium to Eucharistic monstrance underlined the transposition of the form of reverence: the showing.

3 DEATH AND BURIAL

Everything that sings, lives and blooms under the warm sun one day turns to grey ash. As their final end approached, saints would have themselves laid on ash and sprinkled with it in the guilty realisation that they were to return to dry, dark dust. Christians are reminded each year that they will "return to dust" on Ash Wednesday, when their foreheads are marked with the ashes of the once green branches used on Palm Sunday.[1]

---

[110]Stückelberg (1904), 48-54; in this treasure trove of relics there was also a blue band with a gold-embossed side which bore alternately in small Gothic letters the words *Manna* and *Maria*. Was this designed to close a small pouch for carrying relics or the Eucharist?

[111]Braun (1940), 72.

[1]LW I, 193.

No man can avoid death and decay. Death is a profound matter and causes those present to be still; all that counts is to be near one another. Whatever has provided consolation and strength in life also provides the same in the last hours. It must have been at times like this that the primitive and early medieval Christians held fast to the relics that they had kept at home and worn throughout their lives.[2]

People derived strength from the Cross as they did from the book of the Gospels. And from the 12th century onwards, the prayer beads that were later to be called the rosary in the 15th century[3] also constituted a source of consolation. No matter how much reliance may have been placed on the relics during life, there are but a few examples known of them providing support in the hour of death. The principal role was taken from the start by the last communion or *viaticum*. It provided strength as food for the soul on the journey to the Lord, the *migratio ad Dominum*.[4]

The name *viaticum* is pre-Christian and comes from the Greco-Roman culture, whose funerary customs were adopted and adapted in form and significance by the Christians. Jerome had no objection to a husband spreading a variety of flowers over his wife's grave, even though the usage had long been seen in a bad light because of its pagan origin.[5] In the ancient world it was assumed that the living could offer sacrifice to support the dead, a belief that found its Christian counterpart in the prayers for the departed, especially during Mass.

Death was represented as a journey in both Egyptian and Greco-Roman Antiquity, a journey requiring preparation and supplies - the *viaticum*. The Greeks believed the world of the dead to be a world of shades, bounded by a black, misty river, the Styx. From the 6th century BC these shades were seen as gathering by the boat belonging to the ferryman, Charon, a skinny old dimwit who demanded a coin, or obol, for the fare. The obol was placed in the dead person's mouth and quite possibly once symbolised the person's entire possessions.[6] The custom

---

[2]Beissel (1976), II, 92.

[3]LCI 3, 568; Rothkrug (1980), 95.

[4]Grabka (1953), 21; Nussbaum (1979), 70.

[5]CSEL 54, 653, ep. 66.5: "Ceteri mariti super tumulos coniugum spargunt violas, rosas, lilia floresque purpureos et dolorem pectoris his officiis consolantur".

[6]ibid. 20.

found its way into Roman culture, which sometimes called the obol *viaticum*.[7]

During the period when the Christian faith was spreading throughout the Greco-Roman world the dead person's journey through the world of the dead was a generally accepted image in large sections of the population. Archaeological finds in graves dating from the 4th century in countries including Germany, France, Spain and Greece demonstrate that the Christians had not completely abandoned such practices until well into the Middle Ages. The original meaning of the obol was lost but the need remained to be of support to the one who had died.[8]

Old customs die out slowly. St. Monica († 387) followed the custom she was used to in Africa when she carried gruel, bread and unmixed wine into the cathedral in Milan in order to place it at the graves of the martyrs. The doorkeeper stopped her, saying that the bishop, Ambrose, had forbidden the practice. Augustine supplies an explanation of the interdict: it resembled too closely in the externals the pagan meal of the dead and it could, in any case, encourage excessive drinking.[9]

The custom described above whereby Christians placed a coin in the mouth of the corpse was probably not all that widespread, since no protest is recorded on the part of the church fathers or in early conciliar texts. The representation of death as a journey full of dangers was, however, adopted by Christians in general, and another form of *viaticum* gradually took over in this *migratio ad Dominum*: the Eucharist,[10] which was placed on the dying person's tongue in the very last moments. This led to an abuse which did come in for censure on the part of the church in conciliar and synodal prescriptions: the custom of placing the *viaticum*, like the obol, on the tongue of one already dead.

In addition to this 'communion of the dead' the Eucharist was also placed separately in the coffin as a *fylacterium*. Just as those of the

---

[7]ed. Adlington (1566), Apuleius (124), *Asinus Aureus*, VI,18: "nec Charon ille vel Ditis pater, tantus deus, quicquam gratuito facit, sed moriens pauper viaticum debet quaerere"; Grabka (1953), 20, n. 119; Nussbaum (1979), 64 sqq.

[8]Grimm (1876⁴), 2, 694: "es scheinen uralte heidnische Erinnerungen, die um nicht ganz zu erlöschen sich veränderten"; 3, 441: "*Todten* one puts *Geld in den Mund*, so kommen sie, wenn sie einen Schatz verborgen haben nicht wieder"; Ulrichs (1844), 377; Schmidt (1845), 83; Cochet (1857), 329-330; Sartori (1899); Hermann (1953), 1056 sqq.; Nussbaum (1979), 70; RAC II, 1056-1061, 'charon'.

[9]CC SL 27, 74, *Confessiones*, VI, c. II,2: "Itaque cum ad memorias sanctorum sicut in Africa solebat, pultes et panem et merum attulisset atque ab ostiario prohiberetur, ubi hoc episcopum vetuisse cognovit, tam pie atque obedienter amplexa est ut ipse mirarer, quam facile accusatrix potius consuetudinis suae quam disceptatrix illius prohibitionis effecta sit"; Meer v.d. (1947), 452-453.

[10]Grabka (1953), 27.

ancient world feared the demons of the underworld and ordered their funereal rites accordingly, so too the Christian practice of giving the Eucharist in this fashion was intended to keep the devils at bay. And yet this was not the only motive, certainly not in every case. Going down into the grave with Christ implied the promise of resurrection with Him.

The fear of evil spirits is also demonstrated by little bells, amulets and engraved daggers which have been found in the graves. Here too Christian antiquity would seem not to have been totally liberated from heathen practices, something confirmed by the apotropaeic grave symbolism of an 'evil eye' and all its accompaniments.[11] These acts steeped in the pagan spirit gave expression to the links of the living with the dead and to the questions surrounding the final end to life.

The Christians were convinced that once death had taken its toll nothing more could be done to redress the balance of a lifetime. The dead person thus had to rely on the prayers of the living and the intercession of the martyrs and saints who already beheld the glory of God. This the reason for the strong desire in early Christian times to have one's last resting place *ad sanctos*, close to a martyr's grave or the tomb of a saint - something that was, incidentally, "a privilege which (...) many desire and few obtain".[12] As far as the poor were concerned it was nothing more than a pious wish. The burial places of martyrs and saints drew the praying faithful who hoped that the intercession they pleaded for would guarantee them God's mercy and resurrection on the Last Day.[13]

When, from the 4th century onwards, the mausolea or *martyria* rose above the graves of those who had witnessed with their blood, buildings which rapidly took on the dimensions of a burial chapel, the martyrs' graves were ipso facto inside the church building and thus too the last resting places of those buried nearby.

Until around the 5th century a sharp distinction continued to be made between this type of graveyard basilica and the church buildings intended for the gatherings of the community. Later the distinction became less clear. Ambrose began the process as early as 386. He reports to his sister, Marcellina, the *inventio* of Ss. Gervase and Protase, whose

---

[11]Kraus (1886), II, 881; Engemann (1975), 24: "das Bild des von mancherlei Waffen, Tieren und Symbolen duchbohrten, bedrohten oder umringten 'Bösen Auges'(des Phthonos - Neides)"; funeral ritual: Rush (1941).

[12]DACL I, 408, 479; Brown (1982²), 34.

[13]Delehaye (1933), 131-137; Duval (1991), 342: "le sépulcre lui-même qui dans sa matérialité fait du mort un membre du groupe des saints, et lui assure ainsi leur secours pour l'autre vie".

bones were found in a state of good preservation "with a great deal of blood". He had the remains of the two martyrs transferred to the church where he himself had assigned them a final resting place under the altar.[14] At a later date, incidentally, the church was named after Ambrose rather than the two martyrs.

To be buried close to a martyr now started to mean being buried inside a church, a usage which was long the source of some difference of opinion in Christendom, as witness the many synodal decisions on the subject.[15] In this regard there is an interesting statement made by the Council of Braga in 563, which rejected burial in a church as contrary to the reverence due to the martyrs,[16] a reverence expressed with light and incense, signs of reverence that were continued and transposed into forms of reverence shown the Eucharist, something which will be dealt with further in chapter VI.

However in general the principal obstacle was not reverence for the relics but reverence for the Eucharist.[17] The *Decretum Gratiani*, which gives a summary of almost all the decisions taken up to that time, banned the custom around 1143. An exception was made for the atrium (the area at the front of the church) and for other parts of the church building, but within the church itself, close to the altar where the body and blood of Christ were consecrated, it was forbidden to bury the dead.[18] The interdict did not apply to the bodies of bishops, abbots, priests and lay

---

[14]CSEL 82, 127-128, lib. X, ep. LXXVII (22), c. 1-2: "Nam cum basilicam dedicassem, multi tamquam uno ore interpellare coeperunt dicentes: 'Sicut Romanam basilicam dedices'. Respondi: 'Faciam, si martyrum reliquias invenero' (...). Invenimus mirae magnitudinis viros duos ut prisca aetas ferebat. Ossa omnia integra, sanguinis plurimum. Ingens concursus populi per totum illud biduum. Quid multa? Condivimus integra ad ordinem, transtulimus vespere iam incumbente ad basilicam Faustae; ibi vigiliae tota nocte, manus impositio. Sequenti die transtulimus ea ad basilicam, quam appellant Ambrosianam"; ib. 134, c. 12: "Sanguine tumulus madet"; PL 16, 1019-1020, ep. classis I, 22, 1,2; ib. 1023; MGH SRM I,2, 69, *In gloria martyrum,* c. 46; Delehaye (1933), 76-77; Dassmann (1975), 52-57; Brown (1982), 36; J. den Boeft (1988) states that according to the report made to Marcellina of two sermons, which follow the passage in the letter quoted, this translation of the martyrs' remains had an anti-Arian significance.

[15]Kötting (1965).

[16]Mansi IX, 779, c. 18: "ut modo intra ambitus murorum cuiuslibet defuncti corpus humetur, quanto magis hoc venerabilium martyrum debet reverentia obtinere?"; Kötting (1965), 32.

[17]ibid. 33.

[18]ed. Friedberg (1879), *Decretum Magistri Gratiani,* II, 13, q. 2, can. 15: "Prohibendum est etiam secundum maiorum instituta, ut in ecclesia nullatenus sepeliantur, sed in atrio, aut in porticu, aut in exedris ecclesiae. Infra ecclesiam vero, aut prope altare, ubi corpus Domini et sanguis conficitur, nullatenus sepeliantur".

people who had borne witness to great faith.[19] The significance of burial close to the *memoriae martyrum*, stated the decree, lay particularly in the protection afforded the dead by the martyr and the prayer of the faithful thereby intensified.[20]

As well as burial *ad sanctos*, people took relics with them into the grave as a means of support. This was a solution adopted by a certain Asclepia in Salona (Dalmatia), a place rich in early Christian remains. She had managed to acquire the body of Anastasius of Aquileia, who had been killed there in the reign of Diocletian. This saint, who went in search of a martyr's death, was thrown into the bay of Salona with a millstone round his neck. In 304 she had a niche made in the family grave where his body could be placed. Her own final resting place was connected to that of the saint by means of a *fenestella*, from which a small shaft led to the outer world, emerging in the top of a sacrificial table designed to serve in the cult of the dead.[21]

During the pagan meals of the dead this type of shaft served to transport milk, wine or honey to the body so that the dead one could have some share in the memorial meal eaten by the survivors. The funnel-shaped holes found in various Christian tomb coverings once again demonstrate that in the beginning the Christians had failed to shake themselves loose from the practice of pagan libations.[22] The previously cited basket carried by St. Monica was an example. The privilege enjoyed by Asclepia was one that few enjoyed. Most were happy enough if they had a relic of their own to place in their grave.

3.1   Relics by death and burial

It was not realised until she was on her deathbed in 379 that Makrina, the sister of Gregory of Nyssa, wore around her neck as a *fylacterium* a small ring, containing a particle of the True Cross, together with a small crucifix. Her friend Vetania and her brother Gregory were present when she died. After Makrina had expired Vetania was carefully arranging the

---

[19]can. 18: "Nullus mortuus infra ecclesiam sepeliatur, nisi episcopi, aut abbates aut digni presbiteri vel fideles laici".

[20]can. 19: "Quod vero quisque apud memorias martirum sepelitur, hoc tantum mihi videtur prodesse defuncto, ut commendans eum etiam martirum patrocinio affectus supplicationis pro illo augeatur".

[21]Dyggve (1939), 80 sqq.; (1951), 78; Buschhausen (1971), 15.

[22]Wieland (1912), 148-162, with illustr.

dead woman's head when she discovered a chain and the ring in question. She undid the chain and, after discussing the matter with Gregory, she was given the ring to wear as a piece of jewellery and Gregory took the small crucifix. She came off best because when they looked at the ring again more carefully they discovered a hollow containing a particle of the wood of the True Cross.[23]

Although her *vita* fails to report explicitly any support that Makrina may have felt in her final moments from the crucifix and the relic, it is nonetheless mentioned implicitly. Protection against danger to the soul and body was acute in the lonely hour of death. Prudentius sang the praises of the relics of the martyrs at home and on journeys, describing them as a *fidele pignus* or "a trustworthy pledge";[24] Paulinus of Nola qualified the particle of the True Cross that he sent to his friend Sulpicius as "a daily protection and guarantee of perpetual salvation";[25] and Jerome remarked that the spirits of darkness could in no way prevail against the relics.[26] And yet they were seldom reported as providing support at the hour of death. This could be because of their obvious presence in the sleeping quarters and even more by the prevailing role filled by the *viaticum*.

In the *vita* of St. Meinrad († 861) we read how he prepared himself for his violent end by first receiving the *viaticum* and then seeking support from the relics. The event turned Einsiedeln later into a well known Swiss pilgrimage place. Meinrad had a lonely hermitage deep in the forest. One day two vagrants were inspired by the devil to penetrate to the hermit's refuge. At their approach the chickens gave vent to wild and unfamiliar cackling, as if being attacked by a fox. The biographer quotes this as a warning and a sign of their own death. Meanwhile the saint commended himself to God and, as if he felt the close approach of death, received the body of the Lord as *viaticum*. Then like Jesus on the Mount of Olives he remained in prayer, knowing that his enemies were close at hand. While taking the *capsae* one by one in his hands and kissing the relics, he commended his soul once again to God and to the

---

[23] See p. 84.

[24] CSEL 61, 360, *Peristephanon*, VI, 133-135: "Fratrum tantus amor domum referre, sanctorum cinerum dicata dona, aut gestare sinu fidele pignus"; Dölger (1929-50), III, 108.

[25] CSEL 29, 268, ep. 31.1 : "munimentum praesentis et aeternae salutis".

[26] Le Blant (1875), 28, n. 7.

saints whose relics he held.[27] His friendly welcome to the men as they
forced their way in was of no avail. One of the two hit him on the head
with a stick and dispatched him. Two black ravens in the coat of arms of
Einsiedeln recall the fact that these birds later brought the murder to
light.[28] On the site of his hermitage an abbey was built with a beautiful
pilgrimage church.

Emperor Otto III († 1002) is also reported to have been
strengthened in his last hours by a relic of the True Cross which had a
history behind it.[29] One of Otto's predecessors, Emperor Charles III,
known as the Fat († 888), had sent it to his nephew, Arnulf of Carinthia
(† 899), when the latter had proved unfaithful to his uncle. The emperor
thus attempted to remind him in a subtle way that Arnulf had sworn fealty
to him on this very relic. Arnulf understood only too well and burst into
tears. Which did not prevent Charles being deposed and Arnulf being
chosen as his successor.[30]

The relics again appear as a final source of consolation after
receiving the communion of the sick in the life story of Richard of St.
Vannes. As soon as this monastic reformer of the Lorraine felt his death
approaching in 1046, he first received the anointing of the sick and then,
after confessing his sins, the *viaticum*.[31] "Then he lay there upon ash
and dressed in a penitential robe in such a way that he had his face turned
towards the altar of St. Nicholas." He asked his brothers to bring to him
the *fylacterium* that he had brought back from Jerusalem and had always
worn around his neck. He kissed it and begged for the protection of the
saints. When the coldness of death crept into his body, he laid the relic at
his feet and when they grew cold drew them closer to himself. He expired
with the *capsa* clasped to his bosom.[32] His body was stripped and buried

---

[27]AASS 21 ian. II, 384, *Vita s. Meinradi eremitae mart.* c. VII, 12: "corpusque
Dominicum ut praescius futurorum ad viaticum obitus sui, puro corde, ac devota mente
susceperat (...) Strenue ergo orationem complevit, capsasque singulas reliquiarum manu
suscipiens et deosculans, commendabat agonem suum Domino et Sanctis, quorum reliquias
complectebatur reverenter".

[28]KE 17, 'Meinradus'.

[29]Schramm (1962), 26: "Vielleicht handelte es sich um das gleiche Stück des heiligen
Holzes, das Otto III in der Todesstunde tröstete".

[30]MGH SS (1891), 106, *Annales Fuldenses* ad a. 887.

[31]AASS 10 iun. II, 998, *Vita ven. Richardi ab. Virdun.*, n. 79: "et inunctus ab episcopo
oleo sancto, confessione data, viatico caelesti pastus, expositus est lectulo et iacuit in cinere
et cilicio, ita ut altare s. Nicolai eius semper appareret conspectui"; see p. 87, n. 37.

[32]ibid. "Ubi vero coepit iam inferiori parte corpus emori, sanctorum reliquias
apprehendens in lectulo sedit; et ad pedes eas ponens, atque uti vitalis calor deficiebat,
paulatim eas protrahens, tandem in pectore substitit; et reliquias ibidem cum reclinasset,
deposuit (...) Cum ergo (caput) reclinasset, manus reliquiis apposuit, et sic usquequo spiri-

in blessed garments, with the same relics on his body that had consoled him until his last moments.[33] The consolation given by such objects was reported earlier, in the 12th-century chronicle or Ortlieb of Zwiefalten, where it is said that it was the abbot's custom to carry the relics with him when he was travelling "for the benefit of the sick".[34]

When Hugh of Cluny was on his deathbed in 1109 he asked for *capsa* containing the relics of St. Marcellus, so recounts Hildebert of Lavardin, who wrote a *vita* of this famous abbot at the beginning of 1122 based on material made available to him by Hugh's successor. And when David I of Scotland was dying in 1153, a relic of the True Cross brought him the consolation he sought. David's death was recorded by Aelred of Hexham, a Cistercian who had spent his youth as a page at court. When the king sensed that his end was approaching, he asked to be taken to the altar to hear Mass one more time. Then he commanded the costly crucifix to be brought which his mother, St. Margaret, had brought to Scotland. It was possible to open it to reveal a particle of the True Cross. He honoured this crucifix with great reverence and then received the *viaticum* and the sacred anointing, after which he gave up his spirit while those around him sang psalms.[35]

Some decades later, in 1191, there were fears for the life of Louis, the still young son of Philip II Augustus. The monks of St. Denis placed their hopes in a crown of thorns, a nail from the True Cross and the arm of St. Simeon, relics which they used to make the sign of the cross over Louis' abdomen, following which his health was restored.[36] A final example of support provided by relics at a time of mort danger can be found in the account of the death of St. Catherine of Siena in 1380. After

---

tum Creatori redderet".

[33] ibid. n. 80: "Ipsi corpus sanctissimum procuraverunt: vestibus sacratis ex more induit episcopus (...) Reliquiae, quas super pectus commiserat, induto eo sacris vestibus, supra pectus eius repositae sunt".

[34] See p. 88; for 14th-century examples see : Kroos (1985), 32.

[35] PL 159, 890, *Vita s. Hugonis auctore Hildeberto Cenomanensi episcopo*, c. VII, 48: "Dei famulus b. Marcelli capsam sibi iuvet praesentari"; ed. Cowdrey (1978), 23; PL 195, 715, *Genealogia Regum Anglorum*: "Est autem crux illa longitudinem habens palmae de auro purissimo mirabili opere fabricata quae in modum thecae clauditur et aperitur. Cernitur in ea quaedam Dominicae crucis portio (...) Hanc igitur crucem omni Scotorum genti non minus terribilem quam amabilem cum rex devotissime adorasset, cum multis lacrymis peccatorum confessione praemissa, exitum suum coelestium mysteriorum perceptione munivit"; Bridgett (1908), 249-250.

[36] ed. Viard (1920-53), VI, 204: "car il recovra maintenant plaine santé à l'atouchement du saint clou et de la sainte corone et du braz saint Symeon qui li furent atouchié en croiz sur le ventre"; Mély de (1904), 231-232: "les religieux de l'abbaye de Saint-Denis portent *la Couronne d'épines* au jeune fils de Philippe-Auguste, Louis, quand en 1191, il est atteint de la maladie qui le met aux portes du tombeau".

receiving absolution, the Eucharist and the anointing with oil, she fixed her gaze on a crucifix "set in a frame with relics".[37]The crucifix itself was, we assume, the most important factor for her.

The relics that Richard of St. Vannes held in his last hour were placed in his grave. Even after death the relics were relied on to provide the protection of the saints during the journey to the Lord. In the burial chambers of the catacombs in Rome and in various graves in Merovingian France dozens of glass, terra cotta or alabaster vases have been discovered which did not serve exclusively to contain incense, as is shown by a documented study carried out by H. Leclercq.[38] Some vases or phials were qualified as "blood ampoules", since it was assumed that they had contained the blood of martyrs. Martin is said to have filled three ampoules with dewdrops that had turned into blood at the site of the death of the martyrs of the Theban legion († 304). Apparently he made it known that he would like one of these ampoules to be buried with him.[39] In these small bottles earth was also found, and holy water, oil *eulogia*[40] and possibly also Eucharistic wine.

The latter suggestion was proposed[41] because of a gravestone dating from the 5th century discovered at Vix, close to Chatillon-sur-Seine. It carried the following inscription: *Christus hic est.*[42] However it is much more likely that the inscription referred to the monogram of Christ which was also on the gravestone. This was often placed above doors and graves in early Christian times as a protection against the tricks of the devil.[43]

In the introduction to this chapter a link was made between the fear of the forces of Hell and the function off the Eucharist and the relics in funerary customs. In early Christian times this fear is found in such things as the appeal made to Christ - previously referred to - to be present at

---

[37]ed. Cartier (1859), 467: "Enfin elle fixa ses regards sur un crucifix placé dans un petit cadre rempli de reliques"; This had already been reported by her contemporary, Cafarini, who wrote a supplement to the vita written by her father confessor, Raymund of Capua.

[38]DACL I,2 , 1747-1778, 'ampoules de sang'.

[39]AASS 20 sept. VI, 384, *Gloria posthuma s.s. Mauritii et Thebaeorum,* c. XV n. 179: "Super herbas igitur prati illius, ubi sanguis sanctorum martyrum pro Christo fuerat effusus, apparuit ros sanguineus ex quo tres ampullas beatus pontifex replevit".

[40]Le Blant (1858); Engemann (1973), 6, n. 11 and 11-13.

[41]Le Blant (1875).

[42]DACL I,2 , 1756-57.

[43]Engemann (1975), 43-44; Nussbaum (1979), 81, n. 180.

death in the terrifying stories recounted by pope Gregory the Great. A description is given of the devouring fire shooting out of someone's grave and bringing his impurity to light,[44] or of devils shouting and dragging the corpse of a sinner out of the church where he has been buried[45] and of the body of nun who could not hold her tongue being dragged out of the grave and half burned.[46]

As a guarantee for a safe journey the dead one was given such things as holy water, relics or a crucifix. Dölger mentions findings of crucifixes in graves in Egypt which had been worn as *fylacteria* and were possibly inlaid with relics from the 4th century onwards.[47] As far as the West is concerned, he mentions the discovery of a reliquary cross in 1863 on the Agro Virano in Rome. It was found lying on the chest of a corpse and must have been worn around the neck. The hollow in the upper part probably contained a relic of the True Cross, since on the front there is a cryptic engraving on the top and side beams: "The cross is life for *me*, and for *you*, enemy - demon -, death". The words on the back of the cross: "Emmanuel, God with us", seem to be some sort of exorcism.[48]

Small separate leaden crosses, frequently found on the chest of corpses, sometimes bore a name, a formula of absolution or the inscription: "The cross of Christ vanquishes the enemy, the cross of Christ triumphs".[49] The degree of persistence exerted by pagan influence on the cross amulet worn in a Christian sense can be judged from a discovery made in a grave in the cathedral of Lausanne, dating from the 8th or 9th century. In the lead of the cross found there was engraved the pagan magic formula 'Abracax'.[50]

The relics were buried not only contained in crosses but also in late-Roman *scrinia* and other types of reliquaries. These *scrinia* were small cube-shaped boxes measuring approximately 20 by 30 cm. Because of their increased prevalence in graves from the 4th century onwards and the engravings they carried, taken from sarcophagi, Buschhausen assumes

---

[44]SC 265, 110, *Dial.* lib. IV, c. 33; PL 77, 372-373, lib. IV, c. 32.

[45]SC 265,180, lib. IV, c. 55; PL 77, 413-416, lib. IV, c. 53.

[46]SC 265, 178, lib. IV, c. 53; PL 77, 412-413, lib. IV, c. 51.

[47]Dölger (1929-50), III, 91.

[48]ibid. 97-98: "Crux est vita mihi, mors, inimice, tibi"; Kraus (1886), 882.

[49]"Crux Christi pellit hostem, Crux Christi triumphat"; Cochet (1857), 303-318, 323-330, 335-338; Corblet (1885-1886), I, 537 (see n. 152); Murcier (1855), 20-27, 168; Rossi de (1863), 31.

[50]Dölger (1929-50), 89; DACL X,1, 1107, J. Leclercq, "magie", illustr. 7510.

that they were specially made for placing in a grave. In a grave found in
Fének and dating from the 4th century, a *scrinium* was found lying at
knee height between two skeletons. The same circumstances were
discovered in a burial chamber in Lopud and in a tomb in the St. Sophia
basilica in Sofia.[51] H. Leclercq provides an extra interesting detail
regarding the latter: the silver *capsa*, laid between bones which had
collapsed and gold-embroidered material, was locked and contained
organic remains.[52] In the Roman 'Coemeterium Ostrianum' a grave was
opened the bottom of which had a hollowed-out space, covered with a
marble slab and destined to hold relics.[53] In graves dating from the 4th
to the 6th centuries found along the Rhine, in England and in former
Pannonia, the *scrinia* stood in niches at the head of the corpse. Such
niches correspond to those found in Pécs, Nis, Chur, Istanbul, Kozanis
and Carthage, in which relics must have been placed from the 4th century
onwards.[54]

Sozomenos, who continued the work started by Eusebius († 339),
provides an example of a niche of this nature from around the year 430 in
Constantinople. The story tells of Eusebia, deaconess of the sect of the
Macedonians, who denied the divinity of the Holy Ghost.[55] She owned a
relic of the forty martyrs who had been consigned to the flames under the
emperor Licinius († 322) in Sebaste (Asia Minor).[56] She wished to have
these relics buried with her, and such was done. Her final resting place
was on her own estate, not far from the city walls. The relics were placed
in a separate hollow in the sarcophagus, level with her head.[57]
    The same sort of wish was expressed by a certain Jacob, recounted
to us by Theodoretus of Cyrus († 460). This hermit wished to be buried
with the relics of prophets, apostles and martyrs that he had collected "so

---

[51]Buschhausen (1971), 14-15.

[52]DACL 14,2, 2337.

[53]Kraus (1886), 882.

[54]Buschhausen (1971), 16.

[55]Dölger (1929-50), V, 240.

[56]Delehaye (1933), 61; see p. 15.

[57]PG 67, 1598, *Hist. Eccl.* IX, c.II: ["Quae cum moritura iam esset, supradictum locum
monachis eiusdem sectae reliquit, et iureiurando eos obstrinxit, ut ipsam illic sepelirent, ac
supra caput in summa parte loculum ipsius separatim inciderent, et martyrum reliquias una
cum ipsa deponerent, nec ulli rem indicarent. Ac monachi quidem id quod mandatum erat
fecerunt"].

that even after his death he could dwell with them and rise with them".[58]
This is why Gregory of Nyssa († 394) buried his parents in the family
oratory close to his relic of the martyrs of Sebaste.[59] Maxim of Turin
(† c. 470) emphasises the protection afforded by the relics against the
dark forces of the underworld. They can do nothing against us, he claims,
when we lie at rest close to the bones of the martyrs. Christ will cause the
darkness to disappear thanks to the petitions and sanctity of those who
have already attained paradise. The promise made by the Lord was that
the gates of Hell would not prevail against the rock, the martyr and
apostle Peter (Mtt. 16:18).[60]

During the medieval period of the Latin church reports become fewer of
the burial of relics with the dead.[61] The reason may well be that reports
concerning an *elevatio* or *translatio* usually leave us guessing about the
presence of relics in the grave. The mortal remains of those revered as
saints were, after all, themselves relics.

The best known instance is the opening of the grave of
Charlemagne in the cathedral of Aachen. The learned and usually well-
informed writer, Thietmar of Merseburg († 1018), recounts how Emperor
Otto III took the decision around the year 1000. He kept for himself the
cross that hung around Charlemagne's neck and parts of his still
remaining clothing. The rest was put back.[62] The emperor's body must
have been accompanied by at least three reliquaries at his funeral in 814:
the golden cross mentioned alluded to with a particle of the True Cross, a

---

[58]PG 82, 1450, *Hist. Religiosa*, 21: ["Collectis enim undique multis prophetis, multisque
apostolis, et martyribus quamplurimis, omnes una in arca reposuit, cum sanctorum populo
habitare cupiens et cum eis resurgere divinoque conspectu potiri"]; SC 257, 21, c. 30, 115-
117.

[59]PG 46, 783-784, *hom. in martyres quadraginta*: ["Habeo et ego particulam huius sacri
muneris et corpora parentum meorum iuxta horum militum reliquias posui ut tempore
resurrectionis cum opitulatoribus spei et fiduciae plenis resurgant"].

[60]PL 57, 426-427, *hom.* 81: "Nam ideo hoc a maioribus provisum est, ut sanctorum
ossibus nostra corpora sociemus: ut dum illos tartarus metuit nos poena non tangat; dum
illos Christus illuminat nobis tenebrarum caligo diffugiat. Cum sanctis ergo martyribus
quiescentes evadamus inferi tenebras eorum meritis, attamen consocii sanctitate. Ait enim
dominus Petro: '*Tu es Petrus, et super hanc petram aedificabo ecclesiam meam; et portae
inferi non praevalebunt ei (Matth. XVI)*' Si ergo apostolo et martyri Petro inferni porta non
praevalet, quisquis sociatur martyri tartaro non tenetur. Martyres enim inferni porta non
possidet, quoniam eos paradisi regna suscipiunt"; Kötting (1950), 333; Fichtenau (1952), 89,
n. 146

[61]Le Blant (1858); Corblet (1886), I, 537(see n. 154); Kraus (1886), II, 881 sqq.
"Todtenbestattung"; Freestone (1917), 100; Kötting (1950), 332 sqq.

[62]ed. Trillmich (1960), 162-164, *Chronicon*, lib. IV, c. 47: "Crucem auream, quae in
collo eius pependit cum vestimentorum parte adhuc imputribilium sumens, caetera cum
veneratione magna reposuit"; MGH SS IX, 188.

holder with an image of the Virgin Mary in relief and what was known as the 'talisman'. This consisted of two round sapphires placed one against the other and between which, it was said, was a hair of the Virgin Mary. In 1804 this talisman was given by the chapter of Aachen cathedral as a gift to Joséphine de Beauharnais and it is at present in the possession of the cathedral of Rheims.[63]

Reports of the *inventio* and *translatio* of the body of St. Ulrich († 973) state that both relics and the Eucharistic offerings were found in the grave. This was preceded by a fierce fire that broke out in 1183, reducing to ashes the monastery and church of the saint in Augsburg. His body lay on gold and costly topaz with some remains of his episcopal robes that had not rotted away. To the right of his head a silver pyx was found, still with its original gloss. "Therein were concealed, so said some, the blood of the Lord and other sacred things". It could be that the latter referred to the Eucharistic bread. There was also a small chest filled with relics. This was replaced in the same manner in the new coffin together with the pyx.[64]

The "selectively critical" Guibert de Nogent († 1125) believed firmly that the British king, Quilius, was buried in the first century on the site of the abbey that was later to rise, "next to a *reliquarum*" containing costly relics of Jesus. Some considerable time later they were excavated and thus came to belong to the treasury of relics of his abbey.[65]

Like Richard of St. Vannes, a century later even Bernard of Clairvaux († 1153) yearned for the relics after his death. As a great venerator of the Virgin Mary, he was buried in front of her altar. On his breast was the *capsula* containing the relics of the apostle Thaddeus, which Bernard had obtained from Jerusalem in the year of his death, and had given the order for them to be buried with him. This would assure him of a place next to the apostle on the day of the *parousia*. The account

---

[63]Honselmann (1962), 164-165; Grimme (1972), 21-22 with illustr.

[64]AASS 4 iul, II, 131, *Inventio et Translatio corporis s. Udalrici*, c. I,3: "Inventum est igitur corpus sanctissimi confessoris, super aurum et topazion pretiosum, cum quibusdam particulis pontificalium induviarum, necdum vetustate consumptarum, et in dextro latere ad caput, pixis argentea, admodum nitens in sacello holoserico, et in pixide (ut quidam dicebant) sanguis Domini et alia sancta continebantur. Inventa est etiam cistella serata, admodum magna, quae omnia plena erant et referta reliquiis sanctorum".

[65]ed. Labande (1981), 224, *De vita sua*, lib. II, c. 1: "ubi corporis eius gleba monumenti obtinuit requiem, ibi reliquiarum iuxta ipsum habuit loculus sedem"; Lettinck (1983), 67, 69, 157.

is contained in the oldest version of his *vita*, written by Geoffrey of
Auxerre, Bernard's former secretary.[66]

The previously mentioned desire of Martin to be buried with the
relics of the Theban legion is legendary and is contained in a text dated
1186. However his final wish does match that of Bernard and reinforces
the opinion that this custom was not unknown in the 12th century.[67] In
the first place, because Bernard did not support the introduction of novel
forms of piety[68] and, secondly, because others can have been caused to
follow this example because of the widespread interest shown in his
vita.[69] However there is no trace of the fear of demons so evident in the
early days of Christianity, a fear which was sometimes intertwined with
the desire to rise with the saints.

3.2   The viaticum for the living and the dead

The use of the *viaticum* demonstrates the tensions existing between the
fear of Satan and the hope of resurrection. The sacrament of the sick is
actually the sacrament of anointing. It originates from the letter of the
apostle James in which he says: "Is any sick among you? let him call for
the elders of the church; and let them pray over him, anointing him with
oil in the name of the Lord: And the prayer of faith shall save the sick,
and the Lord shall raise him up; and if he have committed sins, they shall
be forgiven him. Confess your faults one to another, that ye may be
healed". (Jm. 5:14-16). This anointing of the sick was originally not
necessarily intended for someone in danger of death. It can have had a
medicinal purpose and have been administered with accompanying prayers
in every case of sickness. It was in the Carolingian era that this sacrament
became specifically the 'last' anointing and was thus linked to confession

---

[66]PL 185, 360, *Vita Bernardi,* lib. V, c. II,15: "Sepultus est autem undecimo Kalendas
eiusdem mensis ante sanctum altare beatae Virginis Matris, cuius fuerat devotissimus ipse
sacerdos. Sed et pectori eius ipso tumulo capsula superposita est, in qua beati Thaddaei
Apostoli reliquiae continentur, quas eodem anno Ierosolyma sibi missas, quo iusserat corpori
superponi, eo utique fidei et devotionis intuitu, ut eidem Apostolo in die communis
resurrectionis adhaereat"; AASS aug. IV, 324; Bredero (1959), 41-42, l. 427-432.

[67]Surius IX, 22 sept. 385; AASS sept. VI, 385; Le Blant (1858), 31.

[68]Thus Bernard opposed the introduction of the feast of Mary's Immaculate Conception
using the argument that the Fathers of the church had made no reference to this 'article of
faith'; ed. Leclercq (1957-1977), SBO VII, 388-392.

[69]Bredero (1960), 15-23.

and the *viaticum*.[70] In contrast to the anointing of the sick, the *viaticum* has always been linked to the approach of death.

Though in the first three centuries there are few witnesses of the practice of receiving communion at such a time, we need have no doubt that those who kept the Eucharist at home made use of it for this purpose.[71] Those living in the same house as the sick person could, in fact, keep the Eucharist wholly or partly to this end and administer it to the sick one at a time when symptoms made the need apparent.[72] It was even permitted that those doing penance should receive communion when their life was in danger. Normally speaking they were excluded from communion, since as public sinners they first had to do penance and reconcile themselves with the church before being allowed to receive communion once again.

This concession to them also emphasised the forgiveness factor as an element of the sacrament of the sick. It was a concession that even applied to the *lapsi*, those who had fallen away out of fear of persecution. In a letter to his fellow bishop, Fabius of Antioch, bishop Dionysius of Alexandria († 265) discusses a certain old man named Serapion. This was someone who, under the emperor Decius, had even gone back to offering sacrifice to the pagan gods. When the greybeard became mortally ill he sent his grandson at dead of night to look for a priest. The latter was himself sick and therefore entrusted the lad with the Eucharist with the advice that he should first soak the bread and then place it in his grandfather's mouth. Serapion died after having received communion in this way.[73] The priest had acted in the manner recommended by his bishop in the case of someone who asked for communion in such circumstances: they should receive absolution and be given back their hope.[74]

---

[70]Browe (1931); Chavasse (1942); Beauduin (1948); Botte (1948); Philippeau (1948); Rush (1974), 11-12.

[71]Browe (1936), 60; Dölger (1929-50), II, 515-535; Grabka (1953), 40-41.

[72]ibid. 30-31; Nussbaum (1979), 74; see p. 44.

[73]PG 20, 634, Eusebius, *Historiae ecclesiasticae*, lib. VI, c. 44: ["Mox puer bucellam intinxit et in os senis infudit. Qui ea paulatim absorpta, continuo animam exhalavit"].

[74]ibid. 631: ["Sed quoniam in mandatis dederam, ut morituris, si peterent, et maxime si antea suppliciter postulassent, venia indulgeretur, quo bonae spei pleni ex hac vita migrarent, exiguam eucharistiae partem puero tradidit"].

According to the correspondence of Cyprian († 258) this was the practice in Rome as well as in his own diocese of Carthage.[75] He makes only one exception: that of repeated offenders who had never shown remorse. The synod of Elvira (in 306),[76] a place close to Grenada, and that held in Arles in 314.[77] The attitude of the early church did, however, tend to great mercy without exception in cases involving death. This was seen yet again at the synod of Ancyra (Ankara), also held in 314, where the bishops weighed to fate of the *lapsi* against the tradition that had grown up of ecclesiastical clemency. It was decided that it was not permitted to withhold communion from *lapsi* in danger of death.[78] The Council of Nicaea in 325 made this a general rule and denied communion to no-one in danger of death.[79] This ruling was, in fact, understood by Christians to mean that everything possible was to be done to ensure that no-one should die without receiving communion. What is more - and in view of the original meaning of the *viaticum* entirely understandable - every effort was made to place the body of the Lord on the tongue of the dying person at the very moment they departed this life for the next. This custom is expressed in the apocryphal *vita* of bishop Basil of Caesarea († 379) who "with the Eucharist in his mouth gave his soul back to God".[80] At the critical moment, Ambrose was given communion in his home by his upstairs neighbour, bishop Honoratus. He died "taking the *viaticum* with him".[81]

Gravestone inscriptions speak of the administration of baptism at the hour of death, which was probably accompanied by reception of the Eucharist.[82] An inscription found in the region of Catania on the island

---

[75]CSEL 3,1, 476, ep. 4,4; CSEL 3,2 , 523-524, ep. 18,1; 525-526, ep. 19,2; 528-529, ep. 20,3; 626-629, ep. 55,5; 636-637, ep. 55,17; 649, ep. 56,2; 650-651, ep. 57,1; 653-654, ep. 57,4.

[76]Mansi II, 6-7, 16, c. 1, 2, 3, 7, 8, 17, 63, 64.

[77]ibid. 473, c. 22; CC SL 148, 13.

[78]CSP 62, 68, 71; Mansi II, 515, c. 6: "Sed si periculum mortisque expectatio ex morbo, vel aliqua occasione evenerit, ii sub definitione recipiantur".

[79]ibid. 674; COD, 12, c. 13: "De his qui ad exitum vitae veniunt etiam nunc lex antiqua regularisque servabitur ita, ut, si quis egreditur e corpore, ultimo et necessario viatico minime privetur"; see also Mansi II, 540, Neo Caesarea (314-319), c. 2; CSP 76.

[80]PG 29, CCCXV: *Vita apocrypha:* "Recumbensque in lecto, cum Eucharistia adhuc in ore, reddidit spiritum Domino".

[81]PL 14, 46, *Vita s. Ambrosii*, autore Paulino eius notario, c. 47: "bonum viaticum secum ferens".

[82]Dölger (1922), II, 515-535.

of Sicily, at present in the Louvre,[83] concerns a two-year-old girl and
begins thus: "For Julia Florentina, the dearest and most innocent child,
taken up in the faith". She was baptised at 2 o'clock in the morning at the
moment death was threatening. However she continued to live for four
more hours, which meant that she received "the usual offering". This
cannot refer to baptism - which is administered only once - nor to
anything profane, but only to the Eucharist, according to Dölger.[84] So
Juliana received the Eucharistic bread twice in rapid succession because
the hour of death came more slowly than had been anticipated. There are
more examples of the same. Gregory of Nazianze († c. 390) writes that
his father received the *viaticum* every hour in the last phase of his life.[85]

The death of Melania, a foundress of convents, is a striking
example from the 5th century. In 437 her uncle, Volusianus, received
communion three times on the day of his death in Constantinople. Two
years later she herself felt death approaching. Her spiritual guide,
Gerontius, provides an eye-witness account in a *vita* which has been
preserved in both the Greek and Latin versions.[86] At first light she
received communion from him. When day had fully dawned she received
communion for the second time, now from the hands of the bishop of
Jerusalem. She took her leave of those at her deathbed and lost
consciousness at three o'clock in the afternoon, a time with eternal
significance for Christians since the first Good Friday. They thought she
was dead and went to stretch out her feet. But she whispered: "It is not
yet time", at which Gerontius asked him to tell him in time. The Latin
version adds the explanation that it was a Roman custom to have the
Eucharist in the mouth at the instant of death.[87] When she told him:
"The end is nigh, as the Lord has willed it", she received the *viaticum* at
that instant.

---

[83]Ducroux (1975), 224, catalogue n. 224; magasin n. 2993. The marble gravestone (h. 49
cm, l. 46 cm, th. 4 cm), which the curator, Mr. M. Baratte ("Conservation Grecque"),
showed us in the museum store, is occasionally exposed; DACL II,2 , 2513, illustr. 2194.

[84]Dölger (1922), II, 522; CIL 10,2 , 729, n. 7112: "supervixit horis quattuor ita ut
consueta repeteret ac defuncta est".

[85]PG 35, 1036, *Oratio* XVIII, c. 38: ["atque interdum etiam horis, ex sola liturgia robur
concipiebat, ac morbus tanquam ex edicto fugatus, se subducebat"].

[86]ed. Gorce (1962), SC 90 (Greek text); ed. Rampolla (1905).

[87]ed. Rampolla (1905), 39: "consuetudo autem est..Romanis ut cum animae egrediuntur,
communio Domini in ore sit"; *An. Boll.* 8, 61; Nussbaum (1979), 77, n. 150; Boglioni
(1979), 193.

The 'Roman custom' made its entry into Gaul, where the same spirit of mercy was maintained as at the Council of Nicaea.[88] In Orange in 441 the text of the Council was used in order to lay down that the 'viaticum', an appropriate name given by the church Fathers, was intended as a source of consolation for the dying.[89] That this, in fact, implied laying the Eucharist on the tongue of the dying person at the moment of death can again be seen from the Statuta Antiqua, probably written or compiled around 480 by Gennadius of Marseilles and addressed to the clerics of Provence.[90] Regarding the moment of death of the Christian it says: "and the Eucharist is placed in his mouth".[91]

As far as the early Middle Ages are concerned, there is repeated reference in the Dialogues of Gregory the Great to the viaticum given at the instant the earthly is exchanged for the eternal. In the second book he describes the death of St. Benedict, who was buried next to his sister Scholastica who had died a few weeks beforehand: "Six days before his departure he had his grave opened. Shortly afterwards the fever took hold of him, a heavy, glowing, destroying fever: he became weaker by the day. On the sixth day he had himself carried to the chapel by his disciples; there he armed himself for his departure by receiving the body and blood of the Lord; and, his feeble limbs held upright by his disciples, he stood there, hands raised to heaven; and, in the midst of the words of his prayer, he breathed his last breath".[92]

In this text Gregory also mentions the monk Eleutherius, who felt death approaching and had told his brothers so. "In the hour of his death he received the body and blood of the Lord".[93] Bishop Cassius of Narnia died in the same manner[94] and in one of his sermons this pope with a

---

[88]See above n. 79; Rush (1974), 21-24.

[89]CC SL 148, 78-79, Concilium Arausicanum I, c. 3: "quod morientis sufficit consolationi secundum definitiones patrum, qui huiusmodi communionem congruenter viaticum nominarunt"; CC SL 148, 96, Conc. Vasense a. 442, c. 2.

[90]Rush (1974), 21; C. Vogel in NCE 13, 682.

[91]CC SL 148, 170: "et infundatur eius ori eucharistia"; PL 56, 882-883.

[92]SC 260, 244, Dial. lib. II, c. 37; PL 66, 202; Gross (1975); Meer v.d. (1979), 102.

[93]SC 265, 118, Dial. lib. IV, c. 36: "Ad horam vero mortis veniens, mysterium Dominici corporis et sanguinis accepit"; PL 77, 377.

[94]SC 265, lib. IV, c. 35: "Qui (...) cum missarum solemnia peregisset, et mysteria sacrae communionis accepisset, e corpore exivit".

fine gift for literature recounts how a female religious, Romula, stricken
by paralysis, received the *viaticum* just before her death.[95]

As has already been noted, in the early Middle Ages priests were
obliged to take the Eucharist with them on journeys in order to be able to
give it to the seriously ill.[96] The regulation bears witness to the great
value attached to the *viaticum*, about which the Council of Aachen in 836
said the following: "When a person falls ill, it should not happen that,
through neglect on the part of the priest, the sick person is deprived of
confession, prayer and the anointing with holy oil. If the priest finally
realises that the end is near, he must recommend to God the soul of the
Christian and give him holy communion".[97]

It was not beyond the imagination that people would wait too long.
In 858 the archbishop of Tours ordered his diocesan clergy to ensure that
the sick received the *viaticum* while they were still alive.[98] Aelfric of
Canterbury, writing in 1005, gave expression to the same thoughts. The
Host must be given while the sick person is still able to swallow and not
if he was in the process of dying.[99] The administration of the sacrament
was the first duty of the cleric and had to be free of any charge. Medieval
synodal prescriptions repeat this frequently[100] and in the hagiographies
the *viaticum* is stereotypically described as the last food for the
journey.[101]

Its importance was stressed to the faithful by way of legends: saints
who had died without the *viaticum* returned to the kingdom of the living
to make good what they had missed. And then fell asleep in peace. The

---

[95]PL 76, 1311-1312, *Homiliae in evangelia*, 40,11: "Qua veniente, viaticum petiit, et
accepit (...) Cumque ante foras cellulae exhiberentur coelestes exsequiae, sancta illa anima
carne soluta est".

[96]See p. 84 sqq; 90 sqq.

[97]MGH Conc II, 712, (29) c. V: "Si autem infirmitate depressus fuerit, ne confessione
atque oratione sacerdotali necnon unctione sacrificati olei per eius negligentiam careat.
Denique si finem urgentem perspexerit, commendet animam Christianam domino Deo suo
more sacerdotali cum acceptione sacrae communionis corpus sepulturae, non ut mos est
gentilium, sed sicut Christianorum"; see also PL 97, 759, *Benedicti Diaconi*, II, c. 75: "Si
infirmitate depressus quis fuerit, vitam sine communione non finiat, nec unctione sacrati olei
careat. Et si finem perspiciat, sacrosancto corpore Deo anima eius a sacerdote praecibus
commendetur"; Browe (1936), 17, n. 13.

[98]PL 121, 765-766 *capitula Herardi*, XXI: "Ut in infirmitate positi absque dilatione
reconcilientur, et viaticum viventes accipiant et benedictione sacrati olei non careant".

[99]ed. Fehr (1966²), 150, ep. 3, n. 11 and 12.

[100]Browe (1931), 527: synods of Tribur (1036), Rheims (1049), Toulouse (1119), Tours
(1163); 524: Trier (1227), Lincoln (1236), Salamanca (1335); see further Browe, 524-526.

[101]See above n. 27, 31, 35, 36; Andrieu (1924), 114-135; Browe (1936); Rush (1974), 26
sqq. ; Nussbaum (1979), 75, n. 137, 140.

tallest story that told of pope John I († 526), a friend of Boëthius. The head of this martyr was cloven in two. He held together both bloody halves with his hands and by divine power made it to a church, where he received the communion, kneeling before the altar in the usual way. Subsequently he was able to give up the gost blissfully.[102]

A no less spectacular story is told by Ordericus Vitalis († 1142) concerning St. Ebrulf († 596) of the abbey of the same name in St. Evroul in Normandy. Abbot Ebrulf blamed himself for not having been present when brother Ansbert left this world. The author takes the opportunity to note that watchfulness is of the essence (I Cor. 16:13) for we do not know on what day the Lord will come (Mtt. 24:42). When he arrived at the bedside of his dead brother, the saint prayed for mercy and called Ansbert back to life, whereupon the dead monk opened his eyes and thanked the abbot for saving him. Condemned at God's seat of judgement to remain outside the company of the saints, he had already fallen into the grip of the devil. He armed himself against this with the *viaticum* and to everyone's amazement breathed his last for a second time.[103]

The 7th-century abbot Albert of Gambron-sur-l'Antion is also reported to have raised someone from the dead for the same purpose[104] and in 720 St. Odilia, much to the horror of her sisters, died alone in the church of the Odilienberg convent which she had founded. The community's prayer was heard and she was returned to life. She herself took the Eucharistic offering and then returned her soul to God. The chalice used in this instance is said to have been kept as a relic.[105]

Legends of this type focus attention in their own particular way on what was regarded as the primary importance of the *viaticum*, given just before death. This occasioned few problems in monasteries. In fact there were always brothers present to perform the service. The custom was maintained in many communities until the 12th century. It had come to an end before that for the laity[106] since no such favourable circumstances

---

[102]AASS 27 maii VI, 707, *De s. Ioanne papa I* c. III,21: "narrat, quod a loco martyrii, capite duas in partes scisso cruento, divina virtute eas ipse propriis sustentans manibus, iunctas detulit ad templum, ibidemque ad altare flexis genibus, susceptis pro more sacramentis, perbeatum emisit spiritum".

[103]ed. Chibnall (1968-83), vol. III, 292-294, lib. VI, c. 9.

[104]AASS OSB III,2, 531.

[105]MGH SRM VI, 49-50; see Hugh of Fleury, 12th-century vita of St. 'Sardos' († 720), bishop of Limoges, whose father had the same experience: PL 163, 988, *Vita s. Sacerdotis*, c. VII,12; AASS 5 maii II, n. 16.

[106]Browe (1936), 18-19.

were available for them. After the disappearance of communion at home
the lay people came to depend on the clergy, who often had objections to
making themselves available precisely at the last moment, especially if the
death throes laster longer than anticipated.

Furthermore the original healing function of the anointing of the
sick lost some of its healing significance and came to be increasingly seen
as a way of wiping out possible remains of punishment for sin. And in
addition the anointing of the lay person took on the character of an
'ordination', which gave rise here and there to the belief that if the sick
person should recover then he should thenceforth abstain from all sexual
activities and should go through life as a penitent and vegetarian.[107]

All these factors contributed, some time around the 12th century, to
the sacrament of the sick no longer being administered before the *viaticum*
but afterwards as the 'last anointing' or *extrema unctio*. Today the
original order has been restored.[108]

The practice of administering the *viaticum* at the very last moment calls
for comparison with the custom of the obol, all the more so in that no
few Christians held on to it for some considerable time afterwards.[109]
Yet there are major differences. While the coin was given to the dead, the
viaticum was administered to the living. The aim, too, was different: the
obol served as far for the ferry in order to be assured of eternal rest on
the other side, whereas the *viaticum* meant more to the Christian: it was
Christ himself, originally seen as the good shepherd, who leads his sheep
(Mtt. 18:12-14).[110] He held the promise of an eternal, transformed life
with God, according to the consoling words spoken from the Cross:
"Today thou shalt be with me in paradise" (Lk. 23:43).[111]

Despite these differences the significance of the obol as guarantee
of a safe journey would seem to have transferred something of its
properties of magic to the practice of giving the *viaticum* come what may.
If the sick person had already died there was a great temptation to place
the Eucharistic bread in the mouth anyway. This practice must have
assumed alarming proportions, to judge from the resistance shown to it by
various councils and synods.

---

[107]Browe (1931), 556-561.

[108]LW I, 229.

[109]See above n. 8.

[110]Angenendt (1982), 217.

[111]Grabka (1953), 37-38; Rush (1974), 33-35; Nussbaum (1979), 78.

When the bishops of Africa met in Hippo in 393 they condemned this deviant form publicly and forbade the giving of the Eucharist to the dead.[112] Four years later in Carthage they again did not mince their words on the subject. After all, the Lord had said: "Take and eat". But corpses can no longer eat. And they advanced a second argument: the fear that the weaker brethren would go on to baptise the dead as well.[113]

Their fears were not unfounded, for in the same period John Chrysostom was fighting both abuses.[114] In the writings of the pseudo-Dionysius, the 5th-century Areopagite, someone dying during the service was anointed with oil, but not a word is mentioned about the Eucharist.[115] A repetition of the interdiction would seem to have been deemed opportune. The Sixth Council of Carthage, held in 525, again quoted the text of canon 6 formulated in 397.[116] The same note was sounded in Gaul. The Council of Auxerre held around 580 laid down that "The Eucharist must not be given to corpses (...)".[117] At the end of the 7th century the Council of Constantinople held in Trullo († 691) referred in its canon 83 to what had been prescribed in Carthage.[118]

The custom was partly encouraged by the keeping of the Eucharist in the home[119] and proved to be very persistent. An 8th-century penitential[120] and the 9th-century pseudo-statutes of Boniface repeat the ruling.[121] Various motives could have contributed to this stubborn

---

[112]CC SL 149, 21: "Illud autem quoniam praesentibus corporibus nonnulli audeant sacrificia celebrare et partem Corporis sancti cum exanimi cadavere communicare arbitror prohibendum"; Mansi III, 850, c. 3; CSEL 36, 84, Augustinus, *Retractiones,* lib. I, c. 16.

[113]Mansi III, 881. Conc. Carth. III, c. 6: "Item placuit, ut corporibus defunctorum eucharistia non detur. Dictum est enim a domino: 'Accipite et edite'. Cadavera autem nec accipere possunt, nec edere. Cavendum est etiam ne mortuos baptizari posse fratrum infirmitas credat, cum eucharistiam mortuis non dari animadverterit"; 919, c. 4; CC SL 149, 51.

[114]PG 61, 347, *Homil.* 40, 1.

[115]PG 3, 556, *De ecclesiastica hierarchia,* c. VII, par. III.

[116]CC SL 149, 264; Mansi VIII, 643.

[117]CC SL 148 A, 267, Concilia Gallia, c. 12: "Non licet mortuis nec eucharistia nec usculum tradi nec de vela vel pallas corpora eorum involvi"; Mansi IX, 913; MGH Conc. I, 180; see below n. 153.

[118]Mansi XI, 979. c. 83.

[119]Nussbaum (1979), 80; Angenendt (1982), 217.

[120]d'Achery, I, 539, *Collectio antiqua canonum poenitentialium,* lib. II, c. 64: De communio privatis et ita defunctis. Ex epistola Leonis I Papae ad Rusticum.

[121]ibid. 508; Mansi XII, 385, *Statuta Bonifatii,* 18: " Hoc autem omnibus modis observari oportet ut post mortem communio eucharistiae in os cadaveris non immittatur, aliquo intuitu misericordiae: quod prohibent valde canones"; c. 20: "Non licet mortuis (...)", see above n. 117.

refusal to disappear. Funerary rites tend to be strongly tied to tradition, so that the obol - though in another form, that of the *viaticum* - was maintained.[122] Or was it perhaps no more than a posthumous gesture of reconciliation, so that the *viaticum*, like the *fermentum*, stood for the community? Was the departed person regarded as being taken into the bosom of the church in this way?[123] The fear of the forces of Hell, also expressed in the giving of crosses and relics to the corpse, was also no stranger here.[124] The Greek Orthodox canonist, Theodoros Balsamon († c. 1195) pointed to this in his commentary on canon 83 of the Council of Constantinople when he wrote that these princes of the church received the *viaticum* to lead them to heaven and to drive off the demons.[125]

In the chronicle of the Cistercian, Radulfus Niger, written around 1200, there is the report of an event showing how eager Satan was to be rid of the *viaticum*. At the prompting of the devil a woman attempted to seize the Host out of the mouth of pope Urban III when he was being carried to his grave in 1187.[126] The author reports the happening with caution, which does not justify the assumption that the custom was still a matter of generalised practice in the 12th century.[127]

Eagerness to circumvent Satan and fear of the demonic forces encouraged the dead person's survivors to place the Eucharist, like the relics, separately in the grave. It was usually laid on the chest of the corpse, perhaps enclosed in a small bottle or some other form of container. This second form of burial together with the Eucharist could have issued from the former, communion of the dead, as a practical solution, especially when rigor mortis had already set in.[128] In its application it shows similarities to the *fylacteria* placed in the grave, as these were discovered during the excavations in the Vatican in 1571. We can only guess as to

[122]Thiers (1697), II, 246; Nussbaum (1979), 78, 79, 82, 83.

[123]Corblet (1886), I, 536.

[124]Dölger (1929-50), V, 257-258; see above n. 11, 44-48, 59.

[125]PG 137, 794: ["Quod autem sanctus panis antistibus post mortem tradatur, et sic sepeliantur, existimo hoc fieri ad avertendos daemonas, ut per ipsum, tamquam viaticum, deducatur ad coelum, qui magna et apostolica professione dignus est habitus. Antiquae consuetudinis fuit corpus et sanguinem Domini mortuorum corporibus impertiri"].

[126]MGH SS 27, 336: "Quo mortuo, sedit ad exequias eius mulier iussu demonum, ut dictum est, prestolans eripere viaticum corporis Domini de ore eius, quia illud in assumptione nondum transmiserat".

[127]Nussbaum (1979), 78.

[128]Binterim (1827-31), VI,3 , 369.

whether the *'encolpia'* discovered at the time contained relics or the Eucharist.[129]

A clearer indication for the situation in the Eastern church is found in a discovery of a grave dating from the 4th or 5th century discovered at Oumm-Thouba near Bethlehem in 1893. It contained a disc only 1 cm thick in the form of a bird, representing a peacock. There was a round opening measuring 5.5 cm in diameter, originally filled with glass, which could have held the Eucharistic bread. No definite conclusion can be drawn because the contents were, for reasons of piety, not studied but probably burned in a neighbouring monastery. A hole bored through the piece indicates that it could be hung.[130] A similar disc, with a small hollow covered with glass, came to light in a Byzantine grave excavated in 1907 at Gezer. It is possible that this too once contained the Eucharist[131] and not a relic, as was originally thought.[132] The hypothesis is not unacceptable, since it is certain that it was the custom in the est up to the 8th century to bury the Eucharist with a deceased bishop,[133] a practice that demonstrably persisted in the Greek orthodox church until the recent past.[134] As well as driving away demons in early Christian times, the burial of the Eucharist also signified being buried with Christ: "to conquer death and to rise with Him".[135]

Basil died in 379. Among the sources his *vita*, written about the year 800, should contain some indication of this usage: "When he first celebrated the Eucharist as bishop of Caesarea he divided the consecrated bread into three pieces: one to receive, one to hang above the altar in a

---

[129]Freestone (1917), 100: "Similar boxes were found in the oratory of St. Ambrose and elsewhere on the breasts of christian bodies. These encolpia were generally used to contain relics of written passages of the scriptures; and similar receptacles were worn on the person to bear about the eucharist".

[130]Nussbaum (1979), 80 with illustr. 1; extensive description: Cré (1894).

[131]Nussbaum (1979), 81; Vincent (1908), 389-393, 401, 393: "The object enclosed in this supposed reliquary is nothing else than the blessed eucharist".

[132]Nussbaum (1979), 81; Stewart MacAlister (1907), 258: "I (...) can only guess that it may be a reliquary".

[133]LW I, 543.

[134]Petrakakos (1905), 105-106: "Indes war es eine christliche Sitte, die Bischöfe mit dem heiligen Brot in der Hand ins Grab zu legen"; Kyriakakis (1974), 57: "In addition, the Byzantines placed the Holy Eucharist in the hands of a dead bishop, as was permitted by the Church canons. This custom (...) is still part of liturgical practice of the Orthodox Church today"; Nussbaum (1979), 81.

[135]Binterim (1827-31), VI,3 , 396, appendic. tom V oper. s. Augustini: "Recte hanc vitam - corpus Domini - nos in nostro sepulchro condimus ut vivificet mortem ut cum ipso a mortuis resurgamus".

dove-shaped tabernacle and one to have buried with him".[136] The latter
was, however, understood by the author - as the text goes on to
demonstrate - to mean dying with the *viaticum* in his mouth.[137] The
phrase "buried with him" is not elucidated any further.

An example from the Western church can be found in pope
Gregory's *vita* of St. Benedict, where a young monk finds no rest in his
grave until the Eucharistic bread is laid there with him. The story goes as
follows: "One day one of his monks, still a boy, and unusually strongly
attached to his parents, left the monastery to visit his home without asking
for a blessing before leaving. The same day, having just arrived at his
parents' house, he died. Several days after his burial his body was found
thrown out of the grave; they buried it again; but the following day they
found it once again unburied outside the grave, just like the first time. In
mortal fear they rushed off to father Benedict, threw themselves at his
feet and asked him tearfully to be merciful to them. The man of God
immediately gave them, with his own hands, a piece of communion bread
saying: "Go home, place this body of the Lord on his bosom, and bury
him with it". When they had done that, the earth retained the body
entrusted to her and threw it out no more".[138]

This legendary tale, told by Gregory, was based on a recognisable
custom. This is further confirmed by an account written by Amalarius of
Metz († c. 852) concerning the exhumation of St. Cuthbert († 681), at
which similar pieces of bread were found. He says that Augustine of
Canterbury († c. 605) had introduced the practice into England when he
was sent there by the pope. He had come to know the custom in
Rome.[139] The holy Irishman, St. Mochoemag († 656), is said to have
buried his 'chrismale' - which, as already noted, usually contained the
Eucharist - and his stick with a certain Foelanus, who had been killed in a
treacherous manner. This was his way of protesting against the abbot's
decision to forbid the burial of this man in the monks' cemetery. The

---

[136]PG 29, 302, *Vita Apocrypha,* c. 2: ["Cumque panem divississet in tres partes, unam quidem cum multo timore et veneratione sumpsit; alteram vero una secum sepeliendam servavit; tertiam denique in columba aurea depositam, desuper sacrum altare suspendit"]; 315, c. 4: ["testamento autem sepeliri sanxit cum tertia illa portione datae sibi a Deo"] ; PL 73, 301, *De vitis patrum,* lib. I, *Vita s. Basilii,* 6.

[137]See above n. 80.

[138]SC 260, 210, *Dial.* lib. II, c. 24; PL 66, 180; Meer v.d. (1979), 92.

[139]ed. Hanssens (1950), 2, 531, *lib. de eccl. offic.* 4, 41: "oblata super pectus sanctum posita vestimento sacerdotali indutus (...) Non est dubitandum quin ipse mos esset apud Romanam Ecclesiam in hac re, qui apud Anglos fuit, praesertim cum ex illa primum episcopum Augustinum haberent Angli Saxones"; PL 105, 1236.

saint was certain that Foelanus was already in the presence of God.[140]
At the *elevatio* of the body of St. Berinus († c. 650) it was discovered
that his attachment to the Eucharist on his journeyings had found
expression in the way in which he had been buried. Next to the stole and
a metal cross on his incorrupt body there lay a simple chalice and a small
pouch of gold brocade woven in a single piece, a detail recalling Christ's
seamless garment (Jn. 19:23). All declared that the pouch contained the
palla with the body of Christ.[141]

The question here is whether the above account is speaking of
consecrated bread or merely blessed bread. Amalarius' source for the
story was a *vita* written by an anonymous biographer, which speaks of the
oblata found on Cuthbert's breast.[142] The monk Iso, of St. Gallen, also
writes about this in connection with the *translatio* of St. Otmar († 759):
"Under the head and on both sides of the breast of the man of God bishop
Salomon found certain round pieces of bread, which are usually called
oblatae. They were still so pure and untouched by any corruption that
they had lost nothing of their colour or external appearance and to those
looking on appeared to be not even a week old". The bishop took part of
the skeleton as a relic and some of the *oblatae*, which he kept in a pyx as
a proof of Otmar's sanctity. He placed the rest back on the body.[143]

The marvellous appearance of the *oblatae* is given such emphasis
that it could be asked whether this does not accentuate more the
consecrated nature of the bread than the sanctity of Otmar. But this
assumption does not fit the period, for it was only in the 11th and 12th
centuries that the belief arose that a perfect state of preservation was
proof that any bread found was Eucharistic bread. At the time of these
translations such miracles were not on the agenda. And thus Binterim

---

[140]AASS 13 mart. II, 284; see p. 94, n. 74.

[141]Surius XII, 70, 3 dec.: "factaque ab abbate potestate, quaesito sepulcro et aperto,
praesentibus abbate et canonicis, invenisse corpus episcopi integrum cum duplici stola, et
infula rubra e panno serico, atque cum cruce metallo confecta, pectori eius imposita: denique
cum calice ad umbilicum eius posito"; DACL I,2, 1758: "Quidam calix parvus (...)
quaedam pera ex una parte auro contexta: asserebant enim omnes quod in ea fuerit palla (...)
cum corpore Christi".

[142]ed. Colgrave (1940), 131, *Vitae s. Cuthberti Anonymae*, lib. IV: "oblata super
sanctum pectus posita vestimento sacerdotali indutus".

[143]MGH SS II, 49, *De miraculis s. Othmaris*: "sub capite autem et circa pectus viri Dei
quaedam panis rotulae, quae volgo oblatae dicuntur, ita illaesae atque ab omni corruptione
extraneae ab eodem episcopo inveniebantur, ut in nulla omnino parte colorem vel speciem
sui amittentes aspicientium oculis infra spatium ipsius hebdomadae viderentur esse con-
fectae"; "Idem tamen episcopus venerabiliter eas assumens sacro corpori apposuit,
ipsumque corpus cum summa cautela obvolutum in lectica superius dicta honorifice
commendavit"; PL 121, 783; 792.

does not make this link[144] and assumes, as did others who followed him,[145] that the *oblatae* were not consecrated Hosts but pieces of bread that had been blessed, known as *eulogia*. Burial of the Eucharist, therefore, would seem to have been on the wane in the 7th century. And yet there is one report dating from 1183 which forms an exception. It is said that when the body of St. Ulrich († 973) was exhumed a pyx was found containing "the blood of the Lord and other sacred things". The force of the statement is somewhat weakened when the author goes on to write "as some said".[146]

Such reports are not available for the later period, which is understandable enough. The repeated interdictions issued by the ecclesiastical authorities regarding the administration of the Eucharist to the dead were at odds with this particular form of burial of the Eucharist.[147] Moreover the practice was difficult to reconcile with the growing devotion with regard to the Eucharist. The use of *eulogia* may perhaps have stilled the objections voiced by the church. In fact the *eulogia* were blessed during Mass in close proximity to the Eucharist and had thus already been endowed with spiritual power as 'contact relics'. In place of the Eucharistic bread they were intended, together with holy water, crosses and relics, to keep the devil at bay.[148]

Thanks to Burchard of Worms († 1025) we know of a funerary custom followed by the laity which resembled that maintained by the clergy. If a baby died immediately after baptism some pious women buried the little body with in one hand a wax paten on which was an *oblata* and, in the other hand, a chalice, also of wax, containing a little

---

[144]Binterim (1827-31), II,2 ,223.

[145]Corblet (1886), I, 536; Freestone 1917), 100.

[146]See above n. 64.

[147]Binterim (1827-31), II,2 , 223: "Vielleicht ist der Gebrauch den Verstorbenen die Oblaten beizulegen, dann erst entstanden, da die Kirche strenger verboten hat, die heilige Eucharistie mit ins Graf zu legen".

[148]Corblet (1866), I, 537: "Dans d'autres tombes on renfermait parfois de l'eau bénite et des eulogies comme un double préservatif contres les embûches du démon. C'est dans le même but qu'on déposait dans les cercueils soit des reliques, soit des croix d'absolution portant cette inscription: *Crux Christi* (...)"; see above n. 49.

wine.[149] Were these priestly props, given as a sign of innocence, the guarantee of a free passage to Heaven?

The *eulogia* did not only offer indirect Eucharistic protection in the grave but they were also symbols of the sacred office of the deceased. In this respect they can be compared to the priestly vestments and sacred vessels which went into the coffin with such personages as Berinus, Cuthbert, Otmar and Ulrich.[150] Iso of St. Gallen adds to his account of the *oblatae* found on Otmar's body the explanatory remark that it was, in fact, an old custom to bury priests with the ornaments and objects that they had use during the sacred actions.[151] A remark of this nature relativises the *oblatae* discovered and includes them in the 'objects' used by the priest Otmar.

There is a remarkable example from the end off the 13th century, where the significance of the bread and wine in the grave appears to be different from that of the remaining clerical symbols. The body of Nicholas Gellent, bishop of Angers, was buried in 1290 wearing a white mitre and with a "chalice and paten made of lead with bread and wine".[152] The body and blood of the Lord are no longer mentioned. It is hardly imaginable that in the 13th and 14th centuries, when the *praesentia realis* was being accentuated by means of many Host miracles and adoration came to occupy a central position, the burial with a corpse of a consecrated Host still occurred in the West.

Yet another aspect is linked to the *viaticum* of the dead: the role of the altar cloth and the corporal in the rite of burial. These too had been in contact with the consecrated bread which had rested on them. Hence there was a protective, sometimes magical power attributed to them, a tendency which brought warnings from the church. At the end of the 6th century the Council of Auxerre added to the interdict concerning communion for

---

[149]ed. Schmitz (1958), 450, *Poenitentiale Burchardi,* c. 185: "Cum infans noviter natus est, et statim baptizatus, et sic mortuus fuerit, dum sepeliunt eum, in dexteram manum ponunt ei patenam ceream cum oblata, et in sinistram manum calicem cum vino similiter cereum ponunt ei, et sic sepeliunt. Si fecisti, decem dies in pane atque aqua poenitere debes"; English translation in ed. McNeill (1990³), 340; PL 140, 975, decr. lib 19, *De poenitentia* c.5; Hain (1956), 47: "Das tote Kind soll wenigstens die Symbole der Eucharistie empfangen, da das Sakrament ihm nicht zuteil wird".

[150]See above n. 141, 142, 143, 64 respectively; Vloberg (1946), I, 74: excavations of 13th-century graves of the bishops of Troyes, Salisbury, York en Chester.

[151]MGH SS II 792: "nempe moris erat antiquis, ut sacerdotes cum iis ornamentis instrumentisque sepeliruntur, quibus in re sacra uti solebant".

[152]DACL I,2, 1759: "Corpus ad tumulum detulerunt et posuerunt honorifice in sarcophage de tupello ex diversis peciis constructo, cum mitra alba in qua fuerat conscratus et crocia de stanno seu cupro, et super pectus eius calix et patena plombei cum pane et vino".

the dead the prescription that the dead must not be wrapped in altar linen.[153] It was no novelty, since the synod of Clermont had, in 535, already voiced its opposition to the covering of the dead with palls or other sacred cloths. Deceased priests were not allowed to be carried to their grave wrapped in altar cloths that had been used to cover the body of Christ during the Eucharistic celebration, the reason being that its further use in the church would mean the profanation of the altar.[154] The pseudo-*Isidorian Decretals* written in the 9th century identify this as an interdict issued by pope Clement I.[155] It can also be found in the statutes of Boniface[156] and in more or less the same words in the writing of Burchard of Worms, who also protested about the abuse.[157] A final example is that of a penitential dating from the 12th century.[158]

***

Parallel applications of the relics and the Eucharist in the customs surrounding death and burial are, as would appear from the above, have been very subtle. Private collections and museums still have objects known as "mortals' crosses" from Oberammergau. These originate from the 17th and 18th centuries and are filled with small relics. They served as a powerful source of strength and intercession for the seriously ill whose end was approaching. The tradition goes back to the earliest days of Christianity. In fact, because of the trust in the saint and the attachment to the *fylacterium* shown by Makrina and others, it can be assumed that in those times too the relics were seen as providers of strength at the hour of death, sometimes together with the *viaticum*, as described in the *vitae* of Meinrad, of Richard of St. Vannes and of David of Scotland. The greatest confidence was placed in the *viaticum* administered at the actual moment

---

[153]See above n. 117.

[154]CC SL 148 A, 106-107, c. 3: "Observandum ne pallis vel ministeriis divinis defunctorum corpora obvolvantur"; c. 7: "Ne opertorio Dominici corporis sacerdotes unquam corpus, dum ad tumulum evehetur, obtegatur et sacro velamine usibus suis reddeto, dum honorantur corpora, altaria polluantur".

[155]ed. Hinschius (1863), 46-47, c. 45: Item epistola preceptorum sancti Clementis papae: (...) "Nemo per ignorantiam clericus palla mortuum credat obvolvendum, aut diaconus scapulas operire velo, quae fuit in altari aut certe quae data est in mensam domini".

[156]See above n. 121.

[157]PL 140, 694, *decr.* lib. III, c. 107: "Ne opertorio Dominici corporis, vel altaris non unquam corpus dum ad tumulum evehitur obtegatur, ne sacro velamine dum honorantur corpora altaria polluantur".

[158]ed. Schmitz (1958), I, 832.

of death or even subsequently, despite church opposition to the latter. With regard to the placing of the Eucharist on the body in the grave, excavations and reports confirm the existence of the practice as being more extensive in the case of relics than of the Eucharist. Apparently it was more common in the Eastern church than in the West to allow the Eucharist to accompany the body to the grave. The underlying motive here was not simply the desire to rise again with Christ and to be assured of the intercession of the saint already in Paradise but it was also the case that the demons so often referred to reveal a deep-seated fear of the uncertainty of death and the forces of Hell. The borderline between life and death was not very clearly drawn. The *Dialogues* of Gregory, popular and much-read in the Middle Ages, have devils leaving the underworld to desecrate the graves of sinners and dead men returning to receive the *viaticum* they had missed or to describe the horrors of death from first-hand experience. A certain Reparatus claimed he had seen a priest named Tiburtius, who was then still alive, bound to a stake in Hell and a soldier returned from the dead who declared that he had been taken over a bridge from which the damned were flung into a black, stinking river. He also saw a priest, Petrus, deceased four years previously, hanging from his feet with an iron weight around his neck.[159] Accounts of this type, of eye-witnesses from the underworld, can also be found in the writings of Gregory of Tours, Bede, Boniface and others. They are depicted in the tympana of cathedrals, where the devils can be seen dragging the damned on a chain into Hell, towards a region crawling with toads, snakes and demonic goblins, who are heating up the flames with bellows. It is this *Divina Commedia* avant la lettre that caused Christians of the first centuries and early Middle Ages to seek at death and burial the protection of Christ and his saints, present in the Eucharist and the relics.[160]

---

[159]SC 265, 108, *Dial.*, lib. IV, c, 32,5: "Paratus fuerat rogus ingens. Deductus autem Tiburtius presbiter in eo est superpositus atque subposito igne concrematus"; ib. 130, lib. IV, c. 37,8: "pons erat, sub quo niger atque caligosus foetoris intolerabilis nebulam exhalans fluvius decurebat"; c. 37,11: "Ibi se etiam Petrum ecclesiasticae familiae maiorem, qui ante quadriennium defunctus est, deorsum positum in locis teterrimis, magno ferri pondere religatum ac depressum vidisse confessus est".

[160]Gurjewitsch/Gurevich (1987), 167-227; (1988), 104-152; Moolenbroek v. (1989).

4   OATH-TAKING ON THE RELICS AND ON THE EUCHARIST*

It must have been a generally widespread practice in the 5th and 6th centuries to take oaths on the relics.[1] It was particularly favoured in the barbarian monarchies founded on the ruins of the vanished West Roman Empire. When certainties disappeared - including that of the written word - people appealed to higher powers.[2] The Germanic practice of swearing on sacred stones was probably continued under the guise of swearing on the gravestone of a saint or at the stone altar containing the bones of a saint. The Dutch expression *'bij steen en been klagen'* (i.e. to complain bitterly, but literally means "complaining by stone and bone") is perhaps a version of a more ancient 'steen en been zweren' - swearing by stone and bone.[3] When the vassal swore to stand by his master in word and deed for life, this 'doing of homage' was shown in concrete visual form by the servant placing his joined hands in those of his master. Then followed an oath which was similarly characterised by the typical medieval tendency to concretise the abstract. The verbal component was underlined by the touching of the *res sacrae*, usually consisting of relics. In addition a cross and a book of the Gospels were popular means of guaranteeing the truthfulness of the oath to be sworn. Around the year 1000 the Gospels began to replace the relics and by the 13th century they had clearly gained the upper hand.[4] The inhabitants of Wales, however, are said to have sworn oaths with greater fear on the relics than on the Gospels.[5] The oath sworn without sacred objects - *solo sermone*, often sworn on God's saints in general - was also practised from the second half of the 12th century.[6]

This generally accepted practice of oath-taking, despite the objections expressed in the Sermon on the Mount (Mtt. 5:34-38), must have come from disillusion with human unreliability. It was impossible to

---

*A list for further reading and sources can be found in: Hofmeister (1957), Hermann-Mascard (1957) and Bartlett (1986).

[1] Hofmeister (1957), 15.

[2] David (1953), 6.

[3] Stoett (1953), 270; Nottarp (1956), 219.

[4] Hofmeister (1957), 36-61; Hermann-Mascard (1975), 249.

[5] Finucane (1977), 26, 221.

[6] Hermann-Mascard (1975), 237.

resist that need to call on what men held as their deepest concern, their own existence, that of their children or God and the saints.[7]

The sources are full of accounts of oath-taking on the saints and on their relics. The literature draws a distinction according to the aim and function of the oath and the place of the oath-taking.[8] For the purposes of this study a rougher division is sufficient: the oath of promise and the oath of truth. The former confirms the seriousness of the obligations taken on while the latter guarantees the truth of the statement made, which was of special importance in the case of a suspect. The suspect had to clear himself of all guilt by an 'oath of purgation', a specialised form of the oath of truth. The risk incurred here was that the saint would see any perjury as a personal insult and punish it with death. People did not even hesitate to call down God's punishments should they be lying.

This 'challenge' to God can be seen as a bridging form to the trial by ordeal, which was even further from the prescriptions of the sermon on the Mount. In this *tentatio Dei* the suspect submitted to a test designed to bring the truth to light whether or not the truth had been confirmed under oath. It was, as it were, a 'requirement made of God' to show demonstrably that he was championing the innocent. From about the 8th century the practice came to be used in legal situations, but it was also used outside this context when the credibility of a promise or a statement was in question.[9] The trial by ordeal, of pre-Christian origin, became associated with Christian belief and was integrated into medieval Christianity for a number of centuries. It was accompanied by liturgical formulations and regulated by synodal and conciliar prescriptions.[10] It was based on the medieval conviction that the result was a divine demonstration of the truth or lack of it which constituted a binding revelation for man.[11] The test could consist of a duel, the form which endured the longest. Other methods included tests by fire, water or the cheese and bread test.[12] If someone took hold of a red-hot piece of metal or walked over hot ploughshares in bare feet and suffered serious burns, guilt was established unless the wounds healed quickly. The cauldron test

---

[7]Boelaars (1968), 179, 182-184.

[8]ibid. 235-270; David (1953); Hofmeister (1957).

[9]Schwerin (1933), 50.

[10]Nottarp (1956), 110; regarding the cultural dynamic and synthesis, from both Christian and non-Christian viewpoint in general, see: Engen v. (1986), 549-551.

[11]Mordek (1986), 45, lit. n. 117.

[12]DTC, 1139-1152, Ordalies.

- seizing an object plunged in boiling water - could lead to the same conclusion. The cold water test proved the suspect's guilt if he floated. When suspected of robbery the prisoner would be put to the cheese and bread test: he was given blessed dry rye bread with cheese. It was assumed that a thief would not be able to swallow the measured quantity or would vomit it out.

The trial by ordeal or 'ordale' led a stubborn existence inmost European countries until well into the 13th century.[13] The growth of the towns and the rise of the commercial law, bad experiences with the 'ordale' and various forms of deception, efforts to find more judicial methods of research and proof, critical noises from individuals within the church and the debates at the universities of Paris and Bologna at the end of the 12th century - these were all factors which led to the disappearance of the trial by ordeal.[14] The Fourth Lateran Council in 1215 gave rise to this gradual disappearance by forbidding clerics to perform blessings or consecrations at the 'ordale'.[15]

The Eucharist fulfilled a function both in the trial by ordeal and in the two types of oath-taking mentioned: the oath of promise and the oath of truth. The oath could be taken on the Eucharist alone - by touching it a few times as with the relics - but it was also possible to reinforce any statement made by signing it with consecrated wine or by receiving the consecrated bread.

This latter was the principal component of the 'communion test',[16] a demonstrative manner of receiving communion on the part of the suspect as a proof of his protestation of innocence. It served as a substitute for the oath of purgation and the trial by ordeal, especially for the clergy around the 10th century when, particularly in Germany, the tendency arose to spare them the 'ordale'. As early as 794 the Council of Frankfurt laid down that a bishop could have his trial by ordeal taken by a substitute, though he was himself still required to take the oath of purgation.[17] A capitulare issued in Aachen in 801 banned priests from

---

[13]Nottarp (1956), 137, 189-210, 222, 317-397; Bartlett (1986).

[14]Leimaier (1953), c. 5, 6; Baldwin (1961); (1970), I, 323-332.

[15]COD 244, c. 18.

[16]Köstler (1912); Browe (1928).

[17]MGH Conc II, 167, c. VIII: "Qui episcopus, dum cum quibus iuraret non invenisset, elegit sibi ipse, ut suus homo ad Dei iudicium iret, et ille testaretur absque reliquiis et absque sanctis evangeliis, solummodo coram Deo, quod ille innocens exinde esset, et secundum eius innocentiam Deus adiuvaret illum suum hominem, qui ad illud iudicium exiturus erat et exivit".

taking the oath.[18] The Council of Meaux in 845 was less general in its tone and confined itself to the bishop, who was forbidden to swear *super sacra*.[19] An explanation for the growing resistance to oath-taking by clerics was given by the Council of Tribur in 895: the hand consecrated by the body and blood of Christ should not be contaminated by the oath.[20] And what is more, the clergy were now in close contact with the Eucharist as a result of the clericalisation off the liturgy.[21] Emperor Henry III, finally, published an edict in 1074 forbidding oath-taking by clergy without any exception.[22]

'Parallel application in concrete use' can be seen in both the oath of promise and the oath of truth, which we are to be discussed consecutively. Within the context of the oath of purgation taken on the Eucharist the communion test will be paid special attention. In view of the frequent references in the sources this is something that must have occurred relatively frequently.

4.1 Oath-taking on the relics

In the taking of oaths on the relics as confirmation of a promise, a few examples of which will now be quoted, in Rome the bones of the apostle Peter played a central role. Standing before the grave of the 'first' among the apostles, Pope Boniface II († 352) appointed the deacon Vigilius under oath as his successor and later burned his order, again using the grave as his witness.[23] According to the *Liber Diurnus*, written at the end of the 8th century, there must have been a custom of earlier date of having the bishops take an oath of fidelity on the body of Peter during their

---

[18]MGH Leges I, 19; "ut nullus sacerdos quisquam cum iuramento iuret, sed simpliciter cum puritate et veritate omnia dicat".

[19]Mansi XIV, 827, canon 38: "Ut nullus deinceps veritatis episcopus super sacra iurare praesumat".

[20]MGH Capit II, 224, c. 21: "Manus enim, per quam corpus et sanguis Christi conficitur, iuramento polluitur"; Mansi XVIII, 143; frequently repeated in subsequent centuries; Hermann-Mascard (1975), 262, n. 209.

[21]See p. 39.

[22]MGH Const I, 96-97: "ut clerici iurare non audeant (...) diffinimus ut non episcopus, non presbiter, non cuiuscumque ordinis clericus, non abbas, non aliquis monachus vel sanctimonialis in quacumque controversia sive criminali sive civili iusiurandum compellatur qualibet ratione subire (...)"; see also PL 140, 655, Burchardi Wormaciensis ep., decr. lib. II, c. 182.

[23]LP I, 281: "Quod constitutum cum cyrographis sacerdotum et iusiurandum ante confessionem beati apostoli Petri in diaconum Vigilium constituit; ante confessionem beati apostoli Petri ipsum constitutum praesentia omnium sacerdotum et cleri et sanatus incendio consumpsit".

consecration, certainly if it was performed by the pope.[24] This practice of taking an oath on the grave continued until the 11th century, when it was replaced by an oath taken on the book of the Gospels.[25] The 'princeps' of the apostles was also called on to bear witness when the pope himself got into difficulties. Pope Hadrian I († 795) called on Charlemagne for support against the Longobard, Desiderius, and together they prayed bowing before the grave of Peter, each reinforcing the other with the oath *ad corpus beati Petri*.[26] Over two centuries later, in 962, when the papacy had become a football kicked around by machinating noblemen, John XII († 964) called on the aid of Otto I against Berengarius of Ivrea and declared his fidelity to the new emperor under oath *supra corpus sancti Petri*. In his turn the emperor took an oath on the wood of the Cross and *per has reliquias*.[27] The pope was to break this oath, which was the reason for the emperor deposing him and replacing him with Leo VIII. Two years later the people swore willy-nilly the oath of obedience on the tomb of Peter to Otto and his protégé, Pope Leo.[28]

Outside Rome, of course, it was not Peter's tomb but the local relics which imparted power to many an oath. Duke Tassilo of Bavaria († 798) swore his vassal's oath to Pepin the Short on local relics apart from its reliability and duration.[29] Pepin's successor, Charlemagne, of whom it is known that he was attached to the relics,[30] required his subjects to take the oath of fidelity on the relics. The capitularia dated

---

[24]ed. Sickel (1966), 79, LXXV: "Promitto ego ill. episcopus sanctae ecclesiae ill. vobis beato Petro apostolorum principi vicarioque tuo beatissimo papae domno ill. successoribusque eius per patrem et filium et spiritum sanctum, trinitatem inseparabilem et hoc sacratissimum corpus tuum"; LXXV, 80-81.

[25]Hermann-Mascard (1975), 249.

[26]LP I, 497: "Et descendentes pariter ad corpus beati Petri tam ipse sanctissimus papa quamque antefatus excellentissimus Francorum rex cum iudicibus Romanorum et Francorum, seseque mutuo per sacramentum munientes (...)".

[27]MGH Const I, 21: "Tibi domno Iohanni papae ego rex Otto promittere et iurare facio per Patrem et Filium et Spiritum sanctum et per hoc lignum vivificae crucis et per has reliquias sanctorum"; 23; Hofmeister (1957), 21.

[28]LP II, 246; "Coangustati autem et afflicti Romani (...) spondentes ei obedientiam et domno imperatori super corpus beati Petri apostoli per sacramentum".

[29]RHF V, 34, *Annales*, a. 757: "Ibique Tassilo venit Dux Baioariorum in vassatico se commendans per manus sacramenta iuravit multa et innumerabilia reliquiis sanctorum martyrum manus imponens (...) Sic confirmavit supradictus Tassilo supra corpus sanctorum Dionysii, Rustici et Eleutherii, necnon et s. Germani, seu sancti Martini".

[30]See p. 18 and 113.

789[31] and 803[32] are examples of this. Charles the Bald also demanded a similar oath.[33] An example of a medieval oath on the relics, all the more expressive because it is illustrated, is that taken by Harold († 1066), the 'oath-breaker'. The Bayeux Tapestry shows him with both hands resting on a reliquary, recognising the rights of William of Normandy from a position of weakness. According to a canon of Bayeux, Robert Wace, in his *Roman du Rou*, William secretly placed a chest full of relics under the altar cloth when the oath was taken. When he drew away the cloth after the oath had been pronounced, Harold was deeply shocked and his fall at the battle of Hastings was regarded as a judgement of God.[34]

The chronicler Galbert of Bruges repeatedly mentions the oath on the relics in his account of the turbulent events of his era. Thus it was that in 1071 Robert the Frisian swore homage to his brother Baldwin VI and "the oath was sworn in the church of St. Donation at Bruges on a great many relics of the saints, which Count Baldwin had ordered to be brought". The Count, William Clito, advanced by king Louis VI of France, promised on 5th April 1127 to leave untouched the privileges of the canons of Bruges. "Binding themselves to accept this condition, the king and the count took an oath on the relics of the saints in the hearing of the clergy and the people".[35] This they did in their capacities as liege and vassal. The oath of fidelity taken by the vassal with respect to his feudal lord, of which Tassilo of Bavaria has provided us with an example, was usually taken *per loca sanctorum vel pignora*.[36] It remained in general force until the 12th century, in northern France until the 13th and in the German Empire even as late as the 15th-16th century.[37]

There is still another aspect requiring our attention: the monastic promise. The richest collection of relics was to be found within the confines of monastery walls, relics of the saints regarded as 'protectors' of the region. The prospective monk called on these 'vassals' of God to bear

---

[31]MGH Cap. Reg. Franc. I, 58, *Admonitio Generalis*, c. 64: "Ideo omnino ammonendi sunt omnes diligenter, ut caveant periurium, non solum in sancto evangelio vel in altare seu in sanctorum reliquiis sed et in communi loquella".

[32]See p. 18, n. 59.

[33]Mansi, XVII, 94, a. 860, tit. 31: "Sic me Deus adiuvet et istae reliquiae".

[34]Lefeuvre (1932), 103; Boussel (1971), 203.

[35]Galbert of Bruges, *The Murder of Charles the Good* (1982), resp. 234 and 204.

[36]MGH *Marculfi Formulae* I, 40; "fidelitatem (...) per loca sanctorum vel pignora (...) debeant promittere et coniurare".

[37]Hermann-Mascard (1975), 253.

witness to his commitment when he bound himself to the abbey for all eternity in obedience and fidelity.

The profession, or monastic promise, to which the oath can to some extent be compared,[38] would seem to be of Benedictine origin in the West. The *Regula Magistri*, which is summarised and modified in the rule of St. Benedict, makes no mention of it in the chapter dealing with the confirmation of the new monk's entry into the community.[39] The promise was made in the monastery church in "the presence of God and all his saints" - *coram Deo et sanctis eius*[40] - or, as the oldest known formulation from 7th-century Albi puts it, "before the relics which rest in the altar".[41] The *promissio* was confirmed by the novice in a handwritten document or at least in a signed request to be accepted into the monastic community. He laid this document on the altar - *super altare* - with the offerings during Mass in the name of the relics reposing in the altar stone.[42] All monastic orders that came into existence after Benedict show similar traits in their ritual of profession. The rule, for instance, of the Carthusians, and order founded in 1084, prescribes a promise made to God, his saints and their relics,[43] as did that of the Cistercians.[44] Around the 13th century the relics are no longer referred to in the profession and the promise is simply made to the saints in general, to the angels of God or to the Gospels.[45]

The oath taken on the relics was, as well as a seal on a promise made by a human being to God or to another human being, was also the usual means of freeing oneself from an accusation or suspicion in the form of an oath of purgation, of which a few examples are given here.

---

[38]ibid. 250; Capelle (1959), 231: "Nous avons donc un voeu proprement dit et une promesse accolés, mais point de serment".

[39]ed. Vogüé de (1964), SC 106, c. 89, 370-378.

[40]RSB c. 58, 17, 18: "Coram deo et sanctis eius, ut, si aliquando aliter fecerit, ab eo se damnandum sciat, quem inridit"; 19: "De qua promissione sua faciat petitionem ad nomen sanctorum, quorum reliquiae ibi sunt, et abbatis praesentis".

[41]Martène (1788), IV, 224; Capelle (1959), 105; Hermann- Mascard (1975), 250, n. 111.

[42]Zeiger (1935); Frank (1951); Hofmeister (1963), 114-137.

[43]ed. Guiges Ie (1984), SC 313, 214, *Consuetudines, c. 23*, professio novicii: "Ego frater ille, promitto (...) coram Deo et sanctis eius, et reliquiis istius heremi (...) in praesentia domni illius prioris"; PL 153, 685.

[44]PL 66, 820, *Regula commentata*, c. 58, formulae cisterciensum: "coram Deo et omnibus sanctis eius quorum reliquiae hic habentur".

[45]Hermann-Mascard (1975), 251.

Augustine was an early seeker of refuge in the oath. In a letter written in 404 he set out this problem: two people living in his house were accusing one another of a misdeed. Although he had the greater trust in one of them, named Bonifatius, he had no clear proof of the guilt of the other. And so he sent them to the tomb of St. Felix of Nola, which enjoyed a certain reputation of strictness with perjurers.[46] The two were expected to swear an oath absolving them of blame, leaving it up to Felix to bring the truth to light. At the time of Ambrose the Milanese had obliged a thief to confess on a similar way. They required that he should swear an oath on the tomb of the city's patron saints, Gervase and Protase, which he refused to do.[47]

Pope Gregory the Great requested of abbots and bishops accused of anything at all to clear themselves by means of an oath taken at "the sacred body of Peter, the first apostle".[48] Gregory of Tours also provides various examples of oaths of purgation, in which the tomb of Maximinus of Trier († 346) or that of his celebrated predecessor Martin, repeatedly play a role.[49] In these examples the perjurer called down upon himself the fatal judgement of God.[50] One such victim is said to have been the sly priest Arboastes, who was commissioned by king Theodebert († 537) to confirm - at the grave of St. Maximinus - false accusations made against a certain Frank. He paid with his life.[51] Another man was accused of arson in a case in which there was no possible doubt. For this reason Gregory refused him admission to the church, at which the man swore an oath on the spot. When he turned around he fell flat on the ground and died of suffocation. This was seen as a warning given by Martin to all who dared to commit perjury on his territory.[52] The oath of purgation was also taken on the grave of the founder of Saint Germain-

---

[46]ibid. 235.

[47]CSEL 34, 333-336, ep. 78, c. 2, 3.

[48]CC SL 140, 469, *Registrum epistularum*, VII, 18: "ad sacratissimum corpus beati Petri apostolorum principis districto fecimus sacramenta praebere"; 115, lib. II, 29.

[49]MGH SRM I,1 , 259, *Hist. Franc.* lib. V, c. 49: "Qui tertio aut eo amplius mihi sacramentum super sepulcrum sancti Martini dederat".

[50]PL 71, 823, *Miraculorum*, lib. II, c. 39: "Est etiam in Turonico vicus (...) in quo beati martyris reliquiae continentur, qui cum magnis virtutibus crebro illustretur, in periuris tamen plerumque agitat ultionem".

[51]MGH SRM I,2, 356, *Liber in gloria confessorum*, c. 91: "Si vera sunt, inquit (Thodebertus) quae prosequeris, hoc super tumulum Maximini antistitis sacramento confirma (...) Et statim ponens manus super sanctum sepulcrum dixit (...) Cumque per viam pariter pergerent, subito dilapsus presbiter solo pessumdedit et mortuus est".

[52]MGH SRM I,1 , 384, *Hist. Franc.* lib. VIII, c. 16: "Et dum haec diceret, spiritum exalavit. Multis haec causa documentum fuit, ne in hoc loco auderent ulterius peierare".

des-Prés, St. Germanus († 576), and on the bones of St. Denis, the first
bishop of Paris who, with his companions Rusticus and Eleutherius, died
a martyr's death in the mid-3rd century.[53] St. Pancratius has gone down
in history as the protector of the oath and the avenger of perjury.[54]

The oath of purgation also had a function in the exercise of justice.
It is mentioned in the tribal laws promulgated in the Merovingian and
Carolingian eras, from the 6th to the 9th century. The *Lex Alamannorum*
required that the oath of the suspect and his oath-helpers should be taken
"on the relics".[55] Other barbarian peoples must also have used the relics
as *res sacrae*, whether those entombed in the altar or not, especially in
serious cases such as witchcraft or manslaughter.[56] In the *Lex Frisionum*
there is mention of swearing oaths *in reliquiis sanctorum*.[57] A series of
witnesses recorded from the 9th to the 11th century in Burgundy and the
Languedoc we read that the oath was taken "on the altar", but mostly "on
the relics".[58] In Artois, south-west France and also possibly in
Normandy the oath of purgation was maintained for only slight
infringements until well into the 13th century and perhaps even later.[59]

In the judicial system of the church, for which the first guidelines
were set down by Regino of Prüm around 906,[60] the oath of purgation

---

[53]ibid. 237, lib. V, c. 32; Martène (1788), II, 330, c. VII, Probatio occultorum criminum
per iuramentum: "In Gallis etiam ad s. Martini, sanctique Germani, ac beatorum martyrum
Dionysii et sociorum eius tumulum divinam periuri vindictam non semel experti sunt".

[54]PL 71, 740, *Miraculorum*, lib. I, c. 39: "Pancratius martyr, valde in periuris ultor. Ad
cuius sepulcrum si cuiusquam mens insana iuramentum inane proferre voluerit prius quam
sepulcrum eius adeat (...), statim aut arripitur a daemone, aut cadens in pavimento amittit
spiritum".

[55]MGH Leges III, 133, *Lex Alamannorum*, c. VI, 4: "Ista sacramenta debent esse iurati,
ut illi coniuratores manus suas super capsam ponant (...) ut sic illi Deus adiuvet vel illae
reliquiae ad illas manus quas comprehendas habet".

[56]ed. Rozière (1871), I, 597, no. 494, Notitia de erbas maleficas: "femina (...) posita
manu sua super sacrosancto altare sancto illo, sic iurata dixit: 'Hic iuro per hunc loco sancto
et Deo altissimo (...) ego herbas maleficas nec potiones malas nunquam temporavi nec
bibere dedi"; Hermann-Mascard (1975), 244.

[57]MGH Leges, III, 666, tit. XII, 1, De delicto servorum: "Si servus rem magnam
quamlibet furasse dicatur (...) dominus eius in reliquiis sanctorum pro hac re iurare debet";
667, tit. XIV, 3, De homine in turba occiso: "Is qui compositionem homocidii quaerit, in
reliquiis sanctorum iuret".

[58]ed. Thevenin (1887), 81, n. 68, (a. 821): "Iurati autem dicimus et iuramus imprimis
per Deum patrem omnipotentem et Jhesum filium eius (...) et ex locum venerationis
ecclesiae s. Iuliani martyris Christi super cuius sacrosancto altario has conditiones manibus
nostris continemus vel iurando contingemus"; 127 n. 93 (a. 858): "Iuramus (...) sive et per
reliquias s. Petri"; 162, n. 109 (a. 887): "Venit Aimoinus ad altare et mittebat manum suam
super altare et super sanctas reliquias et iurabat"; 188, n. 127 bis (a. 928) : "mitentes manus
super altarium eius, dicentes: 'Per Deum Patrem omnipotentem et has reliquias s. Stephani".

[59]Hermann-Mascard (1975), 245.

[60]ed. Wasserschleben (1964), 207, lib. II, c. 2.

was used for, among other things, turning aside the suspicion of incest.[61] Up to and including the *Decretum Gratiani* in the middle of the 12th century the oath on the relics and the oath on the Gospels at the *purgatio canonica* is still mentioned in the canonical collections,[62] after which only the latter survived for any length of time. The oath could also be taken on both relics and Gospels, and not just by clerics, as is shown by the following example. When, after the murder of Thomas à Becket on 27th September in the cathedral of St. Andrew in Avranches, King Henry II was reluctantly reconciling himself with the church, he took an oath not only on the relics but also on the Gospels. He swore in the presence of papal legates, abbots and bishops from Normandy that he deeply regretted the death of the Archbishop of Canterbury, which he had never desired nor willed.[63]

The gesture made by the taker of the oath demonstrated the presence of the 'sacred'. He laid his hands on the tomb, relic or altar table.[64] He could also stretch his arms out in supplication to heaven[65] or hold the relics.[66] Sometimes the relics were simply shown to the one taking the oath.[67]

4.2   The oath on the Eucharist

The concrete expression of the sacred component of the oath consisted not only of the relics but also of the Eucharist. We know of an occurrence in the life of St. Ambrose, for example, when a promise and the Eucharist were quite clearly involved together. In 388 Emperor Theodosius I wanted to oblige a bishop to re-build a synagogue which he had had burned down. He also decided to punish a number of monks who had

---

[61]Hermann-Mascard (1975), 240.

[62]ed. Friedberg (1879-81), 887, causa XXII, qu. 5, c. 16, 17: "in sanctis iurare"; 889, qu. 5, c. 22: "super sacra evangelia iurare"; 1279, causa XXXV, qu. 6, c. 5; iuramentum accusatoris: "Sic te Deus adiuvet et istorum sanctorum reliquiae"; Hermann-Mascard (1975), 241; David (1953), 160 sqq. esp. 166 n. 24 en 167 n. 32; ed. Pontal (1971), 160, Synodal de l'Ouest, c. 35: "Ne tradantur reliquie laicis ad iurandum nisi certis temporibus".

[63]Hefele (1907-42), V,2 , 1054-1055; Foreville (1943), 338-339.

[64]MGH SRM I, *Hist. Franc.* lib. III, c. 14: "Tunc Aregisilius positis super altarium sanctum manibus, iuravit ei ut securus egrederetur"; lib. V, prologus.

[65]MGH SRM I, *Hist. Franc.* lib. V, c. 32: "Tunc (...) elevatisque manibus super altarium iuravit"; PL 71, 755, *Miraculorum*, lib. I, c. 53.

[66]Förster (1942), 16: Aethelred in 997.

[67]Zeiger (1940), 184.

done the same with another Jewish sacred building. Ambrose wrote the emperor a letter pointing out bitterly that many Christian basilicas had suffered a similar fate under Julian the Apostate († 363). He was able to persuade the emperor to give up his first wish but not his second. Ambrose declared that he would approach the altar only on condition that Theodosius gave way on this point too and would keep to his promise.[68]

Here the celebration of the Eucharist in its totality is the price and the seal of a promise made. It is not a question of an oath explicitly made on the Eucharist, nor is it so in the case of the adjuring Eucharistic formulations found on amulets excavated from early Christian graves. On a small lead plate, found in 1886 in Reggio Calabria, there is a text with these last four lines: "And I curse every evil spirit. Depart from your servant of God, Sittisma, you evil and utterly abominable, corrupt and unclean spirit, by the power of the body and blood of Jesus Christ".[69] This plate must have been used as a *fylacterium* as did the scrap of paper, now in the British Library, which bears the words: :For I have bound you with iron, with the spotless bread and blood".[70] This line, written in Coptic, would seem to serve as a reinforcement of a statement or promise with the Eucharist as guarantee.

The earliest trace of an oath takes us to Novatianus, a theologian who set himself as anti-pope to Cornelius († 253) with whom he disagreed on the subject of the *lapsi*. He belonged to the 'precise' (the pure) party while Cornelius chose the side of the 'moderates'. This difference in opinion led to a schism in 251. The father of church history, Eusebius († 339), writes of the accusation made by Cornelius against his opponent. Novatianus had his followers swear on the body and blood of Christ that they would stand by him. At the reception of the bread he clasped the hands of the communicant in his own hands and would not let go until he had sworn: "I shall never again return to Cornelius", a formulation which was used instead of the usual 'amen'.[71]

---

[68]CSEL 82, 161, ep. I (41), c. 28: "Ita ad altare accessi, non aliter accessurus, nisi plene promisisset mihi"; Dölger (1929-50), I, 54- 65; ed. Schaff (1979), X, 450, n. 28.

[69]Dölger, V, 255; Cozza Luzi (1887), 199-200.

[70]ibid. 207; Hyvernat (1888), pl. XIV; this reproduction refers to text OR.1013A (Catalogue no. 369 in Crum, catalogue of the Coptic manuscripts in the British Museum, 1905) kept in the British Museum (now British Library); information provided by Dr. V. Nersessian, curator Christian Middle East, The British Library, London.

[71]PG 20, 627, *Hist. eccl.* lib. VI, c. 43: ["Iura mihi per corpus et sanguinem Domini Iesu Christi, te nunquam meas partes deserturum, nec ad Cornelium esse rediturum (...) Et cum panem illum accipiens dicere debuisset Amen, eius loco dicit: Non revertar deinceps ad Cornelium"].

The pseudo-Chrysostom was very unhappy about oath-taking on the Eucharist. He complained that shameless women enter the church under the pretext of wanting to pray but in fact go to swear on the mysterious body and blood of the son of God or - so he adds in the same breath - on His mother, on a saint or on the wood of the Cross.[72] John the Almsgiver († c. 619) was, according to his *vita*, just as concerned in the early Middle Ages about such practices. Perhaps he was thinking of the punishment meted out to those committing perjury on the grave of a saint when he said: "How many commit perjury by His mysterious body and blood and He suffers it to happen and shows indulgence without striking them with disaster on the spot?"[73]

The oath on the relics, to be found in German tribal law, was supplemented by the Visigoths with an oath taken on the Eucharist. First the oath was taken on the Trinity, then there followed a long series of other possible witnesses, including "all the holy bodies and martyrs' crowns", and finally the Eucharist: "We swear by the holy communion, that the perjurer may be brought to eternal damnation".[74]

We have already seen that the Benedictine made his promise 'to God and His saints', present in the relics. When a monk or priest was ordained, the abbot called on his brothers in the name of the Eucharist to inform him if there was any impediment. So at least prescribed Paul Diaconus around 774 in his commentary on the Benedictine rule. The abbot had to call the chapter together and speak thus: "I swear and beseech you 'by the communion of the body and blood of our Lord Jesus Christ', by the sacred baptism, by the eternal reward of heaven, by the profession we have made, that each of you inform me of any sin he may know of which may be an impediment to the candidate in making his sacrifice".[75] The abbot requested this guarantee from his chapter,

---

[72]PG 56, 536, *In genesim sermo*, III, 4: ["Impudenter illae ecclesias adeunt quasi orandi causa, et iurant per corpus intemeratum et sanguinem Filii Dei vel per matrem eius, vel per aliquem sanctorum, multae etiam per vivificum lignum"].

[73]PL 73, 374, *Vita s. Ioannis eleemosinarii*, c. 40; "quanti peierant corpus et sanguinem eius sacrosanctum et patitur et longanimiter agit, non reddens eis hic aliquid difficile"; Dölger (1929-50), V, 256.

[74]MGH *Leges Formulae Visigothicae*, 592, c. 2,39: "Iuramus per omnia sacra corpora gloriosasque martirum coronas omnesque virtutes caelorum vel haec sancta quatuor evangelia et sacrosancto altario domini nostri ill. martiris, ubi has conditiones superpositas nostris continemus manibus"; "Iuramus per sanctam communionem, quae periuranti in damnatione maneat perpetua".

[75]*Bibliotheca Casinensis*, IV (1880), Florilegium Casinense, 155, LXII, De sacerdotibus monasterii: "Deinde debet venire in capitulum et (...) debet coniurare omnes isto modo. Adiuro vos et coniuro per communionem corporis et sanguinis domini nostri Iesu Christi et per sanctum baptismum et remunerationem caelestis gaudii; et professionem nostram quam

convinced as he was of the sacral status acquired by the monk once ordained.

The signing of documents with a pen dipped in consecrated wine is also reported. The document by which Pope Theodore I deposed the patriarch Pyrrhus in the 7th century was done in this way, with the pope resting his hand on the tomb of St. Peter: it had the character of an oath taken on the Eucharist and on the relics simultaneously. This custom must have still have been practised a century later, according to the sources, since Photius, condemned by a document signed in this way with the sacred blood, was himself witness of the practice.[76]

He had been proposed as patriarch by Bardes, a member of the governing council of Emperor Michael III († 867). But Bardes fell into imperial disfavour when a new favourite, Basil, arrived on the scene. When Bardes was to lead an expedition against the Cretans, Michael and Basil swore that he could leave without danger, even though they had made an attempt on his life. After the reading of the Gospel Photius held "the precious body and blood" in his hand while the emperor and Basil signed the oath in the sacred blood.[77] The guarantee offered by the oath was not worth much since Basil later removed first Bardes and then Michael.

In the West Charles the Bald († 877) was guilty of breaking an oath taken on the Eucharist. This Charles was born of the second marriage of Louis the Pious with Judith of Zwaben, whose appearance made an impression on more men than Louis alone. In fact the mentor appointed by Louis for Charles, Duke Bernard of Septimania, compromised himself by an affair which he is reported to have had with Judith. As a result he was forced to Barcelona and kept out of things when Louis' son's had their armed struggle over how the kingdom should be divided. Although Charles resented Bernard's attitude in this, he nevertheless made a peace agreement with him that was signed by both with the Eucharistic blood. But this agreement also failed: Charles ordered Bernard to meet him in a

---

professi sumus, ut quicumque cognovit illum in tali peccato detentum, quod illum proibet ab oblatione sacrificii, nuntiet michi atque manifestet".

[76]See p. 67.

[77]*Theophanes Chonographia*, ed. Goar-Cambefis (1665), 445-510, *Leonis Grammatici Chronographia res a recentioribus imperatoribus gestas complectans*, 465: "et patriarcha pretiosum corpus et sanguinem Domini nostri Iesu Christi manibus tenente, calamum intingentes imperator et Basilius venerandis crucibus appositis, subscripserunt iuramento"; Vogelius (1713), 10.

monastery in Toledo where he unexpectedly struck him in the heart with a dagger.[78]

It very much open to question whether or not, in 896, the citizens of Rome had the Eucharist in mind when they swore fidelity to Arnulf of Carinthia. The formulation "I swear by all these mysteries of God" is too vague for any definite conclusion to be reached.[79]

The question is more easily answered with regard to the imperial coronation of Henry V on 13th April 1111, where pope and emperor called on the Eucharist to witness their mutual bonds. A bitter history had preceded the coronation. The pope, Paschal II, somewhat aloof on the ways of the life and the world, had been imprisoned by the future emperor during the conflict over the investiture. Henry had been able to force a shaky compromise leaving the way open for the coronation. Standing before St. Peter's, Henry placed his oath in the hands of the pope "before God and St. Peter"[80] and Paschal performed the coronation during the Mass. At the moment of communion the pope is reported to have taken a moment of silence before appealing to the "body of our Lord Jesus Christ", shown by him to the congregation, as a guarantee of the mutual peace. The 'oath on the relics' in front of the church was further reinforced by the Eucharist inside the church.[81]

Sometimes, as was the case in oaths taken on the relics, the Eucharist was merely exposed or touched. It is known that in 1134 Bernard of Clairvaux showed the Eucharist to Duke William of Aquitania and adjured him to discontinue his loyalty to the anti-pope Anacletus. William stood outside while Bernard celebrated Mass. Bearing the consecrated Host in his hands "the man of God" emerged threateningly from the church and addressed William, as if he were a fanatic Saul (Acts 9:3-9; 26:9-16): "Behold the Son of the virgin, who is the head and the

---

[78]Agobardus, 129, *Stephani Baluzii Tutelensis notae ad Agobardum*, ad librum apologeticum, c. II : "Pace itaque cum sanguine eucharistico separatim per regem et comitem firmata et obsignata"; Vogelius (1713), 11.

[79]MGH Cap II, 123, n. 229, *Iuramentum Romanorum Arnolfo Imperatori Praestitutum:* "Iuro per haec omnia Dei mysteria"; Hofmeister (1957), 76-77.

[80]MGH SS V, *Annales Romani*, 475-476; VI, *Sigiberti Chronica*, 373, a. 1111: "Ego Henricus imperator augustus affirmo Deo et sancto Petro".

[81]ibid. III, 112-113, *Annales Hildesheimenses* a. 1111; "Cumque usque ad communicandum missae sollempnitas esset celebrata, apostolicus dato silentio regem sic alloquitur: *'Hoc corpus domini nostri Iesu Christi, natum ex Maria virgine, passum pro salute generis humani, sit confirmatio verae pacis et concordiae inter me et te'*. Et communicantes, invicem osculati sunt".

lord of the church, whom thou persecutest". The duke fell to the ground and submitted.[82]

When Raymond VI of Toulouse had been excommunicated for sympathising with the Albigenses, he was accepted back into the church during the synod of Montelimar in 1209 by the swearing of a simultaneous oath on the Eucharist and on the relics. The latter were spread in considerable numbers throughout the church held by more than twenty prelates. Raymond approached the church barefoot and, with his hand on the book of the Gospels, swore the oath on the holy relics, the Eucharist, the wood of the Cross and the Gospels.[83] The formula of oath of his dukes and barons, addressed to the legate of the Holy See, was more or less of the same kind. It too included mention of the Eucharist, the relics and the Gospels.[84]

The spoken word in the 13th century must have mirrored the Eucharistic oath, since in the oldest statutes of the Sylvestrines the custom of calling on the Cross, the Virgin Mary or the *corpus Dei* under oath is stated to be a moderate sin in the case of a monk. The Sylvestrines, founded in 1231, followed the Benedictine rule strictly, and the rule forbids the swearing of oaths.[85]

There is a treaty still extant that was signed under oath in the 14th century between Duke Simon of Lippe and William of Arnsberg. During the signing they laid their hand on the Eucharist "according to the custom of the time", just as Louis of Bavaria († 1347) and Frederick the Fair of Habsburg († 1330) were reconciled in 1326. These latter went on to

---

[82]PL 185, 289-299, auctore Ernaldo, lib. II: "Ecce ad te processit Filius Virginis, qui est caput et Dominus Ecclesiae, quam tu persequeris (...) Videns comes Abbatem in spiritu vehementi procedentem, et sacratissimum Domini Corpus ferentem in manibus, expavit"; 1181, *Exordium Magnum*, c. 2; AASS 10 febr. II, 454-455.

[83]Mansi XXII, 769: "Adductus est comes nudus ante fores ecclesiae b. Aegidii, ibique coram legato, archiepiscopis et episcopis qui ad hoc convenerant plusquam viginti, iuravit super corpus Christi et sanctorum reliquias, quae ante foras ecclesiae expositae cum magna veneratione, et in multa copia a praelatis tenebantur (...) Ego Raimundus (...) sacrosanctis reliquiis, Eucharistia, et ligno crucis dominicae compositis supra sancta Dei evangelia corporaliter manu tacta, iuro".

[84]ibid. 771, *Iuramentum comitum et baronum* (...): "iuramus tibi magistro Miloni domni papae notario apostolicae sedis legato, coram sancta eucharistia, et cruce Dominica, et sanctorum reliquiis supra sancta evangelia corporaliter manu tacta"; Hofmeister (1957), 77: 'einen änlichen Eid leisten auch seine Anhänger (...) Doch fehlt bei ihnen die besondere Erwähnung der hl. Eucharistie". This remark was probably intended for *Iuramentum consulum Avenionensium*, which follows (772) and in which the Eucharist does not figure.

[85]Weissenberger (1942), 85: "Media culpa est..si cum iuramento, ut in loquendo fieri potest, dicendo per crucem dei, per beatam virginem, per corpus dei vel aliquid simile negaverit vel affirmaverit"; RSB c. 4,27: "Non iurare ne forte periuret".

receive half each of the Host in question in the course of the Mass.[86] In an English rite of coronation from the same century, the king goes to the altar after the sermon to take his oath which he "must confirm with the sacrament of the body of the Lord".[87] In this case we can speak of an oath taken on the Eucharist, but it is also possible that prior reference is made to the communion the king is to receive as a "crowning" of the oath. The Sacrament was of major influence on a promise during the Western Schism when, in 1381, the papal legates representing the two obediences had met in a chapel in Medina del Campo, together with the royal officials of King John of Castille. A promise was made by the parties to keep to the truth while "the body of Christ was present the whole time on the altar".[88] A report from a non-ecclesiastical source, the Florentine bookseller and author Vespasiano da Bistici († 1498) recounts how the leaders of the Medici and the Picti promised mutual reconciliation by taking an oath on the Eucharist. This involved them holding the Host which was split down the middle by a priest in the course of the Mass. Some contemporaries regarded the event too shocking to merit further comment.[89]

The solemn monastic vow also took on a closer relationship with the Eucharist, especially in the mendicant orders, who made such an important contribution to the spread of Eucharistic devotion. It was their custom to profess their vow *in manus* - in the hands of the father superior - rather than *super altare*. Originally this was done in the chapter room, later in the monastery church. The novice knelt at the prior's feet and placed his hands in those of his spiritual father, with the whole community present as witnesses. The symbolism would seem to be inspired by the commendatio of the vassal towards his master.[90]

---

[86]ed. Schaten (1775), 170-171, lib XII: "Sub id tempus Simon comes de Lippa, et Wilhelmus comes Arnsbergensis mutuum quoque foedus iurare, dexteris supra eucharistiae sacramentum positis, quo *ritu tum usitato* etiam ipsi reges Ludovicus et Fredericus postea sibi fidem et concordiam iurasse, auctor est Rebdorsius in annalibus"; RHF 20, 642, *Continuatio Chronici Guillelmi de Nangiaco* a monacho benedictino abbatiae s. Dionysii in Francia (1348): "facto tamen sibi prius iuramento supra corpus Christi, de quo uterque hostia divisa in duas in eadem missa communicavit".

[87]Wordsworth (1892), 66, I *Forma coronationis*, 14: "Item finito sermone accedit rex ad altare ad faciendum iuramentum suum quod debet confirmare cum sacramento dominici corporis".

[88]Seidlmayer (1939), 52: "eratque ibi super altare continue corpus Christi consecratum, quo utrique respondentes eorumque consciencie arcius stringerentur veritatem omnimodam in suis responsionibus reserare" (Paris Bibl. nat. cod. lat. 11745, f. 253).

[89]Vespasiano da Bisticci, *Vite di uomini illustri del secolo*, XV, 496; Trexler (1980), 116.

[90]Zeiger (1936), 161 sqq.; (1940), 175.

The Franciscans regarded the instant of the taking of the vow as
having particular significance. The prescriptions of the general chapter
held in Perpignan in 1331 require the novice to make his profession after
having the communion of the celebrant and before his own communion.
Then the document containing the statement of solemn profession was
placed on the altar and the celebrant said: "If you keep to this, I promise
you eternal life", followed by the liturgical formula usually pronounced at
communion: "May the body and blood of the Lord Jesus Christ preserve
you for eternal life".[91]

During the Counter Reformation this development led to the
professio super Hostiam. The rule of Ignatius of Loyola († 1556)
prescribed that the celebrant should show the Host to the young Jesuit,
who then made his solemn profession and received communion.[92] The
solemn profession made before the exposed Eucharist resembles the oath
taken on the Eucharist or the relics. Zeiger was even of the opinion that
in the subsequent act of receiving communion there was some remnant
left of the communion test, an opinion we regard as questionable. After
all, the communion test belonged to another category: it was the
equivalent of the oath of purgation and replaced the trial by ordeal.

From the 9th century onwards a wide variety of rituals were used by way
of preparation for the trial by ordeal. Originally the ritual consisted of no
more than the blessing of the object to be used as the means of testing.
This simple ceremony gradually developed to become a complex ritual
and included Mass and the reception of communion.[93] The oldest ritual,
originating in the 9th century, is related to the trial by hot water, from
which the hot iron test was developed. The ritual of the cold water trial
followed in the 10th century.[94] The accused usually spent the three days
prior to the trial in fasting and prayer, the last night being spent in the

---

[91]ed. Saturninus (1909), 281, III,8: "Cum autem sacerdos communicaverit, novitius dicat:
'*Confiteor*'. Quo dicto, praelatus celebrans (...) absolvat (...) Et hiis peractis, ipsum
interroget dicens: '*Frater, vis renuntiare saeculo?*' Quo respondente: '*Volo*' (...) Quibus
dictis, novitius professionem faciat, tenens in manu sua verba professionis. Qua facta, ponat
praedictam cedulam super altare, et sacerdos dicat ei: '*Et ego (...) promitto tibi vitam
aeternam*'. Et dans ei corpus Christi addat sic: '*Corpus Domini nostri Iesu Christi custodiat
animam tuam in vitam aeternam. Amen*'".

[92]*Consuetudinarium* S.J, V, c. III, 1-4: "cum sanctissimo sacramento eucharistiae ad eum
qui professionem est emissurus, se convertat. Ille autem, absoluta generali confessione et
verbis, quae ante communionem dici solent, voce alta votum suum scriptum leget, cuius
formulae haec est: '*Ego (...)*.' Post haec sumet sanctissimum eucharistiae sacramentum";
Zeiger (1940), 175-176; 186.

[93]Franz (1909), II, 350-351; Schwerin (1933), 58; Leitmaier (1953), 31-32.

[94]Köstler (1912), 221; Schwerin (1933), 53-61; Nottarp (1956), 230-232.

church.[95] Before receiving communion on the day of the trial the priest adjured him by the Trinity, baptism, the Gospel and the relics contained in the church not to approach the altar nor to receive communion should he be guilty. He was then given communion with these significant words: "May the body of our Lord Jesus Christ serve you as proof".[96]

After the blessing of the iron, the hot water or the rye bread, the actual trial was preceded in no few rituals by an oath of purgation directed against demonic influences.[97] The accused swore on the Cross, the Gospels or the relics. Once communion had been absorbed into the ritual of preparation it replaced or supplemented this oath.[98] The oath on the relics and communion are found both separately and jointly in the rituals. The 'parallel application in concrete use' gave the preparation of the accused for the trial the character of an oath.[99] Sometimes this was emphasised even more: before the start of the trial by ordeal Mass the priest carried outside the church the book of the Gospels, the chalice and the paten together with the relics in order to show them. From the church doorway he warned the accused not to enter if he had anything on his conscience. Sometimes he also left the church after Mass had ended to carry the same objects in procession to the place of the trial.[100]

Apart from being a preparation for the trial by ordeal, the reception of communion served in itself as a means of proving the accusation false and thus became itself the 'ordale' or replaced the oath of purgation. It

---

[95]ed. Liebermann (1904-16), I, 163; Browe (1932), 171, n. 75; Nottarp (1956), 232-233.

[96]Franz (1909), II, 351, 370, 4: "Adiuro vos (...) per vestram christianitatem, quam suscepistis, et per sanctum evangelium et per reliquias, que in ista continentur ecclesia: ut non presumatis ullo modo communicare neque ad altare accedere, si hoc fecistis"; 370, 5: "Deinde sacerdos dat ei corpus et sanguinem domini dicens: Corpus et sanguis domini nostri Iesu Christi sit tibi ad comprobationem"; Ebner (1896), 254-255.

[97]MGH Leges I, 634, Ordines iudiciorum Dei, A, 31 (c), (after: benedictio panis ordeacci vel casei ad iudicium faciendum): "Postea dabis ei quod pansat sol 3 aut den 9, et iurabant omnes testes de furto illo super sanctos"; 638, B, I,2 (c): "Post benedictionem aque qui mittendus est in aquam (...) et dato iuramento"; 676, XIV,1 (r): "Deinde, dato iuramento inmergatur"; 686, XVI,2 (q): "Postea, facto iuramento solito, ligetur et ponatur in aquam"; 616, A, 10 (m): "ego (...) magis credo in Deum patrem..quam in diabolo et in maleficiis"; ed. Rockinger (1858), 378; "si aliqua infidelitatis suspitio in eo habeatur, iuret in altari, aut in cruce vel in evangelio sive capsa"; Franz (1909), II, 352 n. 3; Schwerin (1933), 9, 27-30; Nottarp (1956), 236.

[98]Martène (1788), II, 332, a. 928, ordo I:" Sub ipso (...) die, panem eucharisticum sumito, ac iureiurando"; ordo II: "et eat ad sacrosanctam communionem ipsa die (...) et iuret quod publico sit innocens".

[99]Köstler (1912), 216, 220; Browe (1928), 196; Schwerin (1933), 7-9, 21, 26, 29-30, 37; Nottarp (1956), 233.

[100]Martène (1788), II, 342, ordo XVI: "sacerdos (...) ferens in laeva sanctum evangelium, cum chrismario, et patrociniis sanctorum, caliceque et patena, expectante eum plebe cum fure vel quocumque crimine implicito in atrio ecclesiae et dicat coram astante plebe in ostio ecclesiae"; ed. Rockiner (1858), 347; Schwerin (1933), 49.

was no longer a wrath of disgruntled saint that hung over the head of the accused, but the anger of God himself directed against the guilty communicant if he dared to receive communion as if he were innocent. The words of the apostle Paul were understood literally here: "For he that eateth and drinketh unworthily eateth and drinketh damnation to himself" (I Cor. 12:29).

A first example of communion of this sort, requiring a divine decision, in this case tightly bound up with the judgement of a saint, is provided by the wonderful storyteller Gregory of Tours. A certain Eulalius of Clermont had committed youthful misdeeds which had caused his mother to suffer. This did little to help the relationship between mother and son. When she was discovered murdered, suspicion immediately fell on the errant youth, Eulalius. The bishop, Cautinus of Clermont-Ferrand, excluded him from the community of believers, which the rejected boy complained about on the feast of the martyr St. Julianus. The bishop allowed him to return to the celebration of the Eucharist but left "the judgement of God and of Julianus" the question of the truth or otherwise of the rumour about the young man. Just before the communion he addressed him with these words: "If you really are innocent, as you assure us you are, come closer and receive a piece of the Eucharistic bread. Eulalius took the bread, ate it and went free.[101]

At another time Gregory himself was occasioned difficulties by a rumour monger who accused him of having placed Bishop Bertram of Bordeaux and Queen Fredegund in a bad light. In 580 the synod of Berni decided that the oath of purgation he was required to take should be preceded by the celebration of Mass on three different altars. He would then as priest have sufficiently proved his innocence.[102]

At about the same period in the East, according to John Moschus, the oath of truthfulness or of purgation on the Eucharist appeared at the communion. When a monk in Gervase's monastery was suspected of a misdeed, it cost him the friendship of a deacon there. In order to demonstrate his innocence the monk approached the deacon while he and

---

[101]MGH SRM I,1 , 414, *Hist. Franc.* lib X, c. 8: "Ego vero, utrum perpetraveris hoc scelus, an non, ignoro: idcirco in Dei hoc et beati martyris Iuliani statuo iudicio. Tu vero, si idoneus es, ut asseris, accede proprius, et sume tibi eucharistiae particulam (...) Erit enim Deus respector conscientiae tuae".

[102]ibid. 261, lib. V, c. 49: "Tunc cunctis dicentibus: Non potest persona inferior super sacerdotem credi, restitit ad hoc causa, ut dictis Missis, in tribus altaribus me de his verbis exuerem sacramento".

his fellow monks were drinking from a consecrated chalice and swore by the chalice that he was guilty of no fault.[103]

God's avenging hand is detected by the chronicler in the confrontation between Pope Hadrian II and King Lotharius II in 869. Lotharius was living in an adulterous relationship with Waldrada and had had to promise to Hadrian's predecessor, Pope Nicholas I, that he would take back his lawful wife Thietberga. When the king arrived in Rome the first question put to him by Hadrian was whether he had kept to his promise. Lotharius lied and said that he had, the royal officials confirming his word since they did not have the courage to contradict him. The pope then invited him to celebrate Mass at the bones of St. Peter and to receive communion. Holding the Eucharist in his hands he told him to receive communion without hesitation if he was no longer with Waldrada and would have no further truck with her. "But", continued the pope, "if your conscience is gnawing at you and accusing you of a mortal sin, or if you intend to indulge once again in the swinish practice of adultery, do not dare to receive communion so that you take for your damnation that which divine providence has provided as a remedy for those who believe".[104] The king's retainers were offered the same advice. The chronicler reminds his readers of various pertinent texts, including the letter to the Corinthians already referred to[105], and recounts how the sacrilegious communion proved their undoing. Before the end of that year all the communicants were dead and those who had abstained from receiving communion only narrowly escaped death. King Lotharius left Rome, was overcome by sickness and died, on arrival in Placentia, that same year of 869.

Two decrees issued by the synod held in Worms in 868 provide guidelines for the communion test which, from then onwards, replaced the oath of purgation and the trial by ordeal for clerics in both ecclesiastical and temporal law. This applied particularly in Germany, also in England

---

[103]PG 87,3, 3109 , *Pratum Spirituale*, c. 219; ["Cum ergo ille teneret calicem in manibus fratribusque distribueret, accessit ad eum et iuravit per ipsum calicem nihil me omnium tale gessisse"].

[104]MGH SRM I, *Reginonis Chronicon*, 580-581: "si autem tua conscientia te accusat et letali vulnere sauciatum proclamat, aut iterum redire mente disponis in moechiae volutabro, nequaquam sumere praesumas, ne forte ad iudicium et condemnationem tibi eveniat, quod fidelibus ad remedium praeparavit divina providentia".

[105]ibid. "Horribile est incidere in manus Dei viventis" (Hebr.10,31); "Qui enim manducat et bibit indigne, iudicium sibi manducat et bibit" (I Cor. 12:29).

until the 12th century, but less in France.[106] The first guideline applied exclusively to monks, the second to priests and bishops in general.

"It often happens that robberies take place in monasteries and the culprit remains undiscovered", states the first decree. "In such cases the abbot or one appointed in his place should celebrate Mass in the presence of all the brothers and give them all the body and blood of our Lord Jesus Christ for their purgation. In this way they must demonstrate their innocence."[107] Six months later Regino of Prüm added to this the closing phrase from the 'ordale' Mass, referred to above: "May the body of the Lord be your proof".[108]

The second decree, which constituted a privilege given to priests and bishops until the 13th century,[109] reads as follows: "If a bishop or priest is accused of murder, adultery, robbery or witchcraft, for each crime imputed to him he must celebrate the Mass, saying the Canon out loud, and receive communion, thereby proving that he is innocent of each of the misdeeds".[110] Similar prescriptions were later to be included in Anglo-Saxon legislation promulgated by Aethelred II in 1014 and by Knut († 1034).[111]

The priest was familiar with the whispered and inaudible praying of the Canon. Now he had to change his habits and speak even the words of consecration out loud. If his voice hesitated or wavered at this it was regarded as significant as regards his guilt. How easily he could become

---

[106]Leitmaier (195), 20-23.

[107]ed. Browe (1932-33), I, 35, no. 61, c. 15: "Saepe contingit, ut in monasteriis furta perpetrentur et qui haec committunt ignorentur. Idcirco statuimus, ut quando ipsi fratres de talibus se expurgare debeant, missa ab abbate celebretur vel ab aliquo, cui ipse abbas praeceperit, praesentibus fratribus et sic ultimae missae celebratione pro expurgatione sua corpus et sanguinem D.N.I.Chr. percipiant, quatenus inde innocentes se esse ostendant"; Mansi, XV, 872; ed. Friedberg (1879-1882), I, c. II, q.3, c. 23.

[108]ed. Wasserschleben (1964), 321, lib. II, c. 277: "et sic expleta missa omnes communicent in haec verba: corpus Domini sit tibi ad probationem hodie".

[109]Browe (1928), 199.

[110]ed. Browe (1932-33), I, 35, no. 61, c. 10: "Si episcopo aut presbytero causa criminalis, h.e. homicidium, adulterium, furtum et maleficium imputatum fuerit, in singulis missam celebrare et secretam publice dicere et communicare debet et de singulis sibi imputatis innocentem reddere"; Mansi, XV, 872; ed. Wasserschleben (1964), 321, lib. II, c. 278; ed. Friedberg (1879-82), I, c. II, q. 3. c. 26.

[111]ed. Liebermann (1903-16), I, 265, 19: "Wenn ein Priester, der kanonisch lebt, mit einfacher Anklage bezichtigt wird, so lese er, wenn er es wagt, Messe und reinige allein sich selbst durch den Abendmahlsgenuss"; 19.1: "Und von dreifacher Anklage reinige er sich (...) ebenfalls durch den Abendmahlsgenuss mit zweien seiner Standesgenossen"; 20: "Wenn ein Diakon (...) so nehme er zwei seiner Standesgenossen und reinige sich mit denen"; 20,1: "Und wenn er mit dreifacher Anklage bezichtigt wird, so nehme er sechs seiner Standesgenossen und reige sich mit denen und er selbst sei der siebente [im Eide]"; ibid. 285, 5, 5a.

confused and fear of the *tremendum mysterium* could seal his fate. And when taking communion he was not allowed to choke on the Host, something which recalls the cheese and bread test.[112]

A prayer of preparation preceding the communion test, probably dating from the 11th century, indicates how earnest a request was made for the simultaneous manifestation of God's intervention: "We humbly pray you, Your Majesty, that this priest will be unable to receive the honoured body of Your Son (...) if he is guilty of the misdeed of which he has been accused, and that that which has been given to us as a remedy against our enemies will be to his harm, full of grief and sorrow and bitter sadness".[113]

A single example is known of this type of test taking place in France, even though it was practised numerous times up to the 13th century. The synod of Chalons-sur-Saône in 894 dealt with the affair involving the Benedictine monk Gerfred, who was suspected of having poisoned Adalger, the Bishop of Autun. He denied the charge and there was no proof. The question was postponed to the next synod, in the course of which he was to be required to submit to the communion test. It was made clear to him that he should not do this in a reckless manner because, like the traitor Judas, he would be punished for all eternity. The monk showed no sign of hesitation and fulfilled the requirements made of him.[114]

In the same way Archbishop Frederick of Mainz was able to escape the threat of danger. Emperor Otto I suspected that this prince of the church had joined in a plot organised against him by his brother Henry. The communion test is reported to have absolved him from blame in 941.[115]

The canon laws applying in Wales around the year 940 speak of an oath of truthfulness, separate from the reception of communion, practised annually. Here the Eucharist and the relics were used together as a guarantee. After the celebration of Mass by the *capellanus* to close the year, the judge was required to place his hands in those of the celebrant and make an oath on the Eucharist, the altar and the relics placed on the altar. He then declared, in the presence of eminent personages, that

---

[112]Köstler (1912), 244-248; Nottarp (1950), 231.

[113]Mansi II, 575; Köstler (1912), 214; Browe (1928), 202.

[114]Mansi XVIII, 127-128.

[115]MGH SS I, 619, *Regionis Chronicon*, a. 941: "Fredericus archiepiscopus, quia conspirationis huius particeps videbatur, publice se examinatione, perceptione corporis et sanguinis Domini, coram populo in ecclesia purgavit".

throughout his whole life he had exercised his function without being influenced by intercession or advantage, nor by sympathy or antipathy.[116]

However when clerics were suspected, the communion test was almost always required to break the impasse, especially in cases involving unprovable situations thought to involve love. Bishop Abraham of Freisingen, for instance, was accused by certain individuals out of jealousy because they considered that Judith, the widow of the Duke of Bavaria, looked far too kindly on him. On the day of her burial in 987 the bishop sprang to her defence in no uncertain terms. Just before the communion he related all the good deeds she had performed and made a plea on her behalf and on behalf of himself by calling on the almighty Father and the body and blood of His own Son that he should be acquitted or condemned and that she, at any rate, should be granted eternal happiness. On the grounds of these words he received communion in the presence of all the faithful. They were finally convinced of his innocence, from which any shadow of doubt was removed in the chronicler's mind.[117]

Bishop Sibico of Spiers had to deal with a similar question. He was accused of adultery, a charge he cleared himself of by means of the communion test in 1049. Lambert of Hersfeld relates that he did this in the presence of Pope Leo IX and Emperor Henry III. And yet not everything about Sibico was in order since Wibert of Toul, describing the life of Leo IX, alleges a rumour that his jaw was affected by paralysis and remained permanently crooked.[118]

Even more miraculous is the story told by the imaginative Raoul Glaber in the middle of the 11th century to discourage all clerics from committing perjury. A priest had attempted to conceal his guilt by allowing himself to be put to the communion test "according to clerical

---

[116]PL 138, 473, *Hoeli Dha regis seu principis totius Walliae leges ecclesiasticae*, VII: "et missa celebrata, et oblatione ad missam ab omnibus facta, capellanus faciat eum iurare per sacrum incelebratum, et per altare, et reliquias superpositas".

[117]MGH SRM N.S. IX, 90, *Thietmari chron.* lib. II, c. 41: "Hoc, inquiens delictum, quo diffamata fuit, si hec umquam commisit, faciat omnipotens Pater Filii suimet corporis et sanguinis salutare remedium mihi provenire ad iudicium et ad debitam dampnationem animaeque eius ad perpetuam salvationem. Et tunc cum mentis ac corporis innocentia sumpsit unicum cunctis fidelibus remedium".

[118]MGH SS VII 346, *M. Adami gesta (...)*: "In eo concilio quidam Spirensis episcopus, Sibico, cui criminem adulterii intendebatur, examinatione sacrificii purgatus est"; V, 154, *Lamberti Hersfeldensis annales*; Browe (1928), 203.

usage". His crime was quickly exposed when the Eucharistic bread re-emerged out of his navel.[119]

We know of two communion tests in the 'Canossa' year (1077) relative to the action of Emperor Henry IV in the Investiture Controversy. The first can again be found in Lambert of Hersfeld, but is reported by no other contemporary and is probably based on rumour. Once Gregory VII had lifted the interdict on the emperor, while celebrating Mass and holding the Eucharist he is said to have mentioned the letter which Henry had written at the Diet held in 1076 and in which he accused 'Hildebrand' of having seized the papal throne by heresy and simony. Gregory received communion in a demonstrative manner begging that he either be absolved of the alleged crimes or be killed on the spot. When the emperor was requested by Gregory to do the same, in order to prove his own innocence, he refused.[120] The second test involved the Bishop of Augsburg who had, at first, taken the side of the anti-king, Rudolf of Swabia, but later pledged his loyalty to Henry once again. He declared that he would receive communion in order to have the affair surrounding Henry justified or condemned. Within a few days he fell ill, deteriorated visibly and died.[121]

A perjurer named Galdricus of Laon met an even more unfortunate end in 1112. Guibert of Nogent, who had tried to prevent the nomination of this bishop at the Council of Langres in 1107,[122] describes the terrible way in which the man was lynched. Then before passing on to another subject Guibert expresses the desire to report yet another recent fact concerning Galdricus which greatly contributed to his fall. Two days before he died, some eminent clerics from his immediate circle of acquaintances accused him that he had blackened the name of his clergy to the king who had just been appointed in the city. He replied as follows to the accusation: "May the holy communion which I have just received

---

[119]ed. Prou (1886), 123, *Historiarum libri quinque*, lib. V, c. 1,11: "in clericali habitu, dum iure culparetur quodam crimine, contigit ut sumeret audacter iudicio examinationis donum eucharistiae, calicis videlicet sanguinis Christi"; PL 142, 691.

[120]MGH SS V, 259-260: "praeferensque manu corpus dominicum (...) ecce corpus dominicum, quod sumpturus ero, in experimentum mihi hodie fiat innocentiae meae, ut omnipotens Deus suo me hodie iudicio vel absolvat obiecti criminis suspicione, si innocens, vel subitanea interimat morte, si reus".

[121]ibid. 296, *Bertholdi annales* a. 1077: "Illic etiam missarum sollemniis usque ad locum communionis ab eo peractis, ad regem et caeteros auditores se convertit et (...) coram omnibus sua sponte professus est, se sanctam eucharistiam in probationem et huiusmodi iudicium accepturum fore, quod causa domini Heinrici regis iusta fuerit, Roudolfi autem prorsus iniusta".

[122]Lettinck (1983), 73, n. 145.

at the altar - he had held his hand out to receive it - be my downfall and I
call the sword of the Holy Ghost down upon my life if I have ever used
these words about you".[123] Guibert recounts in another connection that
his mother saw in a dream what a brother of him was to suffer after his
imminent death because he had "taken this terrible oath on the body and
blood of the Lord".[124]

A formulation not susceptible to misinterpretation, used at
communion and derived from the cheese and bread test was, according to
John of Trittenheim († 1516), used in 1124 by the abbot Rupert of
Limburg, who was suspected of superstition: holding the body of Christ
in his hand he swore that this "could stick in his throat, yea, even pinch
his throat closed, suffocate him and exclude him from heaven" if the
accusation levelled against him was true.[125]

The replacement of the oath of purgation by the communion test is
again demonstrated by an experience of Bruno of Trier at the beginning
of the 12th century. Four persons, two priests and two lay people, were
suspected of the heresy of denial of the *praesentia realis*. One lay person
and one cleric demonstrated the truth of the accusation immediately by
taking to flight once the bishop had questioned them. The two remaining
had to purify themselves of the accusation: the lay person took an oath on
the relics presented to him and the priest underwent the communion test.
He held the Host in his hands while the bishop formulated both the pure
and the heretical doctrine for him and asked him to choose. The 'sinner'
subsequently received communication in humble penitence.[126]

---

[123]ed. Labande (1981), 344, *De vita sua*, lib. III, c. 8: "Communio sancta, quam ex illo
pridem altari suscepi (dexteram enim illo protenderat) veniat mihi ad perniciem, et sancti
Spiritus gladium invoco in animam meam, si haec unquam verba regi de vobis dixi"; PL
156, 928, *Guiberti abbatis s. Mariae de Novigento Opera omnia*.

[124]ed. Labande (1981), 152, lib. I,1: "Vidit (...) fratrem meum, horrenda divini Corporis
et Sanguinis per sacramenta iurantem".

[125]Joh. Trithemius, *Opera historica*, II, 118, a. 1124, Monast. Hirsaugiensis: "hoc
corpus Domini nostri Jesu Christi quod in manibus meis teneo (...) si aliter est quam dixi et
iuravi, tunc hoc Domini nostri Iesu Christi venerabile corpus non pertranseat guttur meum
sed haereat in faucibus meis, strangulet me, suffocet me ac interficiat me statim in momento:
et non sit mihi locus in coeli".

[126]MGH SS VIII, 193, *Gesta episc. Treverorum*: "adhibitis sibi sanctorum reliquiis
iuramento verbis fidem fecit"; 194: "Si vivificum hoc salutis nostrae sacramentum quod
manibus tenes, non vere corpus Christi et sanguinem esse ausus es impio ore garrire, cum
ipsius misterii contestatione interdico, ne quomodo praesumas accipere; si vero non ita sed
catholice profiteris, accipe".

**

In the examples quoted the relics and the Eucharist are seen to have been used for oath-taking in parallel and as substitutes for one another. This 'parallel application in concrete use' would seem to be the clearest in the oath of purgation and the communion test. This practice must have been generally widely known: it is, after all, reported not only in the chronicles and in the legislation promulgated by Aethelred and Knut referred to above, but both theologians and canonists pay it some regard. Gratian, for instance, included the two mid-12th-century prescriptions of Worms already quoted in his *Decretum*. The Italian cardinal Laborans, who opposed oath-taking on biblical grounds, nonetheless noted in his collected canons of 1182 that the communion test was "a virtuous and divinely granted judgment".[127] Thomas Aquinas too was familiar with the communion test.

Resistance to it first appeared in France. The historian Richer of Rheims reported at the end of the 10th century a communion test required by the bishops on the nomination of a new metropolitan. His commentary on this is that the test was "seen as no few persons as criminal and contrary to the faith." For the Eucharistic had been given not for a man's damnation but for his salvation.[128] A century later Robert the Pious († 1031), hastening to emphasise the devotion due to the Eucharist, raised anew a critical voice and fulminated against a bishop who had turned the communion test into an habitual practice for his clergy. However Robert's biographer, Helgaud, admits that the usage was already generally widespread.[129]

This form of trial by ordeal was also criticised at the University of Paris where Peter the Chanter († 1197), furious opponent of trial by ordeal, set his face against it as also against other types of ordeal. With regard to single combat, for instance, he commented sarcastically that he as a priest would not offer the relics and the Holy of Holies to a duellist

---

[127]PL 204, 911: "Verum, non temptatur Deus, ubi secundum quod praecepit agitur. Hoc etenim purgandi per eucharistiam genus, sumptum videtur a sacrificio zelotipiae quod dominus in lege constituit"; "Probabile iudicium vel divinum, iuramentum intelligi, vel experimentum in eucharistiae perceptione. Amplius et omnino contra".

[128]MGH SS III, 637-638, *Hist.* lib. IV, c. 31: "Nonnullis tamen quorum mens purgatior erat, nefarium et contra fidei ius id creditum est (...) Asserebant quoque ex decretis patrum, et canonum scriptis, neque invitum   ad eucaristiam impellendum, neque eucaristiam perditionis causa cuiquam offerendam, cum redemptionis gratia et petentibus offerendam, et invitis negandam credendum sit."

[129]ed. Bautier (1965), 66; PL 141, 912.

to touch and to swear on.[130] Duelling, incidentally, proved well nigh impossible to do away with at a time when the other types of ordeal were on their way out. From ancient times it had been the custom in times of war to swear on the relics in order to conduct a just fight. But as we can see from the words of Peter the Chanter the Eucharist was also used in a similar situation - and was subsequently to replace the relics completely: at the end of the 14th century the duellists in the diocese of Lausanne, before engaging in combat, laid their left hand in that of their opponent above the body of Christ and swore the oath of purgation.[131]

Various scholastics later followed Peter the Chanter's example in their criticism of the awesome communion test, which called on the justice of God as the vengeful Yahweh of the Old Testament. The generally based their criticism on Thomas' opinion that man must not put God to the test, and certainly not through the intermediary of the Eucharist, which was instituted for salvation and not for damnation.[132] And yet there were some theologians who, well into the 16th century and even later, retained a fairly liberal attitude towards the communion test, provided that the spiritual atmosphere was appropriate. It is reported to have been practised in Spain until well into the 17th century, but this would constitute an exception. By the middle of the 13th century the communion test had in fact fallen into disuse practically everywhere.[133]

---

[130]PL 205, 226, *Verbum abbreviatum*, c. 88; PL 205, 232, *Petri Cantoris abbreviatum*, c. 78: Sacerdos similiter, non benedicerem aquam vel ferrum, nec reliquias et sancta praeberem, ut super ea iuraret commissurus monomachiam, ne per auctoritatem et occasionem essem reus sanguinis effusionis"; see also Baldwin (1961), 619 sqq.; Bartlett (1986), 82.

[131]ed. Browe (1932-33), II, 84-85, n. 108, n. 3: "duellantibus etiam eucharistiam oblatam fuisse, monstrat legum, quas c. 1368 episcopus Lausanensis dederat (...) sacerdos habitu sacerdotis indutus tenens sacrum corpus Christi interesse debet, super quo appellans et appellatus debent iurare (...) et debent se tenere et tangere manus suas sinistras utriusque modi suasque manus debent habere supra corpus Christi"; according to Thiers (1677), 792, (1697), II, 351, 352, even as late as the 17th century, lawyers in Guyenne, Languedoc and Britanny took the oath with their hand resting on the foot of the ciborium.

[132]*Summa* III, q. 80, art. 6: "In omnibus enim in talibus esse videtur Dei tentatio; unde sine peccato fieri non possunt. Et gravius videretur, si in hoc sacramento, quod est institutum ad remedium salutis, aliquis incurreret iudicium mortis. Unde nullo modo corpus Christi debet dari alicui suspecto de crimine, quasi ad examinationem"; ed. Blacfriars, vol. LIX.

[133]Browe (1928), 204 sqq.

5   PRAYER OF SUPPLICATION

When the monasteries fell prey to violent seizure of power and possessions during the process of feudalisation, they were often scarcely able to offer resistance, if at all. Feeling themselves cornered, the monks sought refuge in begging God and his saints urgently for aid once all earthly means of bringing a usurper to heel had been exhausted. To this end they introduced not only the *clamor*[1], inserted into the Mass between the *Pater Noster* and the *Pax Domini*[2] but also the *humiliatio*[3] of the relics.

The *humiliatio* is the older of the two and was integrated into the *clamor* from the 10th century onwards. It dates from the 6th century and survived until the middle of the 13th century. It was to be found particularly in France. This is understandable since it was in that country that feudalism first came in. There are some sources which mention England[4] and very few that refer to Germany.[5]

The grave of a saint was crowned with thorns by the monks, the candles were extinguished and the shrines placed on the ground, resting on a penitential robe or on a bed, again made off thorns. These latter, recalling the humiliation of Christ's crowning with thorns, symbolised humiliation, sadness and sinfulness. They were also placed around the shrine and at the church door. They thus kept at a distance those coming to pay reverence since visitors always attempted to touch the shrine or tomb.[6]

In this visual way the monks attempted to 'punish'[7] the saint while making their supplication and thus force him to recall and fulfil his

---

[1]Schneider (1927); Bauerreis (1950); Jungmann (1962), II, 361- 363; Little (1979); (1991); Platelle (1980), 387-388; (1980a), 178-181, 201; Pas v.d. (1984), Geary, (1985); in this study the term 'clamor' refers exclusively to the appeal made to God during the Mass and not an appeal made to the saint. The latter, incidentally in the examples quoted by Van de Pas does in fact include the threat of a 'humiliatio'.

[2]i.e. the peace greeting preceding the *Agnus Dei* (LW I, 80-81); the clamor is found after the offertory only in the *consuetudines* of Bernard of Cluny: ed. Herrgott (1726), 231.

[3]Du Cange (1883-87), VII, 112 sqq; Beissel (1976), II, 10-14; Hermann-Mascard (1975), 226-228.

[4]Mansi XIX, 845, Synodus Landavensis, a. 1056: "Et in plena synodo depositis crucibus cum sanctis reliquiis ad terram, et versis cymbalis, simul et clauso ostio ecclesiae, cum stipatis spinis: et ita carens servitio et pastore remansit diebus et noctibus"; ed. Dugdale (1846), VIII (VI,3), 1226, Landavensis ecclesiae cathedralis, num. LVIII; ed. 1665, III, 195-196.

[5]Beissel (1976), II, 12-13.

[6]Geary (1985), 130-131.

[7]See p. 21.

responsibilities as *patronus*. The *humiliatio* also had the character of a demonstrative protest against injustice suffered and aimed at influencing public opinion. It increased the pressure on the usurper's conscience to retreat from his position. If he took no notice, God's vengeful hand was still available, as is suggested by the accounts. The effects mentioned were further reinforced when the *humiliatio* became a component of the *clamor*, made known to the surrounding district by a specific way of tolling the bell. This cry for help which the monks emitted on the floor of the church was not addressed to the saint but rather directly to the almighty God, since it was performed in front of the newly consecrated Host.

The oldest version dates from the 9th century and survived, with very small modifications, until approximately the 15th century. An ordo of the canons of Tours makes a distinction between the 'minor' and the 'major' *clamor*. The minor *clamor* was placed at the end of the Mass while the major *clamor* started in the early part of the morning Office, which was marked by sobriety and sadness, an atmosphere that also marked the Mass.

The emergency which was the reason for the supplication was expressed in the kneeling or lying position assumed by the monks flat on the ground, in the quiet recital of the prayers, in the absence of festive vestments and in the lighting of a single candle. The bells large and small drew attention to their desperate situation.

During the 11th and 12th centuries the *clamor* became intertwined with the *humiliatio*. It was at this period that the relics began to be placed on the floor of the church between the monks and the altar so that the dramatised prayer of the *clamor* was rendered even more urgent.

If the *humiliatio* was combined with the minor *clamor*, the reliquaries were placed on the floor after the *Pater Noster*, just before the *clamor* started, and immediately it was finished they were replaced in the chapels in the apse. If the *humiliatio* was included in the major *clamor*, the process began during the singing of the Office. This meant that the relics were already on the floor before Mass began and remained after it had finished. Sometimes this continued for a year or more in the hope that the prayer would eventually be heard. Supplication during Mass was roughly the same as during the minor *clamor*.

The sad sobriety of the *humiliatio*, expressed in the relics placed on the ground between thorns with little or no candlelight, found in the *clamor* its counterpart in the more sober Office and liturgy of the Mass. The aim of both was the same: to have the prayer heard that those praying would be spared from disaster caused by men. The position of the saint during the *clamor* differed somewhat from that occupied in the separate *humiliatio*. In the former he was a member of the praying community with its attention focused on the Eucharist, although the place occupied by the shrine - between the monks and the altar - helped to express a possible role as mediator. In the separate humiliatio, however, the failed saint was central Attention was focused on him and on his relics, which had been placed in a humiliating position.

5.1 The 'humiliatio'

The *humiliatio* was practised as far back as in the time of Gregory of Tours, who paints the picture of a disagreement between Franco of Aachen and King Sigibert of Austrasia († 575). One of the latter's courtiers had deprived the bishop of some property belonging to the church of St. Mitrias. The bishop complained of this to the king, but he fell foul of the monarch and was even fined for his pains. Franco, in dejection, threw himself on the ground before the tomb of Mitrias saying: "Here no light shall be lit nor psalm sung, o famous saint, until you have justified your servants against their enemies and have restored to the church that which was stolen in an inimical fashion." He then placed thorn branches on the grave and by the door, after which he locked the church.[8] The bishop's actions were, according to Gregory, entirely successful. The usurper became seriously ill, his contrition came too late and he quickly gave up the ghost. The threat made by St. Eligius († 660), Bishop of Noyon, to take the same measure as Franco if St. Columba failed to return to the church the stolen treasures, would seem - according to his 8th century *vita* - to have had a similar effect.[9]

Around the 10th century, as soon as portable shrines became popular, there was no longer any need to feel confined to the site of a grave. It became possible to adapt the ceremony, and a penitential robe or a bed of thorns was laid in the desired place. This happened in 997, when

---

[8]MGH SRM I,2, 339, *In gloria confessorum*, c. 70: " 'Non hic accenditur lumen, neque psalmorum modolatio canitur, gloriosissime sancte, nisi prius ulciscaris servos tuos de inimicis suis, resque tibi violenter ablatas eclesiae sanctae restitutas'. Haec cum lacrimis effatus, sentes cum acutis aculeis super tumulum proiecit; egressusque, clausis ostiis, similiter in gressu alias collocavit".

[9]PL 87, 503, *Audoeni vita s. Eligii*, I, c. 30: "Audi, inquit, sancta Columba, quae dico: novit meus Redemptor, nisi cito ornamenta tabernaculi huius furata reduxeris, equidem spinis allatis faciam hanc ianuam ita obserari, ut nunquam tibi in hoc loco veneratio praebeatur ab hodie".

the Count of Anjou and Touraine had invaded the monastery of St. Martin of Tours by force of arms. He had destroyed a wing of the building and offended seriously against the law of immunity. The canons had little else to defend themselves than to place the reliquaries on the ground next to the crucifix in the midst of thorn branches and to close the door demonstratively in the face of the count and his followers. Pilgrims were granted freedom of passage in order that they might witness the pitiful straits of Martin and the other saints. The count, banned from the monastic sanctuary where his ancestors were laid to rest, begged barefoot for forgiveness before the grave of St. Martin and the other relics. With his hands in those of the bishop, Rainald of Anjou he promised never again to commit such a misdeed.[10]

From the 11th century onwards there is a steady increase in the number of examples of this intimidating ceremony,[11] some of them of great duration, such as that performed at the monastery of St. Medardus near Soissons. The villa Donchéry had been taken from the community by the Capetan King Henry I († 1060) and given as a gift to Duke Gothelo of Lorraine. From that instant the joy off the monks turned to sorrow. The abbot watched the king's abuses with troubled eyes and not knowing who to turn to - the king had turned against him and the *advocati* held out no hope - he joined with the entire community in calling on almighty God's help in 1037. Together with his brothers the abbot went into mourning and clamour to frighten the king. He stopped all official services in the church and put the saints' *corpora* on the floor, as if to 'sigh in commune with them for the wrong they had been done'. His aim was to call God's mercy to his aid, to be given back the land and to restore the saints to their place of honour. The duke had a significant vision. In a dream he say Sebastian, Pope Gregory and the patron saint of the monastery, Medardus, followed by many saints carrying candles and crosses, speaking to one another of the situation which had come about and which they found extremely regrettable. On Gregory's orders Sebastian struck him with a lance, whereupon he woke with a start, bleeding from the nose and ears, and immediately rave back the property. The monks reverently returned the relics to their former places and sang hymns and

---

[10]AOB IV, 108; Halphen (1906), 348-349: "corpora protinus sanctorum et crucifixum terrae deponentes, super ipsum beatissimi confessoris Martini sepulchrum et circa corpora sanctorum et crucifixum spinas adposuerunt. Portae insuper ecclesiae die et nocte continuo clausae, castrensibus etiam non introeuntibus, solis peregrinis patuere".

[11]Du Cange (1883-87), VII, 112 sqq.; Platelle (1980a), 180, 201.

psalms in praise of God such as had not been heard there for a long time.[12] Sometimes it also happened that the *humiliatio* was employed to complement an excommunication order proclaimed by the bishop, as did Remigius, abbot of the convent of St. Eligius in Noyon in 1049. Bishop Fulco of Amiens had already excommunicated the person who had stolen a villa belonging to the monastery and who had, in addition, treated the peasants living there in a totally unacceptable manner. Remigius therefore had the relics placed on the ground in order to encourage the people and to increase the moral pressure.[13]

If a statement issued by the curia failed to have the desired effect, it was always possible to apply the curse and the *humiliatio* as a last resort. In the late 11th century, for instance, the monks of the 'Elnone' monastery (also known as 'St. Amandus'), placed the relics and the crucifix of the high altar on the floor of the church and pronounced Anselm II of Ribemont anathema when the latter, despite his promises made to the court of Count Robert II of Flanders, had refused to compensate damage caused to the monastery.[14]

Even a bishop could get into such difficulties that he resorted to not only the *humiliatio* but also the curse of banning. In 1105 in the diocese of Amiens Geoffrey had been celebrating Christmas elsewhere and while he was returning to his episcopal seat the *princeps civitatis*, Adam, who was riding with him, began to feel uncomfortable. He asked the bishop whether they could not take another road since he feared meeting Guermundus, the *vicedominus* of Péquigny, against whom he had been repeatedly obliged to fight. Geoffry reacted by assuring Adam that Goddemundus had recently sworn fidelity to him. Hardly had he spoken the words than Guermundus appeared and dragged Adam away in chains. Geoffrey's followers had taken to flight and he thus arrived in Amiens alone. The town erupted in indignation and Geoffry placed the bodies of St. Firmin and other saints on the ground, locked the churches in the

---

[12]RHF XI, 456: "Et sanctorum corpora (...) quasi rerum suarum damna secum gementia humi prostravit: quamvis omnipotentis Dei misericordia (...) sanctorum suorum reliquias (...) in proprio recondere faceret honore"; 457: "Sanctorum denique corpora, quae humi prostrata iacuerant cum summa veneratione et nominis Dei glorificatione (...) sui loco restituta sunt; et divinae laudis praeconia, quae diu eadem ecclesia siluerant, cum laudibus et hymnis Deo gratias referentibus fratribus insonuerant"; AASS 12 martii, II, 127-128; AOB IV, 416.

[13]ibid. 509: "quod ut maiori cum sollemnitate fieret, corpora sanctorum de locis suis in terram monachi deposuerunt".

[14]PL 162, 657, *ep. Lamberti Atrebatensis episcopi*, XXIII: "qui nisi ad satisfactionem venerit, monachi et sanctorum reliquiis in terram depositis in huius rei ultionem Deum invocabunt et Anselmum cum suis fautoribus maledictionibus et exsecrationibus anathematizabunt".

territory of Guermundus and pronounced a ban on him and his followers. From that moment a fierce struggle broke out and Geoffry received continual alarming reports about fields abandoned by the people, about the plundering of villages, about men, women and children trampled underfoot and about the burning of churches. 'God's servant' bemoaned having to suffer all these things. The affair took a pragmatic turn when the captive Guermundus turned to Geoffry and begged for mercy. Geoffry decided to reward evil with good and set Guermundus free. Subsequently Adam was released and the relics were returned to their former places.[15]

Just as the Count of Anjou, impressed by the *humiliatio*, had had to end the conflict at Tours by swearing an oath of penitence in 977, so were a certain Gisela and her eldest son, Stephanus, obliged to carry the same yoke in 1152 in their confrontation with the monks of St. Amandus. Gisela was the widow of Herimanus, the monastery 'prévôt'. She and her son had considerably advanced the tradition of usurpation which had already affected her dead husband's father Almannus. Gisela's subjects and her son attacked the monks physically, stole their horses and took expensive wood from the monastery's forests. This was enough for Hugh II, abbot of St. Amandus, and the *humiliatio*, as previously employed against Anselmus II, was again set in motion. He ordered the monks to remove the relics of the protomartyr, St. Stephen, and of St. Cyricus from their places of honour. Even the bier on which the remains of St. Amandus lay was placed on the ground. The monks "prostrated themselves in the dust and, all the while praying, poured out great quantities of incense for the divine Majesty". The two miscreants gave in, whereupon a wide-ranging contract was drawn up which they signed on their word of honour. They swore a costly oath with their hand on the bier of Amandus. With festive songs of praise the monks put the relics back in their rightful places in the chapels of the apse.[16]

---

[15]AASS 8 nov. III, 927, *De s. Godefrido episcopo Ambianensi*, n. 31: "Itaque Godefridus corpora sanctorum Firmini ac reliquorum solo tenus deponit, ecclesias provinciae infidi vicedomini claudit, ipsum cunctosque ipsi faventes ore manuque anathematis virga percutiens, Sathanae tradit in interitum carnis"; AOB V, 482-483; St. Firmin, a 4th-century martyr who had converted the Belgic tribe of Ambiani (from whom Amiens takes its name).

[16]Martène (1717), I, 430-431, *Litterae Geraldi Tornacensis episcopi*: "thecam in qua continentur reliquiae gloriosissimi protomartyris Stephani, et non modica portio membrorum pretiosi martyris infantis Cyrici, feretrum etiam in quo repositum adoratur honorandum atque omni reverentia amplectendum corpus beati Amandi, de sublimi et honorabili sanctuarii loco deponentes, non sine magno gemitu cordis nec sine pia lacrymarum effusione in facie altaris ad terram humiliaverunt, sed et ipsi humiliantes in pulvere animas suas, phialas plenas odoramentorum in conspectu summae maiestatis orantes effuderunt"; 433: "feretrum (...) in voce exultationis et laudis, a terra levaverunt, et cum honore ac reverentia in secretis oraculis reposuerunt"; Platelle ((1965), 99.

In the same year of 1152 Wibaldus, abbot of the monastery of Corvey, preferred to rely on the authority of Emperor Frederic Barbarossa († 1190) than on the *humiliatio*, as we can read in their exchange of correspondence. Widekindus, later helped by his brother Folcwinus, had plundered the monastery's possessions, including the graveyard. Wibaldus first approached the pope, Eugene III, who brought in the Bishop of Paderborn to require the usurper to make amends on pain of excommunication. Unfortunately the threat had the opposite effect and Widekindus simply multiplied his evil deeds, according to Wibaldus. During the abbot's absence the monks had placed the bodies of Ss. Vitrus and Justinus on the ground with the crucifix, had stopped praying the solemn Office and no longer rang the bells. After having described these preparations to the emperor, the abbot asked him to intervene. Barbarossa responded within a month and promised to punish the guilty parties. He also ordered that the monks end their *humiliatio*, which they did.[17]

In France too the increasing royal authority and the improvement in judicial practice removed the need for the *humiliatio*. It is not unheard of in the 13th century, but its occurrence is less frequent.[18] In the church too it was seen as desirable that conflicts be solved via canon law and formal procedures. The prescription of 1215 forbidding clerics to take part in trial by ordeal is a proof of this. The *humiliatio* was seen as old fashioned, hardly elegant and certainly not reverential towards the saints.[19] The Council of Lyon in 1274 issued an implicit condemnation of the practice. It spoke of the "objectionable custom" of placing the crucifix and statues - *imagines seu statuas* - of the Virgin Mary and other saints on the ground and covering them with thorns.[20] The word *imagines* usually referred to the costly reliquaries.[21] However the crucifix is specifically mentioned since it was always placed upon the

---

[17]ed. Jaffé (1864), I, 515-521, *epistolae Wibaldi*, 516, ep. 384: "Pro hac tam atroci contumelia fratres nostri, cum absentes essemus, corpora sanctorum Viti et Iustini, quae apud nos requiescunt, in terram deposuerunt, et humiliatis crucifixi Salvatoris nostri imaginibus, ab omni deinceps sollempni officio divino et a pulsatione campanarum abstinuerunt".

[18]Hermann-Mascard (1975), 234.

[19]Schmitt(1988), 513-516; (1992), 50-51.

[20]COD 323, c. 17: "Ceterum detestabilem abusum horrendae indevotionis illorum, qui crucis, beatae Virginis aliorumve sanctorum imagines seu statuas irreverenti ausu tractantes, eas in aggravationem cessationis huiusmodi prosternunt in terram, urticis spinisque supponunt, penitus reprobantes: aliquid tale de cetero fieri districtius prohibemus"; Mansi XXIV, 92; Hefele (1907-42), 6,1 ,195; Du Cange (1883-87), VII, 114, Statuta synod. eccl. Castrensis, a. 1358.

[21]Hermann-Mascard (1975), 134: "les images des saints sont le plus souvent de précieux reliquaires".

ground when the *humiliatio* was part of the *clamor*.[22] The prescription issued by the Council can perhaps also have come from the resistance, by a hierarchical church that had become more tightly organised, to the monks' independent addition of this ceremony to the liturgy of the Mass.[23]

5.2   The 'clamor'

The *clamor*, or the cry to God in times of need, is a familiar phenomenon in the Bible. In the book of *Exodus* Yahweh speaks: "I have surely seen the affliction of my people which are in Egypt, and have heard their cry by reason of their taskmasters" (Ex. 3:7). Esther put on garments of mourning and sorrow and addressed her cry to God to obtain salvation for her people threatened with annihilation (Est. 4:10-19). Psalm 102 begins with the prayer: "Hear my prayer, O Lord, and let my cry come unto thee"[24] and Psalm 130 with the words: "Out of the depths I have cried unto thee, O Lord. Lord, hear my voice: let thine ears be attentive to the voice of my supplication".[25].

As well as having a literary origin, the *clamor* is also historically based.[26] In early and Carolingian times the term '*clamor*' had a legal tone and implied the appeal that the helpless - monks, the poor, widows and orphans - made to the tribunal. This category of persons were without any form of power, which makes it not so surprising that when central government's judicial and military protection of monastic property disappeared in post-Carolingian times the monks cast their cares before God and the saints. In addition to the curse[27], the liturgical *clamor* came available.

The *clamor* is found in a number of monastic *ordines* or *consuetudines* and in some *sacramentaria*. The oldest known example is the sacramentarium of Tours dating from the 9th century, in which the

---

[22]See p. 170 sqq.

[23]Geary (1985), 137.

[24]*Domini exaudi orationem meam et clamor meus ad te veniat.*

[25]*De profundis clamavi ad te Domine, Domine exaudi orationem meam.*

[26]Bauerreis (1950), 26; Little (1979), 56-58.

[27]See p. 21.

deacon is charged with saying, before the *Agnus Dei*, a prayer to Christ for the church in need, while the celebrant knelt at the altar.[28]

The kneeling or prostrate attitude prescribed, an expression of humility and discouragement, is stereotypical of the *clamor* and is repeatedly emphasised. In an ordo, again from Tours, used by early 12th-century canons, the celebrant knelt before the altar holding the consecrated Host, while the deacon said the prayer for intercession.[29] Further examples are the *consuetudines* of Farfa dated approximately 1040,[30] the prescriptions issued at the general chapter of the Dominicans[31] in 1269 and of the Franciscans[32] in 1359.

The canons' ordo referred to above contains, as already stated, a major and a minor *clamor*. In the minor variant Psalm 25 was recited after the prayer of *clamor*: "O my God, I trust in thee: let me not be ashamed", while the Mass servers rang the bells.[33] After a closing prayer, answered with an *Amen* by all present, the Mass continued.

The ritual of the major *clamor* begins like this: "In order to have the hand of the church weigh more heavily, the Office recited out loud is set aside and the prayers are recited in a hushed voice. This is done as follows: all clerics descend from their choir stalls and the whole text is recited in the usual order *submissa voce* on the floor of the church, the antiphons end *recto tono*[34] and no incense is burned. The *septimanarii*[35] light the double candelabra for only a brief moment and then extinguish

---

[28]Leroquais (1924), I, 53: "Antequam Agnus Dei dicatur, sacerdote ante altare in terra prostrato, diaconus stans ante altare dicat: 'In spiritu humilitatis'"; Bauerreis (1950), 28.

[29]Martène (1788), II, 321: "etiam presbyter genuflexo ante altare tenens in manibus Corpus Domini".

[30]See below n. 47.

[31]Martène (1717), 1269, c. 15: "Item, singulis diebus profestis in missa conventuali, post 'Pater noster', cum prostratione dicatur psalmus 'Deus venerunt gentes' cum versiculis et orationibus ab illo qui dicit missam dicendis et incipiatur post pascha".

[32]*Analecta Fanciscana*, II, 194: "Ordinat Generalis, pro statu pacifico totius Ecclesiae et statu domini Innocentii divina providentia Papae VI suffragia in omnibus locis totius Ordinis ab omnibus et singulis fratribus modo subscripto per obedientiam observanda, videlicet quod, cantato Pater noster in Missa diei sacerdos humiliter genuflectat ante corpus Christi, et idem faciant fratres alii existentes in choro"; Browe (1929c), 48.

[33]Martène (1788), II, 321: "Qua dicta dicunt psal. *Ad te levavi* et sonant clericuli campanas chori".

[34]i.e. without the melodious 'neuma' (a musical notation indicating one or more notes of Gregorian chant, LW II, 1893-94).

[35]Those on duty that particular week.

it. They toll the bell dressed in the cowl."[36] The Mass was as little ceremonial as the choir Office. The deacon and subdeacon did not wear costly vestments but merely a simple surplice.[37]

The texts of the *clamor*, the most recent of which is that taken from the 15th-century missal from Admont (Austria)[38], differ little one from the other and always begin with a phrase in which *humilitas* is the basis: "In a spirit of humility and with a despairing heart we come to you, Lord Jesus, saviour of the world, before your altar and your all-holy body and blood".[39]

While the *clamor* was being spoken, the community knelt or was prostrated in prayer before the newly consecrated Eucharistic gifts. This cry of distress to God always had the aim of supplicating Him in a time of disaster caused by human hand: plundering, pillaging or usurpation. "To you, Lord Jesus, we come and we call to you, lying at your feet, because inimical and vainglorious men, priding themselves in their own strength, are attacking us from every side and are plundering and destroying the lands of this, your sanctuary, and of the rest of church property that they have taken for themselves."[40]

During the Crusades additions were made to the formulation of the *clamor* in the shape of prayers for the Holy Land under threat, as in the

---

[36] or *in cappa chori*, the choir cape rather than the solemn alb; Marténe (1788), II, 321: "Ad aggravandum manum ecclesiae, quandoque deseritur officium altum, et sit submissa voce officium: quod debet fieri in hunc modum. Omnes clerici descendunt de stallis suis ad terram, et in ordine dicitur totum submissa voce, nec finiunt antiphonae cum neuma, nec incensatur: Septimanarii accendunt duplum tantummodo et extinguunt, et sonant in cappa chori".

[37] i.e. large white liturgical outer garment (LW II, 2606).

[38] Bauerreis (1950), 27.

[39] 'In spiritu humilitatis et in animo contrito ante sanctum altare tuum et sacratissimum corpus en sanguinem tuum, Domine Iesu, redemptor mundi, accedimus'; Leroquais (1924), I, 53, sacramentarium van Tours, eind 9e eeuw; 75, sacramentarium van Saint-Père van Chartres, 2nd half of the 10th century; (1937), I, 143, Pontificale van Halinardus, 2nd half or end of 10th century; PL 141, 353, Proclamatio composita a domino Fulberto († 1029); Hallinger, X, 244, consuetudines de Farfa, 11e eeuw; Leroquais (1924), I, 183-184, missale van Saint-Étienne van Caen, end of 11th century; Leclercq (1947), clamor of Saint-Airy of Verdun, early 12th century; Leroquais (1924), I, 190, missale of Remiremont, 12th century; 273- 274, sacramentarium of Arras "a l'usage de Senlis", 2nd half of 12th century; 349, sacramentarium of Sainte-Barbe-en-Auge, end of 12th century ; II, 43, missale of Tours, eraly 13th century; 157, missale of Saint-Corneille de Compiègne, 2nd half of 13th century; 196, missale of Chartres, 14th century; III, 176, missale of Remiremont, 2nd half of 15th century.

[40] Hallinger, X, 245: "Ad te domine Ihesu venimus, ad te prostrati clamamus, quia viri iniqui et superbi suisque viribus confisi undique super nos insurgunt, terras huius sanctuarii tui caeterarumque sibi subiectarum aecclesiarum invadunt, depraedantur et vastant"; Bauerreis (1950), 23.

sacramentarium of St. Amand,[41] dated towards the end of the 12 century, and in the prescriptions drawn up by the general chapter of the Cistercians in 1194, 1195, 1196, 1197 and 1245.[42]

A fixed component was the call made on the intercession of the patron saint(s). In the *Pontificale* of Halinardus, dating from the second half of the 10th century, the saint in question was St. Benignus. The relevant text runs as follows: "This, o Lord, your church, which thou hast founded in the past to the honour of St. Benignus, thy martyr, is imprisoned in grief (...) but for the glory of your name and with the intercession of St. Benignus, thy martyr, in whose name thou hast founded this place, grant us peace and free us from our present straits".[43] In other texts more saints are named, including that of the Blessed Virgin.[44]

The appeal made to the patron saints was not, however, confined to the abstract appeal for their intercession: they were involved in a concrete manner. From the 10th the middle of the 13th century the monks increased the power of the *clamor* by linking the *humiliatio* to it. When they left the choir stalls to throw themselves on the floor of the transept, as has already been noted, they took the relics from the altars in the apse and placed them on the floor of the church between themselves and the altar.

The 11th-century *consuetudines* of the abbey of Farfa, which is situated in the Sabine mountain country, provide a good picture off this interweaving of the *clamor* and the *humiliatio*. After some initial resistance, the monastery had joined with the observance movement of Cluny around the year 1000. The new monastic usages were largely derived from those obtaining in Cluny.[45] Which is why it is assumed that the combining of the cry for help before Christ present in the Eucharist

---

[41]Leroquais (1924), I, 269: "Pro tribulatione terre Ierosolimitane".

[42]Canivez (1933-41), I, 172, n. 10, *Oratio pro terra Hierosolymitana*; 208 n. 57; 210 n. 2; II, 289 n. 2; Schneider (1927), 109, 111; Jungmann (1962), II, 362, n. 91.

[43]Leroquais (1937), I, 143: "Ecclesia tua hec, Domine, quam priscis temporibus fundasti et in honore sancti Benigni martiris tui dicasti, sedet in tristitia (...) sed propter gloriam nominis tui et per interventum beati Benigni martiris tui, in cuius honore locum istum fundasti, visita nos in pace et erue nos a presenti angustiae".

[44]Bauerreis (1950), 28, Sacramentarium van Tours: "in honore sanctae tuae genetricis Mariae et sancti Mauritii omniumque sanctorum"; missale van Admont: "in honorem sancte dei genetricis Mariae et sancti Blasii"; Leroquais (1924), I, 75: "in honore et nomine sanctorum apostolorum Petri et Pauli et omnium apostolorum"; 184: "et in honore sancti Stephani"; 349:"et in honore sanctorum Martini atque Barbare"; Hallinger (1963-1985), X, 247, "in honore genetricis tuae".

[45]Schuster (1907), 383; Hallinger, X, introduction XLIII.

and the urgent appeal made to the saint in the *humiliatio* of his relics occurred more frequently - or was perhaps generalised - in the Cluniac monasteries during the 11th and 12th centuries.[46]

This *humiliatio*, as laid out in the *consuetudines* referred to, is an integral part of the *clamor*. During the Mass, as the time for the *clamor* approached, the clergy officiating at the liturgy spread a rough penitential robe in front of the high altar and placed on it a crucifix, the book of the Gospels and the relics. The monks joined the tangibly present saints, prostrating themselves on the floor, and sang in soft voice Psalm 74: "O God, why hast thou cast us off for ever?" Then the bell was sounded twice and the celebrant intoned the *clamor* prayer, facing the consecrated body and blood of Christ and in the presence of the relics. After the prayer had ended the relics were placed on or near the altar and the celebrant continued the Mass.[47]

So, at least, was the ceremony of *humiliatio* combined with *clamor* in the Cluniac communities. Intertwined with the major *clamor* of the canons of Tours, the *humiliatio* began as a separate ceremony at the early hour of Prime, part of the extremely sober choral prayer as described above. At the sounding of the *irata*, or 'angry' bell, which was the only one allowed to sound at each prayer gathering, all the monks came to the choir and began to sing the seven psalms[48] with the litany, after which followed the *humiliatio*.

The way this happened is described as follows: "Then the principal members of the community with the *ministri* stand up and place before the chair of the *subdecanus* a silver cross and all the shrines in which the saints are at rest. They place thorns on and around the tomb of St. Martin. They also place in the centre of the nave a wooden cross

---

[46]Geary (1979), 29; (1985²), 125.; Little (1979), 53.

[47]Hallinger, X, 244-247: "Ad missam principalem iam dicta oratione dominica ministri ecclesiae cooperiant pavimentum ante altare cilicio et desuper ponant crucifixum et textum evangeliorum et corpora sanctorum. Et omnis clerus in pavimento iaceat prostratus canendo psalmum '*Ut quid deus reppulisti in finem*' sub silentio. Interim duo signa percutiantur ab ecclesiae custodibus. Solusque sacerdos stet ante dominicum corpus et sanguinem noviter consecratum et ante praedictas reliquias sanctorum et alta voce incipiat hunc clamorem dicere (...) Quo clamore facto reportentur reliquiae suis locis et dicat sacerdos sub silentio collecta *Libera nos quaesumus domine*".

[48]This must refer to the Seven Penitential Psalms, nos. 6, 31, 37, 50, 101, 129 en 142 (LW I, 301).

completely surrounded by thorns. All the entrance are securely closed off with thorns, except for one small door".[49]

When the *Pater Noster* had been recited at the end of Mass, before the *Pax Domini* the deacon began the prayer *In spiritu humilitatis* and thus began the *humiliatio*, while all knelt on the ground in the choir and the priest held the body of the Lord in his hands before the altar. After this initial prayer, Psalm 52 *Quid gloriaris* - "Why boastest thou thyself in mischief, O mighty man?" - was recited. The bells rang again, so that the whole region was aware of what was going on. Then followed the chapters and collects, which the choir answered with loud voice.[50]

The difference between the two versions of the *clamor* in relation to the *humiliatio* lay in the time of starting and the duration. In contrast to the minor *clamor*, in the major version the *humiliatio* began in the choir prayer and continued until after the Mass in order to help force a solution to the current difficulties.

Most manuscripts do not elaborate the *clamor*, begun with the prayer *In humilitate*,[51] as fully as those of Farfa and Tours, so that we do not know the extent to which the *humiliatio* was a part of it. However, because of the numbers available, they do indicate that the *clamor* must have been practised in many monasteries.

In the various descriptions of the *humiliatio* in practice there is a noticeable lack of a mention of its relation to the *clamor*. And yet there are indications that point to this link. Indeed, the *humiliatio* occurred in the monastery church where the monks prayed the Office daily and celebrated their monastic Mass. It is difficult to see how the *humiliatio* could have been separate from all of this.

In the events reported from the monasteries of St. Medardus, Elnone and Corvey the link would seem to have been made somewhat more explicitly. There is mention of leaving aside the Office during the *humiliatio*,[52] of the appeal to almighty God and the divine Majesty, of

---

[49]Martène (1788), II, 321: "Et tunc vadunt maiores personae cum ministris ecclesiae, et ponunt ad terram ante formam subdecani crucifixum argenteum et omnes capsas ubi sancti requiescunt, et spinas desuper capsa B. Martini in loco suo cooperta, et spinis circumdata; et in medio navis ecclesiae ponunt crucifixum ligneum spinis undique coopertum omnibus portis ecclesiae fortiter obseratis, parvo ostio ibi relicto".

[50]Martène (1788), II, 34: "et ad missam post *Pater noster* antequam dicatur *Pax Domini* dicit diaconus *Clamorum magnorum*, scilicet *In spiritu Humilitatis*, et sunt omnes terram in choro, et presbyter ante altare tenens manibus Corpus Domini. Qua dicta dicunt ps. *Quid gloriaris* et sonant clericuli campanas et iuvenes omnia magna signa".

[51]See above n. 39.

[52]ibid. n. 12, 17.

the intercession of the saints and of the hymns of praise which were once again heard when the suffering had passed.[53]

It is the same elements as those found in the *ordines* of Farfa and Tours which return in the stories. A tale told by Ordericus Vitalis concerning a *humiliatio* at Le Mans in 1090 is a good example of this. The statues of the Lord and the saints, the crucifixes and the reliquaries were placed on the ground, the doors of the church were barred with thorns, the bells were not allowed to ring and the solemn celebrations neglected. The picture is that of a "grieving widow".[54]

In the *humiliatio* against Anselmus II in the monastery of St. Amandus at the end of the 11th century - which has already been dealt with - its intertwining with the *clamor* is referred to, for each day the monks repeated their complaint 'during Mass before the body of the Lord', having placed the complaint in writing in the hand of the Christ figure on the crucifix.[55]

In a final example, dating from the 12th century, the 'parallel application in concrete use' is again expressly shown. The event took place around the tomb of St. Lifardus in the monastery at Meung-sur-Seine. A certain Eruinus had been cultivating a piece of land for his own benefit for several years, with the permission of the canons, on condition that he paid a yearly tithe and fulfilled his other duties. After his death his son, Eudo Baduinus, claimed the land and took it using violence. He chased away the oxen that the canons had sent for the ploughing, grabbed hold of the ox drivers and mishandled them. One of them, his clothes torn and his body streaming with blood, reached the church during the celebration of Mass and told the canons what had happened. Full of indignation "they threw their cares upon the Lord and as soon as the priest had said the *Pax vobis*, prostrate on the ground they began to proclaim the ritual *clamor*, before the Lord and the tomb of St. Lifardus, against those who had disturbed their peace."[56] Eudo came riding up during the *clamor* and hurled a number of threats at the canons, arrogantly galloping past the monastery. God's lightning punished him.

---

[53]ibid. n. 12, 16.

[54]ed. Chibnall (1968-1983), IV, 194, lib. VIII, c. 11.

[55]Platelle (1962), 132; (1965), 79.

[56]AOB I, 161: "sed super Dominum curam suam iactantes, mox ut sacerdos Pax vobis dixit, de pacis suae perturbatore ante Corpus Domini et sepulcrum venerabilis Lifardi ecclesiastico more clamorem facere coeperunt prostrati".

He gave a shriek, lost his power of speech and died within three days, without the signs of repentance having any effect.

***

We have categorised the combining, at the end of the 10th century, of the *humiliatio* and the *clamor*, which date from the 6th and 9th centuries respectively - as 'parallel application in concrete use'. The argument underpinning this is that both components, in accord with our definition, served the same purpose: that of entreating God either directly or through the mediation o the saint(s) in order to be released from danger. In components radiate sobriety and 'humility' and both were used either separately or in combination. In two respects there is a difference with the forms described up to this point: this 'parallel application' did not come into being until the end of the 10th century rather than in early Christian times or in the early Middle Ages, and the two practices were finally discontinued not because they were regarded as incompatible with respect for and the intention of the Sacrament but rather because of their incompatibility with respect for the relics. When the *humiliatio* - "that objectionable practice" - was forbidden by the Council of Lyon in the 13th century, that put an end to the 'parallel application' but not to the *clamor* used on its own. The *clamor* continued in existence until well into the 16th century. The *Missale Romanum* of Pope Pius V (1566-1572) abolished the practice[57], but this does not mean that it disappeared immediately.[58]

By way of explanation for the late date at which this 'parallel application' came into use we suggested that the solemn rite in this form was not possible earlier than when the practice had arisen of placing the relics in separate portable shrines after the *elevatio*. In addition, the *clamor* itself is of later date than the *humiliatio*. The fact that the *clamor* survived in the 13th century is equally understandable in that its 'reverential' and 'adoration' characteristics, which were present from the start, accorded well with the introduction of the 'elevatio' during the Mass and the other forms of extra-liturgical reverence. But where should we seek the origins of the premature 'adoration' of the Host in the Cluniac monasteries? It would seem that the celebrant kneeling before the altar with the Host in his hands and the monks bowing deeply to the

---

[57]LW I, 420.

[58]See above n. 19; Schneider (1927), 113; Jungmann (1962), II, 363, n. 96.

ground, which appeared at the end of the 9th century, were early signs of the adoration of the Lord shown to the congregation which the 'elevatio' expressed at a later date.

In chapter II it was mentioned that the doctrines of Paschasius Radbertus († 859) had their first really tangible effects on the theologians from the second half of the 11th century, caused by another Eucharistic dispute, and not until the beginning of the 13th century on popular devotion. Paschasius' teaching regarding the *praesentia realis* did, however, find its way in the 10th, 11th and 12th centuries into the beliefs of the Cluniacs and, subsequently, other orders including the Cistercians.[59] They placed this doctrine within the context of "an everlasting intimacy with Christ", expressed in the annual cycle of His birth, death resurrection and ascension, but also in the daily liturgy of the Mass, choral prayer and private devotion.[60] The link between the *praesentia realis* and the *humanity* of Christ actually experienced can be found in the writings of Odo of Cluny († 942). In his *Occupatio* this abbot deals with the former aspect and repeats the saying of Christ - "if you do not eat of my flesh and drink of my blood you will not have eternal life" (Jn. 6:53) - and the reactions to it.[61] In his *Collationes* he deals with the latter aspect: the human Christ as the "shepherd", the "humble God", the "scourged one", the "one crowned with thorns" and the "one comforted with gall".[62] A successor to Odo, the abbot Odilo († 1049) devoted so much attention in his sermons to the earthly life of Christ and His mother that the abbot's biographer regarded his death, on 1st January, the feast of the Circumcision, as a heavenly reward for his devotion to the wounds suffered by the body of the Lord.[63] For Peter Damian († 1072) "the human Christ in the consecrated Eucharistic

---

[59]Devlin (1975), 101-136.

[60]Hallinger (1956), 128-130.

[61]ed. Swoboda (1900), 120, r. 50-51, lib. VI: "Dixerat ille: 'meam nisi carnem habeatis in escam/ Sanguinem et in potum, vitam nec habere valetis"

[62]PL 133, 532, Coll. lib. I, c. 19: "sed *pastor* et episcopus animarum nostrarum Christus non est contemnendus"; 543, lib. I, c. 34: "ut *humilis* Deus doceret hominem non esse superbum"; 582, lib. II, c. 35: "apparuit ei mirabili fulgore portans *coronam spineam*"; 637 lib. III, c. 52: "in siti sua *fellis amaritudinem* accepit"; "*flagellari* autem opus est hominis peccatoris non eius qui peccatum non fecit".

[63]PL 142, 911, *Vita s. Odilonis*, lib. I, c. 14: "et diem suae vocationis circa festivitatem Dominicae Circumcisionis imminere pro certo testatur; memorans illius perfectissimi viri Willelmi abbatis Divionensis in ea sancta Circumcisione obitum qui propterea eadem die coronam accepit divinae remunerationis, quia semper pie compatiebatur tenera vulnera Dominici cruoris, videlicet secundum Hieronymum iniuriam Circumcisionis. Simili modo et iste in *humanitate* Salvatoris, eamdem habebat qualitatem affectionis"; 991-1036: *S. Odilonis Sermones* I-XV.

elements was for him just as real and alive as the Christ on the cross visible to this soul's eye".[64] The widely-read author of works on Christ's humanity, John of Fécamp († 1078), speaks with fear and desire of the loving king Christ - *rex pie* - of "that truly great and ineffable sacrament" in which in truth His body is eaten and His blood drunk.[65] Then came the Cistercians, who continued to prepare the popularisation of the sufferings of Christ. Their principal representative was Bernard († 1153), who left an indelible stamp on the devotion to Christ's humanity, followed by his friend Peter of Celle († 1138) and his fellow monk Herbert († c. 1180). Although there was an increase in the affective element in the monastic Eucharistic devotion described, it was never separated - as was the later popular devotion centred on the 'physical' presence of Christ in the Eucharist - from its liturgical and sacramental origins and context. It is these forms of devotion and contemplation centred on the *praesentia realis* and on the *humanitas Christi* that inspired the monks to concentrate on the Host during the *clamor* and to adore the Lord in all humility.

6 THE 'BURIAL' IN THE ALTAR

During the persecutions in the first centuries of Christendom the Christian martyrs gave their lives for their beliefs. Their constancy and courage earned a great deal of admiration. The 2nd-century bishop of Antioch, St. Ignatius, went to his martyr's death using an image which grips the imagination: he called himself the wheat that was to be ground by the teeth of the animals in the arena so that he would become pure bread for Christ.[1] This sort of self-sacrifice, which went to the utter limit, left such an impression on the survivors that following their immediate dismay and

---

[64]Devlin (1975), 117; PL 145, 432, *Opuscula*, XIX, c. 5: "Saepe cernebam praesentissimo mentis intuitu Christum clavis affixum, in cruce pendentem, avidusque suscipiebam stillantem supposito ore cruorem (...) vel de sacratissima nostri Redemptoris *humanitate*, vel de illa coelestis gloriae inenarrabili specie (...)".

[65]ed. Leclercq (1946), 173, *Confessio Theologica*, tertia pars, c. 28: "Magnum quippe et ineffabile constat esse sacramentum, in quo tua caro in veritate editur, et sanguis tuus in veritate bibitur. O pavendum reverendumque mysterium, ad cuius intuendam altitudinem humanus reverberatur intuitus. Per ipsum sacrosanctum et vivificum mysterium corporis et sanguinis tui, humili prece clementiam tuam deposco rex Christe, rex pie, da mihi gratiam lacrimarum quam multum desiderat et a te petit anima mea: quia sine te non possum habere eam".

[1]SC 10 (1969⁴) *Ad Roman*. IV. 1.: ["Laissez-moi être la pâture des bêtes, par lesquelles il me sera possible de trouver Dieu. Je suis le froment des bêtes, pour être trouvé un pur pain du Christ".]

horror they had to give some expression to their wonder. The tombs of the martyrs, where without doubt in the beginning "bitter tears were shed",[2] became objects of reverence once time had created some distance from their deaths. After all, the tombs contained the remains of those in whom Christ had shared suffering. *Christus in martyre est*, wrote Tertullian († c. 220).[3]

Within the Christian community there was an annual remembrance of the one who had earned the martyr's crown and was, as it were, born anew. In the 2nd century the practice must have come into being of celebrating the Eucharist in the vicinity of the martyr's grave. The words spoken over the grave of St. Polycarp († c. 156) at least point towards this being the case: "There we will come together in joy and happiness in order to celebrate the day of his martyrdom and birth."[4] The martyr's grave and the celebration of the Eucharist were therefore tightly bound together even in pre-Constantinian times. This can be seen in the placing of altars - at first temporary and later fixed - above or in the immediate vicinity of the martyr's final resting place.

In North Africa altars of this kind were called *memoriae*, tombs to the memory of those who had gone before. The altar had, in fact, become a memorial grave because it contained the mortal remains of the martyr. It is to this kind of 'altar grave'[5] Augustine refers in his writings directed against the Manichaean Faustus, when he says that the altars should be built on the *memoriae* of the martyrs.[6] The Council of Carthage (407) used the same word when it named the altars at the roadside *memoriae*.[7] In Rome and much of the neighbouring area altar graves were widespread towards the end of the 5th century.[8]

---

[2] Delehaye (1933), 1: "les premières larmes qui coulèrent sur les tombes des martyrs furent des larmes amères".

[3] CC SL II, 1329, *De Pudicitia*, 22, 6: "Habeo etiam nunc quo probem Christum. Si propterea Christus in martyre est, ut moechos et fornicatores martyr absolvat, occulta cordis edicat, ut ita delicta concedat, et Christus est".

[4] SC 10 (1969[4]), 269, *Martyrium Polycarpi*, 18, 3 :["C'est là, autant que possible, que le Seigneur nous donnera de nous réunir dans l'allégresse et la joie, pour célébrer l'anniversaire de son martyre, de sa naissance, en mémoire de ceux qui ont combattu avant nous"]; ed. Dehandschutter (1979), 231; Rordorf (1972).

[5] Braun (1924), I, 525-662.

[6] PL 42, 384 , *Contra Faustum* lib. XX, c. 21 :" ita tamen, ut nulli martyrum, sed ipsi Deo martyrum sacrificamus, quamvis in memoriis martyrum constituamus altaria"; Saxer (1980), 125-140.

[7] CC SL 149, 359, c. 15 : "Item placuit ut de altaribus quae passim per agros aut vias tanquam memoriae martyrum constituuntur, in quibus nullum corpus aut reliquiae martyrum conditae probantur, ab episcopis qui iisdem locis praesunt, si fieri potest, evertantur".

[8] Deichmann (1970), esp. 145, 168.

The relationship between altar and relic was not confined to these sepulchral monuments. Increasingly in the churches within the city walls and in the countryside, built for the celebration of the liturgy and not as *martyria*, was a tendency to imitate the *memoriae*. The only altar in these churches became the meeting place for the community of believers where they celebrated the Eucharist as the rendering present of Christ's sacrifice on the Cross.[9] In these churches too the people wished to emphasise during the liturgy the closeness to the crucifixion and death of Christ that the martyr had achieved by his death: this they did by placing the martyr's relics in or under the altar. Hence the references in ancient Christian texts to the placing of mortal remains *sub altare*,[10] which can mean either "directly below the altar" or "as nearly as possible under the altar".[11] And thus altars were built for relics, but the other side of the coin was that relics were provided for altars.

Although not all altars had been provided with relics before the 8th century,[12] it was nonetheless a general desire to place the relics of the patron saint at least in the high altar and, if at all possible, in the other altars. The individual church was thus assured of the special patronage of the saint, whose presence was guaranteed by the relics contained in the altar grave. He was near to his people. His role as mediator with God gained in significance following the weakening of the mediating role of Christ by the emphasis placed on his divinity in the struggle against Arianism. The image of the God-man had thus become more abstract, only seldom received in the Eucharist - and then with sacred awe. The final sentence of the *Collect*, even today, reminds us of the accentuation of his divinity "through our Lord Jesus Christ, who lives and reigns as God for ever and ever".[13]

It has already be mentioned that relics in the West were at first not skeletons but contact relics, such as oil from the lamp burning at the original martyr's grave or a piece of material that had come into contact

---

[9]TRE 2, 310.

[10]CSEL 29, 292, Paulinus van Nola, ep. XXXII, c. 17: "Ecce sub accensis altaribus ossa piorum. Regia purpureo marmore crusta tegit"; CSEL 30, 280, *Carmen* XXVII, 400 sqq.: "spectant de superis altaria tuta fenestris, sub quibus intus habent sanctorum corpora sedem".

[11]TRE 2, 316.

[12]Hermann-Mascard (1975), 147-148; Angenendt (1982), 222; "In frühen Mittelalter galt ein Altar ohne Reliquien als befremdliche Anormalität".

[13]Angenendt (1982), 179-181.

with the saint himself or with his tomb.[14] Gregory of Tours relates how, for the consecration of the church at Pernay, he took a few threads of the shroud of St. Nicetius. He placed them in the high altar and, some days later, in other altars, after a blind man had told him that the light had returned to his eyes during prayer at the altar of the saint.[15] Regarding the *brandea*, supplied by Pope Gregory I, it is sometimes emphatically stated that they are intended for use in altars. Relics of this sort contained a living reality for the Christians. They represented the saint in his own very person. Placing them in the altar meant burying the body of the saint himself.[16] From the 6th or 7th century a preference grew for corporal relics.[17]

Space was provided in or under the altar table for these remains. In the case of altars in the form of a table, this space was usually in the pedestal supporting the legs of the table top. Where the table top was supported by right-angled trestles, a small shuttered window was made in the front, known as the *fenestella confessionis*, which made it possible to access the space behind and below. In the case of stipes or tomb altars the actual burial space is situated under the cover on the upper side.[18] Its size depended on the quantity of relics to be placed there.

Again Gregory of Tours provides us with a graphic detail. St. Senoch had set up an altar at a place where St. Martin had prayed long before. He asked Bishop Eufronius († 573) to place the *capsula* with the relics in the space but, alas, it proved too small. A fiery prayer session by both men achieved a miracle: the *capsula* shrank and the space designed for it increased in volume.[19]

Larger-sized spaces for the relics were certainly required when, as we have seen, around the 7th and 8th centuries the popes finally agreed to the *translatio* of the relics from the catacombs which no longer served a function and from graveyards that had been desecrated by the Longobards. The "grave space" in the altar thus had to be large enough

---

[14]Duchesne (1925), 423; see p. 12.

[15]MGH SRM I, 2, 248, *Vitae Patrum* VIII, 8: "lumen ei virtus divina patefecit. Posui, fateor, de his pignoribus et in aliis basilicarum altaribus".

[16]See p. 13; Duchesne (1925), 423; Delehaye (1933), 90-96.

[17]McCulloh (1980), 318.

[18]TRE 2, 310-317; Angenendt (1989).

[19]MGH SRM I,2, 271, *Vitae Patrum*. c. XV.1: "Adfuit tunc Eufronius beatus episcopus, qui, consecratum altare, eum diaconatus honori donavit. Celebratis igitur missis, cum capsula reliquiarum in loculo cupirent collocare, extetit capsa prolixior nec recipere in loculum poterat (...) Mirum dictu. Ita enim loculum divinitus amplificatum capsulaque constricta est, ut in eo spatiosissime non sine admiratione reciperet".

to contain not just a single relic but an entire sarcophagus. This resting place, which eventually was of one piece with the altar itself, is called by various names in the sources:*locus*, *sigillum*, *foramen*, *confessio* or *sepulcrum*.[20]

The name *confessio* came into existence in Rome in the 5th century and at the time meant a space or a crypt, usually between the altar and the grave. Via the *fenestella* the *brandea* could be lowered onto the tomb down the shaft of the grave. From the 9th century it came to mean the resting place of the relics themselves and became synonymous with *sepulcrum*[21] or 'grave', a name which was used in the sources for such spaces only after 1100. After that date the frequency increased, especially in the 14th and 15th centuries. From now on we will use this term in order to avoid confusion with the term *confessio* in an earlier meaning.

The question arises as to why the term 'grave' was not used, while in the pontificals of the 11th and 12th centuries it is said that the relics were "buried". Braun assumes that until the 13th century preference was given to *confessio* because the Eucharist was often placed there. The space in question could hardly be regarded as a 'grave'. When the space came to be used (almost) exclusively for the relics, the term *sepulcrum* came into general use.[22]

This question introduces the general form of usage which is frequently referred to in the sources from the 8th to the 13th century. After that it is found less often until its disappearance in the 15th century. Here were referring to the custom of placing the relics and the Eucharist together in the *sepulcrum* near the altar. Originally the consecration of a church consisted of the first celebration of the Eucharist, and this has always remained the core of the ceremony.[23] In the *martyria*, constructed over the graves, this Eucharistic celebration was ipso facto involved with the remains of the martyr. An early example in the West of expressly involving the relics in the consecration of another church is that found in the consecration of the 'Basilica Ambrosiana' in Milan in 386. The populace had asked Ambrose to consecrate the new church in the same way as the 'Basilica Romana', also known as the 'Basilica Apostolorum'.

---

[20]Braun (1924), I, 549.

[21]LW I, 455.

[22]Braun (1924), 553: "als schon manche Pontifikalien des 11. und 12. Jahrhunderts im Ritus der Reliquienrekondition die Antiphonen kennen *Corpora sanctorum in pace sepulta sunt*".

[23]LW I, 1319; Hermann-Mascard (1975), 148-151; Andrieu (1931-61), IV, 369; TRE II, 317.

The bishop laid down the condition that relics of a martyr had to be available. These must have been part of the consecration ritual - which is not described anywhere - in the basilica in question.[24] Ambrose's wish was fulfilled by the famous finding of the bodies of Gervase and Protase. The martyrs were taken to the small basilica of Fausta the evening before, and then carried to the new church the following day. There they were placed under the altar during the consecration rite. Gregory of Tours also writes of relics being kept on the eve of a consecration in a nearby church, where the faithful spent the night in prayer. He mentions a similar vigil in connection with the consecration of the church of Julianus[25] and of his own private oratory[26] he places the Mass of consecration both before and after the *depositio* in his writings.[27] He even mentions one occasion when an altar was consecrated without a *depositio*.[28] These possible variants show that in his time the consecration of an altar and the *depositio* could be either linked or separate from one another. In the course of time they came to form a single whole. In the second half of the 8th century the consecration of the altar extended to become the consecration of the church building and remained an integral part of the larger ceremony.

Local diversity gave way to a uniform ritual, in which a Gallic and a Roman version can be distinguished. In the original Gallic ritual, as described in the *sacramentarium* of Angoulême[29] dated approximately 800, the 're-burial' of the relics is given less emphasis than in the Roman version, of which *Ordo XLII* is the oldest version. In this mid-8th-century *Ordo* - originally intended as a rite of consecration of the altar - "the oldest Roman tradition of the consecration of a church in combination with the *depositio* has been preserved".[30] The bishop begins the

---

[24]See p. 104; Dassmann (1975), 52-53.

[25]MGH SRM I, 2, 128, *De virtutibus S. Iuliani*, c. 35 : "Depositis ergo super altare (basilicae sancti Martini) sacrosanctis reliquiis, vigilata nocte, cum grande psallentio ad ante-dictam deferebantur basilicam (monasteriis Iuliani)".

[26]MGH SRM I,2, 309, *In gloria confessorum*, c. 20: "Quam (cellulam) diligenter conpositam, altare ex more locato, ad basilicam sanctam vigiliis noctem unam ducentes, mane vero venientes ad cellulam, altare quod erexeramus sanctificavimus. Regressique ad basilicam (S. Martini), sanctas eius reliquias (...) radiantibus cereis crucibusque admovimus".

[27]See above n. 22; MGH SRM I,2, 148, *Vitae patrum*, VIII,8: "Accessi, fateor, sacravi altare, decerpsi fila de lenteo, locavi in templo; dictis missis, facta oratione, discessi".

[28]MGH SRM I,2, 58, *In gloria martyrum*, c. 33; Andrieu (1931-61), IV, 333.

[29]Chavasse (1958), 42; Hermann-Mascard (1975), 153; Vogel (1986), 71.

[30]Mermann-Mascard (1975),151; Vogel (1986), 181.

ceremony with prayer in a neighbouring church next to the relics which he entrusts to a priest. This latter, at a later stage in the ritual, has the relics carried to the new church in procession. The prelate has meanwhile gone to the new building and performed the first acts of consecration. At the *adventus* of the procession he goes outside and prays before the open door. Then follows the entrance and the *depositio* of the relics, together with a few particles of the Eucharistic bread.[31] From the 8th century onwards under the Carolingians a mutual the Roman and Gallic ritual began to influence one another mutually, so that this 'parallel application in concrete use' in the *dedicatio* spread throughout Europe, described in *sacramentaria*, *ordines* and *pontificales*. The mingling of both rituals finally resulted in the *Pontificale* of the bishop of Mende, William Durandus, completed in 1294.[32]

6.1   The relics in the altar tomb

According to the *Liber Pontificalis*, it was Felix I († 274) who issued the decree to celebrate Mass on or near the tombs of the martyrs.[33] This decree, the authenticity of which is disputed, probably referred to the *missae ad corpus*, in which the martyr's death was commemorated.[34]

The erection of all kinds of altars above and adjacent to the martyrs' tombs in the 4th century, once the persecutions had ended, points on the one hand to a manifestation of a practice that had gone on previously in secret and, on the other, to the encouragement given by the bishops to remove heathen practices and abuses from the meals of the dead. And it was only from this date that it became possible to construct *martyria* above the tombs, soon to be followed by larger sepulchral monuments thanks to the increase in devotion to the martyrs. Early examples of this are the memorial churches to Peter and Paul in Rome, containing the altar grave, which came into general use after the decree of the Emperor Constantine (306-337) permitting Christianity. The best known and most frequently visited *memoriae* all contained this altar grave from the 5th century onwards.[35]

---

[31]Benz (1956), 69-74.

[32]Andrieu (1938-41), III, 455-478.

[33]LP I, 158 : "Hic constituit supra memorias martyrum missas celebrare".

[34]Braun (1924), I, 528; DTC XIII 2nd p. col. 2328-2330.

[35]Braun (1924), I, 525-662, "Das Altargrab" esp. 529, 532.

A remarkable fact was the decree of the Fifth Council of Carthage already referred to: the local bishops were required to remove the roadside altars which did not contain relics. This would seem to demonstrate that as early as the beginning of the 5th century there was a close link made between the relics and the altar. Jerome also referred to this relationship when writing the following sharp question to the Vigilantius we have already mentioned: "Could it be that the bishop of Rome does wrong in regarding the tombs of Peter and Paul as altars and celebrates the Lord's sacrifice over their bones, which we regard as objects worthy of reverence and which you see as a simple heap of dust?"[36]

If only because of legal constraints, originally there were no relics in the Roman churches which served only as places where the Christian community celebrated the Eucharist. Such buildings were not, in fact, intended for the cult of the relics.[37] Outside of Rome the *translatio* in Milan to which reference has been made was an early exception. Ambrose regarded it as fitting that the triumphant victims should be given a place under the altar where Christ, who had saved them through their suffering, was present as sacrifice.[38] Ambrose played a role in other *translationes*. According to the *vita s. Ambrosii*, written in approximately 422 by Paulinus of Milan, the bishop had the remains of St. Nazarius, probably martyred under Diocletian (284-305) and buried in a garden outside Milan, removed and taken to the 'Basilica Apostolorum', later re-named 'St. Nazarius'.[39] A year previously in Florence, under pressure from the people, he had placed under the altar of a Florentine basilica the secondary relics of two other victims of Diocletian's regime, Vitalis and

---

[36]PL 23, 346, *Contra Vigilantium*: "Male facit ergo Romanus episcopus, qui super mortuorum hominum Petri et Pauli, secundum nos ossa veneranda, secundum te vilem pulvisculum, offert Domino sacrificia, et tumulos eorum Christi arbitratur altaria"; see p. 73.

[37]Braun (1924), I, 653.

[38]PL 16, 1066, ep. 22: "Succedant victimae triumphales in locum ubi Christus hostia est. Sed ille super altare, qui pro omnibus passus est. Isti sub altari, qui illius redempti sunt passione".

[39]PL 14, 40-41, *Vita s. Ambrosii auctore Paulino eius notario*, n. 32 : "Quo in tempore sancti Nazarii martyris corpus, quod erat in horto positum extra civitatem levatum ad basilicam apostolorum quae est in Romana transtulit (...) Vidimus autem in sepulcro (...) sanguinem martyris ita recentem, quasi eodem die fuisset effusus. Caput etiam ipsius, quod ab impiis fuerat abseissum, ita integrum atque incorruptum cum capillis capitis atque barba, ut nobis videretur eodem tempore quo levabatur, lotum atque compositum in sepulcro. Et quid mirum, quandoquidem Dominus in evangelio ante promisit, quod capillus de capite eorum non peribit" (Luc.21,18); AASS 28 iul. VI, 503 sqq.; DAC XI, 1, 1058, 'Milan'; Dassmann (1975), 53.

Agricola. He was present at the *elevatio* in Bologna and thus had come to possess these relics.[40]

The argument that it was fitting to bury the martyrs under the altar where the celebration of the Eucharist implied the proclamation of Christ's death (I Cor 11:26) can be found in a letter ascribed both to Augustine († 430)[41] and to Maximus of Turin († c. 470)[42]. The plea on behalf of the practice begins with a passage from the *Apocalypse* where St. John sees the Lamb break the seven seals: "And when he had opened the fifth seal, I saw under the altar the souls of them that were slain for the word of God, and for the testimony which they held" (Apoc. 6:9). The Christians concertised this - heavenly - altar described in this passage by creating the Eucharistic altar, on which the body of the Lord was offered in sacramental sacrifice. The souls of the just were for them synonymous with the relics of the blood witnesses who had become one with Christ in their sufferings and now under the altar shared in the union with the Eucharistic gifts on the altar.

Gregory of Tours provides us with rich sources of information on pre-6th-century times. In addition to the *depositiones* already mentioned, he reports many others, spread all over Gaul. For instance, the relics of St. Symphorian in Thiers (Puy-de-Dôme) were placed in a silver *capsa* under the altar.[43] In Pernay and Petit-Pressigny, in Indre-et-Loire, Gregory placed the *pignora* of St. Nicetius in the *sepulcrum*.[44] In the same way relics of St. Stephen found their way to an oratory close to Tours[45] and to the church of St. Stephen in Bourges.[46] Similar reports

---

[40]PL 14, 39, n. 29 : "In eadem etiam civitate basilicam   constituit, in qua deposuit reliquias martyrum Vitalis et Agricolae (...) Quae cum deponerentur sub altari..magna illic totius plebis sanctae laetitia atque exsultatio"; Dassmann (1975), 57-58.

[41]PL 39, 2154-2155, sermo 221,1 : "Recte sub altari iustorum animae requiescunt; quia super altare corpus Domini offertur. Nec immerito illic iusti vindictam sanguinis postulant, ubi etiam pro peccatoribus Christi sanguis effunditur. Convenienter igitur, et quasi pro quodam consortio ibi martyribus sepultura decreta est, ubi mors Domini quotidie celebratur sicut ipse ait *Quotiescumque haec fereritis, mortem Domini annuntiabitis, donec veniat* (I Cor. XI,26): scilicet ut qui propter mortem eius mortui fuerant, sub sacramenti eius mysterio requiescant. Non immerito, inquam, consortio quodam illic occisis tumulus constituitur, ubi occisionis Dominicae membra ponuntur: ut quos cum Christo unius passionis causa devinxerat, unius etiam loci religio copularet"; see also: PL 38, 1425, sermo 313,5; 1437, sermo 318, 1; PL 46, 865, sermo 14,5.

[42]PL 57, 689-690, sermo 77; see also: Gagé (1929), 147.

[43]MGH SRM I,2, 74, *In gloria martyrum*, c. 51.

[44]ibid. 248, 250, *Vitae patrum* VIII, 8 and 1.

[45]ibid. 58, *In gloria martyrum*, c. 33.

[46]ibid. 59, c. 33.

relate to such places as Lyon,[47] Neuvy-le-Roi in Touraine[48] and Bordeaux.[49]

Pope Gregory the Great repeatedly speaks in his letters of relics in relation to the altar grave. Mostly the link is only indirect, such as in his descriptions of the consecration of churches,[50] but once or twice the altar is referred to as the place where the relics are kept. Bishop Palladius of Saintes, for instance, had asked Gregory for relics so that he could provide his basilica with a more fitting appearance. Nine altars already had relics, but four did not, so that the Eucharist could not be celebrated on them. According to a letter which Gregory wrote to Palladius the latter's wish was granted.[51] The generalised nature of the ruling, in 6th-century Rome, that on or under the altar table relics should be kept can be deduced from a letter from Gregory to Abbot Mellitus, bishop of London, in which the pope says that when heathen temples were consecrated for Christian use, the altars should be provided with relics.[52]

The practice was also widespread in 6th-century Spain. One of the canons collected by St. Martin of Braccara († c. 580) prescribed that priests should not celebrate memorial Mass for the dead in the open fields but in the church building where the relics of the martyrs reposed.[53] In the 7th century the placing of relics in the altar was already a familiar sight, expressed in such things as the prescriptions issued by a council held in Paris at the beginning of the century.[54]

In the *Ordo of Saint-Amand*, which describes an early stage of the Gallic rite of consecration of the altar, the *depositio* is no longer an independent entity, as it was in the time of Gregory of Tours, but is part

---

[47]ibid. 71, 72, c. 48, 49; ibid. 131, *De virtut. S. Iuliani*, c. 44.

[48]ibid. 56, *In gloria martyrum*, c. 30.

[49]ibid. 59, c. 33.

[50]MGH Ep I. 78, 107-108, 112-113, 177, 240, 265, 460, 419, Ep. II. 76, 81, 174, 176; resp. Greg. Magnus ep. I, 52; II,9 and 11; III 19; IV 8 and 30; VI 22 and 43; IX 49 and 58; 180 and 183.

[51]MGH Ep I, 423, *ep. ad Palladium*, lib. VI, 48; Hefele (1907-42), III, 208-214.

[52]MGH Ep I, 330-331, ep. lib. XI, 5.

[53]Mansi IX, 857, Capitula collecta a Martino episcopo Bracarensi, can. LXVIII: "Non oportet clericos ignaros et praesumptores super monumenta in campo ministeria portare, aut distribuere sacramenta; sed aut in ecclesia, aut in basilica, ubi martyrum reliquiae sunt depositae, ibi pro defunctis oblationem offerre"; PL 84, 583-584, Concilia Hispania Bracarense.

[54]MGH Conc I, 193, *Concilium incerti loci*, post a. 614, c. II : "Ut altaria alibi consegrari non debeant nisi in his tantum ecclesiis, ubi corpora saepulta".

of an actual ritual of consecration.[55] And in the *Gelasianum Vetus* the rite of consecration of the altar in integrated into the church consecration, this part being added to the original Roman sacramentarium in Gaul in the middle of the 8th-century.[56] The *Liber Diurnus*, a book of liturgical formulae drawn up by the papal chancellery that took on a more fixed form towards the 8th century, though parts of it date from earlier times, provides various texts for this type of consecration rite all of which imply that the *depositio* is in or under the altar.[57]

The frequent reference to this since Carolingian times in the *sacramentaria, ordines* and *pontificales* points to a practice that had already become part of the pattern of the church's liturgical life. In the East the *depositio* had become a sine qua non. The Second Council of Nicaea stated in 787 that the use of relics at the consecration of a church was obligatory and threatened with deposition any bishop who should fail to carry out this decree.[58] Such a rigid regulation did not exist in the West, but efforts were nonetheless made to ensure that every altar had relics. And here was meant not just the high altar but the side altars too. With the same show of industry as Palladius had once demonstrated, Bishop Aldrich of Le Mans set to work in 834 when he placed relics in the six altars of the church of St. Stephen and the fourteen altars of the restored cathedral. This example is but one of many.[59]

The extent of the protection provided by the saints would even seem to have been measured against the number of relics in the altar grave. In 1174, at the consecration of a new church, Bishop Adelog of Hildesheim determined with great precision that there were 118 relics in the high altar and 103 and 97 in the respective side altars.[60] Such numbers, however, pale into insignificance when compared to those provided by Winith, the founder of the monastery of Windberg in the

---

[55]LW I, 123; Duchesne (1925), 478-479; Benz (1956), 69 sqq.; Vogel (1986), 152.

[56]ed. Mohlberg (1981), *Orationes in dedicatione basilicae novae*, 108, r. 693: "benedictio altaris"; 111, l. 710: "Deus, qui ex omni coaptacione sanctorum aeternum tibi condis habitaculum, de aedificationis tuae incrementa caelestia, et quorum hic reliquias pio more conplectemur, eorum semper meritis adiuvemur"; PL 72, 534; Vogel (1986), 65-68.

[57]ed. Foerster (1958), 83-93; Braun (1924), I, 536; LW I, 1520-1521.

[58]Mansi XIII, 751, c. 7: "Quaecumque ergo templa consecrata sunt absque sacris reliquiis martyrum, in iis fieri statuimus reliquiarum depositionem cum consuetis precibus. Episcopus autem posthac templum consecrans sine sanctis reliquiis, deponatur, ut qui ecclesiasticas traditiones transgressus sit".

[59]MGH SS XV, 310, *Gesta Aldrici*, n. 2, 3, 18; Braun (1924), I, 538; II, 545-647.

[60]Hermann-Mascard (1957), 161, n. 111: *Annales Stedeburgenses* S.S., t. XVI, 212.

diocese of Regensburg. He arrived at a total representation of 6200 saints in one altar.[61]

Although the presence of relics in the altar was greatly valued, the *depositio* was not an absolute requirement for the consecration of church and altar. It was omitted when there were no relics available. The walling up of the remains of the saints was, however, regarded as so essential for the validity of the consecration that it was more and more the exception when no relics were placed in the altar. When Pope Clement VIII prescribed the Roman pontifical of 1596 for the whole of the Western church, the *depositio* gained a more obligatory character.[62] This decree, incidentally, also put an end to the long and always current dispute regarding the validity of the consecration of an altar if the *depositio* were omitted. The question was not definitively settled until the church's book of law was brought out in 1917, when canon 1198, paragraph 4 of the Codex made it obligatory to cement relics into the *sepulcrum*.[63] This law has been included in the new Codex published in 1988.[64]

6.2   The Eucharist in the altar grave

The practice of placing the Eucharist in the *sepulcrum* started much later and ended much earlier. The oldest testimony to the custom probably dates from approximately 750. It is rubric 11 of the Roman *Ordo XLII* for the consecration of a church, which was spread all over the West and continued to exist in some places even into the 15th century.[65] The bishop performing the consecration "lays", says the rubric, "three particles of the body of the Lord and three grains of incense - recalling

---

[61]MGH SS XVII, 560, *Historiae et Annales Windbergenses*.

[62]Clemens VIII, *Pontificale romanum*, 211 en 274: "Pontifex parat reliquias in altari consecrando includendas ponens eas in decenti et mundo vasculo cum tribus granis thuris".

[63]DDC I, col. 1461-1462; Jone (1950-55), II, 411 can. 1198, par. 4: "Ad normam legum liturgicarum tum in altari immobili tum in altari mobili sit sepulcrum continens sanctorum reliquias".

[64]can. 1237, n. 2: "Antiqua traditio martyrum aliorumve sanctorum reliquias sub altari fixo condendi servetur, iuxta normas in libris liturgicis traditas".

[65]Andrieu (1931-61), IV, 394: " Mais l'on ne risque guère d'être dans l'erreur en admettant qu'il représente une discipline fixée dès le milieu du VIIIe siècle et peut-être depuis quelques décades"; Vogel (1986), 181: "this document circulated in Gaul around 750 and may represent something worked out around 720-750".

the balsam used at the burial of the martyr[66] - in the *confessio* of the altar. Then the relics are closed up inside".[67]

This prescription made reference to the relics and the Eucharist. It can also refer to the Eucharist alone. According to the late-medieval canonists Guido of Baysio († 1313) and Panormitanus († 1445), during the consecration of a church in the 9th century a certain Pope Leo added part of the corporal to the Eucharist as a substitute for the relics. However the historicity of this piece of information is dubious.[68]

In 816 the Council of Celckyth (Chelsea) formulated a canon (canon 2) regarding the consecration of a church in which the Eucharist is regarded as an accompaniment to or a replacement of the relics. "Together with the other relics" it is placed in a *capsula* and enclosed in the altar or, should there be no relics available, the bishop can make use of the Eucharist alone "because it is the body and blood of our Lord Jesus Christ".[69] The close 'parallel application in concrete use' is very obvious here: the Eucharist is indirectly called a relic, but a unique relic at that: it is the body and blood of Christ himself. And thus, says canon 2, this 'relic' can replace all other relics.

Had this usage anything to do with a scarcity of relics in the Carolingian period, such pragmatism in subsequent centuries would not have weighed very heavily. However according to the many *sacramentaria* and *pontificales* which demonstrate the influence of the Roman ritual on this point the Eucharist is seldom placed alone in the *sepulcrum* but is almost always accompanied by the relics.[70] According to the sacramentarium of Bishop Drogo of Metz († 855), for instance, the relics are placed in the *sepulcrum* together with three particles of the Host

---

[66]Duchesne (1925), 428.

[67]Andrieu (1931-61), IV, 400 : "Deinde ponit tres portiones corporis domini intus in confessione et tres de incenso et recluduntur reliquiae intus in confessione".

[68]Gillmann (1922), 38, n. 2, Guido de Baysio, *Rosarium* (1481): "Sed legitur, quod Leo papa dedit partem corporalis et eucharistiam in dedicatione ecclesie pro reliquiis"; Panormitanus, *Commentaria*, t. VI, fo. 196, de consecr. eccl.: "Fertur tamen quod Leo Papa deficientibus reliquiis dedit partem corporalis et Eucharistiae in consecratione cuiusdam ecclesiae"; Hermann-Mascard (1975), 160, n. 101: "Il s'agit vraisemblablement soit de Leon III († 816), soit de Leon IV († 855)".

[69]Mansi XIV, 356 : "Postea eucharistia quae ab episcopo per idem ministerium consecratur, cum aliis reliquiis condatur in capsula, ac servetur in eadem basilica. Et si alias reliquias intimare non potest, tamen hoc maxime proficere potest, quia corpus et sanguis est domini nostri Iesu Christi".

[70]Braun (1924), I, 625; for a bibliographic review see: Jungmann (1962), Quellen, 589 sqq.

and three grains of incense.[71] The pontifical of Rheims, dating from the second half of the 9th century, prescribes the same, though in reverse order.[72]

Similar formulations are found in the 10th century, as in the pontificals of the monastery of Jumièges in Normandy,[73] of Mainz,[74] of Noyon,[75] of St. Dunstan,[76] of Egbert of York[77] and in the Romano-German pontifical, a synthesis of the Gallic and the Roman ritual which includes *Ordo XLII*.[78] For the 11th century we can quote the lost pontifical of the monastery of St. Lucianus in Beauvais,[79] the pontifical of Narbonne[80] and that of the Cluniac Halinardus, Archbishop of Lyon († 1052).[81] A prescription similar to that seen in the pontifical of Cambray[82] can be found in the 12th-century pontifical of Salzburg[83] and in the abbreviated version of the *Pontificale Romanum*.[84]

This 'parallel application in use' between the relics and the Eucharist in the altar grave occurred in the whole of western Europe - in Italy, France, Spain, England and Germany.[85] The practice is illustrated by a letter dated 1020 from Pope Benedict VIII to the Margrave of Mantua regarding the holy monk Simeon who had died in the neighbouring monastery of Padolinora. The letter empowers the margrave

---

[71]Duchesne (1925), 507 : "Postea ponentur reliquiae in confessione cum tribus particulis corporis Domini ac tribus particulis thimiamatis"; Benz (1956), 72; see also: Braun (1924) I, 624, Ordo van Verona, 823-840, can. 92 and PL 78, 424 : (In s. Gregorii librum sacramentorum notae) "In eodem Ratoldi codice haec sequuntur (...) Et ponat tres portiones corporis Domini intus et tres de incenso. Recluduntur tunc reliquiae".

[72]Martène (1788) II, 261, lib. II, c. 13. ordo 5 : "Deinde ponat tres portiones Corporis Domini intro in confessionem et tres de incenso et recluduntur reliquiae in confessione".

[73]ibid. *Pontificali Anglicano monasterii Gemmeticensis*, 254, lib. II, c. 13. ordo 3; Martimort (1978), 119 n. 137; 395 n. 795.

[74]Braun (1924), I, 624.

[75]Martène (1788), II, 261, lib. II, c. 13 ordo 6.

[76]ibid. 257, lib. II, c. 13. ordo 4; Martimort (1978), 172 n. 236.

[77]ibid. 249, lib. II, c. 13. ordo 2; Martimort (1978), 395 n. 794.

[78]ed. Vogel (1963), I, 88.

[79]Martène (1788), 243, lib. II, c. 13. n. XI.

[80]ib. 268, lib. II, c. 13. ordo 7.

[81]ibid. 270, lib. II, c. 13. ordo 9.

[82]ib. 272, lib. II, c. 13. ordo 10.

[83]ibid. 243, lib. II, c. 13. n. XI.

[84]Andrieu (1938-41), I, 186: "pontifex recondat reliquias in capsa et ponat tres portiones corporis domini et tres de incenso".

[85]Braun (1924), I, 625; Nussbaum (1979), 188 n. 92.

to build a church, to bury the saint in the church and to have an altar consecrated in the vicinity of the grave, an altar in which the relics of earlier saints would be enclosed, together with the body of our Lord Jesus Christ.[86] About the same time an altar was consecrated in the cathedral of Vich in Catalonia, in which both the relics of St. Felicity and her son and the body of the Lord were placed.[87] A contemporary report of the 1096 consecration of the abbey of Marmoutiers, performed by Pope Urban II, confirms that the sacrament of Christ's body was set into the high altar with the *pignora* of the saints, including a particle of the True Cross, pieces from the clothing of the Blessed Virgin and John the Evangelist, together with hairs from the beard and head of the apostle Peter and relics of a number of named martyrs and witnesses.[88] During a consecration rite in Zürich on 10th September 1170, Bishop Otto of Konstanz placed in the altar the body of the Lord and relics, something that came to light in 1320 when it had been decided to repeat the consecration.[89] Bishop Gaufridus of Sorra († 1277) was faced with a similar situation on Sardinia. Conrad of Eberbach († 1277) relates that this bishop wished to restore a ruined church. When he had the altar opened there was found a corroded *capsula* containing relics of the saints, but also including the body of the Lord. The Eucharistic bread still seemed as fresh and unsullied as if it had only just been placed there. The emphasis in this story is on the miraculously preserved bread, which "was not subjected to decay". The fact that the bread was enclosed in the grave drew no special attention and was evidently regarded as the most natural thing in the world.[90]

---

[86]PL 139, 1633, *ep. et decr.* c. 35; AASS iul. VI, 320: "Si ita coruscat miraculis ut vester homo nobis asseruit, aedificate ecclesiam, collocate in ea eumdem, iuxta quem altare consecrari rogate, in quo reliquiae antiquorum sanctorum cum sacratissimo corpore Domino nostri Iesu Christi, et si demum mysteria celebrentur"; Bredero (1994³), 169: the pope intervened in this affair after the margrave had approached him because the local bishop had shown no interest in the canonization of the dead monk.

[87]Braun (1924), I, 625.

[88]PL 151, 275 : "In altari ergo Dominico est ineffabile corporis Christi sacramentum collocatum cum horum pignoribus sanctorum. Particula scilicet victorissimae crucis Christi, et de vestimentis gloriosae Dei Genetricis, de capillis et barba Petri apostoli, de vestimento Ioannis Evangelistae et reliquiis sanctorum martyrum (...) confessorum autem".

[89]Rahn (1901), 66 (30) n. 21, "de communione corporis domini, de lacte S.Marie".

[90]ed. Griesser (1961), 206-207, dist. III, c. 25, *Exordium Magnum Cisterciense*, lib. III, c. 23: "Cum ergo ipsum altare in praesentia sua dirui praecepisset, reperit in eo capsulam scabrosam ac veterem, sanctorum reliquias continentem. Porro inter easdem reliquias corpus Domini repositum erat, quod ita sanum et integrum, ita mundum et candidum, et ab omni corruptione penitus alienum inventum est, ac si recentissime ibi reconditum esset (...) de quo veraciter scriptum est: *'Non dabis sanctum tuum videre corruptionem'*"; PL 185, 1363.

The Franciscan chronicler Salimbene († c. 1290) bears witness to another such discovery in a church in Reggio, where a consecrated Host was found in the *sepulcrum* of an altar, still untouched by the passage of time, though it must have been there for three hundred years.[91] Sicardus of Cremona († 1215) puts the placing in the *sepulcrum* in a biblical context by comparing the church building to the heart of man "who is the temple of God" (I Cor. 3:17). He regards the placing of the Eucharist and the relics in the altar as the closing up of God's commands and the example of the saints in his heart so that he can sincerely claim: "Thy word I have hid in my heart, that I might not sin against thee" (Ps. 119:11).[92]

Frolow reports a reliquary in which the Eucharist and the relics were placed together. The reliquary, in the form of a chest with a flat top, looks very much like a portable altar. It comes from the castle chapel in Quedlinburg and is said to have belonged to the emperor Otto I († 973). Around 1200 it was restored on the orders of Abbess Agnes whose name, together with 18 representations of saints, appears on the bottom of the reliquary. The inscription indicates that the chest contains the body of the Lord, a single particle of the True Cross and some relics of the Virgin Mary, John the Baptist and the saints depicted. The text begins with the words: "In this *capsa*, made in honour of St. Servatius, is hidden the divine body and the divine wood of the True Cross".[93]

In the 13th century the canonists concentrated no longer on the simultaneous burial of the Eucharist but merely on its function as substitute for the relics in the *sepulcrum*, as was once expressed by the Council of Chelsea in 816 already referred to. Hugh of Pisa († 1210), in

---

[91]MGH SS XXXII (1963), 339, *Cronica fratris Salimbene de Adam Ordinis Minorum* a. 1250: "Et longe melius debet conservari hostia consecrata quam non consecrata, tum quia in pulchriori loco servatur, tum etiam quia in ea Deus est, qui est omnium conservator. Patet hoc per exemplum. In Regina civitate destructa fuit quedam ecclesia in cuius altari corpus Domini pro reliquiis positum fuerat, et ita invenerunt hostiam illam consecratam candidam et pulcram ac si eadem die facta fuisset. Et tamen CCC annis steterat ibi".

[92]PL 213, 36 *Mitrale* lib. I, c. 10: "in altari, corpus Domini et reliquiae reconduntur, incensum, et chrisma ponitur"; "in altari corpus Domini et reliquias ponere, est mandata Domini et exempla sanctorum memoriter retinere, ut possit dici: In corde meo abscondi eloquia tua, ut non peccem tibi"; see also Gillmann (1922), 33-34: Simon von Bisiniano in his *Summa* (1179) referring to the *Decretum Gratiani*, c. 24 D. 1 de cons. : "Nam absque reliquiis non videtur, quod possit ecclesia consecrari, quamvis quidam pro reliquiis dominicum corpus ibidem apponant"; 35 : Johannes Teutonicus (after the Fourth Lateran Council of 1215), *Glossa ordinaria*, c. 26 D. 1 de cons. : "Tamen et sufficit corpus domini"; Gottofredo de Trani (1245) ed. 1968, 324, fol 161,7 : "dicunt tamen doctores sufficere corpus Iesu Christi".

[93]Frolow (1961), 345-346, n. 374: "In hac capsa ad honore(m) beati Servatii facta e[st] reconditu(m) corp(us) et lign(um) D(om)inicu(m) et (...)"; Braun (1940), 154; illustr. 67.

his *Summa* of approximately 1188, still regarded it as necessary to maintain the role of the Eucharist in case of a lack of or in place of the relics. He did not, however, make the validity of a consecration dependent on this.[94] However Bartholomew of Brescia, teaching in Bologna in the middle of the 13th century, was of the opinion that the Eucharistic bread could be used instead of the relics only when the latter were not available.[95] Finally, Durandus made this into a prescription not only in his *Rationale* (1268) but also in his *Pontificale* (1294). In fact he was referring back to the pre-8th-century tradition with the rule that only the relics with incense grains should be placed in the *sepulcrum*.[96]

The distinction made by Durandus between the hiding of the relics with incense grains as a rule on the one hand, and the use of the Eucharist by way of exception on the other shows that some hesitation was being felt towards treating a consecrated Host in this fashion. A pointer in this direction could be the fact that as early as the 12th century the Eucharist was no longer mentioned in the *depositio* in the altar nor in the so-called long version of the *pontificale*,[97] nor in the Curia version that was drawn up later on the orders of Innocent III. These documents refer exclusively to the relics and the grains of incense.[98]

Evidently Salimbene was not entirely happy, as can be seen from his *Cronica*, with the discovery made at Reggio referred to above. This, at least, is what he says: "It disturbs me that the body of the Lord should be placed in the altar instead of the relics".[99] According to reports, the decretalist Henry of Segusia († 1271), who as Cardinal-Archbishop of

---

[94]Gillmann (1922), 35 n. 1, quotation from Huguccio, *Summa* c. 24 D. 1 de cons. ad v. 'accipiat': "Set credo, quod reliquie non sint (V.: 'sunt') de substantia consecrationis ecclesie et altaris, et ideo non minus consecrabitur ecclesia vel altare, si (V: 'set') ille non habentur. Quidam loco reliquiarum apponunt corpus domini, quod laudatur (B: 'claudatur') et debet fieri, etiam si habeantur reliquie" (Cod. Bamberg. can. 40 [P. II. 25] f. 245 c. 2; Cod Vat. 2280 f. 330 c. 2).

[95]Braun (1924), I, 626.

[96]Durandus, *Rationale*, 34, lib. I, c. 7. n .23 : "Sane sine sanctorum reliquiis aut ubi illi haberi non possunt, sine corpore Christi non fit consecratio altaris fixi (...) Reliquiae siquidem sunt exempla (...) Haec in capsa recondimus, cum ad imitandum ea in corde retinemus"; Andrieu (1938-41), III, 456, *Pontificale G. Durandi*, lib. II, c. II n. 3.: "Sane precedenti sero ante diem dedicationis, pontifex paret reliquias in altari consecrando includendas, ponens eas in decenti et mundo vasculo vitreo, vel eneo, vel alio, cum tribus granis incensi, vel, deficientibus reliquiis, ponat ibi corpus domini".

[97]*le Pontifical d'Apamée* : Andrieu (1938-41), I, 116-119, 176-195.

[98]Andrieu (1938-41), II, 421-440.

[99]MGH SS XXXII, 339: "Non placet mihi, quod corpus Domini in altari pro reliquiis includatur".

Ostia was also known as 'Hostiensis', made his way to Lyon (First Council, 1245) to Pope Innocent IV († 1254) to ask if it permitted to place the Eucharist in the *sepulcrum*. The pope consulted two prelates from his entourage and answered in the negative, though without advancing any supporting argument.[100] The archdeacon and canonist Guido of Baysio († 1313) took a critical look at the pope's reply. He qualified Innocent's response as absolutely certain because the body of the Lord was food for the soul. It should thus be preserved only to be given to the sick. At the institution of this sacrament the Lord had not said: "Hide it away", but "Take and eat"[101].

This same argument, which was also advanced against the practice of burying the Eucharist in an ordinary grave, was used by his pupil, the Italian canonist Johannes Andreae († 1348).[102] Later canonists followed him in this. The Spanish Jesuit, Francesco de Suarez († 1617) typified Durandus' prescription as "unsuitable and to be rejected".[103] This did not, however, end the usage which was already waning in the 14th and 15th centuries. The canonist Panormitanus († 1445) and the Spanish theologian Juan de Torquemada († 1468) in fact still report its existence, and not in a tone that would suggest they rejected it.[104] Another canonist, Bishop William Lyndwood († 1446) declared at the time that he opposed the custom but was honest enough to admit that this scarcely influenced the general opinion.[105]

And yet in the 14th and 15th centuries a difference with the previous period came into being. While the relevant article in most of the sacramentaria and pontificals from the 9th to the 13th centuries constituted

---

[100]Gillmann (1922), 35, n. 4. quotation from *Summa aurea* (1250-1253) lib. III, t. 40. n. 3. ed. Venet. 1480, f. J. 5. col. 2 ed. Colon. 1612. col. 1041 : "Dicunt etiam aliqui doctores sufficere corpus Christi loco reliquiarum et *hoc innuit liber pontificalis*. Dominus tamen noster per me consultus habito consilio dominorum patriarchiae Constantinopolitani et domini Sabinen., quondam Mutinen. qui ei assistebant Lugduni, mihi respondit contrarium".

[101]ibid. 38 n. 1. quotation from *Rosarium*, 1300, D. I. de cons. c. 26, n. 2 sqq. ed. Lugdun. 1549 f. 381 col. 2: "ubi patet, quod corpus Christi est cibus anime. Item quia non debet servari, nisi ad opus infirmorum (...) et non debet poni ad alium usum, nisi inquantum institutum fuerit, (...) ubi dicit: Accipite et comedite et non dicit: Accipite et *conservate* sive recondite".

[102]Johannes Andreae, *In decretalium libros*, fo. 215; see p. 123, n. 113.

[103]Suarez, *Opera Omnia*, t. XXI, 808 , In tertiam partem Divi Thomae, disputatio 81 art. III, De loco et vasis sacris in quibus sacrificium missae celebrandum est: "Sed hoc indecens mihi videtur, et improbabile".

[104]See p.187; Gillmann (1922), 39.

[105]Lyndwood, *Provinciale*, lib. III, fol. 86, De reliquiis et veneratione sanctorum: "non tamen puto hoc verum (esse) in consecratione altaris, ut scilicet corpus dominicum loco sepeliatur in altari, licet communis opinio faciat contrarium".

a fixed component, this changed from the 13th century onwards and in fact only appears sporadically. Since the first official edition of the *Pontificale Romanum* in 1485 the passage has never appeared again.[106]

The conclusion can be drawn that with the gradual rise of the Eucharistic devotion from the 13th century onwards this 'parallel application' was also gradually disappearing - with some local exceptions. In Catalonia and on Majorca, for instance, the custom continued long after that date, but in the 15th century in must have disappeared even there, again as a result of the 'process of independence of the Eucharist'. The following occurrence in Barcelona is, at least, interesting. In 1432 a particle of a relic, from the skeleton of St. Andrew, was placed in the altar of St. Mark in the cathedral, together with the Eucharistic bread. In 1482 the alter was opened and the Host, wrapped in a corporal, was found to have decayed and become discoloured. Out of reverence the priest consumed it during Mass and a fresh Host was put in its place, but now with a completely different end in view. It was closed in a silver container and placed in the *sepulcrum*, which was 'remodelled' to make a lockable tabernacle. Two sanctuary lamps were left burning there and on major feast days the old Host had to be replaced with a fresh one. Thus a cult of adoration came into being as a special privilege for this altar. The original significance of the *sepulcrum* was pushed completely into the background.[107]

No less worthy of mention is an occurrence in San Juan de las Anbadesas where, in 1426, a crucifix was found that had been placed in the altar at the consecration. A consecrated Host had been placed in the head of the figure of Christ. In line with the usual plot followed by such accounts, the Host was still white and whole. Since that time people have come frequently to venerate "the holy mystery". In 1926 its fifth centennial was celebrated with great pomp and circumstance.[108]

In only a few accounts do we read of crucifixes in which the Host is placed. In the choir of the octagonal palace chapel of Charlemagne in Aachen a bronze crucifix is said to have been found containing the Eucharistic bread in the head of the figure.[109] In a legendary passage of the chronicle written by Thietmar of Merseburg († 1018) a relic of the

---

[106]Andrieu (1931-61), IV, revision carried out on the orders of Pope Innocent VIII by the papal *ceremoniarii*, Augustinus Patricius and Johannes Burchard. ed. Étienne Plannck.

[107]Braun (1924), I, 627-628.

[108]Browe (1938), 150.

[109]Keller (1951), 71; Frolow (1961), 241, n. 148; (1965), 32.

True Cross is added to it. Archbishop Gero of Cologne († 975) was deeply attached to a crucifix (the extant 'Gerokreuz'), the head of which had a crack in it, recounts Thietmar. The bishop prepared the way for a miracle. He placed a particle of the Host and of the True Cross together in the crack. He threw himself to the ground and prayed fiercely and humbly that the break would be repaired. When he stood up he perceived that the crack had closed.[110] The following account dates from around 1340: when the patriarch of Antioch was on the island of Cyprus he was stricken with reverence for a particle of the True Cross and the miracles it performed. For the church of the Holy Cross he had a large cross made out of walnut wood more than a metre long "and put in it a little bit of the Holy Wood, and put in it of the Body of the Lord made on Holy Thursday (...) and put in it relics of the saints, in number forty-six". This silk-covered reliquary was to serve as a processional cross at times of catastrophe.[111]

As in Barcelona, in the late Middle Ages it happened a few times that the Eucharist was kept under the altar in a niche, which also served to contain the relics and vessels and linen used at Mass. But this type of solution was applied only in very exceptional circumstances and by way of an emergency measure, according to Braun. He takes the example from Corblet.[112] Such a niche was made in the tomb or *stipes* of an altar in Notre Dame in Paris, behind the high altar at the time in question. It was used for the Eucharistic bread and the relics, which were not just placed there together since within the stipes itself a separate tabernacle was made for the Sacrament. It was covered with gold and silver brocade and the Eucharistic bread was brought there in a small procession, while acolytes walking backwards waved the censer. The reverence and adoration due to the Eucharist can be seen in this description and explain the hiding of the Eucharist and the relics.

A synod at Liège in 1287 left two options open for reservation of the Eucharist: in a closed cupboard - *armariolo* - or 'under' - *sub* - the

---

[110]ed. Trillmich (1960), 86, *Chronicon*, lib. III, c. 2: "Huius caput dum fissum videret, hoc summi artificis et ideo salubriori remedio nil de(se)presumens sic curavit. Dominici corporis porcionem, unicum in cunctis necessitatibus solacium, et partem unam salutifere crucis coniungens posuit in rimam et prostratus nomen Domini flebiliter invocavit et surgens humili benediccione integritatem promeruit"; ib. MGH SS III, 759; see also: AASS 4 sept. II, 277, *Vita b. Irmgardis Virginis*, c. III, no. 9.

[111]ed. Dawkins (1932), 71, n. 77; Frolow (1961), 506.

[112]Corblet (1885), I, 553; Braun (1924), II, 599; Nussbaum (1979), 326-328.

altar.[113] King points to the unusual nature of the first variant and assumes that a corruption of the written text - *sub* instead of *super* - has occurred. Maffei, however, regards a pyx found under the tomb of the high altar in the church of St. Leonard at Léau in 1860 as confirmation of the prescription of the Liège synod.[114]

In addition to this direct 'parallel application' between the relics and the Eucharist in the *sepulcrum* there is also an indirect one - just as in the act of burial in an actual grave. There is no certainty as to whether the corporal ever performed the function of substitute here. In the 9th century Pope Leo is said to have indicated the possibility of placing it in the *sepulcrum*, with the Eucharist, instead of the relics. However this report is confirmed nowhere else in the sources and is thus regarded by Braun as legendary.[115] Canon 16 of the Council, of Oxford in 1222 does mention it, but not as an accompaniment to the Eucharistic bread: old corporals, no longer suitable for use, must be kept with the relics or burned.[116]

In a completely different situation Eudes of Sully († 1208) puts the corporal with the relics in the *sepulcrum* if "the blood of the Lord has been spilled on it". The same goes for the pall, the chasuble or the alb.[117] These objects are, in fact reckoned to be 'relics' in such circumstances.[118] The same kind of reverence was striven for in the case of remains left after a miracle of Eucharistic change. The chalice with 'flesh and blood' could, for instance, be regarded as a precious relic and be given a place on the high altar. This happened around 1300 at Meerssen near Maastricht.

As already stated in chapter II, in the second half of the 13th century there was a lively debate surrounding the question of whether transubstantiation occurred immediately after the words "This is my body" - that stand taken by the synod of Paris - or not until after the wine

---

[113]Mansi, XXIV, 899, c. 42: "Corpus Domini in honesto loco sub altari vel in armariolo sub clave sollicite custodiatur".

[114]Maffei (1942), 44; King (1965), 78; Nussbaum (1979), 327.

[115]See above n. 68; Braun (1924), I, 629.

[116]Powicke, 111 : "Vetera vero corporalia que non fuerint ydonea in altaribus quando consecrantur loco reliquiarum reponantur vel in presentia archdiaconi comburantur".

[117]PL 212, 65-66, Synodicae Constitutiones, c. 23 : "Si quid ceciderit de sanguine Domini super corporale, rescindendum est ipsum corporale, et in loco reliquiarum observandum. Si palla altaris inde tincta fuerit, rescindenda pars illa, et pro reliquiis servanda. Si super infulam, casulam, vel super albam decurrat, similiter fiat".

[118]The prescriptions formulated by Oxford and Eudes of Sully do not, therefore, refer to "the closing up of the Eucharist in the *confessio* because there are no relics available" in the spirit of Durandus, as Hermann-Mascard (1979), 160-161, writes.

had been consecrated. Caesarius of Heisterbach welcomed the view of
Paris and illustrated his belief with an example. He told of a priest who
had forgotten to put wine in the chalice and at the instant that he broke
the Host above the chalice blood came out of it "as from a cut vein" and
filled the chalice one-third full.[119] This miraculous blood was exposed
for adoration in 1224 and later, as already mentioned, placed under the
high altar in Meerssen.[120] The exposition for adoration had already
occurred half a century earlier in 1171, again in the Normandy town of
Fécamp, after the miraculous blood had been under the high altar for
some time.[121] The miraculous blood of Pavia was also given a place in
the *sepulcrum*.[122] By way of a fourth example we can mention a report
passed down by Lanfranc († 1089). He told his pupil, Guitmund of
Aversa, that when he had been a boy in Italy he had heard how, during
the Mass, a priest was confronted with a miracle of change. In confusion
he sought the advice of his bishop, who had "the flesh and blood of the
Lord" placed in the altar "as great relics".[123]

The Cistercian, Herbert, closes some chapters of his work *On
Miracles*, written in the second half of the 12th century, with the
statement that the miraculous *sacramentum* was kept with all due
reverence in a *sanctuarium* or *sacrarium*, sacred places which could have
been either above or below the altar.[124] It could be that he was not
thinking of the *sepulcrum*, since these miraculous gifts were often kept as
relics in a specially constructed *tabernaculum*, as in Trani.[125] In
Merseburg, Villers and Cologne the *tabernaculum* was a crucifix and

---

[119]ed. Hilka (1937), 20-21, lib I, c. 3: "Sicut de incisis venis sanguis erumpit"; "Qui
(episcopus) precepit, ut, sigillo amoto in testimonium fidei christiane cunctis
supervenientibus et videre volentibus liquor ostenderetur per dies octo. Quod et fecerunt. Est
autem pupurei coloris et ex tempore spissior, utpote duos in calice habens annos, nunc autem
sigillatus est"; synod of Paris: see 55.

[120]Browe (1938), 151, 178.

[121]ibid. 151; ed. Douie (1961), 2, 92-94.

[122]Browe (1938), 39, 151.

[123]PL 149, 1450, *De corporis et sanguinis Christi veritate in eucharistia libri tres*, lib. II:
"calicem illum eadem carne et sanguine Domini diligenter opertum ac sigillatum in medio
altaris inclusit, pro summis reliquiis perpetuo reservandum".

[124]PL 185, 1370, *De Miraculis*, lib. III, c. 20: "et adorantes deificum corpus, cum
honore et reverentia ad ecclesiam detulerunt atque in sanctuario digne collocaverunt"; 1371,
c. 22: " veluti thesaurum incomparabilem, praecepit in ecclesia cum digna veneratione
custodiri"; 1374, c. 28: "et reverentia magna ad ecclesiam reportarunt, atque in sacrario
digne, ut dignum est, reposuerunt".

[125]AASS iun. I, 252, *Acta s. Nicolai peregrini Tranen*. c. 2, n. 87: "Servatur vero haec
reliquia, in tabernaculo argento quod ex speciali affectu fabricavit vir nobilis Fabritius
Cornei. Huic appositae sunt duae particulae Crucis Dominicae".

contained a relic of the True Cross[126] and in Salzburg it was a glass cylinder.[127] In one or two cases small crosses are also found in the *sepulcrum* with the relics, probably as substitutes for the Eucharist.[128]

***

The forms of 'parallel application in concrete use' which we have so far examined came into being in early Christendom or in the early Middle Ages, apart from the combination of the *humiliatio* with the *clamor*, something that was not possible until after the *dismembratio*, when the relics were placed in smaller shrines. The intention of the types of usage have also been discussed: the Eucharist and the relics offered protection to people in their homes, to travellers and to the dying, while they created a 'guarantee' at an oath-taking. But why was it not until the Carolingian era that the particles of Eucharistic bread were placed with the relics in the *sepulcrum*, when the latter had been available since the earliest times? Another question is related to this one: from what point of view or with what intention was this done?

As far as the time of introduction is concerned, a casual reference has been made to the possibility of the scarcity of relics as a reason. However the sources practically always mention a combination of the Eucharist and the relics in the *sepulcrum*. In an attempt to explain this usage Braun makes a few general assumptions which are not placed in any closer relationship with the time the custom came into being. Was the practice an attempt to emphasise the symbolism of the altar as image of Christ? Was there a desire to create permanent residence for the Lord rather than a temporary home during the Mass? Did Christ, king of the martyrs, perhaps belong with the remains of those who had given their blood for him? Were the three particles - or three Hosts - a symbol of the Three-in-One God in heaven, where the martyrs wore their crowns of martyrdom? Was it the desire of Rome, where the custom probably

---

[126]MGH SS XXX 2, 927, *Sigebotonis vita pavlinae*, c. 34: "Stupefactus rex et omnes qui aderant, maxime tamen episcopus, mox lintheo quodam candidissimo sanguinem, qui apparuit, cum magno detersit tremore eumque in crucem, quae pro reliquiis sacris modicum quid Dominici sanguinis retinebat"; for the Cistercian monastery of Villers in Brabant: see Browe (1938), 141 and 151; for the 14th-century cross in the Augustinian monastery in Cologne: Frolow (1961), 521-522, n. 758.

[127]MGH SS IX, 787, *Annales s. Rudberti Salisburgensis*, a. 1238: "hostia corporis et sanguinis Christi in veram carnem et sanguinem transformata est, quae in cristallo perspicaci recepta a fidelibus devote celebratur".

[128] Gillmann (1922), 40; Braun (1924), I, 629.

originated, to emphasise the consecrated character of the altar? Brown shows regret that even Sicardus of Cremona limits himself to mentioning the practice, whereas normally speaking they have no hesitation in providing a mystical explanation. This fact forced Braun to come to the conclusion that we simply do not know.[129]

However in 1926 under an altar in Bellezma in Numidia a vase was discovered which dated at the latest from the 5th or 6th century, and this inspired Gagé to return to the question a few years later. On the lid of the vase the following was indicated: It had served for the *membra Christi*, or the 'limbs of Christ'.[130] The imagery recalls St. Paul who described the relationship between the believers and Christ in the same words in his letter to the Romans (12:4-5) and to the Corinthians (I Cor. 12:27). And yet the inscription on the vase was not speaking of flesh-and-blood believers but of relics that are called *membra Christi*. This should not come as a surprise: after all, were not the relics regarded by the Christians of that time as the martyrs in person?

Gagé demonstrated that the term *membra* was used more often for the relics. A contemporary 5th-century source, *De dogmatibus ecclesiasticis*, stipulates that the Christians worship the *membra Christi* in the relics.[131] The same terminology for the relics can be found in Chrysostom in his commentary on the letters of Paul mentioned above,[132] in Augustine's resistance to the sale of relics,[133] in Gregory the Great's *Liber Sacramentorum*[134] and in the writings of the 12th-century author, Guibert de Nogent, when he criticised the excesses of contemporary veneration of the relics.[135]

---

[129]Braun (1924), II, 661: "Wir wissen es nicht".

[130]Gagé (1929), 139 : "In isto vaso s(an)cto congregabuntur membra X(risti)"; "Ecce locus inquirendi domin(u)m ex toto corde amen Xr(ist)e"; Meer v.d. (1947), 421.

[131]PL 58, 997, *De ecclesiasticis dogmatibus* (Genadii Massiliensis), c. 73 :"Sanctorum corpora, et praecipue beatorum reliquias, ac si Christi membra sincerissime honoranda et basilicas eorum nominibus apellandas. Velut loca divino cultui mancipata, affectu piissimo et devotione fidelissima adeundas credimus"; see also PL 42, 1219, c. 40.

[132]PG 60, 680: "Vellem sepulcrum videre, ubi iacent arma iustitiae, arma lucis, membra nunc viventia, et mortua dum ille viveret, in quibus omnibus vivebat Christus, quae crucifixa erant mundo: membra Christi".

[133]PL 40, 575, *De opere monachorum*, lib. I, c. 28 :"Alii membra martyrum, si tamen martyrum, venditant".

[134]PL 78, 159, c. 152 : "Fac nos Domine, sanctorum tuorum specialiter dicata membra contingere, quorum cupimus patrocinia incessanter habere".

[135]PL 156, 654, *De pignoribus sanctorum*, lib. III, 5 : "Videte ergo ne dum membra Dei quasi pro honore et genio, ac speciali praerogativa ecclesiae vestrae vobis arrogatis".

Gagé emphasised that the suffering of the martyr sanctified his body and turned his relics into *membra Christi*.[136] This close relationship in the community of suffering dominated the comparison, pushed almost to the limits, which Simeon of Thessalonica made between the relics and the body and blood of Christ. This Greek orthodox theologian wrote: "When the sacred relics are placed in the church, this is because they are sanctified as limbs of Christ and as his altars, sacrificed for hi. They are placed on the eminently holy paten because the martyrs share in the same glory as the Lord, now that they have fought the fight for him. They are placed on the consecrated table because they died with Christ and have earned a place at his side on his throne of glory. For this reason too the priest raises the paten above his head, in order to honour them as is honoured the divine mystery itself, the body and blood of the Lord".[137] In this outburst on the part of the author the relics become the personalisation of the martyr and one with the Eucharistic gifts. Gagé also pointed to Ambrose, who had already made the link between the "triumphant victims" and the presence of Christ "as sacrifice". And in a sermon given by Maximus of Turin the altar is said to be the best resting place for the martyrs because the Lord's death is celebrated on it daily.[138] The most compelling reason for the *depositio* of the relics in the altar is, according to Gagé, this mutual relationship of the *membra Christi* with the other *membra Christi*, the Eucharistic gifts. For this reason the consecrated Hosts or particles were able to replace the relics, as expressed in the ritual of consecration used at Vich.[139] We have already noted that the Council of Chelsea implicitly called the Eucharistic gifts relics. Because of their mutual solidarity it was possible for them to be placed together in the *sepulcrum* of the altar and for the Eucharist to replace the relics.

---

[136]Gagé (1929), 145 : "c'est par leur passion que les corps des martyrs sont sanctifiés et leurs reliques devenues les membres du Christ. L'idée de la communauté de la passion domine toute la suite des parallèles entre les reliques et l'hostie eucharistique".

[137]PG 155, 319, c. 116 [*Quare reliquiae martyrum sub altari deponantur*: "Sacrae vero reliquiae prius deponuntur in templum eo quod sanctificata sunt Christi membra et altaria, tanquam propter ipsum immolata. In sacratissimum imponuntur discum, quia parem cum Domino participant honorem, ob ipsum certamina passae. Super consecratam ponuntur mensam, siquidem cum Christo mortuae sunt, et considere cum ipso super thronum gloriae meruerunt. Ideoque super caput cum disco tollit eas pontifex, sicut ipsa divina mysteria, corpus et sanguinem Christi honorans"].

[138]PL 57, 600; Gagé (1929), 147; see above n. 52.

[139]Braun (1924), I, 625 : "Haec sunt reliquiae conditae, videlicet corpus Domini Iesu Christi et cineres S. Felicitatis et filiorum eius".

Nussbaum's assumption - he does not discuss Gagé in this regard -
that the Eucharist was perhaps placed in the *sepulcrum* out of a desire to
decrease the strong religious force ascribed to the relics is supported by
not a single argument. It would also seem to be out of step with the many
forms taken by the reverence, approved by the church, which was paid to
the relics and even more so with the important position occupied by the
patron saint within the community at the period when 'parallel application
in concrete use' came into being.[140]

Although Gagé went deeper into the union in suffering and sacrifice
between the martyr - or his relics - and the Eucharistic gifts, both being
membra Christi, he avoided the question of why this 'parallel application
in concrete use' came into being in the Carolingian period in particular.
He failed to place nuances in the essential significance of the notion of
sacrifice, whether the concept is used by the early Christian writers or by
those working in the 9th century or later.

The change in the theological interpretation of this term round
about 800 can, however, have been of major influence on the change in
the rite of the consecration of the altar which took place at the same
time.[141] The texts taken from Ambrose and Maximus of Turin, quoted
by Gagé, speak respectively of Christ's "presence as sacrifice" and of
"the daily celebration of Christ's death".[142] These descriptions match
those given in the *Leonianum*, a sacramentary going back to Pope Leo I
(† 461), Gelasius I († 496) and Vigilius († 555).[143] The text of the
sacrifice contained in this document goes as follows: " (...) as often as the
commemoration of the sacrifice pleasing to You is celebrated, the work of
our salvation is rendered present or revealed".[144] In the 8th to the 9th
centuries a shift occurred in notions concerning the sacrifice, a shift
which can be illustrated by a change made by the copyists to this text in
the *Gelasianum Vetus*. Whereas originally the sacramental celebration

---

[140]Nussbaum (1979), 188.

[141]Neunheuser (1963); see p. 36.

[142]See above n. 52, 55 and 56.

[143]Martimort (1984), I, 60; II, 61.; Vogel (1986), 37-43.

[144]ed. Mohlberg (1956), 13, 1. 93 : "Da nobis haec quaesumus domine frequentia
mysteria: quia quotiens hostiae tibi placatae commemoratio celebratur, opus nostrae
redemptionis *exeritur*" [Schillebeeckx (1984), 159: "is rendered present" or Casel (1931),
35-36: "is revealed" - *exseritur*].

"rendered present" or "revealed" the sacrifice on the Cross, in Carolingian times the Mass had become "the sacrifice of the Mass".[145]

Furthermore the developments surrounding the 'process of independence of the Eucharist' contributed to this 'notion of sacrifice'. As, indeed, was stated in chapter II, in the early Middle Ages the original prayer of thanks for Jesus' self-sacrifice in the *anamnesis* came to be more and more concentrated on the sacred 'sacrificial gifts' themselves: the bread and wine as the veil over Christ's historical body and blood. Under the carolingian theologians the 'sacrifice' became a dominant theme of the Eucharist.

The liturgical setting reinforced the formation of these views. The preparation of the Offertory gifts was accompanied by private prayer on the part of the priest, which extended in the Roman liturgy to form the Offertory part of the Mass, in which the sacrificial notion of the Eucharist was thrown into even greater relief. The displacement of the altar towards the rear wall of the apse and the position occupied by the priest - between the altar and the congregation - practically eliminated the character of a meal and strengthened the exclusive nature of the sacrificial form.

The desire to see the events of the life of Jesus and His sufferings pictured in the Mass and to explain them in a allegorical fashion, as Amalarius of Metz did, turned the Mass into a 'passion play', a renewal of the historical sacrifice on the Cross.[146]

Moreover both Paschasius Radbertus and the opponents of Berengarius of Tours, who figured in the first and second Eucharistic disputes respectively, only helped to encourage the realistic - not sacramental - view of the Eucharist. Because of not only the realism, but also the allegorical approach and the liturgical context the Eucharistic

---

[145]Schillebeeckx (1984), 159-160 : *exeritur* was changed into *exercitum* and even later *exercetur* (is achieved); The author, following Casel, sees in the expression "the work of salvation" not only the mercy shown but also the timeless elements of the *mysterium*, salvation, the objective deed itself or the suffering and death of Christ as a pneumatic event. This interpretation is a point of theological discussion and is disputed by the theologians who believe that *opus redemptionis* means no more than the *virtus* or the application, the effect of Christ's sacrifice. See: Brou (1959), Vaggaggini (1959), 79 sqq., Diezinger (1961), 137 sqq., Ellenbracht (1963), 45 and Haunerland (1989), 209 sqq. However the 'Effektustheorie' (Gozier, 1986, 28-33) did not appear until Thomas Aquinas and the Scholastic school. This dating thus leaves untouched the suggestion that the 're-writing' in the Carolingian era indicates a shift at the time in the notions concerning the sacrifice; for this notion of the sacrifice and its development, see also: Stevenson (1986), 116 sqq.

[146]TRE I, 90; see p. 34.

bread - "none other than the flesh born of Mary"[147] - entered perhaps into a far more direct relationship with the other realistic remains of the martyrs: the relics in the altar. Once the sacramental sacrifice had become the renewed sacrifice of the Cross, 'space' was created for the placing of the Eucharistic bread, the Jesus essentially present in His act of sacrifice, and the relics, the martyrs really present who had offered themselves up for Him. The altar had, indeed, gone from being a table to becoming most definitely a tomb "in which the relics of Christ and his saints were carefully enshrined".[148]

As regards the disappearance of this 'parallel application in concrete use', which is more obvious than its coming into being, the reasons have already been mentioned: the application did not match the aim of the Eucharist, which was first and foremost instituted to be used as food for the soul. The adoration of the Host, moreover, tended to the 'raising up' of the Eucharistic bread rather than its 'burial'. Finally, therefore, the altar grave was again only used for the relics after centuries during which the particles of the Host had been laid there. Cemented into the altar stone, the relics remained modestly hidden away in the *sepulcrum*. In the end they disappeared almost entirely from the surrounding periphery, where they had decorated the Eucharist, standing in places of honour behind, above and on the altar table. But now we are talking about 1963, or the Second Vatican Council, after which the sacrificial and reliquary altar became once again a table for the Eucharistic meal.

7   THE PLACING ON OR NEAR THE ALTAR

The altar grave formed a single unit with the actual grave of the martyr, or with his relics hidden in a hollow in the altar or in the crypt below. This was not the only way of expressing the relationship between altar and martyr. The relics could also be closely involved with the altar without being an integral part of it. In that case the altar would be known as a 'relic altar' in order to distinguish it from the altar grave. This close relationship between the two was evident, for instance, when an opening

---

[147]Paschasius Radbertus, CC SL 16, 27, *De corpore et sanguine Domini*, c. 3 : "Unde nec mirum Spiritus Sanctus qui hominem Christum in utero virginis sine semine creauit, etiam si ipse panis ac uini substantia carnem Christi et sanguinem inuisibili potentia cotidie per sacramenti sui sanctificationem operatur"; 28, c. 4: "ut sicut de virgine per Spiritum uera caro sine coitu creatur, ita per eundum ex substantia panis ac uini mystice idem Christi corpus et sanguis conscretur"; PL 120, 1277-1278.

[148]Mitchell (1982), 109.

was made in the stipes of the altar where relics could be placed. Only one such altar has remained intact and the medieval sources only make infrequent mention of the type.[1]

A much more usual way of expressing the close link between altar and relics was, from the 6th century, to place the martyr's grave behind the altar as an independent unit. This type of grave was sunk into or stuck out a little above the floor.[2] The oldest example of this type of grave, which are most common in Gaul, is the tomb of St. Martin in the basilica of St. Perpetuus in Tours dated about 470.[3] In order to give added lustre to what was, in fact, a rather unremarkable tomb, pseudo sarcophagi were constructed and placed on top of the grave. Then following the *elevatio* of the relics it became customary to place them definitively above ground in a stone 'coffin', again situated behind the altar. From the Carolingian era onwards this system took over from the floor grave and the latter took a back seat. But some time around the 11th century even this solution was no longer considered adequate. There was an increased desire on the part of the congregation to have eye contact with the saint and this was met by placing the shrine even higher so that, decorated with gold, silver and precious stones, it towered above the altar.

Until the 10th century the mortal remains recovered at the *elevatio* were placed in their entirety in such a shrine, but later a change occurred in this practice at first from the south of France.[4] And thus at the end of that century, for instance, in Tournus the head of St. Valerian was placed in a relic holder in the shape of a head which, the chronicler reports, even bore the features of the saint.[5] Sometimes part of the remains was put back in the original grave or shared among various reliquaries.[6] These could be small chests or cupboards made of wood, ivory or metal but were also of anthropomorphic chape, as in the case of St. Valerian, corresponding to the nature and shape of the relics: heads, arms, hands

---

[1] Braun (1924), I, 207-220; II, 545 sqq.

[2] MGH SS XX, 669, *Casus Monasterii Petrihusensis*, lib. V: "supereminens pavimento quasi duobus palmis " - *elevatio* of St. Gebhard (996) in 1134.

[3] Hubert (1961), 219.

[4] Keller (1951), 82.

[5] ibid. n. 55 a : "Caput vero iuxta memoratum loculum in imagine quadam velut ad similitudinem martyris ex auro et gemmis pretiosissimis decenter effigiata separatim erigitur" (quotation taken from: Pierre-François Chifflet S.J., *Histoire de l'abbaye royale et de la ville de Tournus*, Dijon, 1664, Preuves, 48).

[6] MGH SS X, 351, *Gestorum abb. Trudonensium Continuatio secunda*, lib. IV, c. 1: "Sumptis ergo de ossibus eius (s. Liberti) et sacro cinere necessariis reliquiis, reliqua omnia in sciniolo ad hoc opus preparato cum reverentia reposita"; Beissel (1976), II, 87.

and feet. Statues - known as *majestas* - were also constructed to contain the relics. The *majestas* of the staring-eyed Sainte-Foy at Conques dates from approximately 1000.[7] The two gold hands made to contain the relics of Ss. Germanus and Stephen, ordered by Bishop Goderich of Auxerre, date from 933 and the bust of St. Candidus is from approximately 1150. From around the same period there is also the Madonna of Clermont-Ferrand, which served as a model for many 'statues of pilgrimage' until the end of the 12th century. Usually a space, covered with rock-crystal, was hollowed out in the back, sometimes in the chest, to contain the relics.[8]

These smaller reliquaries were placed above the altar in the retable, also known as the retable.[9] When the altar was moved back against the wall of the apse, as a consequence of the privatisation and clericalisation of the celebration of the Mass as described in chapter II, the opportunity was provided for this kind of separate siting of the reliquary. In addition, the familiar *capsae*, *bursae* and little boxes continued to serve their purpose. These - known as 'separate relics' - were kept in all kinds of places, both inside and outside the church building, until the 9th century. A suitable site for this was the entrance to the church where the church-goer could venerate the relics on entry. The atrium and the sacristy also served as a resting place. Within the church itself preference was given to conspicuous plinths or capitals of pillars,[10] protrusions of the wall around the altar, the choir seats,[11] or a cross hanging in the priests' choir.[12]

The altar table itself was kept free of relics until the 9th century, apart from short periods of time such as the evening and night preceding the consecration of a church or whenever someone passing through required a temporary place to put his *pignora*. From the 9th century onwards a change came about: reliquaries which could be easily handled were accorded a place on the altar during such ceremonies as exposition

---

[7]Keller (1951), 77, 81, 86, 89; Hubert (1982); *Lexicon des Mittelalters* III (1985), 142: "Conques".

[8]Keller (1951), 78-79, 86; (1956), 73; Beissel (1976), 86; Aalberts (1985), 49.

[9]LW I, 108 ; Braun (1924), II, 556-561, 631.

[10]MGH SS III, 748-749, *Thietmari Chron.* lib. II, c. 11 : "In omnibusque columnarum capitibus sanctorum reliquias diligenter includi iussit"; Keller (1975); Bosman (1985).

[11]Appuhn (1961), 80: "Die Inthronisation der Heiligen sollte andeuten, dass die Heiligen unsichtbar an der Feier des heiligen Mahles teilnehmen".

[12]Hermann-Mascard (1975), 175: "Ces croix surplombant le chœur, le lien entre la relique et l'autel était assuré"; Keller (1971), 70-73, examples from the Merovingian and Carolingian eras.

or celebration of the Mass. In the latter case they were in the close vicinity of the Eucharist and the closeness was maintained when the Sacrament was reserved on the altar.

About the same period that the relics were placed on the altar table the Eucharist was also given a place here. Except for here and there in private dwellings, the sacristy had been the only place where the Eucharist had previously been reserved for the sick.[13] Now the Sacrament was given a place inside the church building: either on, close to or suspended above the altar. It was contained in a *capsa* or a pyx, a small 'Eucharistic tower'.[14] Dating from the time of the *Admonitio Synodalis* there is abundant witness to the place of reservation of the Eucharist either on or above the *mensa*, although this place was never imposed as generally obligatory until the end of the Middle Ages.[15]

In general it would seem that in the beginning no particular safety measures were taken, and yet the danger that mice would eat the Eucharist or that it would be profaned would suggest that precautions were required. From the 11th century, for instance, the *columba* or metal dove, hanging on chains above the altar, came into use.[16] A small pyx or linen cloth containing the Eucharist could be placed in a hollow in the back of the dove. Another method was to place the pyx, sometimes together with the relics, in a separate tabernacle or *scrinium*. The fixed altar tabernacle was extremely exceptional in the Middle Ages, though the ambry - *armarium* -mentioned by Rupert of Deutz († 1135) witnesses to the fact that the Eucharist contained in a *fenestra* of this kind was not affected by fire.[17]

These developments were codified in 1215 by the Fourth Lateran Council in the decree issued by Pope Innocent III, which prescribed that the Eucharist should be kept under lock and key in all churches. This

---

[13]and for the *Sancta-Ritus*, see p. 34.

[14]King (1965), 29; Dijk v.(1957), 27-31.

[15]Braun (1924), II, 585 sqq.; Nussbaum (1979), 314-319, 581.

[16]PL 149, 723, *Consuetudines Cluniacenses Udalrici*: "Praedictam autem pixidem (...) diaconus de columba iugiter pendente super altare, bene cum linteolo de pulvere exterius tersa, abstrahit, et super dextrum cornu sub coopertorio ponit, missaque finita in eodem loco reponit"; ed. Herrgott (1726), 226; King (1965), 41-45; Nussbaum (1979), 356-361.

[17]ed. Grundmann (1966), 445, *De incendio*, c. 5: "Pixidem ligneam et in ea corpus dominicum habuerat secus altare de more repositum in fenestra sive absida introrsus in muro tegulis ligneis compacta cum ostiolo et sera"; PL 170, 337; Lengeling (1966), 163; Martimort (1984), II, 263-264.

decree was repeated by many synods in subsequent centuries.[18] The 'tabernacle thus had to conform to this requirement, whether it was a wall tabernacle next to the altar, a separate shrine on the altar table or a hanging pyx. In France and England it was often in the shape of a dove. Moreover during the 14th and 15th centuries in Germany, the Low Countries and Bohemia the tower-shaped housings for the Sacrament came into fashion, the *Sakramenthäuser*, masterworks of wood carving built backing on to a pillar.[19] The Host exposed in these shrines demonstrated how the function of the reserved Eucharist was changing: it was no longer availability of communion for the sick that took centre stage but devotion on the part of the faithful.

The Lateran Council referred to above also prescribed safety measures for the relics in canon 62: they were no longer to be exposed or venerated outside the *capsa*,[20] a regulation issued to prevent desecration, deceit and theft. The *capsa* named in this canon was the most frequently used type of reliquary until 1100. We have already seen mention of it made in canon 2 of the Council of Chelsea in 816, where it was used for both Eucharist and relics.[21]

We have already seen this mutual exchange in usage in the case of the 'chrismale' which became the *chrismarium*. The same phenomenon occurred in the case of the pyx, a term used from the 9th century onwards for a tower-shaped Eucharistic container, usually of precious metal or ivory. The name "tower of ivory" given to the Virgin Mary in her litany which has gone into obscurity possibly refers to this.[22] During

---

[18]COD, 244, c. 20: "Statuimus, ut in cunctis ecclesiis chrisma et eucharistia sub fideli custodia clavibus adhibitis conserventur, ne possit ad alia temeraria manus extendi, ad aliqua horribilia vel nefaria exercenda"; King (1965), 67 sqq.

[19]Braun (1924), II, 588, 599-616; King (1965), 83; Nussbaum (1979), 390-393, illustr. 30, 32; Rubin (1961), 292.

[20]COD, 263, c. 62: "Cum ex eo quod quidam sanctorum reliquias exponunt venales et eas passim ostendunt, christianae religioni sit detractum saepius, ne detrahatur in posterum praesenti decreto statuimus, ut antiquae reliquiae amodo extra capsam non ostedantur nec exponantur venales"; ed. Pontal (1971), 164, Le synodal de l'Ouest, c. 40; Guth (1970), 139; Hermann-Mascard (1975), 214-215.

[21]See p. 187, n. 69; LP 374 : "Hic beatissimus vir in sacrario beati Petri apostoli capsam argenteam in angulo obscurissimo iacentem (...) repperit. Oratione itaque facta (...) eoque ablato, inferius crucem diversis ac pretiosis lapidibus perornatam inspexit"; see also 434; ed. Durandus (1614), *Rationale* lib. I, c. 3. n. 25: "Et not. quod capsa in qua hostiae consecratae servantur, significat corpus virginis gloriosae"; Mansi XXV, 178, Lucana synodus, anno 1308, De Corpore Domini nostri Iesu Christi in capsa tenendo : "Corpus autem D.N.I.C. in cassa vel pixide (...) altari appensa et in sacrario ne ab indiscretis vel bestiis tangi possit cum multa reverentia teneatur "; Braun (1940), 40.

[22]Dijk v. (1957), 30; Bredero (1960), in statement XI, gives a different interpretation and refers us to the text "Collum tuum sicut turris eburnea" (Cant. 7:4), which, in this context, can be explained as a call to Mary as mediatrix.

the 11th century we find a few cases of a pyx as meaning a reliquary and in the 13th and 14th century this was no longer exceptional.[23] We have pointed out that the shape of a closed tower could have originated in the model provided by the tower-shaped rock grave of Christ.[24]

The reliquaries all showed the same preference for the tower shape. They could be closed or open and transparent in order to serve as *ostensorium*. In this guise they seemed more to indicate the Gothic cathedral and the Heavenly Jerusalem than the Holy Sepulchre.[25] The latter is recalled by a closed cylindrical example in the British Museum dating from around the year 1000. The tomb is pictured on it with soldiers keeping watch on Easter morning.[26]

About the same time that the *columba* came into use as place of reservation for the Eucharist it was also used as reliquary. But in this case the hollow was no longer in the back but in front and was protected by a piece of glass so that the whole could function as an *ostensorium*. This was in accordance with the prescription issued by the Lateran Council but also enabled the relic thus venerated to be seen. In the case of one 12th-century *columba* in Lyon Braun assumes that it was first used as a Eucharistic dove and at a later date contained the "milk and hair" of the Virgin Mary.[27] A similar reliquary, part of the treasure of the abbey of St. Caesarius in Arles, changed in reverse order from reliquary to Eucharistic container. A report from 1473 states that in the hollow in the front of this dove-shaped container the body of Christ was placed on the feast day of St. Caesarius. The Eucharist had thus replaced the relics: the

---

[23]Rupin (1890), 202, n. 1: in the 12th-century altar at St-Maurice de Chinon (Indre-et-Loire) an enamel pyx was found "pleine de reliques", the same being true of the Hubert treasure (Belgium) and in the inventory of Boniface VIII († 1303) "unam pixidem rotundam argenteam (...) et sunt in ea reliquie plurium sanctorum"; Braun (1940), 47-48; Maffei (1942), 44; Dijk v. (1957), 33-35.

[24]PL 72, 93, ps. Germanus, *Expositio brevis antiquae liturgiae Gallicanae*, ep.1 : "Corpus vero Domini ideo defertur in turribus, quia monumentum Domini in similitudinem turris fuit scissum in petra"; King ((1965), 41; Mitchell (1983), 51; Raible (1908), 152: he points to the tower being the symbol of the Lord as safe refuge (Ps. 61:4; Prov. 18:10); see p. 34.

[25]Brandmann (1974), 78; Bosman (1985a), 308-312.

[26]registration n.: 55,10-31,1 in Case 2 , Medieval Gallery, Room 42; Dalton (1909), 45-47, n. 47; Dijk v. (1957), 29 and illustr. 2.

[27]PL 156, 1013, *De miraculis s. Mariae Laudunensis*: "Postmodum cruces aureas et phylacteria confringens, inter caetera et etiam unam columbam auream confregit, quae pro lacte et capillis sanctae Mariae, ut et ferebatur introrsus reconditis multum erat famosa et honorabilis, unde et in maioribus festis super eius altare solebat appendi"; Braun (1924), II, 609.

dove stood on a silver pediment and hade become a Eucharistic monstrance.[28]

The 1338 inventory of the church of St. Francis in Assisi lists *ciboria* which did not serve the usual function of container for the Eucharist but instead were meant to contain relics. These *ciborium*-shaped reliquaries came into use in the 13th century at the same time that ciboria began to be used for the Eucharist. They often show such an astonishing resemblance to the Eucharistic ciboria that it is impossible to say for which use they were intended. However a reliquary of this type is rarely referred to in the late medieval sources as a *"ciborium"*.[29]

From the 14th century onwards the *tabernaculum* could also be a reliquary. Originally it had been a cloth hanging over the place where the Eucharist was reserved, whether the latter was a dove, a small cupboard - *arca* -, a *capsa* or a *vasculum* - pyx, *ciborium*. Subsequently the term came to be applied to the containers themselves. The *tabernaculum* then signified a separate shrine standing on the altar, a *Sakramenthaus*, or a niche in the wall, which was known as the wall tabernacle.[30] The *tabernaculum*, in its small cupboard form, usually served only to contain the Eucharist, but the relics could also be kept in it.[31] If a reliquary was meant by the term *tabernaculum* it was usually a pyx-shaped container on a foot, used for the exposition of the relics.[32] Such 'relic tabernacles' were the opposite side of the coin to the *ostensoria* discussed in the next chapter. The association of names and their simultaneous presence on the altar table were both consequence of and encouragement to 'parallel application in concrete use' and 'transposition of forms of reverence', to which the present subject forms a bridge.

---

[28]Gay (1887), 415 : "Unum reliquiarium argenti factum ad modum unius colombe, in quo portatur corpus Christi die fenestivitatis eiusdem, cum uno vitro in pectore, et habet unum pedem argenti" (Inventory of the abbey S. Césaire d'Arles p. 169); Raible (1908), 152; Nussbaum (1979), illustr. 39.

[29]Braun (1940), 59-60, 220-238.

[30]LW II, 2629; Dijk v. (1957), 35-37.

[31]Corblet (1886) II, 158; Braun 1924), II, 567.

[32]Braun (1940), 58-59.

7.1 The 'relic altar'

The altar grave was hardly a source of inspiration as far as veneration of the relics was concerned. The relics were, after all, hidden deep inside and invisible. The floor grave already referred to, with its carved pseudo-sarcophagus, provided greater opportunity. The 7th-century authors, writing in the *vitae*, make frequent mention of graves of this type, such as in the life of St. Gallus († 630)[33], St. Eligius († 660)[34] and St. Audoin[35]

And when graves above ground level became more the trend, the need remained to decorate the tomb with tower-shaped constructions, covered with reliefs, gold and silver. Detailed descriptions of these relic altars, especially from the 8th, 9th and 10th centuries, have come down to us.[36] The tomb monuments were placed close to or up against the altar as a sign if mutual unity, sometimes emphasised by a baldachin or *reba* covering the entire area.[37] Even as late as the 12th century, interest in these graves would seem to have continued. Abbot Suger († 1151) of St. Denis proved this by having a grave prepared behind the altar in the abbey church for the remains of St. Denis and his faithful companions. It became a focus of veneration, and was fitted out with a majestic construction with carvings, jewels and enamel.[38]

Meanwhile a third variant of the relic altar had come into fashion: the mortal remains were placed in shrines which were placed even higher than the sarcophagus, so that they could easily seen from the back of the church. Like the former grave coffins, they stood lengthwise at right-

---

[33]MGH SRM IV, 275, lib. II, n. 32 : "Sepulcrum deinceps inter aram et parietem peractum est"; n. 36 : "sancti corporis gleba in sarcofago digno inter aram et parietem sepulturae tradebatur atque super illud memoria meritis electi Dei congruens aedificabatur".

[34]PL 87, 517, lib. II, c. 6 : "corpus summa cum diligentia citra altare transposuit; tumbam denique ex auro argentoque et gemmis miro opere desuper fabricavit".

[35]AASS 24 aug. IV, 819, *Vita altera*, c. V,43: "Quod sacratissimum corpus tam alienum inventum est ab omni corruptione, quam primum vivens decoratum fuit virginitate. Fecit super eius sepulchrum repam mirifice constructam, in qua misit argentum maximi talenti, aurum plurimum, et gemmas optimas."

[36]The chroniclers gave a name to a grave of this type depending on the situation: *arca* or *mausoleum, memoria, ciborium* or *lectulus, reba, culmen* or *turris*; see Braun (1924) II, 546-554; Nussbaum (1965), 307.

[37]MGH SS II, 268, *Pauli Geta episcoporum Mettensium*: "Hic fabricare iussit una cum adiutorio Pipini regis rebam (feretri operculum, umbraculum) sancti Stephani prothomartyris, et altare ipsius atque cancellos, presbiterium arcusque per girum"; 564, *Vita Chrodegangi* (766), c. 21.

[38]PL 186, 1231, *Sygerii Liber de rebus in admin. sua gestis*, c. 31, 32. en 1238-1254, *Libellus de consecratione ecclesiae S. Dionysii;* ed. Lecoy de la Marche (1867), 192-196; 211-238.

angles to the edge of the altar table. The smaller reliquaries were placed to catch the eye in the rear wall of the altar, the retable or the predella, from where they were solemnly exposed or carried in procession.

The relic altars still existing in churches and crypts give us some idea of the exact position they occupied relative to the altar table in cases where the sources fail to inform us or simply state that they were *super altare*: on the altar. In 1025, for example, on the orders of Abbot Gerard of Fontenelle, the bones of St. Wulfram, Bishop of Sens, were exhumed to be placed in a new monastery church. The bones were placed temporarily in a simple shrine because there were no funds available for an expensive metal chest. The shrine was placed *super sacrum altare*, where the faithful could venerate the saint and would not have to try in vain to implore his intercession.[39]

The saint belonged on the altar. During the *humiliatio* he lost this privileged position. The examples already quoted can be supplemented by the tale of the events surrounding the abbey of Malmédy in the diocese of Liège, a sister foundation of the monastery of Stavelot, where the relics were repeatedly removed from the altar and replaced. Archbishop Anno of Cologne, with the formal support of the emperor, Henry IV (who was still a minor at the time), laid claim to Malmédy.

Two parties arose in the monastery, the majority who wished to accommodate the archbishop and a minority, inspired by the abbot of Stavelot, who were not prepared to budge an inch and wished to remain in the diocese of Liège. When the demands became more acute in 1065, both groups started a prayer campaign around the shrine, placed on the ground, of a prince of the church from the diocese who had died in 670, St. Remaclus. Abbot Theoderik sought support outside the monastery for his point of view and, on his return from the goodwill trip, had the shrine put back in its original place.[40] The affair dragged on and the ceremony with the shrine was repeated in 1066, the year in which the abbot succeeded in getting his monastery back. It was not until Henry returned

---

[39] AASS OSB III,1, 351, *Acta invent. s. Wulframni ep. Senon*: "Inventum igitur, ut praemissum est, sancti Praesulis Vultramni pretiosum corpus, et in ligneo locello pro tempore aptato, (quia nimirum tanta erat adhuc loci pauperies, ut unde decentius fieri deberet pretiosi metalli species deesset) cum reverentia et honore reconditum super sacrum altare repositum est".

[40] MGH SS XI, 442, lib. I, c. 9: "Placuit ergo communi consilio fratrum venerabile corpus domini nostri Remacli exponi in medium, sicque cum eo cui fiebat iniustitia, propensius esse supplicandum"; 443 c. 12: "Interea domnus abbas fratres, quos tristes reliquerat, habuit revisere, veniensque venerandum corpus domini nostri et sanctique Remacli invenit depositum in pavimento iam multos dies iacuisse".

Remaclus' staff that the monks restored the shrine to its place on the altar.[41]

But that did not settle the question. Anno of Cologne refused to concede defeat and in 1068 pleaded his case before the pope. The abbot had anticipated this move, with the result that the pope referred the two parties to the emperor, whereupon Theoderik left no stone unturned in his attempts to justify his standpoint. In 1071 he ordered the relics of Remaclus to be taken to Liège in order to have them reinforce his plea to the court. During the negotiations, in which Anno of Cologne naturally took part, the monks had placed the relics on the altar of the church of the Holy Trinity. There they chanted litanies, penitential psalms and the *Veni Creator Spiritus* - "Come Holy Spirit, Creator".[42] Then they went in procession to the crypt of St. Lambert, to the church of Our Lady and then back to the Holy Trinity altar where they once again placed the relics.[43]

Finally the monks, shrine and all, presented themselves to Henry, who was at the time taking a meal with Archbishop Anno and other imperial notables. Indignant at feeling that they had been left standing at the door, they forced their way in and plonked the shrine down on the table. Although this somewhat rude gesture caused no small measure of consternation, the result was that Theoderik got his way for the second time.[44] Remaclus retained a place of honour in Stavelot. In a 17th-century drawing of his altar in something like 1150 (the altar has long since disappeared) his shrine can be seen occupying an extremely privileged position in the middle of retable measuring 9 square metres. All around it there are depictions of scenes from his life.[45]

On the occasion of an *elevatio* it could happen that part of the relics were placed inside and part on the altar. This was a method employed by Abbot Theomar († 1125) of the monastery of St. Mansuetus in Toul. An anonymous monk has left us the account of a precious find that was made

---

[41]ibid. 446, c. 18: "cum apud nos esset cum regina, bonum hoc ipsi sancto Remaclo per baculum ipsius reddiderat, cum etiam sacrum lipsanum expositum hac de causa in medio, ipse revehens in loco eius condignis laudibus relocaverat".

[42]ibid. 452, lib. II, c. 6: "Itaque assistentes in spiritu humilitatis sanctae Trinitatis altari, super quod iacebat venerabile corpus piisimi patroni nostri, *Veni Creator Spiritus* usque ad finem ymnificavimus".

[43]ibid. 452, c. 7: "Etenim scrinium sancti, quod impositum erat sanctae Trinitatis altari, cum repentino sonitu visum est in aera sublevari".

[44]MGH SS XI, 433-461, *Triumphus S.Remacli de Malmudariense coenobio*; another example MGH SS XI, 156; XV 2, 642-644; AASS 5 febr. II, 676.

[45]Koldewij (1985a), 38, 51 illustr. 6 a.

when the high altar was being demolished: a gravestone decorated with gold and precious stones on which was carved the following inscription: "In this grave relics of the apostles Peter and Paul lie, together with a particle of the True Cross of the Lord". Other relics were also found. Theomar ordered the first find to be placed in the new high altar and the second the be placed in a gilded shrine on the altar of the apostles.[46]

Another altar dedicated to the apostles, this time in Vicogne near Valenciennes, was built as a relic altar in 1150 by the Premonstratensians after they had come into possession of the relics of three companions of St. Ursula. The bones were placed in three separate shrines which were mounted above the altar in a retable, painted in beautiful colours and decorated with shining gold.[47]

Sometimes a procession went all the way through the town before the shrines were set in their final resting places on the altar. This is what happened with the relics of Ss. Eucherius and Trudo, that were discovered in 1169 under the vault behind the altar. The wooden shrines were replaced by brand new ones made of gold, and after the procession they again occupied their privileged place behind the altar under a shared baldachin.[48]

Usually it was the miraculous cures that legitimised the *elevatio* and installation. Even the birds acquitted themselves well. During the *elevatio* in 1320 of the Franciscan, St. Gandolf, who had died in 1260 on the island of Sicily, swallows burst into song. The saint's mortal remains were carried to the steps leading up to the high altar, where the bishop had ordered that they be purified by priests. During the night the birds, in their nests attached to the roof beams, began to twitter as if singing in choir, since they had been very attached to the saint whom they had obeyed by falling silent during one of his sermons. He asked the animal kingdom to keep silent, otherwise the people would not hear his words. This orchestra caused the priests to break into the *Te Deum Laudamus* -

---

[46]MGH SS XV, 933-934, *Narratio rerum in monasterio S. Mansueti gestarum*: "In hoc conditorio sitae sunt reliquiae sanctorum apostolorum Petri et Pauli, insuper etiam de ligno Domini (...) Inventa sunt ibi, opitulante misericordia Dei, praeter undecim de ossibus capitis dentes septem, sexdecim etiam frusta in modum tesserae quadratae de ligno triumphali vivificae crucis, quae omnia extunc et modo in scrinio deaurato super altare sanctorum apostolorum conservantur".

[47]MGH SS XXIV, 300, *Historia Monasterii Viconiensis*: "desuper altare apostolorum in ipso fronte capitis ecclesiae, ut intuentibus facile patet, cum reverentia et timore collocaverunt"; see also: MGH SS XVII, 26, *Annales S. Dissibodi* a. 1143.

[48]MGH SS X, 296-297, *Gesta abb. Trudonensium*, lib. X, c. 16; 353-354, *Continuatio secunda*, lib. IV, c. 6: " Indicto itaque tam fratribus quam populo celebri ieiunio, eos circa civitatem sollempni processione ferri fecit, et post missarum sollempnia de eis rite celebrata, post altare capellae vola inclusos ad perpetuum nostri munimen eos recondidit".

"We praise Thee, o God". The bones were placed on the altar and the fame of the miracles attributed to them spread from the altar throughout the length and breadth of Sicily.[49]

These accounts are taken from the hagiographies. But the inventories and the reliquary altars still in existence - whose richly decorated predellas and retables have long since disappeared - also provide us with information. An ancient inventory drawn up in 1382 relating to the abbey church of Cluny includes the fact that the high altar comprised a shrine of Pope Marcellus († 309) and one of St. Hugh († 1109) with silver relief.[50]

A somewhat spectacular example is that provided by the 14th-century panelled altar or tryptych in the church of the Cistercian abbey in Marienstatt, consisting of three horizontal sections: twelve above a row of statues, in the centre twelve reliquaries - busts with circular windows - and below thirteen spaces closed off with Gothic tracery, also intended for relics.[51] This is just one example of reliquary altars which are still in existence here and there in churches and treasure houses, constituting major attractions for the astonished tourist.

The development of the relic altar demonstrates an increase in the number of relics which were accorded an increasingly important position around the altar table, encouraged by an irresistible desire to see the relics. From the simple grave in the floor behind the altar, via the more elevated tomb and then the shrine above the altar, from the 12th century onwards the relic altar finally became an impressive retable, in which the ever-multiplying numbers of relics came to represent the saints, the apostles and the martyrs, all commemorated in the Canon of the Mass. The next step was the presence of the relics on the altar table itself.

---

[49]AASS 10 sept. V, 710, *Vita b. Gandolphi confessoris*, c. III,38: "Elevatio itaque corpore et in altare cum reverentia posito quanta devotione ubique Siciliae miraculorum eius divulgata est fama".

[50]*Revue de l'art chrétien 38* (Paris, 1888), 199; n. 155, 156.

[51]Koldeweij (1986a), 38; illustr. 11; Raible (1908), 234-236: built in 1324, presently in a museum in Wiesbaden; Legner (1989), 92 sqq.; other examples in: Braun (1924), II, 555-573, Beissel (1976), II, 19-40, Keller (1965), Ehresmann (1982) and Decker (1985).

7.2 Altar table relics and altar Sacrament

In the previous paragraphs we saw that even in the time of Gregory of Tours the relics were placed on the altar during the vigil of the consecration of the church of St. Julian. Elsewhere Gregory tells of his own experiences regarding an itinerant confidence trickster who carried around what purported to be the relics of St. Felix and of the deacon Vincentius. The man also carried a cross from which dangled ampoules filled with holy oil. The bishop of Tours was in the middle of dinner when the pseudo-prophet arrived at the church of St. Martin and sent him a message to say that he should come quickly to view his treasury of relics. It was not until the following day that Gregory realised, from the insolent behaviour of the man, that he was dealing with a charlatan. On the evening in question he was not yet aware of the fact and he had thought it too late an hour to go to the church so he had passed on the message to the confidence trickster: "Just place the sacred relics 'on the altar' and I shall come and have a look tomorrow".[52]

In these two examples the relics were only briefly present on the altar table. The many relics brought back to the abbey of Glastonbury by Abbot Ticca were somewhat longer on the altar. However Braun warns that it is possible that the storyteller, William of Malmesbury († 1143), could have been tempted by the lively manner of recounting events usual at the time and identified with habits current in the 8th century.[53]

From the 9th century onwards there is such an increase in sources telling of relics being placed on the *mensa* of the altar, sometimes for long periods of time, that the custom must have become general. An early example from the 9th century is found in the account given by Einhard of the translation of the relics of Bishop Marcellinus and of Peter the Levite, both of whom were martyred under Diocletian in the early 4th century. In 827 the biographer of Charlemagne previously mentioned had contacted the "relic merchant", Deusdona, in order to obtain the martyrs' relics from Rome. They were intended for his basilica which had recently been constructed near Michelstadt. The dealer, who was also a deacon, left Aachen for Rome in the company of Einhard's *notarius*, Ratlecus. They visited the monastery of St. Medardus at Soissons where Hilduin was

---

[52]See p. 180; MGH SRM I,1, 418, *Hist. Franc.* lib. IX, c. 6: "Cui nos, quia hora iam praeterierat, diximus: Requiescant beatae reliquiae super altarium, donec mane procedemus ad occursum earum".

[53]PL 179, 1693, *De antiquitate Glastonensis ecclesiae*: "Haec igitur super altare locatae reliquiae non parum reverentiae loco adiecere"; Braun (1924), II, 554.

abbot, and he in his turn entered into a contract with the deacon to obtain the relics of St. Tiburtius, also to be brought back from Rome. For this reason, at their departure three people left Soissons, one representing Hilduin. However when they were returning home with the relics, that they had obtained thanks to a dream, the companion from Soissons is said to have stolen part of the precious baggage from the *capsa* and to have taken it to Hilduin. After some time had passed, Einhard discovered what had happened and immediately began to pressurise Hilduin to return the stolen relics. The place chosen for the handing over was the Palatinate church in Aachen, where Hilduin was to lay the relics on the altar of the Virgin Mary. Einhard then took them in solemn procession to Mulinheim, which was re-named 'Seligenstadt', for it was to here that the relics were translated which Ratlecus had brought back with him. On arrival the *capsa* was given pride of place on the altar table directly in front of the ancient shrine whose contents had been interfered with. Later the relics were placed together in a single shrine at the request of the saints made during an apparition.[54]

At the end of the 9th century on the occasion of the *translatio* of St. Walburga - who had been Boniface's helper and was also related to the saint - a few particles of the skeleton were placed on the *mensa*. The particles were taken to the monastery of Monheim at the request of a certain Sister Liubila, where in the presence of the people they were given a central place on the altar in the church of the Saviour.[55]

An anonymous 9th-century document, the *Admonitio Synodalis*, reports that in addition to the relics the Eucharist was also placed on the altar. The text reads: "The altar should be covered with pure linen; nothing lese may be placed on it except the *capsae* containing the relics, the four Gospels and the pyx with the body of the Lord as *viaticum* for the sick; other things should be placed elsewhere in a suitable place".[56] This prescription was given papal sanction by ascribing it to Pope Leo IV

---

[54]MGH SS XV,1, 246, *Einardi translatio et miracula ss. Marcellini et Petri*, lib. III, c. 3: "Hildoinus (...) memoratis reliquiis de oratorio suo ubi servabantur sublatis atque basilicae sanctae Dei genetricis inlatis altarique superpositis, me, ut eas susciperem, fecit acciri (...) Exin sublatam de altari eandem capsam manibus meis inposuit (...) Processimus inde paulatim cum crucibus et caereis, laudantes Domini misericordiam, usque ad oratorium quod erat in domo nostra vili opere constructum"; Geary (1978), 52; Schefers (1990).

[55]MGH SS XV,1, 542, *Ex Wolfgardi Haserenensis Miraculis Walburggis Monheimensibus*, 10: "Postquam vero eiusdem virginis sacrosancta xenia in basilicam, quae sita est in honore opificis et salvatoris domini Iesu Christi, cum populi laude plenaria sunt super altare locata".

[56]PL 132, 456; PL 115, 677, *Leonis Papae IV Homilia*, VIII: "Super altare nihil ponatur nisi capsae, et reliquiae, et quatuor Evangelia, et pixis cum corpore Domini ad viaticum infirmis; caetera in nitido loco recondantur"; Nussbaum (1979), 314.

(† 855).[57] It was not without influence since it is quoted in several sources. The first time was at a synod in Reims in 867, chapter five of which must have been written in practically the same terms. The precise text has not come down to us but both Abbot Regino of Prüm († 915)[58] and Bishop Burchard of Worms († 1025)[59] cite it in the 10th and 11th centuries respectively as a prescription issued by the Rheims synod. Ulrich of Augsburg († 973) also quoted the *Admonitio Synodalis* in a pastoral sermon.[60] In the same period it was repeated at a synod by the remarkable but awkward prince of the church, Ratherius of Verona († 974).[61] The authors named here all agreed with the position taken by the *Admonitio*.

These statements made by church leaders and the accounts of translations and expositions mention the placing of the relics on the altar so often that it would seem that since the 9th century there was no problem in breaking with the tradition of the early Middle Ages that this was one thing that one should not do. And yet there are signs of resistance. The scholaster of Fulda, Rudolf († 865), describes at the time of the issuing of the *Admonitio Synodalis* the miracles that accompanied some translations in the diocese. What is remarkable is that he sketches various situations in which the relics were placed near the altar but not on it, not even for a short time.[62]

[57]Dijk v.(1957), 47.

[58]ed. Wasserschleben (1964), 52: *Ex Consilio Remensi*, c. 5: "Observandum est, ut mensa Christi, i.e. altare, ubi corpus dominicum consecretur, ubi sanguis eius hauritur, ubi sanctorum reliquiae reconduntur, ubi preces et vota populi in conspectu Dei a sacerdote offeruntur cum omni veneratione honoretur et mundissimis linteis et palliis diligentissime cooperiatur nihilque super eo ponatur, nisi capsae cum sanctorum reliquiis, et quattuor evangelia. Expleta missa, calix et sacramentorum liber cum vestibus sacerdotalibus in mundo loco sub sera recondantur".

[59]PL 140, 693, *decr.* lib. III, c. 97.

[60]PL 135, 1071, *Sermo Synodalis*.

[61]PL 136, 559; d'Achery, I, col. 377, *Synodica ad presbyteros*: "Nulla foemina ad altare accedat, nec calicem Domini tangat. Corporale mundissimum sit. Altare coopertum de mundis linteis, super altare nihil ponatur nisi capsae et reliquiae, aut forte quatuor Evangelia, et pyxida cum corpore Domini ad viaticum infirmis, caetera in nitido loco recondantur".

[62]MGH SS XV,1, 332, *Rudolfi miracula sanctorum in Fuldenses ecclesias translatorum*: "iuxta altare in parte meridiana feretrum cum sacris cineribus posuerunt"; "abbas (...) ossa sanctorum martyrum (...) intulit in ecclesiam (...) atque in arca saxea inclusis eorum plumbeis oculis, ad orientem altaris collocavit"; 333: "Reliquorum vera sanctorum ossa (...) in basilica beati Bonifacii martyris in absida orientali posuerat (...) anno ab incarnatione Domini 835"; "Nam cum adhuc feretrum cum sacris ossibus (sancti Venantii) iuxta altare esset positum"; 334: "ac per hoc sub divo loco editiore altari erecto, ac feretro iuxta illud posito, rursus missarum solemnia celebravimus".

This could, of course, be explained by the tradition still existing at the time, but the reports given by Rudolfus were perhaps manifestations of his own attitude, that the altar table was not a suitable place for the relics. Odo of Cluny († 942) leaves no room for doubt in his tendentious story regarding the relics of St. Walburga already mentioned. These remains had for several days been exposed on the altar of a church dedicated to this abbess who was so widely revered in Europe. Yet from the moment they were placed there the miracles expected from her intercession failed to happen. She solved the impasse personally by appearing to a sick person to reveal the reason: her relics did not belong on the altar table, which was intended exclusively for the celebration of the holy Mass. The hint was more than clear, and once the church warden had removed the reliquary the miracles began to happen with their accustomed frequency.[63]

Another indication of this conviction can be found in the chronicler Heriger of Lobbes of the southern Netherlands. This abbot, writing some time around 980 about the *translatio* of St. Servatius, performed at the behest of Charles Martel or Charlemagne (so in the 8th or 9th century)[64], states that at the time the relics were placed in front of the altar and not on it. He does not fail to mention the argument behind the practice: it was still usual at the time to use the altar table exclusively for the celebration of the Mass.[65] Two documents dating from the 11th century contain similar messages. These again deal with the Bishop of Maastricht: the *Actus Sancti Servatii* written by the northern French monk Jocundus, and the *Miracula Sancti Bercharii,* by an anonymous scribe.

The performance given by Bercharius († 916) has a great deal in common with that of Walburga in the tale told by Odo. Because of a fear that the pedestal on which the saint's shrine stood would collapse, the church warden had got up in the night to place the relic on the altar table. Once he was back in bed, however, the former abbot of St. Vannes appeared to him and told him that the mortal remains should not have

---

[63]PL 133, 573, *Collationum libri tres,* II, c. 28: "Contigit autem (...) ut eiusdem sanctae Gualburgis reliquiae super altare per aliquot dies manerent. Sed mox miracula cessaverunt. Tandem vero ipsa virgo cuidam ex infirmis apparens: Idcirco, inquit, non sanamini, quia reliquiae meae sunt super altare Domini, ubi maiestas divini mysterii debet solummodo celebrari".

[64]Koldeweij (1985), 26, 38, 289 n. 121, 290 n. 133.

[65]AASS 13 maii, III, 218 B, *Acta Servatii ab Harigero abbate Lobiensi conscripta ex editione Chappiavillae,* n. 30 : "Tolluntur interim que inveniuntur luctuque mixto cum inerarrabibli gaudio ante altare ponuntur; necdum enim praesumi fas erat, ut quidquam super altare poneretur praeter sacrificium, quod mensa est Domini exercituum".

been placed on the altar of our Lord Jesus Christ and, said the indignant saint, the shrine had to be restored immediately to its original location.[66]

In his veiled pleading the anonymous writer who told of Bercharius' miracles must have felt that he was a voice crying in the wilderness - like Jocundus, who completed his work in 1088 at the best of the chapter of the church of St. Servatius in Maastricht. This monk too was little pleased with the change in ideas regarding the place of the relics with regard to the altar table. He wrote with regret that the current practice of placing the relics on the altar were out of harmony with the customs dating back to the Carolingian era. At present, he wrote, compared to the reverence shown at the moment of the *translatio* far too little respect is shown for the altar. In the past more honour had been paid to the sacred altar which, following the example of Pope Gregory the Great, had to be approached with extreme piety.[67]

But even though the tradition supported by Jocundus continued in some places until well into the 16th century, the resistance noted from the 9th to the 11th centuries to having the relics on the altar merely serves to confirm that the custom had become a fixture. An opportunity par excellence for exposing the relics was the feast day in their honour, which was introduced for the first time in the monastery of Echternach on 13th December 1059.[68] This example was followed in France, England and Germany in various monasteries, cathedrals and other churches on a wide variety of dates.

The old monastic *consuetudines* prescribe that on these days the relics should be placed on the altar for veneration.[69] At the same time the illumination that usually surrounded the altar and the relics from early Christian times appeared on the altar in the form of candles.[70] According to the 11th-century *consuetudines* of the Cluniacs in Farfa, during the

---

[66]AASS OSB II, 858, lib. II, c. 26, *Mirac. s. Bercharii abb. Dervensis*: "B. Pater Bercharius (...) cum fremebundo vultu tangens eum vocavit (...) Ad quem beatus cum increpatione haec intulit: Ego sum ille, cuius super Creatoris et Salvatoris nostri Domini Iesu Christi mensa Corporis composuisti cinerem. Ergo propera surgens, et inde corpus meum ad priorem transvehito locum".

[67]MGH SS XII, 95, *Iocundi translatio s. Servatii*: "omnes (...) ante altare ponunt quod afferunt. Nondum enim in ecclesia mos iste adoleverat, ut in altari vel reliquie sanctorum vel aliquid poneretur, quia mensa est Domini exercituum, unde et apostolici viri ante sacrificium vix accedunt. Beatus vero Gregorius papa apostolorum principis in basilica Romae quotiens missam celebraturus erat, ante altare, ut aiunt, tabulam erexerit, Christum christo porrexit, iudicans se indignum proprius accedere ad eum".

[68]Berlière (1927); Hermann-Mascard (1975), 174.

[69]Martène (1690), 431: "et altaria ornanda fuerint linteaminibus, palleis, capsis et diversis reliquiarum: crucibus et philacteriis, buxis quoque, et pixidibus et textis".

[70]Dendy (1959), 17-43, *Lights around the altar*; 44-71, *Lights upon the altar*.

sung Office there were three candles lit in front of the altar and, on major feast days, two on the table itself. On the feast of the Ascension the relics were also placed there,[71] and on 2nd February, the feast of the Purification of the Virgin Mary and the presentation of the child Jesus in the Temple (also known as Candlemas) a candlelight procession was held in which the smaller reliquaries were carried.[72]

The Cistercians - who contrasted with the Cluniacs by their strictly sober customs - kept candles off the altar as much as was possible. Their 1152 *consuetudines* speak of two candlesticks on either side of the altar and, if necessary, one source of light on the table itself.[73] The general chapter of 1185 allowed the crucifix and the relics on major feast days but no candles.[74] Four years later it was laid down that on the feast of saint light was allowed during the whole of the night at the altar dedicated to him but candles were forbidden.[75] In 1197 the presence of *fylacteria* and the absence of candles on the altar was again confirmed.[76]

In the discussions on this point there was as yet no link made with the presence of the Eucharist. This began to make its influence felt only from the middle of the 13th century, when devotion to the Sacrament began to grow, and especially from the 14th century onwards, when the 'Masses with exposition' came into being. In the period prior to his pontificate, before 1198, Innocent III gave an allegorical explanation for the papal court custom of having two candles on the altar with a crucifix between them: they represented the shepherds and the Magi, enlightened

---

[71]Hallinger X, 108: "Tunc secretarius det vascala aurea minoris vel phylacterias ad quattuor seniores"; Albers I, 23; 100; Dendy (1959), 23.

[72]Hallinger X, 40: "Ante Primam sint tres calices aurei super altare et duo candelabra aurea quae iugiter ardeant in ipso die"; 41 (De processione): "accipiant quattuor seniores reliquias minores"; LW II, 1535-1540.

[73]Séjalon (1892), 125, *Ecclesiastica Officia*, lib. LIII: "Finita tertia exeant, et unus ministrorum qui adiuverunt eos ad induendum pulset signum et accendat duas candelas, quae solent ardere iuxta altare hinc et inde, et absconsam cum lumine super altare si necesse fuerit praeparet".

[74]Canivez (1933-41), I (1116-1220), 98, *Statuta ord. cisterciensis* 1185, n. 4: "Unam tantum crucem licet super altare ponere praeter communem ligneam cum vase reliquiarum, sine cereis, in praecipuis festivitatibus tantum ad missas"; Martène (1717), 1257.

[75]ibid. I, 112, n. 12: "Quando festum alicuius sancti fuerit, in cuius honore altare aliquod praecipue consecratum fuerit, liceat abbati ad altare illud lumen sola nocte illa accendere, cereos tamen interdicimus".

[76]ibid. I, 210, n. 4: "De philacteris ponendis super altare in festis praecipuis, quod definitum est teneatur (...) Cerei omnino interdicuntur".

in their faith by the birth of Christ.[77] Usually, however, the light was related to the altar and the relics, the presence of which on the altar required some type of regulation. The danger of theft was not unreal. And for their exposition the relics were taken out of their holders, with all the attendant dangers of damage or sacrilege.[78] In order to fulfil the prescriptions of the Fourth Lateran Council, *ostensoria* were developed in all shapes and sizes from around the 13th century so that, on the one hand, canon 62 was adhered to and, on the other, the relics could nonetheless be viewed by the faithful. Another variant was the opening of the doors of a moveable reliquary. "Unattached" relics were also kept in the sacristy just as was done here and there with the Eucharist until the end of the Middle Ages. On special days they were then placed on the altar.[79]

The 13th-century monastic customs of the ancient Saint-Benoît-sur-Loire monastery at Fleury confirm the Benedictine tradition. On the vigils of Christmas, Easter and Whitsunday candles burned throughout the night before each altar. For the Office of the night the warden lit two more on the altar of St. Benedict and incensed all the others.[80] On the feast of Candlemas, during the Rogation Days and at the Ascension the relics were also given a place of honour, were incensed and carried in procession.[81] Another day of procession with a similar ritual was 25th

---

[77]PL 217, 811, *De sacro altaris mysterio*, c. 21: "Ad significandum itaque gaudium duorum populorum, de nativitate Christi laetantium, in cornibus altaris duo sunt constituta candelabra, quae mediante cruce, faculas accensas (...) Inter duo candelabra in altari crux collocatur media, quoniam inter duos populos Christus in Ecclesia mediator existit (...) ad quem pastores a Judaea, et magi ab Oriente venerunt"; according to Durandus in the 13th century it became a general custom to have two candles and a crucifix on the altar, *Rationale,* I, c. 3 fol. 27; The number of instances increased so that uniformity was achieved; see Dendy ((1959), 51 sqq. esp. 67-71; LW I, 1201 B.

[78]Hostiensis, *In primum Decretalium*, lib. III, fo. 173; Hermann-Mascard (1975), 214.

[79]Freestone (1917), 188-189; Dijk v. (1957), passim; King (1965), 71-75; Nussbaum (1979), 292-308; Bosman (1986), 38.

[80]Hallinger IX, 14: "Vigilia Natalis Domini post Completorium mittat capicerius ante unumquodque altare (cereos) qui accensi possint sufficere tota nocte donec diescat. Priusquam surgatur ad Nocturnos, sacrista maturius ceteris surgens, accensis cereis super altare patris Benedicti, revestitus cuncta altaria thurificet qui sunt in monasterio"; ibid. 84; 109; 115; 242; 264; 270; 301; 304; 305 sqq.

[81]Hallinger IX, 149, Purificatio Beatae Mariae: "Deinde incensato altari cum reliquiis fit processio preeunte aqua benedicta cum crucibus et ymagine beate Marie"; 101-102, In Rogationibus: "Tunc domnus abbas, vel si forte abfuerit vice eius ebdomadarius sacerdos, albatus thurificabit altare et reliquias. Thurificatione autem facta sacerdos cum diacono et duobus subdiaconibus duobusque conversis (...) tollent reliquias, cereos et textum ita ut sacerdos spongiam, levita a dextris, subdiaconus a sinistris eius alias sanctorum reliquias"; 108-109, In Ascensione Domini: "Ad finem Tertie ornamenta et reliquie a sacrista super altare ponuntur. Post Tertiam ab abbate et altero sacerdote qui baiulatu(ru)s est dexteram capis induti(s) thurificantur cum duobus thuribulis (...) Novissime portatur maxima crux aurea cum sex philacteriis et spongia in medio ponatur".

April, the feast of St. Mark the Evangelist.[82] In the 14th-century constitutions of Monte Cassino the warden was expected to light a separate candle for each relic on the altar and to keep them alight for as long as the relics remained exposed.[83]

Such customs prevailed not just in monastery churches: in parish churches the relics stood on the altar during the Mass; originally this would happen only on the appropriate feast day but later it applied to every solemn celebration of the Mass. A prescription dated 1350 in the register of documents and records of Bremen required the celebrant to place the head of St. Secundus on the altar before Mass began.[84]

A ruling laid down by the provincial synod of Rouen in 1445 shows that the relics still appeared daily on the altars: they were to be locked away after the liturgy was completed.[85] The situation remained the same until the post-Tridentine era. In 1588 Pope Sixtus V divided the Roman Curia into a number of congregations,[86] including the Congregation of Rites, which was to occupy itself with questions regarding indulgences and relics. Again in 1669, for this purpose Pope Clement IX called into being a separate congregation which continued to exist into the 20th century.[87] These congregations issued further prescriptions regarding the placing of relics on the altar. They were no longer permitted to stand in front of the Sacrament nor in front of or on the tabernacle. Even though they lost some ground, the relics were able to maintain their place on various altars between the candlesticks or in the retables[88] until the 1960s, at which stage altars were turned to face the people.

---

[82]ibid. 164: "Post Tertiam fit processio per cimeterium. Dicta Tertia domnus abbas (...) thurificabit altare et reliquias"; "Et nominato sancto Johanne bis recedit processio eo ordine quo venerat per claustrum in navi ecclesie et sic in chorum venientes depositis sacris reliquiis super armariolum iuxta altare beatae Marie".

[83]ibid. VI (1975), 238, l. 1-14: "Item debet dictus sacrista, quando alique relique ponuntur super altare, unam candulam ante ipsam reliquiam accendere et tandiu accensam manere quamdiu ibi reliquie steterint".

[84]Browe (1931a), 383: "Sacerdos celebraturus missam portabit caput b. Secundi in processione et ipsum caput ponetur super altare maius in choro" (quote taken from: *Bremisches Urkundenbuch*, 2, 1876, n. 620.)

[85]Mansi XXXII, c. 33: "Item ordinat ipsa synodus quod expleto servitio divino ponantur reliquiae in locis honestis et firmentur ecclesiae"; Hermann-Mascard (1975), 174, n. 193.

[86]i.e. colleges of cardinals supported and aided by consultors.

[87]*In ipsis*, dated 6th July 1669. This Congregation for Remains and Relics was once again merged with the Congregation of Rites by Pius X on 28th January 1904 in: *Quae in Ecclesiae bonum;* see NCE XII, 239.

[88]DDC VII, 571; DTC XIII,2, 2375-2376.

What associations were created with the Eucharist by the presence of the relics on the altar? Let us take another look at the *Admonitio Synodalis*. This document allowed only the *viaticum*, the relics and the book of the Gospels on the altar. Exceptions to this were the prominent candles accompanying the relics, which the Cistercians objected to. It is possible that this extension of the 'ornaments' reinforced the 10th- and 11th-century objections to altar table relics that we have already noted. Similar objections to the presence of the pyx are not found. But there are remarks concerning the care to be taken. Regino of Prüm insisted that his visitors ensured that the *viaticum* was present on the altar. The pyx had to be securely closed as a protection against mice and to prevent sacrilege. The consecrated bread had to be renewed every three days.[89] The fact that this is repeated by Ratherius of Verona in 966, by Burchard of Worms († 1025) and by Ivo of Chartres († 1116)[90] confirms the presence of the pyx *super altare* without it being possible to conclude from the texts whether the pyx was suspended above or standing on the altar.

In the 10th-century *Ordo Romanus II* the bishop is held to bow before the Eucharist or *Sancta* on reaching the altar, which must mean that the Eucharist was already present there.[91] In this regard a piece of information provided by Rupert of Deutz († 1135) in his description of the fire in the church of St. Urbanus in 1128 is a good illustration. The wall tabernacle was consumed by the flames together with all the objects it contains. Only the pyx with the consecrated bread was spared. The following Sunday they were carried solemnly in procession and placed on the high alter, together with the corporal, "as the most sacred relics".[92]

Originally it had probably been regarded as sufficient to place the pyx with the relics. No extraordinary measures were taken, apart from practical matters such as the suspending of the pyx from chains or the use

---

[89] ed. Wasserschleben (1964), 20, lib. I, Notitia 9: "Inquirendum, si pixida semper sit super altare cum sacra oblatione ad viaticum infirmis"; ibid. 56, de synod. caus. c. 71: "Ut omnis presbyter habeat pixidem aut vas tanto sacramento dignum, ubi corpus dominicum diligenter recondatur ad viaticum recedentibus a seculo"; "semperque sit super altare obseratum propter mures et nefarios homines et de tertio in tertium diem semper mutetur".

[90] resp. above n. 61; PL 140, 754, decr. lib. V, c. 9; PL 161, 165, *decr.* II, 19.

[91] Andrieu (1931-61), II, 211-212, *Ordo Romanus* V, 17: "Tunc procedit pontifex et antequam veniat ad scolam (...), inclinato capite ad altare, primo adorat Sancta"; ed. Hanssens (1948-1950), III, 234, Amalarii episcopi Eclogae 6: "Episcopus veniens ante altare adorat primo sancta"; PL, 78, 970.

[92] ed. Grundmann (1966), 447, *De incendio*, c. 6: "Ego una vobiscum, fratres karissimi, supra dictum corporale et pixidem illam pro summis reliquiis transferre ad maius altare et hoc monosticum superscribere dignum duxi: Hac corpus Domini flammas in pixide vicit"; PL 170, 338.

of a separate 'tabernacle shrine'.[93] It was an obvious move to house both pyx and relics in the same shrine when they were both present on the same altar table. Caesarius of Heisterbach († c. 1240) reports this solution implicitly in one of his reports of Eucharist miracles. Thieves had broken into a church at night and stolen the *scrinium*. When they noticed that it contained nothing more than the pyx and the relics, they left their 'booty' without further thought in a new furrow in a field that had been half ploughed. Early the next morning, while it was still not fully light, the oxen drawing the plough refused to take another step forward, not matter what the farmer said or did, when they reached the spot where the robbers had abandoned the *scrinium*. He left the oxen where they were and ran back into the village to tell everyone what had happened.[94] The lack of interest shown by the thieves in the *scrinium* and pyx is not all that strange since they could be made of wood or cork rather than precious metals.[95]

Similar information is provided by the liturgist Durandus, writing at the end of the 13th century. Following in the footsteps of his 12th-century predecessor, Honorius of Autun[96], he called the separate tabernacle the *propitiatorium* (Ex. 25 and 27) by way of analogy with the golden table top above the Ark of the Covenant where Yahweh was present as a sign of reconciliation. In the 'altar ark' Christ was to be found, Christ our *propitiatio*, reconciliation, and there the relics were also placed.[97] It is worthy of note here that we again encounter the notion of sacrifice which we assume to have had a role to play in the placing of both Eucharist and relics in the altar grave around the same time that the relics were given a place on the altar table.

Braun points to a number of tabernacles still in existence, which Durandus must have meant. They date from the 13th, 14th and 15th

---

[93]Nussbaum (1979), 314-319.

[94]ed. Strange (1851), II, 172, *Dial.* IX, c. VII: "nocte fures ecclesiam infringentes inter cetera etiam scrinium cum Corpore Domini inde tulerunt. Qui cum nihil aliud in eo praeter reliquias et pixidem cum sacramento reperissent".

[95]Dijk v.(1957), 32; Nussbaum (1979), 320; Freestone (1917), 210 n. 6.

[96]PL 172, 587, *Gemma animae*, lib. I, c. 136, De propitiario.

[97]Durandus, *Rationale*, lib. IV, c. 1, n. 15: "Et inde tabernaculum sive locus super posteriori parte altaris collocaturus in quo Christus propitiatio nostra, id est hostia consecrata servatur, hodie propitiatorium nuncupatur"; ibid. lib. I, c. 2, n. 5: "Super arcam vero factum est propitiatorium (...) In cuius rei imitationem in quibusdam ecclesiis super altare collocatur arca seu tabernaculum, in quo corpus Domini et reliquiae ponuntur"; c. 3, n. 26: "Phylacteria vero est vasculum de argento vel auro vel chrystallo, vel ebore et huiusmodi, in quo sanctorum cineres vel reliquiae reconduntur (...) Super altare etiam quibusdam ecclesiis collocatur tabernaculum de quo sub tit. de altari dictum est".

centuries and are of small dimensions. The one to be found in the treasury of the parish church of Siegburg is 28 cm wide, 21 cm deep and 41 cm tall. In comparison with the four others he describes, this is the largest. In the course of time it went from being a Eucharistic shrine to being a reliquary. Nussbaum mentions a few examples of these "extremely simple small cupboards".[98]

A document dated 1429 also mentions Eucharist and relics placed together namely in a *Sakramenthaus* in Ingolstadt. The document confirms the privilege, granted by Duke Louis of Bavaria to the women's convent of Our Lady, of the daily celebration of a 'Mass with exposition'. The priest was expected to give a blessing with the Sacrament after Mass and then to carry it, together with the relics, to the 'sarg', in which he locked both Eucharist and relics. This custom continued until 1525 every Thursday Mass of the Blessed Sacrament was celebrated.[99] The reservation of both Eucharist and relics in the tabernacle must have been practised until some time in the 16th century, at which period the Congregation of Rites was obliged to forbid the reservation of the relics *in tabernaculo* if the Sacrament was present there.[100]

Towards the end of the Middle Ages in Germany a tabernacle of this sort would sometimes be placed in the retable or - more frequently - the predella. In the monasteries of Isenhagen and Ohrdorf (near Wittingen) we can find 'double predellae', in which the relics and the Eucharist were kept separately.[101] Normally speaking, however, the niches in the predella served for the exposition of the relics, though sometimes the pictorial decorations and the short inscriptions permit the conclusion that a niche of this sort served to hold the Sacrament: angels with censers and texts such as "Behold the Lamb of God" (Jn. 1:29) or "This is the living Bread come down from heaven" (Jn. 6:51) indicate unmistakeably that the Eucharist was once present there.[102]

The original function of the wall niches in medieval churches is just as unclear. Any niche sited on the Gospel side of the high altar usually

---

[98]Braun (1924), II, 624-626; Nussbaum (1979), 320: "äussert einfachen Kästchen aus Holz".

[99]Buchner (1918), 686-688: "darunter sol der Priester mit dem Sacrament den Segen geben und dann das Sacrament und ander Heiligtum wider zu dem Sarg tragen und darein setzen und bewaren"; Greving (1908), 103.

[100]Ferraris, II, col. 1568: "In tabernaculo, ubi asservatur S.S.Sacramentum, non sunt retinendae reliquiae, nec vasa sacrorum oleorum, nec aliud".

[101]Appuhn (1961), 84 sqq.; ibid. 103; Raible (1908), 236-237: a predella-tabernacle dating from 1483 in a museum in Braunschweig 1483.

[102]Braun (1924), II, 631-633.

indicates a former tabernacle. The rest are mostly places for keeping relics or other consecrated objects. In Westphalia it would seem that there were even *Sakramenthäuser* used for holding relics.[103] We have already indicated this tendency to place both relics and Eucharist in the same container in the case of various types of reliquary or Eucharistic holder. The similarity of form implied and identity of name, such as: *capsa, arca, pyxis, cuppa, columba* or *ciborium*.

The presence of both relics and Eucharist on the altar table also perhaps affected the transposition of forms of reverence 'in the reverse direction'. It can be seen in the *missa sicca*, in which the relics took the place of the Eucharist at the 'elevatio'. The *missa sicca* was a ritual resembling the Mass, but without Offertory, Canon, Consecration or Communion, though the latter was not always left out. It was a ritual generally familiar in the 12th century and must have existed for some time before that date, ever since the bination interdict was brought in in the second half of the 11th century. The 'dry Mass' replaced the actual Mass on such occasions as a burial or marriage in the afternoon or at the arrival of a pilgrimage.[104]

In his *Manipulum curatorum* dated 1333 Guido of Montrocher recommends that on such occasions the priest should put on the Mass vestments and read the formula of the Blessed Virgin or of the Holy Ghost or of the saint in honour of whom the pilgrimage is being undertaken. The celebrant could show some relics to the people during this *missa* by way of compensation for the fact that consecration and 'elevatio' of the body of Christ was not permitted.[105]

And yet things went further than merely the *elevatio* of relics. The similarity with the Mass gained much greater emphasis when not a relic but the *ciborium* containing the Sacrament was elevated. A gesture such as this related better to the current Eucharistic devotion which had already become disengaged. The synod held in Cologne in the autumn of 1348

---

[103]Raible (1908), 174: "Eine sehr reich verzierte Nische im Breisacher Münsterchor, welche sogar an Ornamentik die nebenan befindliche Tabernakelnische übertrifft, lässt durch ihre Inschrift erkennen, dass sie die Reliquien der hll. Gervasius und Protasius enthielt"; ibid. 195-196: "In Westfalen waren die Sakramentshäuschen so beliebt, dass sich in manchen Kirchen drei (...) oder doch zwei (...) vorfinden, von denen noch dazu einige mehrere Schränke enthalten, ersichtlich also, da sich der provinzielle Geschmack eimal für diese Form der Depositorien entschieden hatte, auch zur Aufbewahrung der Gefässe mit den heiligen Ölen und von Reliquiarien dienten".

[104]Pinsk (1924), 94; LW II, 1738.

[105]Montrocher, *Manipulorum curatorum*, tractatus VI, c. 7: "non tamen dicit canonem nec consecrat sed ostendit eis reliquias aliquas loco elevationis corporis Christi".

deals with this 'elevatio' during the *missa sicca*[106] and it appears in the *ordo missae* drawn up by the liturgist John Burckard in 1502 - which condemns the practice.[107] Luther gave a retrospective review of the *missa sicca* in a speech made at table[108] and the Council of Trent, which finished in 1563, picks out Hungary as a land where the Host, reserved in the *ciborium*, is shown to the people for veneration during the *missa sicca*.[109] The 'elevatio' of the relics rather than of the Eucharistic bread, the practice[110] which stemmed from the recommendation made by Guido of Montrocher, would seem to have given way rapidly to the 'elevatio' of the Sacrament itself. Intended as a replacement, it was replaced by what it itself had replaced.

***

In the foregoing paragraphs the placing of the relics on or near the altar has been discussed. The relics were placed in beautiful shrines, decorated with costly gold, silver and jewels. These glittering decorations seem to have fulfilled a dual function: to cover an inglorious death and to reveal a glorious eternity. On the one hand, indeed, the bones of the martyr, hidden inside the container, are a tangible sign of death and, on the other, offer a view of eternal life, the price of martyrdom for belief in Christ. The beauty of the shrine symbolise simultaneously earthly decay and eternal life. The death and eternal happiness of the martyr are a reflection of Christ's death and resurrection, celebrated and commemorated on the altar. Hence the external manifestation of the inner bond that was created between the relics and the altars in 'the relic altar' and the 'altar table relics'.

---

[106]Schannat-Hartzheim, IV, 460, Coloniae synodus autumnalis, c. 1: "aliqui presbyterii induti sacris vestibus coram populo missae legunt officium sine tunc sacramenti confectione ostendentes tamen ipsis hostiam antea alio tempore consecratam".

[107]ed. Wickam (1904), 174: "ut premittitur paratus missam huiusmodi siccam legere (...) et non debet in ea sacramentum ostendere etiam si illud in ecclesia ibidem in loco suo sacro habeat paratum propter periculum ostensionis".

[108]Quirin (1952), 130, n. 608: "Da war ein solch Meshören, das, wenn grosse Herrn und Gewaltige des Morgens keine Messe hatten gehort, so musste man ihm ein truckene Messe halten. Alle Gebete, die Epistel, das Evengelium, den Canon, die consecrirte Hostien, aus dem Ciborio mit dem Kelch aufheben" (quoted from Luther, *Tischreden oder Colloquia*, gesammelt von Johannes Aurifaber, Eisleben, 1566, S.385)

[109]CT VIII, 922, 15-19: "Tollique abusum mandat missarum, quas siccas vocant, in quibus nulla fit consecratio neque sumptio, sed sacramentum, quod in ciborio asservatur, populo ad adorationem ostenditur, quod saepe fit ab iis, qui plures parochias aut capellas in diversis ecclesiis habent, maxime in Ungaria".

[110]Franz (1902), 81.

CHAPTER FOUR

THE TRANSPOSITION OF FORMS OF REVERENCE[*]

The four major forms of reverence that first appeared in the cult of the relics and later were introduced into the reverence shown for the Eucharist are the *visit*, the *procession*, the *exposition* and the *blessing*. These four forms are the basis of the subdivisions of this chapter. During these various types of reverence the one paying homage kissed the sacred object, knelt before it or lay prostrate on the ground. Illumination and incense add to the solemnity of the occasion. And even these subsidiary phenomena were first to be observed within the cult of the relics and only later were they applied to Eucharistic devotion. Prior to the four substantial subjects already listed, this introduction will devote some attention to the 'accompanying' expressions of reverence which, to some extent, can also be regarded as transpositions, at least to the extent to which it is possible to speak of this in such 'omnivalent' forms of cult.

Incense and light were both part of pre-Christian cults. The ancients saw light as symbolising - among other things - an apotropaic power. In the pagan mysteries, which were accompanied by incense, the presence of lighted torches was a sign of the union with the godhead. In the Old testament incense belonged to the Jewish temple ritual and Yahweh's glory appeared time and again as a fire and light, symbolically present in the Ark of the Covenant in the eternal flame.[1]

Incense and light also played an important part in funerals held in the Greco-Roman world.[2] At the time of Augustus, for instance, it was customary to light torches and candles on the tombs in a cloud of incense. The light was intended to offer a protective power to the dead one, sometimes accompanied by the *obolus*, against the demonic darkness in his fraught journey through the kingdom of the dead. This custom did not disappear at the coming of Christianity but continued, even among Christians, just as did in some places the custom of burying lamps and other apotropaic objects with the deceased.[3] Despite the negative attitude of the

---

[*]A list for further reading is can be found in: Atchly (1909); Dendy (1959).

[1]LW I, 2915; II, 1528; Martimort (1984) I, 205-208.

[2]LW II, 1533.

[3]Cumont (1946); Dendy (1959), 97; see p. 104.

early Fathers of the church and of the Council of Elvira[4] around the year 300 because of the Jewish but also - and more especially - the pagan origin of such practices, the use of candles and incense gained ground and was taken up into the Christian symbolism surrounding the liturgy of the dead.

A first report of such things can be found in the account of the burial of the martyr Cyprian († 258), the authoritative bishop of Carthage, who was carried to his final resting place at night accompanied by candles and burning torches.[5] At the funeral of Peter of Alexandria († 311) incense was also burned in the procession.[6] In addition to having a practical use, the light also had a symbolic meaning: 'the victory' and the entry into eternal light. This symbolism also included the long journey of the soul after death, a journey full of dangers, represented by the lion and the dragon.[7] It was reflected in the prayers and hymns of the church. After the Edict of Milan, when the church came out into the open, candles and torches very quickly became part of the normal pattern of the church's funeral rites.[8] Lights were also lit at the grave side in memory of the deceased one. Perhaps the Council of Elvira was referring to this custom when it expressed disapproval of the lighting of candles in cemeteries during daylight hours. Light and incense is also mentioned in the *acta* of the most revered martyr of the Byzantine church, St. Demetrius of Thessalonica († c. 306) who was probably killed in Sirmium during the reign of the Emperor Maximian.[9] We have previously alluded to the fact that Peter the Iberian is said, in his *vita*, to have prayed by the relics "in the midst of lights and the odour of incense".

In the 5th century the practice of keeping lamps or candles burning at the graves of the saints had become a stereotypical expression of

---

[4]Mansi II, 11, can. 34: "Cereos per diem placuit in coemeterio non incendi; inquietandi enim sanctorum spiritus non sunt. Qui haec non observaverint, arceantur ab ecclesiae communione"; Dendy (1959), 2, 99, 108.

[5]ed. Musurillo (1972), 174, Acta Procunsularia s. Cypriani episcopi et martyris, c. 5: "Ita Cyprianus passus est eiusque corpus propter gentilium curiositatem in proximo positum est. Per noctem autem corpus eius inde sublatum est ad cereos et scolaces in areas Macrobii Candidiani procuratoris (...) cum voto et triumpho magno deductum est et illic conditum"; CSEL III,3, CXIII; LW I, 1201.

[6]PG 18, 465, *S. Petri Alexandrini episcopi Acta sincera*: "Tum victricia signa palmas gerentes, flammantibus cereis, concrepantibus hymnis, flagrantibusque thymiamatibus, coelestis victoriae triumphum celebrantes, deposuerunt sanctas reliquias".

[7]LW I, 573-574.

[8]Dendy (1959), 99-107.

[9] PG 116, 1242: ["Atque illi (...) in quodam, in quo et sacras sese inventuros reliquias existimabant, venerandi templi fodientes in terram, hymnis et canticis et lampadibus et thymiamatibus utentes, descendebant"].

reverence. Jerome speaks of it in his writings against Vigilantius[10] and in a letter to Riparius the priest, where he also finds it difficult to get around the pagan origin of the practice.[11] An even clearer message is given by Paulinus of Nola († 431), who sings the praises of the beauty provided by the candles and flowers that grace the tomb of St. Felix day and night.[12] The grave of St. Martin of Tours was given the same signs of reverence. Indeed, on his death in 491 Bishop Perpetuus left a piece of land whose earnings were to be used for the illumination of Martin's tomb.[13]

Pope Gregory the Great and the historian Gregory of Tours are important sources of information about the 6th century. In one of his letters the pope mentions the offering of incense with aloes and balsam to the *corpora* of the holy martyrs.[14] In the *Historia Francorum* written by Gregory of Tours we read of Bishop Eufronius placing relics, at the request of St. Radegunde († 587), in her convent in Poitiers, relics she had been able to obtain in the East. A processions with candles and incense is an important component of the installation described.[15] In the 6th century the practice of burning lamps and candles at a tomb or next to a reliquary was already widespread, since both authors speak of it repeatedly. Candles were lit, for instance, at the tomb of St. Sollemnis († c. 510) at its discovery.[16] Legend tells that this saint was present at the baptism of Clovis. St. Mitrias, as already mentioned, had to do without this show of reverence until he had proved himself as a heavenly protector. The custom is also indirectly alluded to in the report of oil from these lamps being used as a secondary relic and as a valued

---

[10]PL 23, 357, *Contra Vigilantium*, 4: "Prope ritum gentilium videmus sub praetextu religionis introductum in ecclesiis, sole adhuc fulgente, moles cereorum accendi, et ubicumque pulvisculum nescio quod, in modico vasculo pretioso linteamine circumdatum osculantes adorant".

[11]CSEL 55, 352, ep. CIX: "et quotienscumque apostolorum et prophetarum et omnium martyrum basilicas ingredimur, totiens idolorum templa veneramur accensique ante tumulos eorum cerei idolatriae insignia sunt? plus aliquid dicam, quod redundet in auctoris caput et insanum cerebrum vel sanet aliquando vel deleat, ne tantis sacrilegiis simplicum animae subvertantur"; Dendy (1959), 109.

[12]CSEL 30, 49, *Carmen* XIV, 99-101: "clara coronantur densis altaria lichnis, lumina ceratis adolentur odora papyris, nocte dieque micant"; PL 61, 467.

[13]AASS 8 apr. I, 751, *Testamentum s. Perpetui*, c. 16: "Villam (...) lego. Ita tamen ut de eorum proventibus oleum paretur pro Domni Martini sepulcro indeficienter illustrando".

[14]MGH Ep II, 147, lib. IX, indict. II, ep. 147, *Gregorius Secundini servi Dei incluso*: "Aloa vero, thimiama, storacem, et balsamum, sanctorum martyrum corporibus offerenda latore praesentium deferente transmisimus".

[15] MGH SRM I,1, 464, lib. IX, c. 40: " Qui (Eufronius) (...) cum grandi psallentium et caereorum micantium ac thymiamatis apparatu sancta pignora (...) in monasterium detulit".

[16]MGH SRM I,2, 311, *In gloria confessorum*, c. 21: "lumen accendite cultumque debitum exibete".

medication.[17] Legends also mention its use. They show the value placed by the saints on the lamps hanging by their graves on a cord suspended from the wall or ceiling. They continued to burn even when the oil was not replenished, they lit themselves in a miraculous fashion[18] or they fell to the stone floor without breaking.[19] There was also a custom of giving a candle, sometimes of the same height as the giver,[20] as a votive offering.[21]

The use of incense and light to honour the relics continued in subsequent centuries. When, in 684, St. Audoin was carried to his final resting place, bearers of crucifixes, lamps and incense walked in the procession.[22] The is reported a century later of the funeral of St. Sebald.[23] The Councils of Toledo in 597 and 688 regarded the use of

---

[17]MGH SRM I,2, 338, *In gloria confessorum,* c. 68: "Ex quo oleo plerumque infirmi medicamenta suscipiunt"; ibid. c.69: "Praestat ex oleo virtus Domini medicinam infirmis"; MGH SRM II, 333, Vitae Galli auctore Walahfrido, lib. II, c. 39: "Memento fili ut, luce terris reddita, oleo, quod in cripta ante altare consuevit ardere, vulneris locum perunguas".

[18]MGH SRM I,2, 338, *In gloria confessorum,* c. 68: "Ad huius sancti (Marcellini) sepulchrum lychnus assidue lumen praebet; sed accensus semel multis noctibus sine ullo additamento perdurat. Et plerumque contingit, ut extinctus a vento, divinitus iterum accendatur"; II, 338, *Passio s. Sigismundi Regis,* c. 10; "In quo loco nocturnis temporibus a sanctis viris divinitus lampadam accensam per totum illum spatium, quod ibi sancta corpora quieverunt, visa est"; see also SC 260, Gregorii Magni *Dial.,* III, 30, 6: "Die vero alio, cum in ea lampades sine lumine dependerent, emisso divinitus lumine sunt accensae, atque post paucos iterum dies, cum expletis missarum sollemniis, extinctis lampadibus, custos ex eadem ecclesia egressus fuisset, post paululum intravit et lampades quas extinxerat lucentes repperit".

[19]MGH SRM I, 161, *Hist. Franc.* lib. IV, c. 28: "Lyghnus enim ille, qui fune suspensus coram sepulchrum eius ardebat, nullo tangente, disrupto fune, in pavimento conruit et, fugientem ante eum duritiam pavimenti, tamquam in aliquod molle elimentum discendit, atque medius est suffossus nec omnino contritus".

[20]MGH SRM I,2, 148, *De virtut. s. Mart.,* c, 18: "quidam paralyticus adveniens, et cereum in status sui altitudine nocte tota vigilans retenuisset, mane facto, ut lux reddita est mundo, ipse absolutis gressibus, populo teste incolomes exilivit"; ibid. 48, *In gloria martyrum,* c. 15: "Nocte vero sequenti fecit cereum in altitudinem status sui. Tunc in oratione pernoctans, tentum tota nocte manu propria cereum, restinctis ardoribus, incolomis est egressa"; PL 88, 509, *Vita s. Radegundis reginae:* "Goda, puella saecularis (...) facta candela ad mensuram suae staturae, Domino miserante in nomine sanctae feminae, qua hora frigus speraret, lumen ascendit et tenuit, cuius beneficio ante fugata sunt frigora quam esset candela consumpta".

[21]MGH SRM I,2, 311, *In gloria confessorum,* c. 21: "acceptis ex hospiciolo suo cereis surrexit cum uno tantum puero, accessitque ad locum. Fusa vero oratione, accensis cereis manu propria per totam noctem detentis, vigilias celebravit"; ibid. 48, *In gloria martyrum,* c. 14; 303, *De virtutibus s. Mart.,* IV, c. 15; PL 88, 426, *De Vita s. Martini,* 692-693.

[22]Surius VIII, 24 aug., 599: "Episcopus (...) cum crucibus et lampadibus atque thymiameteriis (...) sunt ingressi, summoque cum honore beatum corpus humeris gestantes".

[23]AASS 19 aug. III, 772: "Cum devote eius celebrarentur exsequiae, incenso redolente et accidit casualiter, ut una candelarum non solide posita de basi caderet".

light to accompany the sacred relics as quite normal[24], and this remained so throughout the rest of the Middle Ages and right up to the present time. Before the tomb of St. Remaclus[25] († 670), of Liudger[26] († 840) and of Otmar[27] († 770) the light was lit in a miraculous manner. Charlemagne († 814) gave to the basilica of Metz a 'villa' (manor) dedicated to his predecessor, St. Arnulf, so that its earnings could be used to pay for lamps burning day and night for the salvation of the soul of his wife, and Charles the Bald († 877) assured the tomb of St. Martin of continuous light with a donation.[28] King Alfred of Wessex († 899) is known to have had wax candles burn day and night by the relics which he always had with him.[29] In 916 the tithes were spent on the illumination of the grave of St. Emmeranus, who had passed through Bavaria as a missionary and was martyred in approximately 650. His body was taken to Regensburg, where the abbey of Sankt Emmeran rose near his grave.[30] The relics on the altar were incensed. The sick lit a candle there in order to be healed through the saint's intercession, as mentioned in the 11th-century *Miracula* of St. Trudo.[31] This was also an expression of devotion used by the pilgrims who put the *majestas* of Sainte-Foy de

---

[24]Hardouin, III, 536, a. 597: "Certe si minus est census, ostiarius a sacerdote sit electus, qui nitorem infra sinus sanctae ecclesiae faciat; qui et sanctarum reliquiarum luminaria omni subsequente nocte accendat"; Mansi XII, 29, a. 688, can. XL: "Reliquiae sanctorum venerandae sunt, si potest fieri, candela ardeat per singulas noctes; si vero paupertas loci non sinit, non nocet eis".

[25]AASS OSB, II, 501: "cerei, qui ante loculum quo b. Remacli corpus asservabatur, ferebantur, paulo ante vi ventorum exstincti, rursus accensi sunt divinitus".

[26]MGH SS II, 422, Ex Vita s. Liudgeri II, lib. II, c. 28: "ad extinguendas ex more lucernas accessit. Quo facto quandam ex eis post paululum rede accensam luce ardere clarissime vidit. Ille negligentius se eam extinxisse suspicatus, iterato eam extinguere emunctorio curavit. Sed cum post haec secunda quoque vice pristinae luci cerneret restitutam (...) Denique tertio quoque accessit, et ita extincta candela carbunculum de lichino emunxit, ut nihil prorsus in eo lucis remaneret. Vix paululum abscessit, cum rursus eandem lecernam clariori resplendere luce contemplatus est".

[27]ibid. 45, Miraculi s. Otmari, auctore Walafrido, c. 11: "Ut vero discessit, lux, quae per se venerat, per se etiam substracta est".

[28]AOB II, 265: "Hoc diplomate Carolus praedictae sancti Arnulfi basilicae donat villam (...) pro remedio animae ipsius coniugis suae tum ut die noctuque luminaria ad eius sepulcrum ardeant"; Martène (1733), 118-120, Miscellanea, *Diploma Caroli-Calvi*.

[29]ed. Rock (1905), III, part. I, chap. X, 294, n. 22: "Sex illae candelae per viginti quatuor horas die nocteque sine defectu coram sanctis multorum electorum Dei reliquiis quae semper eum ubique comitabantur, ardentes lucescebant"; Förster (1943), 10.

[30]Ried (1816), I, 94.

[31]MGH SS XV, 827, Miracula s. Trudonis, lib. II, c. 66: "Ephebus quidam de Reinbretesdalo Wenezo appellatus, ferens ad mensuram sui status cereum, sanctissimi viri devotus adiit tumulum".

Conques in a sea of candlelight.[32] Sometimes the candles represented
that for which the supplicant was praying. It is said that Abbot Hugh of
Cluny burned a wax peacock when one of his birds was sick.[33] The life-
size candle, offered as early as in the time of Gregory of Tours, is seen
once again in the 12th-century miracle story of the Irish saint Virgilius
(† 784), the apostle of Carinthia. When a pregnant woman of Regensburg
had been in acute labour for several days, she had placed on the saint's
grave a candle of the same size as herself. As soon as it had been lit she
swiftly gave birth and recovered immediately.[34] This type of votive
candle could also be in the shape of a part of the body that was sick or of
objects connected with someone's safety. If someone had been saved from
a storm at sea by the intercession of a saint, gratitude was expressed with
a candle in the shape of a boat. In 1331 ninety examples of such things
were found at the tomb of Ivo of Chartres († 1116).[35] In the late Middle
Ages gifts and legacies were given for the provision of light, that often
burned day and night at the tombs, reliquaries and altars of the saints.[36]

At that time, however, such gifts no longer guaranteed light at the
relics but also served to keep the flame burning before the Eucharistic
bread, which was both revered and visited. An example of transposition
of this form of reverence is a tale from the early 14th century from the
Cistercian monastery of Villers in Brabant. A gift had been given of a
handsome candlestick and a sum of money to provide candles. But,
decided the abbot, the candle was "justifiably" to burn perpetually before
the Holy of Holies and no longer - as was previously the custom - before
the relics in the sacristy.[37] Sometimes , too, when a gift was made the
giver had an eye to providing light not only for before the relics but also
for the Eucharist. A sick man promised the patron of epilepsy, Blessed

---

[32]ed. Bouillet (1900), 483-484, lib. I, c. 24: à cause de la multitude des pelerins qui offrent des cierges.

[33]Dendy (1959), 116.

[34]AASS OSB III,2, 215; "Mulier de civitate Saltzburg, cum in partu multis diebus laborans periclitaretur, per revelationem nocturnam admonita candelam ad mensuram sui corporis super famuli dei sepulcrum transmisit candelaque incensa statim puerum enixa convaluit"; see Franz (1909), II, 457-458.

[35]Dendy (1959), 115; Vauchez (1981), 534, n. 49, 536.

[36]Dendy (1959), 116-119; Appuhn (1961), 98: gifts in 1299, 1313 and 1344 for perpetual light at the sacred blood relic at Wienhausen.

[37] MGH SS XXV, 214, *Chronica Villariensis Monasterii*, c. 19: "Ego frater Conrardus dictus abbas de Villari notum facio (...) Sciant etiam presentes et futuri, quod acquisite fuerint nobis, sicut seniorum nostrorum relatione didicimus, 10 libre bone monete pro candela illa cerea que iugiter ardet in presentia eucharistie: que quidem ardere debebat coram reliquiis in sacristario, sed postea visum est magis expedire eam lucere continuo coram sancto sanctorum"; Martène (1717), III, 1300.

Joachim Piccolomini († 1258) that if cured through his intercession he would travel barefoot from Florence to Sienna. In Sienna he would then place a wax image, as large as himself, near the holy places and in addition would donate a candle to provide illumination before the Sacrament.[38]

The first reports of light and incense being used in honour of the Eucharist date, however, from earlier. Incense was being used as early as the late 7th and early 8th centuries to show reverence for the *Sancta* already alluded to - the Eucharistic bread remaining from the previous liturgy that was carried solemnly into church. The communion of the sick was also accompanied by incense and lamps, as was - in the life of St. Ulrich, the procession on Easter morning towards the end of the 10th century. In Lanfranc's *decreta*, drawn up around 1080 for the abbey in Canterbury, incense and candles demonstrate the reverence shown to the Eucharistic gifts on Good Friday and Palm Sunday. The shrine containing the Eucharist has become the new focus of the procession of the palms rather than the reliquary cross.[39]

The perpetual light burning before the Eucharist is reported for the first time in the West around the middle of the 11th century, again within the context of the independent role played by the consecrated bread in the symbolic burial during Holy Week.[40] In the rubrics laid down for the Cluniacs for Maundy Thursday, the monk Bernard prescribed in 1068 that "for three days" the Sacrament "was not to be left without light for a single hour" after it had been incensed and taken to the altar of repose.[41] Lanfranc incorporated this direction into his *decreta* around 1080[42] as did Sigibert. The latter ordained that after Mass the deacon, the verger

---

[38]Browe (1933), 5, n. 35 ; for more examples see: 1-11; Bridgett (1908), 182-183; Dendy (1959), 16, 54, 56, 61, 67-71; Nussbaum (1979), 170-174.

[39]Palm Sunday: see p. 46; Good Friday: Hallinger III/IV, 37, *Feria sexta ebdomadae sanctae*: "Vadant ad locum ubi quinta feria corpus Domini fuit repositum, et posito incenso thuribulo incenset illud. Cum appropinquant altari adorent omnes fratres flexis genibus corpus domini. Collocato super altare Christi corpore (...) incenset sacerdos corpus Christi et calicem".

[40]In the East this was somewhat earlier, at the synod of Seleucia in 904, Mansi, suppl. I, 1092; Nussbaum (1979), 170.

[41]Hergott (1726), 313; "His enim tribus diebus non est ignis in ecclesia nisi ante corpus Domini"; ibid. 259, I, c. 67: "corpus Dominicum (...) a diacono et a sacerdote incensatum, cum candelabris et thuribulo defertur retro maius altare (...) nec una hora sine luminaribus manet".

[42]Hallinger III/IV, 29: "Interea sacerdos praecedente processione, cum qua ad altare venit, vadat ad locum constitutum decentissime praeparatum ibique reponat corpus domini incensato ipso loco et ante repositionem et post repositionem. Ante quem locum lumen continue ardeat".

and the *conversi* should carry the body of Christ between two patens, wrapped in a linen cloth, to the altar of repose, accompanied by candles and incense. There lights should burn the whole day and night.[43] The liturgical task was carried out no less thoroughly in St. Martin's monastery in Lyon. The two patens were placed between two silver dishes, laid in the book of the Gospels and carried to their destination in the same way as directed by Sigibert, where the entire monastery knelt and a candle was lit.[44] At the end of the 11th century, however, the light kept burning in the presence of the Sacrament was still an exception, whereas it was the rule in the case of the relics. A miracle story from the Benedictine abbey of Corbigny near Lyon is at least illustrative of this. When the relics of St. Markulf were in Picardy in 1085 and thus were not in a church, the person responsible for looking after them came to believe that there was not further use keeping light burning by the relics and so he put it out. However, "stupidly enough" he failed to take account of the equally important presence of the body of the Lord. When he returned he saw the lamp he had extinguished emitting an angelic light and was thus reminded of the actual function of the reliquary lamp: to grace the place where the Holy of Holies was present.[45] The fact that this was still not the custom in mid-12th-century can also be seen in a contemporary report in an appendix to the *Ordo Romanus XI* regarding the number of at least 115 candles at night in St. Peter's Basilica and another 250 in the city churches, without any mention being made of the light burning before the Eucharist.[46]

Around 1200 in many parts of England, and at a later date on the European mainland, it was the custom to light candles and lamps at the side of the holy sepulchre. In the cathedral of Bamberg from the 13th to the 15th century the altar of St. George served as a holy sepulchre. The

---

[43]Albers, II, 93, *Consuetudines Sigiberti abbatis,* XXX: "Post missam veniet diaconus et secretarius atque conversi cum candelabris et turibulo accipiantque calicem et patenam, que habet corpus dominicum, imponentes aliam patenam super illam et involvant super aliquod altare aut in arca mundissima sitque lumen ante ipsum tota die et tota nocte usque ad Matutinam".

[44]Browe (1931d), 97-98.

[45]PL 151, 729, *Sermo de s. Marculfo*: "Is itaque qui ecclesiae officio praeerat, coepit secum cogitando dicere quoniam idem luminare in vanum ardebat, eo quod corpus beati Marculfi in praesenti non esset, non considerans ibidem Dominicum corpus (quod maius et praecipuum erat) cum angelorum adesse custodia. Quod cum prave et inaniter cogitasset, exstincta lucerna abiit; sed post transactum horae spatium, causa cogente aliqua reversus, dictu mirabile! illico oculis eius apparuit. Vidit namque eamdem lampadem angelica claritate fulgentem"; AASS maii VII, 532.

[46]ed. Mabillon (1724), II, 161: "Omnes igitur candelae, quae quotidie ardent in ecclesia beati Petri, sunt CXV ad minus omni nocte, in stationibus vero sunt CCL".

Holy of Holies - together with the relics - was placed there while two candles burned before it.[47] This occurred not only in Holy Week but also at other times, for during the same period there was an increase in the number of donations given for the 'eternal flame' before the Sacrament throughout the whole year. Originally the practice was found in France, Flanders and England, but from the mid-13th century it was introduced in Germany and the rest of Western Europe. The increase corresponded to the extension - already alluded to - of the expressions of devotion towards the elevated Host: incense, candles and the tolling of bells.[48] I the course of the 14th century the light before the Sacrament gradually came to be a sign, in many monastery and collegiate church, of the recognition of Christ's presence in the sacred stillness of the church. One or two synods, such as that of Meaux in 1365, made attempts to introduce the divine lamp into parish churches, burning "before the body of Christ, the brightness of the eternal light".[49] But material resources were not sufficient at the time. This obstacle was also felt in the 15th century, for even though the synods were increasingly insistent on the use of the sanctuary lamp they also took a lack of resources into account. The prescription was thus tempered with a limitation recognising the facts: "to the extent that resources permit".[50] Sometimes in such cases the church was invited to hold a special collection among the parishioners, as was requested by the synod of Eichstätt in 1453.[51] In the 16th century almost every synod required that the sanctuary lamp be used without any escape

---

[47]Browe (1931d), 105; Haimerl (1937), 23, (in the cathedral of Bamberg) : "Auf diesen Altar wurde das Allerheiligste mit dem Reliquien - eine genaue Pozessionsordnung für die Grablegung in 15 Jahrhundert: *parvam crucem cum digito S. Gertrudis, clavum Domini, parvum plenarium, et pacem* - gestellt. Es brannten dort zwei Kerzen. Das Grab wurde mit einer Tür verschlossen, vor dieselbe, wie bereits im 12 Jahrhundert bezeugt ist, ein Stein gelegt, und dann aussen *(foris ante capsam S. Cunigundis)* das Adorationskreuz angebracht"; Nussbaum (1979), 148, n. 351.

[48]Browe (1933), 1-11; Dendy (1959), 68, n. 6: light before "the reserved Sacrament", synod of Rouen (1198), council of York (1195), canons of Hubert Walter of Canterbury (1200), Odo of Paris (1200), Edmund of Canterbury (1236); 27: council of Oxford (1222), synod of Exeter (1287); Nussbaum (1979), 171-174.

[49]Martène (1717), IV, 930, *Statuta synodalia ecclesiae Meldensis. Instructio decanorum*: "Item et continue lumen seu lampas ardeat ante corpus Christi, qui est candor lucis aeternae".

[50]Browe (1933), 8; Nussbaum (1979), 172.

[51]Schannat-Hartzheim, V, 435: "Et siquidem ecclesie adeo egeant, quod de suis facultatibus lumen huiusmodi tenere nequeant, volumus, ut ad hoc opus specialem inter parochianos vestros collecturam fieri disponatis, eosdem ad contributionem huiusmodi seriosus adhortantes".

clause,[52] which led to the first general ruling in the 1614 version of the *Missale Romanum*.[53]

Even more so than in the attributes of incense and light the praying devotee's desire for forms of reverence was expressed in the kneeling position and the tendency to place a kiss on the sacred object. Kneeling[54] and kissing[55] are both general primary human expressions, in the liturgy, of honour, emotion and devotion. Within the Christian religion these expressions of devotion manifested themselves once again first in the case of the relics and then later towards the Eucharist, to the extent that the latter gained in independent status.

We have already mentioned that at the beginning of the 4th century Lucilla of Carthage kissed her private relic before receiving communion. Prudentius[56] († c. 405) and Paulinus of Nola[57] († 431) relate how people kissed the threshold on entering the *martyrium*, knelt before the relics or threw themselves flat on the ground in the position known as *prostratio*. Prudentius, visiting the grave of St. Cassian († c. 304) in Imola, sings the praises of another type of kiss, the greeting given to the altar tomb, so that in the following lines of the poem the kiss given to the altar and that given to the grave coincide: "I embrace the grave and shed tears; the altar is warmed by my mouth, the stone by my bosom".[58] Though this kiss was a sign of respect given to the relics in the *sepulcrum*, it is not the derivation of the kissing of the altar at the beginning of the celebration of the Mass: it comes rather from the pre-Christian custom of kissing the altar in greeting at the beginning of the service of sacrifice. Because of this tradition the kiss given to the altar has retained in the liturgy the significance of a greeting given to the *mensa Domini*, the Lord's table, and because of the presence of the relics in the

---

[52]Nussbaum (1979), 172, n. 550, more than 25 synods.

[53]Browe (1933), 11, n. 77: "Coram tabernaculo ss. Sacramenti lampades plures vel saltem una diu noctuque perpetuo collucere debet".

[54]DACL VI,1, 1017-1021; LW II, 1359-1362.

[55]DACL II,1, 117-130; LW II, 1421-1423.

[56]CC SL 126, 275, *Peristefanon* II, 519-520: "apostolorum et martyrum exosculantur limina"; CSEL 61, 314.

[57]CSEL 30, 108, *Carmen* XVIII, 248-251: "ingressusque sacram magnis cum fletibus aulam sternitur ante fores et postibus oscula figit et lacrimis rigat omne solum, pro limine sancto fusus humi"; ibid. 102-103; 260, *Carmen*, XXVI, 387-388.

[58]CC SL 126, 329, *Peristefanon* IX, 99-100: "conplector tumulum, lacrimas quoque fundo, altar tepescit ore, saxum pectore"; CSEL 61, 370.

altar tomb it took on a secondary meaning of greeting to the martyrs of the 'church triumphant'.[59]

For Gregory of Tours the kiss was directed towards the altar tomb present at the altar. A woman was given back the power of speech by touching with her lips the grave of St. Aredius immediately after his burial.[60] Another woman, suffering from an issue of blood (Mtt. 9:20) lay for several days on the threshold of Martin's sacred place begging for healing. At one point she approached the tomb, kissed it and prayed to the saint. In doing so she touched the cloth that hung over it and was cured from that instant.[61]

We have previously seen how St. Gallus prayed prostrate on the floor before his *fylacterium* and how Pope Hadrian († 795) together with Charlemagne bowed forward on the ground and poured out his prayer at Peter's tomb. Pope Nicholas I († 867) made purity of heart conditional on the bearing and kissing of relics. Ss. Meinrad († 861) and Richard of St. Vannes († 1046) found consolation in this form of veneration in their last hours. St. Wulstan († 1095), bishop of Worcester, demonstrated excessive kneeling in his lifetime: this holy Benedictine knelt seven times per day before the eighteen altars in his church.[62] An account given by Suger († 1151) witnesses to exaggerated efforts to kiss the relics: an indescribable tumult broke out at the fair of St. Denis when women began to push and shove one another and to climb over the backs of the crowd in order to be the first to reach the monks when they appeared carrying the relics for veneration. The monks finally had to seek refuge by climbing through the window.[63] After the edict of 1215 which forbade the exhibition of unprotected relics, the smaller relics were offered for veneration behind glass windows in portable reliquaries. In this veneration the relic of the True Cross was given a certain prominence, especially on

---

[59]Dölger (1929-50), II, 191-221; Jungmann (1962), I, 402-409; LW I, 118-119.

[60]MGH SRM I,1, 525, *Hist. Franc.*, lib. X, c. 29: "Post celebrato vero funere mulier quaedam rictu patulo sine vocis officio ad eius accessit tumulum, quod osculis delibato, elocutionis meruit recipere beneficium".

[61]ibid. I,2, 162, *De virtutibus s. Martini*, lib. II, c. 10: "Quae diebus singulis ad sancti confessoris limina iacens prostrata opem sanitatis poscebat. Factum est autem, ut quadam die accedens ad sanctum sepulchrum, orans et osculans, de palla quae super est posita aures sibi et oculos tangeret. Protinus, siccato rivo sanguinis, ita sanata est".

[62]PL 179, 1741, *Wilhelmi Malmesburiensis Vita s. Wulstani*, lib. I, c. 3: "Ante unumquodque XVIII altarium, quae in veteri ecclesia erant, septies in die prosterni".

[63]ed. Lecoy de la Marche (1867), 217, *De la consécration de Saint-Denis*, lib. II: "Fratres etiam insignia Dominicae passionis adventantibus exponentes, eorum angariis et contentionibus succumbentes, nullo divertere habentes, per fenestras cum reliquiis multoties effugerunt"; further examples: Kroos (1985), 30-32.

Good Friday.[64] The *Liber ordinarius* of the cathedral of Notre Dame in Amiens[65] in 1291 and that of the collegiate church of Tongeren[66] in 1435 give a characteristic detail: not only the crucifix but also the relic of the True Cross was kissed after the devotee had made the usual genuflections.

The *prostratio* and the act of kneeling happened only occasionally during the *humiliatio* since the relics were usually denied all forms of reverence in this humbled state. But such gestures were an integral part of the *clamor* when performed both on its own and in combination with the *humiliatio*. In the latter case the whole monastic congregation would not kneel facing the relics but rather together with the relics: in the midst of the reliquaries the monks knelt or lay prostrate on the floor of the church before the consecrated bread that was being venerated. As already said, the *clamor* was an element inserted into the liturgy of the Mass, the oldest version dating from the end of the 9th century. In the *prostratio* and the kneeling position the overwhelming atmosphere was one of submissiveness and supplication "before the holy altar and the all-holy body and blood".[67]

As a mere act of reverence and veneration we find kneeling before the Eucharist again first in the West on the taking of the *viaticum* to the sick. The *consuetudines* of Farfa state: "When they - the monks with the *viaticum* - enter the house, all kneel before the body of the Lord".[68] Lanfranc uses similar terms when dealing with both the communion of the sick[69] and the solemnities of Good Friday just mentioned and the ceremonies of Palm Sunday. Singing children, choir members and congregation knelt before the Eucharist, which was carried round on a litter. From the 12th - and even more in the 13th - century the rules of

---

[64]Klauser (1969), 114.

[65]ed. Durand (1934), 227: "Crux itaque et reliquie sancte Crucis adorantur (...) et deosculantur".

[66]ed. Lefèvre (1967), 161: "Debet autem feretrum coopertum stare in medio ecclesie, sub crucifixo cooperto in medio templi, et iuxta feretrum erit locata cathedra (...) supra quam erit locata capsa velata, in qua lignum dominice crucis continetur (...) ut ab omnibus osculetur, et omnes faciant oblacionem suam ibidem, flexis genibus osculando pavimentum".

[67]See p. 168 sqq.

[68]Hallinger X, 271, lib. II: "Cum domum intrare coeperint, omnes flectant genua contra dominicum corpus"; In the East the Nestorian synod of 585 speaks of the practice, as does Lucas Thaumaturgus († 946), who supported the use of incense and a tripple genuflection at communion; Browe (1935a), 43.

[69]Hallinger, III/IV, 98: "vadat sacerdos, praecedentibus duobus conversis cum candelabris vadat et tertius ad thuribulum deferendum. Quibus reverentibus flexis genibus adorent omnes corpus Domini quod a sacerdote affertur".

the orders and the synodal decrees insisted "countless times" on people kneeling in the street when the 'procession' passed by with the *viaticum*.[70]

The act of kneeling outside the Mass was mirrored from the 11th century by the congregation's kneeling at the 'elevatio' and communion. The *consuetudines* of some orders describe how the monks no longer limited themselves to bowing before receiving communion, which had been the custom from the 7th century[71], but that they first genuflected or prostrated themselves on the ground. In 1086, in addition to genuflecting, the Cluniacs showed reverence for the Sacrament by kissing the hand of the priest giving communion.[72] According to the *Liber usuum* dated 1119 it was usual for the Cistercians to practise the *prostratio*, after which they received communion in a kneeling position.[73] The reason for this, Browe assumes, was originally of a practical nature: during the Carolingian period the practice of receiving the Eucharist on the tongue made its appearance.[74] As long as the communicant received communion in the hand, this was possible in a standing position, of which the prescription contained in the *Regula Magistri* is an example.[75] It is, incidentally, impossible to say when this change of posture was introduced.[76] What can be stated with certainty is that it is illustrated in the *evangelarium* of Bernward of Hildesheim († 1022), an art-loving bishop of the Ottonian era, who was possibly an artist himself. The illustration shows Judas kneeling before his Master, who is placing the bread in his mouth.[77] The prescription contained in the *Liber usuum* referred to above, to be followed by rubrics drawn up by other orders, followed the existing tradition.[78] Subsequently, from the 12th and 13th centuries, it became the custom outside the monasteries to receive communion in a kneeling

---

[70]Browe (1936), 41-44.

[71]Browe (1935a), 42.

[72]PL 149, 721, *Udalrici (...) consuetudines*: "antequam communicent cuncti veniam petentes, et manum sacerdotis osculantes".

[73]PL 166, 1432, c. 58: "Venientes vero ad gradum altaris proximum, incumbant super articulos manuum: ascensoque gradu, flexoque genu iuxta cornu altaris et suscepta eucharistia, cum se erexerint, inclinent".

[74]Browe (1935a), 46.

[75]ed. Vogüé de (1964), SC 106, c. 21: "Ergo post modicam orationem erecti communicent".

[76]Browe (1935a), 46.

[77]Tschan (1942-52), III, Album, Codices, no. 70, The Last Supper; see also Vloberg (1946), 88 sqq.

[78]Browe (1935a), 47.

position. Abbot Egbert of Schönau († 1184) used it in a sermon preached to a number of Cathars and later the number of references increases.[79]

In the 13th century the act of genuflection was also generalised among the laity at the 'elevatio'. Again the origin is to be found in the monasteries. As early as 1152 the Cistercians prescribed the *prostratio* when the bell rang to announce the 'elevatio' - which was chest-high at the time - not only for all those present in the church but also for anyone anywhere in the monastery, with the exception of the dormitory.[80] The general chapter of 1215 changed the *prostratio* into kneeling, so that the raised Host could be prayed to while looked at.[81] Sometimes members of the congregation would stretch out their hands, but usually they simply knelt - eventually from the *Sanctus* to the communion - and this was also prescribed for the laity, as seen in the regulations drawn up by the synod of Oxford in 1222.[82] Towards the end of the 13th century, as already stated in chapter II, the bells in the church tower even invited those living in the immediate vicinity of the church to participate in the Consecration in this way.

In the midst of the kneeling clerics the celebrant, of course, remained standing in order to be able to perform the 'elevatio'. He showed reverence by first bowing deeply. It is only at the end of the 14th century that we find the first reports of the celebrant genuflecting before and after the 'elevatio'. This had not become a general custom even in the 15th century.[83] This type of reverence, moreover, would seem to have been regarded in the Middle Ages as fitting only for a temporal monarch but not for the King of Heaven.[84] As well as making a bow, the celebrant could show reverence with a kiss. The *Ordo Romanus Primus* dating from the 7th-8th century does not mention the kissing of the Host but does say that the chalice and paten were kissed, a practice repeated at the beginning of the 12th century by some, including the monk, Honorius

---

[79]PL 195, 90, Sermo XI, c.10: "et multo humilius caeteris genua tua ad altare incurvas".

[80]Canivez (1933-41), I, 49: "Quando campana pulsatur in elevatione hostiae salutis, omnes petant veniam praeter eos qui sunt in dormitorio".

[81]ibid. 434: "omnes flectant genua (...) orationem quam inspiraverit Deus facientes".

[82]Mansi XXII, 1175: "Frequenter moneantur laici, ut ubicumque videant corpus Domini deferri, statim genua flectant (...) et hoc maxime fiat tempore consecrationis in elevatione hostiae".

[83]Jungmann (1962), II, 265.

[84]Browe (1929c), 45-50, esp. 46, n. 171.

of Autun, who probably came from Regensburg.[85] In the 13th century, it would appear that Eucharistic devotion had become so intensified that the celebrant now even kissed the Host itself, either before and after the consecration or at the *Pater Noster*.[86] This expression of devotion, which was reflected in the kissing of the *viaticum* of communion was impossible, was one the one hand encouraged in some French missals[87] it was, on the other, forbidden as a measure against superstitious practices. The interdict issued by a synod held at Sarum in 1217[88] and the resistance to the practice expressed by Bonaventure[89] († 1274) are early witnesses to this in the century in which the practice was introduced.

As already stated at the beginning of this introduction, candles, lamps and incense surrounded the relics and, later, the Eucharist, when people knelt before them on the occasion of a *visit*, during *exposition* and a *procession* or at when they were used to give a *blessing*. It is these four forms of devotion which, once again, took on concrete forms in the devotion shown towards the Eucharist around 1300 in the gradual process of the uncoupling of the Eucharist from the celebration of the sacrament.

1   VISITS TO THE RELICS AND TO THE EUCHARIST

Whenever anyone took candles and incense to the *martyrium*, kissed the tomb and knelt before it, this expression of reverence signified ipso facto a visit to the saint in question, present in his relics. The visit was made so that the visitor could request the saint's intercession with God or ask the saint himself directly for a favour. Because of the close relationship between the sacrifice of the Mass offered on the altar table and the martyr's grave, early on in the Middle Ages piety towards the altar

---

[85]Andrieu (1931-61), II, 97, n. 94: "vertit se archidiaconus et osculatam patenam dat eam tenendam diacono secundo"; PL 172, 560, *Gemma animae*, I, c. 56: "Confecto ergo corpore Christi, labia calicis tangimus"; Dölger (1929-50), III, 238-239: in the East the practice of kissing the Eucharistic bread is reported as early as around the year 500; Nussbaum (1969), 17-19.

[86]Durandus, *Rationale*, 187, lib. IV, c. 46, n. 24: "In quibusdam ecclesiis sacerdos hic (after the Pater Noster) etiam hostiam osculatur, innuens quod Nicodemus idem fecerit".

[87]Leroquais (1924), II, 299, n. 477, missal of Rheims (14th century): "Hic elevet panem (...) hic ponat ad os."; III, 160, n. 728, missal of Evreux (15the century): "Hic deosculetur hostiam et postea elevet".

[88]Mansi XXII, 1119, can. 37: "hostiam consecratam, pacem daturus sacerdos, ore suo non adveniat, quia ante perceptionem, ore suo tangere non debet".

[89]*Opera omnia*, VIII, 600, Opusculum I, speculum disciplinae, c. XVII,10: "nec post nec ante elevationem osculentur eandem (hostiam)"; Browe (1929c), 62-64; (1933) 65; (1936), 225.

predominated in monastic circles. It was expressed in 'going from altar to altar' inside the church building in order to show reverence towards the martyrs and saints whose relics lay within or close by.

In 789 Charlemagne decided that monasteries containing the *corpora* of saints, which attracted many visitors, needed a separate oratory where people could pray undisturbed.[1] His son, Louis, set a time during the sung Office for the visiting of the altars.[2] However they make no mention of reverence towards and visits to the Eucharist. Indeed, the Sacrament was generally reserved in the sacristy, available for the sick. Even after the publication of the *Admonitio Synodalis* at the end of the 9th century the gradually increasing presence of the Eucharist on or close to the altar table did not lead to this form of reverence. The passage from visit to altar grave or relic altar to devotion to the Sacrament only occurred once the reverence paid to the raised Host at the 'elevatio' had become general practice in the 13th century.

The first reports of visits to the Blessed Sacrament date from approximately 1220. The introduction and extension of the feast of Corpus Christi eventually turned the altar into the pedestal on which rested the Sacrament which the faithful visited and pushed into the background the practice of visiting the relics.

1.1   Visits to the relics

From the middle of the 4th century people of all types visited the graves of the martyrs. The attraction of the tomb of Felix of Nola was so great that sick and healthy pilgrims came daily from far and wide to ask for healing or to fulfil a promise made.[3] In Antiochia the *martyria* drew such hordes of pilgrims that it was worth the beggars' while to stand at the entrance door to ask for alms from a generous visitor come to take his candle or other gift inside.[4] The *martyria* functioned as safe havens,

---

[1] Albers, III, 67, *Documenta,* 17,7: "Ut ubi corpora sanctorum requiescunt aliud oratorium habeatur ubi fratres secrete possint orare".

[2] MGH Ep V, 304, ep. variorum, 4, XXXI: "Ut intervallum post matutinos et ante primam hiemis vel aestatis tempore eo proteletur spatio, quo se fratres apte parare et convenienter orando altaria circuire possint".

[3] CSEL 30, 260, *Carmen* XXVI, 385: "omni namque die testes sumus undique crebris coetibus aut sanos gratantia reddere vota aut aegros varias petere ac sentire medellas"; PL 61, 647; CSEL 30, 107 *Carmen*, 198: "videas etiam de rure colonos non solum gremio sua pignora ferre paterno, sed pecora aegra manu saepe introducere secum"; PL 61, 495.

[4] PG 62, 466, Chrysost., *In ep. ad Thessal.* c. V, hom. XI,4: ["et in ecclesiis et in martyriis ante vestibula sedent pauperes"].

where the intercession of the saints and martyrs was requested by those in spiritual and material need. The earliest witness to this prayer for the intercession of a saint with God dates from the year 260. It is scratched in the catacomb of San Sebastiano in Rome and reads: "Peter and Paul, pray for me".[5] The following prayer was addressed to St. Genesius, martyred in Arles around the year 300 and reverenced in the town: "Save us because of your holiness".[6] His tomb was one of sixty or so in Gaul which were often visited *in corpore* and which can be found in the works of Gregory of Tours.[7] The numbers of visitors were sometimes so great that the monks had no opportunity to pray in peace and quiet. Following the example of Charlemagne's capitularium, the Council of Frankfurt in 794 repeated that in such circumstances the monasteries should have a separate oratory on the premises.[8]

From the 3rd century onwards the altar became the centrepiece of the church building. As already said, it was reverenced with a kiss of greeting as the Eucharistic table of the Lord, the symbol of Christ, but also - from the 4th century on - also as resting place of the martyr[9], given shape in the altar grave or relic altar. In the early Middle Ages, from the 8th century on, there are examples of monks who prayed to God and the saints before these altars in their churches. This custom of paying a visit was greatly encouraged by Benedict of Aniane[10] († 821), the initiator and leader of the Frankish monastic reform. The procession from altar to altar usually took place three times daily: before evening prayer, before the Office of the night and after morning prayer.[11] It became a monastic tradition, described as a valued practice in the life of many a monk and bishop. Ulrich of Augsburg († 973) knelt before the various altars praying to the Lord "out of the depths" (Ps. 130) "for mercy" (Ps.

---

[5]Jounel (1987), 30.

[6]MGH SRM I,2, 84, *In gloria martyrum,* c. 68: "Genesi beatissime, eripe nos propriae sanctitatis virtute".

[7]Vieillard-Troiekouroff (1976), 435-437.

[8]MGH Conc II, 168, can. XV: "De monasterio, ubi corpora sanctorum sunt: ut habeat oratorium intra claustra, ubi peculiare officium et diuturnum fiat".

[9]LW I, 105-108.

[10]Browe (1933), 11-25; Couneson (1935-36), 8-9.

[11]Halliger, I, 302-303, *Institutio Angilberti Centulensis* (ca. 800), XVII, De circuitu orationum : "ubi per singulos cotidianos dies ac noctes (...) Vesperos, Nocturnos et Matutinos ob memoriam omnium fidelium defunctorum persolvant"; Albers, III, 103, Documenta, 22,31; V, 74, *Consuetudines Einsidlenses* (10th century); IV, 223-224, *Consuetudines Vallumbrosae Congregationis* (late 12th century); Gougaud (1925), 58; 63, n. 34.

56).[12] We have already mentioned the oft-repeated kneeling undertaken by Bishop Wulstan of Worcester in the late 11th century. In the middle of the 12th century in his *Explicatio* of the liturgy the Parisian theologian, John Beleth, dealt with the visit to and greeting of the altars during the sung Office. He set the time for it at a particular moment: just before the night Office.[13] The visit to the altars was again mentioned in the 13th century by the Cistercian, Caesarius of Heisterbach and by the Premonstratensian, Peter of Dacia († 1288), without any reference to the Eucharist.[14]

The custom was not entirely confined to the monasteries: Bishop Jonas of Orleans († 844) criticised those lay folk who neglect to enter a church where the relics are available for reverence, a complaint repeated by the Council of Paris in 829.[15] The *vita* of Benedict, abbot of a monastery in Piedmont, we read of a man who takes his son into a church dedicated to St. Michael. The little boy secretly takes a piece of wax candle while his father is devoutly visiting each altar in turn. The Sacrament is not mentioned, neither here nor in the continuing story of the little boy's theft. For on the road back home St. Michael causes the boy's arm to swell and he confesses his fault. Father and son return to the sacred place to clear up the problem with the archangel.[16] Similarly neither Regino of Prüm († 915) nor Burchard of Worms († 1025) make any connection whatsoever with a visit to the Eucharist when quoting the *Admonitio Synodalis* or when issuing further prescriptions regarding keeping the church building clean. Their argument is "that the body and blood of the Lord are consecrated there and the relics are present for

---

[12]MGH SS IV, 391, *Gerhardi Vita s. Oudalrici ep.*: "Sexta autem hora expleta, altaria circuibat cum venia, cantans *miserere mei Deus et de profundis.*"

[13]PL 202, 35-36, *Rationale divinorum officiorum explicatio*, c. 24 : "Cum ecclesiae ministri ad nocturnum officium surgunt (...) ecclesia aperta est, quam simul atque ministri ecclesiae ingressi sunt, debent se ante omnia ad sanctorum altaria conferre, ibique pressa voce prostrati eos implorare".

[14]ed. Strange (1851), I, 12, 80, 354 and *Dial.* I, c. 6; II, c. 12; VI, c. 5; Browe (1933), 13.

[15]PL 106, 149-150, *De institutione laicali*: "Sicut sunt nonnulli, qui orandi gratia ecclesiae limina frequentare negligunt, ita e contrario existunt plerique, qui pro eo, quod basilicas adire nequeunt et reliquias sanctorum praesto non habent, idcirco vota precum suarum ad Dominum, ut oporteret, supplici devotione non fundunt"; MGH Conc II, 666, can. XIII.

[16]MGH SS XII, 205, *Vita Benedicti abb. Clusensis*: "Longobardus quidam causa orationis ad Sanctum Michaelem venerat cum proprio filio, qui attentius agens curam orationis, cuncta oratorii circuiret altaria".

veneration".[17] When Peter Damian († 1072) mentions greeting the church when passing he is referring to a greeting given to the altar and not to the Sacrament.[18] For the 12th century the account in the *vita* of the Scottish St. Walthenius († 1159) of the appearance of a ghost could be an indication of the connection made between a visit to the altar and the Eucharist present there. The saint is bothered by the devil and prays "with his gaze directed straight at the altar". Then he takes the pyx from the altar, makes a sign of the cross with it and Satan disappears.[19]

Browe analyzed even more examples of the visit to the altars than the above, taken from his work. His analysis caused him to form the opinion that the piety shown towards the tabernacle did not take form earlier than the 13th century, when it came into being parallel to the spread of the adoration of the Host at the 'elevatio'. This conclusion agrees with the arguments advanced by the synod held in Paris around 1208 and repeated by that held in Lerida (1238-1247) regarding the "greatest reverence" to be shown to the altar: it was there that the body of Christ was to be found and where the Mass was celebrated. The safety precautions drawn up by the Fourth Lateran Council also implied reverence of this type.[20]

1.2   Visits to the Blessed Sacrament*

The earliest document containing unmistakeable the visit to the Blessed Sacrament is the *Ancrene Riwle*, written around 1220 in England for three female recluses.[21] This rule states that the prayer said on visiting the

---

[17]ed. Wasserschleben (1964), 51, c. 59: "Ubi enim corpus Domini consecratur, ubi angelorum praesentia non dubitatur adesse, ubi sanctorum reliquiae reconditae venerantur"; PL 140, 691, Burchardi Wormaciensis ep. *decr.* lib. III, c. 85.

[18]PL 145, 528, op. 30, *De sacramentis per improbos administrandis,* c. 3; Browe (1933), 16.

[19]AASS 3 aug. I, 264, *Vita s. Waltheni abbatis,* n. 65, 66: "Cum enim quadam vice Sanctus staret orans coram magno altari oculis et manibus in caelum intentus, ante conspectum eius in varias formas se transfiguravit angelus malus (...) Sanctus autem in impetu spiritus concito gressu, prout potuit, pergens ad altare pyxidem eburneam sacrosanctum corpus Domini continentem reverenter assumpsit, et secum illo signans".

[20]Mansi XXII, 677, Capitula de sacramenti altaris: "Summa reverentia et honor maximus sacris altaribus exhibeatur, et maxime ubi sacrosanctum corpus Domini reservatur, et Missa celebratur"; Browe (1933), 18-19; Couneson (1935-36), esp. 9-12.

*A list for further reading and sources can be found in: Browe (1933), 11-35; Nussbaum (1979), 139-142.

[21]ed. Salu (1955), XX.

Sacrament should also be prayed at the 'elevatio' and communion. The visit to the saints, their altars and relics follows then.

Daily the recluses were expected first to dress, praying the while, and then direct their thoughts to the body and blood of the Lord above the altar, kneel before it and greet Him thus: "Hail, author of our creation! Hail, price of our redemption! Hail, *viaticum* of our journey! (...) Be Thou our joy, who art to be our reward; let our glory be in Thee throughout all ages for ever. O Lord, be always with us, take away the dark night, wash away all our sins, give us Thy holy relief".[22]

Then the sisters were required to pray the same prayer at the 'elevatio' during the Mass and before the confession of guilt at communion. Then they knelt before the crucifix, meditating on the five wounds, and before the statue of the Virgin Mary where they said five "Hail Marys". Finally they were recommended: "(...) bow or kneel before the other images and before your relics, especially those of the saints to whom you have dedicated your altars out of devotion, more particularly if any of them have been consecrated".[23]

Prayer said at the altar of the saint had now been relegated to a lower level. The Eucharist reserved in the church above the high altar was given pride of place. A small indication of this change in emphasis is perhaps to be found in the biography of St. Hedwig († 1243), Duchess of Silesia. She was highly regarded for her charitable works and founding of monasteries, especially following the death of her husband, whom she had married when she was thirteen. "At night she would go from altar to altar", so her biographer writes. He continues with a remark that she kissed the ground as had Mary Magdalene, because she herself was not allowed to touch her Saviour.[24] However, this does not necessarily mean the Eucharist but can refer to the altar, symbol of Christ. Pachasius Radbertus had already recounted how at night abbot Wala († 835) prostrated himself before the altar at his Master's feet.[25] The new tendency is expressed much more convincingly around 1250 in the words of Humbert Romanus, the then Father General of the Dominicans. He

---

[22]ibid. 7.

[23]ibid. 8.

[24]AASS 17 oct. VIII, 236, *Vita s. Hedwigis viduae*, n. 50: "orando per singula circuibat altaria (...) in terramque cadens ad pedes Domini Iesu cum Magdalena humiliter se prostravit".

[25]AASS OSB IV,1, 471, *Vita V. Walae abb.*, lib. I: "nocte vero (...) ad pedes Domini Iesu coram sanctis altaribus prostratus humo iacebit".

states - and the Franciscan Salimbene agrees with him on this[26] - that people should go to church to pray because the crucifix and the statue of the Virgin Mary are to be found there, but also because it is there that the body of the Lord and the relics are kept permanently.[27] Elsewhere he recommends kneeling before the altar "because of the relics and the statues (...) but *especially* because of the body of the Lord, that is reserved there".[28] We have already seen how Louis the Pious on his return journey from Syria in 1254 withdrew into the tabernacle tent he had on board ship and prayed "before the Blessed Sacrament and the holy relics".[29]

From the 13th century onwards there was a growing tendency to pay a visit to the the holy sepulchre during Holy Week. Although sometimes relics were contained in it, in this case it was a question of a visit to the Lord really present.[30] Other examples no longer mention the relics and the greeting is wholly centred on the Eucharist. Around the year 1250, for instance, Salimbene's fellow Franciscan, Bishop Odo of Rouen, decided in the course of his visitation of the cathedral of Séez that the Eucharist should be reserved on the high altar so that everyone kneeling there would be able to see the Sacrament.[31] The miraculous

---

[26]MGH SS XXXII, 338, *Cronica*, 350: "Quod viri ecclesiastici dominicum corpus reservant in ecclesiis et oratoriis suis propter tria (...) Primo, ut pro infirmis possit haberi (...) Secundo, ut exhibeamus ei reverentiam debitam et devotam (...) Tertio, quod Dominus promisit habitare nobiscum, quod facit in sacramento altaris".

[27]ed. Berthier (1956), I, 175, *Expositio Regulae b. Augustini*, c. II, 54: "Item, ibi ut frequentius est corpus Domini et reliquiae sanctorum".

[28]ibid. II, 170, *Expositio (...) super constitutiones fratrum praedicatorum*, c. II, 56: "Profunde autem sunt faciendae huiusmodi inclinationes ante altare, propter altaris ipsius sanctitatem (...) Item, propter reliquias et imagines sanctas, quae solent in eo vel iuxta esse; maxime autem propter Corpus Domini, quod ibidem reservatur".

[29]See p. 97

[30]Arens (1908), *Liber Ordinarius*, written in the 14th century for the canons of Essen, 57-58, *In Parasceve*: "Deinde fit processio ad sepulchrum cum scolaribus, qui ibi tunc presentes erunt, sic. Dyaconus cum cruce precedet, deinde scolares, deinde canonici cum reliquiis, deinde ceroferarii ante sacramentum, deinde sacerdos cum sacramento, et subdyaconus cum pleonario iuxta eum, deinde conventus, ultimo populus (...) ad sepulchrum, quod ante altare sancti Michaelis preparatum erit (...) Tunc aperto sepulchro scilicet archa in tentorio posita, in qua munda palla erit strata seu expansa, sacerdos flexis genibus ponat intus sacramentum, reliquias et pleonarium, et replicata palla desuper et thurificatione facta et reverenti inclinatione recludat archam clave assignando clavem thezaurarie ad reservandum postea"; 71, *In nocte sancta Pasche*: "deinde, sepulchro aperto scilicet archa et iterum thurificatione facta et amota palla de sacramento et aliis reliquiis intus positis, presbiter recipiat sacramentum, subdyaconus pleonarium, alii alias reliquias, singuli singulas".

[31]ed. Bonnin (1852), 81: "Invenimus quod sacrosanctum et venerabile corpus Christi circa maius altare non habetur, quod transeuntibus per chorum et ibidem orantibus haberi deberet pre oculis, ut ipsorum devotio augeretur"; Dumoutet (1942), 96; Browe (1933), 21; Nussbaum (1979), 141.

events described in the *vitae* of Beguines and Cistercian sisters, whose visions have already been referred to, also serve to confirm the existence of the practice of visiting the Eucharist. The father confessor and biographer of Ida of Louvain († 1260) reports her mystical vision of a pyx returning her greeting in the church.[32] The previous link between altar and relics, with its obvious roots in the early Christian cult of the martyrs, would thus seem to have been modified: the altar is become the chosen place for the 'unique relic' of Christian faith.[33]

***

The visits to and devotion directed towards the Host outside the Mass was, however, far from being general practice at the time. We have already seen that neither Caesarius of Heisterbach nor Bonaventure († 1274) made mention of it, in contrast to the latter's brothers Salimbene and Odo. The argument of Bonaventure, laid out extensively, consisted of a recommendation to the mendicant Franciscans to go first to the church on entering a village and pray before the altar. In this way they were continuing the Gospel tradition of first going to visit the Temple on entering Jerusalem. He did not, however, motivate his recommendation with any mention of the presence of the Holy of Holies.[34]

The turning point in the transposition we are discussing must have occurred in the 13th century, in which this 'second founder of the Franciscans' lived. The above would thus seem to indicate that the reason for kneeling before the altar was about to change. This expression of devotion no longer applies only to the altar and the relics but also - and sometimes exclusively - to the Eucharist. The sisters for whom the *Ancrene Riwle* was written knelt in church in order to greet the body and blood of the Lord. It was only later on the day that they turned their attention to the statues and relics. Caesarius of Heisterbach, Peter of Dacia and Bonaventure, on the contrary, make no mention whatsoever of

---

[32]AASS 3 apr. II, 172, *Vita ven. Idae virg. cisterc.*, lib. II,6: "sacramentum, in altaris superficie reverenter in vase reconditum (...) salutavit: Ave (...) pie et dulcis Iesu. Quo dicto (...) ictus (...) pyxidem ab interiore suae parte vehementius impulit; sonitumque faciens validum et excussum, hunc ipsum, vice resalutationis (...) ex eodem habitationis suae vasculo, delegavit".

[33]Mitchell (1982), 169.

[34]*Opera Omnia*, VIII, Opusculum, I, c. XXIX,1, 610: "Pervenientes ad religiosorum vel saecularium loca, cum ad ecclesiam si in loco fuerit, veniunt, in ingressu ecclesiae illum secum versiculum memorantes: *Introibo in domum tuam, adorabo ad templum sanctum in timore tuo*".

the presence of the Eucharist when they speak of visiting the church. Odo of Rouen changes the emphasis and connects reverence for the altar with the Sacrament, while Ida of Louvain and like minds concentrated solely on greeting the pyx. Between these two extremes is the prescription of Humbert Romanus and the prayer of St. Louis: their devotion was directed at both Eucharist and relics, but "especially" - *maxime autem* - to the *corpus Domini*, for which Louis had caused a fine tent to be erected on the stern deck.

A century later the balance changed definitively in favour of the Sacrament when the effects brought about by the feast of Corpus Christi became clear, the Eucharistic devotion that had become institutionalised by the Church. The theophoric procession which emerged from this happened also to provide an opportunity to pause at the altars of repose before the exposed Eucharist as also during the Mass followed by exposition. These instants of devotion were in all likelihood prompted visits to the Blessed Sacrament at other times, a practice familiar in various women's convents in South Germany in the 14th century.[35] And yet this form of private visit to the Lord did not remain confined geographically: in 1343 a Franciscan lay-brother in Palermo is stated to have obtained the healing of a brother who had been given up for lost by praying for an hour before the Eucharist.[36] This form of veneration was infrequent among the laity in the 14th century. An exception to this was the mystic, Dorothy of Montau († 1394), wife of a manual worker from Dantzig from her sixteenth year. She visited "before the dawning of the day" a small chapel of the Blessed Sacrament close to Dantzig where the Eucharist was exposed.[37]

In the 15th century some bishops of Northern Germany accorded indulgences to anyone making this type of visit before the closed tabernacle. The church with the sanctuary lamp has become the 'dwelling' of the Lord, which should only be approached with reverence. The popular preacher, Bernardino of Siena, gave seven reasons for this in a sermon preached in 1424: it is the house of God; the divine Sacrament is

---

[35]Nussbaum (1979), 141.

[36]ed. Wadding (1931-64), VII (1932), a. 1343, n. XXIV: "Domum regressus Dei servus, protracta per integram horam oratione coram sanctissimo altaris sacramento, meruit exaudiri".

[37] ed. Stachnik (1978), 269, Processus canonisationis, 1404 , October 30 : "et ex nimio huiusmodi desiderio compellebatur ire ad ecclesias, ut saltim videret hoc venerabile Sacramentum (...) ideo ipso desiderio impatiens solebat ire ad ecclesiam Corporis Cristi, que est ante oppidum Gdanczk, ante diluculum, ut videret ibi Eukaristie sacramentum, quod aperte in una monstrantia ibi servabatur, et sic fervorem sui desiderii in aliquo refrigeraret".

present there; there are angels; it is the place where the sacraments are received; Christ cleared the Temple of buyers and sellers (Mtt. 21:12-13); the relics are present; God is praised there as if it were Paradise.[38] The preacher relegated the relics to sixth place in order of importance. The focus of the church building has now become the tabernacle with "the divine sacrament of the Eucharist", before which the Cistercians of the Pforte monastery in Saxony knelt and prayed the 'Our Father' and 'Hail Mary'. The Bishop of Magdeburg mentioned the visit to the Sacrament in a long list of other 'good works', to all of which he accorded forty days' indulgence.[39] The visit to the Blessed Sacrament remained an exception for the laity in this century. A major obstacle was the fact that the churches were usually locked.[40] This was to change in the 16th century when the devotional forms known as 'perpetual adoration' and 'Forty Hours' (Quarant'Ore) involved de facto a visit to the Holy of Holies. This met the desire felt at the time to feel close to Christ as in the past the faithful had wished to feel close to the saint present in the relics.

2   THE PROCESSION WITH THE RELICS AND THE EUCHARIST

"The fact that every age, every race, civilisation and religion has recognised and used the procession as a religious rite bears witness to its universal significance".[1]

The people of God in the Old Testament is a people on the road in messianic hope towards the Promised Land, and the *Apocalypse* (7:21-22) shows to the people of the New Testament processional images of the view of a new heaven and a new earth. The procession in the Christian church is a symbolic expression of feeling a stranger on this earth, going to meet Christ, just as fasting - often preceded by rogational and penitential processions - witnesses to the realisation that there are values

---

[38]*Opera Omnia*, I, 238-245, sermo XX, art. I, cap. I: "quia ibi est praesentia Dei"; cap. II: "quando est ibi praesentia Dominici Sacramenti"; cap. III: "quia ibi astant multitudines angelorum"; cap. IV: "quia in eis suscipimus multiplicia beneficia Dei"; cap. V: "Quod in nullo ostendit Christus sic fervidum zelum, sicut pro honorando dominico templo"; cap. VI: "cum ibi sint multa divina et sacra (utpote reliquiae sanctorum)"; cap. VI: "Quod in ecclesia fiunt officia paradisi".

[39]Geschichtsquellen der Provinz Sachsen (1870 sqq.), vol. 34 (1909), 202-203, *Urkundenbuch des Klosters Pforte*, n. 259: "qui flexis genibus coram divinissimo eukaristie sacramento unum Pater noster cum Ave Maria dixerint (...) quadraginta indulgenciarum dies de iniunctis eis penitenciis in domino misericorditer relaxamus".

[40]Nussbaum (1979), 142.

[1]Doncoeur (1955), 29.

in life higher than food and drink.[2] This does not detract from the fact that it is precisely the rogational and penitential processions that have the aim of begging God and His saints - whose relics were borne in the procession - to turn aside the *pestilentia igneria* and other disasters of this earthly existence and to safeguard the crops. This really was a question of life and death since the vulnerable inhabitant of the Middle Ages had no defence against a failed harvest coupled to the phantom of hunger.[3] There were specific relic processions for the harvest on the 'Rogation Days' and on 25th April, the feast of St. Mark. The procession on this day originated in the pagan Roman tradition where the procession was led past the fields in order to ask the gods for a good harvest.[4] Ecclesiastical feast days were scarcely imaginable without a procession. Even Sunday was considered appropriate. A breviary from Eichstätt contains regulations covering no less than thirty-three processions per year. Need and joy were, indeed, reasons for holding a procession throughout the whole of the Middle Ages, processions in which the Cross and the relics had gained a regular place.[5]

'Theophoric' processions, or processions in which 'God' under the sign of bread was 'carried' were not part of the usual pattern before the 14th century. The first signs date from the end of the 10th century in the liturgy of Passiontide and when the *viaticum* was taken to the sick. The theophoric processions came to be called 'Blessed Sacrament processions' at the time they were linked with the feast of Corpus Christi instituted in 1264. They were born "in the wake of the processions of the relics".[6]

2.1   The procession of the relics[*]

In the West, Ambrose († 397) relates how the relics discovered by chance with approval of the people were translated to a neighbouring basilica. He

---

[2]LW I, 710; II, 2281.

[3]Le Goff (1982), 205-218.

[4]LW II, 1551-52; see p. 220-221.

[5]Buchner (1912), 118; Browe (1933), 89.

[6]Martimort (1955), 69.

[*]A list for further reading and sources can be found in: LMD 43 (1955) *Les processions*; H. Leclercq, *Procession*, in DACL XIV,2, 1895-1896; W. Pax, *Bittprozession*, in RAC II, 422-429; Boeren (1962); Hermann-Mascard (1975), 193-203; Heinzelmann (1979), 29 n. 58.

organised this type of *translatio* , which Augustine also mentions[7], on the Eastern model. For the early Middle Ages the procession, already described, to the monastery of St. Radegunde, is one of the many translation processions appearing in the works of Gregory of Tours. The people sang as they walked, carrying crosses, candles and incense to solemnize the *translatio*, which shows close resemblances to the ceremonies surrounding the consecration of a church. The procession, in fact, was an integral part of the consecration ritual. Gregory mentions it in connection with such occasions as the consecration of the church of St. Julianus and of his own private oratory.[8] The procession of consecration also figures in the writings of Pope Gregory the Great, as also in the later Roman and Gallic versions of church consecration, which in the end were all combined in the *Pontificale* of Durandus.[9]

The colourful procession of the relics was described in connection with the translations from Italy to the north at the beginning of the 8th century, the *adventus* of St. Nazarius in Lorsch being only one of many examples. The whole village came out to greet the approaching relics and it was an unwritten law that the relics were accompanied for some distance until the next village took over the responsibility.[10] The local or regional translation of relics to a more suitable place was also done under the form of a procession. We have seen how Einhard brought the relics he claimed and obtained from Aachen to Seligenstadt accompanied by hymns of praise, and how the relics of Ss. Eucherius and Trudo were carried around the town in procession before they were given their new resting place behind the altar.

Events of this sort must have been impressive to see. The people came in from far and wide, sometimes even crossing the sea as in the case of the translation of Thomas à Becket in 1220, when his remains were removed from the crypt to a place of honour behind the high altar of

---

[7]CC SL 48, *De Civitate Dei*, XXII, c. 8,2; CC SL 27, *Confessiones,* IX,7, c. 16.

[8]See p. 180, n. 25 and 26: see further: MGH SRM I,1, Hist. Franc., lib. II, c. 14; MGH SRM I,2, 60, 72, 94, resp. *In gloria martyrum,* c. 34, 48, 82; ibid. 128, *De virtutibus s. Iuliani,* c. 33; ibid. 246, 248 resp. *Vitae patrum,* c. 6, c. 8.

[9]PL 78, 159, *Oratio quando elevantur reliquiae*: "Finita hac oratione elevent eas (reliquias) cum feretro, et cum magno honore cantando (...) cum crucibus, et thuribulis, et candelabris multisque luminaribus. Et veniant ad basilicam in qua deponendae sunt".

[10]See p. 19; MGH SS XV, 287-288, *Translatione ss. Alexandri et Iuliani presbyteri,* c. 3: "Huiusmodi quapropter gratiarum rumore comperto, quaque proficiscebamur neminem vicinorum civium oppidanorumque sua tecta tenebant. Et erat iam quadam lege sanccitum, non necessitatis alicuius, sed omnino promtissimae voluntatis, ut ab occurrentibus catervarum turmis eo usque per octo ferme vel amplius spatia milium sancti deducerentur donec quoque aliarum villarum plebes cum crucibus obviam properarent".

Canterbury Cathedral. "It is reported that the people of England had never seen such a large number of people gathered together in one place".[11] The sources speak of the translations as drawing huge crowds to the church square, in the streets and in the trampled fields round about. All attention was focused on what was going to arrive, as the bells began to ring to signal that the procession was moving off. A sea of silver and gold crosses rose above the uncovered heads, a long line of monks, priests, deacons and subdeacons made its way forward, with each in their distinctive garments and carrying torches in their hands; then came the candle-bearing abbots, bishops and archbishops, clad in richly ornamented choir capes and wearing magnificent mitres that glittered with precious stones. Hymns and harps rang out and the people sang with gusto as each hymn was begun. Then a "sweet smelling mist" became visible as up-curling smoke of incense arose from the thuribles, swung by young men in a festive show of perfumed clouds. Through the incense smoke, finally, the outlines of a beautiful reliquary, borne by monks, princes of the church or kings, was seen approaching.[12] Thus in 1239 St. Louis carried the Crown of Thorns into Paris in procession, Henry III († 1272) bore on his shoulders the relics of Edward the Confessor along the paths of Westminster Abbey and Edward I († 1307) regarded it as an honour to be permitted to carry the body of St. William, archbishop of York.[13] In the descriptions quoted, the shrine only needed replacing by the Sacrament under a baldachin for the transposition into a procession of the Blessed Sacrament to be complete. In addition to monks, priests and bishops, kings too bore witness of their reverence. During the Council of Vienne in 1311 the baldachin was carried by four kings: Louis IV († 1314) of France, his son in his capacity as king of Navarre, Edward II († 1327) of England and James II († 1327) of Aragon. The same devotion to the Sacrament was shown in 1424 in Barcelona by Alfonso V the Magnanimous and in 1535 by Charles V.[14]

The procession was not only employed on the occasion of translations: the aim could also be a manifestation in honour of God or the saints or an attempt to influence them in order to have an enemy

---

[11]ed. Rock (1905), III, 404: "Ad cuius translationem tam grandis conventus utriusque sexus de diversis mundi partibus convenerat, ut nunquam retroactis temporibus, ut dicitur, tam magna multitudo hominum ad unum locum in Anglia coadunata fuerat".

[12]ibid. 405-407, a compilation taken from the report of the translation of such saints as Albanus in 1129 and Guthlac in 1136.

[13]See p. 26; ed. Rock (1905), 309-310.

[14]Corblet (1885-86), II, 380-381; Matern (1962), 106; Stemmler (1969), 202.

driven off or a disaster avoided. The procession with the tunic of St. Vincent along the town defences of Saragossa in the 6th century (already referred to) and the procession bearing the bones of St. Germanus and Genoveva in 886 to the parts of Paris threatened by the Norsemen are examples of relic processions in time of war.[15] To this same category could be added the attempts on the part of the monks to put pressure on a usurper when they processed with their relics to a disputed territory. The relic processions to the truce of God councils or on the occasion of the consecration of a monastery had the character of a manifestation. When the Hasnon monastery on the Flemish border was to be consecrated in 1070, the local abbots attended with as many relics as possible so that the saints could personally witness the consecration.[16]

During natural disasters the people sought refuge in penitential and rogational processions with the relics. In order to be spared from the deadly clutch of the bubonic plague, as Gregory of Tours relates, the people of Rheims gathered around the tomb of St. Remigius, spending the night their in prayer and hymn-singing surrounded by burning lamps and candles. Then the cloth covering the tomb was removed and carried through the town - in *modum feretri* - as if it were a litter.[17] In order to avert a similar plague epidemic in 590 and 603, Pope Gregory the Great organised the *litania septiformis*,[18] the sevenfold litany. These were penitential processions starting from seven churches in Rome to the church of St. Mary Major.[19] In later years the separate relic processions were often to make for the main church where a re-grouping took place and then the real procession set out. On the occasion of processions Pope Gregory emphasised the power of the relics and made reference to the cloak of St. Eutychius. Every time the rains failed to come and the crops dried up, he stated, the people gathered together and carried the saint's

---

[15]See p. 11 and 20; Gaier (1966); Hermann-Mascard (1975), 218-219.

[16]MGH SS XIV, 157, *Tomelli historia monasterii Hasnoniensis*: "adiunctisque eis quam plurimis abbatibus cum quam plurimis sanctorum patrociniis, saepe memorati encaenias coenobii non modicis transegit solempniis".

[17]MGH SRM I,2, 346, *In gloria confessorum*, c. 78: "Adsumpta igitur palla de beati sepulchro, conponunt in modum feretri; accensisque super cruces cereis atque cereferalibus, dant voces in canticis, circumeunt urbem cum vicis".

[18]Biraben (1969), 1493, 1498.

[19]Matern (1962), 40-41.

tunic through the fields. The rain was subsequently not long in coming.[20] Processions of this type were on the increase from the 11th century onwards. In 1021 the people of Amiens and Corbie were at the end of their tether and went to meet one another bearing the relics when the plague afflicted the region for seven years. This same procession was subsequently repeated annually for some years.[21]

In 1053 the plague struck again in Neustrië and threatened Rouen. Fifteen Benedictines from the monastery of Fontenelle, picked for the task, carried the bones of St. Wulfram to the town, from where the canons came to meet them bearing the relics of St. Romanus. In this way they attempted to invoke the intervention of the saints in order to keep the plague out of the town.[22] According to an 11th-century source, rich in miracle stories, the people carried the *majestas* of Sainte-Foy in procession at Conques on several occasions when disaster threatened.[23] These acts were regarded as so effective that at one stage the monks were no longer able to meet the demand for processions. They had to apply to Pope Urban II for his help in putting a stop to these sometimes presumptuous demands.[24] Basing himself on the opinion of Gregory the Great, Thiofried of Echternach († 1110) stated that on the occasion of natural disasters God's miraculous powers worked through the linen relics of the saints. It was not without reason, he said, that these were carried through the fields at times of drought or flood.[25] However when the Seine broke her banks in Paris in 1206, the reliquary of Genoveva herself was carried out. This was compared to the might shown by Yahweh's Ark, which permitted the Israelites to cross the Jordan dry-shod

---

[20]SC 260, 326, Dial. lib. III, c. 15: "Nam quoties pluvia deerat, et aestu nimio terram longa siccitas exurebat, collecti in unum cives urbis illius eius tunicam levare (...) Cum qua, dum per agros pergerent exorantes, repente pluvia tribuebatur, quae plene terram satiare potuisset".

[21]AASS OSB IV, 280: "ad quam (pestem) sedandam ambo illi populi humani auxilii inopes, ad vota precesque confugere, indicta in medio inter utrosque itinere processione, in qua Sanctorum utrimque reliquiae ad placandam divini Numinis iram deferrentur, idque singulis annis continuaretur".

[22]ibid. 541: "Fontanellenses coenobitae (...) sancti Wulframni corpus Rotomagum sollemni pompa deferre constituerunt. Condicto itaque die (...) electi quindecim fratres sacrum loculum efferunt, et Rotomagum appulsi, canonicis cum sancti Romani corpore obviam progressis in ecclesiam sanctae Dei genetricis Mariae festivo ritu inferunt".

[23]ed. Bouillet (1900), 474-475, *Liber miraculorum s. Fidis*, c. 14: "A l'occasion d'un fléau"; c. 15: "A l'occasion d'une calamité".

[24]ed. Jaffé (1885-88), I, 701, no. 5802, "Ad hoc nos".

[25] PL 157, 377-378, *Flores epitaphi sanctorum*, lib. III: "In sancta Romana Ecclesia antiquitus mos inolevit et in indissolubilem consuetudinem devenit, ut pro reliquiis sanctorum consecrati brandei rogantibus fidelibus transmitterentur"; Guth (1970), 124.

(Jos. 3:17). The people crossed the river safely with her relics and the water level fell until the Seine was again running in its usual bed.[26]

From the 13th century onwards there was an increase in the regulations governing the holding of processions. The church tried to place processions under the authority of the bishop, an attempt which did not lead to general rules governing processions. A great deal of liturgical liberty was available, all the more so because a procession was also an event for the town itself. The same freedom was given to the local populace in the organisation of the Blessed Sacrament procession, which could be held on the feast of Corpus Christi or on a subsequent day, as the people wished. The lack of regulation expresses to some extent the fact that this procession was never officially prescribed by any pope.[27]

The processions referred to up till now all took place under more or less exceptional circumstances. But there were also relic processions which, from the 8th century onwards, were part of the familiar pattern of the liturgical year and for which a detailed procession liturgy was laid down. Processions of this type included the *rogationes*, penitantial litanies on the three 'Rogation Days' preceding the feast of the Ascension, which were connected with prayers to ensure that the earth brought forth her fruit. Originally they had been designed to ensure safety in situations of acute need. They are said to have been initiated in the mid-5th century by Bishop Mamertus of Vienne († 474) on the three days preceding the Ascension after earthquakes had occurred with all the subsequent dangers as the wolves emerged from their dens and made the whole region unsafe.[28]

The processions on these days became part of tradition, while their aim slowly turned towards the ensuring of a good harvest. Their

---

[26]PL 221, 94-95, *Relatio insignis miraculi*: "Praecedente quondam arca testamenti populus Israel per medium Jordanis sicco pede pertransiit; praecedente etiam b. Genoveva cum sanctorum reliquiis per pontem confractum et ruinae proximum, subsecutus est eam universus populus imminenti periculo inundantium aquarum et pontis per collisionem aquarum fluctuantis, sub eius securus protectione (...) aquae abeuntes decrescebant, usquequo Sequana fluvius intra alveum suum se collegit".

[27]Browe (1931d), 112; Ter Reegen (1956), 196 [8]; Matern (1962), 88; Stemmler (1970), 207; Hermann-Mascard (1975), 223.

[28]PL 59, 289, *Alcimi Aviti homilia de rogationibus*; MGH SRM I,1, 83, *Hist. Franc.*,lib. II, c. 34: "has ipsas rogationes (...) a Mamerto ipsius Viennensis urbis episcopo (...) instatutas fuisse, dum urbs illa multis terreretur prodigiis. Nam terrae moto frequenti quatiebatur, sed et cervorum atque luporum feritas portas ingressa, per totam, ut scripsit, urbem nihil metuens oberrabat"; on the origin of the rogation days see: Franz (1909), II, 7-8; Bruyne de (1922), 14-18; Martimort (1961), 638-639; Bailey (1971), 95-98; Le Goff (1977), 229 n. 18; Vauchez (1987), 145-155.

established practice can be seen in such accounts as that contained in the *vita* of St. Hubert († 727)[29] and in the *Institutio* of Angilbert, the confidant of Charlemagne already mentioned in chapter II. This abbot of the Centula-St. Ricquier Monastery, which was situated between Amiens and Boulogne, describes how things went. Centula possessed the most important *capsa maior*, reputed to contain relics of Christ and the Virgin Mary.[30] These formed the focus of the procession. On either side of the *capsa* three priests walked with smaller reliquaries. Then came the members of the clergy, the monks, the temporal lord's representatives, boys and girls singing, the local worthies and finally the congregation. Leading the procession and bringing up the rear were bearers of crucifixes and incense.[31]

A further example of a similar description can be found in the 11th-century *consuetudines* of the abbey of Farfa, which contain regulations regarding the manner in which the relics were to be taken from one place to another in procession.[32] The permanent position which the relics had gained in the rogation processions and the forming of the tradition can be read clearly in the formulation: "a long-established tradition", found in the 11th-century *passio* of St. Leudegarius[33] and in the *vita* of St. Winnocus.[34] The relics borne in procession represent the saints invoked in the litany. The custom grew up of reading the beginning of the four Gospels to the four points of the compass at each station, based on the belief that these pericopes were of exceptional aid against tempest and

---

[29]MGH SRM VI, 486, c. 6: "Per idem namque tempus, quo triduanum ieiunium universalis celebrare consuevit ecclesia, vir sanctus Dei athleta per oppida et castella praedicando pergebat, veniensque Triiecto iuxta consuetam ordinem cum crucibus et sanctorum reliquias (...) orando extra civitate egrediens (...) dicebat"; see also: Bock (1873), 40.

[30]Heitz (1987), 622.

[31]Hallinger, I, 296-297: "Tunc cruces septem sequantur, ex quibus sit media crux sancti Salvatoris, quas sequatur capsa maior ipsius Salvatoris. Ad cuius dextram partem vadant sacerdotes tres cum aliis capsis minoribus tribus, ad levam similiter"; Heinzelmann (1979), 52.

[32]Hallinger X, 240: "*De sanctorum reliquiis qualiter deferantur ad locum ubi necesse sunt deportande processionaliter aut qualiter recipiantur cum laude*".

[33]MGH SRM V, 361, c. 34: "Est etenim ibi consuetudo ex tempore antiquo, ut in rogationibus, quas invenit sanctus Mamertus (...) extrahantur de latibulis omnes reliquiae et deportentur".

[34]MGH SRM V, 781, *Miracula Winnoci*, c. 3: "Preterea quodam tempore rogationis, dum more solito processionem faceremus cum populo (...) Ibi quoque portabatur viri sancti inter cruces cambuta cum reliquiis"; AOB IV, 368, a. 1031: "Tunc moris erat ex condicto Ambianensum et Corbeiensum, ut reliquiae sanctorum quique suorum ad medium viae inter utramque spatium octavis rogationum unoquoque anno deferrent"; see also n. 28 and 82 and Martène (1788), III, 185, 190.

thunderstorms.[35] The imagination displayed by people and clergy ensured a colourful pageant. At Angers in the 13th century the 'guardians of the relics' bore the shrine of St. Serenus, bedecked with flowers, to three different places on the three Rogation Days and on Ascension Day they participated in the procession that wended its way through the town.[36] Jacob of Voragine mentions in his *Legenda aurea* dated approximately 1265 an enormous dragon which joined the procession as a symbol of evil and sin. The beast had a long straw-filled tail. On the first two days it walked in front of the Cross but on the third day the monster was forced to creep behind the Cross with a floppy empty tail, as a sign that the devil had been banished from his kingdom by Christ.[37] Durandus confirms that an underlying notion in these processions was that the Cross and the relics would serve to drive off the demons.[38]

As well as on the Rogation Days, the annual feasts of the martyrs and saints were marked by a procession of the relics. In Spain there must have been one such on those days as early as in the 7th century, since the Council of Braga held in 675 notes that the bishops have themselves carried into the church with the *capsae* around their necks "on the martyrs' feast day". Such a feast day could serve to celebrate either the death of the saint, the *inventio* of the relics, the *translatio* or the *depositio*. Thus 11th July and 4th December were feast days in Fleury monastery because on those dates the monks celebrated the translation and burial respectively of St. Benedict's relics. From the 9th century on both days a procession was held in honour of Benedict.[39] The 'arrival' of the relics of Saint Maurus in Paris in 868 also gave rise to an annual procession in which the relics of the saint were carried.[40] From the 11th

---

[35]Franz (1909), II, 57: the earliest account dates from the 12th century and the practice became relatively generalised in the 13th-14th centuries; Browe (1933), 108-109, 124, 127, 128, 129-130; Haimerl (1937), 8-21: "Bittprozessionen".

[36]Farcy de (1901), III, 178, n. 2; Hermann-Mascard (1975), 198.

[37]ed. Graesse (1969), 315, cap. LXX, *De letania maiori et minori*: "In quibusdam autem ecclesiis et maxime in ecclesiis Gallicanis consuetudo habetur, quod draco quidam cum longa cauda et inflata, plena scilicet palea vel aliquo tali duobus diebus primis ante crucem et tertio cum cauda vacua post crucem defertur"; Vauchez (1987), 152.

[38]Durandus, *Rationale*, 394, lib. VI, *De rogationibus*, c. 107, no. 7: "Caeterum in processione ipsa praecedunt crux et capsa reliquiarum sanctorum, ut vexillo crucis et orationibus sanctorum daemones depellantur".

[39]See p. 89 and Hermann-Mascard (1975), 199.

[40]AASS-OSB IV,2 , 166, *Historia translationis corporis s. Mauri abbatis*: "Anno dein DCCCLXVIII, cum corpus s. Mauri (...) tandem delatum est in Monasterium Fossatense. Aenea Parisiensi Episcopo sacram pompam ducente et sanctum corpus humeris gestante (...) Processio ista fiebat adhuc inito saeculi XI, ut patet ex litteris Rainaldi Parisiensis episcopi eam confirmantis anno millesimo sexto"; MGH SS XV, 451-472: *Ex Odonis miraculis s.*

century the procession of the relics on the feast of the saint became
customary as also on the general feast day of the relics, which arose at
the same time following the example of Echternach. And even if there
was little or no information regarding the identity of the relics, this did
not stand in the way of a procession. For instance, in Angers a "large
capsa" was carried, containing relics of both identified and unidentified
saints.[41]

Even more ancient than the rogation processions is the procession
held on Palm Sunday, which was known in Jerusalem as early as the 4th
century.[42] Here too the relics were part of the ritual. The reports that a
book of the Gospels and a *fylacterium* were also carried date from the
Merovingian period.[43] This is mentioned in the *Pontificale* of Besançon
about the year 600[44] and in the *ordinarium* of Le Mans. And in "no few
other places" the custom was to be found: Langres and the monastery of
St. Martin in Tours.[45] The relics were placed on a litter, which is again
stated in the *Pontificale* of Poitiers in approximately 800.[46] Hincmar of
Rheims († 882) is reported to have had a beautiful shrine made to contain
the relics of many martyrs "which is carried by two priests".[47] Gerbert,
abbot of Sankt-Blasien, provides various examples in his *Vetus alemanica
liturgia* of palm processions after 800 and notes that the custom arose of
carrying rh relics in the procession. He refers to documents such as the
consuetudines of William of Hirschau († 1091) who prescribes that the

---

Mauri sive restauratione monasterii Glannfoliensis.

[41]Farcy de (1901), III, 179: "On lit dans l'inventaire de 1255: *Item capsa magna
processionalis, in qua plurimorum sanctorum reliquiae continentur*"; Hermann-Mascard
(1975), 200.

[42]Stemmler (1970), 194.

[43]Martène (1706), 192-193: "Processio in quibusdam ecclesiis hac die duplex erat;
scilicet Palmarum et Dominicalis solita (...) Duplicem etiam processionem praescribit
antiquum Rituale ms. monasterii S. Remigii Remensis annorum 400"; "Mane in Palmis
custodes praeparent diligenter quoddam portatorium in modum feretri, in quo reponantur
parvae capsae sive textum Evangeliorum. Desuper quoque appendantur philacteria sive buxae
reliquiarum".

[44]ibid. 204, *Ex. ms. Pontificali Ecclesiae Bisuntinae*: "Primum aqua benedicta (...) tunc
feretrum cum reliquiis (...) inter hos medius diaconus, indutus dalmatica portans brachia
domni Stephani".

[45]ibid. 194: "An vero de huiusmodi ritu intelligi debeat ordinarium ecclesiae
Cenomanensis ubi ait: Deinde processionibus ordinatis, scilicet processione s. Petri primo,
nostra subsequente *cum feretro*, quod portatur a duobus diaconibus (...) An vero sacris
reliquiis, quas etiam nonnulli deferebant, ut *Lingonenses, Turonenses* s. Martini et alii?"

[46]ibid. 201, Ex ms. *Pontificali Ecclesiae Pictaviensis*: "accipiunt duo diaconi desuper
altare feretrum reliquiarum et evangeliorum".

[47]MGH SS XIII, 479, *Fleoderdi Historia Remensis ecclesiae*, lib. III, c. 5: "Locellum
etiam quendam, hoc est capsam maiorem, quae a duobus clericis ferri solet, fieri iussit".

most conscientious *conversi* (lay brothers) should be appointed to carry the relics as was the custom ón the three Rogation Days.[48] Another example can again be found in the *consuetudines* of Farfa, where *conversi* and priests carry crucifixes, statues and relics of popes and other saints in the procession.[49] Even the processional cross itself was decorated with relics enclosed in costly *capsae*.

From the 10th century in some places north of the Alps the Palm Sunday procession took on the character of a dramatisation of the entry of Christ into Jerusalem. A statue of Christ was carried, sometimes seated on a donkey, in the procession. In the *vita* of St. Ulrich († 973) the people are said to have received the blessed branches and walked in the procession to the top of the hill. Others from surrounding villages joined in, waving the branches and spreading their clothes over the roadway for the approaching Messiah seated on the donkey.[50] The presence of Jesus was given even more emphasis when the Eucharist itself was carried in the procession.

2.2   *The procession of the Blessed Sacrament*

The use of the Eucharistic bread as centre point of the Palm Sunday procession would seem to have started in England. At any rate it is from Lanfranc that we have the first report dated 1084. It is contained in his *decreta* and reads as follows: "two priests, dressed in albs, carry the litter on which the body of Christ - in a shrine - is placed, preceded by the Cross and standard bearers".[51] This description is a prelude to the

---

[48] Gerbert (1776), 995-996, dist. X, c. VII,4; PL 150, 1092, Constitut. Hirsaug. lib. I, CXXXII : "In die quoque Palmarum debet aliquos diligentiores de conversis eligere, qui capsas et arcas ss. reliquiarum ad processionem humeris sciant portare (...) quod et in tribus diebus rogationum faciunt"; see also Martène (1788), III, 71, 74, 77.

[49] Hallinger, X, 68: "Tunc conversi accipiant quattuor cruces (...) unus ex sacerdotibus brachium sancti Mauri. Et tres alii ex sacerdotibus cum reliquis ornamentis, vel etiam octo. Sedecim alii conversi, ex quibus portent duo vel quattuor imaginem sancti Petri cum reliquiis et alii duo vel quattuor corpus sancti Marcelli papae, et bini vel quattuor alii cassa sancti Gregorii papae et duo vel quattuor alii sanctorum reliquias multorum patrum"; Albers, I, 44.

[50]Albers, V, 117, *Consuetudines s. Vitonis Virodunensis* (10th century) : "Imaginem nostri Salvatoris per processionem cuncti adorabunt salutantes Ave rex noster"; Stemmler (1970), 194; Nussbaum (1979), 146; Broekaert (1985).

*A list for further reading and sources is can be found in: Browe (1929a); (1931d); (1933), 89-140; Ter Reegen (1956); Niedermeier (1974-75), to a large   extent taken from Browe (1931d); Haimerl (1937), 32 sqq.; Matern (1962); Stemmler (1970), 191 sqq.; Nussbaum (1979), 142-149; 154-161; Zika (1988), 37-48; Rubin (1991), 243-271; Caspers (1992), 103-126.

[51]See p. 47, n. 68; Stemmler (1970), 195-196; Devlin (1975), 97-99.

procession of the Blessed Sacrament, as is Lanfranc's description of the exposition of the Eucharist on a *mensa* at a station or resting place. He would seem to have used the royal palm procession as a means of giving form to his ideas on the *praesentia realis*, which he had already set out in a theological statement opposing Berengarius. This theophoric procession of palms spread rapidly in England and in Normandy, the region where Lanfranc had formerly headed the Le Bec monastery school. The Eucharist does not yet figure in the palm procession in Rouen of approximately 1065 described by John of Avranches.[52] This fact tends to confirm the suspicion that England was indeed the source of the practice around 1080,[53] though its spread from Normandy to England cannot be entirely excluded.[54]

In the procession itself the litter took on another function: it carried the reliquary on which the pyx containing the body of the Lord was hung. Two clerics carried it, preceded by candle bearers. This is how it is described in the *Consuetudinarium* of St. Osmund of Salisbury, a document that served as a guideline in many churches and monasteries in England throughout the 13th century.[55] The commentator on the *Ordo of Sarum* speaks of "the shrine with the Blessed Sacrament and relics",[56] thereby putting into words this dual function. The *Hereford Missal* says of the body of the Lord that it was placed on the altar of repose "together with the relics".[57] Although the carrying of the Eucharist in the procession of palms never became a hard and fast rule, and the custom - to the extent that it existed - disappeared once more,[58] it is still reported in Hereford and Melford up to the 14th century and in Rouen up to the

---

[52]PL 147, 9 sqq. *Liber de Officiis Ecclesiasticis ad Maurilium Rotomagensis Archiepiscopus*; Bailey (1971), 116, n. 11.

[53]Benoît-Castelli (1961), 299.

[54]Browe (1931d), 108; Vloberg (1946), II, 237: "Angers et Rouen dès le XIe siècle"; Stemmler (1970), 199; Niedermeier (1974-75), 419-420.

[55]ed. Jones (1883-4), RS, 78,I, 120-122, c. 70: "et dum distribuuntur rami benedicti, praeparetur feretrum cum reliquiis a quo Corpus Domini in pixide dependeat et ad locum stationis a duobus clericis (...) deferatur, lumine in lanterna precedente"; ed. Rock (1905), IV, 269; Stemmler (1970), 196: in at least 11 English monasteries; Nussbaum (1979), 146, n. 339.

[56]ed. Rock (1905),IV, part II, chap. XII, 267: "The priests who bore the shrine with the Blessed Sacrament and relics, stepped forwards"; Nussbaum (1979), 146.

[57]Bridgett (1908), 269, *Hereford Missal*, Rev. W. Henderson (1874), vol. II, 80; see also: Benoît-Castelli (1961), 299.

[58]Bailey (1971), 117.

16th.[59] In York there was a prescription for the carrying of the Eucharist in procession which stated that it should be done "in the manner of Palm Sunday".[60] In a 14th-century *ordinarium* of the cathedral of Rouen the same comparison can be traced between the procession of the Blessed Sacrament and the theophoric procession on Palm Sunday: the Holy of Holies is placed on a litter and carried by two clerics, a custom which persisted until the 15th century.[61]

Palm Sunday was not the only day - in England and Normandy at least - where a theophoric procession was organised in Passiontide. It was known at an earlier date on Whitsunday, at the *depositio* on Good Friday and at the *elevatio* on Easter morning. On the latter two days it must have existed in Augsburg as early as the 10th century, since the biographer of St. Ulrich († 973) speaks of a procession, "hallowed by tradition", with the Eucharist to the church of St. Ambrose, returning to the church of John the Baptist on Easter morning.[62]

On Good Friday the *missa praesanctificatorum* was celebrated, a liturgy in which the Eucharistic gifts 'pre-sanctified' on Maundy Thursday were used. After 700 the Eucharist consisted only of the consecrated bread. The custom was jealously guarded since the people received communion on Good Friday - something that was reserved mostly to the priest alone throughout the rest of the year.[63] For this purpose on Maundy Thursday the priest took the Eucharistic bread to the *sacrarium*, the place where from the 10th century the holy sepulchre was situated. This originally ritual-free reservation was, as already stated, gradually solemnised in mid-11th century - though not everywhere - to become a

---

[59]PL 147, 123: "et portetur feretrum in quo sit corpus Christi honorifice a duobus sacerdotibus indutis casulis albis"; Browe (1931d), 109; Stemmler (1970), 198.

[60]ed. McLachlan (1936-51), II (1937), 344-345, *De Solempnitate Corporis Christi* : "et sacerdote quodam (...) parato, qui portabit Corpus Domini in media processione, modo quo dictum est Dominica in Ramis Palmarum, vadat processio circa ecclesiam"; Bailey (1971), 90 and 117.

[61]PL 147, 117-119; 123-124, *Acta Vetera* (processiones (...) in ecclesia cathedrali Rotomagensi), 117: In ramis palmarum: "Finitis Matutinis deferatur corpus Domini ad locum destinatum in feretro a duobus sacerdotibus"; 123, In festo Corporis Christi: "et portetur feretrum in quo sit corpus Christi honorifice a duobus sacerdotibus"; Braun (1932), 355; Ter Reegen (1956), 210.

[62]See p.45 .

[63]Browe (1930a), 65-73; in the course of time, however, the "bitter sadness" was to gain the upper hand over the "joy" of the resurrection, so that this day was deemed less appropriate (CSEL 82, 227, ep. s. Ambrosii, 13 (23), c. 12: "Ergo non solum passionis diem etiam resurrectionis observari oportet a nobis ut habeamus et amaritudinis et laetitiae diem: illo ieiunemus isto reficiamur").

procession with candles and incense as described by Sigibert and Lanfranc.[64]

Although the original significance was different - namely, the 'translation' of the Sacrament - these theophoric processions in Holy Week, as also the solemn entrance with the *Sancta*, might still be regarded as modest predecessors of the subsequent procession of the Blessed Sacrament. This applies even more strongly to the small procession of the *viaticum* for the sick, since this 'procession' was not confined to the church building but, like the Blessed Sacrament procession of later date, ventured outside and, from around 1250, synods right across Western Europe ordered that the faithful should not only kneel when the *viaticum* procession was approaching but should even join it. Indulgences granted on such an occasion were of a later date.[65] In this context Browe refers to another example: Rupert of Deutz, who after the fire of 1128 seized on the usual Sunday procession to carry to the high altar the pyx and corporal that had been spared from the flames as "the most elevated of relics". Browe also reports a theophoric procession, organised by Louis VIII († 1226) from Avignon to a chapel outside the town after the victory over the Albigenses. It should be noted that neither of these events were followed up.[66]

When the feast of Corpus Christi was introduced in 1264 the theophoric procession was, therefore, no unfamiliar phenomenon and it would have been able to have helped to prepare the minds of the faithful for the procession which was to become a permanent feature of the *festum Eucharistiae*. But to what extent did the ages-old tradition of the procession of the relics have an influence? Were any elements taken from the processions of translation, intercession, prayer, penance and feast days and transposed to the procession of the Blessed Sacrament? Was it originally perhaps a 're-shaped' relic procession?

Information available regarding the oldest known procession on the feast of Corpus Christi would seem to point in this direction. It was probably held between 1264 and 1277 in the collegiate church of St. Gereon in Cologne. The deed of establishment (1275-1277) of the feast

---

[64]Browe (1931d), 98; Kettel (1953); LW II, 2926-27.

[65]for similarities between the viaticum procession and the procession of the Blessed Sacrament see p. 44 and Caspers (1992), 87-95; the influence of this 'small procession', however, on the shape taken on by the procession of the Blessed Sacrament would seem to be far less than that of the 'democratic' procession of the relics. After all, the form was ready-made in the latter. The reliquary only needed to be replaced by the Sacrament (see e.g. p. 253). This aspect is not discussed by Caspers; see Snoek (1995).

[66]See p. 222 and Browe (1933), 90-91.

included the procession, in which the carrying of the *corpus Christi* -
together with the head of St. Gereon and the crown of St. Helen - appears
as "nothing new". For the rest of the ceremony the document refers to
the procession of the relics on the feast days of St. Christopher and St.
Quintinus. The major relics were generally carried at the front of the
procession, where the Eucharist also was probably placed at the time.
Later the Sacrament was to be preceded by crucifixes, banners, candles
and incense, just like the costly reliquary on the occasion of a translation.
It looks as if the canons of Cologne simply added the Eucharist to the
procession of the relics "so that the Lord would turn aside all evil from
them because of the honour shown to his all-holy body".[67] This
formulation shows to some extent the transposition of the aim
characteristic of the rogational procession in times of need with the relics:
turning aside disasters. The 'obvious' combination of Eucharist and relics
in the deed of establishment is typical of later processions of the Blessed
Sacrament: the relics were usually part of the ceremony.

Thus a *directorium*, probably from 14th-century Liège, stating that
the six or eight *capellani* should walk with the relics before the
Sacrament, which was carried under a baldachin.[68] Here the position and
function of the relics has undergone a change: they have been moved to
second place; the saints pray together with the clergy and the people. All
attention is focused on the new centre: the Sacrament. In 1381 in
Würzburg the head of their patron saint, the Irishman Kilian († 689) was
carried before the Blessed Sacrament.[69] Flowers scattered on the road or
worn on the head contributed to the colourful scene. A Dominican
carrying the relics in a procession of the Blessed Sacrament held in

---

[67]Schnitzler (1973), 358-360; 354-355: "Ante missam ipsa quinta sollempnis fieri debet
processio cum cappis purpureis choralibus circa claustrum cum corpore Christi deportato et
capite sancti martyris et corona sancte Helene, sicut decet ipsam sollempnitatem, (et) ad
sanctum Christophorum cum canticis et laudibus est eundum, proxima vero dominica cum
predicta sollempnitate et reverenicia, ut supradictum est, cum processione et reliquiarum
portacione circa claustrum et ad sanctum *Quintinum* est eundum, ut dominus propter
memoriam et reverenciam sui sanctissimi corporis omne malum et (a) nobis et a nostra
ecclesia avertere dignetur"; see also Siben (1949), 351, 353, 357, 358, 360.

[68]AASS 5 apr. I, 904, *Appendix de officio Venerabilis Sacramenti*, 5: "vadantque singuli
in suo ordine. Primo crux nostra cum cruce s. Remacli exeant (...) postremo sex capellani
vel octo reliquias deferentes, ante quas portentur octo torticia ecclesiae; tandem venit
decanus, qui missam celebravit, deferens corpus Christi, una cum duobus ministris eum
deducentibus, deferanturque duo baldechina supra Sacramentum et duo scholares stent
ibidem cum duobus turibulis thurificantes"; Browe (1933), 108, n. 111.

[69]Monumenta Boica, 43 (1978), 394, n. 169: "Hic est autem ordo processionis (...) et
stantibus in gradibus cum crucibus et reliquiis sancti Kyliani".

Frankfurt in 1395 had a crown of roses and other flowers on his head.[70] This function of honouring the Sacrament was also given to the relics in Freising. There in the early 15th century the procession started in the cathedral after the end of the singing of the Office. The monks of the 'Weihenstephan' and 'Neustift' monasteries joined the choristers with their "relics and standards".[71]

Finally, an account which is of major importance for the secondary role now accorded to the relics in favour of the Eucharist is the description given by Beissel of the *deportatio S. Victoris* in Xanten in 1464. The climax of a relic feast held their irregularly from the end of the 13th century was the majestic procession with the reliquary of St. Victor, surrounded by many other reliquaries. The participants in the procession, estimated to number 200.000 (!), who included the Duke and Duchess of Cleves, climbed the hill to the monastery church. From there emerged a second procession with the Blessed Sacrament, also surrounded by reliquaries, to join up with the first procession. Just as the parish priests from the surrounding district had brought their relics so that all the saints of the region could do honour to St. Victor, "so begegnete jetzt der hl. Victor seinem höchsten Herrn und Könige, um ihm seine Huldigung darzubringen. Sein Schrein wurde eine Zeitlangf auf den eine Estrade vor das heilige Sacrament gestellt".[72]

Very distinguished members of the clergy were expected to carry the chests of relics, thereby adding to the colourful nature of the procession. A regulation governing processions issued in Mainz around 1400 contains a prescription to this effect,[73] which was applied in various places including Magdeburg in 1451. There an abbot and a provost walked in the procession carrying the relics in front of the

---

[70]ed. Froning (1884), I, 188, Bernhard Rorbach's *Liber gestorum*: "Anno domini 1395 in festo corporis Christi (...) frater Johannes dictus Rosenbeimchin ordinis Predicatorum portavit loco decani sancti Bartolomei sacrum ecclesie, habens in capite suo sertum rosis et floribus diversis".

[71]Mitterwieser (1930), 11: "Sie beginnt nach dem Chorgebet im Dom unter Zuziehung der Chorherrn von den beiden Nebenstiftern St. Veit und St. Andreas und der beiden Klöster Weihenstephan und Neustift mit ihren Reliquien und Fahnen".

[72]Beissel (1889), 68.

[73]Bruder (1901), 503: "Alle Übrigen Canoniker oben genannten Kirchen ziehen bessere Chormäntel an, und jeder soll ein Reliquienkästchen in seinen händen tragen"; 503-504: "Hinter diesen (Schüler) wird die grosse Monstranz der seligsten Jungfrau einhergetragen; auf diese folgen nach ihrem Range geordnet die Canoniker mit den Reliquien".

cardinal-legate, Nicholas of Cusa, who carried the Blessed Sacrament.[74]
At Spiers around the same time the relics were literally 'subordinated' to
the Eucharist: a white relic chest decorated with angels was carried in the
procession, at the end of which the Eucharistic monstrance was placed on
top of the chest. It stood there, surrounded by candles, throughout the
Mass and the remainder of the octave.[75] From the 12th century onwards
in Bamberg the relics of the founders of the bishopric were carried at the
front of the procession of rogation: the head of Kunigonde († 1033) and
the "sarcophagus" of her husband, Emperor Henry II († 1024), followed
by other reliquaries. The transposition can be found in a 15th-century
directorium that indicates in detail the order of participants in the
procession. One of them is a priest, again with the head of Kunigonde,
and three others with that of the emperor. At the end of a long line of
participants in the procession come two young men scattering roses before
the Eucharist, which is borne by the bishop under the baldachin. After the
procession is finished there is High Mass, with the Blessed Sacrament and
the relics laid out on the altar.[76] The Passau *breviarium* speaks of "the
solemn procession with the relics and the body of the Lord". The
reliquaries were also included at Ingolstadt in 1522, where they were also

---

[74]ChrDSt VII, 401: "und de cardinal droch dat sacrament sulven, dat to vorn nue gehort
was (...) und unse here van Magdeborch droch dat hilge cruze, und de abbet van Berge und
de provest van unser leven vruwen drogen ok hilgedom (...) des namiddages (...) dar gingen
de cardinal und unse here van Magdeborch mede up dem gange und stunden bi dem preister,
de dat hillichdom vorkundigede, so lange went dat geschen was. do gaf de cardinal over dat
volk de benediccien"; Browe (1933), 118; MGH SS XIV, 469-470, *Gesta archiepiscoporum
Magdeburgensum*, a.d. 1451: " et dominica infra octavas corporis Christi cardinalis ivit in
processione cum archiepiscopo et portavit sacramentum corporis Christi et in ostensione fuit
presens et dedit benediccionem super populum".

[75]Mitterwieser (1930), 15: "Vor dem Dekan geht 'der die rote laden dreit' und hinter ihm
der mit der weissen Reliquienlade mit den Engeln (...) Auf der weissen Lade mit den Engeln
bleibt die Monstranz die ganze Oktav stehen (...) und darneben vier silbern lichter mit vier
kerze".

[76]Haimerl (1937), 10: "Dem Charakter der Bittprozession entsprechend wurden Reliquien
mitgefürt (so auch in Essen, Ingolstadt, Hilpoltstein und Biberach). Der Offiziator trug das
kleine goldene Kreuz mit dem Finger der hl. Gertraud (*parvam crucem auream cum digito
S. Gertrudis*), der Diakon den Arm des hl. Georg (*brachium S. Georgii*), der Subdiakon das
Haupt der hl. Margarete (*caput S. Margaretae*). Vor ihnen her wurde das Haupt der hl.
Kunigunde - *cum suis candelis* - und der Sarkophag des hl. Heinrich getragen"; ib. 36: "Das
Mittragen von Reliquien und Kelchen (...) treffen wir auch für das Bistum Bamberg an";
38-39: "Vor Beginn der Prozession wurden sämtliche Reliquien am Petersaltar ausgesetzt
(...) Hierauf teilten zwei Kapitulare (...) die Reliquien aus. Vier Kanoniker der
Kathedralkirche erhielten die kostbareren, die anderen Reliquien verteilten sie an die übrigen
Kanoniker"; 40: "Das Allerheiligste und die Reliquien wurden sodann auf dem Hochaltar
gestellt, und dan begann das feierliche Hochamt"; Mitterwieser (1930), 15-16: "Es folgten
ein Priester mit dem Haupte der hl. Kunigungund (...) dann kommen die Dekane der drei
Stiftskirchen oder in ihrer Vertretung die 'Amter' (*sumissarii*) vom Dom, das Haupt des hl.
Kaisers Heinrich tragend (...) zwei Jünglinge in seidenen Tüchern Rosen tragend, die sie vor
dem Sakrament ausstreuen, dann endlich der Bischof(...) mit dem Allerheiligsten unter
einem Himmel (*sub tapeto*)".

present in considerably larger numbers "according to custom" than in other theophoric processions.[77] We can conclude that the 'procession of relics with the Blessed Sacrament' in the church of St. Gereon very rapidly elsewhere became a 'Blessed Sacrament procession with relics'.

Apart from this presence as evidence of transposition, it was also characteristic that the Eucharist was borne in a similar manner to that used for the relics. The litter was used, which we have already noted as figuring in the Palm Sunday procession, during which - in England and Normandy - the Eucharist was carried with the relics on a *feretrum*.

The litter was a familiar object in relic processions. At the 7th-century Council of Braga all bishops drunk on pomp and circumstance were reigned in by the issuing of a regulation that the priest or 'levites' should carry on their shoulders the *arca* with the relics rather than the prince of the church. If a bishop wanted to carry relics in a procession he should do it on foot.[78] In the course of the translation the 'brancard' was a practical piece of equipment in addition to the cart drawn by horse or hinny.[79] It appears in the short rite of reservation of the *dedicatio* in *Ordo XLI*[80] of the late 8th century and in the *Sacramentarium of Drogo* (son of Charlemagne and Bishop of Metz) which was produced between 830 and 850.[81] The litter with relics is characteristic of the ceremony of consecration of a church. In rogational and penitential processions the litter is also mentioned as well as the cart. At the end of the 11th century the monks of Fleury carried the relics of St. Maurus on a litter round a region struck by the plague. The population came in droves with pots and buckets in order to pour water or wine over the *feretrum* and collect it as medication.[82] A begging procession called on the generosity of the

---

[77]ibid. 16: "Im Sommerteil eines Breviers von Passau aus dem 15 Jahrhundert (...): Heute vollziehe sich (...) die feierliche Prozession mit Reliquien und dem Leibe des Herrn"; Greving (1908), 99, 122-123: *pro more* on church feast days and Thursdays.

[78]Mansi XI, 158, c. 6: "Et ideo antiqua in hac parte et solennis consuetudo servabitur, ut in festis quibusque arcam Dei cum reliquiis, non episcopi, sed levitae gestent in humeris"; *feretrum*: see e.g. p. 47, n. 68; p. 164, n. 16; p. 252, n. 9; p. 259, n. 43-46; below, n. 81; below, n. 85; p. 330, n. 88; p. 335, n. 114.

[79]Heinzelmann (1979), 50.

[80]Andrieu (1951-61), IV, 346-347, n. 28: "Deinde vadunt ad locum in quo reliquiae praeterita nocte cum vigiliis fuerunt et elevant eas cum feretro cum honore et laude decantando cum crucibus et turibulis et luminibus multis".

[81]Benz (1956), 66: "sequendo feretro reliquiarum"; 69: "subleventur reliquiae cum feretro"; Heitz (1987), 611.

[82]Franz (1909), II, 454; see also Martène (1788), III, 190, *Ordo processionis rogationum*: "et portentur tres cruces (...) et unum feretrum reliquiarum sanctorum".

population for the construction or refurbishing of a church or monastery. With this in mind the monks of Elnone travelled the roads with their litter in 1066.[83] The canons of Laon criss-crossed the countryside around Sens, Tours and Bourges with dubious relics in order to collect money for their cathedral, a practice that Guibert de Nogent was not very happy with.[84]

Various sources report that the Eucharistic bread was carried in a similar manner in England and Normandy during the procession of the Blessed Sacrament, which leads to suspicions of influence on the part of the Palm Sunday procession. The *consuetudines* of St. Augustine's abbey in Canterbury, set down around 1340, prescribe the following: "The litter of St. Letardus, with the body of Christ placed upon it, must be carried by a priest of St. Andrew and St. Paul".[85] The chronicler Thomas Walsingham († c. 1422) describes a procession held in the late 14th century in Canterbury, where again two priests carried the body of Christ *in feretro* on their shoulders. He noted that a seven-year-old boy could have done the same, so light was the litter.[86] We have already mentioned the processions in York and Rouen above.

Later not only the closed pyx but also the monstrance was placed on the litter or on a 'palanquin' - just like the bishops carrying their relics in Braga - and carried on shoulders. In "many places" in Spain this task was performed by two priests, and sometimes even by four or eight, depending on the size of the monstrance. In 1430 in Gerona a silversmith was commissioned to make a new monstrance on which he worked for twenty-eight years. It was 185 cm tall and weighed 185 kg.[87] The Congregation of Rites objected to this manner of carrying the

---

[83] AASS 6 febr. I, 900, *Historia miraculorum s. Amandi corpore per Bragbantum delato*; see also Heliot (1965); Hermann-Mascard (1975), 296-312.

[84] ed. Labande (1981), 378, lib. III, c. 12: "Interea secundum qualemcunque morem ad corrogandas pecunias coeperunt feretra et sanctorum reliquiae circumferri"; Heliot (1965), 819.

[85] ed. Thompson (1902), 115: "Similiter et feretrum beati Letardi, cum Corpore Christi superposito, preparet, a presbiteris videlicet sancti Pauli et sancti Andreae portandum, cum lumine a clerico sancti Pauli portando, in laterna posito".

[86] ed. Riley (1967-69), RS 28, II, 185-186, Thomas Walsingham, *Gesta abbatum*: "in processione per parochiam deferebatur Corpus Dominicum, super duorum humeros sacerdotum, in feretro non ponderoso, sed tam levi, ut a septenni puero, sine vexatione, portari tota machina potuisset".

[87] Matern (1962), 178.

Eucharist,[88] though its objections had little effect since in some places the monstrance itself was given the form of a litter. This could be observed in the 15th century in England,[89] an example that was followed in the 16th and 17th centuries in Paris and Chartres. In these cases too the Congregation objected. Necessity took precedence over the law in Narbonne where the monstrance was so heavy that it could only be lifted by eight priests. In Valencia two groups of twelve bearers were required so that they could relieve one another.[90]

Continuing the customs of the already current theophoric processions, the Eucharist carried during the procession of the Blessed Sacrament was originally enclosed in a pyx. However the monstrances referred to fulfilled the desire to see the Host, a desire already fulfilled for an instant at the 'elevatio' during Mass. The monstrances were derived from the relic ostensoria, which were as different in form as they were in name. In the 14th century they were not all that common, but later their use increased[91], something which will be dealt with in greater detail under 'exposition'.

The transposition process can also be seen in the organisation of the procession. Just as we have seen in the previous example that the relics of Ss. Eucherius, Trudo and Vincent were carried around the town or along the fields in penitantial or rogational processions, so also was the practice as far as processions of the Blessed Sacrament were concerned.[92] In imitation of the *litania septiformis*, the main church was the assembly point, while the progress of the main procession smaller groups could join in as in Freising mentioned above. The result was that more than one Eucharistic monstrance figured in the procession as if they were reliquaries. The *Liber ordinarius* originating in the second half of the 14th century in Essen mentions this: not only was there a procession on the

---

[88]ed. Gardellini (1856), I, 190, no. 931: "supplicarunt pro licentia deferendi S.S. Sacramentum processionaliter super humeros Sacerdotum, iuxta eorum antiquam consuetudinem. Et S.C. respondit: nullo modo permittendum sed deferendum esse manibus celebrantis"; in addition to this, an interdict dated 1631 in Ragusa (Sicily) and 1632 on the island of Corfu, ibid. 193, no. 951; 1640 in Brixen, ibid. 220, no. 1198: "an liceat in die Parasceve deferre Sanctissimum Eucharistiae Sacramentum processionaliter in quadam bara humeros? Et Sac. C. respondit: nullo modo licere, neque permittendum"; Matern (1962), 183-184.

[89]ed. Dugdale (1846), VIII, 1279; Bridgett (1908), 184.

[90]Browe (1933), 121; Browe (1933), 121, n. 204; Matern (1962), 183-184.

[91]LW II, 1778; Browe (1927a); (1933), 100.

[92]Mitterwieser (1930), 12: Munich in 1360 (*in circuitu civitatis*); 10: Würzburg in 1381 (*circueundo civitatem*); 13, Regensburg in 1463: "an den drei Toren, duch welche die Prozession ging".

feast of Corpus Christi but a second and more extensive theophoric procession took place on a subsequent Friday. On the latter occasion the citizens left the town to process through the fields until they came to the monastery of Stopenberg, where the monks joined them also carrying the Sacrament, so that two 'Eucharistic shrines' participated.[93] This was no coincidence but rather reposed on a custom current at the time which was expressly objected to in the prescription issued in Mainz - already mentioned - in 1400: "It should also be noted that in no other monstrance than that under the baldachin may the Blessed Sacrament be carried, though the other monstrances may contain relics".[94]

Whenever people left from the various parish churches to assemble at the main church, the number of Eucharistic monstrances could equal the number of participating parishes. The modern devout, John Busch († 1479) noted on his visit to Halle that the procession of St. Mark, held since time immemorial, included five Eucharistic monstrances, a number he reduced to one from fear that it could lead to misunderstanding about the presence of the one unique God.[95] A similar ordnance was required in Meissen, directed at the monks who were determined to take their own monstrance along. In Münster in 1482 Bishop Nicodemus decreed another solution as a compromise in the efforts made by various groups to gain the upper hand: the subordinate groups left their monstrances in the main church, after which everyone left together with just one monstrance. The function of assembly point was shared in alternate years by the churches of St. Peter and Our Lady.[96] The Augsburg chronicle, on the contrary, records the traditional pattern once again in 1500: each parish joined in

---

[93]ed. Arens (1908), 94: "Feria sexta, que est crastino Sacramenti, consueverunt opidami cum sacramento corporis Christi circuire rura (...)"; "Cum autem prope conventum de Stopenbergh, ut dictum est, pervenitur, ibi concurret conventus ibidem cum processione etiam cum sacramento".

[94]Bruder (1901), 504-505: "Auch ist zu merken, dass in keiner anderen Monstranz das Sacrament getragen werden darf ausser in jener unter dem Baldachin, wohl aber dürfen in den übrigen Monstranzen Reliquien getragen werden".

[95]ed. Grube (1886), 445, *Liber de reformatione monasteriorum*, I, cap. XVI: "Animadverti, quod hec venerabilis sacramenti delatio in monstrantiis diversis pariter incedentibus fidei catholice multum esset nociva imo et contraria, tanquam singuli plebani, sicut singulas habent monstrantias, sic etiam singuli proprium haberent deum, et unum non esset corpus dominicum, quod in diversis monstrantiis portaretur. Mandavi igitur plebanis per totam civitatem quod non nisi unum sacramentum et unam monstrantiam per civitatem et circuitum eius portare deberent".

[96]Browe (1933), 103, n. 78: *Cod. diplomat. Saxoniae reg.* 4 (1873) n. 323; Mitterwieser (1930), 16-17; Zika (1988), 40-41.

the procession with its own monstrance and relics accompanied by the triumphant sound of trumpets, flutes and kettledrums.[97]

As in Essen, from the 14th century onwards no few parishes in present-day Germany, Austria, Switzerland and the Low Countries held a second procession during the octave of the feast of Corpus Christi. This custom was also found in Spain, but usually the Latin countries kept to a single procession on the day itself. The actual procession of the Blessed Sacrament went through the town in joy and triumph, while the second wended its way through the fields and took on the character of a rogation. The people prayed that they would be spared from hailstone and lightning and besought God's blessing on house, hearth and cattle. In this procession of rogation and penance the Eucharist had taken over the role formerly played by the relics. The reading from the Gospels and the blessings to the four points of the compass at the stations completed the resurrection of the rogations in the procession of the Blessed Sacrament.[98] The transposition was put into words in the Havelberg *breviarium* where, in 1469, the bishop prescribed a second procession after the feast of Corpus Christi. The Eucharist and the relics were to be carried "as during the rogations".[99]

Frequently no need was felt for a second procession with this aim, since the procession on the feast of Corpus Christi took on the character of a rogation procession. It also sometimes happened that the procession on the 25th April and on the Rogation Days was theophoric. In the Germanic countries mentioned there were doubtless only a few parishes in the 15th-16th centuries where no processions with the Sacrament were held around the time of Easter and Whitsun. The popularity of such events was perhaps partly due to the fact that they were familiar 'field processions', from which it was hoped protection would be obtained against tempest, hail and thunderstorm.[100]

---

[97] ChrDSt XXIII, 83: "An unsers herrn fronleichnamstag ist alle priesterschafft und pfarvolck mit irem hochwirdigen sacrament mit ainer process in unser liebe Frauenkirchen komen. daselben hat man ain gemeine process angefangen und ist durch den Fronhoff gangen auff den Perlach (...) da sind auch gewessen des kinigs und aller fürsten thrumether, pfeiffer und baugenschlager (...) auff dem Perlach haben sich die processen getailt, und ist ain jedliche process widerumb in ir pfarr und kirchen gangen".

[98] Browe (1933), 109, n. 117, 118; Caspers (1992), 69 sqq.

[99] ed. Riedel (1838-69), I,3, 253: n. 12 des Havelberger Brevir: "processio cum Reliquiis et Sacramento, sicut in diebus Rogationum".

[100] Franz (1909), II, 73; Browe (1933), 127-128; Haimerl (1937), 14-15: "In ausführlicher Weise sind wir auch über die in Hof um das Jahr 1479 abgehaltenen Bittprozessionen unterrichtet. Hier wurde am Markustag das Allerheiligste verhüllt mitgetragen (...) Wie letztere (der Fonleichnamsprozession) ihrerseits durch die Bittprozession beeinflusst und - vor allem in Deutschland - zu einem Flurumgang wurde, so

There were other processions of relics of the time on feast days, days of thanksgiving, Rogation Days and penitential days which took on a mainly theophoric character, while maintaining the presence of the relics. In mid-14th-century Cologne a magnificent procession was held annually in honour of the sacred lance and sacred nail of the True Cross, leaving the cathedral to process round the city on the second Friday after Easter. The relics shared the procession with the Eucharist.[101] Coronations and victories of princes were celebrated with a theophoric procession, but even the casting of a church bell could be the occasion for such a celebration. Previously the procession containing the relics had processed around the bell as it was being made;[102] now the Eucharist was added to the procession. In 1486 in Magdeburg, at least, there is a report of the "cathedral dean" and other prominent clerics approaching the bell in procession with both the Eucharist and the reliquary of Our Lady, the head of St. Moritz and the finger of St. Catherine.[103] On the feast of St. Michael in 1568 in Paris a whole series of relics was processed before the Eucharist: the reliquaries of the Sainte Chapelle and those of Ss. Denis, Rusticus, Eleutherius, Louis, Genoveva, Marcellus and a reliquary from each parish.[104]

When death occurred on a large scale in Augsburg in 1358, the people went around the town in a theophoric penitential and rogational procession after first fasting on bread and water. The chronicler reports that their prayer was heard, but four years later he was again recounting the tale of a famine that followed an icy winter and a sweltering summer, a famine so bad that people were cutting straw so that they would have at

---

wurden anderseits Wetter und Flurprozessionen vielfach in der Form van Sakramentsprozessionen abgehalten, was am Ende nicht ohne Missbrauch abging"; 16: "Diese Prozession am Markustag unterscheidet sich nicht wesentlich von der später geschilderten Fronleichnamsprozession. Sie hatte wie diese den Charakter einer theophorischen Flurprozession"; ibid. 34 sqq.

[101]ed. Knipping (1898), II, 42, 43, 79 : I Die Gesammtausgaben von 1375-1380; Browe (1933), 122, n. 210.

[102]Martène (1788), II, c. 21: "dum aes conflatur"; Browe (1933), 123, n. 214.

[103]ChrDSt VII, 412: "als nu de spise gesmolten unde gar was, dat de spise lopen scholde, do quam de domdeken und etlike domheren mit on und ein deils der vicarien mit einer processien, mit cruzen und vanen, mit dem hilgen sacramente unses hern Jhesu Christi und unser lever vruwen schrin und sunte Mauricius hovet und sunte Katherinen vinger. mit dieser processen gingen se umme de kulen, dar de forme und dat belde de clocken inne stunt"; Browe (1933), 123.

[104]François Grin (1554-70), 49-50.

least something to eat.[105] In early 1374 in Cologne attempts were made
to prevent a flood by holding a procession of the Blessed Sacrament.[106]
In May 1491 a disastrous spell of cold weather was seen as justification
for carrying the Blessed Sacrament and the relics of St. Severinus out into
the cold, an act which was unable in that same year to prevent some
people from "having tasted or seen no bread in four weeks".[107] In the
15th century in Gerona a theophoric procession was organised to protect
the people from earthquakes.[108] In 1479 the King of France, Louis XI,
deemed it necessary to perform a similar act in his conflict with
Maximilian of Austria regarding ownership of the Franche Comté, Artois
and Flanders. He asked the prior of St. Léonard-de Noblac near Limoges
to organise a procession of the Blessed Sacrament with all the relics,
especially that of the popular Saint Leonard, so that he and his people
could live in peace.[109]

The entry of the Sacrament into the procession caused the presence of the
relics to be questioned in some places. First of all there was the general
question of whether beautifully decorated reliquaries were fitting in a
procession whose principal theme was penitential grief. In the procession
held in Frankfurt in 1467 to turn aside the plague, the relics were omitted
for this very reason.[110] However elsewhere the chronicler reports this
event without further comment. In 1502 in Dortmund the "hoechwerdigen
hillegen sacrament" was present with the "villen hilligedombs" in a
penitential procession which visited seven churches, in which many joined

---

[105]ChrDSt XXIII, 29: "Anno domini 1358 ist hie ain fast grosser sterbent gewessen, und
ist das ganz statvolck zusammen komen und haben mit wasser und brot gefastet und sind
barfuss mit dem hochwirdigen sacrament mit ainer process um die stat gangen und got den
hern andechtigklich um barmhartzigkait angeriefft, welcher gepett got der her erhört, und
der sterbent auffgehört".

[106]ed. Knipping (1898), II, 143, 147; Browe (1933), 125, n. 225.

[107]ChrDSt XIV, 880: "Item up den 16. dach des meies droich men dat hillige sacrament
ind sent Severin umb ein goiden vreden ind goit wedder zo der vrucht, want it ein sere kalt
wedder was ind die vruchte waren sere dure"; " In dem selven jair (...) men vant wail lude
, die in 4 wechen nie broet gekoirt of gesien hatten"; Haimerl (1937), 80-86.

[108]Matern (1962), 58.

[109]Bruel (1905), 11-12: "et ad ce present jour fust fecte procession generalle en
Champmaing et porté le précieux corps de nostre Seigneur pour la paix et conservation de
nostredict seigneur et pour tout le bien (...) Et pour ce que désirons de tout nostre cuer la
fin des dictes guerres, nous vous prions que (...) vous faictes processions generalles,
èsquelles vous ferrez pourter tous les reliquaires de vostre esglise et prier monss. sainct
Lieunard (...) affin que puissions vivre en bonne paix et repos et soubzlager nostre peuple".

[110]ed. Froning (1884), I, 216: "Anno 1467 2 octobris habebatur valde venerabilis
processio pro pestilentia; et portabatur corpus Christi sine velamine et non reliquiae
sanctorum et duxerunt portantem sacramentum".

barefoot.[111] But it was not only in the case of penitential processions that doubts were raised. It was also feared that the baroque decoration of the reliquaries could be apt on occasion to overshadow the Blessed Sacrament. For instance, the *Liber ordinarius* of the church of Our Blessed Lady in Tongeren (1434-1436) contains a description of the annual procession of the Blessed Sacrament which makes no mention of the relics. No further explanation is given, as was the case in later years. The provincial synod held in Cologne in 1549, for example, and the Haarlem synod of 1564 insisted that the processions should be kept modest, without being turned into exhibitions of statues. They did not, however, forbid the inclusion of relics and compared the procession to Christ's progress through Judea, surrounded by His disciples. Hence it was a good thing to include statues and relics since these objects referred to the triumph of the saints with the Lord.[112] In contrast to this, the bishops of Milan and Ermland took up a rigid stance and excluded the relics from the procession in (to name but two dates) 1576 and 1610.[113] In the post-Tridentine atmosphere of the time the reverence accorded to the exposed Host reached an apogee. However it was not until the 19th century that the relics completely disappeared from the procession of the Blessed Sacrament.

***

In the transposition at present under discussion there was, on the one hand, the influence of the already existing processions in which the Eucharist figured and, on the other, of those which focused on the relics and which were part of the church's processional inheritance. The extent of this latter influence cannot be seen separately from the contribution made by the faithful themselves. Indeed, large crowds always attended an

---

[111] ChrDst XX, 373: "Und ist ouch dis jaers binnen Dortmunde so ein devoten, innigen beweechlichen bedemisse gehalten worden, der gein mensche belevet hadde, want man genk mit dem hoechwerdigen hilligen sacrament sampt villen hilligedombs in die seven kerken, alle menschen wullen und barvoets volgende".

[112] Schannat-Harzheim VI, 557-558: "videlicet simul repraesentans itineris Christi historiam, qui dum quaereret salutem nostram, in medio populi versatus est, et universam Judaeam circumambulavit, docens, et aegrotos sanans, discipulis comitantibus: quam ob rem et sanctorum reliquias et imagines eorum, qui vestigia eius secuti sunt, simul circumferimus, significantes, illos nunc cum ipso regnare et triumphare in coelis"; VII, 11, 12; ed. Lefèvre I (1967), 231-233.

[113] Browe (1933), 119, n. 193-194, *Ach. Ratti, Acta ecclesiae Mediolanensis ab eius initiis usque ad nostram aetatem*, II, (Mediolani 1890), 355: "In solemni illa processione, in qua ss. Domini Corpus (...) defertur, ne reliquiae ullae, sed illud solum (...) feratur"; Schannat-Harzheim, IX, 120.

event of this type, people participated in a creative fashion and the individual had an 'interest' in the affair, all the more so when the reason for organising it was to avert some sort of disaster. As far as the participation of the people in the earlier theophoric processions is concerned, they did take some part in the procession of the *viaticum* in the 13th century, but they were hardly - if at all - present at the procession to the holy sepulchre on Maundy Thursday, the *depositio* on Good Friday and the *elevatio* on Easter morning. But the people did have an active part in the veneration of the Cross and in the procession on Palm Sunday. To explain this Stemmler points out that the two latter solemnities date from before the Carolingian era, a time when the clericalisation of the liturgy had not yet led to passiveness on the part of the people. In addition, the Palm Sunday procession was not limited to the interior of the church building but, as in Ulrich's *vita*, it went outside thereby allowing the people to play the role of the crowd at Christ's triumphal entry into Jerusalem, waving olive or palm branches and singing *Osanna filio David*.[114] In Spain a raised platform was built before the city gate to represent Calvary, with at its foot the altar, on which lay the palm branches given to the people after they had been blessed. The Cross and the book of the Gospels used in the procession were symbolic of Christ, carried triumphantly into the church.[115]

The victorious decorations, with standards and candles and crucifixes, was not unfamiliar in other processions held for translations or on feast days, but in this case they were directly targeted on Christ the King and His triumph, which was also the context of the feast of Corpus Christi. The expectantly worded decree establishing the feast in 1264 speaks of the jubilation and happiness of the "faithful flock": the clergy and the people.[116] During the procession of the Blessed Sacrament the Psalm (147:12) *Lauda Jerusalem* and the Sequence *Lauda Sion* bear witness to the same atmosphere of the Palm Sunday procession. When the procession with the Sacrament entered the church in Mainz around the year 1400 the choruses which resounded were even taken from the second

---

[114]Martène (1706), 195: *De Dominica Palmarum, Crucis adoratio*: "in statione fiebat Crucis adoratio, iteratis crebris ante ipsam genuflexionibus, quibus nonnulli pium subiugebant osculum. Ita fere habet antiquus ordo Romanus: (Ut autem pervenerint cum psalmis, ubi statio est sanctae Crucis, clerus populusque reverenter stent per turmas in ordine suo cum baiolis et reliquo ornatu, et infantes paraphonistae in loco competenti subsistentes imponant antiphonam)"; Stemmler (1970), 204.

[115]Matern (1962), 44.

[116]Mansi XXIII, 1079: "et tam clerici, quam populi gaudentes in cantica laudum surgant. Tunc enim omnium corda et vota, ora, et labia, hymnos persolvant laetitiae salutaris".

antiphon of the Palm Sunday procession: "This is He who is to come for the salvation of His people. He is our salvation and the saviour of Israel. How great is He, whom the Thrones and Dominions come to meet". [117]

In general the transposition of the Palm Sunday procession is evident in the similarities mentioned, but more especially it comes to the fore in England and Normandy, where it became theophoric with the carrying of the Sacrament together with the relics on the litter. Retention of the litter in the procession of the Blessed Sacrament and the express reference to the Palm Sunday procession in the guidelines published for the feast of Corpus Christi in York and Rouen reinforce this assumption. Detailed studies will be needed to show why the Eucharist eventually disappeared from the Palm Sunday procession. Did the procession of the Blessed Sacrament in these regions take over the theophoric role and thus restore the Palm Sunday procession to its original form? [118]

In addition to the Palm Sunday procession the processions of the relics served as 'models' for the procession of the Blessed Sacrament, which could hardly have come into existence out of nothing in the midst of such a rich tradition of processions dating back to early Christian times. Concrete signs of bringing the practices up to date betray this: the transitional forms, the entourage, the organisation and the continued presence of the relics. Needless to say, this cannot have been a one-way process: there must have been mutual interchange. The *rogationes* became 'Blessed Sacrament processions' by including the Eucharist, and when the processions on the feast of Corpus Christi wended their way through the fields they automatically turned into *rogationes*, doing 'penance', although less emphatically. This mutual interchange is confirmed by the presence of the dragon, without which no medieval procession would have been complete. [119]

Matern seeks the prayer and penance element in the link with Passiontide and relates it to one of the aims of the decision to establish the procession: reparation for dishonour done to the Eucharist. It strikes us that this relationship is too artificial as an explanation for the less festive aspect. The Blessed Sacrament procession could perhaps take on this character particularly because of the increasing significance being given to piety towards the Host and because of the easy link with the existing

---

[117]"Hic est qui venturus est in salutem populi. Hic est salus nostra et redemptio Israël. Quantus est iste, cui Throni et Dominationes occurrunt"; Bruder (1901), 506; Fürstenberg (1917), 322.

[118]Matern (1962), 44, n. 17; Niedermeier (1974-75), 421.

[119]Haimerl (1937), 35; Matern (1962), 78.

tradition of processions. Once introduced, the Blessed Sacrament procession easily gave form to the other processions, in this case the *rogationes*. It constituted the crowning glory of the feast of Corpus Christi and was both a manifestation, a 'translation' of the Sacrament - originally the only aim of the theophoric process - and in some regions a procession of intercession for favours sought. Thanks to this omnivalent nature no few festive, thanksgiving and penitential processions gained a theophoric element whether the procession was held in Cologne in 1401 to celebrate the departure of the Roman king, Ruprecht III, to the Eternal City, or in celebration of the lection of Pope Martin V at the Council of Konstanz in 1417 or, in 1447, as a rogation procession to beg for good weather to make the crops grow.[120] Just as prior to the introduction of the feast of Corpus Christi a procession was often a procession of the relics, so there gradually came into existence the tendency to turn a procession into a procession of the Blessed Sacrament.

3   THE EXPOSITION OF THE RELICS AND OF THE EUCHARIST

From the 11th century onwards the relic shrines towered over the altars and the smaller reliquaries were 'exposed' in the retable or on the altar as a matter of course. When the relics were accorded a place of honour during church feasts or they were held in the hand on similar occasions, this was known as an 'exposition'. Both forms were the aim of what were called as 'jubilee processions', processions of prayer which were held on regular occasions. Attendance at such an event was a condition for obtaining the jubilee indulgence or cancellation of punishment for sin. This privilege was even attached to some local celebrations with exposition in the 13th century.

We have already seen how, since the safety precautions prescribed by the Fourth Lateran Council, little windows were fitted to the locked reliquaries. In addition the *ostensoria* fitted to a foot were developed. This opened the way to exposition and veneration of the relics without their being touched. The oldest examples known dates from the second decade of the 13th century, a common type being a vertical cylinder with a pointed top, somewhat resembling the tower shape of the pyx.

The instance of exposition of the Eucharist can also include the 'elevatio', its timing during the Consecration carefully laid down in the

---

[120]ibid. 51-52; 57.

synodal statutes of Paris (1205-1208), as already referred to in chapter II. For a long period this was the only time that the people had the opportunity of seeing the Host unveiled. Otherwise it was kept and laid out in a closed container. Around 1300 a change occurred when the practice came about of exposing the Sacrament in *ostensoria*. An impressive example of this was the solemn showing of the Eucharistic monstrance by the priest during the singing of the Sequence on the feast of Corpus Christi - the *Lauda Sion Salvatorem*, a "jewel of Scholastic poetry".[1]

3.1 The exposition of the relics*

A fine example of the exposition of the relics is the event reported to have taken place in 386 in Milan. For two whole days the people flocked to see the newly discovered mortal remains of Gervase and Protase before they were taken on the evening of the second day to the basilica of Fausta for the all-night vigil.

'Expositions' of this kind on the occasion of the *inventio*, the *elevatio* and the *translatio* could be brief, as could the verification of the presence of certain relics in a monastery or church.[2] But this in its turn was not a general rule. Around the year 700 the body of St. Amandus († c. 678) remained exposed 'above the earth' for 32 days after the *elevatio*,[3] and the remains of St. Bathilde was exposed for 18 days before her *translatio* to Paris began in 833. She had been buried in the convent of Chelles, which she had founded, and the abbess, Helgilwich, had had the *elevatio* performed at the request of Louis the Pious.[4] Such expositions also occurred at the opening of the grave of Charlemagne in

---

[1] LW II, 2538); *Praise, o Sion, the Saviour*, ascribed to Thomas Aquinas (LW II, 1438); Bruder (1901), 506; Mitterwieser (1930), 19.

*A list for further reading and sources is can be found in: Mayer (1938): Boeren (1962), 60-68 and passim; Hermann-Mascard (1975), 206-216; Kroos (1985), 37-38.

[2] Hermann-Mascard (1975), 207-208.

[3] AASS 6 febr. I, 892, *De elevatione*, c.I,11 : "Corpus vero venerabile (...) per triginta duos dies supra terram manere permisit".

[4] AASS 26 ian. II, 748, *Historia translationis*, c. 8: "Octavo decimo autem die, postquam corpus venerandum a terra effosum fuerat, secundum postulationem sacratissimae abbatissae Helgilwich, evocatus sacer episcopus Erkanradus, qui tunc sedem Parisiacae urbis regebat (...) venit (...) vidensque sanctissimum corpus, ut positum fuerat, integrum (...) gratias agit omnipotenti Domino"; MGH SS XV,1, 285, lectio 7.

the year 1000[5] and at the *elevatio* of St. Bertha, whose head was brought
back from Erstein in Alsace to her abbey of Blangy-sur-Ternoise near
Lille in 1032. Her body, which the translation account states restored the
light to the eyes of a blind girl, was ordered by the *praesul* to be carried
by a crowd of monks, men and women to a hill top "so that a precious
treasure of this sort could be seen by all". After the sermon the *praesul*
once more raised the head of St. Bertha above the multitude so that all
could see it, whereafter they all returned home after the blessing filled
with joy.[6] The exposition of a single relic at the *elevatio* was repeated,
for instance, in 1151 on the opening of the shrine of the widely venerated
abbess Aldegonde († c. 700). The bishop of Cambray first showed the
foot of the skeleton to those present, after which he blessed the crowd,
and then he held the saint's head aloft while all bowed in wonder.[7] The
consecration of a new altar in honour of St. Lawrence in 1112 was
accompanied by the exposition of the famous grill on which the martyr
was roasted alive. It remained exposed for several days in full view of the
people.[8] The customary nocturnal vigil by the relics destined for the
church to be consecrated could also be regarded as a form of exposition,
just as the exposition of relics when the general interest was threatened.
The exposed shrine of St. Denis was used, when Philip II Augustus set
out on crusade in 1191, to encourage the people of Paris and the pilgrims
to pray not only to the saint but especially to the Virgin Mary and the
Lord for the freeing of the Holy Land.[9]

---

[5]Pognon (1947), 172-173: "On l'éleva et on l'exposa à la vue du peuple".

[6]AASS 4 iul. II, 58, *Liber de miraculis et translatione s. Bertae*, III,18: "egressus
Praesul cum monachorum caterva, seu non modica populi utriusque sexus multitudine,
ferentes humeris sanctissimum corpus, monachis psallentibus populisque laetantibus,
ascenderunt ad supercilium cuiusdam montis, ut tam desiderabilis thesaurus ab omnibus
posset videri. Completo autem ad populum sermone, ostendit ipse praesul populo caput
beatissimae Bertae (...) Accepta autem Praesulis benedictione, populus ad propria
revertebatur".

[7]ibid. 30 ian. II, 1051, *Historia II translationis* c. 4: "Accessit propius Cameracensis
episcopus manu tractans, et unum de pedibus corio imputrescibili et ungulis sicut viventes
incorruptibiliter vestitum, a corpore segregavit, et sustulit, et omnibus adstantibus ostendit,
et facta benedictione omnibus se humiliter inclinantibus, in loco a quo sustulerat reposuit
reverenter. Similer et caput sanctum ex maxima parte cute incorruptibili coopertum, et
capillulis quibusdam adhuc vestitum, sustulit et ostendit inclinatibus se flebiliter".

[8]AOB V, 570, lib. LXXII: "quae craticula, postquam aliquot diebus Romano populo
ostensa fuisset, per manus Leonis Ostiensis episcopi sub novo altari recondita est".

[9]ed. Viard (1920-53), VI, 206: "l'on voloit que li pelerin et li poples, qui là venroient et
verroient presentement le glorieus martyr et la sainte congregation, fussent plus esmeu et
plus devot à prier Dieu et la benooite Virge et les glorieus martyrs pour la delivrance de la
sainte Terre, pour le roi et pour toute sa compegnie (...) A la feste saint Denis (...) fu la
fierte deseelée et overte, et en quoi les precieuses reliques du glorieus martyr reposent (...)
Lors fu li cors trovez toz entiers, o tout le chief, et fu mostrez au pople par grant devotion
et à touz ceus qui là estoient venu en pelerinage de divers païs".

As well as the 'special' type, 'ordinary' expositions had also come into fashion. The Benedictine, Adrewald, of Saint-Benoît-sur-Loire, refers to "the old custom" of exposing the relics for veneration in a tent under the trees by the church on certain Sundays, which would draw great crowds from the surrounding area either out of devotion or in order to obtain some spiritual or physical favour.[10] Towards the end of the 11th century, expositions at the altar, in the nave or outside the church took on a periodic character at Easter and on other major feast days. Other suitable occasions were the commemoration of the consecration of the church itself, the feast of the relics or the actual feast day of the saint.[11] On the annual relic feast the expositions attracted innumerable crowds to Vienne, Mayence and Trèves in France, and to Halle, Lübeck and Osnabrück in Germany, all come to venerate the relics.[12] The shrine of St. Serenus in Angers was carried round the town on the saint's feast day and exposed before his altar on a table in the nave of the church.[13] The *Liber ordinarius* of 1291 put together for the cathedral of Amiens speaks of a 'Mass with exposition' - not of the Eucharist but of the relics - mentioning the exposure to the public gaze of the *capsula* of the 9th-century martyr, Firminus, and other relics.[14] The ordinal of Chartres reports the same custom.[15] We have already seen how the head of St. Secundus was carried to the altar before Mass began and was exposed there during the Mass. "Scarcely any of the larger churches or abbeys did not possess major relics and showed these to the people on important feast days" confirms Beissel. If the blessing was given with the relics at the

---

[10]ed. Certain (1968), 64-65, lib. I, c. 28.: "ut extra portam monasterii, ad orientalem plagam, in loco nemoribus consito, tentorium extendi iuberet, quo memoriae sanctorum, certo tempore, hoc est vigilia Dominici diei deferrentur, manerentque sub reverenti vigilum custodia ibidem tam monachorum quam clericorum, usque ad eamdem horam Dominici diei, iterumque sacris referrentur aedibus. Quod cum impletum fuisset, multitudines plebium, non solum ex contiguis, verum procul positis locis, medelam animarum ac corporum consecuturae, eo confluxere. Operabatur denique Dominus per clarissimos martyres suos incredibilia virtutum dona".

[11]Hermann-Mascard (1975), 124-125.

[12] Berlière (1927), 339.

[13]Farcy de (1901), III, 178, n. 2; see also p. 258.

[14]ed. Durand (1934), 46: "ad idem altare, altari textato, capsula beati Firmini martyris, tabula altaris et corporibus sanctorum discoopertis, ab episcopo canitur (...) Intr. Sapientiam"; p. 30, 38, 108.

[15]Kroos (1985), 37-38; Scribner (1987), 21: In the first half of the sixteenth century in catholic Germany relics were placed on the altar during the mass on solemn feast days. According to the Constance *Processionale* there were eight occasions when relics were set on the main altar of the minster: Christmas, Easter, Pentecost, the Assumption, the Birth of the Virgin and the feasts of SS Pelagius, Martin and Conrad.

end of Mass, such expositions were a weekly or even daily occurrence.[16] The 12th-century *Guide for Pilgrims*, written for pilgrims going to Compostela, gives a wide range of holy places and relics to be visited on the way. It recommends such places as Orleans, where one could find the miraculous chalice and the grave of St. Evurtius († c. 340). Here too a particle of the True Cross and the bread knife used at the Last Supper were to be seen. And the place that owed its name to the head of John the Baptist, Saint-Jean-d'Angély, should not be missed. This priceless relic stood there in a "gigantic" basilica, perpetually exposed, as was to happen in the case of the Eucharist from the end of the 14th century. It brought about "countless miracles" and was "venerated day and night by a choir of a hundred monks".[17]

The 1215 restriction on exposing the relics outside the *capsae* had to be repeated on several occasions and obviously had no absolute force. Here and there it was ignored because of the desire to have more direct contact and the allied local tradition.[18] A council held in Budapest in 1279 placed two restrictions: the relics could be exposed outside of their holders on major church feast days and at times when pilgrims crowded in to reverence them.[19] It hardly needs to be said that the pilgrims wanted to see with their own eyes that for which they had undertaken such a journey. In the later Middle Ages the expositions held on the occasion of jubilees were from a gallery, a chancel, a higher place or a podium. In Aachen there was an annual exposition of holy cloths of Jesus and Mary which, according to legend, had been brought there personally by Charlemagne from Constantinople.[20] These expositions, preceded by a sermon, were held inside the cathedral until 1320, after that from the gallery of the tower so that they were clearly visible to the crowd on the cathedral square. When the relics were shown, a priest fulfilled the

---

[16]Beissel (1976), II, 124; see below p. 296.

[17]ed. Vieillard (1963), 58: "in urbe Aurelianensium lignum dominicum et calix beati Evuricii episcopi et confessoris, in ecclesia Sancte visitandum est"; 60: "item (...) beati Evurcii, episcopi et confessoris, corpus visitandum est. Item (...) cultrum qui ad cenam dominicam veraciter extitit"; 62: "Item (...) beati Johannis Baptiste venerandum caput quod per manus quorumdam religiosorum virorum a Jherosolimitanis horis usque ad locum qui nuncupatur Angelicus, in terram scilicet Pictavorum, defertur; ubi ingens basilica sub eius veneratione miro opere componitur, in qua idem caput sanctissimum a centeno monachorum choro, die noctuque veneratur, innumerisque miraculis clarificatur".

[18]Boeren (1962), 64-66; Hermann-Mascard (1975), 216, n. 178; Sumption (1974), 339-340, n. 215.

[19]Mansi XXIV, 283, c. 27: "In concilio statutum est, ut amodo reliquiae extra capsam nullatenus ostendantur, nisi in praecipuis festivitatibus vel ad hoc ex devotione concurrentibus peregrinis".

[20]Boeren (1962), 28.

function of 'announcer'. In a loud voice he commanded the pilgrims to pray for forgiveness of their sins, for the spread of the glory of God, for God's blessing and "that they might never be separated from Him".[21] In 1347 the 'tower exposition' was turned into a seven-yearly affair. It was characteristic of the entire region, which had places of pilgrimage such as Kornelimünster, Maastricht, Tongeren, Trier, Gladbach, Düsseldorf, Düren and many others.[22]

In Limoges, the town where the dukes of Aquitania were crowned, possessed the relics of St. Martial who, a Carolingian legend tells, was sent there by Peter. The head of this person regarded as an apostle was exposed in the 12th century every seven years for a 50 days' period of grace. In 1388 one of the intentions was the ending of the Western schism. In Chartres the veil of the Virgin Mary was the centre of attention of the solemnities. In 1300, the first 'Holy Year', the exposed cloth of Veronica was in competition with the grave of Peter as focus of pilgrimage. Countless numbers of pilgrims took home with them an image of the sweat-soaked cloth bearing the features of Jesus. The solemn exposition during a Holy Year took place in Holy Week and in other years on the Sunday following the Epiphany. To see it meant gaining thousands of years of indulgence.[23]

Expositions were also held in places of pilgrimage such as Compostela,[24] Oviedo[25] and Canterbury.[26] On the island of Rhodes the pilgrims travelling through to Palestine could see a thorn from the Crown of thorns, of which it was said that it bled on Good Friday.[27] One among many travelling to Weingarten to see the sacred blood was the consort of Rudolf of Hapsburg, Queen Anna, who visited the place in 1273. Weingarten had been in possession of this blood relic from the middle of the 11th century. To see it meant the remission of punishment for sin and it had a wonderful healing power. The benefits of seeing such a relic were not limited to the spiritual sphere: in the 14th century it was said of a relic of blood preserved behind crystal in Weissenau that it

---

[21]Beissel (1976), II, 125-126.

[22]ibid. 123; Koldeweij (1985), 64; Mayer (1938), 247-248.

[23]Boeren (1962), 63, 134-137, 146; Beissel (1976), 117.

[24]Mayer (1938), 247.

[25]Bruyne de (1927), 95: "crux ibi monstratur opere angelico fabricata"; Boeren (1962), 143: "kruis der engelen" (the cross of the angels).

[26]Sumption (1974), 340.

[27]Dersch (1931), 465.

remained invisible for whoever was to die in that year.[28] During the expositions in Aachen it was custom for the pilgrims to hold bread and meat aloft so that they could take it home with them. It should be said that as far as the relics are concerned there are few examples of this sort relative to material matters.[29] However the hope of obtaining a cure caused many a pilgrim to look up to the exposed relic and also to the raised Host.

3.2   The exposition of the Eucharist[*]

The procession of the Blessed Sacrament could be regarded as a single continuous exposition, in the course of which certain instants are chosen for explicit exposition. Such an instant preceded the blessing, given at the various stations and at the end of the procession. The priest, standing, held the Sacrament in both hands, showed it to the participants and they praised the Eucharist with hymns. This accord between the exposition of the relics and that of the Sacrament is discussed further in the description of the transposition of the fourth form of reverence, the 'blessing'.

Once the Blessed Sacrament procession had become popular, people wanted to see the Eucharist not only on that occasion but also at other times. We have already described, for instance, how on the feast of Corpus Christi in Spiers and Bamberg the monstrance remained exposed during the Mass and the whole of the octave of the feast. Quite separate from the feast day itself other 'Masses with exposition' had come into being, which recalls the 'Mass with exposed reliquaries': the shrine of St. Serenus on the altar at Angers, the *capsula* of St. Firminus at Amiens and the head of St. Secundus at Bremen. The earliest recorded example of a Mass with exposition of the Sacrament dates from 1372, the year that the bishop of Brandenburg gave permission for the practice on major feast days.[30] Subsequently the same type of development occurred in the exposition of the Eucharist as we have observed in that of the relics. Just

---

[28]Nagel (1956), 201.

[29]Boeren (1962), 41.

[*]A list for further reading ans sources is can be found in: Browe (1933), 141-181; Andrieu (1950); Devlin (1975).

[30]ed. Riedel (1847), 298-299, n. CCXCI: "In nova civitate Brandenburg (...) concedimus (...) eucaristiam, hoc est hostiam consecratam, sex diebus festivis infra scriptis, ad monstranciam cristallinam a nobis benedictam ante horam solempnis processionis ponere (...) et post processionem quamlibet in altari, in quo tunc summam missam contigit celebrare".

as the desire was expressed to see the relics exposed on the altar not only on the saint's feast day and on major feasts but also on Sundays or even during the week, so also was the same desire expressed with regard to the Eucharist. As early as 1416 in Passau it was the custom to expose the Sacrament several days per week. However the bishop thought it necessary to limit the number of days for fear that people would become habituated and irreverent.[31] The two examples quoted are symptomatic for the development outlined in chapter II: in the 15th century 'Masses with exposition' were a fact of life.

Since Maundy Thursday was the day on which the church celebrated the institution of the Eucharist, Thursday was regarded from the 14th century onwards as being the most appropriate day for this sort of Mass. It was usually celebrated in early morning so that everyone had the opportunity to attend. The Sacrament was brought in procession from the *Sakramenthaus* to the high altar. And often an 'altarist' sang or read the Mass at a side altar which be in the care of a guild or a Corpus Christi fraternity. Papal legates and bishops granted indulgences to encourage church attendance. In 1382 the cardinal legate in Dresden confirmed a Corpus Christi fraternity "so that a Mass might be celebrated every Thursday by its priest in honour of the Sacrament". He attached a 100-day indulgence to attendance at the Mass. At the end of the Sequence *Lauda Sion* the priest was to show the Sacrament, in a transparent shrine made of beryl, to the people, accompanied by the singing of *Ecce panis angelorum*.[32]

The examples in which the relics form a part of the ceremony support the fact that the process of transposition did actually occur. In 1399 a *capellanus* in Plassenburg obtained, as one of his many privileges in *capella et castro*, the right to expose "the Sacrament and the relics" during the Thursday Mass.[33] The rubrics drawn up in 1423 demonstrate the particular solemnity attached to the Mass and procession held at

---

[31]Schannat-Harzheim, V, 154: "ex qua frequenti expositione, ut percepimus excrescit indevotio multorum, minoratur reverentia, tepescit charitas et ut locorum vicinorum pericula edocent, ex ea hereses insurgere, et pullulare formidamus: et quia quod ad salutem pie indulsimus, cum ad noxam tendere perspicimus, consultius revocamus".

[32]Browe (1933), 153; 151: "In fine sequentiae per ipsum presbyterum (...) ipsum sacramentum dominicum in birillum consecratum positum christifidei populo astanti cantante presbytero Ecce panis angelorum demonstratur", quotation from the Dresden cartulary, n. 361, *Cod. diplomat. Saxoniae regiae* II 5 (1875) n. 85.

[33]Monumenta Zollerana, VI, 45: " Et idem cappellanus (...) habeat et habere debeat plenarium potestatem (...) corporis domini sacramenti in dicta capella continue retinendi et qualibet feria quinta infra missarum solempnia ipsum sacramentum et alias reliquias ostendendi"; 50: "in dicta capella et castro predicet et ewkaristiam et reliquias populo ostendet".

Straubing. Every Thursday the priest was required to open the 'sarg' - the tabernacle - in the early morning so that the monstrance could be seen. After the Mass of the Virgin Mary the clerics went to the place of exposition and carried the "Eucharist with the other relics" in procession, accompanied by the singing of hymns, to the high altar for the Mass of the Blessed Sacrament. Once arrived at the high altar the celebrant turned towards the people, holding the monstrance so that they could see it. During the Mass, at the *Ecce panis* of the Sequence he again turned to the people, and again for the third time before returning to the tabernacle. The Sacrament remained exposed all that morning in the sarg until the end of the last Mass.[34]

Another document, dated 1429 and promulgated by the bearded Duke Louis of Bavaria, contains approximately the same prescriptions. These were laid down for the church of Our Blessed lady in Ingolstadt. The Mass began between 6 am and 7 am. The celebrant did not only expose the Sacrament but also acted as announcer by holding the monstrance in his hands and requesting the people to praise "the true body of Christ" and to pray for the forgiveness of sin, eternal peace and the welfare of temporal princes. Both Sacrament and relics remained exposed on the side until the last Mass was finished.[35] The relics in question were a particle of the True Cross and a thorn from the Crown of thorns, given by the Duke, who was therefore remembered in the prayers. In a later parish book dated 1525 by Pastor Johannes Eck the rubrics are again found, in an abbreviated but unchanged form.[36]

---

[34]Browe (1933), 152-153: "Danach soll der Pfarrer alle Donnerstage in der Frühe den Sarg, in dem der Fronleichnam in einer Momstranz steht, aufschliessen (...) Wenn Unser-Frauen-Amt (...) gesungen ist, sollen die Priester (...) zum Sarg gehen und mit dem Sacrament und anderen Heiltum (...) um den Chor herumgehen. Am Altar soll sich der Priester der das Sacrament trägt, zum Volke hinwenden. Wenn man..die Sequenz singt soll er den Vers Ecce panis angelorum anstimmen und sich mit der Monstranz dem Volk zuwenden, wie man das am Fronleichnamstag zu tun pflegt. Nach dem Amt soll sich der Priester mit dem Sacrament zum Volke umkehren"; cit. *Straubing cartulary* (1911/18) n. 326.

[35]Buchner (1918), 687: "und sol der priester mit dem sacrament stillstan und darauf pitten das gemain volk, das si anrufen das hailwirdig sacrament, den waren gotsleichnam unsers herrn Jesu Christi (...) für uns hertog Ludwigen (...) das uns got durch sein parmherzigkeit all unser sünd wolle vergeben und zu den ewigen frewden nemen, auch füden allerdurchleuchtigsten fürsten (...) Darnach sullent dann die caplan, psalteristen und schüler das amt gar aussingen und wann das gar volbracht und der segen geben ist so sol sich dann der priester mit dem sacrament aber umbkeren und den vers anvahen (...) und darunter sol der priester mit dem sacrament den segen geben".

[36]Greving (1908), 103: "Dieser Altarist trug in der Prozession das Sanktissimum (...) die sieben Schüler trugen Wandelkerzen und den Reliquien einher, die der Herzog für diese Prozession geschenkt hatte. Das Amt schloss mit feierlichem Segen, und dann sollten Sakrament und Reliquien im Sakramentshäuschen so lange zur Verehrung ausgestellt werden bis das letzte Amt am Tage gesungen war".

Sometimes this Thursday procession was not confined to the interior of the church but, as on the feast of Corpus Christi, wended its way to the cemetery. In Breslau, according to the 1471 rubrics, when the bell rang for the morning Office the church warden had to prepare a monstrance and two 'small pax tables'[37] with relics. During the Office the Eucharist was exposed on the high altar and at the end of the Office, before the Mass began, the congregation went in solemn procession to the cemetery, bearing the Eucharist and the relics.[38]

Browe believes that these solemnities on Thursday were a reflection - on a small scale - of the feast of Corpus Christi. He leaves unanswered the question of whether the exposition of the Sacrament originated on the feast of Corpus Christi itself or on the Thursday celebrations. Whatever may be the case, the ceremony was part of the customary ritual on both occasions and is repeatedly mentioned in rubrics applying to both. A text referring to the feast of Corpus Christi and originating in Oldenzaal in 1495 reads as follows: "The celebrant shall sing devoutly the *Ecce panis angelorum* - "behold the bread of angels" - three times and intone the *corpus Domini* while the choir responds".[39] The exposition of the Eucharist behind clear glass had already been introduced in the theophoric procession on Easter morning in England. The abbess of the abbey of Barking, Sibille Fenton, prescribed it in the rubrics she presented in 1404. The priest must, states the temporale, carry the body of the Lord from the grave to the altar while singing the antiphon *Christus resurgens* - "The risen Christ" - and "he then stands before the altar facing the people, with the body of Christ, behind crystal, in his hands".[40]

The exposition of the Eucharist early on in the morning Office made its appearance from the middle of the 14th century. An *ordinarium* originating in Strasbourg mentioning exposition outside of the Mass dates from 1374. The exposition was gradually extended to the entire day, at first on the feast of Corpus Christi and then subsequently on other feast

---

[37]That is, a small metal plate with a handle, kissed by the celebrant, assistants and faithful at the prayer for peace (LW II, 2185).

[38]Browe (1933), 149: "Jeden Donnerstag sollte der Sakristan beim Läuten der Matutingglocke eine Monstranz und zwei silberne Paxtäfelchen mit Reliquien bereithalten (...) Nachdem die Matutin in der üblichen Weise gebetet war, fand die Prozession durch die Kirche oder über den Friedhoff Statt".

[39]ed. Geerdink (1887), 181: "Et ipso die sacerdos celebrans cantabit devote tribus vicibus *Ecce panis angelorum* Corpus Domini demonstrando, choro sibi respondente"; Browe (1933), 152.

[40]ed. Tolhurst (1927-28), I, 108: "et interim asportabit copus dominicum de sepulcro incipiendo Ant. *Christus resurgens*, coram altari verso vultu ad populum tenendo corpus dominicum in manibus suis inclusum cristallo".

days of the church. The Cistercians of Kaisheim in Bavaria exposed in 1394 the Sacrament the whole day at Christmas, Easter and Whitsun.[41] Around the year 1400 the canons of Mainz had the monstrance standing on the altar from 6 o'clock in the morning, preceding the procession.[42] At the end of the 15th century in Germany, Austria and Scandinavia evening services were held in praise of the exposed Sacrament. Belgium and Holland followed in the 16th century and France in the 17th. In addition, from the end of the 14th century, particularly in what was then German territory, there was a form of exposition that lasted several days or even the entire year, known as the 'perpetual adoration'. This obviously had an effect on visits to the Blessed Sacrament, as already indicated.

In these forms of exposition the monstrance was placed on the altar, in a niche in the wall or in the *Sakramenthaus*. An exception mentioned by Browe was the Spanish town of Lugo, known from a document dated 1579. The tabernacle doors were made of crystal glass so that the Sacrament was visible throughout the entire day. Less exceptional were the statues of angels and of the Virgin Mary in which the Eucharist, in imitation of the anthropomorphic reliquaries, was sometimes contained. Like the reliquary-Madonna-statues of the Clermont-Ferrand type, they were usually fitted with a small window. A crucifix, adorned with precious stones, made in 1324 for the cathedral of Rheims, had a crystal window in the centre through which the Eucharist was visible. In a document of donation dated 1334 the donor gave a costly statue of Mary to St. Stephen's church in Vienne to serve as a *ciborium* for the Eucharist. A citizen promised the Dominicans of Lübeck a similar statue in 1418.[43] In the previous Benedictine church of Sainte Marie at Pornic on the lower reaches of the Loire there was a statue of the Madonna more than a metre tall. The mother of God is depicted holding the infant Jesus on her left arm and pointing significantly with her right hand to her breast where there is a hollowed-out space across the width of the statue designed to contain the Host. The foundation of 1554 expresses the desire

---

[41]Martène (1788), IV, c. 29 n. 6: "Ponatur corpus Christi super altare in prima vespera et in matutinis et in missa"; Browe (1933), 154-155.

[42]Bruder (1901) 502: "Um sechs Uhr setzte man das Sacrament in einer schöneren Monstranz auf dem Altare in Chore der Herren (Canoniker) aus".

[43]Browe (1933), 101, 161, 163; in 1425 the monastery of Goldenkron (Böhmen) also had in its possession a *crux cristallana* in 1425 used for processions with the Host; Urkundenbuch-Lübeck (1843-1905), VI (1881), 15, n. XV: "dat werde hilghe sacrament des hilghen lichames unses Heren Jhesu Christi in ener monstrancien edder in enen marienbilde".

to have a lamp burning continually in front of the statue 'servant le sacraire'.[44]

Even more commonly than Mary, she who gave birth to the Word made flesh, the figure of the Saviour, the Risen Lord, was used as a place for reserving the Eucharist. The monastery of Wienhausen, founded in 1221 by a son of Henry the Lion, has such a statue that must have stood on the altar from the end of the 13th century. Through an opening in the side it was possible to catch a glimpse of the Eucharist - or at least the desire to do so was thereby awakened. The somewhat tapered opening in the back was large enough for a small pyx. A reliquary chest containing a blood relic served as a seat for the statue of the Saviour. The same situation was maintained in the new altar of 1519: the blood relic was placed in the foot of the predella-tabernacle and once again acted as support for the pyx or monstrance, visible when the tabernacle doors were pushed aside. The statue in Wienhausen was somewhat smaller than two other anthropomorphic containers for the Sacrament: the statues of Christ and Thomas, almost 3 metres tall, in the nunnery of Frankenberg in Goslar.[45]

"Every means imaginable to guarantee that the faithful could remain close to and see the relics was employed afresh in order to show the body of Christ and offer it for veneration", writes Andrieu.[46] This is seen even more clearly in the use of the *ostensorium* or 'monstrance'. Up to this point we have used these words somewhat interchangeably, although at present the word 'monstrance' refers exclusively to the Eucharistic monstrance. Both names clearly indicate the function: they were designed to 'expose' the sacred object behind glass. When around the year 1215 there was an increase in the existing tendency to provide reliquaries with a 'peep-hole', the goldsmiths designed models that were more manageable, consisting of glass cylinders, placed vertically or horizontally on a foot. Although they were originally intended to contain only partial relics, they were later used for exposing the Eucharist. This happened around 1300, when the 'elevatio' was no longer the only instant that the faithful were allowed to look at the exposed Host. Before that time not even the procession provided such an opportunity since the Eucharist was

---

[44]Rupin (1890), 217 sqq. According to report dating from 1678 the statue was still being used at that time for the same purpose. Two more drawings of statues of the Virgin Mary dating from the 13th century show a hollowed-out space at knee-height.

[45]Appuhn (1961), 92, 101-103; illustr. 76, 82.

[46]ibid. (1950), 398: "Tous les moyens imaginés pour procurer aux fidèles l'approche et la vue des reliques, on les reprit pour leur montrer et leur faire vénérer le Corps-Dieu".

carried in a closed container. A synod held at Liège in 1287 mentions not a monstrance but a pyx in connection with the feast of Corpus Christi.[47] When the *viaticum* was taken to the sick or in the course of the theophoric processions, to the extent that these occurred during the Eastertide, the Eucharist was carried in a closed pyx. What was still being treated as an exception in 1300 was by 1350 more of a general rule. Around 1400 the Host was carried and exposed in a fairly general way *in pixide cristallano*.[48]

A glass container of this type for the Host usually started out as a 'rebuilt' relic ostensorium. The adaptation required consisted of a *lunula* for the Host. These glass cylinders were, in fact, designed to hold long objects - a finger, arm or leg, which made them less suitable for the Host. And yet the traditional cylinder continued its existence from the 14th to the 16th century in the monstrance, even when this was built exclusively to contain the Eucharist. Often, therefore, it is impossible to tell whether examples of these objects which have come down to us were a Eucharistic or a relic monstrance, all the more so since the *lunula* was easily removed. Sometimes there is not even any need to pose the question, since the monstrance in question will have been used for both purposes depending on circumstances.

The naming of objects also carried the marks of the process of transposition. In some of the text quoted above the "Eucharist and the other relics" are mentioned in the same breath.[49] The Eucharist monstrance can be found listed in various ecclesiastical, monastic and princely inventories as *reliquarium*. Andrieu quotes ten or so instances dated between 1380 and 1580. The word "reliquaire" is repeatedly used when the subject of carrying the Lord's body is mentioned. Whether these also served to expose the relics cannot be determined. A second category was designed for simultaneous exposition of Eucharist and relics, which were somehow included in the monstrance. Andrieu quotes something like 25 instances in support of this. A third group clearly had a double function: they were suitable for exposition of either Eucharist or relics. These are horizontal cylinders for the relics with a medallion mounted higher up for the Eucharist. Angels support the cylinder or keep watch on the medallion.

---

[47]Schannat-Harzheim, VII, 691, c. 5 n. 33; Braun (1932), 355.

[48]Browe (1927a), 83-84.

[49] see above n. 33, 34, 38 and p. 247, n. 30; Andrieu (1950) en Zika (1988), 46: As late as 1489 the church of Ss. Ulrich and Afra in Augsburg had a monstrance made for the sudarium of St. Ulrich but also used to carry the body of the Lord.

The foot of an *ostensorium* of this type, property of the parish of St. Quentin in Hasselt, carries the date 1286 and has six small recesses for relics. The *ostensorium* came from the abbey of Herkenrode near Liège where, around the year 1317, a Host is reported to have bled. It has a double *lunula* so that both the Sacrament and the miraculous Host could be exposed.[50] This 'solution' was opted for more often as a preventive measure against idolatry during processions and expositions. *Latria* or adoration is due only to God. This pragmatic form of regulation bears witness to the influence of St. Thomas Aquinas and scholastic theology, which stated that the miraculous Eucharistic bread and wine should not be regarded as the body of Christ. Hence the practice in Alkmaar of carrying a recently consecrated Host with the miraculous Host. In 1346 the bishop of Amsterdam, Jan van Arkel, gave permission for the miraculous Host to be replaced by a newly consecrated Host, without any trouble being caused.[51] In addition to Herkenrode, Alkmaar and Amsterdam there are various places to which thousands of pilgrims made their way to venerate, request healing or offer some other form of prayer: Andechs, Augsburg, Daroka, Orvieto, Paris, Walldürn, Deggendorf, Wilsnack and Boxmeer. There a Host would be exposed that had undergone some miracle or other: found in a miraculous way, having withstood fire or showing visible signs of the blood of the Lord. The 'evidence' was often venerated in a separate chapel. Pilgrims were granted generous indulgences, especially in Orvieto, Wilsnack and Andechs. In this latter pilgrimage place there were three miraculous Hosts, to which a newly consecrated one was added. During the exposition a cleric would read aloud the history of the miraculous Host. If the original object of devotion had become unrecognisable, as has been the case in Orvieto since the 15th century, the devoutly venerated remains were regarded as a relic and were exposed and carried in procession as *summae reliquiae*.[52]

---

[50]Braun (1932), 356; Andrieu (1950), 403; Browe (1938), 175.

[51]for Thomas see p. 49; Browe (1929f), 327-328; Caspers (1992), 255-256; for the controversy in this matter at Pulkau: see Browe (1929d), 327, (1938), 163 and for Wilsnack: Zika (1988), 51-52.

[52]Browe (1938), 115, 123, 152, 153, 198; Herwaarden v. (1978), Wilsnack: esp. p. 413-414, 705; (1980).

***

We have already made the acquaintance of an announcer such as the one present in Andechs - and Ingolstadt - at the 'exposition of the relics' in Aachen accompanying the sermon in the cathedral. Sermons and explanations were part of the usual pattern of expositions on pilgrimage days. These and other parallels in the above are aspects which could point to a process of transposition. Indeed, the relics of a particular saint were the object of special attention on the saint's feast day: they would be carried in procession, exposed and set out during the Mass. It also happened that they were exposed for longer or 'perpetually': the shrine of St. Denis in Paris, the relic of John the Baptist in St-Jean d'Angély and Veronica's towel in Rome. In the same way, on the feast of Corpus Christi the Eucharist was carried in procession, exposed and stood on the altar during Mass. The exposition on the feast day was extended to the octave, major feast days, Thursdays with episcopal permission and, here and there, 'perpetually'.

While the efforts made to explain 'the sacred object' - the relic or Host - in a visionary manner on such feast days must have been a common background to the exposition itself, it does not explain the similarities we have pointed out between these efforts in the case of the relics and of the Eucharist. Just as with the tradition of processions, it is obvious that we can assume here too that the then current practices surrounding the exposition of the relics were brought up to date in the exposition of the Eucharist. The following details already reviewed point to this: the procession as an extended form of exposition, the placing on the altar and the combination of both types of exposition at Plassenberg and Ingolstadt; then the presence of relics in the Eucharistic procession to the high altar at Straubing and Breslau, and the references to this in the 'procession' described; the *ostensoria* also confirm transposition: the 'misericordiae' and the reliquary *ostensoria* were turned into Eucharistic monstrances, their original form as designed to contain the relics being preserved, the monstrance continued to be designated as *reliquarium* and the possibility was maintained of placing both Host and relics in the monstrance. Finally the material expectations of a venerator of the relics such as at St-Benoît-sur-Loire, St-Jean d'Angély, Weissenau and Aachen are reminiscent of the *ex opere operato* effectiveness of the raised or exposed Host. In both cases the people expected to be freed from hunger, sudden death or some other disaster.

In a spiritual sense in both cases diminution of punishment due to sin could be obtained by means of indulgences, but here the ways divided:

the seeing of the raised or exposed body of Christ came to be the *manducatio spiritualis*, or 'spiritual communion', which had become general practice. The path leading to this practice had been prepared by such people as the 12th-century authors who enlarged the difference that had caused so many problems since Berengarius of Tours: *sacramentum* and *res sacramenti*. The theologian Alger of Liège († 1130) mentions two ways of receiving the body of Christ: physically, by way of the mouth and spiritually by way of the heart.[53] Stephan of Autun († 1140) stated the same: "Both the good and the bad communicate sacramentally, but only the good also communicate spiritually".[54] Hugh of St. Victor († 1141) again put it slightly differently. He who eats and unites with Christ, he concludes, "participates in the *sacramentum* and in the *res sacramenti*", but he who receives but with an inappropriate attitude "participates in the *sacramentum* but not in the *res sacramenti*".[55]

Caesarius of Heisterbach expressed the positive significance of spiritual communion in an example in which a lay brother is granted the gift of prophecy in return for his spiritual communion.[56] The chancellor of the University of Paris, Guiard of Laon († 1258), later bishop of Cambray, bore witness to even more generous gifts. In his sermons he held out twelve spiritual gifts before the faithful, gifts in which they could share. Later writers and preachers were to imitate him by often quoting these rich opportunities.[57]

The 13th-century theologians continued to elaborate on the basic assumptions of the preceding century. To see the Host was regarded by them as a means of achieving union with Christ. William of Auxerre († 1231) called the desire to see the Host "an appeal to the love of

---

[53]PL 180, 797, *De sacramentis corporis et sanguinis Dominici* lib. I, c. XX: "Sunt etiam duae comestiones corporis Christi in ecclesia, una corporalis, altera spiritualis; una fit ore, altera fit corde".

[54]PL 172, 1296, *De sacramento altaris* c. XVII: "Sciendum est quod duplex est sumptio corporis et sanguinis Domini, sacramentalis et spiritualis. Sacramentali communicant boni et mali, soli boni spirituali".

[55]PL 176, 465, *De sacramentis christianae fidei* lib. II, c. V: "Qui manducat et incorporatur, sacramentum habet, et rem sacramenti habet. Qui manducat et non incorporatur, sacramentum habet, sed rem sacramenti non habet".

[56]ed. Strange (1851), II, dist. IX, c. 45: "Habebat enim maximum desiderium communicandi. Eadem nocte et sequenti die, omnia quae intra monasterium spiritualiter agebantur, divinitus ei sunt revelata. Et licet absens corpore, spiritu tamen praesens fuit, communicans spiritualiter, et si non sacramentaliter. Reversis fratribus ipse eis per ordinem indicavit, quis missam maiorem celebrasset, quis legisset Epistolam, quis Evangelium; similiter ad vigilias qui monachi quas lectiones vel quae responsoria cantassent".

[57]ed. Boeren (1956), 130-134; 341-344: "*Des XII fruits du sacrament*".

God".[58] Bonaventure († 1274) emphasised the need for the right attitude[59] in words similar to those used by Stephen of Autun. Albertus Magnus († 1280) distinguished three ways of union with Christ's mystical body, but linked spiritual communion inextricably with the sacramental.[60]

For the lay person the 'communion with the eyes' implied no confession and no danger of receiving communion unworthily. He was freed from the fear of "eating and drinking to his own damnation" during the sacramental communion - for which, it was said, "a thousand years' preparation would not be sufficient". "Anyone receiving the Host made, as it were, a statement regarding their own worthiness".[61] The transposed exposition of the relics within the context of Eucharistic devotion gained for its content the exposed Sacrament, which offered the people a divine dimension: affective eye-contact and spiritual union with Christ truly present.

4   THE BLESSING GIVEN WITH THE RELICS AND THE EUCHARIST

A blessing is a prayer, accompanied by a gesture of tion, containing the wish that the creation in its own function may serve man to fulfil his Christian existence or that he himself should develop positively in that existence. It is based on the belief in the effective presence of God in His world. For this reason a sick person is blessed and a prayer is uttered that he might be strengthened and cured. In this the mediation of God's chosen ones, the saints, be called on for help. As far back as the early Middle Ages the *capsae* containing secondary relics were placed on the sick and used to make a gesture of blessing over them. Thus Herman of Auxerre († 448), "filled with the Holy Spirit", prayed first to the Triune God before placing his *capsula* on the eyes of a blind girl. We again find this gesture of benediction in Gregory of Tours, who recounted that he was relieved of grievous stomach ache by praying at the grave of St. Martin. He had a sign of the cross with a thread taken from the grave

---

[58]ed. Pigouchet (1964), 260: "aspicere corpus Christi provocatio est ad dilectionem Dei".

[59]Bonaventura *Opera Omnia*, 201, Sententiarum, lib. IV, dist. IX, 1.1, : "quidam accedunt male dispositi, et hi manducant sacramentaliter; quidam bene, et hi spiritualiter".

[60]Albert Magni *Opera Omnia, Sententiarum*, IV, IX, 2, : "Et haec manducatio spiritualis numquam separatur a sacramentali".

[61]See p. 54, n. 103; Caspers (1992), 220.

cloth and touched the site of the pain with it. The blessing and healing power of Martin was seen as present in the *virtus* of this contact relic.[1]

This type of blessing took on a public character in the weather blessing: a gesture of exorcism with accompanying prayer formulas in which prayer was offered to God and the help was invoked of certain saints believed to have special powers against fire and lightning, such as St. Barbara († c. 306) Cyril († 444),[2] Bridget († c. 523) or Columba († 597). The extent to which people could place their confidence in a relic off a saint is reported in the *vita* of St. Mathilda († 1160) written by a contemporary. In the Bavarian convent of Diessen this nun's long hair, which she had never had cut during her lifetime, was hung outside during thunderstorms to still the thunder.[3] A more detailed study is told in the 13th-century *vita Hildulfi* († c. 707). During a terrible thunderstorm the monks of the Moyenmoutier monastery rushed to the altar with relics, crucifixes and corporals while the bells rang to drive off the weather demons. When this proved of no avail, they called on their patron, St. Hidulfus, and carried his relics outside. The storm subsided, but once they had replaced the shrine in the church the thunder began afresh, so that they had to repeat the process three times, each time with the same brief result. Finally they opted for the most radical solution: they left the saint standing on guard, and this sufficed.[4]

The weather blessing with a reposes on this trust in the *virtus* of the saint against the 'weather gods'. Another public blessing using relics was that in which the believer crossed himself. This form of reverence was easily derived from the showing of relics after Mass or a procession.

It is imaginable that in the private sphere a gesture of blessing was also made with the pyx or the Host when *viaticum* was brought.[5] From the 12th century onwards, in addition, the custom arose of placing the communion on the breast of the sick who could no longer receive or of

---

[1]See p. 84; MGH SRM I,2, 200-201, *De virtutibus s. Martini*, lib. IV, c. 1: "Accessi temerarius ad locum sepulchri, proiectusque solo, orationem fudi atque, secretius a pendentibus velis unum sub vestimento iniectum, crucis ab hoc signaculum in alvo depinxi; protinus dolore sedato, sanus abscessi".

[2]Franz (1909), II, 61: in the prayer formulas this name is not detailed any further, so that it is not sure whether Cyril of Alexandria is meant.

[3]AASS 30 mai VII, 457, *De b. Mathilde virgine*, c. IV,32: "Certissimo autem sunt remedio contra tempestates et fulgura, et surgentibus ventis atque minitantibus, capillos Sanctae suspendunt in aera; sicque tempestates conquiescunt, conticescunt tonitrua, ac si Dominus Iesus imperet eis".

[4]AASS-OSB, III,2, 483-484, c. 20 (anno c. 707?).

[5]Thurston (1901), 192-193; the author assumes that the blessing of the sick according to the then current *Rituale* refers to this ancient practice.

allowing them to touch the Eucharist.[6] In the 13th-14th centuries the transposition of the weather blessing took place: instead of using the relics, it was the Eucharist that was used to make the sign of the cross on the clouds. The transposition of the blessing with the Sacrament over the faithful is derived from the feast of Corpus Christi, and was given during and after the procession in the 14th century. The 'Mass with exposition', which followed, was again brought to an end with the Eucharistic blessing. It was analogous to an already existing tradition: the blessing withe the relics.

4.1   The blessing with the relics[*]

From the 9th century onwards it was customary on Ascension Day in south-west Germany to curse the demons so that they would not cause "storm, rain or any destructive natural disaster whatever". The priest made the sign of the cross on the clouds with raised hand, holding a crucifix containing when possible, a relic of the True Cross or some saint. The oldest rubric known prescribes the singing of Psalm 147, *Lauda Sion*, after the blessing.[7] Preceding this blessing, or following it, from the 10th century onwards the Litany of the Saints was recited, and from the 12th century onwards the reading of the beginning of the four Gospels was also part of the ritual, elements to be found in the processions held on the 25th April and the Rogation Days.

The weather blessing to protect against thunder and lightning was given on set days. Using the prayer formulas and *consuetudines* of Hirsau and Cluny Franz describes how fear struck at the onslaught of a thunderstorm. The warden at Hirsau set out the crucifix and the relics, sprinkled holy water and rang the bell. If the threat increased, more bells were brought in while the monks gathered in the church to recite the litany and the seven Penitential Psalms. The activity showed similarities to the *clamor* in a situation which actually was more threatening than a usurpation. During 'demonic' thunderstorms the church also used all the

---

[6]Browe (1936), 225-225.

[*]A list for further reading and sources can be found in: Browe (1931a).

[7]Franz (1909), II, 50-52, 75-76: "Adiuro vos, angeli satane (...) ut in loco isto dei et ista parochia neque per tempestatem neque per aquam malignam neque per ullam corruscationem neque per ullam artem venire et nocere possitis in nomine domini nostri Iesu Christi, qui venturus est iudicare vivos et mortuos et te, inimice, per ignem. Signo vos, nubes, signo sancte crucis"; "Deinde Lauda Ierusalem (ps. 147) totum decanta".

sacred means available in parish churches to turn aside the evil: incense, holy water, the paschal candle and the text of the Canon laid out on the altar with a stole laid crosswise over it. The priest stood in the church doorway surrounded by fearful parishioners and at each flash of lightning he raised the crucifix, a relic or an *Agnus Dei*, intoned his prayer of exorcism and with the sign of the cross signed the sky, where the bells were doing their utmost to prevail over the thunder.[8] The fixed days for the weather blessing were: Ascension Day, the feast of the Finding of the True Cross on 3rd May and the Ember Days. Weather processions, designed to persuade the natural forces to serve man rather than harm him, were no exception on these days as a counterpart to the *rogationes*.

While the weather blessing was directed towards the forces of nature, the blessing with the relics on the feast of the saint was aimed at the latter's venerators, asking for his intercession with God. From the 11th century onwards many places were familiar with the custom of closing the Mass with a blessing with the relics, which had stood on the altar throughout the Mass.[9] In 1010 in Limoges the bishop blessed the crowds with the head of John the Baptist after celebrating solemn high Mass on the saint's feast day.[10] This sort of thing came into daily use in one or two places. In 1157 Otto of Freising made the following appreciative remark about Emperor Barbarossa in this regard: "He heard Mass and, after having been blessed with the relics, set to work".[11] In the monastery of St-Guilhelm-le-Désert it was the custom for the people to be blessed with a relic of the True Cross after the morning Mass, a

---

[8]PL 150, 1093, *Constitutiones Hirsaugienses*, lib. II, c. 35: "Surgente tempestate a sacrista in claustro crux est ponenda contra tempestatem eamdem versa, et reliquiae cum aqua benedicta. Statim duo signa maxima pulsantur, quousque instantia tanti periculi transisse videatur at si in tantum videret increscere periculum, (...) tunc sine mora pulsat duo maxima grandinem significantia (...) fratres (...) mox litaniam incipiant. Qua finita septem psalmos (...) adiungant"; Herrgott ((1726), 524; Franz (1909), II, 89, *Ordo X contra auram levatam, contra aereas potestates*: "Cum primo videtur aura inmoderata levari, proiciat sacerdos contra illam aquam benedictam et mox cum clericis ante altare accumbit dicens VII psalmos"; 70, n. 2: "sacerdos (...) cum libello coniuracionum procedat, stans in porticu ecclesie maiori cum thuribulo incensi benedicti, cum scrinario eciam et aqua benedicta et cereo paschali vel candelis purificacionalibus et Agnus Dei - si potest habere - et fiat pulsus campanarum et explicetur canon super altare et stola per modum crucis superponatur".

[9]Browe (1931), 383; Jungmann (1962), II, 551-552.

[10]MGH SS IV, 142, *Adamani Hist.* lib. III, c. 56: "et post missam episcopus cum capite sancti Iohanis benedixit populum".

[11]MGH SS XX, 490, *Gesta Frederici I imperatoris*, lib. IV, c. 76: "Peractis votis et post missarum solempnia divinis consignatus reliquiis, mane reliquum curae regni administrandi deputat".

relic given as a gift by Charlemagne.[12] Even just before the 15th century the Benedictine monasteries of Saint Saveu in Charroux and Saint Isidore in the diocese of Clermont had a similar blessing each Sunday.[13]

Another moment set aside for the blessing with the relics was the Offertory, while people were bringing their offerings to the altar. In Belgium this practice can still be found, with the people kissing the relics. In a document dated 1399 originating in Jena the Dominicans took on the self-imposed duty of keeping a brother available for a particular altar. Each Wednesday he was expected to celebrate a sung Mass in honour of the True Cross. On the altar there stood a tiny monstrance with the relic of the True Cross, which he used to bless all those approaching the altar.[14]

When we looked at the exposition of the relics we saw how the people was blessed with the head of Bertha of Blangy after the sermon and how the bishop of Cambray blessed the devoutly bowing congregation with the relics of Aldegonde. These devotional blessings performed for the benefit of the faithful were derived from the exposition after an incidental *elevatio*. As well as after Mass, the blessing with the relics was often given during and after a procession. Around the year 1100 in Paris the custom came into being whereby the bishop blessed the crowd with the relics during the long procession held in mid-June to open the fair of St. Denis. At the cemetery 'des Innocents' there was a resting place where the crowd sang hymns before a reliquary cross with a particle of the True Cross and the bishop or his representative preached from a tribune. Once this was over the prelate used the cross to give a blessing towards the East, where the relic had come from, and then towards the remaining three points of the compass. Other relics were then brought, including a shrine containing the arm of St. Simeon.[15] It sometimes happened that

---

[12]AASS OSB IV,2, 557, *Mirac. s. Willelmi*: "Interea venit hora quando vigiles Orationes beati Guillelmi expleta matutinali missa, illo benedicto ligno populus more solito a sacerdote peteret benedictionem".

[13]Dénifle (1965), I, 167, n. 414: "et de septennio in septennium omni populo de longinquis partibus ibidem affluenti ostenditur (praeputium Iesu Christi), cum multis aliis magnis et notabilibus reliquiis"; n. 1: "item in ecclesia monasterii S. Ysidori O.S.B. Claromont. diocc., et cum illo qualibet die dominica fiebat solemnis benedictio populi inibi confluentis".

[14]Urkundenbuch-Jena (1888-1936), 474, n. 522: "Czum erstin solle wir und wollin darczu schicken eynen pristir unser bruder eynen, der alle tage ewiglichen obir dem alter halden und sundirlichin alle mittewoche eyne mesze von dem hl. crucze sal singen, und sol dy monstrantczen(!) (...) uf den alter tragin und dy dy masze uz darauf sten lasin, und dy lute, dy ir offer uf den alter reichen, sal man sy damete bekreiszin".

[15]DACL VIII,1, 1258, "Landit".

the reliquary was already in place to be kissed or to be used in blessing, as is reported of the arm of the Irish saint Gibrianus († c. 515) in Rheims in 1145. Since 890 the town had had in its possession the relics of this saint, who is reported to have 'peregrinated' to continental Europe with six brothers and three sisters.[16] Usually the blessing as a form of veneration was to be found in the context of the procession or the Mass. The 13th-century ordinal of the cathedral of Bayeux mentions a procession which, following Terce, made its way to the altar of St. Stephen, after which the blessing was given with the arm of the saint.[17] The arm, in the guise of a fixed gesture of blessing, was the favourite relic for the *benedictio*. It recalls the anthropomorphic reliquary of St. Firminus which, as it were, itself gave the blessing on major feast days. During the procession the deacon, preceded by two acolytes, bore the relic solemnly to the bishop, who made the gesture of blessing in the sign of the cross.[18] The feast of Bishop Basil the Great, whose arm was in the possession of the canons of Essen, coincided with the feast of the Circumcision, 1st January. On that day, according to the mid-14th-century *Liber Ordinarius*, the canons carried the arm in procession to the high altar, in front of which the priest stood holding the shrine in his hands. The priest intoned the oration hymn, in which God was asked in the customary manner to accept the prayers of the congregation and take away their sins for the sake of this confessor bishop. The celebrant than made the sign of the cross with the shrine over the people and pronounced the following blessing: "*Benedictio Dei Patris descendat super vos et maneat semper*".[19] He then placed the arm on the altar, where it remained throughout the Mass,[20] as later it became the custom to do with the Eucharist. In 1395 the clerics of Paris organised a large-scale

---

[16]AASS 8 maii VII,1, 634, *Miracula s. Gibriani*, lib. II,7: "Brachium autem Sancti, quod ad deosculandum et benedicendum populo semper paratum deforis erat".

[17]ed. Chevalier (1902), 68: "Post terciam fit processio ad Sanctum Stephanum (...) et facta oblatione ad brachium et data benedictione cum eodem ut prius".

[18]ed. Durand (1934), 47: "Ad processionem, que fit in cappis sericis per claustrum, fit cum eo (...) Ab episcopo datur benedictio cum brachio beati Firmini martyris, quod ei defertur a dyacono revestito, duobus cereis precedentibus"; 551: "In processione (...) diaconus revestitus brachium (...) cum quo prius osculato ab episcopo, dat benedictionem episcopus"; see p. 280.

[19]"May the blessing of God the almighty Father descend upon you and remain for ever".

[20]ed. Arens (1908), 30: "Presbiter cum brachio stabit ante summum altare versa facie ad occidentem, canonici circa eum, conventus ante gradus inferius. Tunc finito responsorio conventus cantabit unam antiphonam de sancto Basilio, presbiter collectam (...) Qua collecta finita presbiter benedicet populum faciendo cum dicto brachio crucem super eos, dicens: *Benedictio Dei Patris omnipotentis descendat super vos et maneat semper. Amen.* Quo facto ponet brachium super altare. Ad summam missam ministratur".

procession for the ailing King Charles VI when his illness showed no improvement. At the front of the procession were six monks carrying on their shoulders the relics of St. Louis, the Virgin Mary and the hand of St. Thomas, all encased in gold and precious stones. Behind the monks of St. Denis walked "almost three thousand" men and women. At the city gate two other processions joined them and the whole mass moved off towards the Sainte Chapelle. There the prior celebrated a solemn Mass and the ceremony closed at the city gate with the giving of the blessing with the relics.[21]

And yet around the year 1400 this sort of thing had become the exception since another type of blessing had come to prevail: that given with the corporal, the paten or the chalice. In addition to the gesture of blessing made with the hand, formerly reserved exclusively to the bishop, this practice had originated in the south and developed in the course of the 13th century. It was directly related to the Eucharist. Just as in the Middle Ages the corporal, chalice or paten had been placed in the tomb as objects that had been in contact with the body and blood of Christ, so for the same reason were they used in order to beseech God to grant His blessings to His people.

The synod of Albi in 1230 prescribed a prayer formula[22] and Durandus regarded this type of blessing, performed by the priest, a suitable way of distinguishing it from the blessing given by the bishop's hand.[23] Many French sacramentaria and missals contain a description of it. The tradition was continued into the 15th and 16th centuries, and not just in France. During the nuptial Mass celebrated in England the couple were given the extra gloss of a blessing with the chalice.[24] A blessing was seldom given with these consecrated objects outside of the context of the Mass.

---

[21]ed. Bellaguet (1839-52), II, *Chronicon Karoli sexti*, lib. XVI: "Qua peracta, cum prefati domini duces usque ad portam civitatis pervenissent, et benedictionem sanctarum reliquiarum percepissent, conventus ad ecclesiam rediit".

[22]ed. Lagger de (1927), 433, VIII, c. 28: "Item, precipimus quod sacerdotes in fine missae semper benedicant populum cum cruce vel calice vel patena vel corporali, dicendo simpliciter: *Benedicat vos Omnipotens Deus, Pater et Filius et Spiritus Sanctus*"; Browe (1931a), 384.

[23]ed. Berthelé (1900-1907), 77, *Instructiones*: "Missa vero completa (...) volvens se ad populum, benedicit simpliciter facto signo crucis super illum cum cruce vel cum patena vel cum corporali (ad differentiam episcopalis benedictionis, que fit cum manu)".

[24]Browe (1931a), 385-386.

4.2   The blessing with the Eucharist*

Caesarius of Heisterbach recounts in one of his examples, intended to convince the doubter of the presence of Christ in the Eucharist, what happened during the night after a priest had taken the *viaticum* to a sick person. A violent thunderstorm broke out, with lightning that turned night into day. The priest went through the house carrying the pyx and made the sign of the cross before the windows.[25] Franz recounts a similar 14th-century miracle story of a priest from Aquileia who quelled the thunder with a Eucharistic blessing.[26]

These legendary reports could be an indication that in the 13th and 14th centuries in some cases on the outbreak of a thunderstorm the weather blessing was given with the Eucharist rather than with the relics. A non-legendary source is constituted by information coming to us from the 15th century: in some dioceses in the south of Germany, northern Italy, Spain and France this Eucharistic blessing had become a controversial custom. As early as the first decades of that century a certain Rudolf Artzat or Medicus of Augsburg wrote a tract opposing the custom. He writes: from the feast of Corpus Christi to the gathering of the harvest in a number of regions the Sacrament is carried to the church door to bless the air. The same is done when bad weather threatens, whereas the Sacrament was instituted as food for the soul and should not be used for other ends. The Viennese theologian, Thomas Ebendorfer of Haselbach († 1461) agreed with Rudolf and added a supplementary argument that experience had shown that lightning had struck a church where the Sacrament was reserved and also a priest who was giving the weather blessing with the Sacrament in his hands. Similar arguments were used by the prior of Tegernsee, Augustin Holzapfler. One of the supporters of the practice, however, was Felix Hemmerlin who, as provost of Zurich, was close to the people and could thus easily share their feelings. In 1451 he suggested that Jesus had stilled the storm and that the hand of the priest holding the Sacrament could do much more than with it. He thus approved of the blessing given at the church door. The authors of the 1487 *Malleus maleficarum* agreed with this, provided

---

*A list for further reading and sources is to be found in: Franz (1909), II; Browe (1929a), 386-391; (1933), 181-185.

[25]ed. Hilka (1937), 92, lib. II, c. 14: "Sacerdos vero pyxidem cum sacramento tollens, cum   domum circuiret et contra fenestras singulas cum eo signum crucis ederet, contemplatus est in angulo eiusdem domus quasi umbram humanam stantem".

[26]Franz (1909), II, 71-72; Browe (1933), 131 (example from 16th century).

that the Sacrament was veiled. They described the weather blessing as "a very old custom of French and some German churches".[27] The blessing given during thunderstorms remained controversial: in Spain a rituale published in Burgos in 1497 prescribed excommunication for anyone taking the Sacrament out of the *sacrarium* during a storm. The priest was, however, allowed to leave the *sacrarium* open and take the usual measures such as lighting the paschal candle and ringing the bells.[28] A rituale from Lyon in 1542, on the other hand, bade the pastor carry the Sacrament to the front of the church and drive away the tempest in the name of Christ.[29]

This discussion is often interwoven with processions through the fields and the weather blessing, which was given with the Sacrament during such processions once they had become theophoric. The blessing with the Eucharist took over from that performed with the relics and also implied a prayer for the fertility of the earth. The rubrics of 1388 of the Bavarian monastery of Osterhofen in the diocese of Passau speak of the burning of a candle in honour of St. Albanus to guard against inclement weather. This continued from Easter to 8th May, the feast of the apparition of St. Michael, while on the feast of Corpus Christi a monk carried the Sacrament through the monastery gardens "to bless the fruits".[30] This represented an attempt to 'safeguard' the growing period of the crops. The weather blessing given to the four points of the compass with the same end in view has already been mentioned, a practice rejected by the synod of Passau in 1470: "In many places the four Gospels are read, accompanied by ceremonies against lightning and thunder. This can give rise to dangerous doubts that God is not present everywhere but only in those places where He is called on in this manner". The bishop of

---

[27]*Malleus maleficarum*, 197: "diverse consuetudines ecclesie in cultu divino in nullo veritate repugnant (...) antiquissime consuetudines ecclesiarum gallie et quarumdam germanie cum decreverint eucharistiam ad auram deportare, non poterit hoc esse illicitum, verum quod non in patulo, sed in sacrario abscondito et incluso"; ed. 1600, IIq. 2c; ed. Schmidt (1906), 268; Franz (1901), 91; (1909), II, 101-123.

[28]ibid. 104, *Ordo contra tempestates*: "Primo et ante omnia sacrista attendat ad nubes et ad dispositionem tempestatis et, cum viderit moveri tempestas, statim pulset cimbala. Et sacerdos cum superpellicio et stola veniat ad sacrarium et aperiat altare (...) Et incendat luminaria et cereum paschale, et aperiat sacrarium, ubi est corpus Christi, sed non extrahat corpus Christi a custodia vel a pixide pro nulla tempestate, quoniam esset excommunicatus, sed solum aperiat sacrarium, et sit sic apertum, donec tempestas fuerit quietata".

[29]Thiers (1679), II, 354.

[30]*Monumenta boica*, 12 (1775), 445-446: "et a festo Pasche inclusive usque ad festum beati Michaelis, in honorem beati Albani, contra malignitatem aerearum tempestatum, una candela ardens, ad missam choralem per custodem procuretur, que etiam post finem misse ante corpus Christi infra ambitum benedictionem frugum per ministrum deportetur".

Spiers also forbade the blessing given in the open air in the years 1479 and 1488.[31]

Despite these protestations the processions through the fields increased in the 15th-16th century and, in consequence, so did the blessing given with the Eucharist. In southern Germany, Austria and in a number of Swiss dioceses the parish pastors even went round individually on foot or mounted on horseback with the Eucharist around their neck in order to bless the fields. After all, the clerics were children of their age, an age in which the practice of fighting fire was still regarded as valid - a practice we still have to look at and one which was also forbidden by the same synod of Passau. Moreover the parish priest was often under heavy pressure to carry out these ceremonies: refusal could mean that he would be blamed for damage caused by heavy rainfall, hail and failed crops, with the attendant famine, sickness and death. During a synod held in 1456 in Salzburg there was opposition both to this custom and to the habit that many parishes had of holding a 'weather procession', with the Eucharistic blessing, around the church every Sunday between Ascension Day and 10th August, the anniversary of the death of Lawrence. Opinions must have remained divided and the practice not amenable to abolition since more than 150 years later the Council of Konstanz expressed absolutely no opposition to it.[32] The weather blessing, originally a sign of the cross on the clouds with a crucifix and a relic, was finally also transformed into the blessing with the Eucharist at the end of Mass. In various places in Germany this blessing was not, as at the Sequence, intended for the churchgoers but for the forces of nature: it was given towards the four points of the compass, as the example of Biberach in 1530 shows.[33]

---

[31]Schannat-Harzheim, V, 486, c. XLII: "Dudum in nostra dioecesi inolevit (...) quod nonnullis temporibus almum Corpus Christi per campos, et segetes ad diversa loca, etiam ad ignem deportatur (...) in pluribus etiam locis leguntur quatuor Evangelia, ad quatuor mundi partes cum suis ceremoniis contra fulgura, et tonitrua. Inde surgit dubietas multum periculosa ac si Deus non esset ubique praesens, et imploratus (...)"; ibid. the synod of Antwerp in 1610: VIII, 991: "Quoniam in processionibus, quas vocant Dedicationum, contingit multas insolentias plerumque committi, et quaedam inepta et lasciva immisceri, (quae tamen non esse toleranda decernimus) omnino prohibemus in illis Ven. Sacramentum circumferri"; for Spiers: see Browe (1933), 128.

[32]Salzburg: Schannat-Harzheim, V, 944; similar objections including: V, 486, synod of Passau in 1470; V, 646, synod of Schwerin in 1492 and VII, 170, synod of Augsburg in 1567; Konstanz (1609), VIII, 860; more reports of synods limiting the practice in: Franz (1909), II, 120-123; Scribner (1987), 42; Zika (1988), 35.

[33] Schilling (1887), 153: "underm Sequenz so hat der prüester herumb gekhört mit dem Sacramendt und auch gesungen, und die Schuoler nach Ihm, und den Segen geben mit Sacramendt"; 154: "Nach dem Ambt so hat sich der prüester aber herumbkhert mit dem Sacramendt und gesungen und die Schuoler nache, und hat den Seegen geben zue den Vier Orthen und das Sacramendt hinein Tragen".

Usually, however, it was the congregation and not the forces of nature that were blessed at the end of Mass and during the procession of the Blessed Sacrament. The earliest report of this devotional blessing with the Eucharist is found in the ritual of 1301 accompanying the feast of Corpus Christi in the abbey of St. Gotthard in Hildesheim. The priest on duty that week, the regulations read, walks at the front of the procession robed in a red chasuble and carrying the pyx, preceded by two acolytes. From the steps of the altar of repose he then blesses the people while the choir kneels humbly and sings an antiphon.[34] The placing of the Sacrament at the head of the procession shows the early developmental stage of this ceremony. Indeed, it was there that the major relics - and also the Sacrament in the beginning - were carried from the church or abbey, something that is not mentioned here. In another example, that of Warburg in 1331, the sacramental blessing during and after the procession, in which two violinists walked in order to "fiddle to the praise and honour of the Blessed Sacrament".[35] The focus of the procession is now no longer that arm or some other relic of a saint but the body of Christ, which overshadows every other type of blessing.

During the great theophoric field procession, already mentioned, after the feast of Corpus Christi in Essen the blessing was repeatedly given to all who knelt along the roads and stations. The close of the procession resembled a transformation of the ceremony involving Basil's arm on 1st january: just before the start of Mass the celebrant, standing before the altar facing the people, exposed the Sacrament once more while the monastery sang in praise of the Eucharist. This was followed by the trusty formula: *Benedictio Dei Patris*.[36] The rubrics of Mai"z of around 1400 paint the same picture, with an extra detail about the relics that accompanied the procession. Once back in the church the people in

---

[34]ed. Doebner (1980), I (ca.996-1346), n. 558, 306: "Item in circuitu sacerdos ebdomadarius indutus ornamentis sacerdotalibus cum rufa casula precedet processionem, pixidem cum hostia salutifera ducibus faculis cereis se praeeuntibus ferens reverenter. In stacione medii monasterii stabit supra gradus ante altare s. Crucis cum ipsa hostia sacratissima populum benedicens. Chorus cantabit antiphonam *O ammirabile precium* (...) ad terram humiliter se prosternens".

[35]Fürstenberg (1917), 321; 323: "videlen to love und to ere deme hilgen lichamen".

[36]ed. Arens (1908), 95: "Presbiter cum sacramento stabit ante summum altare versa facie ad populum. Conventus manebit apud sepulchrum fundatoris cantabitque antiphonam (105) unam "de Sacramento", presbiter collectam, sequente benedictione cum sacramento super populum. Clerici cantabunt missam "de Sacramento" sollempniter. Et nota, quod presbiter faciet frequenter in via cruces cum sacramento super homines de novo advenientes et genuflectentes sacramento. Et in singulis stationibus supradictis finito ewangelio, scilicet: "In principio" et in monasterio finitis collectis, in statione dicet sic, tres cruces super populum faciendo: *Benedictio Dei Patris et Filii et Spiritus sancti descendat super vos et maneat semper. Amen*"; see above n. 16-17.

the procession fell into two lines. The celebrant then stood opposite the choir of canons with, on the front row, "the gentlemen with the relics". The saints are once more no longer the centre of the procession. They have joined the praying congregation facing the Eucharist just as, in their shrines on the floor of the church, they joined the monks beseeching the consecrated Host when the *humiliatio* and the *clamor* were fused. Before the blessing a responsory sung with the choir, *Ego sum lux mundi* - I am the light of the world - was intoned by the priest holding the Eucharistic monstrance. After this exposition he made the sign of the cross with the Eucharist over the people, turned around and took the Eucharist back to the high altar, where it was left displayed during the Mass.[37] The blessing with the Eucharist, given once or even more often during the procession of the Blessed Sacrament, is rare in the 14th century but by the 15th had become common practice in present-day Germany, Austria and Switzerland.[38]

Just as the blessing had been given after Mass with the relics that had been standing on the altar, the *ciborium* or monstrance encouraged the same gesture during the 'Mass with exposition', in order - among other things - to mark the end of the procession. This blessing with the Sacrament was originally confined to the German empire. It occurred at the *Credo*, the Sequence and especially at the end of Mass. Again it would seem to have first appeared in Bavaria, since it occurs as a derivative of the Thursday expositions in Ingolstadt in 1429 which have already been referred to. The celebrant was also required to give the sacramental blessing once more, so the document says, when the Mass had finished.[39] This was performed in the same way at Neuffen in Würtemberg in 1446,[40] in Magdeburg in 1451,[41] in Hamelen in

---

[37]Bruder (1901) 505-506: "Beim Einziehen stellen sich im Innern des Domes die Jungfrauen und Schüler, die Vicare und die übrigen prozessionsmässig in zwei Reihen getheilt auf. Nachdem alles still und ruhig geworden ist, stellt der Priester, der das Sacrament trägt, vor den Chor der Stiftsherren; vor ihm stehen, mit dem Gesicht zu ihm gewandt, jene Herren, welche Reliquien tragen. Alsdann hebt der priester an zu singen: *Ego sum lux mundi* (...) Hirauf wird zusammen geläutet; der Priester macht das Kreuzzeichen mit dem Sacrament über das Volk, wendet sich um, schreitet durch den Chor zum Hochaltar, stelt das Sacrament darauf".

[38]Browe (1933), 182-183; 106, n. 98.

[39]See p. 285.

[40]Browe (1933), 144, n. 17; 183.

[41]See p. 266, n. 74.

1498[42] and in 1491 in the convent of the Poor Clares at Villingen in the diocese of Konstanz after the Mass and procession with the Sacrament and the relics.[43] At the end of the 15th century in Bamberg the solemn Mass was interrupted at the *Credo* while the relics, which had been carried in the procession, were grouped around the altar.[44] Around 1500 the sacramental blessing was generally practised in these regions before and after the Mass, which in most cases was extended to include a short ceremony of praise, during which the *Tantum ergo*[45] was sung and the blessing was given. This is described in detail in two documents from Hildesheim, dated 1493 and 1500.[46] This brief ceremony also occurred detached from the Mass during afternoon and evening services held in honour of the Sacrament. After the middle of the 16th century, in the Romance countries and England, the blessing with the Eucharist was to increase in frequency outside the context of the feast of Corpus Christi and the octave.

***

In the above we made a distinction between two public blessings: the weather blessing and the devotional blessing, both of which were originally given with the relics. The weather blessing with the relics was the Christian response to the heathen weather gods carried round in procession. A mirror image of the Roman origin of the *rogationes* is the ancient practice of carrying a statue of Freya, the Norse fertility goddess,

---

[42]Urkundenbuch-Hameln (1887-1903), 10 (1903), n. 643, 462: "Darvor schullen se synghen in der capellen sunte Jostes in tween choren solemniter *Te Deum laudamus* und dat versch *Salvum fac populum tuum domine* schal de deken edder we dat werde sacramente pro tempore dragende worde, drye repeteren unde gheven dem volke de benedictiones myt dem werden hilligen sacramente".

[43]ed. Glatz (1881), c. 32, 91-92: "Und als solches mit aller andacht vollendet war, nam sein wol erwirde also angelegt in heiliger priesterlicher geziert das allerheiligste, hochwirdigst sacrament in der silberen monstranz uss dem tabernacul und drug das selbig mit aller erwirdigkait uss den kirchen (...) Der ganz erwirdig convent güeng vor mit brinenten körzen, mit vill schenen hailthum und hohem, herlichem lobgesang (...) Nach vollender predig war das ampt loblich usgesungen. Alsdan füengen sie widerumb an gehn den creüzgang hinumb, bis sie mit aller ortnung widerumb kamen in den kor in unser kirchen. Da war der seegen geben mit dem heiligen, hochwirdigen sacrament und das herlich *Te deum laudamus* gesungen".

[44]Mitterwieser (1930), 16: "Alle Reliquien kommen zum Hochaltar (...) Vor dem Credo scheint es gibt man den Segen mit dem Allerheiligsten und vor dem Evangelium wird die Sequenz des Aquinaten *Lauda Syon* gesungen".

[45]*Tantum ergo sacramentum veneremur cernui* (Let us kneel and venerate that great sacrament).

[46]Browe (1933), 160; 184.

in procession and a similar 4th-century 'procession' for a blessing on the earth in Gaul, while in Saxon territory the statues of the idols were carried around until the forcible Christianisation by Charlemagne. In thunder and lightning, hail and storm the Christians saw the demons at work, and from the early Middle Ages they were combated by the raising of the relics into the air in a sign of the cross or carrying them through the fields while the bells tolled. The reading from the four Gospels had the function of driving disaster away from the crops just as the carrying of a Gospel text - and relics - in the *fylacterium* gave protection to the individual.[47]

The transposition of the weather blessing occurred before that of the devotional blessing. The question may be asked whether the exorcising blessing performed with the Sacrament is not of earlier date than the 13th-14th century in the legendary accounts. Franz assumes that it was already in existence in the early Middle Ages.[48] This would be in accord with the use of the paten, chalice and corporal in sickness and when fire broke out and with the burial of the Eucharistic bread in the ground to ensure a good crop or for superstitious ends. The latter category, condemned by Jacob of Edessa († 708), Peter Damian († 1071) and others as an abuse did, however, belong to the private sphere. It is not likely that it had a great deal of influence on a public weather blessing given by the priest, standing in front of the church building. The use of the Eucharist when fire broke out or for the sick - a use which was confined to the Eucharistic vessels and the corporal - came in from the 11th century onwards when the Sacrament began to be endowed with a miraculous power similar to that possessed by the relics, something which we deal with in the next chapter. In the 9th and 10th centuries a custom of this sort practised by the church outside the Mass and involving the Eucharist had not yet come into being. For this period only one text could be found, in which the Sacrament appears in the ceremony of exorcism directed against storm and hail.[49] And it still had a somewhat modest role in the ceremony. After the litany, some psalms including *Lauda Jerusalem*, the *Pater Noster* and the , "the chalice with the body and

---

[47]Franz (1909), II, 42, 69; Browe (1929a), 744-747.

[48]Franz (1909), II, 71-72.

[49]ed. Rozière (1859), II, 895, no. 628: "Primum celebretur letania, postea conveniens psalmodia, *Pater noster* et *Credo in Deum*. Calix cum corpore et sanguine Domini, crux sancta, evangelium, reliquie sanctorum cum reverentia deportentur, et aqua benedicta. Psalmus *Deus auribus nostris, Exurgat Deus, Notus in Iuda Deus, Qui regis Israel, Lauda Hierusalem*. His ita peractis, stola benedicta mox imposita, dicat (...)".

blood of the Lord, the holy cross, the book of the Gospels, the relics of the saints and the holy water were brought with reverence". To conclude the ceremony the priest pronounces the prayer formula after the consecrated stole "has been placed in position" - which will refer to the placing of it in the form of a cross on the text of the Canon. However there is no word of a blessing being given with the Eucharist, which is present along with the other consecrated objects. Therefore if the miraculous power of the Eucharist assumed by the parish clergy inspired them to substitute the Eucharistic weather blessing for the weather blessing with the cross and relics, we cannot state that this occurred any earlier than the 11th century. But this too would seem unlikely: the prayer formulas quoted by Franz say nothing of the matter; indeed, they call on the Lord God and the intercession of the saints rather than on their power to perform miracles; in addition the criticism of the weather blessing performed with the Sacrament, as far as we can assume, would have been expressed earlier than the 15th century. This blessing, performed during the *rogationes* or other field processions, is without doubt of a later date: the period in which the procession of the Blessed Sacrament became generalised - the 14th century.

The transposition of the devotional blessing occurred in the same period. The blessing - previously performed with the relics and now with the Eucharist - can be added to the many similarities between the relic procession and the Eucharist procession. It would seem justified to assume that the blessing given with the Sacrament came into being in imitation of the blessing with the relics, during the procession and at the end of Mass.[50] But the new blessing far outstripped that given with the relic of a saint. It was given with the "Word made flesh", "which we venerate kneeling",[51] the 'unique relic' adored at the 'elevatio', the visit, the exposition and the procession.

---

[50]Browe (1931a), 386: "Wohl in Nachahmung dieses Brauches hat man ihn am Fronleichnamsfeste während oder nach dem feierlichen Umgang mit dem Sanctissimum erteilt".

[51]The *Tantum ergo* is part of the *Pange lingua*, taken from the Office for the feast of Corpus Christi, and is ascribed to Thomas Aquinas: *Verbum caro, panem verum, Verbo carnem efficit* (The Word made flesh makes the bread into His flesh with a single word).

CHAPTER FIVE

SIMILARITY IN MIRACULOUS POWER

The Medieval miracles reflect the then current world of religious imagination. They penetrate the natural order in a supernatural manner, usually in a situation fraught with danger. In some Eucharistic miracles the Host seems to manifest itself more as a relic with its own particular *virtus*. It shines like the Star of Bethlehem, it escapes from someone's hands or it jumps out of fire. This chapter will deal with these *similar miraculous traits in the presentation of the phenomena*, which we have established as the third form of relationship. This occurred increasingly after the 11th and 12th centuries. The relationship between the relics and the Eucharist here is the most 'external' and the least 'close' when compared to the other two relationships we have established: the 'parallel applications in concrete use' and the 'transposition of forms of reverence'. For this reason the description given of it is somewhat limited.

The notion of 'parallel applications in concrete use' is linked to this third relationship to the extent that the similarity in miraculous powers has actually provided justification for so doing. Indeed, when the conviction arose that not only the relics but also the Eucharist was proof against fire did people begin as if automatically 'to use' It to combat fire. And when a relic or the Eucharist were employed in order to bring about a healing, the separate or joint application of both was inspired by the presumed medicinal powers of both. The emphasis in this 'parallel application' deviates from the other forms of use, dealt with in chapter III, in the weight it gives to the miraculous effect sought, that we were persuaded to place this use under the heading of the third form of relationship.

This form of 'parallel application' made its appearance when most of the other types of 'concrete use' had passed their zenith. Indeed, it could only take form in the period when the Eucharistic miracles were being at a premium. In early Christian times and in the early Middle Ages there were very few such, in contrast to the innumerable relic miracles, known from the beginning of the veneration of the bones of the martyrs. The authors who described Eucharistic miracles at that time simply took over the arsenal of the few existing miracle stories and added very little that was new. These were, moreover, generally 'liturgical' miracles, which concentrated mainly on the sacrificial mystery and only infrequently on the Eucharistic gifts as such. Such accounts were familiar only in the refectories of the monasteries where they were read aloud, but they never achieved great general popularity nor did were busy places of pilgrimage caused to come into being by the summoning up of bleeding Hosts. It was only after the late 11th century that they began to gain in importance, which increased in the course of the 12th century, to become 'countless' in the 13th when a veritable explosion of miracles occurred following the prescription that the Host be raised up during the Consecration.

The explanation for this must be mainly sought in the consequences of the second Eucharistic controversy surrounding Berengarius of Tours († 1088). Many opponents of his thesis had inexhaustible supplies of Eucharistic miracles, advanced in *vitae*, sermons, parables and even theological tracts as 'proof' of the *praesentia realis*. Durandus of Troarn († 1088)[1] told of the miracles of Paschasius Radbertus, and Guitmund of Aversa († 1095)[2] followed his example in order to disprove Berengarius' contention that these were merely 'fables'. In the 12th century such figures as Alger of Liège and Hugh of St. Victor[3] wove the Eucharistic miracles into their theological tracts. Herbert of Clairvaux († 1180) brought them closer in time by naming the witness and place of occurrence. In 1197 Giraldus Cambrensis included a number miracles in his *Gemma ecclesiastica*, though the number he quoted was amply beaten by Caesarius of Heisterbach († c. 1240) in his well known *Dialogus Miraculorum*, which includes more than fifty, and in his unfinished *Libri octo miraculorum*. He too followed Herbert's method for bringing the occurrences closer to the time of the reader. The same literature includes the *Bonum universale de apibus* by Thomas of Cantimpré († 1272),[4] although this work contains fewer examples concerning the Eucharist than that written by Caesarius. Miracles evoked miracles which concentrated on the 'independent' Host and wine. The understandable consequence was that the Eucharist began to be 'used' for magical and miraculous ends, once the many miracles had brought about general acceptance of the *virtus* of the Sacrament, which the relics had long been credited with.

---

[1]PL 149, 1418-21, *Liber de corpore et sanguine Christi*, with the subtitle given to it by Migne: *contra Berengarium et eius sectatores*, pars octava.

[2]PL 149, 1469-80, *De corporis et sanguinis Christi veritate in eucharistia*, lib. III.

[3]resp.: PL 180, 727-856, *De sacramentis corporis et sanguinis Dominici*; PL 176, 461-480, *De sacramentis christianae fidei*, pars octava.

[4]ed. Colvenerius (1597), 325 sqq.; ed. Stutvoet (1990), 172 sqq.

The miracles described were categorised by Browe.[5] They deal with subjects such as the presence of angels and doves during the Mass, the distribution of communion by these creatures or even by Christ Himself, the Host which turns into a red-hot coal or becomes ash when received unworthily, the Eucharist as the only means of nutrition or the changing of the bread and wine into the suffering Christ, the child Jesus or flesh and blood. This latter category created in an almost crudely realistic manner a picture of the physical *praesentia realis* and served to reward those of steadfast faith or to punish whoever failed to believe, doubted or communicated unworthily. The reward is usually found in *vitae*, the punishment in sermons, examples, chronicles and theological tracts.

Most of these miracles are not relevant in demonstrating the similarity in miraculous power between the Eucharist and the relics. The parallelism we infer does not, in fact, consist of the simple that miracles occurred because of the Eucharist as well as the relics but that in the miracles associated with the Eucharistic bread - and sometimes the consecrated wine - these two components started to 'behave' *like relics* and were *used* as such. This happened when, for instance, a relic and a Host were able to resist earthly decomposition, gave out light, were seen to withstand fire or showed healing powers. These categories listed by Browe can be used as a point of departure for comparison with relevant relic miracles, as also what are known as *blood miracles* - which we will deal with first. For there too there is a degree of parallelism to be found in the sense that we have defined it.

1   BLOOD MIRACLES

Many instances of the miracle of the 'bleeding Host' or the overflowing chalice are reported after 1150. To the extent that the theological opinion regarding the *praesentia realis* or real presence of Christ under each of the sacramental species - of which the average believer will have had little understanding - was demonstrated by a miracle of this kind, this shows no relationship to the miraculous power of bleeding relics. But we can underline the parallelism in the 'bleeding' of itself as a demonstration of the 'reality' of both Host and relic. In the one case this the 'reality' demonstrated is the true and human presence of Christ and in the other

---

[5]Browe (1938).

the presence of the saint thanks to God's mercy. In order to increase the closeness in time to contemporaries, in both cases the accounts speak of the still 'living' and 'fresh' blood. However it is also possible to point out a parallelism in another significance attached to these miracles: they both were quoted as punishments for sacrilege and unworthy use. After 1300 this even becomes the most frequently quoted significance of the Eucharistic blood miracles, which thus showed parallelisms in presentation and significance with the following relic miracles in illustration.

1.1   Bleeding relics

The action of Pope Leo I in cutting the *brandea* and thereby causing blood of the martyrs and apostles to appear was intended to convince the Empress Constantina of the reality and value of such secondary relics, something that Sigibert of Gembloers († 1112) took from a letter of Gregory the Great.[6] The genuine nature of the bones of Gervase and Protase was proved for Ambrose in the state of preservation and "great amount of blood".[7] Gregory of Tours provided the following additional detail concerning the translation of these two saints, a detail which again underlines the verification of the relics: during the Mass of dedication following the *inventio*, a plank fell from the church ceiling and struck the head of one of the martyrs lying there. Blood is reported to have flowed from the wound and it was collected on cloths and spread as a relic all over Italy and Gaul.[8] We have already mentioned a blood miracle reported as a punishment by Gregory of Tours: the drops of blood flowing from the finger of John the Baptist by way of solace in answer to the prayer offered by the three bishops, but perhaps also as a protest at their attempts to break off a particle from the finger.[9] It is recounted of Clovis († 511) that he insisted on gaining possession of a tooth of Regulus, bishop and patron of Senlis, because miracles were still

---

[6]See p. 13 .

[7]PL 16, 1019-1020, ep. 22 : "Invenimus (...) viros duos (...) ossa omnia integra, sanguinis plurimum" 1023: "sanguine tumulus madet ; PL 20, 663, sermo 17; "tenemus enim sanguinem qui testis est passionis"; Delehaye (1933), 76-77; see p. 105, n. 14.

[8]MGH SRM I,2, 69, *In gloria martyrum*, c. 46: "Aiebat enim quod cecidisse e camera tabulam unam, qui inlisa capitibus martyrum, rivum sanguinis elicuerit. De quo infecta lenteamina vel pallulae sive vela eclesiastica beatus cruor collectus est".

[9]See p. 22-23.

happening at the grave of this 3rd-century saint. Despite the resistance offered by the local bishop, Clovis got his way and had the grave opened. What then happened was a warning to Clovis: as the pliers did their work a rush of fresh blood appeared "as if from a living body". The tooth brought no good fortune and was eventually returned to the grave.[10]

This is not the only account of the bloody drawing of a tooth at an *elevatio*. In 641 St. Eligius had the body of the 4th-century martyr Quintinus exhumed. Apart from wishing to possess some iron nails and the martyr's hair, Eligius was also interested in two teeth, to be used in curing the sick. Quintinus demonstrated his lively presence: a few drops of blood flowed from the roots. Was this a sign of appreciation for a noble aim?[11] In a similar manner the relics of Amandus showed their miraculous powers at their *elevatio* in 809: a little blood flowed from his guns "against all nature".[12]

A real punishment for theft and ill-treatment of heavenly things was handed out by St. Patricia († 660) when, a century after her death, a pilgrim attempted to remove a tooth from her mouth, thinking that he would thus obtain constant protection from the devil. At night he forced his way into the church in Naples, lifted the lid of her tomb and carried out his plan. Then he stood still, as if nailed to the ground, as the blood flowing from the gum coloured his hand and the tomb purplish-red. The following day the nuns were able to gather two ampoules of it, as reported by the biographer.[13] The saints who revealed to Einhard in an apparition that their relics should be transferred from Michelstadt to Seligenstadt, gave persuasive force to their request by the blood which flowed from their bones.[14]

---

[10]AASS 30 mart. III, 825, *Vita s. Reguli episcopi*, c. IV,21: "Mox miro modo et prius inaudito miraculo dentem exanimi corporis, viventis more, unda recentis prosecuta est sanguinis quem mirabilis Deus ad laudem fidelis sui producere voluit".

[11]MGH SRM IV, 699, *Vitae Eligii*, II,6: "dentes etiam pro languentium medella ex maxilla sancta abstulit, atque in radice dentis gutta sanguinis exivit".

[12]MGH SRM V, 479, *Vita Amandi*, c.II,7: "Mirum dictu fidelem quaerens auditorem, quod contra naturam est! Mortui cadaveris de dentibus eductis stillae fluxerunt cruoris, huiusque monimenti usque in diem hodiernum testimonium acerra praebet eborea, adhuc eodem quo infusa fuerat sanguine, cum ibi servandi mitterentur, mirabile dictu cruentata"; AASS 6 febr. I, 892, *Historia elevationis*, n. 7 and 8.

[13]AASS 25 aug. II, 208, *De s. Patricia virgine*, c. IV,40: "Et ecce profluus e gingivis sanguis ac vividus, furacem manum, ac loculum purpurat".

[14]MGH SS XV,1, 243, *Einardi translatio et miracula ss. Marcellini et Petri*, lib. II, c. 10: "Cum ille hoc facturus caereum accenderet et circum pendentia pallea, quibus idem loculus tegebatur, sublevaret, animadvertit loculum mirum in modum umore sanguineo undique distillantem (...) sic loculus ille, qui sacratissima corpora continebat vero cruore madens et omni parte perfusus inventus est"; see p. 215, n. 54.

In an example given by Caesarius of Heisterbach the arm of John the Baptist plays a central role. Caesarius had seen it with his own eyes with a certain priest, Theoderik of Groningen. When one of the eminent men of the city fell ill, the cleric put his faith in the aid of John the Baptist and went to take the saint's arm to the man. But when he went to remove it from the reliquary both it and the cloth in which it was wrapped were seen to be drenched in fresh blood. The author heard of this manner of legitimising demonstrated by John the Baptist from Theoderik's own mouth. Another example deals with a female recluse who owned a tooth that had once belonged to Bartholomew. The apostle punishes the priest who forces the recluse to allow him to split the tooth in half. As soon as the cleric puts his knife to the relic there appeared "droplets of blood as if the saint were once more being obliged to suffer".[15]

A less modest bloodletting occurred when St. Luchesius († 1260), revered for his penitential practices and alms-giving during his life, lay dead on his bier. A certain person coming to pay respects to the mortal remains decided on devotional grounds to amputate the big toe of the dead saint's feet and "there suddenly came out of it a stream of great quantities of blood".[16] The next few examples mainly concern the honouring of the sanctity of the dead one. Miraculous blood is said to have flowed from the arms of Nicholas of Tolentino († 1305), blood which was subsequently preserved behind glass in a silver vessel.[17] Raymond of Capua reports a similar event in his *vita* of Agnes of Montepulciano († 1317), who entered the convent at the age of nine and was mother abbess by the age of fifteen.[18] The need for miracles sometimes seemed to call up the phenomenon automatically. Around 1340 the Bishop of Terviso, Pier Domenico de Baone, wrote a *vita* of the poor penitent, Henry of Treviso. He could still remember how, in his youth, the people

---

[15]ed. Strange (1851), II, 126, dist. VIII, c. 53: "tam brachium quam purpuram cui fuerat involutum, reperit recenti sanguine infectum"; ibid. 133, c. 60: "Mox enim ut sacerdos cultellum denti superposuit, ac si denuo sanctus pateretur, guttatim de illo sanguis erupit".

[16]AASS 28 apr. III, 596, *De b. Luchesio Tertiario*, Epitome vitae antiquioris, c. 6: "Quidam ad eius corpus inhumatum accederet, ob devotionem pollicem pedis amputavit, et continuo ex eo magna sanguinis vivissimi copia emanavit".

[17]AASS 10 sept. III, 678, *Gloria posthuma s. Nicolai Tolentinatis*, n. 84: "Quod attinet ad sanguinem, quem ex praesectis brachiis effluxisse diximus (...) mappam vero eodem sanguine tinctam, et repertum in eo manna alteri inclusa theca ex argento pariter ac crystallo confecta servari".

[18]AASS 20 apr. II, 814, *De s. Agnete de Monte-Politiano*, c. II,10: "Accidit autem ut cum aliquando arca praedicta aperiretur coram primoribus oppidi multisque aliis assistentibus ut sacrum corpus sudarit sanguinem"; see Loomis (1948), 213, n. 24, for more examples.

came from far and near to see and touch the dead man. The burial took place in a tense atmosphere which ended in collective hysteria, with miracles occurring and the people believing that they saw the body bleed. Many ampoules were filled with this blood.[19]

1.2 Bleeding Hosts

Parallel to this type of phenomenon, the Host demonstrated a similar miraculous power as a proof of the *praesentia realis* and also as a punishment for lack of belief, doubt and an unworthy attitude. But the blood now in question is no longer that of a saint but of Christ himself. And thus throughout the entire medieval period the tale known as the 1 Gregory legend was passed on and elaborated. This story tells how a piece of Eucharistic bread changed into a very small piece of bloody flesh to the shame of a female communicant receiving communion from Gregory and who was unbelieving the meaning of the words "This is my body". During the second Eucharistic controversy the same tale was told not of one woman but of a whole crowd who needed convincing. The miraculous bread was said to have been preserved in Andechs as one of the three Hosts kept as relics.[20]

As already remarked, miracles of this type - with a few exceptions - are not found in the early Middle Ages until the late 11th century, when Peter Damian († 1072) presented his miracles more with an eye on the reverence due to the Eucharist than on providing proofs of the *praesentia realis*. The following case is an example of the latter. Because of his doubts as to the real presence the bishop of Amalfi was punished at the breaking of the bread: the bleeding Host coloured his fingers red.[21] The unmasking of negligence is the subject of a happening that Emperor

---

[19]AASS 10 iun. II, 374, *Vita b. Henrici Baucensis*, n. 18: "Aliud maius mirabile apparuit manifeste, et omnes viderunt. Ipso sic manente, sanguis ex corpore ipsius coepit affluere: et in tanta copia perfluit, in vasis argenteis collectus, quod plures ampullae impletae fuerunt, et adhuc hodie in sacristia conservantur"; Vauchez (1981), 277.

[20]ed. Colgrave (1968), 106, c. 20: "Qua peracta oratione, sanctus vir invenit super altare quod posuit ut digituli auricularis particulam sanguilenti. Ad quod mirabile spectaculum vocavit incredulam, quo iam viso satis obstipuit. Cui sanctus vir ait: Nunc carnalibus considera oculis, quod prius obcecata celestibus minime potuisti conspicere et disce ei esse credula qui dixit, *Nisi manducaveritis carnem filii hominis et biberitis eius sanguinem non habebitis vitam in vobis*"; Paschasius: CC SL 16, 87-88, *De corp. et sang. Domini*, XIV.

[21]PL 145, 573, *Opusc.*, XXXIV: "sed super sacramento Dominici corporis incredulus haesitaret, in ipsa confractione salutaris hostiae, rubra prorsus ac perfecta caro inter eius manus apparuit, ita ut etiam digitos illius cruentaret, sicque sacerdoti omnem scrupulum dubietatis auferret".

Henry IV († 1106) is said to have experienced at Merseburg. He had attended Mass there, celebrated by Bishop Werner. When the liturgy had ended, the chalice was cleaned in a careless fashion and put away. However the king asked if he could see it again, as it was a fine piece of work. To everyone's horror it was seen to "contain fresh blood, as if it had just flowed out of Christ's side". The end of the story shows parallels with the blood of Gervase and Protase, caught on cloths with a view to being reverenced. The bishop wiped the chalice with a clean cloth and placed it in a reliquary cross where it could be paid the due reverence. The nonchalance previously displayed was a thing of the past.[22]

We have already seen how the miraculous blood that appeared in Meerssen in 1224 became an object of veneration.[23] The same thing happened a year later at St. Truiden. An example taken from Caesarius of Heisterbach lies behind it. The story goes that a woman had kept the Host in her mouth and taken it home in order to kiss her lover with it and thus tie him to her. However, she was unable to swallow the Host and thus wrapped it in a cloth and hid it in a crack in the church wall. Ten years later she confessed her sin. The Host was found completely preserved and "three drops of fresh blood" appeared on it. The relic was taken to St. Truiden and placed behind glass for veneration. This story related by Caesarius is not the only one in which a woman is reprimanded for having secretly taken the Host home for dishonourable ends. In another example she hides the Host in a chest. After some time, the cloth in which the Host is wrapped is again stained with blood, and she burns both Host and cloth for fear of being excommunicated.[24] These are no more

---

[22]MGH SS XXX,2 , 926-927, *Vita*, auctore Sigebotone, c. 34: "Quo interim perspecto, quia repositus erat illotus, ut dictum est, cruor ita recens in eo apparuit ac si hora eadem a latere Christi calici videretur infusus (...) episcopus, mox lintheo quodam candissimo sanguinem (...) in cruce, quae pro reliquiis sacris modicum quid Dominici sanguinis retinebat (...) Itaque iste ministrantium excessus maioris fidei patebat occasio et tam presentibus quam futuris diligentiam et sollicitudinem vigilantiorem in administratione celestium indixit sacramentorum".

[23]See p. 196.

[24]ed. Hilka (1937), 17, lib. I, c. 1: "Qui cum pannum exteriorem coram eisdem clericis explicasset, apparuerunt in eo tres gutte sanguinis recentis"; 18: "Unde et LX armati viri ad resistendum destinati sunt, per quos comitante populo ac clero ad ecclesiam sancti Trudonis delatum est et cum honore debito susceptum atque in vase cristallino repositum"; 19, c. 2: "Quam cum revoluto panno considerasset et totam sanguineam reperisset (...) ignem faciens modicum in loco mundo sacramentum cum panno super carbones vivos posuit (...) Sacerdos vero sacrum pulverem recipiens, sicut homo negligens negligenter satis iuxta altare posuit cum tamen magis ac salubrius debuisset in calice vino mixtum sumpsisse vel ad minus iuxta reliquias condidisse"; 19-20: "Tunc omnes premissa oratione cum multo timore ac reverentia ligaturam panniculi solverunt, et ecce ! iam non pulverem, sed hostiam Christi virtute reintegratam repererunt"; see further: 87-88, lib. II, c. 12; 88-90, c. 13; 94-95, c. 15; ed. Strange (1851), II, 179-180, dist. IX, c. 18-21; 183, c. 25; it should be noted that the Eucharistic miracles recounted by Caesarius deal far more frequently with receiving

than a few examples taken from the many related by Caesarius with reference to Eucharistic flesh and blood miracles - which, incidentally "ziemlich eintönig widerholt (...) in allen Berichte".[25]

Miracles designed to punish and similar to those recounted by Caesarius are reported from Florence in 1230, from Binderen near Helmond at the end of the 13th century, from Boxtel in 1380, around 1400 from Boxmeer and in 1429 from Alkmaar.[26] The Cistercian monastery in Zehdenick in the diocese of Brandenburg was said to be built on a place of pilgrimage where, in the 13th century, earth was found soaked in blood from a consecrated Host placed by a woman under a beer barrel to push up sales.[27] Until well into the 18th century in Herkenrode reverence was paid to a miraculous Host which was said to have bled to such an extent that it stuck to the linen and could no longer be given to the sick person as *viaticum*. The priest was thus paid back for having placed the Eucharist in a side room while he heard confession. From 1330 onwards, writes Browe, the Host showed this miraculous power almost exclusively in cases where it had been handled unworthily or had been used as a source of magical powers and not so much because of insult or physical damage.[28]

Here Browe is alluding to the desecration of the Host which, since the 13th century, the Jews were constantly accused of making - along with ritual murder and the poisoning of wells. All the accounts show stereotypical characteristics. The torture of Christ is brought up to date, just as that of Bartholomew was in the miracle recounted by Caesarius of Heisterbach. Practically always around Eastertide the Jews managed to obtain a Host, thanks to the mediation of a Christian serving girl, in order to carry out their foul practices. The woman in question was persuaded or forced to carry off a Host in her mouth and hand it over to the Jews, who then insulted, tortured and made holes in the Host so that it began to bleed. Thus there are at least thirty versions of what was said to have happened in Paris in 1290. The Host pierced by the Jews fell into three

---

communion worthily or unworthily than with the *praesentia realis*.

[25]Browe (1938), 113.

[26]Foppens (1721), 285-286 (Binderen); Browe (1938), 174; Lauwerijs (1952-1954) (Boxtel); Carosso-Kok (1981), 47-49 (Alkmaar); Dorenbosch (1986), 115-217 (Boxtel).

[27]Escher (1978), 120.

[28]Browe (1927), 183; *Herkenrode 800 jaar*, Hasselt, 1982.

pieces which continued to bleed.[29] It was said that in Röttingen the Host was thrown onto a dunghill, a sacrilege that was revealed by the great amount of blood that flowed out.[30] Other stories tell of the Host - like the relic - offering resistance to the dagger or knife and producing in identical fashion just a few drops of blood.[31] In Austria and Franconia, and in Schwabia - but especially in Bavaria - more than twenty places of pilgrimage grew up around bleeding Hosts.[32]

The placing in the *lunula* of a freshly consecrated Host in addition to the miraculous one or the carrying of both in procession emphasised the distinction made between the two by 'disciples' of Thomas Aquinas. The former was the Eucharistic bread under the form of which Christ's presence was real, while the latter was usually regarded as a relic. A 'miracle' Host of corporal of this type was also revered as if it were a true relic. The really slight difference in the then current ideas about the two can be seen in various examples given by Caesarius, in which Hosts of this type (or corporals or cloths) were placed "among the relics", a custom recommended by his contemporary, Alexander of Hales († 1245).[33] We have already mentioned this phenomenon in the account concerning the altar grave and during the exposition at Orvieto.[34] Parallel forms of reverence can be drawn with the blood of St. Stephen in Naples, Besançon, Metz and Cologne or with that of St. Maurice in the Swiss town of Agaunum, where this saint was said to have been tortured with his Theban legion at the end of the 3rd century.[35]

---

[29]MGH SS XXV, 578, *Iohannis de Thilrode Chronicon*, c. 25: "Tandem quidem ex ipsis magnum arripiens cultellum, hostiam percuscit, et in tres partes hostia se divisit, et continuo sanguis exivit".

[30]MGH SS XVII, 597; Browe (1938), 135.

[31]Browe (1938), 135; Oberman (1981), 129-134; 197-200: "Ein wunderbarlich geschichte, 1510".

[32]Rothkrug (1980), 64, n. 214: Iphofen (1294); Röttingen (1299); Munich (1315-1350) Ehingen (1320-1330); Deggendorf (1337); Pulkau (after 1338); Würzburg (1349); Lauingen (1404); Regensburg (1519); ibid. p. 84-87.

[33]ed. Strange (1851), II, 177, dist. IX, c. 14: "pulverem ponens *inter reliquias*; 183, c. 24: "sed purum sanguinem reperit. Quo allato (...) *inter reliquias* positus est; ed. Hilka (1937), 18, lib. I, c. 1: "Tertiam vero guttulam idem magister Iohannes prescidit *inter reliquias suas* illam honorifice recondens ad ostendendum populis, cum crucem predicaret"; Pijper (1907), 48; J.M. Schröckh, *Christliche Kirchengeschichte*, Leipzig, 1799, Theil XXVIII (1073-1303), 69, *Transubstantiation*: "sondern man muss es (das Fleisch Christi) in einem sehr reinen Gefässe als eine Reliquie aufbewahren (Lib. IV, Sententt. Quaest. LIII. Membr. IV. Artic. I, fol. CCXVIb)".

[34]See p. 196-197, n. 120-128 and p. 290; Browe (1938), 152; Matern (1962), 25.

[35]Beissel (1976), I, 138; II, 22; MGH SRM III, 20-41.

A 13th-century account relates how the miraculous power of the head of St. Cyriakus, with its container, kept near Rome, could be guaranteed to turn "blood-red" on the anniversary of the saint's death.[36] A current miracle is that accompanying the blood of St. Januarius, preserved in Naples, which is said to have liquified anew every year since 1389 on the saint's feast day and on his translation days.[37]

2   INCORRUPTIBILITY

A second aspect demonstrating the parallelism between the miraculous powers attributed to relic and Host is that of *incorruptibility*. Whenever a grave was opened and it was discovered that the body had not been reduced to dust or bones (*corpus incorruptum*), this was regarded as an unmistakeable sign of the sanctity of the one buried there and contributed to his *fama sanctitatis*: it meant that the body had been protected from putrefaction (Ps. 16:10) in expectation of the resurrection of the dead. Medieval man did not shrink from verifying the phenomenon nor from gazing at parts of a skeleton. Indeed, the people of that era were much more familiar with death than we are, and the realities of death were not masked from view nor were they left to doctor or undertaker to deal with. Even if only part of the body was still intact it was seen as a gesture of divine approval of the excellence and holiness of the saint,[38] who shared in Christ's victory over death and decay, consequences of the Fall of Adam. And thus the saint's body, a 'temple of God' (I Cor. 3:17; 6:19), had a share in the new heavenly - not earthly - nature. This basing of the veneration of relics in the Bible and dogma represents an effort on the part of such men as Thiofried of Echternach († 1110) to justify their value.[39] However when a Host was discovered in an incorrupted state after a lengthy period, this was also regarded as a miracle. Indeed, the Eucharistic bread was Christ himself, whose body was protected from decay between death and resurrection. The unearthing of an incorruptible

---

[36]AASS 8 aug. II, 336-337, *Insigne miraculum, quod Romae ad reliquias s. Cyriaci contigit*; see also Kötting (1950), 185-187: Euphemia († 307); 223, Demetrius († c. 306); 256, Cyprian († 258).

[37]Delehaye (1933), 300; PL 53, 861.

[38]Finucane (1977), 22-23. The 'natural' explanations offered by the author, such as balsam, mummification, the formation of adipocere and suchlike is not regarded as relevant in this context; as regards mummies found in Christian graves, Angenendt (1989, p. 12; 1991, p. 340-341) indicates the possible influence of the Egyptian culture.

[39]PL 157, 313-404, *Flores epitaphii sanctorum*; Guth (1970), 114-118.

body meant that it was that of a saint; an incorruptible Host could not but be consecrated.

2.1 Incorruptible relics

Reports of the finding of 'incorruptible' bodies are a matter of course in the hagiographies. When Nazarius was disinterred at the end of the 4th century, Ambrose's biographer Paulinus reported that the saint's hair and beard were still perfectly preserved: "not a hair of his head had been lost" (Lk. 21:18)[40] The same was said of the mortal remains of Bishop Severinus († 482), the mediator between Catholics and Arians in Noricum (present-day Austria) where the latter had the upper hand. When, in 488, Odoacer drove the Romans out of the region, monks took the remains of Severinus with them to Naples. At the *elevatio* the saint's hair was in as fine a state as when he had lived, whereas the body had been laid to rest without any use of preservatives, as emphatically stated by his disciple and biographer, Eugippus.[41] The same phenomena removed any doubt in the mind of Gregory of Tours that Bishop Valerius must have been "a friend of God".[42] Even more convincing 'proofs' were advanced in the *vita* of St. Eligius († 660): his hair and beard, shorn for burial, were reported to have grown again a year later.[43] At the *elevatio* of Amandus († 678) the saint's grey hair and pale, thin face gave the impression that he was merely asleep.[44] In 833 thanks was given to the Lord at the *elevatio* of the body of Bathildes for its state of preservation, and when

---

[40]See p. 182, n. 39.

[41]MGH AA I, 1-2, 29, *Vita S. Severini*, c. XLIV: "Ob quod miraculorum immensas gratias retulimus omnium conditori, quia cadaver sancti, in quo nulla aromata fuerant, nulla manus accesserat condientis, cum barba pariter capillis usque ad illud tempus permansisset illaesum"; CSEL IX, 2, 64.

[42]MGH SRM I.2, 352, *In gloria confessorum*, c. 83: "repperit venerabile corpus valde integrum, de quo non caesaries decidua, non barba fuerat diminuta, neque aliquid in cute corruptum aspiciebatur aut tetrum; sed erant omnia inlaesa (...) tantusque odor suavitatis flagrabat a tumulo, ut non dubitaretur, ibique quiescere Dei amicum"; *In gloria martyrum*, c. 16.

[43]MGH SRM IV, 728, c. 48: "Quodque ita erat solidum et inlibatum atque absque ullius membrorum diminutione incorruptum, ut vivere adhuc putaretur in tumulo; et (...) ita barba et capilli eius, qui tempore abitus sui iuxta morem fuerant abrasi, mirum in modum creverant in tumulo".

[44]AASS 6 febr. I, 892, *De elevatione*, c. I,5: "Et ecce obtulit se obtutibus illius vir cano capite reverendus, abstinentiae ac ieiuniorum macore, quibus comitibus vixerat, pallidus, sanctitate morum, meritorumque praecipuus, incorruptione quoque membrorum suave fragrantium quasi aromaticus, ac toto corpore incontaminatus, hoc solo quod in sepulchro iacebat dormienti simillimus"; MGH SRM V, 462, 478.

the shrine of Aldegonde was opened in 1151 it was noted that her head was still largely covered with scalp and hair, as stated in the report of the *translatio*.[45] A somewhat gruesome tale is told by Herbert of Clairvaux († c. 1180). A pious woman named Margaret was beaten by her cruel husband. He ended up by killing her and hanging her from a beam in the house to make the death look like suicide. The people cast her body aside like that of a dead dog next to the bodies of two robbers who had been hanged. Cures which were effected at the site two years after the event caused further investigations to be made. The corpses of the robbers gave of a horrific stench, while Margaret's body smelt sweet and was preserved "from head to toe".[46] When Francis died his face shone like that of an angel and "his members had taken on the softness and pliability of an innocent child's members" and they "were not rigid, but they could be turned this way and that, however one wished", according to the *vita prima* of Thomas of Celano († c. 1260).[47] In 1281, when the body of the Dominican, Bernard of Caux, was exhumed and found still intact, his confreres hurried to venerate him surrounded by the people. And - a final example - the body of St. Villana dei Botti († 1361) was laid out for veneration for thirty-seven days without showing the least sign of decay.[48]

2.2 Incorruptible Hosts

The earliest example of this miraculous power being assigned to a Host is to be found in the account of a miracle related by Raoul Glaber in mid-11th century. The story goes that someone in the region of Dijon lost a Host, which was only found again a year later at the roadside. It still looked so fresh and pure "as if it had been dropped there the same hour".[49] When the *sepulcrum* - which had served to contain particles of the Host - of a ruined altar was opened, it was usually the occasion for a

---

[45] See p. 278, n. 4 and 279, n. 7.

[46] PL 185, 1379-1381, *De miraculis*, lib. III, c. 34: "ita a planta pedis usque ad verticem incorruptum ac venustrem apparuit (...) ex eo suavitatis fragrantia exhalabat".

[47] ed. Habig (1973³), ch. IX,112, p. 326; ed. Grau (1955), 191.

[48] Vauchez (1981), 500, n. 3: Bernard Gui, *De fundatione et prioribus conventuum provinciarum Tolosanae et Provinciae ordinis praedicatorum*, ed. P. Amargier, Rome, 1961, 109-112; 283 n. 324: S. Orlandi, *La Beata Villana dei Botti, Terziaria domenicana fiorentina nel sec. XIV*, Florence, 1955, 39.

[49] ed. Prou (1886), 123: "Post annum vero evolutum repertum est iuxta viam publicam, ubi sub divo ceciderat, ita candidum atque incontaminatum ac si hora eadem cecidisset".

similar sort of miracle. We have already mentioned the case of Bishop Gaufridus of Sorra († 1178) on the island of Sardinia, when the words of the psalmist were thought appropriate: "neither wilt thou suffer thine Holy One to see corruption" (Ps. 16:10). The discovery made in Reggio after 300 years caused Salimbene († 1190) to state that consecrated Hosts could be kept longer than unconsecrated because of God's presence in the former, he who is the *conservator* of all.[50]

In legends and parables the Host also resists decay in order to expose the use of magic. There is a well known tale told by Herbert of an intact Host found in a beehive, having been placed there by the farmer to prevent disease and increase the honey yield. However the bees showed the reverence due to the Host.[51] The legend was embroidered on and expanded by others, including Caesarius of the same religious order. We have already alluded to the example quoted by the latter of a miraculous Host found and reverenced at St. Truiden.[52] The Host's miraculous resistance to the ravages of time led to the devotion - already mentioned - to the "sacred mystery" in the Catalonian town of San Juan de las Anbadesas from 1426 onwards. Other places of pilgrimage where 'incorruptible' Hosts were venerated included Andechs, Ferrara, Offida and Herkenrode.[53]

The incorruptible *oblatae* and *eulogia* which were unearthed constituted a sort of halfway house between relics thus found and consecrated Hosts. They did not turn to dust in the grave because in their capacity as consecrated 'Eucharistic contact relics' they were affected by the same miraculous powers, for that which is sacred has eternal value.

3   MIRACLES INVOLVING LIGHT

The symbolic power of light as the opposite side of the coin to the powers of darkness is something found in all ages and cultures. It would therefore be surprising if there were not many miracles related involving both the relics and the Eucharist with light. The visions of saints are accompanied by serene light. Saints are assumed to dwell in the vicinity of God's

---

[50]See p. 188-189, n. 90 and 91.

[51]PL 185, 1374-75, *De miraculis*, lib. III, c. 30 : "quod ita sanum et integrum, ita mundum et candidum, et ab omni corruptione penitus alienum inventum est".

[52]ed. Hilka (1937), 17, lib. I, c. 1: "vidi illam (hostiam) et apparuit incorrupta".

[53]See p. 193 and 290; Browe (1938), 150.

eternal light, both before and - especially - after their death. The halo placed above their head is a symbol of this and their relics emit light. In the *vitae* we find the saints' dwelling places and graves are illuminated with light, and it is very often difficult to state when precisely the authors pass from concrete reality into allegory, all the more so because the medieval writers frequently use tangible realities which, to us, are no more than an image of inner reality.[54] Until the 12th century the Eucharistic miracles were mainly signs of God's blessing on the offerings. The light surrounded the celebrant more than the Eucharistic offerings. However after that date the accent starts to shift to the Host itself, which lights up like a relic, "Trägerin wunderbaren Glanzes".[55] The light functions as proof of reverence at communion of blessed sisters or as a means of finding the Host after it has incidents of desecration or theft, events also exposed by light-emitting relics.

3.1 Miraculous light and relics

Remains of the incinerated martyrs of Sebaste († 320) thrown into the headwaters of the river are said to have shone with stars so that they were easily found - though Basil the Great in his sermon devoted to these blood witnesses does not allude to the legend.[56] Gregory of Tours turns to the traditional biblical vocabulary when he speaks of a "heavenly light" filling the basilica when the relics of St. Julianus were carried in (I kings 8:10; II Cor. 5:13).[57] The light surrounded the relics from 'without' as a sign of reverence, but the relics themselves could also emit light in order to indicate the place where they could be exhumed.

Many descriptions have already been given of the "sacred theft" of the relics, belonging to Benedict and his sister Scholastica, from Monte Cassino between 690 and 707. The place where they were discovered was revealed by a clear light, which enabled the deputation from Fleury to pip

---

[54]Loomis (1948), 143-144, n. 15 and 16 approximately 100 examples; 145, n. 18 approximately 75 examples; Vauchez (1981), 509.

[55]Browe (1938), 18.

[56]Günter (1906), 63.

[57]MGH SRM I,2, 128, *Liber de virtutibus S. Iuliani*, c. 34: "Referebat autem mihi vir fidelis, qui tunc eminus adstabat, cum nos basilicam sumus ingressi, vidisse se pharum inmensi luminis e caelo dilapsam super beatam basilicam discendisse"; see also 331, *In gloria confessorum*, c. 58.

their competitors from Le Mans at the post.[58] A supernatural intervention has also been known to 'throw light' on the murder of a saint. One example of this is that of the head and feet of the murdered Theodardus († c. 670), disciple of Remaclus and Bishop of Tongeren-Maastricht, which were illuminated with light.[59] When the bodies of the two Irish martyrs known as the 'Two Hewalds', murdered in Westphalia in 695, were thrown into the headwaters of the Rhine and floated "against the current", a brilliant light shone throughout the night to indicate where they could be found.[60] In the *vita* of St. Romuald († 1027), a man who had become a hermit in order to make recompense for a duel that ended fatally, the murder of two monks is related. The robbers who killed them attempted to get rid of the bodies, but a "flood of light" and angelic song recalling Christmas night prevented them from doing so.[61]

The burial of saints was also accorded extra gloss. During the funeral of St. William, bishop of Bituric († 1031) a fireball is said to have been visible from near and far.[62] The posthumous honours accorded to St. Arnulf († 1087) consisted of a twinkling planet, visible in the heavens from the first to the sixth hour. It remained suspended above the saint's body, turning into an all-illuminating cross, the four arms of which shone against the sky in a golden glow.[63] A similar type of honour was said to have been accorded at the grave of the writer and visionary, Hildegard of Bingen († 1179), who had served as advisor to pope and bishop alike.

---

[58]AASS 17 oct. VIII, 158, *Vita s. Berarii*, auctore anonymo, c. 6 and 7: "Tunc senex ait: (...) cumque aliquem locum huius solitudinis clarissimo lumine radiare conspexeritis ad similitudinem lucidissimi montis, locum diligenter notate (...) de domo egrediuntur (...) concpiciunt quemdam locum, lumine claro, veluti diversis facibus et innumeris luminibus, illustratam, praefulgide micantem" ; DACL V,2, 1720-24; Geary (1978), 146-147: PL 95, 621-622, Pauli Diaconi *De gestis Longobardorum*, lib. VI, c. 2.

[59]AASS 10 sept. III, 591, *Acta inedita*, c. II. n. 13: "luminaria bina flammarum globos scintillantia intueri, quae altrinsecus sita sancti Martyris caput pedesque perlustrabant".

[60]ed. Colgrave (1979), *Hist. Eccl*, V, 482, c. 10: *Passio*, n. 5: "Sed et radius lucis permaximus, atque ad caelum usque altus omni nocte supra locum fulgebat illum, ubicumque ea pervenisse contingeret, et hoc etiam paganis, qui eos occiderant, intuentibus. Sed unus ex iis (...) indicans, quod eo loci corpora eorum posset invenire, ubi lucem de caelo terris radiasse conspiceret"; AASS 3 oct. II, 206, n. 5.

[61]AASS 7 febr. II, 114, *Vita s. Romualdi abbatis*, c. IX,50: "Ubi vero sanctorum iacebant corpora, copiosum lumen usque in diem splendescere, et dulcissimae Angelicae cantilenae non desiit suavitas resonare".

[62]AASS 10 ian. I, 635, *Vita s. Guilielmi archiepiscopi Bituric*, c. X,36: "quasi globus igneus in aere suspensus, supra sancti Protomartyris Stephani ecclesiam instar stellae coruscantis apparuit: quem non solum illi qui aderant, sed etiam nonnulli aliunde ad nostram urbem properantes".

[63]AASS 15 aug. III, 258, *Gloria posthuma s. Arnulfi confessoris*, n. 135: "visa est in caelo sphaera ardens, quasi flamma ignis, quae incumbebat super sanctum corpus beati Viri (...) signum sanctae Crucis, quae crux suo splendore vincebat omnem solis decorem (...) per quattuor cornua ultra tendens et nimio fulgore velut aurum rutilans".

Two arches of light intersected at their highest points, where a small cross appeared that expanded to take on enormous proportions in the midst of rotating circles of multi-coloured light.[64]

Separate relics are also sometimes reported to have radiated light. The *capsa* containing a relic of St. James of Compostella is said to have driven away the darkness at night and prevented the monks from sleeping.[65] The head of Guido of Cortona († 1245) was found in a well out of which "light like that of the sun" was shining. It had been placed there by the verger who wished to find a place of safety during enemy action in the saint's birthplace, near which he had lived as a poverty-stricken hermit.[66] A miraculous healing took place in the church where the relics of Thomas of Cantiloupe († 1282) were kept, and the event was once again bathed with brilliant light.[67] The people of the town of Trier venerated St. Werner, a fourteen-year-old Christian boy, whose death was blamed on the Jews. In the story that was put together 150 years later, the boy's murderers were said to have thrown the body into a crypt overgrown with thorn bushes, but the town watch saw a bright light shining there are night to point out the fateful site.[68] Finally, in a legend concerning a relic of the True Cross there is no lack of miracles. A Flemish pilgrim returning from the Holy Land in 1440 with such a relic is attacked by robbers. He quickly makes a deep cut in his leg and hides the costly treasure there. The wound heals immediately, but once the man is home again a bleeding cross appears above the wound, surrounded by a bright glow.[69]

---

[64]AASS 17 sept. V, 696, *Vita s. Hildegardis virginis*, n. 58: "In hac luce crux rutilans visa est, primum parva, sed crescendo postea immensa, circa quam innumerabiles varii coloris circuli".

[65]AASS 15 iul. VI, *Alia miracula s. Jacobi Majoris*, c. I, n. 255: "quid domum perlustratis tota nocte? Lumina vestra extinguite, et longo itinere fatigati quiescite atque dormite, nosque dormire cupientes dormire permitte. Ipsi vero nullum lumen habentes nec cur eis hoc dicebatur intelligentes, afferebant, se lumen ignis minime habuisse, suasque lampades iam dum exstinxisse quod enim capsam, id est reliquias beati Jacobi veraciter dicitur fuisse".

[66]AASS 12 iun. II, 606, *Miracula b. Guidonis Cortonen.*, n. 16: "Aperto itaque puteo tantum ex eo lumen processit, ac si alius ibi sol fuisset".

[67]Vauchez (1981), 511, n. 39.

[68]AASS 19 apr. II, 701, *De s. Werhero puero mart.* n. 9: "Nam cunctis circum vigilibus castrorum, claritas luminum illuxit tempore noctium; quod illi non absque admirationis stupore declaraverunt. Inde corpus mox repertum".

[69]Boussel (1971), 237.

3.2   *Miraculous light and Hosts*

There are a few sparse legends dating from Christian antiquity - and
already referred to - in which the Eucharist is said to have emitted light:
the aggressive flames that kept Eudoxia's Eucharistic bread out of the
hands of pagans and the two examples given by Cyprian († 258) and John
Moschus († 619). In Cyprianus' account the fire coming from the *arca*
made a woman aware of her sin; the flash of light which Moschus reports
as having prevented further desecration by a heretic by taking up the Host
from the mud. All three examples are in the context of abuse of the
practice of communion in the home.[70]

When the Host increasingly became an object of veneration through
the process whereby it gained independence and was drawn into the
miraculous atmosphere surrounding the relics, the way was smoothed for
it to function as an illuminating relic 'bringing to light' examples of
sinfulness and crime, pinpointing its own location or honouring a pious
communicant. Peter Damian († 1072) talks about sparks shooting out of
the Host and striking a celebrant in the chest at the breaking of the bread
because the victim was addicted to usury.[71] In a legend retailed by John
of Trittenheim the son of a converted Jew was struck down. According to
the tale, in 1153 the young man attempted, with evil intent, to take a Host
from a church in Cologne. When he grew afraid of what he had done, he
buried the Host in a cemetery, but his deed did not go unnoticed since the
priest who had been distributing communion had grown suspicious and
followed him. When the priest tried to recover the Host it turned out to
have changed into a child, which escaped from his grasp and rose to
heaven in brilliant light.[72]

The 'arca legend' turns up again in accounts given by such people
as Giraldus Cambrensis and Herbert of Clairvaux. Their story tells of
how, in 1176, a woman took the Eucharist away with her as if to give it
to a sick person at home. She wrapped it in a head scarf and placed it in
an *arca*, which was surrounded by a "blaze" of light that filled the entire

---

[70]See p. 33, 76 and 79.

[71]PL 145, *Op. varia*, XL, c. 6: "Hic aliquando dum missarum celebraret officium, inter
ipsam Dominici corporis fractionem, tres repente favillae ignis ex ipso coelesti sacramento
prodeuntes emicuerunt, et in pectus sacrificantis terribiliter impegerunt".

[72]Johannes Trithemius, *Opera historica*, II, 136, Monast. Hirsaugiensis, a. 1153:
"cumque manibus reverenter elevans (...) luce coelitus emissa (...) in ipsa luce ascendens
coelos penetravit".

house.[73] The Host-light reported in the legend of a pious Andalusian herdsman had the same function of signal. The event, which happened in 1183, concerned the secretion by the herdsman of the Host in his crook in order to protect his sheep from wolves. But the crook began to glow and light was seen over his hut every evening.[74]

After having been received, the Host retained its miraculous power as a guide in the visions of the saints. Hildegard of Bingen, "who was listened to and respected as a sibyl", was said to have been able to tell by looking whether communicants were in the appropriate state. She assessed this on the basis of the amount of Eucharistic light present,[75] and St. Mary of Oignies († 1213) was able to do the same in the case of priests receiving communion.[76] Caesarius of Heisterbach wrote that the Brabant Beguines also had this gift. Very few were found worthy of communion according to the criterion thus set. 'Unworthiness' is, it should be said, not the least of grounds quoted for the infrequent sacramental reception of communion.[77] In the *vitae* it is told how the saints themselves were blessed by the light. Gertrude of Helfta († 1302) saw "her soul shining like a crystal with a snow-white light".[78] In the 13th century Dominican sisters in southern Germany are reported to have seen the lower arm of the celebrant illuminated by the glowing Host, and in Töss near Winterthur Elli of Elgau is said to have seen a Eucharistic glow as from crystal shining out from her sisters.[79]

---

[73]ed. Brewer (1861-64), 40, *Gemma eccles.* I, c. 11: " matrona quaedam hostiam consecratam quasi infirmo deferendam sibi per sacerdotis incuriam incaute traditam, in capite pepli cuiusdam serici nodatam in cista reposuit (...) nocte quadam mulier evigilans vidit cistam eandem lumine magno circumfusam"; PL 185, 1370, *De miraculis*, lib 3, c. 20: "unus ex puerilis eius vidit immensa luminaria circa eamdem arcam divinitus accensa, quae totam domum ingenti claritate perlustrabant".

[74]Corblet (1885-86), I, 470-471; Browe (1938), 176, n. 27.

[75]CC SL 43, 231, *Hildegardis Scivias*, pars secunda, visio sexta: "alii in corpore lucidi et in anima ignei erant, alii autem in corpore pallidi et in anima tenebrosi videbantur"; Ward (1992), XXIII, *Saints and Sybils: Hildegard of Bingen to Teresia of Avilla*, 107.

[76]AASS 23 iun. IV, 655, *Vita b. Mariae Oigniacensis*, c. VII, n. 71: "Quando vero post confessionem, hostiam sacerdos reciperet, ipsa videbat in spiritu Dominum in anima sacerdotis remanere, et eum mirabili claritate illustrantem, vel, si indigne sumeret, videbat quod, Domino cum indignatione recedente, anima miseri vacua et tenebrosa remaneret".

[77]ed. Hilka (1937), 22, lib. I, c. 4: "cepit corpus eius lucidari et sacre vestes, quibus indutus erat, miro candore decorari"; 23: "beata illa vidit corpus sacerdotis tam clarum et tam perspicuum, ut quasi in phialam cristallinam corpus Christi demitti videretur"; ed. Griesser, Exordium magnum (1961), 228-231, dist. IV, c. 4.

[78]ed. Molenaar (1951-52), I, 333, book III, ch. 37.

[79]ed. Vetter (1906), 83, c. 27: "Sy sach och ainest ab aler engel tag, do der cofent unsern heren enpfieng, das ieckliche schwester, so sy von dem altar gieng, als durchluchtet was als ain kristall. Ir hailig leben zaiget folleklich das die götlich min in irem hertzen bran"; Browe (1938), 19, 20.

The Host indicates faultlessly its own location when it has been hidden, desecrated or thrown away after a robbery. In the accounts we have already examined, attempts said to have been made by Jews to make the Host disappear completely once they had subjected it to torture were frustrated by such phenomena as light shining out from the Eucharistic bread. A few examples are given here, taken from Bauerreis, which show the link between local legend and the "Host-church" in the German language region. In 1243 at Belitz Jews are said to have been frightened to such an extent that they gave the Host to a girl, asking her to accept money and kind words if she would hide it somewhere in an attic. The attempt was in vain: lights and candles betrayed the hiding place in an unmistakeable fashion. At Iphofen in 1294 they threw the Host into a privy. And just as in Werner of Trier's account, it was the night watchmen whose attention was drawn to the hiding place by the light emitted by the Host. The Host shone in the darkness like a ray of sunshine above the well in which the head of Guido of Cortona was found. The account of events in Lauda in 1300 is no less subtle: there the Eucharistic bread was placed under stone on a dung heap, making its presence known subsequently by a bright light.

Robbery is the subject of the legend surrounding the Host-churches in Erfurt in 1248, Zlabing in 1280 and Rulle in 1347. At Erfurt the thieves threw the silver box containing the Host into a fish pond, which subsequently never froze over, while a local deacon had long seen signals of light coming from the pond. In Zlabing the thieves had had their eye on a monstrance, which they hid under a pile of stones overgrown by bushes. A fierce fire broke out spontaneously at the site and revealed their plans. The grazing cattle fell to their knees as if in front of the crib holding the infant Jesus. At Rulle near Osnabrück we see once again Moschus' ear of corn motif: the ivory container with the Host was supported by three ears of corn and surrounded by three lights.[80]

4   RESISTANCE TO FIRE

The parallels can again be seen in the ability of both relics and Eucharist to *withstand fire*. In the Old Testament the purity of heart of the three men consigned to the oven by Nebuchadnezzar prevented the scorching

---

[80]Bauerreis (1931), 33, n. 26; 45, n. 51; 46, n. 54; 52, n. 76; 54, n. 81; 61, n. 98; 63, n. 107; 77, n. 139; see also Corblet (1885-86), 479; Browe (1938), 57, n. 90; 134.

flames from harming them (Dan. 3:19-97). The truth was also regarded as being able to withstand the flames in the trial by ordeal. Relics were therefore subjected to the fire test to see whether they were genuine. The basis for this practice was that the flames would be unable to harm a real relic. The power of the saint would guarantee resistance to the flames.

In the case of the Eucharist there is a tale which vividly calls to mind the story in the book of Daniel. It concerns St. Dominic, said to have thrown a Host into a glowing oven in the presence of some Albigenses. It was left there for three days without showing any signs of being consumed. In this way Dominic hoped to convince the heretics of the unmistakeable presence of Christ in the Eucharist, something they denied.[81]

Rudolf of Schlettstadt provides an example of a test by fire to see whether or not a Host was consecrated. No matter how far-fetched or unreliable the stories told by this Dominican prior might be, the historical reality of a test of this nature cannot necessarily be excluded. The background to it, in fact, agrees with that underlying the trial by fire for relics: the belief in the power to resist the flames - not, in this case, of the saint in question, but that of the body of Christ Himself. The pious dread with which the Eucharist was approached because of the *praesentia realis* will, however, mean that an act of this nature would have been very exceptional. Usually the fireproof nature of a consecrated Host was not tested deliberately but demonstrated by accident. The characteristic appears in documents written after the 12th century and giving accounts of fire in churches and monasteries in the course of which the consecrated Host was subjected to fire, which proved unable to consume the Eucharistic bread.[82]

4.1 Fireproof relics

An early example of the belief in the ability of relics to resist fire is the requirement made by the 2nd Council of Saragossa that relics originating in Arian churches should be subjected to the fire test.[83] A pilgrim named

---

[81]Thiers (1679), II, 337-338; (1677), 800.

[82]ed. Kleinschmidt (1974), 47 sqq. *Historiae memorabiles* (bis ca. 1303), c. 5; fires in churches and monasteries: see Browe (1938), 72-77.

[83]Mansi X, 472, can. 2: "ut reliquiae in quibuscumque locis de ariana haeresi fuerint, prolatae a sacerdotibus in quorum ecclesiis reperiuntur, pontificibus praesentatae igne probentur"; Browe (1938), 75.

Arculf, reporting from Jerusalem, is said by Bede to have stated some
time around 670 that people there no longer had any doubt about the
genuine nature of the cloth with which Veronica is supposed to have
wiped the face of Jesus since it had been shown that fire could not harm
it.[84] From the 9th to the 12th century the 'test' was frequently applied.
After the *inventio* of the skeleton of St. Celsus in 979 a finger joint was
placed on the coals in a censer and withstood the ordeal.[85] A piece of the
cloth used during the washing of the feet at the Last Supper was tested at
Monte Cassino in 1012: thrown into the censer with the glowing charcoal
it at first glowed and melded with the coals, but when later cooled down
it assumed its original shape.[86] In 1031 Bishop Meinwerk of Paderborn
took the same precautions by laying the relic of St. Felix on three
separate bonfires in full view of the people and the monks before placing
it on the high altar.[87] Around 1080 Abbot Walter of Evesham followed a
suggestion made by Lanfranc and tested all the dubious relics of the
church. The fire left not a mark on the relics of the former abbot
Credanus and the martyr Wistanus. And things did not stop at a single
miracle: light and 'blood' added their contributions. When the urn
containing the head of Wistanus slipped from the abbot's hands a large
"puddle" formed on the floor, according to the chronicler. The relics of
Credanus provided their own witness:they shone like the purest gold.[88]
Towards the end of the same century the arm of the martyr Arnulf is said

---

[84]PL 88, 786, *Adamni de locis sanctis*, lib. I, c. 10: "Et haec dicens, sacrum Domini sudarium proiecit in flammas, quod nullo modo ignis tangere potuit, sed integrum et incolume de rogo surgens, quasi avis expansis alis coepit in sublime volare"; see also: PL 94, 1183, c. 4.

[85]AASS 23 febr. III, 400, *Inventio*, n. 22: "accepto in oculis totius cleri panniculo tenuissimi fili, et involuit illi articulum de compage digiti sacrati, et iniecit prunis thuribuli vivis, quibus thymiamata incendebantur, et totum illud horae spatium, per quod canonem mysticum ex integro peregit, illaesum atque ab igne intactum permansit".

[86]MGH SS VII, 649, *Chronica monasterii Casinensis*, lib. II, c. 53: "protinus praedictam particulam in accensi turibuli igne desuper posuerunt: quae mox quidem in ignis colorem conversa, post paululum vero amotis carbonibus ad pristinam speciem mirabiliter est reversa".

[87]MGH SS XI, 156, *Vita Meinwerci*: "rogum maximum in medio claustri sub divo fieri praecepit, in quem cum tercio corpus misisset, totiensque in favillam redactus ignis extinctus fuisset, cum maxima omnium exultatione et laudum iubilatione corpus manibus propriis excipiens super principale altare detulit".

[88]ed. Macray (1863), 323-324: "Superadditur autem miraculum miraculo, quod quum praenominetus abbas testam capitis sancti Wistani deportaret, casu de manibus eius subito in terram cecidit, tantumque rivum sudoris emisit quantum aliquis virorum quolibet accidente de se emittere posset (...) Postmodum (...) invenerunt reliquias eius in medio duarum personarum positas velut aurum purissimum coram oculis cunctorum resplendentes. Quo signo perterriti omnes cum maxima devotione et reverentia honorifico feretro eas collocantes signaque pulsantes (...) in ecclesiam transtulerunt".

to have jumped unharmed out of the flames,[89] and the cloth in which the body of Stephen of Muret had been wrapped disregarded the fire, even when thrown into it several times. A piece of wood, said to have come from his table, is also reported top have withstood the heat.[90] The rubrics and prayers used during the tests were borrowed from the ritual of the trial by ordeal and contained a prayer for God to use the test as a means of indicating whether the relic in question was "true or false".[91]

In view of the power attributed to relics in this way, at the same time miraculous tales were doing the rounds, tales of relics being spared from the flames when a church or monastery set on fire. In Burgundy the flames failed to affect the ampulla containing St. Martin's oil when the church and monastery at St. Roman de Joux went up in flames.[92] A burning candle that fell over during the night at the grave of Hilary of Poitiers threatened the whole fabric of the building, but the saint intervened and made flammable materials fire-resistant: linen taking on the properties of marble and wax those of water.[93] A relic of the Virgin Mary, thrown into fire by thieves out of disappointment that the *capsa* contained no gold was, according to an account given by Gregory of Tours, unharmed.[94] Among the *miracula* of the emperor Henry II († 1024) we read of a verger who found his carefully stored relic

---

[89]PL 156, 959, *Guiberti, abb. s. Mariae de Novig, de vita sua*, lib. III, c. 20: "Brachium beati (...) ad probationem ignibus est iniectum, sed exinde saltu subito est ereptum"; more examples in Browe (1938), 75-77; Hermann-Mascard (1975), 134-136.

[90]CC SL VIII, Continuatio Mediaevalis, 130, *Vita Stephani*, c. 43: "Pannus etiam quo sacrae ossium eius reliquiae involutae fuerant, a sacerdote qui decentiori panno eas involuerat semel et iterum atque iterum proiectus in ignem comburi non potuit"; 133, c. 45: "lignum autem pannumque lineum et pellem candidam quibus illud erat involutum divina potestas penitus ab igne protexit".

[91]Martène (1788), III, 496: "concede nobis (...) ut pannus iste, vel filum istud, quibus involuta sunt ista corpora sanctorum, si vera non sint, crementur ab hoc igne; et si vera sint, evadere valeant"; Browe (1938), 76; Delehaye (1927), 205; Franz(1909), II, 348, n. 5.

[92]MGH SRM III, 162, *Vita s. Eugendi*, c. 18: "Sic igitur et Condatescense monasterium exustum quondam est flammis, sed tamen Martini oleum nullo flammarum est voratus incendio".

[93]MGH AA IV, 11, *Liber de virtutibus s. Hilarii*, c. XII,34: "Item cum iuxta consuetudinem quadam nocte cereus inluminatus fuisset, casu super sepulchrum eius, qui intercessione sua vivificat ardens corruit (...) in virtute confessoris quas didicit cera flammas extinxit, et converso ordine illud a quo vorari potuit praefocavit. Diversae species suam visae naturam mutasse: ne quid hic incendia laederent, pallium pro marmore, cera fuit pro flumine".

[94]MGH SRM I,2, 49-50, *In gloria martyrum*, 18: "Sed cum nihil in eam pecuniae repperissent, extracta pignora in ignem proiciunt, caesoque homine, discesserunt. At ille semivivius exsurgens, ut vel cineres exustorum collegeret pignorum, invenit super carbones accensos inlaesas iacere reliquias"; this is not, therefore - as suggested by Hermann-Mascard, a 'procedure' designed 'to verify' the genuineness of the relics of the Virgin Mary, (1979, 134); see also 215, *Vitae patrum*, lib. I, c. 3.

smouldering, without showing any signs of damage.[95] The hair
belonging to Hildegard of Bingen, to whom we alluded above, which
were kept in a silken *pyxidula* on the altar, escaped the flames.[96] Even
more wondrous are the claims regarding the resistance to fire shown by
the mortal remains of Catherine of Siena. When, during a fire, it was
feared that nothing of her relics would remain, neither her body nor her
clothing suffered any damage, while the saint "according to an accurate
calculation must have been in the flames for several hours". There was
not the slightest sign of any ash nor was there even a smell of fire.[97]

4.2   Fireproof Hosts

A miracle that tells us of the Host's resistance to fire is said to have
occurred in Pommeren, where the wooden chapel of St. Adalbertus in
Wollin went up in smoke in 1125 while the *ciborium* survived.[98] The
story told by Rupert of Deutz concerning the fire that broke out in 1128
and the pyx and corporal that were unharmed has already been discussed
several times in other contexts. The corporal escaped the inferno even
when separated from the Host. In the monastery of St. Vincent in Laon in
1148 a fierce fire broke out during Compline and two monks were killed.
But the large palla or corporal on the high altar was spared.[99] Herbert of
Clairvaux tells us of an occurrence in Toul. In the church of St. Martin a
somewhat carelessly placed candle was set up to replace the sanctuary
lamp during the Easter Vigil because of a lack of lamp oil. The altar
cloths caught fire and were totally consumed. The body of the Lord and

---

[95]AASS 14 iul. II, 768, *Miracula s. Henrici imperatoris*, n. 23: "invenitque ostiolum a
flamma tangi et fumum dare, sed non laedi. Cuius haec meritis, nisi eius, cuius illic
reliquiae servabantur".

[96]ed. Bruder (1883), 123: "Wilhelmus (...) cui cum crines beatae Hildegardis dati pro
reliquiis essent, et in pyxidula serica recondisset (...) ecclesia et iis quae erant altari, exustis,
pyxidula serica permansit illaesa".

[97]AASS 30 apr. III, 885 n. *Vita s. Catharinae Senensis*, n. 127: "Heu! Catharina est tota
combusta. Accedensque velociter proprius et ipsam de igne trahens, invenit et corpus et
indumenta in nullo penitus laesa fuisse ab igne, imo nec vestigium nec odorem ignis
apparere in eis. Et quod plus est, nec cineres applicati vestibus apparebant, dum tamen
diligenti computatione facta postea, pluribus horis in igne fuisse credatur"; see further: 4
sept. II, 425, *De s. Rosa virgine*, a. 1357: "venerabile corpus praefatum, quod intactum
illaesumque a praedicto igne fuit miraculose conservatum"; Loomis (1948), 149, n. 67.

[98]Browe (1938), 72: Phil. Jaffé, *Bibliotheca rerum germanicarum*, Berolini, 1865-73, V,
660.

[99]MGH SS VI, 390, *Sigeberti chronicon contin. Gemblacensis*: "Accidit autem ibi
quiddam mirabile, quia maior palla, quae desuper totum altare ambiebat, aliis pallis
ardentibus, ardere non potuit".

the corporal were untouched.[100] Browe also mentions Wales, Liège and St-Florent-le-Viel near Saumur as places where a similar miraculous power was demonstrated.[101]

The 13th and 14th centuries are not without reports of the Eucharist's ability to withstand fire. In the Rhineland a church was burnt to the ground. When the sad results of the fire were inspected, a pyx containing the Eucharist was found standing unharmed, "a manifestation to man, beast and all creation of the *virtus* belonging to this divine sacrament", as Caesarius puts it.[102] In the diocese of Brandenburg provost Henry gave permission for a chapel to be built at Nauen in honour of the *corpus Domini* which, "men say, was re-discovered in a miraculous fashion" after the parish church had burnt down.[103] The village of Wilsnack in the same diocese gained fame when three Hosts were recovered from the ashes, each of the three bearing a mark in the centre that closely resembled a drop of blood. Wilsnack became the most visited Eucharistic pilgrimage place. A dozen or so other places were known for similar miracles, including Amersfoort in 1340, Stiphout in 1342 and Dordrecht in 1457.[104] The most famous case recorded in the Low Countries was Amsterdam, though it was not inconsequence of a church burning down. It concerned a person seriously ill who, in 1345, was given communion at home and then vomited. The vomit was cast into a fire but the Host remained untouched. On the site of the miracle a chapel, known as the 'Heilige Stede' (the sacred place), was erected.[105]

Other accounts of Hosts remaining undamaged are contained in the stories already referred to, such as when Jews were said to have desecrated a Host and then thrown it in the fire, placed it on a hot stove

---

[100]PL 185, 1369, *De miraculis*, III, c. 19: "In villa territorii Tullensis (...) eucharistia cum sacra pixide et corporale flammas evasit, circumiectis omnibus rebus incendio absumptis"; Browe (1938), 73, n. 11; Nussbaum (1979), 316.

[101]Browe (1938), 73.

[102]ed. Strange (1851), II, 178, dist. IX, c. 16: "Cumque omnia quae cremari poterant in cinerem fuissent redacta, flammis sopitis homines intrantes solam pixidem cum corpore Christi illaesam super altare reperunt (...) Ecce habes ex his quae dicta sunt, evidentissima argumenta, quod omni creaturae, rationabili, ut homini, irrationabili, ut animalibus, insensibili, aquae scilicet, terrae, aeri et igni, manifestata sit virtus divini huius sacramenti".

[103]ed. Riedel (1847), VII, 310: "in quo olim cum parrochialis ecclesia per incendium destrueretur, sanctum domini corpus fuit, ut dicitur, miraculose repertum"; Browe (1938), 73, further examples: Pierrefonds near Compiegne (1221); Bayonne (1290); Plaisance in the diocese of Auch (1386); Elbing in the diocese of Ermland (1400).

[104]Rosweydus (1623), 155; Hermans (1847), 354-360; Browe (1938), 74; 166-169; Zika (1988), 48-64; 74, other examples: Praag (1336); Nordlingen in the diocese of Augsburg (1381); Elbing (1400); Hillentrop in the diocese of Paderborn (1446); Meerssen (c.1475).

[105]Post (1955); Carosso-Kok (1981), 46-47; Magry (1988).

or closed it up in an oven. In the miracle story recounted by the
Dominican prior, Rudolf Schlettstadt, the Host twice jumped out of the
fire into which the Jews had cast it,[106] and a convert Jewess in Breslau
told of a similar miracle: there too, in 1453, the Host is said to have
liberated itself several times from the flames just like Arnulf's arm.[107]
Hosts which were said to have originated in similar contexts were
preserved and reverenced in a number of places for some considerable
time, such as in Triani in 1220, Konstanz in 1332 and Passau in
1477.[108]

5   FIGHTING FIRE

The sources provide far more examples of relics, Hosts and corporals
being active in their miraculous power than merely passively resisting
when it came to being involved with fire. In our eyes fire can destroy in a
few tragic instants something that has perhaps taken years to achieve.
Medieval man had little effective remedy against fire. Danger was round
every corner in a high fire-risk environment. In their impotence, the
people placed their trust in the protective powers of the relics and the
Eucharist. If the worst happened and the flames scorched and destroyed
everything around them, a last resort was sought in these sacred remedies.
Resistance to fire and fire-fighting are closely interwoven.

5.1   Fighting fire with relics

Paulinus of Nola sings the praises of the Cross that is master over
fire[109] and fighting fire using relics is a constantly recurring theme in
the works of Gregory of Tours. Was it not the finger joint of Sergius that
saved the house of Eufronius from fire in Bordeaux? A *chrismarium* filled

---

[106]ed. Kleinschmidt (1974), 80-81, n. 35, *De Judeis in Tunowerd* (Donuauwörth or
Donauried): "de igne saltum dedit et se caloribus liberavit (...) secundario longius elevavit
ac seipsum laudabiliter liberavit (...) Tunc hostia conspectu eorum evanuit"; 47-49, n. 5.

[107]AASS 23 oct. X, 467, *De s. Ioanne de Capistrano confessore*, C. VII,88: "in medio
ignis proiecta est, sed in nulla ex sua parte laesa statim miraculose exivit; secundo et tertio
similiter in ignem coniecta integerrima de igne exilivit".

[108]AASS 12 iun. I, 258, *Acta s. Nicolai peregrini Tranen.*, n. 87; Browe (1927),
173-175, 182, further examples: Deggendorf (1337); Segovia (1408); Sternberg (1492);
Knobloch (1510).

[109]CSEL 30, 297, *Carmen*, 28, 130-131: "quanta crucis virtus! ut se natura relinquat,
omnia ligna vorans ligno crucis uritur ignis".

with dust from Martin's grave turned the wind around and saved the church from burning.[110] During a fierce fire that partly reduced Paris to ashes, a certain person took all his precious possessions to the prayer house of the saint close to the city gates, in full confidence that Martin would help on this occasion as had been his wont during his lifetime. His trust was not betrayed: the fire died down and spared the church and his possessions.[111]

St. Cuthbert († 687) was famous for this specialisation. On Lindisfarne he saved the day during a fire, and the same service was expected of his relics.[112] The effect of the relic is sometimes expressed in a graphic way. In 1027 the monks of the Benedictine monastery of Saint-Géry near Cambray carried the relics of their patron to the flames and the fire went out "as if it had started to rain".[113] The chronicles of the abbey of Evesham describe three events occurring around 1080, when the shrine of St. Egwin placed on the *feretrum* doused the flames "as if a hundred bags of water had been emptied over the crackling flames".[114] In 1177 in Rochester there was a report of a pilgrim putting out a fire using an ampulla filled with ablution water that derived its power from the grave of St. Thomas à Becket. The man had attached the pewter receptacle to a forked staff and, standing on the roof of the house where he was a guest, he was able to resist the flames leaping around him.[115]

---

[110]See p. 73 and 85; MGH SRM I, *Hist. Franc.*, VII, 12; I,2, *In gloria martyrum,* lib. II, c. 10 and 11; *De miraculis s. Martini*, lib. I,2.

[111]MGH SRM I,1, 402, lib. VIII, c. 33: "Ibique cecidit incendium (...) Verumtamen ecclesiae cum domibus suis non sunt adustae"; see also: AASS 25 iul. VI, 195-196, Vita s. Ebrulfi, n. 9: "corpus beati confessori aperto sepulchro, contra ignem extulit; et sic flamma incendit in se ipsa reflexa ulterius tansire nequivit"; Sigal (1985), 163, n. 289.

[112]ed. Colgrave (1940), 89-90; AASS 20 mart. II, 120, *Tertia vita sancti Cutberti*, n. 6 and 7.

[113]MGH SS VII, 458: *Gesta episcorum Cameracensum*, lib. II,7 : "Moxque duo ex clericis (...) thecam argenteam sanctissimi corporis extrahunt, cursimque tollentes flammis furentibus obviam ferunt. Statim ergo divina clementia operante meritisque sancti viri suffragantibus, ita totus ignis submisso furore obtorpuit, ut rorulento desuper imbre respersum estimares".

[114]ed. Macray (1863), 66: "nec ultra ausus est ignis suum protelare incendium quam quo sancti Ecgwini deportatum fuerat feretrum"; "ecce! tantum crepitum reddidit incendium quasi super ignem aquam infunderent utres centum".

[115]MB II, 186-7: "Attulerat autem secum peregrinus (...) ampullam stagneam, aqua sancta Cantuariensi repletam (...) cui hastam vel longum aliquid postulanti furca porrigitur. Accipiens igitur sanctuarium, quod a collo sibi dependebat, cuius etiam, ut credi potest, munitus refrigerio tantae tamque propinquae flammae calorem sustinuerat, summitati furcae colligatum propius opponit incendio".

The veil of St. Agatha, protectress against fire, is said to have driven into the sea a rain of fire coming from Mt. Etna.[116] Sometimes relics were carried around objects on fire in order to quench the flames. Such an occurrence was recorded in the *Liber miraculorum* of the Flemish abbey of St. Cornelius in Nieuwenhoven, written between 1184 and 1199. When the shrine of St. Cornelius was carried out from the church "the flames died down as if forced by divine power", as the writer puts it.[117]

To end these examples, let us return to Caesarius of Heisterbach and his account of the arm of John the Baptist, whose miraculous power would appear to have been capable of quenching fire at a distance. The relic of Theoderik, already referred to, came from a Rhineland merchant who had managed to acquire it - in a dubious fashion - from a verger by bribing the man's mistress. After having settled in Groningen, he secreted the arm in a pillar in his house. When the city went on fire he retired to an inn and had no worries about his possessions. His boast was that he had "left a good watchman at home".[118] Finally, bread that had belonged to Nicholas of Tolentino († 1305) was said to have doused a fierce fire on the spot.[119]

5.2   *Fighting fire with the Host*

Fighting fire using the Host or the corporal, recommended by Raoul Glaber († 1050),[120] was sometimes performed in conjunction with use of the relics. The Benedictines of St-Benoît-sur-Loire, for instance, worried about the danger to which they were exposing their precious relic, carried

---

[116]MGH SS XXVII, 116, *Gesta Henrici II et Ricardi I*: "cum ignis vehemencius solito arderet et exiret a fornace Montis Gebel et appropinquasset civitati Catinensium, ubi corpus sanctissimum beatae Agate virginis requiescit, paganorum multitudo fugiens ad sepulchrum eius tulerunt velum eius contra incendium, et ignis reversus est in mare".

[117]ed. Rockwell (1925), 29, 105: "nam cum scrinium sancti Cornelii circumferretur (...) subito flamma, quasi vim desuper pateretur, in se ipsam recolligebatur"; Loomis (1948), 30.

[118]ed. Strange (1851), II, 125, dist. VIII: "Domui meae non timeo, bonum ibi reliqui custodem".

[119]AASS 10 sept. III, 731-732, *Gloria posthuma s. Nicolai Tolentinatis*, n. 481: "Quare demum ut panis s. Nicolai de Tholentino in locum incendii portaretur, miserant; illumque repente intra accensiores totius validissimi vastissimique illius ignis flammis iniecerunt, atque statim exstinctus evanuit, friguitque ignis".

[120]ed. Prou (1886), 123, *Hist*, lib. V: "De chrismale etiam, quod a quibusdam *corporalis* appellatur, plurimum expertum est praestare remedia, si fides exigentium non fuerit dubia. Nam contra incendia saepius elevatum, aut exstinguendo compescuit, aut retrorsum pepulit, seu in partem alteram retorsit. Membra quippe aegrorum dolentia multoties sana restituit, febricitantibus nihilominus impositum salutem contulit"; Browe (1938), 67-72 further examples and a list of sources.

both Benedict and the corporal to the fire, reasoning that it was on this cloth that the body of Christ was consecrated. They achieved a favourable result in that the wind that had been fanning the flames dropped.[121] At Bourges the population rushed to the monastery to help when a fierce fire, fed by hay and straw, threatened to spread frighteningly quickly. The monks proceeded to the fire armed with the corporal and the arm of St. Gundulf, throwing both objects into the flames with immediate results.[122] The miracles led to the growth of a custom which brought a frown to the collective face of the bishops assembled at Seligenstadt in 1023. The synod forbade "certain stupid priests" henceforth from throwing the corporal into the flames.[123] If this interdict had any effect at all, it must have been no more than local, since during a fire that broke out in Deutz in 1128 a monk went to confront the flames bearing the corporal tied to a stick, as would later be done with the relic of Thomas à Becket in Rochester. He threw the stick into the fire and Rupert reports that the corporal withstood the heat.[124] The *consuetudines* of the Benedictines of Cluny and of the monastery of St. Benignus in Dijon prescribed towards the end of the 12th century that a corporal should always be laid out ready on the corner of the altar as an emergency aid in case of fire.[125] According to one report, it was not unknown for the Eucharist to be thrown into the fire. Abbot Giraldus is said to have done that at the end of the 11th century when lightning struck his abbey in Castres in the south of France.[126] In 1280 the prior of the Carthusian monastery near Condrieu in the diocese of Lyon put out a fire by making

---

[121]ed. Certain (1968), 112, lib. II, c. 9: "Effertur denique lugentium moerentiumque manibus illud admirabile margaritum, et cum palla, super quam pridie sacrosanctum corpus Iesu Christi fuerat confectum, circumducitur".

[122]AASS 17 iun. III, 381, *De s. Gundulpho episcopo*, n. 8: "Accipientes itaque corporalia ecclesiae, super quae Dominici Corporis sit sacratio, et brachium s. Gundulphi piissimi confessoris (...) contra incendium deferunt, et flammis ferventibus obiiciunt".

[123]MGH Const I, 637, c. 6: "Ut nemo corporale ad extinguendum incendium in ignem proiciat. Conquestum est in sancto concilio de quibusdam stultissimis presbiteris, ut quando incendium videant, corporale dominico corpore consecratum ad incendium extinguendum temeraria presumptione in ignem proiciant. Ideoque sancitum est sub anathematis interdictione ne ulterius fiat".

[124]PL 149, 716, lib. II, c. 30: "nam et unum simplum semper iacet in sinistro cornu altaris, ut a prioribus nostris accepi, propter hoc ut ad manum possit esse contra periculum ignis"; Herrgott (1726), 220; Browe (1938), 69.

[125]PL 149, 716; Herrgott (1726), 220; Franz (1902), 89-91; Browe (1938), 69.

[126]d'Achery, III, 572, *Chronicon episcoporum Albigensium et abbatum Castrensium*, XVIII: "Fulgure tacta reliquas incendit, et imber miscetur flammas: ignis et unda furit. Incassum tentant exstinguere flammas. Namque ardentem ignis provocat unda sitim. Iamque monasterium furibunda incendia volvit cum Christi oblato corpore flamma cadit".

the sign of the Cross over it with the Eucharist.[127] A similar miraculous effect is reported in the chronicle of Dortmund where, in 1459, the Sacrament was carried to a fire where no less than fifteen houses had already been reduced to ashes by lightning and it succeeded in quelling the flames.[128] Thomas of Haselbach, strong opponent of the practice of the 'weather blessing' using the Eucharist, also objected to this development because, as he said, the Eucharist was not intended for quenching the fire in the houses but rather the sinful passions. Furthermore this profane use of the Eucharist was out of tune with the respect required.[129] By way of contrast the popular preacher, Geiler of Kaisersberg († 1510), had no objections to the practice and even after his death it continued to be applied in Germany - with varying success - even after his death.[130] Making the sign of the Cross with the Eucharist against a wall of fire, as at Condrieu, very closely resembles the 'weather blessing'. 'Transposition of forms of reverence' and 'parallel application in concrete use' overlap here because of the miraculous effect being sought.

6   MIRACLES OF HEALING

Miraculous healings, of which there were countless numbers in consequence of the *miraculous medicinal power* of the relics in the medieval miracle cult, have in recent literature been again described and catalogued.[131] Such miracles were supposed to demonstrate the fact that God worked through the mediation of the saints who, now dead and

---

[127]ed. Le Couteulx (1887-91), IV, a. 1280, n. 12: "Ignis aliquando aedificia Domus huius invadens, cuncta iam consumpserat a claustri porta usque ad foenile. Ad aquas nonnulli, ad alia remedia currebant alii. Sed et Prior ad locum incendii praesto adfuit, afferens Creatorem omnium stipantibus Angelis et comitantibus Religiosis. Mirabile dictu! Cum signum Crucis versus flammas cum sacro vasculo Prior edidisset intercessori cito paruit ignis, suae virtutis oblitus, flammaque subito disparuit, amarum fumum ibidem tantum relinquens et fervidos cineres".

[128]ChrDst 20, 326: Uf der Bruggestraten binnen Dortmunde (...) seint (...) vijftien huser gebrant, und man genk mit dem hilligen sacrament gegen dat vuer mit groter devotion und innigen gebedde, und ist gedaelt worden"; see also vol. 10, 144, Nürnberg, 1426: "das man sorghet, es würd die gantz stat verprinnen von des wints wegen und man gieng mit dem sacrament umbs stat feur"; Browe (1938), 70.

[129]Franz (1902), 91; see also p. 302, n. 31: the prescription of the synod held at Passau.

[130]Freudenthal (1931), 388-389:   Zittau (1473); Basel (1495); Dortmund (1515); Osnabrück (1613); Rastatt (1750); Langendorf (early 19th century); Thiers (1677), II, Andreas Hyperius, 1562: "Coena Dominici usurpari posset ad avertendas tempestates restinguendas ignes".

[131]among others: Finucane (1977); Sigal (1985); Ward (1981), (1982); Head (1990).

resting with the Lord, could achieve even more than during their earthly existence. Based on the model to be found in the *vita* of Benedict in the *Dialogues* of Gregory, the miracles often show similarities to the wonders recorded in the Gospels.[132] The saints shared in the charisma of Jesus: contact with their relics made the blind see, the lame walk and expelled demons. The Eucharist does not figure so prominently as a source of healing power. Indeed, until approximately the 11th century it is the saints who are the great miracle workers, not the Eucharistic gifts. In order to demonstrate the parallelisms, first a choice was made of the Eucharistic miracles of healing and then analogous examples were taken from the catalogue of miracles recorded in the cult of the relics. The miraculous medicinal power of the relics and the Eucharist was mainly tested by bringing them into contact with the sick.

6.1   The relics' powers of healing

In what we have already examined, the healing power of the relics has been seen on several occasions. The *capsula* of Herman of Auxerre († 488) was placed on the eyes of a blind girl so that she was able to see once again. The *chrismarium* of Gregory of Tours placed around the neck of a corpse is said to have caused the dead man to open his eyes, and by laying a single thread from Martin's grave cover Gregory himself recovered from fierce stomach ache.[133] The relics of St. Julian were able to expel the devil when the *capsa* was placed on the head of the one possessed.[134]

The *Dialogues* of Pope Gregory record an instance of someone being restored to life thanks to dust taken from St. Peter's altar in a church in Rome.[135] In one of his letters Gregory speaks of Peter's key and chains that he sent: these relics had wrought "many miracles" when

---

[132]Ward (1981), 3-4; Browe (1938), 56.

[133]See p. 84-85 and 293.

[134]MGH SRM I,2 131, *De virtutibus s. Iuliani*, c. 45: "Clero vero haec audiens, positam super caput eius capsulam cum pignoribus sanctis, fide plenus orare coepit attentius; ipse quoque cum vomitu sanguinem daemoniumque proiciens, purgatus abscessit"; see also c. 43 and 42, *In gloria martyrum*, c. 5.

[135]SC 260, 338, lib. III, c. 17,3: "ab altaris crepidine pulverem collegit, atque (...) ad defuncti corpus accessit".

laid on the sick.[136] Bede († 735) describes how a hair of St. Cuthbert had caused an eye swelling to disappear.[137] The shoes belonging to the same saint, taken from his uncorrupted body when this was exhumed, are said by one of his *vitae* to have caused a lame man to walk; his stole was also laid on the heads of the sick.[138]

The head of the holy hermit Guthlac († 714), around whose grave the great abbey of Crowland rose probably in the early 10th century, was said to be an effective remedy against insanity. In a 12th-century *vita* the story is told of how a bishop placed Guthlac's reliquary on the head of an architect, a certain Alwoldus, and cured him of this affliction.[139] There is a legendary story, dating from the same century, concerning a girl called Mathilda, whose insanity caused her to reject the embraces of her husband and to be afflicted by the devil several times daily. She received communion at Gournay, kissed the relics of St. Hildevert and of the True Cross, following which the devil left her. Her faculty of speech was restored when her tongue was touched by one of Hildevert's teeth.[140] The hair of Hildegard of Bingen enjoyed fame even during her lifetime. One single hair which she gave to a woman threatened by the devil and her husband is said to have made the demon protest loudly.[141] A much-valued relic for use against all kinds of terrible sicknesses was the cape worn by Peter the Martyr, a Dominican murdered in 1252 by the Cathars.

---

[136]MGH Ep I, 42-43, n. 29 and 30: "Praeterea sacratissimam clavem a sancti Petri apostoli corpore vobis transmisi, quae super aegros multis solet miraculis coruscare; nam etiam de eius catenis interius habet".

[137]PL 95, 228, *Historica Ecc.*, IV, c. 32: "presbyter (...) cum accepisset capillos sancti capitis, adposuit palpebrae languenti (...) ita sanum (oculum) cum palpebra invenit, ac si nil unquam in eo deformitatis ac tumoris apparuisset".

[138]AASS 20 mart. III, 124, *Tertia vita*, n. 17: "Ideo namque deposco ab abbate calceamenta quae circumdederunt pedes sancti martyris Dei incorruptibilis et (...) pedibus suis nocte illa circumdedit et requievit. Surgens in matutinis, quod dictu mirum est, Domino laudem stans cantavit, qui prius pene absque lingua nullum membrum movere potuit. Crastina autem die circuibat loca sanctorum martyrum, gratias agens Domino"; Beek (1974), 65 with illustration.

[139]AASS 11 apr. II, 56, *Translatio s. Guthlaci*, n. 8: "arbitror, quod archtectum quondam (...) Alwoldum nomine, pestifera passio diutine intolerabili languore, scilicet capitis vertigine dementatim torquebat (...) Hic ab episcopo pura mentis devotione impetravit, quatenus scrinium cum s. Guthlaci capite cervici suae desuper imponeret. Quod ut factum est, ita omnis capitis dolor et amaritudo evanuit"; ed. Colgrave (1956), 9.

[140]AASS 27 maii VI, 716, *De s. Hildeverto episc. Meldensi*, 11 n. 15 c: "Tunc sacerdos quidam linguam eius dente b. Hildeverti tetigit, et resumpta inter os lingua cum dente sancto os clausit et labia strinxit. Nec mora os ipsa laxavit et sacerdos dentem sanctum solerter abstraxit: et illa sedata, sacerdos dixit illi: Mathilde clama, Sancte Hildeverte. Et continuo soluto linguae vinculo clamavit"; further examples: Sigal (1985), 42; Beek (1974), 65.

[141]ed. Bruder (1883), 124: "Ipsa vero partem crinium suorum eidem tradidit; et illa secundum eius mandatum suis crinibus innexuit. Quod daemon sentiens, marito dixit: Me decepisti; nihil iuris in ea habeo propter incantationes Hildegardis".

Even during his lifetime he had proved to possess an exceptional power of healing.[142]

6.2 The healing power of the Host

In contrast to the innumerable accounts of healing achieved by contact with the relics, the number of similar miracles performed by the Eucharist is thin on the ground. Christian antiquity again provides us with a few 'lonely' examples to the rule that such miracles are usually reported after the time of the second Eucharistic controversy. Gregory of Nazianze and Augustine happen to describe the miraculous cure achieved by spreading finely ground Eucharistic bread on the eyes of Gorgonia and Acatius respectively. Another report is to be found in an anonymous appendix to the works of Prosper of Aquitaine († 455) where the expulsion of a devil from an Arab girl was achieved by placing the chalice on her throat (I Cor. 10:20-21; II Cor. 6:15), since she was no longer able to swallow the Eucharistic bread.[143]

After that we do not encounter any comparable action until the 12th-13th century, mainly with regard to those possessed by demons, however ambiguous that condition may be. We have already seen Bernard of Clairvaux, Host in hand, adjuring the Duke of Aquitania. There is a further report of when Bernard was celebrating Mass in Milan: after the *Pater Noster* he laid the paten with the Host on the head of a woman possessed by demons. The woman, grinding her teeth, was a terrible sight. He said a prayer over her, returned to the altar, broke the Host and gave the kiss of peace to the Mass server, who then gave it to the woman. She was, according to the biographer, cured on the spot.[144] Caesarius of Heisterbach reports an occurrence similar to that involving Augustine - and which recalled Jesus, who made mud with his saliva and spread this

---

[142]AASS 29 apr. III, 696, *Vita s. Petri mart.* n. 33: "puer iam (morti) devotus, suo languenti collo, tamquam aliquod salutare remedium, eius cappam adhibuit; et benedictione recepta, recepit pariter sanitatem"; "cappam ipsam (...) reverenter afferri fecit; qua suo apposita pectori, mox vermem, duo capita habentem et pilorum densitate villosum, evomuit".

[143]PL 51, 842, c. 6, 10: "ut calicem salutarem gutturi eius pontifex applicaret. Quod ut factum est, statim locum illum quem diabolus obsederat Salvatoris imperio reliquit".

[144]PL 185, 276, lib. II, c. 3,14: "Expleta autem oratione dominica, efficacius hostem aggreditur vir beatus. Patenae (...) calicis sacrum Domini corpus imponens (...) rediens pater sanctus ad altare, fractionem hostiae salutaris rite complevit, diffundendamque in populum pacem ministro dedit; et confestim pax et salus integra reddita est mulieri"; ed. Griesser (1961), 343, dist. VI, c. 2; PL 185, 1180-84.

on the eyes of a man born blind (Mtt. 9:29; Mk. 8:23). A Westphalian priest, writes Caesarius, wet his finger with saliva, touched first the consecrated Host and then the mouth of a sick girl, whose speech was restored and she was able to stand up fit and well.[145] The legend of Giraldus Cambrensis († 1223) perhaps bears witness to a certain degree of scepticism with regard to this approach. First attempts are made to get rid of the devil using the relics, and then if this fails the Eucharist has to be called in. However the devil hoots with derision that this food for the soul is unable to accomplish anything against him![146] In this case a Host and a relic are used together, but it would seem that more was expected of the Host. In exorcisms performed in the late Middle Ages the "pyx with the Sacrament or the relics" was sometimes placed on the head of the subject by way of reinforcement for the exorcism formula.[147] The rituale published in 1614 by Pope Paul V banned the use of the Eucharist in such cases in order to avoid all possibility of irreverence.[148]

The miraculous healing power of the Eucharist was expressed much more in its reception than when it was laid on am person's head. One the one hand, this demonstrates a sharp distinction between Eucharist and relics since it is not possible to 'eat' the latter. On the other, when used in this way the act of communion sometimes lost so much of its communal liturgical significance that the wine or Host thus 'applied' took on the aspect of a relic, a source of miraculous power. There is yet another difference in this and other Eucharistic miracles: the saints effecting cures by means of their relics were following in the footsteps of Jesus, but now it was Jesus Himself who was again effecting cures as in the Gospel narrative. The Eucharistic gifts increasingly took on the aspect of being 'like a relic' the more the liturgical background was lost and medicinal powers were ascribed to the wine or the Host *as such*.

---

[145]ed. Strange (1851), II, 205, dist. XI, c. 50: "Sacerdos vero hostiam quasi pro remedio mittens in os eius non benedictam, cum nihil ei prodesset, digito saliva madefacto corpus Domini tetigit. Quem cum in os misisset mulieris, illa sensum recepit, locuta est et sana surrexit".

[146]ed. Brewer (1861-64), 54, *Gemma eccles.* I, c. 18: "posito super guttur inflatum libro evangelico vel reliquiis sanctorum statim in ventrem descendebat (daemonium) (...) Tandem vero cum corpus Christi mulieri offerrent ad sumendum, respondit daemonium: Stulti, nihil est quod agitis, non enim cibus est corporis quod ei datis sed spiritus; mihi vero non in animam eius sed in corpus est data potestas".

[147]Browe (1938), 59, n. 20; E. Bacha, *La chronique Liégeoise de 1402*, Brussels, 1900; Franz (1909), II, 570.

[148]Browe (1938), 60, n. 26: "ss. eucharistia super caput obsessi aut aliter corpori non admoveatur, ob irreverentiae periculum".

However the sacramental communion was a rare occurrence, which can explain why there are so few examples to be found. As far as Christian antiquity is concerned, we turn again to Gregory of Nazianze, who reported that his father was cured of bad pains by receiving the Eucharist.[149] The *Dialogues* of Gregory the Great mention a dumb cripple who was brought by members of his family to Pope Agapetus († 536). Then pope questioned them as to their beliefs (Mtt. 9:28), took the man by the hand after the Mass and caused him to stand (Acts 3:7; 9:41). "In the power - *virtus* - of the Lord and on the authority of Peter" (Mk. 7:32-37).[150] A dying man is said to have been revived when Sulpicius Pius of Bourges († 646) dripped the consecrated wine into his mouth.[151] And Magnobus of Angers († c. 650) used the *Dominici corporis mysterium* to cure a girl of a fever that she had suffered from for three years.[152]

Here again the miracles mostly involve those suffering from insanity, epilepsy or demonic possession, concerning whose admission to the Eucharist there was no clear general opinion in the early Church.[153] The ascetic John Cassian († c. 434) took their side by referring to the miraculous cure of Abbot Andronicus[154] and the Council of Orange in 441 permitted them to receive communion under certain conditions.[155] In the early Middle Ages miracles in this context were reported

---

[149]PG 35, 1036, *Oratio*, XVIII, 38.

[150]SC 260, 268, III,c. 2: "ab altari exiens, claudi manum tenuit, atque, adsistente et aspiciente populo, eum mox a terra in propriis gressibus erexit. Cumque ei dominicum corpus in os mitteret, illa diu muta ad loquendum lingua soluta est".

[151]AASS OSB II, 177, *Vita s. Sulpicii pii episc. Bituricensis*, c. 34: "Tunc (...) reperit eum semivivum (...) vique dentibus reseratis, sacrificium in ore eius propriis manibus Dei sacerdos infudit. Et (...) surrexit incolumis, acsi nihil mali habuisse putaretur".

[152]AASS 16 oct. VII, 945, *Vita s. Magnobodi*, c. III, n. 21: "Dominici corpus mysterium, quod sanctis manibus tractabat, in os puellae intromisit: quae absque mora veneno diutini languoris deposito, pristinaeque sanitati concessa, laetabunda cum comitibus ad urbem qua venerat regressa est".

[153]Beek (1974), 165-171; Browe (1938), 57; Dölger (1929-50), 130-137.

[154]SC 42, 270-272, *Conlatio*, VII, c. 30: "Hoc namque modo curatum et abbatem Andronicum nuper aspeximus aliosque conplures. Magis enim ac magis inimicus insultabit obsesso, cum eum a caelesti medicina viderit segregatum, tantoque dirius ac frequentius adtemptabit, quanto eum a spiritali remedio longius senserit abdicatum".

[155]CC SL 148, Concilia Galliae, 82, Concilium Arausicanum, can. 13: "Energumeni baptizati, si de purgatione sua curant et se sollicitudini clericorum tradunt, monitisque obtemperant, omnimodis communicent, sacramenti ipsius virtute vel muniendi ab incursu daemonii quo infestantur, vel purgandi quorum iam ostenditur vita purgatior".

sporadically,[156] but from the 11th century they increase in number, with
the devil resisting the power of the Eucharist in every way available to
him (Mtt. 8:28-34; Mk. 5:2-20; Lk. 8:26-29). In a letter to Bishop
Adebold of Utrecht († 1026) we read that seamen brought one of the crew
possessed by the devil and wrapped in a cowhide, to the monastery of St.
Walburgis in Tiel. As he lay on the altar steps his kicking and screaming
died away during Compline, and the next morning he was so calmed after
Mass that he was able to receive communion and was released from the
devil's grip.[157] When St. Ulrich († 1093), a Benedictine from the
Freiburg region, was preparing to give communion to a man possessed by
the devil, the man is reported to have opened his mouth emitting a noise
"like a whole herd of animals".[158] The devil is also said to have left a
possessed girl with no less showmanship when Bernard of Clairvaux gave
her water served from the paten.[159]

7   THE ABLUTION WATER

In addition to direct contact with the relics or the Eucharist, the miracle
often revolve around a more indirect means of contact, namely the
ablution water. This was wine or water that had been in contact with the
relics or the Eucharist. In the course of a funeral or the *elevatio* it was the
custom to wash the *corpora* and regard the water as having the power of
healing. It had a similar power when the relics had been plunged into it.
This water was probably so highly prized precisely because it could be so
easily 'prepared', replenished and transported. As far as the Eucharist is
concerned, the healing power of the water was deemed to be at its
strongest after the third *ablutio digitorum*: this water and wine which the
priest had used after communion to wash his fingers above the chalice and

---

[156]Corblet, 452, St. Auxentius (5th century); MGH SRM IV, 199, *Vita Austregelii ep. Biturgi* († 624): "Ipse prius percepit deditque puelle (...) Ex illa hora, fugato demonio, puella illa pristine sanitate restituta est"; 267, *Vita Galli* (650), c. 21: "inposita mihi manu, signo crucis me munivit nec non et demoni, ut recederet, imperavit (..) Deinceps corpus Domini incolomis accepi".

[157]AASS 25 febr. III, 547, *Miracula s. Walburgis, ep.* I,2: "et missa pro infirmo celebrata (...) traditum est ei corpus et sanguis Domini. Quae postquam gesta sunt (...) purgatus daemone, solutus est".

[158]AASS 10 iul. III, 162, *Vita s. Udalrici conf. ord. s. Bened.* n. 43: "non cessavit intonare, ut multarum bestiarum greges coadunatos crederes"; For the cure of Louis VI, the Fat, see RHF XII, 60, 813, 865, Suger, *Vita Ludovici Grossi*.

[159]PL 185, 275, c. II, n. 11: "Patenam igitur calicis, in quo divina celebraturus erat mysteria, accipit: et digitis latice superfuso, orans intra se, et de Domini confidens, ori puellae salubrem potum applicat et corpori eius stillam medicinalem infundit".

wherein minute particles of the Host and traces of the consecrated wine could be present. Even without that, the water had been in indirect contact with the Host via the priest's fingers. The first and second ablutions in the medieval liturgy, before Mass and before the Preface respectively, were therefore of far less importance in this context.[160]

7.1   Ablution water from the relics

An 11th-century occurrence involving ablution water possessing miraculous powers has already been quoted with respect to the use of the *feretrum* in the procession of the Blessed Sacrament, namely the relics of St. Maurus that were carried around and which the people doused with wine or water.[161] This was 'water' that served for both internal and external use. A perfect example of how the use of ablution water could assume a 'Eucharistic' character was the custom maintained in the monastery of St. Medardus near Soissons. On the feast day of St. Gregory the monks allowed the faithful to drink from a secondary relic: the drinking mug used by this holy pope. When the *pestilentia igneria* struck the fear of death into the neighbouring village of Septmons, the people clung on to the protective force of the mug. It was placed on the altar and begged for salvation "with offerings of peace and a heart full of devotion". The mug was then filled and the congregation drank from it "to strengthen their souls and bodies". Subsequently each took some of the contents home and sprinkled the house, fields and gardens "like dew from heaven".[162]

The custom of regarding relic-water as having healing properties dates from as early as Christian antiquity. According to the apocryphal *vitae* the apostle John died at the age of 120 at Ephesus and was buried on the hill where he had spent his final days. His tomb became an object of devotion almost immediately and remained so throughout the whole of

---

[160]Franz (1902), 105-108; Sigal (1985), 50-51; the 'Preface' is the first part of the great prayer of the Mass recited by the priest preceding the *Sanctus* and forming, as it were, a single unity with the latter. (LW II, 2261).

[161]See p. 267.

[162]AASS 12 mart. II, 750, *Miracula s. Gregorii papae*, n. 7: "Et est consuetudo ut in festo eius de eo bibatur a populo"; 151, n. 8: "Ponitur scyphus in altari, requiritur cum hostiis pacificis et cordis devotione: deinde vino infuso in scyphulo sancti, corpora sua et animas corroborant: et reverentes, de liquore infuso vini vel aquae secum ferunt, et per domos, rura, et hortos quasi de rore caeli desuper satagunt irrigare"; for the drinking mug of Saint Servatius and those of other saints see: Koldeweij (1985), 226-231.

the Middle Ages. A legend came into being which drew its inspiration from "Then went this saying abroad among the brethren that that disciple should not die" (Jn. 21:23). The belief arouse that John was not dead but merely sleeping until the Second Coming. His breath blew dust to the surface so that it became visible during Vespers celebrated on 7th May, the eve of his feast day, and on his feast day itself. This "manna" was distributed to all the pilgrims. Dissolved in water it was regarded as a remedy for fever, gall stones and difficult labour. It also caused storms and the wild ocean to die down.[163] Water was even diverted from the grave into a well, from where it was taken as a miraculous fluid. Paulinus of Nola sings the praises of a similar situation at the grave of St. Felix. Great masses of pilgrims crowded there in order to obtain the water.[164]

The work of Gregory of Tours also contain innumerable passages witnessing to the practice. A certain person anointed his wounds with water that had run over the grave of St. Martin at Easter and even drank it, which produced rapid results. Another dissolved dust from the tomb in wine, a potion which cured him of dysentery. A priest named Aridius washed his face with water from the well into which the blood of St. Julian had flowed. He filled his ampulla with it and used this as a relic in the consecration ritual of a church.[165] Earth soaked in the water with which the body of St. Cuthbert was washed after his death in 687 released a young Lindisfarne man from demonic possession. After he had drunk some water to which a little of the earth had been added he stopped his moaning that very night, as the anonymous biographer reports.[166] In a *vita* written by a certain Felix a blind father from Wissa had the light restored to his eyes thanks to ablution water with a different composition. Pega, the sister of the dead saint, dissolved in water a few grains of a

---

[163]Foss (1979), 36, 127.

[164]CSEL 30, 177, *Carmen*, 21, l. 583 sqq.; 30; PL 61. 594; Kötting (1950), 176-177, 251.

[165]MGH SRM I,2, 190, *De virtutibus s. Martini*, lib. III, c. 34: "Tunc transmissum est ei de aqua, qua beatum tumulum in pascha Domini est ablutum. Denique delibutis ex ea vulneribus, ipsa exinde potui sumpsit. Mox igitur restincta febre, decurrentibus sine dolore visicis, sanata est"; ibid. c. 51: "vidi unum in desperatione a disenteria iacentem..diluculo vero accedens ad tumulum, potato cum vino pulverem, sanus rediit e sepulchro"; see also lib. II, c. 1; ib. 130, *De virtutibus Iuliani*, c. 41: "Inde veniens ad fontem, in quo beati sanguis effusus est, abluta aquis facie, parvam ab his pro benedictione conplevi ampullam"; see also 85, *In gloria martyrum*, c. 70.

[166]ed. Colgrave (1940), 134, c. 15: "puer vero degustata aqua benedicta, a garrula voce nocte illa desinit".

lump of salt blessed by her brother. She placed drops of it under the man's eyelids and so made him to see again.[167]

Monks were known to prepare ablution water for their own personal use. At the end of the 10th century the Count of Champagne, Heribert the Old, was struck down by fever. The abbot of Montier-en-Der celebrated Mass with the community for the Duke's intentions and after the Mass poured a little water over the chain of St. Peter and a relic of St. Bercharius († 696). He placed the water in a small container and sent it to the Duke, who drank it and fell into a deep sleep, waking later free of fever.[168] During en epidemic that struck Lorraine in 1042, Richard of St. Vannes († 1046) prepared a whole barrel for the population, so that they were not necessarily obliged to resort to ablution water prepared during the "ablution of the relics, which was usual at the end of Mass".[169] In both of these examples the relic-water is accorded an 'added Eucharistic value': the ablution took place after the *usual* celebration of the Mass - in the case above celebrated for the intentions of the sick person. The remark made by Gregory of Tours must also refer to this practice: the fact that water was made to run over the grave of St. Martin "at Easter".

Whenever necessary, however, ablution water could be 'prepared' on the spot, as witness the *vita* of Bernard the Penitent. While travelling to England in 1182 a monk of St-Bertin took with him a hair from the head of St. Bernard. He came into contact with a sick man, whose mouth and throat were so infected that he could scarcely draw breath. The monk dipped his relic in water and dribbled a little of it between the patient's teeth and the man was cured. Bernard had acquired his name because of a penance placed on him by his bishop because of his sinful life. He took the penance so seriously, with an iron band around his waist, that even during his sinful life he was generally regarded as a saint. At his funeral

---

[167]ed. Colgrave (1956), 168, c. 53: "Illa quoque partem glutinati salis a sancto Guthlaco ante consecratam arripiens, in aquam offertoriam levi rasura mittebat; ipsam denique aquam, cum intra palpebras caeci guttatim stillaret, mirabile dictu (...) lumen redditum est".

[168]AASS 16 oct. VII,2, 1024, *Miracula s. Bercharii*, c. III: "abbas missa peracta, catenam s. Petri cum aliqua parte reliquiarum s. martyris lavans, ei in vase parvissimo transmisit ad potandum".

[169]PL 154, 262, *Chronicon Hugonis abbatis Flaviniacensis*, lib. II: "Videres monasterium eximii patres ardentium turbis refertum quos ipse sanctorum reliquiis aqua benedicta respersis et vino lotis, et pulvere qui de petra sepulchri Domini radebatur vino ipso consperso, et ad potandum miseris dato, pace firmata et iurata, pristinae sanitati reddebat. Pro innumeris autem turbis confluentium infirmorum vas potui illi paratum erat, ut si advenirent egroti, potus salutis non deesset, ne fallerentur si hora incompetenti venissent; neve tunc foret necessitas recurrendi ad ablutionem reliquiarum, quod post expletionem missae inpleri mos est".

the iron band, his penitential garment and his body were washed so that ablution water could be prepared that would serve as a medication.[170]

The general acceptance of ablution water as a substance with medicinal powers was again expressed by Caesarius of Heisterbach with reference to the remains of the Theban legion, discovered during the restoration of the cathedral in Bonn. "These sacred bones", wrote Caesarius, "have such a great *virtus* that water poured over them is an effective medication against all kinds of sicknesses, especially swellings and infections".[171] And it retained its power in the general popular devotion of the time.

7.2   Ablution water from the Host

The Eucharist demonstrated its indirect miraculous powers not only via the paten, preferred by Bernard of Clairvaux, but also through the corporal and the ablution water. Often, according to Raoul Glaber († 1050), the fever is banished or sick limbs are healed by the laying on of the corporal. Patients were touched with the corporal or paten until well into the 15th century. However in particular the healing power was, as in the case of the relics, regarded as being present in the ablution water obtained after the Communion, particularly if the celebrant had the reputation of living a holy life. The water cured cripples, the blind and those afflicted with fever. One example, dating from around 1050, is the ablution water of John of Monte Cassino, a much sought after liquid. Whoever drank it was guaranteed freedom from fever for life, something that Anselm of Lucca, later Pope Alexander II († 1073) was happy to be able to discover for himself.[172] A blind woman is said to have had her

---

[170]AASS 19 apr. II, 691-692, *Vita b. Bernardi Poenitentis*, n. 50: "monachus reliquias sancti, quae secum habebat, capillos scilicet eius, aqua intinxit; apertisque cum cultello aegri dentibus, ex eadem aqua modicum in os eius instillavit"; 680, lib. I, n. 31: "et cilicio et vinculis ferreis, quae adhuc circa collum et corpus erant cum magno reverentiae timore eum exuentes; et corpus in aqua mundissima abluentes, infirmitatibus haec ad remedium procuravimus".

[171]ed. Strange (1851), II, 136, dist. VIII, c. 65: "Tantae enim virtutis sunt eadem sacrata ossa, ut aqua superfusa variis infirmitatibus sit medela. Maxime tamen sanat tumores ac inflationes"; Loomis (1948), 213, n. 16-18, approx. 20 references.

[172]MGH SS XXXIV, 344, *Chronica Monasterii Casinensis*, II, c. 90: "Ferebatur (...) vir Dei huiusmodi gratia praepollere, ut si ex aqua, qua post missarum sollemnia manus ablueret, aliquis in potum febreticus fideliter sumeret, nullum deinceps in eo febris ius exercere potestatis valeret. Anselmus..cum quodam tempore ardore febris vehementissimo estuaret, repente memoratus est hoc (...) Misitque continuo, qui ex aqua eadem clanculo sibi deferret. Quam mox ut in potum accepit, nulla interposita mora omnis ab eo valitudo illa febris aufugit"; see also PL 173, 1101, *Petri Diaconi, de ortu et obitu iustorum casin.* c. 33:

sight restored by washing her eyes with the ablution water of St. Heribert of Cologne.[173]

Ablution water figures in the *vitae* of popes and abbots[174], including that of Gerard of Brogne († 959), written in the middle of the 12th century[175], and of Hugh of Cluny († 1109). A fellow-brother of the latter, a certain Theoderic, "had a serious condition in the joint of his foot, which no herb could cure and which was called cancer". After the Mass celebrated by Hugo the altar server gave him the ablution water, which he poured over the affected foot. Healing occurred instantly and the flesh which had fallen away grew back again.[176] The ablution water was also distributed after Mass, although this practice grew less frequent after 1300. It was a much sought after remedy for children. The *Liber ordinarius* of the collegiate church in Tongeren makes clear how easily the ablution water derived from Eucharist and relics 'merge together': in 1435 it prescribed simultaneous ablution of chalice and relics. This was supposed to be performed after vespers on Good Friday and the water was then available to the sick throughout the ensuing year.[177]

Meanwhile in Germany a custom, recorded long ago by Cyril of Jerusalem, had come back into force. There no few priests were accustomed to touch the eyes and other senses of the sick with their wet fingers after the ablution (Jn. 9:11). And the mouths and eyes of children

---

"Alexander papa cum febre valida aegrotaret (...) Delata igitur aqua, statim ut eam in potum accepit, omnis ab eo infirmitas febris recessit"; PL 149, 972, Victor III; Franz (1902), 108.

[173]PL 170, 410, *Vita Hereberti*, c. 19: "si ex vino quod idem sanctus Dei post Dominici corporis et sanguinis communionem digitos de more lavisset, sibimet oculos intingeret, amissum protinus lumen reciperet".

[174]Leo IX († 1054) and Gregory VII († 1085), resp. Muratori (1723-51), III,1, 295: "Cui per revelationem ostensum est, ut de lympha, qua Beatus Pastor sacras abluerat manus, et post celebrationem Missarum hauriret, et absque mora sospitatem reciperet" and 324: "cum de more sacras manus ablueret, ipsa ablutionis aqua (...) aegrum quemdam (...) ab aegritudine liberavit"; this latter is not within the context of the Mass; for further examples of healing ablution water from "holy hands": see Loomis (1948), 212, n. 12-15, approx. 35 references.

[175]AASS 3 oct. II, 313, *Vita s. Gerardi abbatis Broniensis*, n. 56: "ut fiat in te fons aquae salientis in vitam aeternam, quatenus mihi misellae digneris illam concedere aquam, qua manus diluet servus Christi Gerardus post perceptam eucharistiam".

[176]ed. Cowdrey (1978), 130, *Hugonis monachi vita sancti Hugonis Abbatis*, lib. II, c. 17: "Huius articulum pedis laetalis infirmitas quae cancer dicitur occupavit, qui cum nullum invenerit remedium fide plena ad patris Hugonis se convertit auxilium. Abbate itaque missas peragente, de aqua qua digitos suos post eucharistiam lavit Theodoricus clanculum accepit et de magistri virtute confisus infudit exesis articuli partibus; statimque pes totus convaluit caroque depasta ilico recrevit"; 75, Gilo, *Vita sancti Hugonis Abbatis*, c. 29; 23: "The *Life* by Hildebert was written with knowledge of Gilo's before 1122. There is every likelihood that Gilo wrote his *Life* in 1120".

[177]ed. Lefèvre (1967), I, 162, c. 20: *De feria sexta in Parasceve*, "Post vesperas lavantur et intinguantur calices et reliquie in aqua, et illa reservetur per totum annum ad opus infirmorum".

gathered round the altar were also thus anointed, a practice which led to the rise of superstitions.[178] A certain healing power, separate from the ablution, was also ascribed to the four fingers which the priest used to hold the Host during Mass. At least Caesarius of Heisterbach, whom we call on once more to close this section, speaks of this in a report of a visit that he made together with his abbot to the abbey of Walberberg near Brühl. There he met a woman who suffered from a throat infection. The abbot touched the sick woman's neck with the four fingers in question saying: "As true as I today have touched the body of Christ with these fingers, so say I to you, recover from this affliction."[179]

***

The remarks made in passing by the authors quoted in the introduction to this book, who spoke of the Host as a "focus of power" have been the subject of our research in this chapter. The miraculous power has been traced in time, elaborated, explained and confirmed by a number of miracles ascribed to relics and Eucharist, miracles which can be compared from this point of view. The parallelism in the miraculous power ascribed to Eucharist and relics has been demonstrated in *presentation*, *effect* and *use* in cases of: incorruptibility, radiation of light, resistance to fire, the dousing of fire, healing both direct and indirect, and to a certain extent in the miracles involving blood. The material we have compared leads to the conclusion that in the aspects noted there was little difference between the miracles effected by Host, corporal, paten or the ablution water on the one hand, and by the relics on the other. In the six types of miracle described it would seem that in every case the point at which a miraculous power similar to that ascribed to the relics was also ascribed to the Host is situated in the 11th-12th and reached its high point in the 13th. This miraculous power would have been unthinkable in the 10th century and prior to then on this scale and in this form - the Host *itself* possesses the characteristic - because in that period the 'process of independence', whereby the Host was separated off from its liturgical context, as described in chapter II, had not gone sufficiently far. The implicit accord in details with the presentation of the relic in the relevant relic miracles examined is sometimes so striking that it is difficult to rule out influence

---

[178]Franz (1909), II, 111-115; Jungmann (1962), II, 519, n. 77 with references.

[179]ed. Hilka (1937), 28, lib. I, c. 9: "Tam veraciter sicut hodie digitis istis corpus Christi tractavi, tam veraciter de infirmitate hac convalescas".

by one on the other. There is, moreover, a difference in the position of the Host, depending on whether the account concerns merely the miracle and the miraculous power or whether it is a question of 'opportunistic' use. When, in fact, it is a question of a Eucharistic miracle as such, the Host occupies centre stage and is presented in a manner almost identical to that of the relic: they are proof against fire and decay, they emit light and they give off blood. In the two parallel uses - combating disease and putting out fire - the Host seldom functions as a 'relic', this task being taken over by the 'secondary relics' - the corporal, the paten or the Eucharistic ablution water. As far as the use of the Host is concerned, the following is worth noting: external medicinal applications of the Eucharist are found practically exclusively in cases of demonic possession and the use of the Host to fight fire was also somewhat limited geographically. Only one report is extant from France and the rest all originate in Germany. According to Thiers such a practice appeared once more in France in 1600, thanks to the activities of a Capuchin friar of Toulouse.[180] These data agree with the *Malleus maleficarum*, which also qualifies the weather blessing as being an ancient practice of the German and French churches.[181] When fire and lightning threatened it would seem that in these regions there was a tendency to use every imaginable aid, including the Host, to quell the unwelcome forces. The cause of this 'parallel application in concrete use' of Host and relics remaining limited in its extent is discussed in the next chapter.

Finally we note that an open question remains regarding the *extent* of the incidence of the parallelism exposed and a magical experience of belief. We have done no more than describe these phenomena, since they are also an aspect in the mutual relationship between veneration of the Eucharist and veneration of the relics. By concentrating our attention on the similarities, however, we risk creating the impression that the exceptional - the miraculous - was characteristic of day-to-day belief. This could lead to the creation of a false picture of the actual reverence paid to the saints, who were daily called on with great trust to mediate between God and man. Once more this would mean a disservice to the rich Eucharistic piety of the Middle Ages, where respectful prayer addressed to the really present Lord, the *praesentia realis* and also His *passio*, were central for the believer and a source of great consolation.

---

[180]Thiers (1677), II, 794.
[181]See p. 300.

CHAPTER SIX

THE 'UNIQUE RELIC'?

"Baptism and the Eucharist are the pillars of our belief. The form taken by these sacraments is the same everywhere. In addition the Church preaches and permits pious usages which can vary from place to place and are not essential for our salvation. Such practices include the reverence paid to the bodies of the saints and their *pignora*."[1] With this qualification Guibert of Nogent († 1125) gave to baptism and the Eucharist pride of place within Christian belief and placed the veneration of relics among the subordinate practices of piety.

The question arises as to whether the relics did indeed play such a subordinate role in the various relational forms identified here. Within that context was the Eucharist primary and always considered as such in popular piety? To what extent is it possible to trace increase or change depending on the image people had and the opinions they held with regard to the *praesentia realis*? In this chapter we will attempt to provide an answer to such questions by interpreting the information we have gathered in the order we have examined it: *parallel application in concrete use, transposition of forms of reverence and similiraty in miraculous power*. The guiding principle in all this will be the way in which the Eucharist was understood. Was it a sacrament to be received or a means of protection? Was it the body of Christ to be worshipped or a guarantee against disaster? Was it seen as Christ Himself, who drove out the devil, or was it regarded as a relic with unique miraculous power? However we will first examine whether the relativisation of the relics in Guibert's writing and in that of other critics can throw any light on the matter.

The quotation from Guibert, given above, can be found in his book, *De pignoribus sanctorum*, which was directed against all the excesses of relic veneration in his time, a criticism which had resounded more than once in the centuries preceding him. Despite the blossoming of the cult of the relics in the Middle Ages and the support given to it by the Church,

---

[1] PL 156, 613, *De pignoribus sanctorum*, lib. I, *"Absque baptismale et eucharistia fides constare nequit, quorum par est forma"*: "Praeterea sunt quaedam, quae etsi inter summe necessaria saluti nostrae, de quibus agimus, non computantur, sine quibus vivi recte non potest, tamen et tenentur et in ecclesiis praedicantur, sine quorum plane usu, et praesentia multi vitas bene transegerunt, et transigunt, ut sunt cadavera sanctorum, ut pignora, de iis videlicet quae fuerunt in usibus ipsorum".

ever since Christian antiquity there have been authors prepared to express
their reservations, doubts and even rejection with regard to the cult.[2]
Basil the Great († 379) rejected the veneration of the saints and their
relics in the *martyria* as an unessential fringe phenomenon: "As the sun
does not need the lamplight, so also the church of the congregation can do
without the remains of the martyrs. It is sufficient to venerate the name of
Christ, for the Church is His bride, redeemed by His blood. The Church
does not owe her glory to the martyrs but it is the martyrs who owe their
glory to the Church".[3] Not all the Fathers of the Church shared Basil's
view. Did not Vigilantius cause Jerome († c. 420) launch a fierce attack
on him when he qualified the cult of dust and bones, the kissing of the
ashes and the lights placed at martyrs' graves as idolatry and a sullying of
God's holy place?[4]

"Superstition unfortunately remains the shadowy twin of every
religion."[5] Alcuin († 804), in a letter to Bishop Aethelred of Canterbury,
emphasised that following in the footsteps of the saints was better than
carrying the remains of their bones or Gospel texts around the neck,
which he characterised as "Pharisaical superstition". Strict limits should
be placed on such practices.[6] His criticism was shared by others. The
veneration of statues and relics found no favour in the eys of two Spanish
bishops, Claudius of Turin († 877) and Agobard of Lyon († 840).
Agobardus, who has already been mentioned in connection with an attack
similar to Alcuin's made on *fylacteria* , remarked: "Between God and
man there is no other mediator than He who is God and man", through
whom we are directly blessed. Agobardus regarded statues and relics as
concessions made to popular taste, which could very quickly slide into

---

[2]A reasoned overview with bibliography and list of sources can be found in: Guth (1970);
Schreiner (1966); (1966a).

[3]ed. Riedel (1968), 250-251, Canones Basilii, 33; Jungmann (1962), I, 336, n. 32.

[4]See p. 73, 182 and 229.

[5]Guth (1970), 16: "Aberglaube bleibt einmal der heimliche Zwillingsbruder jeder
Religion"; for the historical development of the concept of 'superstition', see: Schmitt
(1988), (1992).

[6]MGH Ep IV, 448, ep. 290: "Multas videbam consuetudines, que fieri non debebant.
Quas tua sollicitudo prohibeat. Nam ligaturas portant, quasi sanctum quid estimantes. Sed
melius est in corde sanctorum imitare exempla, quam in sacculis portare ossa; evangelicas
habere scriptas ammonitiones in mente magis, quam in pittaciolis exaratas in colle
circumferre. Haec est pharisaica superstitio; quibus ipsa veritas improperavit philacteria
sua"; see Riché (1991), 221.

superstition and heresy.[7] His fellow-countryman, Claudius, stated that spiritual worship of God did not rhyme with the veneration of creatures and their relics.[8]

This critical undertone, to be heard throughout the Middle Ages, was against the veneration of lifeless bodies and bones. Peter the Venerable († 1156) was far from agreement with this negative approach and tells of someone who preached in the following words: "What is thew use in venerating bodies whose soul has left them? Where is the profit in hymns and songs of praise addressed to dry bones?" The "venerable" abbot of Cluny had not a good word for the so-called questioner and regarded such godless practices - *impii* - as not being part of the life of the Church.[9] The same thing could also be said regarding the later Cathars, who rejected the cult of relics with the scornful remark that this represented an empty reverence of dead bones.[10]

Usually any gesture of rejection did not encompass the cult of the relics as a whole but was directed against certain parts of it or fringe phenomena such as the theft of relics. And although an act of this kind was often explained away[11] - Ratherius of Verona († 974) regarded the good intention as decisive in the matter - the canonists declared that such

---

[7]PL 104, 202, *Liber de imaginibus sanctorum*, c. 3: "Quod inter Deum et homines nullus sit alius mediator quaerendus, nisi ille qui Deus et homo est"; "verum etiam beatificum bonum non oportere quaeri alios mediatores per quos arbitremur nobis perventionis gradus esse moliendos, quia beatus et pacificus Deus, factus particeps humanitatis nostrae, compendium praebuit participandae divinitatis suae"; c. 17: "Non solum vero divinum deferre honorem, quibus non licet, sed et ambitiose honorare sanctorum memorias ob captandam gloriam popularem, reprehensibile est"; c. 31: "Quicumque aliquam picturam, vel fusilem sive ductilem adorat statuam, non exhibet cultum Deo (...) Agit hoc nimirum versutus et callidus humani generis inimicus, ut sub praetextu honoris sanctorum rursus idola introducat, rursus per diversas effigies adoretur"; c. 33: "Nunc autem error invalescendo tam perspicuus factus est, ut idololatriae vel Anthropomorphitarum haeresi propinquum aut simile sit adorare figmenta, et spem in eis habere. At quae huius erroris causa? Fides de corde ablata, tota fiducia in rebus visibilibus collocata".

[8]MGH Ep IV, 611, ep. 12: "Certe si adorandi fuissent homines, vivi potius quam mortui adorandi esse debuerunt, id est, ubi similitudinem Dei habent, non ubi pecorum, vel, quod verius est, lapidum vel lignorum, vita sensu et ratione carentem"; "Et ideo sciendum est summopere, quia non solum qui visibilia figmenta atque imagines colit, sed etiam quamlibet sive caelestem sive terrenam, sive spiritalem sive corpoream creaturam vice nominis Dei colit et salutem animae suae quae a solo Deo est, ab illis sperat, de illis est, de quibus dicit apostolus: *Et coluerunt et servierunt creaturae potius quam creatori*".

[9]ed. Constable (1954), 265-266, *Sermo cuius supra in honore sancti (Marcelli) illius cuius reliquiae sunt in presenti*: "Sed dicet aliquis: Quid prodest exanimata corpora honorare; quid confert ossa sensu carentia ymnis et laudibus frequentare?"

[10]Borst (1953), 220: "Die Verehrung der Heiligen galt den Katharen als müssige Anbetung toter Knochen. Dennoch haben sie die sterblichen Überreste ihrer verbrannten 'Vollendeten' mit Ehrfurcht gehütet und das Andenken dieser Märtyrer immer hochgehalten".

[11]Schreiner (1966), 163: "Die Quellen nennen es *sancta rapina, sacratissimum furtum, pium et laudabile furtum*".

thievery was sacrilege, even if carried out *devotionis causa*.[12] And like Guibert of Nogent, whose response to the existence of the double relic of the head of John the Baptist was that the saint could have had but one head,[13] Innocent III († 1216) left it to God's wisdom to decide which of the three churches - in Rome, Aachen or Charroux - laying claim the relic really possessed Christ's foreskin. He also entrusted to the same divine wisdom the question as to whether the foreskin had not already risen with Christ.[14] Miraculous Hosts, according to Alexander of Hales († 1245) could be the product of demonic or human deception.[15] John of Montreuil († 1418) called the cult of the 11.000 virgins of St. Ursula in Cologne "old women's" superstition.[16] The 15th-century preacher, Bernardino of Siena, was no less subtle in his remark that 100 cows could not produce as much milk as that of the Virgin Mary in reliquaries all over the world. He advised the faithful: "Go to the high altar when you enter the church and adore Him - the body of Christ - rather than going straight to the statues".[17] The last piece of criticism we can take from Erasmus († 1536) who, while not condemning the cult of the relics, attached greater value to imitating the exemplary life of the saints.[18]

However any such critical noises were merely rare "dissidents" in the mighty choir of the Middle Ages that sang with one voice the praises of the "ancient Christian practice of the cult of the relics".[19] The humanly close saints were, after all, a "temple of the Holy Spirit", "precious" and "radiant with a divine light". They dwelt close to God

---

[12]PL 136, 470, Ratherii episc. *Invectiva de translatione s. Metronis*, c. 13: "Tuorum sane pignorum qui temerare sunt ausi sacrarium, interiorem adire moneo consiliarium, et diligenter ab eo disquirere, quem intentionis in tanto facinore secuti sint impetum; et proprium laxare ipsius discrimine factum".

[13]PL 156, 624.

[14]PL 217, 876-877, *De sacro altaris mysterio*, lib. IV, c. 30: "Quid ergo de circumcisione praeputii vel umbilici praecisione dicetur? An in resurrectione Christi similiter rediit, ad veritatem humanae substantiae? Creditur enim Lateranensi basilica scilicet in Sancto sanctorum conservari. Licet a quibusdam dicatur, quod praeputium Christi fuit in Jerusalem delatum ab angelo, Carolo Magno qui sustulit illud et posuit Aquisgrani. Sed post a Carolo Calvo positum est in ecclesia Salvatoris apud Carosium. Melius est tamen Deo totum committere, quam aliud temere diffinire".

[15]Browe (1938), 151, 162; further examples 163-166.

[16]ed. Martène (1733), I, 1417: 120 "anilitates".

[17]Hefele (1912), 258: "Geh an den Hauptaltar, wenn du in die Kirche kommst. Mache vor ihm deine Anbetung und stelle dich nicht gleich vor die gemalten Bilder".

[18]Erasmi *Opera Omnia, Enchiridion*, 27 sqq.

[19]Guth (1970), 14: "Es ist die urchristliche Tradition des Reliquienkultes".

and provided succour in every emergency.[20] The theoretical debates failed to put off the people, who knew that they had contact with an unworldly reality through the relics. The constantly recurring criticism usually left aside the place of the Eucharist with reference to the relics, as Guibert of Nogent had done, and yet they contained a note of concern that the veneration of the relics would draw attention away from the adoration of God or that deception and superstition would gain the upper hand. In this area, therefore, the critics did not possess a kind of separate 'scientific faith' but rather a different 'concept of belief'. Indeed, the basis underlying the veneration of the relics belonged to the Christian heritage generally accepted: the dwelling of the saints with God as mediators on man's behalf, the integral role of the relics at the consecration of a church and their link with the altar table, on which Christ's death and resurrection were celebrated. The concept of faith held by the critics, however, which had different points of emphasis and took the excesses of veneration with a pinch of salt, was different from the collective belief or that which existed at every level of society, from the lowest to the highest. The criticism of the few we have quoted merely confirms and illuminates the extent to which we can say that there was a mass veneration of the relics, encouraged by monasteries, bishops and popes.[21] In short, "the cult of relics was accepted as a natural integral part of Christian tradition, and even Claudius (of Turin) himself admitted that in his opposition he stood alone".[22]

The excesses and the side effects went there all-embracing way. In addition to the theft of relics already alluded to, we can mention the donation, the exchange and the collection of innumerable relics by private individuals, monasteries, churches and royal courts.[23] There is no phenomenon relative to the Eucharist that parallels these practices: Hosts were seldom traded,[24] were not stoled for veneration elsewhere, nor

---

[20]PL 106, 327-328, Jonae Aurelianensis, *De cultu imaginum*, lib. I: "sed aperi oculos fidei, et vide eos divina virtute et gratia Spiritus sancti amictos, et divini luminis claritate radiantes." "Pretiosa enim sunt martyrum corpora".

[21]Vroom (1981), 125.

[22]Geary (1978), 36-37.

[23]Fichtenau (1952), 84-88; Guth (1970), 8 n. 41; ed. Douie (1985), II, 167.

[24]ed. Hauréau (1890), I, 245, no. 3833: in a 12th-century sermon of unknown origin certain parochial clergy were accused of giving away Hosts for magical ends, though it is not stated that they received any reward for doing so: "Corpus etiam dominicum proh nefandum! tradere dicuntur meretricibus ut cum illo amicos suos deosculentur. O rem execrabilem! Ipsum Christum ad negotium immundum portant". A second dubious source is mentioned by Nussbaum (1979), 114. at the beginning of the 7th century Patriarch Benjamin of Alexandria said in a sermon that two priests "einen ausgedehnten Hostienhandel betrieben

were they the subject of exchange or collection. Their physical form alone excluded any such activities: they were the same shape and size everywhere and, in addition, bread and wine could always be consecrated anew.

Guibert of Nogent not only criticised excesses such as the exaggerated decoration of reliquaries, the deception and the gullibility but also and especially the relics of which it was claimed that they came from the body of Jesus. He believed that the presence of Christ in the Eucharist was sufficient argument to prove the falseness of that category of relics and to remove them from pious practice. Why, he reasoned, would Christ have left something as tangible and visible on the earth if He were to give to us mortal beings his flesh as an everlasting guarantee in *figurata hostia*? In such a case the Host could no longer possess its characteristic of substitute mystery.[25] In this way he undermined the claim made by the monks of St. Medardus at Soissons that they possessed one of Christ's milk teeth. The justification for the Eucharist would simply collapse, according to Guibert, if this were a fact. Other less convincing arguments were that Christ would not be fully risen, that the Bible and tradition say nothing about it and that Mary would not have needed the tooth since she had Jesus around her all day. Despite arguments of this kind such relics did not disappear from common devotion. Let us recall not only the statement made by Innocent II concerning a similar relic but also Bruges, Fécamp and Weingarten, much visited places of pilgrimage where Christ's blood was said to be kept.[26]

Although Guibert relativised the significance of the veneration of relics of the saints with reference to the Eucharist, he was also able to detect, in his dialectic approach, similarities - also pointed out by Brian Stock. The relics are, on the one hand, objective, physical, tangible reminders of the historical saint and invite the faithful to contemplation and repentance. The water of baptism and the wine are also physical signs, *sacramenta*, which call to repentance, penance and closeness to

---

hatten" with the consequence that these Hosts began to bleed. The idea behind the sermon - to warn people off from engaging in such practices - seems to have determined the form.

[25]PL 156, 631, lib. II, c. 2: "Et cum Deum non lateat amorem eorum quae videntur et sensibus adiacent, affectuosius in hominum sedere ac haerere iudicio, nunquam decuit ut qui in eius semper possumus delectari proprie proprio, impenetrabili multis subtilitate fatigemur potius quam iucundemur umbratico. Cum ergo sufficeret tantillum illud residui, si tamen tantillum dici potest, quod toti mundo praeponderat, ad gaudii universalis fideique tenorem, quid Jesus Dominus in figurata rursus hostia carnem suam mortalibus dat obsidem?".

[26]Nagel (1956), 201; Bredero (1994³), 92.

God. The imperishable Eucharist, however, possesses an extra dimension: it is the *manna* that is consumed - while the relics are, of course, not-: "Whoever eats of this bread shall live for ever" (Jn. 6:58).[27]

The distinction, quoted above, which Guibert made between this unique *mysterium* of the faith and something purporting to be a relic of Christ's historical body points us in the direction of a similar difference between the Eucharistic gifts and the relics of the saints. The latter are naturally related to the dead one, they are 'remains' of him that can be directly or indirectly touched. But the Eucharistic gifts are not: they do not bear the same relationship to Jesus' body, they are not 'remains' of it and even, according to Guibert, exclude this. The *corpora* and *pignora* were 'by nature' able to satisfy the longing expressed in devotional practice for concrete evidence. They constituted a tangible, recognisable medium for contact with the saint. The sacred and the immaterial in the world view then prevalent easily linked together. The saint was experienced as still present as if still alive. He stretched out a helping hand to the believer or punished him from another real world, where he too would at some stage receive 'wages according to his work'. Have we not seen how St. Bertulf made knocking noises, Gertrude held out her hand to accept the gifts presented to her and Gaugerik's relics once more occupied his episcopal throne five centuries after his death? This "remarkably strong and for us incomprehensible value placed on relics" is seen by Gerken as an expression of the basic thought processes of the Germanic peoples, which he typifies as *dinglichen Realismus*, targeted on the statically graspable. Bread and wine did not lend themselves in such an obvious way to a similar type of tangible, naturally recognisable contact, since they were 'merely signs' of the presence of the 'All Holy One'.

However it is not beyond our powers of imagination that the realistic belief in the presence of the saints - who gave 'signs of life' when their relics were venerated - lent stimulus to the realistic approach to Christ's presence in the bread and wine. "Just as a bone from the physical remains of a saint, in popular belief, *was* in fact the saint himself, so the Eucharist, believed to be the physical and spiritual presence of Christ, constituted the ultimate, the most precious, of all relics."[28] This way of thinking, in fact, went so far that the historical body of Jesus was

---

[27]PL 156, 632, lib. II, c. 2, par. II, *Quod in sumptione corporis Christi efficiat meritorum inaequalitas*: "ab eo ipso Domino alibi dicitur: *Qui manducat me vivit propter me"*; Stock (1983), 241-259; see also Geiselman (1929); Guth (1970), 72-110; Morris (1972).

[28]Rothkrug (1979), 36; Wegman (1989), 115-116.

identified with the Eucharistic body. The 'presence' was not, however, the primary focus of attention during Christian antiquity and the early Middle Ages, when the merciful and communitarian value of the sacrament was in the foreground. Old testament figures such as 'the Paschal Lamb', 'the Ark of the Covenant' or 'water from the rock' were applied to the Eucharist in the writings of the Fathers of the Church and in the symbolic representations, and were thus given a new significance.[29] The *praesentia realis*, which was to become the stimulus for and the object of the most widespread and most typical of all medieval devotions, finds explicit expression there. When the *patres* speak of the "body and blood of Christ" they are not using a clear or unified idea of what they understand by the expression. Theological debates over fine shades of meaning such as "the historical body of Jesus", "His risen body" or His presence "in a spiritual sense" were unheard of. In a general way it can be said that the Fathers of the Church regarding the Eucharistic event as something containing the total history of salvation, in which Christ was present, offering Himself in the bread and wine. The realisation of that presence was sufficient for the Christians and it was absolutely real - "eine selbstverständliche Gegebenheit".[30] However it was already being depicted in a concrete and realistic way in the didactically coloured stories told to the people. We noted the legend of Gregory in the West, preceded by similar stories in the East. The communicants receiving flesh and blood in the *vitae* of Basil and Arsenius are examples. The theme in the latter's biography can be found as early as the 4th century in the *Apophthegmata Patrum*: an old monk came to consider the Eucharist as no more than a representation of Christ until, in the bread on the altar, he saw the child Jesus being slaughtered by an angel and found himself consuming blood-soaked flesh.[31]

Following that tradition in the early 9th century Paschasius Radbertus identified the real presence with Christ's physical historical body. While the doctrine was accepted by the Cluniacs, who laid the partial foundations for the subsequent devotion to the *humanitas* of Christ, it did in fact entirely escape the attention of popular Eucharistic piety. Until the 11th century the *praesentia realis* was shown no theological interest on a wide scale and, until the 12th century, was never the focus of any sort of mysticism or a devotional form treasured by the people.

---

[29]Corblet (1885-86), I, 1-38.

[30]Nussbaum 1979), 18, 102 -115; Gerken (1973), 73,98.

[31]PG 65, 158, 7; more of such examples are to be found in Nussbaum (1979), 113-115.

The real 'swing', with consequences for devotion, did not occur until Berengar († 1088) launched his denial of the possibility of a substantial change in the Eucharistic offerings.[32] His position, in fact, challenged his 11th- and 12th-century opponents on all fronts to refute his arguments. The theological approach led to the crystallisation of not only the doctrine of transubstantiation but also to the development of the later devotion to the Host because of the great - sometimes extreme - emphasis laid by the authors on the *praesentia* of Christ's physical historical body. "In this respect the importance of Berengar, at least as a catalyst, cannot be overestimated, for the Eucharistic devotion of the thirteenth and later centuries was in many respects merely a cult of the real presence",[33] expressed in new liturgical forms and underlined by Eucharistic miracles.

The period in which the *parallel application in concrete use* - described in chapter III - came into being corresponds very largely with that in which this development took place. It started in Christian antiquity and continued through the early Middle Ages to somewhere around the 13th century; which signalled the breakthrough of the liturgical Eucharistic devotion and the end of the *parallel application*. Though there are still texts referring to the relics, many sources at this time show increased emphasis and more frequent repetition of the respect required by the Eucharist, a plea which was certainly not superfluous following on the Edict of Milan.[34]

The *Didache*, probably written in the 1st century, states: "Let only those who are baptised in the Name of the Lord eat and drink of your Eucharist", and follows this with the following justification: "For the Lord has said of this: Give not that which is holy unto the dogs" (Mtt. 7:6).[35] Hippolytus († 235) - together with Tertullian - not only made a plea that communicants should abstain from other foods before receiving communion but also issued a general warning against reckless behaviour towards the body of Christ.[36] Origen († 254) warned against letting any

---

[32]Devlin (1975), 39: "There is no doubt that he rejected on metaphysical grounds the type of eucharistic presence of Christ associated with the concepts of the real presence and transubstantiation, thus absolutely denying the possibility of any substantial change taking place in the eucharistic elements"; ed. Beekenkamp (1941), 4 sqq., 60-61, 115, 140; Montclos (1971), 142-148.

[33]Devlin (1975), 45.

[34]See p. 53, n. 95; 88-89, n. 47-57; Browe (1936a); Hermans (1983).

[35]*Didache*, IX,5.

[36]SC 11 bis, 120, c. 37, *Quod oportet custodire diligenter eucharistiam*: ["Corpus enim est Chr(ist)i edendum et non contemnendum"]; see also p. 75.

of the Eucharistic bread fall to the ground[37], an admonition later elaborated by Cyril of Jerusalem († 386) in his prescription: the left hand should serve as a throne for the right in order to prevent crumbs falling to the ground. A contemporary of Origen, the strict Novatian, expressed his scandal at someone who, having first attended Sunday Mass, repaired to the theatre carrying the Eucharist amidst a worldly gathering.[38] And Cyril of Alexandria († 444) regarded it as madness to state that the Eucharist would no longer possess its saving power if kept until the following day.[39] The miracle stories referring to the punishment of misuse of the Eucharist during home communion, found in the writings of Cyprian († 258) and of Moschus († 619), as also the prescriptions aimed at preventing abuse bear witness to one and the same concern, a concern which did not disappear in subsequent centuries.[40]

In the 7th century Theodore of Sykeon raised his voice in the East against all those who went off to the bath house immediately after communion, and in the West a list of tariffs of punishment was drawn up for reckless handling of the 'chrismale'. Jacob of Edessa († 708), when the question was put to him, replied that the Eucharist was "food for the soul" and did not belong with the relics in *fylacteria*, beds, nooks and crannies in the wall or vineyard. Around the year 800 there was the introduction of unleavened bread - in order to prevent the formation of crumbs, the Eucharist vessels were consecrated as a sign of greater reverence and the Host was laid directly on the tongue of the communicant. In addition to the increase in reverence, the 8th and 9th centuries saw a growth in resistance to the placing of relics on the altar in close proximity to the Eucharist, and in the 10th century there were the first theophoric processions, while the *viaticum* was carried to the sick and dying wrapped in "snow-white linen". From the 11th century onwards the *columba*, the *scrinium* and the *fenestra* began to appear

---

[37]PG 12, 391, *In exodum homilia XIII*: "Volo vos admonere religionis vestrae exemplis: nostis qui divinis mysteriis interesse consuestis, quomodo cum suscipitis corpus Domini, cum omni cautela et veneratione servatis, ne ex eo parum quid decidat, ne consecrati muneris aliquid dilabatur".

[38]CSEL III, 8, *De Spectaculis*, c. 5: "ausus secum sanctum in lupanar ducere, si potuisset, qui festinans ad spectaculum dimissus e dominico et adhuc gerens secum ut assolet eucharistiam inter corpora obscoena meretricum Christi sanctum corpus infidelis iste circumtulit plus damnationis meritus de itinere quam de spectaculi voluptate".

[39]PG 76, 1075, *Epist. ad Calosyrium*: ["Insaniunt vero, qui haec asserunt: neque enim alteratur Christus, neque sanctum eius corpus immutatur; sed benedictionis vis ac facultas, et vivificans gratia, perpetua in ipso exsistit"].

[40]See p. 33; 76 n. 60, 62; p. 79-80, n. 73-78; p. 81, n. 84; Nussbaum (1979), 107-112, mid-5th-century prescriptions regarding the quality of the bread and wine and related to the materials to be sued for the Eucharistic vessels.

above, on or next to the altar in order to prevent desecration or contamination by vermin, which ended up in 1215 with the Fourth Lateran Council prescribing that the Eucharist be kept under lock and key. These early measures failed to exclude the use of the Eucharist for magical purposes. The complaint made by Peter Damian († 1071) about the smuggling out of the Eucharist for amorous ends was repeated by Caesarius of Heisterbach († c. 1240). According to Herbert of Clairvaux († c. 1180) the Eucharist was taken home secretly for other ends: to increase fertility or for material gain.[41] The *Liber exemplorum*, written for preachers around 1275, gave the following example: advised by a female friend, a woman retained a fragment of the Host in her mouth at the Christmas Mass and took it home with her; she placed it in a wine barrel in order to increase production; however she was unable to obtain a single drop of wine from the barrel and when she attempted to measure the amount of liquid using a measuring rod plunged into the barrel, to her amazement she merely succeeded in pulling out the Host. The warning note in the story is unmistakeable: thus will God punish each and every one who tries to use the Host for material ends.[42]

These complaints, statements and measures, summarised in a 'bird's eye view',show clearly that respect for the Eucharist was explicitly and repeatedly pleaded for and encouraged. But does this now mean that the Eucharist, in the *parallel application in concrete use* with the relics, has always and everywhere been clearly distinguished from the latter and that the relics were always regarded as 'different'? The need to emphasise the respect to be shown to the Eucharist would seem to indicate that little distinction was drawn, a similar conclusion being possible on the basis of the complaints made to Jacob of Edessa about the practice of sewing the Eucharist into articles of clothing as a means of protection at home and while travelling. Was not the Eucharist placed on a corpse next to the relics? And did not the Council of Chelsea in 816 speak about the walling up of the Eucharist in the altar *sepulcrum* "together with the other relics"?

In his opposition to the placing of the relics on the same level as the Eucharist in some forms of devotional practice, the learned man of Edessa used the argument which also underpins most of the texts quoted above:

---

[41]See p. 39, 49, 50, 77, 95, 205 and 322; Nussbaum (1979), n. 13.

[42]Little (1966), 55-56, no. 99; further examples: Gurjewitsch/Gurevich (1987), 290-291; (1988), 195-196.

the Eucharist is intended to be 'received'. It was mainly from this critical point of view that home communion was attacked, that "the Eucharist as travelling companion" was emphasised rather as *viaticum* than as *apotropaeon* and that the Eucharist was recommended as preferable to the relics at the hour of death. Because of its unique property the communion test was a touchstone par excellence for priests, communion of the dead was forbidden and objections were raised to its immuring in the *sepulcrum*. The command to "Take and eat" was at daggers drawn with the fabricated "Hide it away". The chronicler attached greater value to the communion received by Lothair II and Henry V than to the oath on Peter's grave. As soon as *reception of communion* within the 'parallel application in concrete use' determined the situation wholly or partially, the Eucharist assumed a higher profile than did the relics.[43]

But how seldom did the laity receive the sacramental communion? From as early as the 4th century the tendency to communicate began to decline and the minimum requirement, set in 1215, of receiving communion at least once a year at Eastertide turned out all to often to be no more than a pious wish. Far more desires and needs underlay the practices of keeping the Eucharist at home, taking it on journeys, its use at the hour of death, burying it and swearing oaths on it than could be encompassed by reception of the sacrament. And in such cases the aims for which the Eucharist was used coincided with those sought in the application of the relics and the mutual differences seem to have become blurred. Both of them served as *apotropaeon* at home, in the bedroom and on journeys, were used as *res sacrae* in the taking of an oath and, placed in the grave, kept demons at bay after death. In such circumstances the forms of use were identical and it can hardly be expected of the Eucharist that it would be seen as 'the sacrament to be received with reverence': it was simply "the most worthy" of the relics serving personal needs.[44] Gurevich is right to note that everything depended on the way in which the people understood the Eucharist at the moment in question. In the comprehension of the uses to which it was put the Eucharist could be perceived as having the characteristics of a "magical means",[45] something we will return to later. Even as late as during the 11th century

---

[43]See p. 123, 152 and 192.

[44]Geary (1978), 28.

[45]Gurjewitsch/Gurevich (1986), 388: "Wozu müsste man dann den Glauben an die Sakramente zählen? Alles hängt davon ab, wie ihn die einfachen Menschen verstanden. Sie konnten zum Beispiel (und haben es wahscheinlich auch fast immer getan) die Sakramente auf ihre Weise deuten: als eine Art magisches Mittel".

Burchard of Worms saw himself obliged to oppose the practice - which he regarded as superstitious - of burying babies with the symbols of the Eucharist: an *oblata* with a little wine. The oath sworn on the Eucharist was still extant here and there until well into the 14th century.[46]

The types of use in question here experienced within general popular devotion no psychic or religious 'obstacle' such as characterised the later emphasis placed on the realistic presence of Christ as the physical historical body of Jesus. The awareness of the *praesentia realis* in this sense was, in fact, not widely accepted in broad strata of the population until the 12th-13th century, because of such phenomena as the 'elevatio', prepared for long centuries in the gradual clericalisation of the liturgy, monastic spirituality and the preaching against the heretical movements, which also drove the Church to reformulation and proclamation of belief.[47]

The placing of both relics and Eucharist in the altar *sepulcrum* from mid-8th century and the linking of the *humiliatio* with the *clamor* from the 10th century onwards were of a different order: they were liturgical in nature and were carried out inside a church building. The joining of Christ's body with those of the martyrs and saints as *membra Christi* was hidden from the churchgoers' eyes. The practice was outside the limits of day-to-day religious experience and its possible excesses. Perhaps it is precisely because of this that such practices gradually began to disappear after the 13th century. According to the Council of Chelsea the Eucharist could replace the "other relics" in its capacity as an exceptional relic, "the body and blood of our Lord Jesus Christ". The gradual change in the value placed on relics and Eucharist is seen not just in this statement but also in the quantities employed: it was sufficient to use the symbolic number of three for particles of the Host, while the number of relics placed in an altar sometimes appeared to be unlimited.

The linking of *humiliatio* with *clamor* occurred during a period when the first theophoric processions came into being and the clericalisation of the liturgy was pushed even further. In addition the 'parallel application in concrete use', like the communion test, was

---

[46]See p. 128, 146.

[47]Devlin (1975), 155-171, heretical movements in Orleans, Arras, Liège and Monteforte, to the south of Turin, around 1025 which implicitly or explicitly contained a denial of the praesentia realis; the Donatists including Tanchelm († 1115), Petrus Bruys († 1130); around 1150 in places such as Soissons, Cologne, Trier, Toulouse; in the late 12th century: Waldenses and Albigenses.

realised in the course of the Mass. The place occupied by the Eucharist here is clearly distinguished from that of the relics. The humiliating gestures were directed exclusively at the latter and not towards the Eucharist. Sometimes the *humiliatio* was extended for a considerable time after the Mass and was thereby designed to raise the pressure on the saints in an atmosphere of punishment and reprisal. On this point there was no similarity with treatment of the Eucharist. Any similarity was even further removed in the excesses of the unlettered that could occur during a separate *humiliatio*, excesses which, it should be pointed out, looked back on the same basic notion as had been present with the monks, namely one of reciprocity. Those present expected something back from the holy *patronus* in return for the honours paid. The world of religious imagination and the forms adopted by the unlettered were in this case once again somewhat different from those of the monks.[48] One example of this was the woman who used an altar cloth to beat the shrine of St. Benedict of Fleury because the saint had failed to prevent her being robbed.[49] The verger known as Christianus reacted in a similarly disturbed manner when bangles had been stolen from the shrine. He struck it with a stick, accused Benedict of falling asleep and threatened never to light another candle if the saint failed to restore the jewellery to its place.[50] In another tale referring to Saint-Calais-sur-Aille similar scenes are painted. A number of serfs who had been exploited by their landlord flung themselves on the ground, praying and shrieking, in front of the grave of St. Calais. Then two of them tugged off the altar cloth and used it to strike the altar containing the relics of the saint, shouting the while: "Why do you not defend us and free us from our enemy?"[51] We have encountered no sources relating such exceptional behaviour towards

---

[48]Jong de (1986), 27.

[49]ed. Certain (1968), 283, *Miracula s. Benedicti*, lib. VIII, c. 6: "Denique cuidam mulierculae aliquid abstulerat, quae currens ad ecclesiam, sublatisque quibus operiebatur lineis, altare diutissime flagris cecidit, increpans quasi praesentem patrem Benedictum his verbis: Benedicte vetustissime, piger, lethargice, quid agis? ut quid dormitas?"

[50]ibid. 59, lib. I, c. 26: "O, sancte Benedicte, ut quid pigrescendo dormitas? (...) Crede mihi si armillas tuas non restituerint mihi, nec unam tibi candelam accendam. Haec et alia multa in hunc comminans modum, simulque baculo petram ante sepulcrum positam percutiens tristis abscessit".

[51]AASS OSB I, 650-651, *Miracula s. Carilefi ad ipsius sepulcrum facta*: "Verum illi cum orationibus diutius incubuissent, lacrymosos addentes gemitus, surgunt altari nudato a duobus, qui gemitus forte constiterant lateribus, fasces virgarum manibus tenentes, altare sacrum verberare coeperunt simul clamantes, cur nos, Domine, non defendis piissime? cur hic obdormiscens nostri oblivisceris? cur famulos tui iuris ab hoste non liberas immanissimo?"

the Host, with the exception of the acts of desecration of which Jews were accused.

In contrast to the joint enclosure of relics and Eucharist in the altar *sepulcrum*, the joining of the *humiliatio* with the *clamor* in the liturgy shows a clear subordinate role accorded to the relics with reference to the Eucharist. The entire action of adoration does, in fact, focus exclusively on the consecrated Host held in the kneeling celebrant's hands. The monks prayed not *to* but *with* the saints, present in the relics spread out before them on the church floor. Situated between the altar and the community, they had become allies and mediators. The monks and saints together, united in the same posture of humiliation, directed their attention to the untouchable 'relic', Christ himself, raised high above the practices of the *humiliatio*.

By referring above to the distinction between the liturgical *clamor* and the *humiliatio* performed by the monks on the one hand, and the physical punishment meted out to the saints by the serfs on the other, we touched on an aspect that has to do with current discussions on the popular, 'culture folklorique', and the official-ecclesiastical, 'culture cléricale' or 'savante' in the Middle Ages, two concepts brought into the world by Jacques Le Goff and Jean-Claude Schmitt. At the risk of simplification, in can be stated in brief that the first is of an ambiguous nature, tied to traditional customs, the world of oral tradition and of the *illiterati*, who ended up no longer understanding Latin. The second is the rational culture of the *literati,* the writing and the Latin language. The gap between these two is said to have increased between the 5th and 8th century, when intellectual culture gradually became the exclusive property of the Church, based on the aristocratic inheritance handed down by Greece and Rome. It was this culture that possessed the greatest means of power, driving the 'culture folklorique' onto the defensive and making of it a subculture. Seen from this point of view, a gulf widened between the clerics and the unlettered lay people, a gulf which turned from 'barrier' to 'blockage' in the high Middle Ages.

A great deal of criticism has been voiced of this supposed opposition, with its turning point in the 12th century, when it is said that not only did the two once again start to approach one another but that it is possible to speak of a new effort at definition and delineation. John van Engen, for instance, writes as follows: "Gregory of Tours described peasants and bishops alike attempting to gain access to the holy power of relics; and Carolingian reliquary shrines attracted the veneration of learned monks and bishops as well as lords and peasants". He suggests that there had been no clerical elite for some considerable time in large areas and for that reason alone such an elite could not have functioned as an instrument of "oppression", let alone the question of whether it can be said that there was a homogenous group. He also says that the presence of "residues of peasant religious folklore" and the Church's use of a language the people did not understand is somewhat different from arguing "that the people had a wholly distinct religious culture, not somehow amalgamated into Christian practice". He pleads for the "religious man" to be taken seriously, for the dynamic of the Middle Ages to be kept in mind and for closer attention to be paid to the elements of belief that were or were not held in common.[52]

M. Lauwers regards most of what Van Engen says to have already been recognised by the authors at whom the criticism is directed, but cannot bring himself to disagree with Van Engen's objection that the facts offered are too exceptional and too isolated within the whole body of extant sources.[53]

At the same time, others including Mayke de Jong regard the 'opposition' alluded to a more useful "heuristic tool" in studying religious practice after approximately 1150 but not prior to that date. Indeed, from the middle of the 12th century the Church grew in power and influence, leading to an increase in the number of ecclesiastical ordinances in many areas of life.[54]

With reference to the present study the following are illustrative: the synodal decrees issued in Paris by Eudes of Sully (1208) regarding the moment of the *elevatio*, the prescription issued by the Fourth Lateran Council making confession and communion obligatory at Easter as also the regulations regarding the exposition of relics and the limiting of trial by ordeal, the mid-13th-century growth in ecclesiastical opposition to the private ownership of relics, against the Host as 'travelling companion', against the cementing up of particles of the Host in the altar grave and the test by communion, and the forbidding of the *humiliatio* by the Second Council of Lyon in 1274.[55]

De Jong quotes texts in support of her thesis that before 1150, and therefore during the first half of the Middle Ages, the conceptual universes of clergy and lay people show far more similarities that presumed by the authors in question - indeed, that the rise of the

---

[52]Engen v. (1986), 528 sqq.; esp. p. 530, 532, 544.

[53]Lauwers (1987), 255, 257.

[54]Jong de (1986), esp. p. 20, 24.

[55]See p. 50, 53, 55, 70, 99, 134, 158, 165 and 191.

sacerdotal class and of the phenomena of blockage were partly encourage by the *illiterati* as a means of setting their own limits to the sacred.

Though we have approached the sources from another angle, we nonetheless maintain the impression that the picture as described is confirmed by *parallel application in concrete use*. It is a fact that little distinction was made between lay people and clerics with regard to the reservation of the Eucharistic bread at home, taking it on journeys, finding consolation in it at the hour of death or having it placed in the grave. This applies even more strongly to the relics than for the Eucharist, which gradually became more and more the exclusive sacral domain of the priest. We have looked at such things as the gradual decrease of communion at home for lay people, the taking of the Eucharist on journeys as *viaticum* by priests and no longer by the laity as also the custom of being buried with the Eucharist, which ended up as an incidental privilege granted to bishops. Here the sacral, accepted in both cultures and in which the consecrating power of the priest - and thus the *praesentia realis* - plays a dominant role, creates specific expectations and conditions with reference to the priest. Finally, a significant commentary on this is the report given by Bruno of Trier where, for the same act, the priest has to purify himself by the communion test and the layman by an oath taken on the relics.[56]

It should also be noted that Le Goff too points to a certain degree of "accueil" granted the 'culture folklorique' by the 'culture cléricale', partly because of the internal structure common to both, under which he includes such things as: the mingling of the earthly and the heavenly, of the material and the spiritual. To clarify this he quotes the cult of the relics and the use of phylacteries. However he regards as essential the "refusal" - "*refus*" - of the culture folklorique by the culture ecclésiastique.[57]

The *clamor* and the *humiliatio* bring us to still yet another subject: the extent to which the people participated in the liturgy or not. The *clamor* raised to the Lord in the Eucharist in the midst of the humiliated relics originated as a ceremony reserved exclusively to monks. The faithful, to the extent that they participated and communicated within the liturgy, were forced into an outwardly passive attitude by the clericalisation of the liturgy from the middle of the 9th century onwards. We have already

---

[56]See p. 156.
[57]Le Goff (1977), 229.

noted how the mass of the faithful also failed to be given a active role in the Good Friday *depositio* and the Easter Sunday *elevatio*, both introduced at a later stage. But by way of contrast the churchgoing public had an active part in the veneration of the Cross and the Palm Sunday procession. People regarded the processions, of which the relics were important elements, as familiar happenings on feasts and Rogation Days, on the occasion of translations, during epidemics, and during natural and man-made disasters. Happenings such as these gave the people the opportunity to escape from their liturgical isolation, in which they had been placed during the *mysterium depopulatum*, until the introduction of the 'elevatio' in the 12th-13th century, with its clouds of incense and many candles and the tolling of bells provided a less infrequent diversion. And so the people were given an opportunity, within the Mass, to participate to some extent: the sight of and reverence paid to the raised up Host. The liturgical show surrounding the 'elevatio' encouraged the faithful to devout reverence, which was accompanied by visions reported in no few *vitae*, such as that of Mary of Oignies († 1213), Juliana of Cornillon († 1258),[58] Ida of Louvain († 1260) and of many Beguines and Cistercian nuns.[59]

The introduction of the feast of Corpus Christi in 1264 can be regarded as an almost essential climax to this devotional development. It subsequently became a means of promoting frequent *visits to the Blessed Sacrament* and the introduction of the *procession*, the *exposition* and the *blessing with the Eucharist*. The retreat of the relics to the advantage of the Eucharist, as had already occurred in the *clamor*, once more appeared centre stage within these transpositional forms, described in chapter IV. The reason is that - just as at the 'elevatio' - the *latria* - adoration - belonging to God alone became the prime goal. The link between *latria* and the visit to the Blessed Sacrament was made in the *Ancrene Riwle*, which required the sisters to repeat during the 'elevatio' the prayers recited during the morning visit to the reserved Sacrament. When the time came they were to stand up and begin the prayer to the raised Host as follows: "Behold the salvation of the world. The Word of the Father, a true sacrifice, living flesh, the whole Godhead, true Man." Falling to their knees they repeated the greetings of the morning: "Hail, cause of

---

[58]AASS 23 iun. IV, 661, *Vita b. Mariae Oigniacensis*, n. 92: "et plerumque sub pueri specie, sub mellis sapore, cum aromatum odore (...) Dominum suum feliciter admittebat"; 660, n. 91: "puerum cum maxime claritate circa pyxidem, in qua ponitur corpus Christi, videbat"; AASS 5 april. I, 446-455, *Vita Julianae virg.* c. 2-5.

[59]See p. 58, 248.

our creation".[60] The most perfect expression of the viewing of the Eucharist was the procession, in which the four transpositional forms coincided: the procession itself, the blessing, the exposition and - by way of greeting - the visit to the Blessed Sacrament in the church building itself, something so infrequently performed by the people of the Middle Ages. But during this manifestation the faithful greeted and adored the exposed Host in the open air at the stations. And the blessing, given before the procession continued on its way as a continuous exposition, was given as the crowd knelt in adoration before the "Sacrament of sacraments".[61]

The procession of the Blessed Sacrament was an occasion for the entire local community. It enjoyed a great deal of liturgical freedom, "left to the devotion of priests and people" motivated by "divine inspiration" by the synods of Sens and Paris in 1320 and 1323 respectively.[62] Episcopal permission was required for the procession to be held on the day of the octave rather than on the feast day itself. There were no generally applicable rubrics for the procession, which meant that its nature and form could differ according to local tradition. The Corpus Christi fraternities, which "had the pretension of themselves representing the activities of all others"[63] from the 15th-16th century onwards, contributed to the organisation as did the committees set up for this purpose. An instance of this is the initiative taken by the municipal authorities of Barcelona in 1424 by which they entrusted responsibility for the procession to a number of canons, four prominent citizens and representatives of the guilds. The determining of the order in which participants walked was not without some measure of competition: one's place in the procession was significant for the prominence accorded to the participant in the community. Of the guild members, the bakers enjoyed the greatest prominence, and it was the clerics who walked nearest to the Blessed Sacrament, with or without the relics which had now been pushed into the wings. The carrying of the baldachin was reserved to kings, counts, town councillors or other high functionaries. The predilection

---

[60]ed. Salu (1955), 13; see p. 245.

[61]Monumenta Boica, 12 (1775), 446: "ob reverentiam sacramenti sacramentorum".

[62]Mansi XXV, 649: "Circa vero processionem sollemnem quae dicta quinta feria fit a clero et a populo in delatione dicti sacramenti his diebus, cum quodammodo divina inspiratione introducta videatur, nihil quoad praesens iniungimus, devotioni cleri et populi relinquentes"; ibid. 727.

[63]Browe (1933), 107-108; (1936), 53-54; Le Bras (1956), 436; Matern (1962), 71-75 in 1317 in Pamplona the first Blessed Sacrament brotherhood in Spain; Zika (1988), 42 n. 53 information regarding 15th-century Germany; see also Rubin (1991), 232 sqq.

shown in the organisation of processions meant that such events assimilated elements taken from popular and reliquary processions, so that the whole event became a veritable pageant, and included statues and tableaux. The city archive of Ingolstadt reports more than thirty-three in the procession held in 1507, including the banishing from paradise, the burial of Christ and the Day of Judgement.[64] In southern countries whole streets were transformed into gigantic, shady canopies, biblical tableaux were acted or figured on 'floats', giants and demons walked by setting off fireworks, while religious dances accompanied the procession to the music of the flute, the violin or the drum.[65]

Although these developments gave rise to deviations and abuse, the central focus of the procession, in which the people were able to function as 'liturgs' in a wide variety of ways, remained the Host in the monstrance: flowers were strewn before it, bells were rung and incense burned. The Host was not just an 'object' of veneration and adoration but was also 'subject', a *virtus* of mercy, of spiritual and material favours. It was from the Host that Christ joined in a spiritual manner with the spectator in the *manducatio spiritualis*, but it is understandable that in addition prayers were said to ensure earthly security - indeed, that the people saw in the Host the warranty of their own welfare, both spiritual and bodily, in the future. Who can unravel what a believer thinks and what a thinker believes? The Eucharist was exposed in its capacity as source of adoration and power during Mass, on the octave of Corpus Christi and on many other days. The viewing of the Eucharist, fed by devotion and expectations, assumed such an importance around the 1400 that some theologians began to show concern. Henry of Hessen († 1397), former chancellor of the University of Paris, recalled the words spoken by Jesus: "Blessed are they that have not seen and yet have believed" (Jn. 20:29). Which convinced him that it was better for some individuals not to see the Host rather than to do so, since they would be more inclined to become bogged down in externals without any trace of internal conversion.[66] Jean Gerson († 1429) was no less critical, with his

---

[64]Mitterwieser (1930), 13; 19-20.

[65]Matern (1962), 79, 148, 162-166, 229, 231 and passim; Sengspiel (1977).

[66]Dumoutet (1926), 29, n. 3: *Secreta Sacerdotum*: "si sacramentum oculi fidei et pure mentis conscientia intus non cernunt, modicum profuerit foris quod viderunt".

conclusion that: "It is not what our bodily eyes see but what the eyes of our heart see that is our God".[67]

In this way the authors were attempting to contradict the material favours that John Mirk had attached to the sight of the Eucharist in his instruction to the parochial clergy.[68] Their efforts were in vain: a few decades later in northern Italy Bernardinus de Bustis († 1500) included Mirk's instructions in his collection of sermons. The *Rosarium sermonum predicabilium*, as he called it, contains a homily on the twelve fruits of the Mass, the 10th of which states that anyone who has seen Christ will not become blind on the day in question and the 12th guarantees the departure of the devil from his heart as well as sufficient to eat. Anonymous 15th-century sources in from Germany and France speak in the same terms.[69] The struggle to preserve an exposed and insecure existence, which is evident from such sources, must have been the inspiration for carrying the Blessed Sacrament past the growing crops, the farm animals and the buildings and to trust in the Sacrament's almighty power to protect the owners from lightning and other natural disasters. Any opposition to such practices from the 'university' ecclesiastical side was ineffective: once the Host in its transposed forms of veneration had been promoted over the relics as the venerated "Son of the living God", it was accorded additional and exceptional material powers of protection.[70]

Within the context of this form of veneration the unique significance of the Host was usually safeguarded and distinguished from that accorded to the relics - it was recommended that only one monstrance be carried per procession - since the people were so thoroughly soaked in the conviction of Christ's presence under the appearance of bread: "the Word of the Father, the true Man". The transition to 'levelling' was swifter, where it was no longer the veneration as expressed in the *Adoro te* that was at the forefront but the use of the Host against fire, disease and storm: the Host

---

[67]*Opera Omnia.* III, pars II, 609, *De exercitiis devotorum simplicium (...) Qualiter et quare orandum sit spiritu, sine imaginibus:* "id quod oculis corporis nobis representat non est deus noster, sed quod oculis cordis est dominus deus noster. Hoc ergo cogitate et hoc vos figite".

[68]See p. 59.

[69]Franz (1902), 57-58, 10: "illo die quo quis videt corpus Christi lumen oculorum conservatur, et quod pro illo tempore, quo quis audit missam, non senescit"; 12: "In illa hora visionis corporis Christi diabolus exit (e corde) cuiuslibet peccatoris devote illud aspicientis. Et qui missam integre et devote audierit, non deficiet sibi in illo die cibus corpori necessarius"; ibid. 103; Dumoutet (1926), 31.

[70]See p. 58 and 301.

was on such occasions much more easily seen as a relic with exceptional *similar miraculous powers*, just as it appeared in certain Eucharistic miracle stories from around 110, emitting light signals or meting out punishment. When, in the process of the Eucharist gaining its independence, the 'elevatio' had turned the Host into the focus of the Mass liturgy, the number of Eucharistic miracles increased and, with them, the tendency to use the Host outside the confines of the Mass against such emergencies as fire and disease.

More often and more general than the use against fire was the confidence placed in the Host during exorcisms, the driving out of a devil from an individual, just as the weather blessing was intended to short circuit the powers of the demons active in the natural world. The demon, scorned as the dragon with the weak tail in the *rogationes*, in caricatures and in parodies, was also feared in parables and plays, and was regarded to be as present on earth as are his opposite numbers, Christ and His saints. In *De remediis peccatorum*, written in the closing years of the 8th century, everyone was admonished to do everything in their power to ensure that no-one died unbaptised and thereby fall prey to the evil spirit. The *viaticum* was always ready at hand in sacristy or church to be used against the devil at the hour of death. Satan's fear of Christ in the Eucharist is expressed in the story of Radulfus Niger, in which the devil is said to have tempted a woman to seize the Host from the mouth of the dead pope Urban III. The sly devil appeared from his hellish dwelling under appearances that were sometimes dazzling in their numbers, disguises ranging from horned monkey-like creatures to snakes, dogs, cats or even as a human being. He was the tempter par excellence and the despot of evil, the opposite pole to God's chosen saints.[71] The tooth that the pilgrim planned to take from Patricia's body was intended to be carried as a means of protection against Satan. In order that he be given no opportunity to twist the results of the trial by ordeal to his own wicked ends, the oath of purgation was sworn on the relics before the trial began. In the legends the devil was always conquered by the saints. One hair from the head of Hildegard of Bingen was said to have caused the demon to seethe.[72]

From the 12th century onwards it is no longer only the saints (with his relics) in the legends and *vitae* who resists the demonic powers but people are depicted as also seeking safety in the power of the Host. Did

---

[71]Gurjewitsch/Gurevich (1987); 274-289; (1988), 184-194.

[72]See p. 83 , 124 and 313.

not St. Walthenius († 1159) drive off the devil using the Eucharist?[73] Peter Martyr († 1252) did the same, according to his biographer: he took the pyx out from under his cloak and rendered a heretic incapable of calling up deceitful visions with the aid of the devil in a church.[74] The story is a variant on similar legends which circulated among German and Spanish Cistercians from around 1200. As in many Eucharistic miracles the Host proved its *virtus* against heretics who were assumed to be in league with the devil. We have already mentioned the account, described in the chronicle of John of Winterthur, of the mendicant monk's fight with the devil in Brandenburg: it too fits into this genre.[75]

The stories of the miracles that were handed down can only have served to reinforce the tendency to use the Host against the demons in cases of possession and during storms. In the formulae employed in the weather blessing they are called "satanic angels", "satanic demons" or "the devil and all his - fallen - angels".[76] Hence the bad reception given to the efforts of Thomas Haselbach who sharply attacked the 'superstitious' weather blessing. The practical-minded village clergy set his words aside, knowing only too well how fearful were their parishioners for their goods and chattels and that they "most certainly expected" the protection afforded "by the Sacrament". In the ceremony of exorcism it was, once again, the devil who had to be driven out. If the saints were capable of delivering a knock-out blow to Satan by means of their relics, how much more so could this not be expected of the Lord, who Himself drove out demons during His life and was now present in the Host, which was laid on the possessed by persistency?[77] Little or no distinction was any longer made between relic and Eucharist in the

---

[73]See p. 245.

[74]AASS 29 april. 694 C, *Vita s. Petri mart.* c. III,27: "Tunc b. Petrus pyxidem in qua Christi posuerat corpus, quam sub cappa detulerat, protulit et ipsam aperiens, dixit ei: si es vero mater Dei, adora hunc filium tuum. Ad huius vocem et corporis Christi ostentatione omnis illa phantastica visio disparuit, cum strepitu terribili et foerore, pariesque ecclesiae malignantium a summo usque deorsum scissus est".

[75]See p. 96; MGH SS XXX,1, 570: *Chronica Reinhardsbrunnensis*, a. 1206: "Effigies autem querens quid Johannis teneret sub clamide, cepit a fulgore pristino paulatim nigrescere et terrorem quem potuit ipsi Johanni ingerere, et nisi prius quod teneat sub clamide abiceret, se non posse secretorum fieri participem constanter asseverabat. Hiis dictis ipsa ymago evanescendo disparuit"; XXIII, 931: *Chronica Albrici Monachi Trium Fontium*, a. 1233: "Et ultra Coloniam fuit quedam synagoga hereticorum, ubi responsa dabat ymago Luciferi, sed ubi catholicus clericus advenit et pixidem cum corpore Domini de sinu suo protulerit, pestifera ymago corruit".

[76]Franz (1909), II, 75: "angeli satanae"; 77: "ut diabolum et omnes angelos eius..repellas"; 82: "demones satane".

[77]ibid. 116; Browe (1938), 60.

geographically circumscribed use of both against fire, with the basic belief in the miraculous power itself and the desired material effect.

The use of the Eucharist at home, during the burial service, while travelling, at oath-taking and during the ceremony of entombment in the altar *sepulcrum* was generally a thing of the past - or even the distant past - by the 13th century. The respect owed to the Sacrament and the function accorded to it by Christ - as a food - were usually advanced as arguments by the ecclesiastical critics. It is understandable that no new 'types of concrete use' of this sort developed as regards the Eucharist because of the collective change that took place in the people in the 14th and 15th centuries relative to Christ's presence in the Eucharist and the accompanying liturgical and personal 'forms of reverence'. In the devotional enthusiasm of the viewing and adoring of the Eucharist at the 'elevatio', during the procession and at the exposition and blessing was the expression of belief in the *praesentia realis* , which was underpinned by the popularised spirituality of the *imitatio Christi* and the related devotion to His suffering.[78] The Man of Sorrows, also sometimes called the *Imago Pietatis*, had a Eucharistic sacrificial character. The "Pie Jezu" was seen on Eucharistic containers, tabernacle doors and monstrances.[79] The emphasis on the secrets of the Humanity of the Lord gave rise to the veneration paid to His 'Name', His crib and His cross. The frequent occurrence of blood miracles, of which there were fewer than ten before 1150, can be partly explained by these devotions. In addition to being a 'translation' of a theological aspect - the full presence under each species - for the faithful and a warning against doubt and heresy, in view of their numbers they must also have been answering a need: the revelation of the Jesus truly present. Against the background of this devotion, directed towards the God-Man present in the Eucharist, it is understandable that it was mostly the corporal, the paten or the ablution water that was used, rather than the 'sacred' Host, to relieve human needs.

Did the Host's miraculous power, described in parallel with the relic miracles, undergo any other pragmatic elaboration than in the weather blessing, during a fire and exorcism, which would have been in a form performed by a priest? The miracles show that from the end of the 11th century various short cuts must have been found for the use of the Host by private individuals for what were called 'magical' end and 'witchcraft', deviations that are punished in the stories. The examples

---

[78]Herwaarden v. (1982).

[79]Bauerreis (1931), 5.

found there were obviously needed as a deterrent. Other facts too demonstrate that misuse of the Eucharist was not infrequent. The prescription of the Fourth Lateran Council (1215) stating that the Eucharist must be kept safely locked up had to be repeated ad nauseam by the western European synods. In an article on the subject[80] Browe mentions eight dioceses where, around the year 1300, the culprit committing such an offence was threatened with excommunication. German, French and north Italian bishops withdrew the offence from the confessional and stated their desire to deal with it personally. Many a penitential warns the parochial to question the penitent about the sin of *sortilegium*, against which the late 11th-century writers repeatedly raised their condemnatory voices - and this continued until the end of the Middle Ages. 'Magical' use, to the extent that it occurred - to win someone's love, to improve the harvest, as had been usual with the relics - turned the Host itself into a magician's tool.[81]

Could we, therefore, say that there was a similar 'equal footage' where the miraculous Host and the relics were concerned? The forms of reverence - visits, exposition, procession and blessing - concord, but as far as the 'Sacrament of Miracle' was concerned the 'Eucharistic miracle' played a special part, which meant that It was not only reverenced by pilgrims but also prayed to. And how did a miraculous Host relate to a normal day-to-day Host consecrated in the course of the Mass? Understandably enough, within theological discourse the increasing devotion to the miraculous, often 'bleeding' Host gave rise to critical questions.

In the first place, the position of a miraculous Host was ambivalent. While the Host consecrated daily served for an 'elevatio' lasting an instant and for spiritual food, the miraculous Host did not have the latter function and the "showing" in the form of an 'elevatio' did not take place during the Mass. The miraculous Host was, however, exposed and carried about in a procession. Furthermore, the Host consecrated daily during the Mass was not tied to place or time - the consecration could take place in any church any day of the week - while in the case of the miraculous Host the miracle was a fact determined by date and place, inseparably bound to the place of pilgrimage. On the one hand the miraculous Hosts had therefore turned into relics, reverenced and borne in procession as *summae*

---

[80]Browe (1930); Habiger-Tuczay (1992), 87-91.

[81]See e.g. p. 77 and 88-89.

reliquiae and, on the other, they were still bound up with the Eucharistic context from which they had sprung.

This gave rise to the question of the theological value of a Host of this kind, spotted with red. We have, indeed, already referred to Thomas Aquinas' opinion that the risen Lord was only present in heaven and that we could not, therefore, speak of the presence of Christ's bodily blood.[82]

In the 15th century Nicholas of Cusa showed his agreement with this point of view and turned against the reverence paid to such Hosts in a letter addressed to the German bishops and the whole of the clergy.[83] With his own eyes he had seen the faithful gathering in droves to pay honour to the precious blood of the Lord which they regarded as being present in this type of Host. This same belief is put into words in the litany used at Wilsnack: "Stand by me, o holy blood, free me" and the prayer said in 1944 in the parish church of Boxmeer destroyed in war, where a blood-stained corporal was involved: "Komt menschen wyt en veer, En valt dyn Heer te voet, Gy siet hier te Boxmeer, Nog druppels van zyn bloet" (Come, people, from far and near and fall on your knees before the Lord: here in Boxmeer you see drops of His blood).[84]

Within this sort of context the cardinal legate took measures against such practices at the synods held in Mainz in 1451 and in Cologne in 1452. In a sermon preached in Haarlem he encouraged the faithful to honour the Host in their own parish church and not to set off on pilgrimage to Wilsnack.[85] This and other pilgrimages, indeed, had the tendency to set the value of the Host in the home church at a lower level than the Host conserved in the places of pilgrimage. In addition there was the threat of adoration (*latria*), when the appearance of bread - and thus the *praesentia realis* - had disappeared, with the result that a compromise was sought: either retain the miraculous Host side by side with a recently consecrated Host in a double *lunula* or even replace the former with the latter.[86]

---

[82]See p. 49.

[83]Browe (1938), 165-166.

[84]Browe (1938), 190; Schannat-Harzheim V, 35 (Synod of Maagdenburg, 1412): "Adiuva me, sacer sanguis" vel "sacer sanguis me liberet".

[85]AAU 31 (1906) 88; 38 (1912) 22; Browe (1929d), 315-316

[86]See p. 290.

Just as the weather blessing with the Blessed Sacrament had its supporters and opponents,[87] there were also theologians who sided with the view expressed by Nicholas of Cusa - and therefore with that of Thomas Aquinas - but there was no lack of those taking the opposing view. Duns Scotus and his followers, for instance, defended a bodily presence of Christ in the miraculous Host.[88]

Charles Zika has investigated the 15th-century opinions on this subject in parts of Germany. He paid particular attention to the miraculous Hosts of Wilsnack. His research shows that the higher clergy of the time placed little value on the expressions of piety paid to the miraculous Hosts. This resistance was not based only on the theological grounds mentioned above but are believed to have had a pragmatic background: there was a desire to reinforce the position of the local priest-celebrant in whose hands the Host was consecrated daily. Opposition to the pilgrimages to miraculous Hosts served to strengthen the local ecclesiastical hold on the faithful. The encouraging of local processions of the Blessed Sacrament could also be linked with this.[89]

Whatever the case, the debates of the time between theologians and church leaders betray a way of thinking quite different from the practices engaged in by broad layers of the population, where the parochial clergy could have played a bridging role. The priest who gave the weather blessing, standing in front of the church door or riding on horseback past the fields, is an example. Even if he was familiar with ecclesiastical "elite" thought, he still had to take account of the beliefs and needs of his people. The same tension can be detected in the use of the Eucharist to fight fire or sickness.[90]

***

The above considerations are designed to seek an answer containing some nuances to the question of the extent to which the Eucharist set itself apart from the relics in its 'uniqueness' in the three forms of relationship we

---

[87]See p. 300 sqq.

[88]Browe (1938), 185-187; Caspers (1992), 242-243.

[89]Zika (1988), Caspers (1992), 235 sqq. The link made by Zika between the theological objections and efforts on the part of the Church to establish its influence and control requires further study which, obviously, should not be influenced by current ecclesiastical power structures.

[90] See p. 300 sqq, p. 336 sqq, p. 341 sqq; Vovelle (1988), 126-141: "*Cultural intermediaries*" or "*Les intermédiaires culturels*", the title of a contribution to a congress of the same name held in June 1980 in Aix-en-Provence.

have defined. In summary the answer would seem to be: in the case of parallel applications under the earliest forms the Host was generally seen as a relic unless its use emphasised its reception, but in the forms of reverence practised the relic was pushed into the background by the Host when it was a question of the adoration due only to Him who is Son of God become Man. In addition the Host also functioned as a centre of sacred power as the relic previously had done when material favours were being asked for, as in the case of the *rogationes*. In many accounts of miracles the Host showed a miraculous power which ran parallel to that of the relics in presentation, effect and application. The 'parallel application in concrete use' in cases of sickness or fire occurred in a limited fashion because of a distancing, already alluded to, from the relics, caused by *latria* and the realisation of the human *praesentia realis*. The clarification of the real presence aimed at in the miracles probably only appealed to the people to the extent that it really was a question of Christ's real presence.

To conclude: gradually, as the bread and the wine gained their independence from the liturgical context, the people received the sacramental communion less and less frequently. The enthusiasm shown for the Eucharist at the 'elevatio' within the framework of the Mass and the other forms of reverence outside the Eucharistic liturgy brought about no change in this. On the contrary: complaints about the infrequency of sacramental communion showed no diminution, and 'spiritual' communion became a habit for the people, providing them with the opportunity to unite spiritually with Christ without any risk of "eating and drinking unworthily to their own condemnation". The miracles would seem to have increased this fear by the warning discounted in them, just as some holy women, led by the light emitted by the Host, stated that they could detect whether or not the communicant was in a fit state. The forms of application and reverence involving the Host outside the Mass turned it into something 'un-sacramental'. The tracts, the chronicles, the *vitae* and the examples all reveal in the clear light of day the extent to which the Host functioned as a substitute relic in the altar grave, as *apotropaeon*, as *res sacra*, as miraculous Host and as body of Christ carried in procession and adored, and thus lost its sacramental role within the context of the Mass, its role of mercy-giver, of unifying factor throughout the whole congregation in the celebration of salvation and communion, in thanksgiving and eschatological expectation.

SUMMARY

The reverence of the mortal remains of the martyrs dates from the second century. Since the Edict of Milan in 313 permanent altars were built above the graves of saints in *martyria*, small buildings which expanded into mortuary basilicas. Among the other churches as well there was a wish to show the connection between the altar and the martyrs. The problem of the shortage of relics was solved by moving the mortal remains (*corpora*) to the place (*translatio*) or by dividing them (*dismembratio*), in the East from the 4th century. In the West originally, for lack of corporal relics, the people contended themselves with indirect relics (everything that had been in contact with the martyr, confessor or his grave). In the 7th and 8th century, the *translatio* no longer belonged to the exception, with the result that the *corpora* were scattered over the entire Frankish Empire. The exhumations (*elevationes*) of the relics from their graves, commonly occurred continuing into the 12th century and (as told in the descriptions of them) was accompanied by emotions and miracles. The purpose of the *elevatio* was to transport the relics to other places or to place them locally in a handsome shrine behind the altar, which became the focal point of the veneration. People had to rely on this local saint (*patronus*). His intercession with God would not only look after all sorts of favours but would also come to the aid in unstable political situations. From the 10th century on in the West the *dismembratio* contributed not only to the scattering but also to the division of the relics among the smaller shrines which were exposed in the back wall (retable) of the altar for the purpose of reverence. The numbers strongly increased after the Fourth Crusade when the Byzantine relics were transported to the West. In the Middle Ages the shrines formed irreplacably tangible and recognizable means of coming into contact with the saint who was thought to be present there. (*Chapter I*)

Three linked forms can be distinguised between this veneration and that of the Eucharist: *the parallel application in concrete use* since the Christian antiquity and early Middle Ages until the 13th century, the *transposition of forms of reverence* from the 13th and 14th century, and the *similarity in miraculous power* since the eleventh and twelfth centuries. This marking out in time is connected to the fact that the Eucharist became 'independent': the bread and wine gradually lost their sacramental and liturgical context in these forms of devotion. Over the centuries attention shifted increasingly from the *activities surrounding* the bread and wine within the Lord's supper - "Do this in memory of *Me*' (Lk. 22:19; I Cor. 24:25) - to *reverence for* the bread and wine themselves. The Eucharistic bread was moreover taken to the sick, kept at home and partaken of there, while the allegorical explanation of the celebration of the Eucharist made the communal altar table into a tomb for the body of Christ since the Carolingian period. Because of the clericalisation of the liturgy, the Mass gained furthermore the outward character of the *mysterium depopulatum* in which the holy fear for the Host increased: only the priest could touch the Eucharist, the seldom received sacramental communion was given on the tongue, the Mass was celebrated by the priest having his back turned to the congregation and the unintelligible Latin was whispered by the celebrant during the Canon. It was in that time that the first cultic form of reverence of the Eucharist outside of the Mass was known: the bringing of the communion to the sick at home with some display. A controversy in the 9th and 11th century about the presence of Christ in the Eucharist, the combatting of heresies that denied this and the growing desire of the people to participate in the celebration and veneration led in the 13th century to a manifest hommage for the elevated Host during the Mass ('elevatio'). Incense was burnt, an extra row of candles was lighted and the bell was rung in support of the adoration and the beholding of the Host in which shape the Lord was hidden. This moment, which quickly grew to the point of culmination in the Mass, called for forms of reverence outside of the Mass: the 'visit' to the Blessed Sacrament, the 'exposition' of the Host, the 'procession' and the 'blessing'. (*Chapter II*)

The Eucharist and the relics could go together in *concrete use* when this was not yet considered as being incompatible with the respect required for the Sacrament and its purpose of being consumed. Thus both were kept at home in the bedroom as a 'home relic' and 'home communion'. The Eucharistic bread was partaken of at home, but it was also thought of as being a means of protection (*apotropaeon*), in which respect the purpose of home relics and home communion coincided. This was not only valid for the house, but also for 'use on journeys'. The accounts about relics worn on the neck in a *phylacterium* are more numerous than those about the Eucharist. This was worn in the same manner in a *bursa* or *pendula*. This served as usual for protection in general and for consumption in the danger of death (*viaticum*), in which respect this distinguished itself from the relics. It was characteristic of the Anglo-Saxon missionaries to carry the 'chrismal' with the Eucharist with them. Popes also carried the bread of fortification (*panis fortium*) around their necks. Of Robert the Pious († 1030) and Saint Louis († 1270) it is reported that they venerated the Sacrament while travelling. Preferably at the moment of death, and if necessary, afterwards (the communion of the dead which recalls the obol), the *viaticum* was given for the journey to the Lord (*migratio ad Dominum*). The relics offered comfort in that hour as well since one clapsed them in his hands. Both were given into grave in order to resist demons and to be resurrected with Christ. It is not always clear in the matter of grave finds and reports about the *elevatio*, whether the object found, served the purpose of storing a relic or a Host. There is sometimes uncertainty whether the bread found there had been sacred (*eulogia, oblata*) or consecrated. Probably this custom came to an end around the 10th century or even earlier. Eucharist and relics also went together in concrete use for the oath of promise and the oath of truth. The first established the seriousness of the duty which one took upon oneself, the second guaranteed that one spoke the truth (oath of purgation). In the latter case the oath had the character of a trial by ordeal. The swearer of the oath placed his hands upon the tomb of the saint, the relic shrine or held the relic in his hands. The oath taken upon the Eucharist was sworn in the same manner. A sworn declaration was also signed with consecrated wine, but the most usual was the communion test. This consisted of a demonstrative manner of receiving communion on the part of the suspect - for priests, instead of the trial by ordeal or the oath of purgation - as a proof of his protestation of innocense. In a account given by Bruno of Trier at the beginning of the 12th century, a layman suspected of heresy, had to swear upon relics and a priest, who was under the same suspicion, had to take the communion test. This trial endured a long while in spite of theological objections.

At the end of the 10th century primarily the Cluniacs combined the humiliation of the relics (*humiliatio*) with a cry of distress to God (*clamor*), which date from the 6th and the 9th century respectively. In the first case, the shrines were placed on the ground, which were covered with thorns in order to place the saint under duress; in the second case, the Mass was interrupted and all the monks lay on the church floor while the celebrant knelt before the altar with the consecrated Host in the hand. When these two customs became interwined, the relics stood between the monks and the altar. This prayer of supplication was a cry for help addressed to God by monks during Mass asking Him to save them from a bad situation ensuing from injustice committed by others. In the 13th century, the *humiliatio* was forbidden by the Council of Lyon. Another common form of custom was the cementing in of the relics and three particles of the Host into the altar grave (*sepulcrum*) within the church building on the occasion of the consecration of the church. This custom took place frequently from the 8th to the 13th centuries. The particles of the Host could be used as a replacement of the relics. Both were limbs of the 'body of Christ' (*membra Christi*). The one who had offered Himself and those who had offered themselves for Him. (*Chapter III*)

We may speak of a *transposition of forms of reverence* when a relationship is realized which we define thus: *the bringing up to date of forms of reverence towards the Eucharist which had already occured at an earlier date with regard to the relics.* The lamp by the shrines became the sanctuary lamp by the Holy of Holies. Light, incense and gestures of respect, such as the kissing of the relics and the kneeling before them are expressions of respect which originally were bestowed upon relics and in a later stage upon the Eucharist. The four most important transpositions are the 'visit', the 'procession', the 'exposition' and the 'blessing'. From Christian antiquity up until the 13th century (the century of the 'elevatio') the church building was visited for the purpose of venerating the altars and the relics, but not for the Eucharist. Later the presence of the Eucharist became the reason for visiting the church. In the 14th and 15th centuries it was practically only in the monasteries that there was interest in that respect while the Eucharist had gained extra splendour by the establishment of the feast of Corpus Christi in 1264. In the 14th century, the custom grew of holding a procession with the Blessed Sacrament on this feast. This displayed the triumphal character of the palm procession, in which Christ was carried in the form of a statue upon a donkey or as a pyx on a relic shrine (in England and Normandy). In addition to this palm procession the rich tradition of the relic procession was the modal for the Blessed Sacrament procession as can be seen in the transitional forms, the entourage, the organization and the presence still of relics in the procession of the Blessed Sacrament. An exchange even developed: the relic processions on penitential days and the Rogation Days became processions of the Blessed Sacrament by taking the Eucharist with them, and the procession on the feast of Corpus Christi took on the character of a rogation procession 'doing penance' by carrying the Eucharist through the fields. Just as on the festival of a saint his relics were carried, shown and exposed during Mass, so also the Eucharist was carried, shown and exposed upon the altar during Mass. The monstrance in which it was carried was usually a renovated show-case for relics. By beholding the relics or the 'sacred-Host', one expected material or spiritual benefits. In the Eucharistic piety the spiritual communion (*manducatio spiritualis*) gained the 'status' of a form of communion 'equal in value', although different from the sacramental communion. After the procession and the Mass were completed, the blessing was given with the Sacrament just as this had taken place earlier with the relics. Still another transposition took place: the weather blessing (an exorcising gesture against thunder, lightening and further danger) with the Sacrament, around the 14th century, was analogous with that with the relics since the 9th century. (*Chapter IV*)

In refutation of the teachings of Berengarius (1088) who denied a substantial change of the bread and the wine at the consecration, the theologians strongly emphasized the *praesentia realis*, a teaching which they considered as being supported by the Eucharistic miracles whose numbers were innumerable in the 13th century. These miracles were concentrated on the 'independent' Host, that in the narratives was attributed with a *similarity in miraculous power* of miracles in presentation, effect and usage as if it had been a relic. Thus it was immune against decay and fire, it gave signals of light, it bled and had healing power. The power of miracles was transported to the paten, corporal and holy water. The understandable result was that the Host itself - although less emphatically - and these 'secondary eucharistic relics' were used against disease and fire, while there were attempts made by stealth to profit from them in a magical manner. (*Chapter V*)

The relics satisfied naturally the longing in the popular religion for concrete forms. They were directly or indirectly the objective, physical, tangible reminders of the historical saint. The Eucharist gifts had as a sign of Christ's presence these qualities in a smaller degree. The realistic approach to Christ's presence in the bread and wine increased by the emphasis on the *praesentia realis*, which - connected to the veneration of the humanity (*humanitas*) of Christ - became the source of the Eucharistic forms of devotion since the 13th century. In the earliest forms of *parallel application in concrete use* the Host was generally experienced as a relic when both were used as a *apotropaeon* at home or on a journey, and as a holy object (*res sacra*) when swearing an oath upon it or for defense against demons in the grave. It distinguished itself however from the relic when the sacramental element was emphasized by consuming it (food for the soul). In the forms of reverence, the relic was pushed aside by the Host because it was the adored 'body of Christ'. In addition it acted as a holy 'power center' as in earlier days the relic had done when one expected material benefits from it in the rogationes. In many miracles, the

Host demonstrated a strength of miracles which in presentation effect and use went parallel with those of the relics. The usage- and veneration forms of the Host outside of the Mass caused it to become a 'relic', unique in as far as it was the most precious as the 'body of Christ', but alienated from its sacramental function and meaning. (*Chapter VI*)

A BRIEF EXPLANATION OF SOME TECHNICAL TERMS

A

ablution water:	water or wine that has come into contact with the relics or with the Eucharistic offerings
absolution:	sacramental forgiveness of sins
acolyte:	originally a cleric, later a lay person whose principal function was to act as server during Mass (LW I, 36-39)
Adoro te:	(I adore you) a hymn* in honour of the Blessed Sacrament, probably written in the 14th century and ascribed to Thomas Aquinas (LW I, 51)
Advent:	the start of the ecclesiastical year, beginning on the fourth Sunday before Christmas (LW I, 52-58)
adventus:	arrival (of the relics)
Agnus dei:	1. a hymn sung during Mass, originally at the breaking of the bread, later at the kiss of peace or as a Communion hymn (LW I, 80); 2. sacramental*, a small disc, circular or oval in shape, bearing on one side a depiction of the Lamb of God, on the other that of one or more saints and marked with the papal stamp (LW I, 81)
alb:	a long, white robe worn during Mass
altar grave:	space in the altar designed to contain relics
altarists:	the name given to priests, especially in the towns, whose daily task consisted of saying Mass and reciting the Office* (LW I, 125-126)
anathema:	a cursing
antiphon:	a verse with its own melody following a psalm; it expresses a core idea (LW I, 169)
apotropaeon:	a means of defence against catastrophe
apse:	semicircular projection of the church building with a shell-shaped roof (see 'side chapel')
arca:	small box used for taking the Eucharistic bread in the home

B

bination:	the celebration of two Masses by the same priest on the same day
blood witnesses:	martyrs
brandeum:	linen cloth that has been in contact with the dead body, the bones or the tomb of a saint

C

Canon:	1. law, rule; 2. the Eucharistic prayer of offering in the Roman and Ambrosian liturgies (LW I, 347-350)
canonisation:	inclusion in the canon or list of saints, the fact of being declared a saint
canonist:	expert in canon (ecclesiastical) law
capsa (capsella, capsula):	reliquary; it could also contain the Eucharist
celebrant:	bishop or priest playing the main part in a liturgical celebration, especially the Mass or the sung Office* (LW I, 379)
chapter:	clerics attached to a cathedral or collegiate church, the canons or choristers as a group
chasuble:	a liturgical garment worn by bishop or priest during the celebration of the Eucharist (LW I, 1247-1251)
choir prayer/choral prayer:	the daily communal recital of the Office* by canons, monks or nuns (LW II, 1372-1376)
chrisma:	holy oil (LW I, 392-396)
'chrismale':	1. a purse or pendant containing the Eucharist; 2. white linen cloth used to cover areas anointed with chrism
chrismarium:	reliquary
ciborium:	1. separate ceiling to cover the altar (LW I, 409-410); 2. liturgical vessel in which the Hosts were kept for distribution during Communion
clamor:	a "shout", a cry for help addressed to God by monks during Mass asking Him to save them from a bad situation ensuing from injustice committed by others
community:	the group of monks or nuns constituting a monastery or convent
Compline:	the Church's evening prayer (LW I, 443-447)
confrère:	a fellow monk
consecration:	1. dedication, blessing; 2. the changing of bread and wine into the Body and Blood of Christ by the words* spoken by the priest (LW I, 460-469)
convent:	1. the body of monks or nuns constituting a community; 2. the monastery or convent itself
conversi:	lay brothers who were part of the monastic community
corporal:	the small piece of altar linen on which the Eucharistic offerings are placed during the Mass and on which the monstrance* stands during exposition; originally it covered the entire altar (LW I, 478)
corpus Christi (Dei, Domini):	the body of God (in this case, the consecrated Host)
Credo:	'I believe', statement of belief included in the celebration of the Eucharist (LW I, 482-483)

crucifix:	a cross bearing the figure of Christ crucified

D

deacon (RC):	cleric who has received the second of the three higher orders (subdeacon*, deacon, priest) (LW I, 523-526)
dedicatio:	the consecration of a church
depositio:	the placing of relics in the altar grave*
diocese:	territory over which a bishop has responsibility
dismembratio:	the taking apart of the mortal remains of a saint
doxologie:	praise directed towards God

E

'elevatio':	the raising of the Host and the chalice in both hands after the words* of consecration have been pronounced
elevatio:	the disinterment of relics from the grave
Ember Days:	days of penance occurring at the beginning of a season (LW II, 2338)
Epistle:	reading taken from the letters (*epistolae*) of the Apostles (LW I, 693-696)
eschatological:	concerned with 'the four last things' (death, judgement, heaven and hell) but here related to the *parousia** or Second Coming of Christ
Eucharist:	'thanksgiving', 'the Sacrament', the Mass, the Eucharistic offerings themselves (bread and wine) (LW I, 711-715)
eulogia:	pieces of blessed bread distributed to the faithful on Sundays and feast deays after Mass (a custom still preserved in the Eastern rite) (LW I, 717-719)

F

feretrum:	stretcher
fermentum:	originally a piece of the Eucharist bread sent by the pope verey Sunday to priests at other churches in Rome (LW I, 749)
firmata oblata:	consecrated 'fortifying' bread kept by the newly ordained priest or professed nun for 40 days in order to eat part of it each day
Forty Hours:	the devotion of Quarant'Ore* consisting of the exposition of the Blessed Sacrament for adoration and prayer for forty successive hours
fylacterium:	see phylactery

G

Gospel:	reading taken from one of the four Gospels ("Gospel":Old English *gōdspel* = "good news") (LW I, 721-726)

H
Holy of Holies: 'Sacrament', the consecrated Host
holy water: water that has been blessed (a sacramental*) (LW
                                   II, 2893-2896)
Holy Week: the week preceding Easter
humiliatio: the 'humiliation' of a saint in his or her reliquary;
                                   the latter was placed on the ground and covered
                                   with thorns in order to oblige the saint to come to
                                   the aid of those (monks) placed in a bad situation
                                   ensuing from injustice committed by others
hymn: song of praise (LW I, 1032-1038)

I
indulgence: remission of punishment due for sins

L
lapsi: ex-believers unable to face the terror of persecution
leavened bread: bread baked with yeast
legacy: gift left in a will, in this context left to an
                                   ecclesiastical institution (church, monastery)
legate: papal representative
litany: liturgical prayer containing a certain number of
                                   separate prayers or appeals (LW II, 1556-1565)
lunula: two sheets made of precious metal in the shape of a
                                   waxing moon, holding the custode with the Host

M
Mass of Presanctified (missa praesanctificatorum):
                                   a liturgical service enabling the faithful to receive
                                   communion, though not a complete Mass,
                                   Praesanctificata (sanctified beforehand) indicates
                                   the Eucharist, consecrated in the course of a
                                   previous Mass.
manna: bread from heaven
manducatio spiritualis: spiritual communion
martyrium: final resting place of a martyr; the church building
                                   placed on top of a martyr's grave (memoria) (LW
                                   II, 1674)
membra Christi: 'members' or 'limbs of Christ', those bound to
                                   Christ by their belief
metropolitan: archbishop
monstrance (ostensorium):   liturgical vessel designed to expose the Host or a
                                   relic to the congregation (LW II, 1778-1779)
mysterium depopulatum: a celebration of the Eucharist in which the
                                   congregation hardly participates
mysterium tremendum: 'the awe-inspiring mystery'

N
novice: aspirant monk or nun before final profession*

O
obol: coin placed in the mouth of a corpse as payment to
                                     Charon the ferryman of the dead
octave: the celebration of a major feast on the feast itself
                                     and the seven days following the feast
Offertory: 1. the part of the Mass in which the bread and wine
                                     are offered; 2. the hymn* sung during the Offertory
                                     procession
Office: choral or hours (*horae*) - prayer
Ordo, ordo: the order of a service, description of a liturgy
ostensorium: see 'monstrance'

P
parish: local Roman Catholic community
parousia: the Second Coming of Christ at the end of time
paten: originally a large tray used for distributing the
                                     leavened* bread; when unleavened bread was
                                     introduced and small Hosts came to be used the
                                     paten lost its original form and became a small,
                                     flattened dish used for the celebrant's* Host
Pater Noster: the "Our Father", the 'Lord's Prayer', the prayer
                                     taught by Jesus (Mtt. 6:9-13) to His disciples
phylactery: reliquary worn around the neck
pignora: indirect or secondary relics
pilgrimage: visit to a sacred place, often regarded as sacred
                                     because of the relics there
pontifical(e):   a book containing non-Eucharistic celebrations and
                                     prayers as used by a bishop
praesentia realis: the real presence of Christ under the appearances of
                                     bread and wine
predella: broad decorated edging at the back of the altar
                                     between the altar table and the retable*
Preface: first part of the great priestly prayer during the
                                     Mass. It precedes the *Sanctus** and forms, as it
                                     were, a whole with the latter
prior: head of a monastery
profession (*professio*):   1. (*promissio*) monastic vow; 2. ceremony in the
                                     course of which a monk or nun takes the vow
prostratio: showing honour to a divinity or a superior by lying
                                     face down flat on the ground
provost: head of a chapter*
pyx (*pyxis*):   1. usually another name for *ciborium**; 2. small
                                     container used by the priest when taking
                                     communion to the sick

Q
Quarant'Ore: see 'Forty Hours'

R
relic: sacred object which has been in contact with Christ
                                      or his saints
res sacrae: 'holy things' on which an oath would be taken
responsory (*responsorium*):   part of the Office* connecting up with the readings
                                      and the *capitula*
retable: 'rear table'; decorated raised portion or wall behind
                                      the altar, usually joined to the altar (LW I, 120-
                                      121)
Rogation Days: the three days preceding Ascension Thursday on
                                      which processions of prayer and penance are held
rogations: 1. penitential litanies* used during the processions
                                      of prayer and penance on the Rogation* days; 2.
                                      the procession; 3. the days themselves

S
sacramentals: sacred symbols (prayers or objects) which by some
                                      sort of analogy with the sacraments indicate mainly
                                      spiritual values, a significance they acquire by
                                      virtue of the Church's invocation
sacramentarium: book of prayers used by the celebrant* during the
                                      liturgy
sacristy (*sacrarium, sanctuarium*):
                                      room attached to a church close to the priests' choir
                                      where the vestments* are stored and the priest
                                      dresses for the celebration of the Mass
Sakramenthaus: a gabled Gothic structure often approached by steps
                                      and railings in which the Eucharist was kept but
                                      also exposed (Rubin, 1991, 292)
Sancta: consecrated bread left over from a previous
                                      Eucharistic celebration and placed in the chalice as
                                      a symbol of the continuity of the one Eucharist
                                      within the local church
sanctuary lamp: lamp kept lit by the tabernacle*
Sanctus: 'holy', a fixed hymn* sung during Mass at the end
                                      of the Preface (hymn of thanksgiving and praise to
                                      the Lord)
scrinium: shrine, reliquary
secular: 'worldly', a priest who does not belong to an order
                                      or congregation
sepulcrum: see 'altar grave'
Sequence (*Sequentium*):   a hymn* sung after the Alleluia during Mass (LW
                                      II, 2538-2539; *prosarium*, 2293-2296)
side, separate chapel: small apse* containing an altar and/or shrines

station church:	church in Rome where the pope or his representative celebrated a solemn Eucharist on major Sundays and feast days
stipend (*stipendium*):	originally an offering (later money) made by the faithful during Mass; at a later date (and at present), a gift of money given to a priest as a guarantee that he would offer Mass for the intentions of the giver (LW II, 2592)
stipes:	underside (tomb) of the altar
subdeacon:	cleric who has been ordained into the first of the three major orders (subdeacon, deacon*, priest) (LW II, 2772-2773)

T

tabernacle:	small box-like cupboard used for reservation of the Eucharist
theophoric:	'God-bearing'; a theophoric procession involves the carrying of the Eucharist
titular church:	originally any church designated by Christians by the name of the owner (*titulum*); later a basilica or other parish church in Rome (LW II, 2678); small regional churches in town where the presbyters celebrated the liturgy in the pope's name (Wegman, 1991, 58)
translatio:	the transfer of the mortal remains of a saint from the original grave to another place
tryptych:	a retable* with side panels (sometimes designed to open and close)

U

usurper:	one who unlawfully seizes power by force

V

Vespers:	part of the evening Office*
vestments:	garments worn during the liturgy
viaticum:	communion given to someone in imminent danger of dying (LW II, 2810-2812)
vigil:	1. the day or evening preceding a major feast; 2. night watch
virtus:	(supernatural) power
vita:	the biography of a saint
votive Mass:	a Mass that falls outside the cycle of the ecclesiastical year and is celebrated for the intention of the celebrant* or the giver of a stipend*

W

words of consecration: the words spoken by Jesus over the bread   and wine at the Last Supper when He instituted the Eucharist" (...) for this is my Body (...) for this is the chalice of my Blood".

ABBREVIATIONS

AQ	Ausgewälte Quellen zur deutschen Geschichte des Mittelalters
AASS	Acta Sanctorum Bollandistarum, Anvers-Meursium, 1643 sqq.
AASS OSB	Acta Sanctorum Ordinis Benedicti, ed. Mabillon, Luteciae-Paris, 1668-1701
AAU	Archief voor de geschiedenis van het Aartsbisdom Utrecht
AFH	Archivum Franciscanum Historicum
An. Boll.	Analecta Bollandiana, Bruxelles
ANK	Archief voor de Nederlandse Kerkgeschiedenis
AOB	Annales Ordini Benedicti, 6 vol., Mabillon/Martène, Paris, 1703-1739
AQ	Ausgewählte Quellen zur deutschen Geschichte des Mittelalters
BHL	Bibliotheca hagiographica latina antiquae et mediae aetatis, 2 vol., Bruxelles, 1898-1901, supplément, 1911.
BKV	Bibliothek der Kirchenväter
CC SL	Corpus Christianorum Series Latinae, Turnholti
CC SG	Corpus Christianorum Series Graeca, Turnholti
CIL	Corpus Inscriptionum Latinarum, Berlin
CF	Cahiers de Fanjeaux.
ChrDSt	Die Chroniken der deutschen Städte vom 14-16 Jahrh. Leipzig, 1862 sqq. (Nachdr. Göttingen, 1961 sqq.)
CNRS	Centre National de la Recherche Scientifique, 15 Quai Anatole France, Paris Toulouse, 1976
COD	Conciliorum Oecumenicorum Decreta, Bologna, 1973[3]
CSEL	Corpus Scriptorum Ecclesiasticorum Latinorum
CSP	Les canons des synodes particuliers, Grottaferrata, 1962
CT	Concilium Tridentinum
DACL	Dictionnaire d'archéologie chrétienne et de liturgie, Paris.
DDC	Dictionnaire de droit canonique, Paris, 1935-65
DS	H. Denzinger and A. Schönmetzer eds. Enchiridion Symbolorum Definitionum et Declarationum, 33 rd. edition, Rome, 1965
DTC	Dictionnaire de Théologie Catholique, Paris, 1931
HJ	Historisches Jahrbuch
JbAC	Jahrbuch für Antike und Christentum, Münster WF
JLw	Jahrbuch für Liturgiewissenschaft
KE	Katholieke Encyclopedie
LCI	Herder, Lexikon der christlichen Ikonografie, 8 vol., Rom, Freiburg, Basel, Wien, 1968-76; 1990
LMD	La Maison Dieu, Revue trimestrielle du Centre de Pastorale Liturgique
LP	Liber Pontificalis: L. Duchesne, Le Liber Pontificalis, Paris, 1886-92, 1965
LJ	Liturgisches Jahrbuch
LW	Liturgisch Woordenboek
MB	Materials for the History of Thomas Becket, ed. J.C.Robertson (I-VI) and J.B.Shepard (VII), RS 67, London, 1875-85.

MGH	Monumenta Germaniae Historica	
	- AA	Auctores Antiquissimi
	- Cap	Capitularia
	- Conc	Concilia
	- Const	Constitutiones
	- Ep	Epistola
	- NS	Nova Series
	- SRM	Scriptores rerum Merovingicarum
	- SS	Scriptores rerum Germanicarum
NCE	New Catholic Encyclopedia	
PG	J.P.Migne, Patrologia Graeca (Paris, repr. Turnhout)	
PL	J.P.Migne, Patrologia Latina (Paris, repr. Turnhout)	
RAC	Reallexikon für Antike und Christentum, hg. Th. Klauser, Stuttgart	
RHF	Recueil des historiens des Gaules et de la France	
RQS	Römische Quartalschrift für christliche Alterthumskunde und für Kirchengeschichte	
RS	Rolls Series	
RSB	Regula Sancti Benedicti, ed. Hanselik, CSEL 75; ed. de Vogüé, SC 181-186	
SBO	S. Bernardi Opera	
SC	Sources Chrétiennes	
TQ	Theologische Quartalschrift	
TRE	Theologische Realencyclopedie	
TvT	Tijdschrift voor Theologie	
TW	Theologisch Woordenboek	
ZkTh	Zeitschrift für katholische Theologie	
[ ]	Text translated, not original	
i/j	Where the letter (j) replaced (i) in Latin texts, the letter i was retained.	
capitals	In the interest of legibility the number of capitals has been restricted in the Latin texts	

BIBLIOGRAPHY

Sources quoted

Albers, B. Albers, *Consuetudines monasticae*, 5 vol., Stuttgart-Wien-Monte Cassino, 1905-12.

Alberti Magni Opera Omnia ed. Honsfeld, 37. vol., Monasterii Westfalorum in aedibus Aschendorff, 1971-87; 38 vol., ed. Paris, 1894.

Accursius, *Codices sacratisissimi imperatoris Justiniani libri II Accursi commentarii*, Lyon, 1612.

d'Achery, L. d'Achery, *Spicilegium sive collectio veterum aliquot scriptorum*, 3 vol., Paris, 1723 (repr. Farnborough, 1967-68)

ed. Adlington (1566), *Apuleius, The Golden Ass., being the Metamorphoses of Lucius Apuleius*, with an English translation by W. Adlington (1566), revised by S. Gaselle, Cambridge, Massachusetts, 1971.

Agobardus, *Sancti Agobardi Archiepiscopi Lugdunensis Opera. Item epistolae et opuscula Leidradi et Amulonis episc. Lugdunensium. St. Baluzius Tutelensis in unum collegit, emendavit notisque illustravit*, 2 prts. 1 vol., Parisiis, 1666.

Analecta Franciscana, ed. Ad claras aquas, Quaracchi, 1887.

Andrieu (1938-41), M. Andrieu, *Le Pontifical romain au Haut Moyen Age*, 4 vol., Citta del Vaticano, 1938-41.

Andrieu (1931-61), M. Andrieu, *Les Ordines Romani du Haut Moyen Age*, 5 vol., Louvain, 1931-61.

Antonius Pierozzi, *Summa Theologica Sancti Antonini Archiepiscopi Florentini*, Veronae, 1740.

ed. Arens (1908), F. Arens, *Der Liber ordinarius der Essener Stiftskirche*, Paderborn, 1908.

Assemanus (1749-66), Joseph Aloysius Assemanus, *Codex Liturgicus eccelsiae universae in quo continentur libri rituales, missales, pontificales, officia, dypticha (...) ecclesiarum occidentis et orientis*, ed. iterata, ad editionis principis exemplum, Ab Huberto Welter, 13 vol., Parisiis et Lipsiae, 1749-66 (repr. 1902; 1968-69).

ed. Bakhuizen van den Brink (1954), J.N. Bakhuizen van den Brink, *Ratramnus, De corpore et sanguine Domini*, texte établi d'après les manuscrits et notice bibliographique,

Verhandelingen der Kon. Ak. v. Wetenschappen, afd. Letterkunde, Nieuwe Reeks, d. LXI, no. 1, Amsterdam, 1954.

ed. Bartelink (1986), G.J.M. Bartelink, *Na de schriften. Twee apologeten uit het vroege Christendom, Justinus en Athenagoras*, Kampen, 1986.

ed. Bautier (1965), Helgaud de Fleury, *Vie de Robert le Pieux, Epitomae vitae regis Roberti Pii*, texte edité, traduit et annoté par Robert-Henri Bautier et Gilette Labory, Paris, 1965.

ed. Beekenkamp (1941), W.H. Beekenkamp, *Berengarius Turonensis, De Sacra Coena adversus Lanfrancum*, Den Haag, 1941.

ed. Bellaguet (1839-52), L.F.R. Bellaguet, *Chronique du Religieux de Saint Denys*, 6 vol., Paris, 1839-52.

Bernardinus van Siëna, S. Bernardini Senensis *Opera Omnia*, 9 vol., Ad Claras Aquas, Florentiae, 1950-65.

ed. Berthelé (1900-07), J. Berthelé, *Les instructions et constitutions de Guillaume Durand* (Instructiones et constitutiones), Montpellier, 1900-07, 1-149.

ed. Berthier (1956), B. Humberti de Romanis opera *De vita regulari*, edita curante Joachim Joseph Berthier, 2 vol., (Torino), Marietti, 1956.

Bibliotheca franciscana scholastica, *Bibliotheca franciscana scholastica medii aevi, Alexander de Hales Glossa in quattuor libros Sententiarum Petri Lombardi*, I-IV, Florentiae, 1951-57.

Bibliotheca Casinensis , *Bibliotheca Casinensis seu Codicum Mansuscriptorum, qui in tabularis Casinense asservantur*. Series per paginas singillatim enucleata notis, characterum speciminibus ad unguem exemplatis aucta, cura et studio monachorum ordinis s. Benedicti abbatiae Montis Casini, 5 vol., Typis Montis Casini, 1873-94.

ed. Bieler (1963), L. Bieler, *The Irish Penitentials*, Dublin, 1963.

ed. Boeren (1956), P.C. Boeren, *La vie et les oeuvres de Guiard de Laon*, La Haye, 1956.

Bonaventura, S. Bonaventurae *Opera Omnia*, ed. Ad Claras Aquas (Quaracchi), 11 vol., 1882-1902.

ed. Bonnin (1852), Th. Bonnin, *Rigaldus Odo, Regestrum visitationum archiepiscopi Rothomagensis*, Rouen, 1852.

ed. Boor de (1883-85), Carolus de Boor, *Theophanis Chronographia*, 2 vol., Leipzig, 1883-885 (repr. ed. anast. Roma, 1964).

ed. Bouillet (1900), A. Bouillet et L. Servières, *Sainte Foy vierge et martyre (Liber miraculorum s. Fidis)*, Rodez, 1900.

ed. Brewer (1861-64), J.S. Brewer, J.F. Dimock, G.F. Warner, *Geraldus Cambrensis Opera*, 8 vol., RS 21, London, 1861-1864.

ed. Brooks (1904), E.W. Brooks, *The sixth book of the select letters of Severus, Patriarch of Antiochie*, London, 1904.

ed. Browe (1932-33), P. Browe, *De Ordaliis*, I, Decreta Pontificum Romanorum et Synodorum, II, Ordo et rubricae - Acta et facta - Sententiae theologorum et canonistarum (Textus et documenta in usum exercitationum et praelectionem academicarum, Series theologica 4 et 11), Romae, 1932-33.

ed. Bruder (1883), P. Bruder, "Acta inquisitionis de virtutibus et miraculis S. Hildegardis", in: *An. Boll.* 2 (1883) 118-129.

Canivez (1933-41), J.M. Canivez, *Statuta capitulorum generalium Ordinis Cisterciensis ab anno 1116 ad annum 1786*, 2 vol., Louvain, 1933-41.

ed. Cartier (1859), E. Cartier, *Vie de Sainte Catherine de Sienne par le B. Raymond de Capoue suivie du supplément du B. Thomas Cafferini et des témoignages des disciples du Sainte Catherine au procés de Venise*, Paris, 1859.

ed. Certain (1968), E. de Certain, *Les Miracles de Saint Benoît, écrits par Adrewald, Aimon, André, Raoul Tortaire et Hugues de Sainte Mairie*, Paris, 1858, repr. New York, 1968.

Chavasse (1958), A. Chavasse, *Le sacramentaire gélasien*, Paris-Tournai, 1958.

ed. Chevalier (1902), U. Chevalier, *Ordinaire et Coutumier de l'église cathédrale de Bayeux*, Paris, 1902.

ed. Chibnall (1968-83), M. Chibnall, *The Ecclesiastical History of Orderic Vitalis*, 6 vol., 1968-83.

Clemens V, *Regestum Clementis Papae V (...) nunc primum editum cura et studio monachorum ordinis s. Benedicti*,Romae, 1885-92.

Clemens VIII, *Pontificale Romanum Clementis VIII. Urbani P.P. VIII auctoritate recognitum primum. Nunc denuo ac demum ad plurimum usum, in commodiorem formam redactum*, Antverpiae. Ex architypographia Plantiniana, 1765.

Codex (1983), *Codex iuris canonici, auctoritate Joannis Pauli P.P. II promulgatus* (Editio tertium), Citta del Vaticano, 1983.

ed. Colgrave (1940), B. Colgrave, *Two lives of St. Cuthbert*, Cambridge, 1940.

ed. Colgrave (1956), B. Colgrave, *Felix's life of Saint Guthlac*. Intoduction, text, translation and notes, London, 1956.

ed. Colgrave (1968), B. Colgrave, *The earliest life of Gregory the Great*. By an anonymous monk of Whithy, Lawrence, 1968.

ed. Colgrave (1979), B. Colgrave and R.A.B. Mynors, *Bede's Ecclesiastical History of the English People*, Oxford, 1969 (repr. 1972, 1979).

ed. Colvenerius (1597), Georgius Colvenerius, *Thomae Cantipratani, S.Th. Doctoris, Ordinis S.Dominici, et Episcopi Suffraganei Cameracensis, Miraculorum, et exemplorum memorabilium sui temporis, libri duo. In quibus praeterea, ex mirifica APUM Repub. universa vitae bene et Christianè instituendae ratio (quò vetus, BONI VNIVERSALIS, alludit inscriptio) traditur, et artificiosè pertractatur*, Duaci: Ex officina Baltazaris Belleri, 1597.

ed. Constable (1954), G. Constable, "Petri Venerabilis sermones tres", in: *Revue Bénédictine*, 64 (1954) 224-272.

Consuetudinarum S.J., *Consuetudinarum Provinciae Germaniae Societatis Jesu*, Ratisbona, Paris, 1913.

ed. Le Couteulx (1887-91), *Annales Ordinis Cartusiensis ab anno 1084-1429* auctore D. Carolo Le Couteulx, 8 vol., Monstrolii, 1887-91.

ed. Cowdrey (1978), H.E.J. Cowdrey, *Two studies in Cluniac History 1049-1126*, M. Sticker, Studi Gregoriani, per la storia della "Libertas Ecclesiae", XI, Roma, 1978.

ed. Dawkins (1932), R.M. Dawkins, Leontios Makhairas, *Recital concerning the Sweet Land of Cyprus entitled 'Chronicle'*, I, Oxford, 1932.

ed. Dehandschutter (1979), B. Dehandschutter, *Martyrium Polycarpi*,Bibliotheca Ephemeridum Theologicarum Lovaniensum, Leuven, 1979.

Didache, eingel. hrsg. übertr. und erläut. von Klaus Hengst, Darmstadt, 1984.

ed. Dimock (1867), James Dimock, *Giraldi Cambrensis Topograhia Hibernica et Expugnatio Hiberna*, 1867 (repr. Rerum Brittannicarum Medii Aevi Scriptores (RS), 21, Geraldus Cambrensis Opera, 5).

ed. Doebner (1980), Rich. Doebner, *Urkundenbuch der Stadt Hildesheim*,9 vol., Hildesheim, 1881-1901 (Nachdr. Aalen, 1980).

ed. Douie (1985), Decima L. Douie and David Hugh Farmer,*Magna Vita Sancti Hugonis. The Life of St. Hugh of Lincoln*, 2 vol., London, 1961; Oxford, 1985.

ed. Dugdale (1846), W. Dugdale, *Monasticon Anglicanum 1665-73*, new English edition by John Caley, Henry Ellis and Bulkeley Bandinel, 6 vol. in 8 bd., London, 1846.

ed. Durand (1934), Georges Durand, *Ordinaire de l'église Notre-Dame cathédrale d'Amiens par Raoul de Rouvroy (1291)*, Amiens, Paris, 1934.

Durandus, Gulielmus Durandus, *Rationale Divinorum*, Antverpiae, 1614.

ed. Fehr (1966), B. Fehr, *Die Hirtenbriefe Aelfrics in altengl. und latein. Fassung* (Bibliothek der angelsächs. Prosa), 1914 (repr. 1966).

Ferraris, L. Ferraris, *Promptae bibliothecae canonica et juridica, moralis, theologica*, ed. Migne, 1852-57.

ed. Foerster (1958), H. Foerster, *Liber diurnus Romanorum Pontificum*, Bern, 1958.

Foppens (1721), J.F. Foppens, *Historia Episcopatus Silvaeducensis, Continens Episcoporum et Vicarium Generalium Seriem, et Capitulorum, Abbatiarum, et MonasteriorumFundationes; Nec non Diplomata varia ad rem hujus Dioecesis spectantia*, Bruxellis: Typis Francisci Foppens, 1721.

Francois Grin, *Journal de Francois Grin, religieux de Saint-Victor (1554-70)*, Mémoires de la société de l'histoire de Paris et de l'Ile-de-France, t. XXI, Paris, 1894.

ed. Friedberg (1879-81), A. Friedberg, *Corpus Iurus Canonici*, 2 vol., Lipsiae, 1879-81.

ed. Froning (1884), R. Froning, *Frankfurter Chroniken und annalistiche Aufzeichnungen des Mittelalters*, Quellen zur Frankfurter Geschichte a. M., 1884.

Galbert of Bruges, *The Murder of Charles the Good*, translated and edited by James Bruce Ross, Toronto, Buffalo, London, 1982 (repr. ed. Harper, 1967, original ed. New York, 1959).

ed. Gardellini (1856), *Decreta Authentica Congregationis Sacrorum Rituum*ex actis eiusdem collecta cura et studio Aloisii Gardellini editio tertia, 2 vol., Romae, 1856.

ed. Geerdink (1887), E. Geerdink, "Calendarium et Necrologium Ecclesiae", S. Plechelmi in Oldenzalia 4,31, in: *AAU* 15 (1887) 128-212.

Gerbert (1776), M. Gerbertus, *Vetus Liturgia Alemannica*, II, III, St. Blasien, 1776 (Nachdr. 1967).

Gerson, *Opera Omnia* Joannis Gersonii, opera et studio M. Lud. Ellies du Pin, Hagae Comitum aoud Petrum de Hondt, 5 vol., 1728.

Geschichtsquellen der Provinz Sacksen (1870 sqq.), Geschichtsquellen der Provinz Sacksen und angrenzender Gebiete, Halle, 1870 e.v.

ed. Giles (1844), J.A. Giles, *Sancti Aldhelmi Opera*, Oxoni, 1844.

ed. Glatz (1881), K.J. Glatz, *Chronik des Bickenklosters zu Villingen, 1238 bis 1614*, Bibliothek des Litterarischen Vereins in Stuttgart, CLI, Tübingen, 1881.

ed. Goar-Combefis (1665), *Theophanis Chronographia. Leonis Grammatici Vitae recentiorum Impp. (Graeca et Lat.). Jacobus Goar Latine reddidit, Theophanem notis illustravit, varias lectiones adiecit. Franciscus Combefis iterum recensuit, notis posterioribus Theophanem; intergris, Leonem Grammaticum strictim discussit, exque fide Codd. auxit, emendavit*, Parisiis, 1665.

Goffredus Tranensis, Gottofredo da Trani, *Summa super titulis decretalium*, Lyon, 1519 (repr. Darmstadt, 1968).

ed. Gorce (1962), D. Gorce, *Vie de Sainte Melanie*, SC 90, 1962.

ed. Graesse (1969), Th. Graesse, Jacobo a Voragine, *Legenda Aurea*, vulgo historia Lombardica dicta, Reproductio phototypica editionis tertiae 1890, Osnabrück, 1969.

ed. Grau (1955), P.E. Grau, *Thomas von Celano, Leben und Wunder des heiligen Franziskus von Assisi*, Werl/Westf., 1955.

ed. Grau (1960), P.E. Grau, *Leben und Schriften der heiligen Klara*, Werl/Westf. 1960.

ed. Grégoire (1930), H. Grégoire et M.A. Kugener, *Marc de diacre, Vie de Porphyre, évêque de Gaza*, Paris, 1930.

ed. Griesser (1961), B. Griesser, *Exordium magnum cisterciense sive narratio de initio ordinis, auctore Conrado*, Rome, 1961 (series scriptorum s. Ordinis Cisterciensis, II).

ed. Grube (1886), K. Grube, *Des Augustinerpropstes Iohannes Busch Chronicon Windeshemense und Liber de reformatione monasterium*, Halle, 1886.

ed. Grundmann (1966), H. Grundmann, "Der Brand von Deutz 1128 in der Darstellung Abt Ruperts von Deutz". Interpretation und Text-Ausgabe, in: *Deutsches Archiv für Erforschung des Mittelalters*, 22 (1966) 385-471.

Guibert de Baysio, *Rosarium seu decretum volumen commentaria*, ed. Franciscus Moneliensis, Venise, 1481.

ed. Guiges Ie (1984), Guiges I, *Coutumes de Chartreuse*, SC 313, 1984.

ed. Habig (1973³), Marion A. Habig, *St. Francis of Assisi, Writings and early Biograhies*, Chicago, Illinois, 1973.

Haddan-Stubbs, A.W. Haddan en W. Stubbs, *Councils and ecclesiastical Documents*, 4 vol., Oxford, 1964; 1969-73.

Hallinger , K. Hallinger, *Corpus Consuetudinum Monasticorum*, I-XII, Siegburg, 1963-87.

ed. Hanssens (1948-50), J.M. Hanssens, *Amalarii episcopi opera liturgica omnia* (Studi e Testi, 138-140), 3 vol., Citta del Vaticano, 1948-50.

Hardouin , J. Hardouin, *Acta Conciliorum et epistolae decre tales ac Constitutiones Summorum Pontificum*, 12 vol., Parisiis, 1714-15.

ed. Hauréau (1890), B. Hauréau, *Notices et extraits de quelques manuscrits latins de la Bibliothèque Nationale*, 2 vol., 1890.

Hermans (1847), C.R. Hermans, *Verzameling van Kronyken betrekkelijk de stad en Meijereij van 's Hertogenbosch*, Tweede Stuk, 's-Hertogenbosch, 1847.

ed. Herrgott (1726), M. Herrgott, *Vetus disciplina monastica*, Paris, 1726.

ed. Hilka (1937), Alfons Hilka, *Die Wundergeschichten des Caesarius von Heisterbach*, Bonn, 1937.

ed. Hindo (1943), P. Hindo, *Disciplina Antiochena Antica*, Siri 4, Fonti 2, 28, 1943.

ed. Hinschius (1863), P. Hinschius, *Decretales Pseudo-Isidorianae*, Lipsiae, Tauchnitz, 1863.

Hostiensis, Henricus de Segusio, Card. Hostiensis, *In primum Decretalium librum commentaria, doctissimorum virorum quampluribus adnotationibus illustrata, hac novissima ed. summo studio (...) expurgata (...) Recens accesserunt summaria et index (...) Venetiis*, 1581 (repr. Torino, 1965).

ed. Huygens (1963), R.B.C. Huygens, *Lettres de Jaques de Vitry*, edition critique, Leiden, 1960.

ed. Huyskens (1908), Albert Huyskens, "Des Caesarius von Heisterbach Schriften über die heilige Elisabeth von Thüringen", in: *Annalen des historischen Vereins für den Niederrhein* 86 (1908) 1-59.

ed. Jaeger (1952), W. Jaeger, *Gregorii Nysseni Opera*, vol., VIII,1, *Opera ascetica*, 347-414: *Vita S. Macrinae*, Leiden, 1952.

ed. Jaffé (1864), Ph. Jaffé, *Bibliotheca rerum Germanicarum*, Berolini, 1864.

ed. Jaffé (1885-88), Ph. Jaffé et G. Wattenbach, *Regesta Pontificum Romanorum ab condita Ecclesia ad annum post Christum natum, MCXCVIII*, 2. vol., Lipsiae, 1885-86 (repr. Graz, 1956).

Johannes Andreae, Johannes Andreae Bononienesis, *In decretalium libros nevella commentaria*, Venise, 1581 (repr. 1963-66).

Johannes Trithemius, *Opera historica omnia*, 2 vol., Ex Bibl. Marquardi Freheri, Francofurti, 1601.

ed. Jones (1883-84), W.H.Rich. Jones, *Register of St. Osmund*, RS 78, I en II, 1883-84 (repr. 1965).

ed. Kayser (1866), C. Kayser, *Die Canones Jacob's von Edessa*,Leipzig, 1866.

ed. Kleinschmidt (1974), Rudolf von Schlettstadt, *Historiae Memorabiles*, hersg. von E. Kleinschmidt, Köln-Wien, 1974.

ed. Knipping (1898), R. Knipping, *Die Kölner Stadrechnungen des Mittelaters mit einer Darstellung der Finanzverwaltung*, 2 vol., Bonn, 1898.

ed. Kristenson (1974), G. Kristenson, *John Mirk, Instructions for parish priests*, London, 1974.

ed. Labande (1981), E.R. Labande, *Guibert de Nogent, Autobio- graphie* (Les Classiques de l'Histoire de France au Moyen Age, XXXIV), Paris, 1981.

ed. Lagger de (1927), A. de Lagger, "Statuts synodaux inedits du diocèse d'Albi au XIIIe siècle", in: *Revue historique de droit français et etranger*, 6 (1927) 418-466.

ed. Leclercq (1946), J. Leclercq et J-P. Bonnes, "Confessio Theologica", in : *Un maître de la vie spirituelle au XIe siècle, Jean de Fécamp*, Paris, 1946, 109-183.

ed. Leclercq (1957-77), J. Leclerq et H. Rochais, *S. Bernardi Opera*, 8 vol., Rome, 1957-77.

ed. Lecoy de la Marche (1867), A. Lecoy de la Marche, *Oeuvres complètes de Suger*, Paris, 1867.

ed. Lefèvre (1967), Pl.F. Lefèvre, *L'Ordinaire de la collégiale, autrefois cathédrale de Tongres*, 2 vol., Leuven, 1967.

ed. Leipoldt (1903), J. Leipoldt, *Schenute von Atripe*, Texte und Untersuchungen, N.F. X,1, Leipzig, 1903.

Leroquais (1924), V. Leroquais, *Les Sacramentaires et les Missels manuscrits des bibliotheques publiques de France*, 4 vol., Paris, 1924.

Leroquais (1927), V. Leroquais, "L'Ordo Missae du sacramentaire d'Amiens", in: *Ephemerides Liturgicae* 41 (1927) 435-455.

Leroquais (1937), V. Leroquais, *Les Pontificaux des bibliothèques publiques de France*, 4 vol., Paris, 1937.

ed. Liebermann (1903-16), E. Liebermann, *Die Gesetze der Angelsachsen*, Halle, 1903-16.

ed. Little (1966), A.G. Little, *Liber exemplorum ad usum praedicantium*, Aberdeen, 1908 (repr. 1966).

Lyndwood, Gulielmo Lyndwood, *Provinciale (seu Constitutionis Angliae) continens Constitutiones provinciales quatuordecim Archiepiscoporum Cantuariensium*, Oxoniae, 1679.

ed. Mabillon (1724), J. Mabillon et M. Germain, *Museum Italicum*, 2 vol., Lutetiae Parisiorum, 1724.

ed. Macray (1863), W.D. Macray, *Chronicon Abbatiae de Evesham ad annum 1418*, London, 1863.

ed. Mai (1838), Angelo Mai, *Scriptorum veterum nova collectio 10*, Roma, 1838.

Malleus Maleficarum, maleficas et earum heresim ut phramea potentissima conterens, Iacobi Sprengeri et Henrici Institoris, Lugduni, 1519; Francofurti, 1600.

Mansi, J.D. Mansi, *Sacrorum conciliorum nova et amplissima collectio*, 31 vol., Florence-Venetië; 59 vol. Parijs, 1901-23 (t. 1-48), Arnheim, 1923-27 (t. 49-50); repr. Graz, 1960-61.

ed. Mansi (1761), J.D. Mansi, *Stephani Baluzii Tutelensis Miscellanea, nova ordine digesta opera*, Lucae, 1761 (original ed. 1678/1715).

Martène (1690), E. Martène, *De antiquis monachorum ritibus*, Lyon, 1690.

Martène (1706), E. Martène, *Tractatus de antiqua ecclesia disciplina*, Lyon, 1706.

Martène (1717,), E. Martène - U. Durand, *Thesaurus novus anec dotorum*, 5 vol., Paris, 1717 (repr. Farnborough, 1968-69).

Martène (1733), E. Martène - U. Durand, *Veterum scriptorum et monumentorum historicorum dogmaticorum moralium amplissima collectio*, 9 vol., Paris 1733 (repr. New York, 1986).

Martène (1788), E. Martène, *De antiquis ecclesiae ritibus*, 4 vol., Venetiis, 1788.

ed. McLachlan (1936-51), *The Ordinal and Customary of the Abbey of Saint Mary (York)*, ed. by Laurentia McLachlan and J.B.L. Tolhurst, Henry Bradshaw Society, 3 vol., 73 (1936), 75 (1937), 84 (1951), London.

ed. McNeill (1990[3]), John. T. McNeill, Helena. M. Gamer, *Medieval Handbooks of Penance. A translation of the principal libri poenitentiales* and selections from related documents, New York, 1990[3] (1938[1], 1965[2])

ed. Mingana (1927-34), A. Mingana, *Woodbrooke Studies, Christian documents edited and translated with a critical apparatus*, 7 vol., 1927-34.

ed. Mohlberg (1956), L.C. Mohlberg, *Sacramentarium Veronense*, Rome, 1956.

ed. Mohlberg (1957), L.C. Mohlberg, *Missale Francorum*, Rome, 1957.

ed. Mohlberg (1981), L.C. Mohlberg, *Liber sacramentorum romae ecclesiae ordinis anni circuli* (Rerum eccl. documenta series maior, 4) Rome, 1960, 1981.

ed. Molenaar (1951-52), M. Molenaar, *Werken van de heilige Geertruid van Hefta*, I; de drie eerste boeken van de Heraut der Goddelijke Liefde II, boek 4 en 5 (Legatus divinae pietatis), Bussum, 1951-52.

ed. Mollat (1904-47), G. Mollat, *Jean XXII (1316-1334), Lettres communes*, 16 vol., 1904-47.

Montrocher, Guido de Montrocher, *Manipulum curatorum, 1333*, Argentoranti, 1483.

Monumenta Boica, Academia Scientiarum electa Maximilianea, 27 vol., Munich, 1763-1829; 60 vol., 1763-1956.

Monumenta Zollerana, Rudolp Freiherrn von Stillfried, Dr. Fraugott und T. Maercker, 6 vol., Berlin, 1852-60.

Muratori (1723-51), L.A. Muratori, *Rerum Italicarum sriptores*, 25 vol., Milaan, 1723-51.

ed. Musurillo (1972), H. Musurillo, *The Acts of the Christian Martyrs*, Oxford, 1972.

Panormitanus, Abbas Panormitanus (Nic. Tudescus vel Tudeschi), *Commentaria in decretalium libros*, 9 tom. in 5 vol. fol. Venetiis, apud Juntas, 1617.

ed. Pez (1931), B. Pez, Ven. *Agnetis Blannbekin Vita et Revelationes*, auctore anonymo Ord. F.F. Min., Viennae, 1731.

ed. Pigouchet (1964), Ph. Pigouchet et Fr. Regnault, *Magistri Gillelmi Altissiodorentis Summa Aurea*, Paris, 1500 (repr. Minerva, G.m.b.H., Frankfurt a. Main, 1964).

ed. Plummer (1968), C. Plummer, *Vitae Sanctorum Hiberniae*, London, 1910, 1968.

ed. Pontal (1971), O. Pontal, *Les statuts synodaux français du XIIIe siècle, précédés de l'historique de synode diocésain depuis ses origines. I. Les statuts de Paris et le synodal de l'Ouest* (XIII e siècle), Paris, 1971.

Powicke, F. Powicke and C. Cheney, *Councils and Synods*, Oxford, 1964.

ed. Prou (1886), Maurice Prou, *Raoul Glaber, Les cinq livres de ses histoires (900-1044)*, Paris, 1886.

ed. Quasten (1936), J. Quasten, *Monumenta eucharistica et liturgica vetustissima*, Coloniae, 1936.

ed. Raabe (1895), R. Raabe, *Petrus der Iberer* (Syrische Überzetsung einer um das Jahr 500 verfassten Griechischen Biographie), Leipzig, 1895.

ed. Rampolla (1905), *Gerontius: Santa Melania giuniore, senatrice Romana*. Documenti contemporanei e note. M. Card. Rampolla del Tindaro. Roma, Tipografia Vaticana, 1905 (text in Latin, Greek and Italian).

ed. Ricciotti (1931), G. Ricciotti, *Disciplina Antiochena (Siri): I, Nomocanone di Bar-Hebreo, Tipografia Poliglotta Vaticana*,1931.

ed. Ried (1816), Th. Ried, *Codex chronologico diplomaticus episcopatus Ratisbonensis*, 2 vol., Regensburg, 1816.

ed. Riedel (1838-69), Ad.F. Riedel, *Codex diplomaticus Brandenburgensis*,7 vol., 41 Bände, Berlin, 1838-69.

ed. Riedel (1968), W. Riedel, *Die Kirchenrechtsquellen des Patriarchats Alexandrien*,Leipzig, 1900 (Nachdruck, Aalen, 1968).

ed. Riley (1867-69), H. Th. Riley, *Gesta abbatum monasterii Sancti Albani, a Thoma Walshingam, regnante Ricardo II compelata*, 3 vol., London, 1867-1869.

ed. Rock (1905), D. Rock, *The Church of our Fathers*, as seen in St. Osmunds Rite for the cathedral of Salisbury; a new edition, edited by G.W. Hart and W.H. Frere, 4 vol., London, 1905.

ed. Rockinger (1858), L. Rockinger, *Quellen und Erörterungen zur bayerischen und deutschen Geschichte, Bd. VII, 313-409, Qellenbeiträge zur Kenntniss des Verfahrens bei den Gottesurtheilen des Eisens, Wassers, geweihten Bissens, Psalters*, München, 1858.

ed. Rockwell (1925), W.W. Rockwell, *Liber miraculorum Ninivensium Sancti Cornelii Papae*, Göttingen, 1924.

Rosweydus (1623), *Kerkeliicke Historie van Nederlandt, vervattende d'outheyt des gheloofs inde XVII Provincien, stiften der bisch-dommen, fondatien van cloosters, de synoden, heylighen ende ketters; ghetrocken uut authentycke registers en chronycken*. T'Antwerpen: By Ian Cnobbaert, 1623.

ed. Rozière (1859-71), E. Rozière, *Recueil général de formules usitées dans l'Empire des Francs du Ve au Xe siècle*, 3 vol., Paris, 1859-71.

Sacchetti, Franco Sacchetti, *Il Trecentonovelle*, a cura di Emilio Faccioli, Torino, 1970.

ed. Salu (1955), M.B. Salu, *The Ancrene Riwle*, London, 1955.

ed. Saturninus (1909), P. Saturninus Mencherini O.F.M. "Constitutiones generales Magistri Geraldi de Equitania Ministri Generalis Ordinis Minorum, editae et confirmatae in Capitulo Generali celebrato apud Perpignianum anno D.Mi. 1331", in: *AFH* 2 (1909) 276 sqq.

ed. Schaff (1979), Philip Schaff and Henry Wace, *A Select Library of Nicene and Post-Nicene Fathers of the Christian Church*, Second Series, Grand Rapids Michigan, 1979.

Schannat-Hartzheim, J. Hartzheim, *Concilia Germaniae*, 8 vol., Aalen, 1970-82 (Nachdruck der Ausgabe Köln, 1759-1790).

ed. Schaten (1775), N. Schaten, *Annalium Paderbornensium*, II, 1775.

ed. Schmidt (1906), J.W.R. Schmidt, *Der Hexenhammer von Jakob Sprenger und Heinrich Institoris*, 3 vol., Berlin, 1906.

ed. Schmitz (1958), H. Schmitz, *Die Bussbücher und das kanonische Bussverfahren*, Düsseldorf, 1898 (repr. Graz, 1958).

ed. Séjalon (1892), H. Séjalon, *Nomasticon Cisterciense seu antiquiores Ordinis Cisterciensis Constitutiones*, Solesmes, 1892.

ed. Sickel (1966), Th.E. van Sickel, *Liber diurnus Romanorum Pontificum*, Darmstadt, 1966.

ed. Stachnik (1978), R. Stachnik, A. Triller und H. Wetspfahl, *Die Akten des Kanonisationsprozesses Dorotheas von Montau*, Cologne-Vienne, 1978.

ed. Strange (1851), J. Strange, Caesarius von Heisterbach, *Dialogus miraculorum*, 2 vol., Coloniae, 1851 (repr. New Jersey, 1966).

Suaerez, R.P. Suaerez, *Opera Omnia*, 26 vol., Paris, 1856-61.

ed. Stubbs (1965), W. Stubbs, *Vita s. Dunstani archiepiscopi Cantuariensis auctore Eadmero*, ed. in RS 63, London, 1874 (repr. New York-Vaduz, 1965, 162-222).

ed. Stutvoet (1990), C.M. Stutvoet-Joanknecht, *Der Byen Boeck. De Middelnederlandse vertalingen van Bonum universale de apibus van Thomas van Cantimpré en hun achtergrond*, Amsterdam, 1990.

Surius, Laurentius Surius, *Historiae seu vitae sanctorum*, 13 vol., 1875-80.

ed. Swoboda (1900), A. Swoboda, *Odonis Abbatis Cluniacensis Occupatio*, Leipzig, 1900.

ed. Symons (1953), T. Symons, *Regularis Concordia*, New York, 1953.

ed. Thevenin (1887), M. Thevenin, *Textes relatifs aux institutions privées et publiques aux époques mérovingiennes et carolingiennes*, Oaris, 1887.

Thomas van Aquino, *Sancti Thomae Aquinitatis doctoris angelici opera omnia iussu impensaque Leonis XIII P.M. edita; cura et studio Fratrum praedicatorum.* Ex Typographia Polyglotta, S.C. De Propaganda Fide, ed. Romae, 48 vol., 1882-1972;

ed. Blacfriars (1963-1973), *St. Thomas Aquinas Summa Theologiae, Latin text and English translation, Introductions, Notes, Appendices and Glossaries*, Blacfriars, London, New York, 1963-1973.

ed. Thompson (1902), Edw.M. Thompson, *Customary of the Benedictine Monasteries of Saint Augustine, Canterbury and Saint Peter, Westminster*, vol., I, Henry Bradshaw Society, 23 (1902), London.

ed. Tolhurst (1927-28), J.B.L. Tolhurst, *The Ordinale and Customary of the Benedictine Nuns of Barking Abbey*, 2 vol., Henry Bradshaw Society, 65 (1927), 66 (1928), London.

ed. Tonneau (1966), R. Tonneau et R. Devresse, *Les homélies catéchétiques de Théodore de Mopsuesta*, Roma, 1966.

ed. Trillmich (1960), W. Trillmich, *Thietmari Merseburgensis Episcopi Chronicon*, Darmstadt, 1957 (AQ 9).

Urkundenbuch-Jena (1888-1936), *Urkundenbuch der Stadt Jena*, Thüringische Geschichtsquellen, 3 vol., hrsg. Jena, 1888- 1936.

Urkundenbuch-Hameln (1887-1903), *Urkundenbuch des Stiftes und der Stadt Hameln*, 2 vol., Hannover, 1887-1903.

Urkundenbuch-Lübeck (1843-1905), *Urkundenbuch der Stadt Lübeck*, 13 vol., Lübeck, 1843-1905.

Vespasiano da Bisticci, *Vite di uomini illustri del seculo XV*, a cura di Paoli d'Ancona ed Erhard Aeschlimann, Milano, 1951.

ed. Vetter (1906), T. Vetter, *Das Leben der Schwestern zu Töss*, beschrieben von Elsbert Stagel, deutsche Texte des Mittelalters, 6, Berlin, 1906.

ed. Viard (1920-53), J. Viard, *Grande chronique de France*, 10 vol., 1920-53.

ed. Vieillard (1963), J. Vieillard, *Le guide de pèlerin de Saint-Jacques de Compestelle*, Mâcon, 1963.

ed. Vogel (1963), Cyrille Vogel, *Le Pontificale romano-germanique du dixième siècle*, Citta del Vaticano, 1963.

ed. Vogüé de (1964), A. de Vogüé, SC 106, *Regula Magistri*.

ed. Wadding (1931-64), *Annales Minorum seu Trium Ordinum A.S. Francisco institutorum*, auctore Luca Waddingo Hiverno. Editio tertia accuratissima auctior et emendatior ad exemplar editionis Josehi Mariae Fonseca, 32. vol., Ad Claras Aquas (Quaracchi), 1931-64.

ed. Walker (1957), G.S.M. Walker, *Sancti Columbiani Opera*, Dublin, 1957.

ed. Wartelle (1987), A. Wartelle, *Saint Justin Apologies*, introduction, texte critique, traduction, commentaire et index, Paris, 1987.

ed. Wasserschleben (1964), F.W.H. Wasserschleben, *Regionis Abbatis Prumiensis Libri duo de synodalibus causis et disciplinis ecclesiasticis*, Leipzig, 1840, Graz, 1964. .

ed. Wickam (1904), J. Wickam Legg, "Ordo Missae Joannis Burckardi", in: *Tracts on the Mass*, London, 1904, 119-178.

ed. Woude v.d. (1951), Gerard Zerbolt van Zutphen, *Over de hervorming van de krachten der ziel*, intoduced and translated by S. van der Woude, Amsterdam, 1951 (Klassieken der Kerk. tweede reeks: De Kerk in de middeleeuwen, dl. 3; original title: *De reformatione virium animae*).

Editions of the Bible

The Holy Bible, containing The Old and New Testaments, Revised Standard Version, translated from the original languages being the version set forth A.D. 1611, revised A.D. 1881-1885 and A.D. 1901; compared with the most ancient authorities and revised A.D. 1946-1952; second edition of the New Testament A.D. 1971, New York and Glasgow (...).
Biblia Sacra iuxta Vulgatam versionem, R. Weber, ed. 2 vol. (Stuttgart 1975; original edition 1969).

Literature consulted

Aalberts (1985), T. Aalberts, "Reliekverspreiding", in: A.M. Koldewey en P.M.L. Vlijmen, *Schatkamers uit het Zuiden*, Utrecht, 1985, 44-56.

Albert (1990), Jean-Pierre Albert, *Odeurs de Sainteté*. Le mythologie chrétienne des aromates, Paris, 1990

Andrieu (1950), M. Andrieu, "Aux origines du culte du Saint Sacrament. Reliquaires et Monstrances Eucharistiques", in: *An. Boll.* 68 (1950) 397-418.

Andrieu (1924), M. Andrieu, *Immixtio et Consecratio*, Paris, 1924.

Angenendt (1982), A. Angenendt, "Die liturgie und die Organisation des Kirchlichen Lebens auf dem Lande", in: *Christianizzazione ed organizazzione ecclesiastica delle campagna nell' alto medioevo: expansone e resistenze* (Settimane di studio 28), Spoleto, 1982, 169-275.

Angenendt (1983), A. Angenendt, "Missa specialis", in: *Frühmittelalterlichen Studien*17 (Berlin, 1983) 153-221.

Angenendt (1989), A. Angenendt, "Der Kult der Reliquien", in: Legner (1989), 9-25.

Angenendt (1990), A. Angenendt, *Das Frühmittelalter*, Die abendländische Christenheit von 400 bis 900, Stuttgart, Berlin, Köln, 1990

Angenendt (1991), A. Angenendt, "Corpus incorruptum", in: *Saeculum* 42 (1991) 320-348.

Appuhn (1961), Horst Appuhn, "Der Auferstandene und das heilige Blut zu Wienhausen", in: *Niederdeutsche Beiträge zur Kunstgeschichte* 1 (1961) 73-138.

Atchley (1909), E.G.C.F. Atchley, *History of the Use of Incense in Divine Worship*, London, 1909.

Bailey (1971), T. Bailey, *The processions of Sarum and the Western Church* (Studies and texts no. 21), Toronto, 1921.

Baldwin (1961), J.W. Baldwin, "The intellectual preparation for the canon of 1215 against ordeals", in: *Speculum* 34 (1961) 613-636.

Baldwin (1971), J.W. Baldwin, *Masters, Princes and Merchants*. The social views of Peter the Chanter and his circle, 2 vol., Princeton, 1971.

Bandmann (1974), G. Bandmann, "Zur Bestimmung der romanischen Scheitelrotunde an der Peterskirche zu Löwen", in: *Beiträge zur Rheinischen Kunstgeschichte und Denkmalpflege*, II (Festschrift Albert Verbeek), Düsseldorf, 1974.

Bartlett (1986), R. Bartlett, *Trial by fire and water. The medieval judicial ordeal*, Oxford, 1986.

Bauerreis (1931), R. Bauerreis, *Das Schmerzensmann. Bild und sein Einfluss auf die mittelalterliche Frömmigkeit*, München, 1931.

Bauerreis (1950), R. Bauerreis, "Der 'clamor', eine verschollene mittelalterliche Gebetsform und das Salve Regina", in: *Studien und Mitteilungen zur Geschichte des Benedictiner Ordens* 62 (1950) 25-34.

Beauduin (1948), L. Beauduin, "Le Viatique", in: *LMD*15 (Paris, 1948) 117-129.

Beaujard (1991), Brigitte Beaujard, "Cité's, évêques et martyres en Gaule", in: Tilliette (1991), 175-191.

Beek (1974), H.H. Beek, *Waanzin in de Middeleeuwen*, Hoofddorp, 1974.

Beekenkamp (1940), W.H. Beekenkamp, *De avondmaalsleer van Berengarius van Tours*, 's-Gravenhage, 1940.

Beck (1978), P. Beck, *Le coeur du Christ dans la mystique Rhénane*, Imprimerie Alsatia Sélestat, 1978.

Beissel (1889²), S. Beissel, *Die Bauführung des Mittelalters*, Studie über die Kirche des hl. Victor zu Xanten. Bau-Geldwerth und Arbeitslohn-Ausstattung, Freiburg im Breisgau, 1889² (Nachdr. Osnabrück, 1966).

Beissel (1976), S. Beissel, *Die Verehrung der Heiligen und ihrer Reliquien in Deutschland im Mittelalter*, I,II, Freiburg im Breisgau, 1890-92 (Nachdr. Darmstadt, 1976).

Benoît-Castelli (1961), Georges Benoît-Castelli, "Un Processional Anglais du XIV ème siècle", in: *Ephemerides liturgicae* 75 (1961) 181-326.

Benz (1956), S. Benz, "Zur Geschichte der römischen Kirchweihe nach den Texten des 6. bis 7. Jahrhunderts", in: *Enkainia*. Gesammelte Arbeiten zum 800 jährigen Weihegedächtenis der Abteikirche Maria Laach, Düsseldorf, 1956, 62-109.

Berlière (1927), D.U. Berlière, "La fête des saintes reliques", in: *Revue liturgique et monastique* 12 (1927) 337-343.

Bernos (1985), Marcel Bernos, Jean Guyon, Charles de la Roncière Philippe Lécrivain, *Le fruit défendue*, Les chrétiens et la sexualité de l'antiquité à nos jours, Paris, 1985.

Betz (1955), J. Betz, *Die Eucharistie in der Zeit der Griechischen Väter*, Band I,1 : Die Aktualpräsenz der Person und des Heilwerkes Jesu im Abendmahl nach der vorephesinischen griechischen Patristik, Freiburg, 1955.

Binterim (1827-31), A.J. Binterim, *Die vorzüglichsten Denkwür digkeiten der Christ-Katholischen Kirche aus den ersten, mittlern und letzten Zeiten*, 16 vol., Mainz, 1827-31.

Biraben (1969), J.N. Biraben et J. Le Goff, "La Peste dans le Haut Moyen Age", in: *Annales*(1969) 1484-1510.

Le Blant (1858), Edmond Le Blant, *La question: Vase de Sang*, Paris, 1858.

Le Blant (1875), Edmond Le Blant, "Sur une pierre tumulaire portant les mots 'Christus hic est'", in: *Revue de l'art chrétien* 19, 28e jrg. t. II (1875) 25-31.

Blouet (1953), L. Blouet, *Le chrismale de Mortain*, Coutances, 1953.

Blumenfeld-Kosinki (1991), Renate Blumenfeld-Kosinki and Timea Szell, *Images of Sainthood in medieval Europe*, New York, 1991.

Bock (1873), Fr. Bock et M. Willemsen, *Antiquités sacrées conservées de S. Servais et de Notre-Dame à Maestricht*, Maestricht, 1873.

Bock (1989), U. Bock, "Kontaktreliquien, Wachssakramentalien und Phylakterien", in: Legner (1989), 154-161.

Boeft den (1988), J. den Boeft, "Milaan 386: Protasius en Gervasius", in: A. Hilhorst (red.), *De heiligenverering in de eerste eeuwen van het christendom*, Nijmegen, 1988, 168-177.

Boelaars (1968), H. Boelaars, "Riflessioni sur giuramento", in: *Studia Moralia*, VI, Roma, 1968, 175-205.

Boeren (1962), P.C. Boeren, *Heiligdomsvaart Maastricht*, Maastricht, 1962.

Boglioni (1979, Pierre Boglioni, "La scène de la mort dans les premières hagiographies latines", in: C. Sutto, *Sentiment de la mort au Moyen Age*, Québec, 1979, 183-210.

Borst (1935, A. Borst, *Die Katharer*, MGH, Schriften, Band XII, Stuttgart, 1953.

Bosman (1985), L. Bosman, "Schatkamers, relieken en architectuur", in: Koldewey (1985a), 27-43.

Bosman (1985a), L. Bosman, "Turris sanctorum locus est". Over de vorm, inhoud en betekenis van de ostensoria, in: *Antiek* 19 (1985) 306-314.

Botte (1948), B. Botte, "L'Onction des malades", in: *LMD* 15 (1948) 91-107.

Boussel (1971), P. Boussel, *Des reliques et de leur bon usage*, Paris, 1971.

Brandmann (1974), G. Brandmann, "Zur Bestimmung der romanischen Scheitelrotunde an der Peterskirche zu Löwen", in: *Beiträge zur Rheinischen Kunstgeschichte und Denkmalpflege*, II (Festschrift Albert Verbeek), Düsseldorf, 1974.

Brandt (1924), O. v. Brandt, *Bertholds von Regensburg deutsche Predigten*, Jena, 1924.

Le Bras (1956), G. Le Bras, *Etudes de sociologie religieuse*, Paris, 1956.

Braun (1924), J. Braun, *Der christliche Altar in seiner geschichtlichen Entwicklung*, 2 vol., München, 1924.

Braun (1932), J.Braun, *Das christliche Altargerät*, München, 1932.

Braun (1940), J. Braun, *Die Reliquiare des christlichen Kultes und ihre Entwicklung*, Freiburg im Breisgau, 1940.

Bredero (1959), A.H. Bredero, "Un brouillon du XIIe s.: l'autographe de Geoffrey d'Auxerre", in: *Scriptorium, revue internationale des études relatives aux manuscrits*, vol. 13, Brussel, 27-60.

Bredero (1960), A.H. Bredero, *Etudes sur la Vita prima de Saint Bernard*, Rome, 1960.

Bredero (1994³), A.H. Bredero, *Christendom and Christianity*, Michigan, 1994³

Bridgett (1908), T.E. Bridgett, *A history of the holy Eucharist in Great Britain*, London, 1908.

Broekaert (1985), Marijke Broekaert, Kristus op de palmezel, Bijdrage tot een kultuurhistorische en ikonografische betekenis van een processiebeeld, in: *Oostvlaamse Zanten* 60 (1985) 125, 215.

Brooks (1921), N.C. Brooks, *The sepulchre of Christ in Art and Liturgy*, Illinois, 1921.

Brou (1959), L. Brou O.S.B., *Les oraisons des dimanches après la pentecôte*, Bruges, 1959.

Browe (1927), P. Browe, "Die Hostienschändungen der Juden im Mittelalter", in: *RQS* 34 (1927) 167-198.

Browe (1927a), P. Browe, "Die Entstehung der Sakramentsandachten", in *JLw* 7 (1927) 83-103.

Browe (1928), P. Browe, "Die Abendmahlsprobe im Mittelalter", in: *HJ* 48 (1928) 193-207.

Browe (1928a), P. Browe, "Die Ausbreitung des Fronleichnamsfestes", in *JLw* 8 (1928) 107-143.

Browe (1929), P. Browe, "Die öftere Kommunion der Laien im Mittelalter", in: *Bonner Zeitschrift für Theologie und Seelsorge* 6 (1929) 1-28.

Browe (1929a), P. Browe, "Die eucharistischen Flurprozessionen und Wettersegen", in: *Theologie und Glaube*, 21 (1929) 742-753.

Browe (1929b), P. Browe, "Die Kommunion in der Pfarrkirche", in: *ZkTh*53 (1929) 477-516.

Browe (1929c), P. Browe, "Die Elevation in der Messe", in: *JLw* 9 (1929) 20-66.

Browe (1929d), P. Browe, "Die scholastische Theorie der eucharistischen Verwandlungswunder", in: *TQ* 110 (1929) 305-332.

Browe (1929e), P. Browe, "Die eucharistischen Verwandlungswunder des Mittelalters", in: *RQS* 37 (1929) 137-169.

Browe (1929f), P. Browe, "Die scholastischen Verwandlungswunder", in *TQ* 110 (1929) 305-332.

Browe (1930), P. Browe, "Die Eucharistie als Zaubermittel im Mittelalter", in: *Archiv für Kulturgeschichte* 20 (1930) 134-154.

Browe (1930a), P. Browe, "Die Kommunion an den drei letzten Kartagen", in: *JLw* 10 (1930) 56-76.

Browe (1931), P. Browe, "Die letzte ölung in der abendländische Kirche des Mittelalters", in: *ZkTh* 55 (1931) 515-561.

Browe (1931a), P. Browe, "Der Segen mit Reliquien, der Patene und Eucharistie", in: *Ephemerides liturgicae* 45 (Rome, 1931) 383-391.

Browe (1931b), P. Browe, "Wann fing man an die Kommunion ausserhalb der Messe auszuteilen", in: *Theologie und Glaube* 23 (Paderborn, 1931) 755-762.

Browe (1931c), P. Browe, "Die Nüchternheit vor der Messe und Kommunion im Mittelalter", in: *Ephemerides liturgicae* 45 (1931) 383-391.

Browe (1931d), P. Browe, "Die Entstehung der Sakramentsprozessionen", in: *Bonner Zeitschrift für Theologie und Seelsorge* 8 (1931) 97-117.

Browe (1932), P. Browe, "Zum Kommunionempfang des Mittelaters", in: *JLw* XIII (1932) 161-177.

Browe (1932a), P. Browe, "Kommunionriten früherer Zeiten", in: *Theologie und Glaube* 24 (Paderborn, 1932) 592-607.

Browe (1932b), P. Browe, "Die Kommunionvorbereitung im Mittelalter", in: *ZkTh* 56 (1932) 375-415.

Browe (1933), P. Browe, *Die Verehrung der Eucharistie im Mittelalter*, München, 1933 (Nachdr. 1967).

Browe (1934), P. Browe, *Beiträge zur Sexualethik des Mittelalters*, Breslauer Studien zur historischen Theologie (23), 1934.

Browe (1935), P. Browe, "Die Kommunionandacht im Altertum und Mittelalter", in: *JLw* 13 (1935) 45-64.

Browe (1935a), P. Browe, "Mittelalterliche Kommunionriten", in : *JLw* 15 (1935) 23-66.

Browe (1936), P. Browe, "Die Sterbekommunion im Altertum und Mittelalter", in: *ZKTh* 60 (1936) 1-54; 211-240.

Browe (1936a), P. Browe, "Liturgische Delikte und ihre Bestrafung im Mittelalter", in: *Theologie und Glaube* 28 (1936) 53-63.

Browe (1938), P. Browe, *Die eucharistischen Wunder des Mittelalters*, Breslau, 1938.

Browe (1938a), P. Browe, *Die häufige Kommunion im Mittelalter*, Münster i. W., 1938.

Browe (1940), P. Browe, *Die Pflichtkommunion in Mittelalter*, Münster i. W., 1940.

Brown (1982²), P. Brown, *The cult of the Saints*, Chicago, 1981; 1982.

Brown (1982a), P. Brown, *Society and the Holy in Late Antiquity*, London, 1982.

Brown (1992), P. Brown, *Power and persuasion in late antiquity. Towards a christian empire*, The University of Wisconsin Press, Madison, 1992.

Bruder (1901), P. Bruder, "Die Fronleichnamsfeier zu Mainz um das Jahr 1400", in: *Der Katholik*, 81,I (1901) 489-507.

Bruel (1905), M. Bruel, "Processions demandées par Louis XI aux religieux de Saint-Léonard en 1479", in: *Bulletin historique et philologique du comité des travaux historiques et scientifiques*,Paris, 1905, 10-13.

Bruyne de (1922), D. de Bruyne, "L'Origine des processions de la chandeleur et des rogations à propos d'un sermon inédit", in: *Revue Bénédictine* 34 (1922) 14-26.

Bruyne de (1927), D. de Bruyne, "Le plus ancien catalogue des reliques d'Oviedo, in: *An. Boll.* XIV (1927) 93-96.

Buchner (1912), Fr. X. Buchner, "Liturgische Prozessionen im Mittelalter", in: *Pastoralblatt des Bistums Eichstätt*, 1912.

Buchner (1918), Fr. X. Buchner, *Archivinventare der kathol. Pfarreien in der Diöz. Eichstätt*. Veröffentlichungen der Ges. für fränkische Gesch. V,2, 1918.

Buschausen (1971), H. Buschausen, *Die spätrömischen Metallscrinia und frühchristlichen Reliquiare*, Wien, 1971.

Cahen (1930), Maur Cahen et Magnus Olsen, *L'inscription runique du coffret de Mortain*, Paris, 1930.

Capelle (1959), C. Capelle, *Le voeu d'obéissance des origines au XIIe siècle*, Paris, 1959.

Carosso-Kok (1981), M. Carosso-Kok, *Repertorium van verhalende bronnen uit de middeleeuwen. Heiligenlevens, annalen, kronieken en andere in Nederland geschreven verhalende bronnen*, 's-Gravenhage, 1981.

Casel (1931), O. Casel, "Ein orientalisches Kultwort in abendländischer Umschmelzung", in: *JLw* 11 (1931) 1-45.

Caspers (1992), Carles M. A. *De eucharistische vroomheid en het feest van Sacramentsdag in de Nederlanden tijdens de late middeleeuwen*, Leuven, 1992.

Cauteren v. (1985), J. van Cauteren, "Relieken en reliekhouders", in: Koldeweij (1985a), 8-26.

Chavasse (1942), A. Chavasse, *Etude sur l'onction des infirmes dans l'Eglise latine du IIIe siècle a la Réforme carolingienne*, Lyon, 1942.

Cochet (1857), J. Cochet, *Sépultures gauloises, romaines, franques et normandes faisant suite à La Normandie souterraine*, Paris, 1857.

Corbin (1960), S. Corbin, *La déposition liturgique du Christ au Vendredi-Saint*, Paris-Lisbonne, 1960.

Corblet (1885-86), J. Corblet, *Histoire dogmatique, liturgique et archéologique du Sacrament de l'Eucharistie*, 2 vol., Paris, 1885-86.

Couneson (1935-36), D.S. Couneson, "La visite des autels dans la tradition monastique", in: *Revue Liturgique et Monastique* 21 (1935-36) 8-21, 142-54, 378-87.

Cozza Luzzi (1887), J. Cozza Luzzi, "Ein altchristliches Phylacterium aus Blei", in: *RQS* 1 (1887) 197-208.

Cré (1894), L. Cré, "Une découverte eucharistique", in: *Revue Biblique* (1894) 277-291.

Cumont (1946), F. Cumont, "Cierges et lampes sur les tombeaux", in: *Miscellanea Giovanni Mercati* V (1946) 41-47.

Dalton (1909), O.M. Dalton, *Catalogue of the Ivory Carvings of the Christian Era in the British Museum*, London, 1909.

Daniélou (1963), J. Daniélou, "Van de stichting van de kerk tot de 4e eeuw", dl. I of: *Geschiedenis van de kerk*, red. L.J. Rogier et al., Hilversum, 1963-74.

Darrouzès (1963), J. Darrouzès, "Le mémoire de Constantine Stilbes contre les Latins", in: *Revue des études Byzantines* 21 (1963) 50-90.

Dassmann (1975), E. Dassmannn, "Ambrosius und die Märtyrer", in: *JbAC* 18 (Münster i. W., 1975) 49-68.

David (1953), M. David, *Le serment du sacre du IXe au XVe siècle*, Chartres, 1953.

418   MEDIEVAL PIETY FROM RELICS TO THE EUCHARIST

Decker (1985), B. Decker, *Das Ende des mittelalterlichen Kultbildes und die Plastik Hans Leinbergers*, Bamberg, 1985 (Bamberger Studien zur Kunstgeschichte und Denkmalpflege 3).

Deichmann (1970), F.W. Deichmann, "Märtyrerbasilika, Martyrion, Memoria und Altargrab", in: *Mitteilungen des Deutschen Archäologischen Instituts* (Abt. 77), Rom, 1970, 144-169.

Deichmann (1983), F.W. Deichmann, *Einführung in die christliche Archäologie*, Darmstadt, 1983.

Dekkers (1950), Dom Eligius Dekkers, "De reservatie der eucharistie", in: *Pro regno sanctuario* (Miscellanea, G. van der Leeuw), Nijkerk, 1950, 141-156.

Delaruelle (1975), E. Delaruelle, *La piéteé populaire au moyen âge*, Turijn, 1975.

Delehaye (1927), H. Delehaye, *Sanctus*. Essai sur le culte des saints dans l'Antiquité, Bruxelles, 1927.

Delehaye (1930), H. Delehaye, "Loca sanctorum", in: *An. Boll.* 48 (1930) 5-64.

Delehaye (1933), H. Delehaye, *Les origines du culte des martyrs*, Bruxelles, 1933.

Dendy (1959), D.R. Dendy, *The Use of Lights in Christian Worship*, London 1959 (Alcuin Club Collections, 41).

Denifle (1965), H. Denifle, *La désolation des églises monastères et hopitaux en France pendant la guerre de cent ans*, 2 vol., Bruxelles, 1965 (original ed. Paris, 1897-99).

Dersch (1931), W. Dersch, "Hessische Wallfahrten im Mittelater", in: *Festschrift Albert Brackmann*, Weimar, 1931, 457-491.

Devlin (1975), D.S. Devlin, *Corpus Christi: a study in medieval eucharistic theory, devotion and practice*, The University of Chicago, 1975.

Diezinger (1961), W. Dietzinger, *Effectus in der römische Liturgie*, Bonn, 1961.

Dijk v. (1957), S.J.P. van Dijk and J. Hazelden Walker, *The myth of the aumbry*, London, 1957.

Dinkler (1980), E. Dinkler, "Petrus und Paulus in Rom", in: *Gymnasium* 87 (1980) 1-37.

Dix (1945), G. Dix, *The shape of the Liturgie*, Westminster, 1945.

Dölger (1922), F.J. Dölger, *Ichthys*, I-II, Münster, 1922.

Dölger (1929-50), F.J. Dölger, *Antike und Christentum*, I-VI, Münster, 1929-50 (repr. 1974-76).

Doncoer (1955), P. Doncoer, S.J., "Sens humain de la procession", in: *LMD* 43 (1955) 29-36.

Dorenbosch (1986), P.Th.A. Dorenbosch, *De Boxtelse St. Petrus. Kerk van de parochie Sint-Petrus Stoel te Antiochië te Boxtel*, II, Boxtel, 1986.

Dossat (1976), Y. Dossat, "Les confréries du Corpus Christi dans le monde rural pendant la première moitié du XIVe siècle", in: *CF* 11 (1976) 357-383.

Duby (1976), Georges Duby, *Le temps des cathédrales*, Paris, 1976.

Du Cange (1883-87), Ch.D. Du Cange, *Glossarium mediae et infimae latinitatis*, ed. L. Favre, 10 vol., Niort, 1883-87.

Duchesne (1925), L. Duchesne, *Origines du culte chrétien*, Paris, 1925.

Ducroux (1975), Serge Ducroux, *Catalogue analytique des inscriptions latines sur pierre, conservées au Musée du Louvre*, Paris, 1975.

Dumoutet (1926), E. Dumoutet, *Le desir du voir l'Hostie et les origines de la dévotion au Saint-Sacrament*, Paris, 1924.

Dumoutet (1932), E. Dumoutet, *Le Christ selon la chair et la vie liturgique au moyen âge*, Paris, 1932.

Dumoutet (1942), E. Dumoutet, *Corpus Domini*. Aux sources de la Piété Eucharistique Médiéval, Paris, 1942.

Duval (1946), A. Duval, "Le concile du Trente et le culte eucharistique", in: *Studia Eucharistica*, Bussum, Antwerpen, 1946, 379-414.

Duval (1991), Yvette Duval, "Sanctorum sepulcris sociari", in Tilliette (1991), 333-351.

Dyggve (1939), Ejnar Dyggve und R. Egger, *Forschungen in Salona*, III, Wien, 1939.

Dyggve (1951), Enjar Dyggve, *History of Salonitan Christanity*, Oslo, 1951.

Ebner (1896), A. Ebner, *Quellen und Forschungen zur Geschichte und Kunstgeschichte des Missale Romanum im Mittelalter. Iter Italicum*, Freiburg, 1896.

Ehresmann (1982), D.L. Ehresmann, "Some Observations on the Role of Liturgy in the early winged Altarpiece", in: *The Art Bulletin* LXIV,3, (1982) 359-369.

Ellenbracht (1963), M.P. Ellenbach, *Remarks on the vocabulary of the ancient orations in the Missale Romanum*, Utrecht, Nijmegen, 1963.

Engels (1965), P. Engels, "De eucharistieleer van Berengarius van Tours", in: *TvT* 5 (1965) 363-392.

Engemann (1973), Josef Engemann, "Palästinensische Pilgerampullen im F.J. Dölger-Institut in Bonn", in: *JbAC* 16 (1973) 5-27.

Engemann (1975), Josef Engemann, "Zur Verbreitung magischer Übelwehr in der nichtchristlichen und christlichen Spätantike", *JbAC* 18 (1975) 22-48.

Engen v. (1986), J. van Engen, "The Christian Middle Ages as an Historiographical Problem", in: *The American Historical Review* 91 (1986) 519-552.

Escher (1978), F. Escher, "Brandenburgische Wallfahrten und Wallfahrtsorte im Mittelalter", in: *Jahrbuch für die Geschichte Mittel- und Ostdeutschlands*17 (1978) 116-137.

Farcy de (1901), L. de Farcy, *Monographie de la cathédrale d'Angers*, Angers, 1901.

Fichtenau (1952), H. Fichtenau, "Zum Reliquienwesen im früheren Mittelalter", in: *Mitteilungen des Instituts für österreichische Geschichtsforschung* 60 (1952) 60-89 (repr. in: *Beiträge zur Mediävistik. Ausgewählte Aufsätze*, Bd.1, Stuttgart, 1975, 108-144).

Finucane (1977), R.C. Finucane, *Miracles and pilgrims. Popular beliefs in medieval England*, London-Melbourne-Toronto, 1977.

Flandrin (1983), Jean-Louis Flandrin, *Un temps pour embrasser.* Aux origines de la morale sexuelle occidentale (VIe-IXe siècle), Paris, 1983.

Foreville (1943), R. Foreville, *L'Eglise et la Royauté en Algleterre sous Henri II Plantagenet (1154-1189)*, Paris, 1943.

Förster (1943), M. Förster, "Zur Geschichte des Reliquienkultus im Altengland", in: *Sitzungsberichte der Bayerischen Akademie der Wissenschaften* Heft 8 (1943).

Foss (1979), Clive Foss, *Ephesus after Antiquity, a late antique, Byzantine and Turkisch city*, London, 1973.

Frank (1951), H. Frank, "Untersuchungen zur Geschichte der benediktinischen Professliturgie im frühen Mittelalter", in: *Studien und Mitteilungen zur Geschichte des benediktinenordens und seiner Zweige* (Salzburg) 63 (München, 1951) 93-139.

Franz (1902), A. Franz, *Die Messe im deutschen Mittelalter*, Freiburg im Breisgau, 1902.

Franz (1909), A. Franz, *Die kirchlichen Benediktionen im Mittelalter*, 2 vol., Freiburg im Breisgau, 1909.

Freestone (1917), W.H. Freestone, *The Sacrament Reserved*, London 1917 (Alcuin Club Collections, 21).

Freudenthal (1931), H. Freudenthal, *Das Feuer im deutschen Glauben und Brauch*, Berlin und Leipzig, 1931.

Frolow (1961), A. Frolow, *La Relique de la Vraie Croix*, Paris, 1961.

Frolow (1961a), A. Frolow, *La culte de la relique de la Vraie Croix à la fin du VIe - et au début du VIIe - siècles*, Byzantinos la vica (Praha 12), 1961, 320-339.

Frolow (1965), A. Frolow, *Les Reliquaires de la Vraie Croix*, Paris, 1965.

Fürstenberg (1917), P. Fürstenberg, "Zur Geschichte der Fronleichnamsfeier in der alten Diözese Paderborn", in: *Theologie und Glaube* 9 (1917) 314-325.

Gagé (1929), J. Gagé, "Membra Christi et la déposition des reliques sous l'autel", in: *Revue archéologique* 5 ser. t. 29 (1929) 137-153.

Gaier (1966), "Le rôle militaire des reliques et de l'étendard de Saint Lambert dans da principauté de Liège", in: *Le Moyen Age* LXXII (1966) 235-249.

Geary (1978), P.J. Geary, *Furta Sacra, Thefts of Relics in the Central Middle Ages*, Princeton, 1978.

Geary (1985), P.J. Geary, "Humiliation of Saints", in: S. Wilson, *Saints and their cults*, Cambridge, 1983, 1985, 123-140.

Geiselmann (1929), J. R. Geiselmann, "Die Stellung des Guibert von Nogent in der Eucharistielehre der Frühscholastiek", in: *TQ* 110 (1929) 66-84; 279-304.

Geiselmann (1933), J.R. Geiselmann, *Die Abendmahlslehre an der Wende der christlichen Spätantike zum Frümittelalter*, München, 1933.

Gerken (1973), A. Gerken, *Theologie der Eucharistie*, München, 1973.

Gillmann (1922), F. Gillmann, "Von der Hinterlegung des Allerheiligsten im Altarsepulchrum", in: *Archiv für katholisches Kirchenrecht* 102 (1922) 33-41.

Gougaud (1925), L. Gougaud, *Dévotions et Pratiques ascetiques du moyen-âge*, Paris, 1925.

Gozier (1986), A. Gozier, *Odo Casel, Künder des Christusmysteriums*, Regensburg, 1986.

Grabar (1946), A. Grabar, *Martyrion*. Recherches sur le culte des reliques et l'art chrétien antique, 2 vol., Paris, 1946 (repr. London, 1972).

Grabar (1958), A. Grabar, *Ampoules de terre sainte*, Paris, 1958.

Grabka (1953), G. Grabka, "Christian viaticum, a study of its cultural background", in: *Traditio* 9 (1953) 1-43.

Graus (1965), F. Graus, Volk, *Herrscher und Heiliger im Reich der Merowinger*, Praag, 1965.

Greving (1908), J. Greving, *Johann Ecks Pfarrbuch für U.L.Frau in Ingolstadt*, Münster i. W., 1908.

Grimm (1876⁴), J. Grimm, *Deutsche Mythologie*, 1-3, Berlin, 1876⁴.

Grimme (1972), Ernst Günther Grimme, *Goldschmiedekunst im Mittelalter. Form und Bedeutung des Reliquiars von 800 bis 1500*, Köln, 1972.

Gross (1975), K. Gross, "Der Tod des hl. Benedictus", in: *Revue Bénédictine* 85 (1975) 164-176.

Gschwend (1965), Kolumban Gschwend OSB, *Die depositio und elevatio crucis im Raum der alten Diözese Brixen*, Sarnen, 1965.

Günter (1906), H. Günter, *Legenden-Studien*, Köln, 1906.

Gurjewitsch (1978), A.J. Gurjewitsch, *Das Weltbild des mittelalterlichen Menschen*, München, 1978.

Gurjewitsch (1987), A.J. Gurjewitsch, *Mittelalterliche Volkskultur*, München, 1987.

Gurevich (1988), A. J. Gurevich, *Medieval popular culture. Problems of belief and perception*, Cambridge, New York, 1988 (repr. 1990).

Gurjewitsj (1992), "Middeleeuwse volkscultuur: een herwaardering", in: *Millennium*, 6e jrg. 1 (1992) 4-16.

Guth (1970), K. Guth, *Guibert von Nogent und die hochmittelalterliche Kritik an der Reliquienverehrung*, Ottobeuren, 1970.

Guyon (1985), J.Guyon, "D'Auguste à Charlemagne, La montée des interdits", in: Marcel Bernos (1985).

Gy (1987), Pierre-Marie Gy, "La doctrine eucharistique dans la liturgie Romaine du haut moyen-âge", in: *Segni e riti nella chiesa altomedievale occidentale*, 11-17 aprile 1985, vol. II, Spoleto, 1987, 533-557.

Habiger-Tuczay (1992), Christa Habiger-Tuczay, *Magie und Magier im Mittelalter*, München, 1992.

Haimerl (1937), Xaxer Haimerl, *Das Prozessionswesen des Bistums Bamberg im Mittelalter*, Münchener Studien zur Historischen Theologie, München, 1937.

Hain (1956), Mathilde Hain, "Burchard von Worms (1025) und der Volksglaube seiner Zeit", in: *Hessische Blätter für Volkskunde* XLVII (1956) 39-50.

Hallinger (1956), K. Hallinger, "Le climat spirituel des premiers temps de Cluny", in: *Revue Mabillon* 46 (1956) 117-140.

Halphen (1906), L. Halphen, *Le Comté d'Anjou au XIe siècle*, Paris, 1906 (repr. Genèva, 1974).

Haunerland (1989), W. Haunerland, *Die Eucharistie und ihre Wirkungen im Spiegel der Euchologie des Missale Romanum*, Münster i.W., 1989

Haupt (1849), M. Haupt, "Herzog Ernst", in: *Zeitschrift für deutsches Altertum* 7 (1849) 193-303.

Hauser (1975), A. Hauser, *Sociale geschiedenis van de kunst*, Nijmegen, 1975, (original title: *The Social History of Art*).

Häussling (1973), A. Häussling, *Mönchskonvent und Eucharistie feier. Eine Studie über die Messe in der abendländischen Klosterliturgie des frühen Mittelalters und zur Geschichte der Messhäufigkeit* (Liturgiewissenschaftliche Quellen und Forschungen, 58), Münster, 1973.

Head (1990), Thomas Head, *Hagiography and the cult of Saints*, The Diocese of Orléans, 800-1200, Cambridge, New York, 1990.

Hefele (1907-42), C. Hefele et H. Leclercq, *Histoire des Conciles*, Paris, 1907-42.

Hefele (1912), K. Hefele, *Der hl. Bernhardin von Siena und die franziskanische Wanderpredigt in Italien während des XV Jahrhunderts*, Freiburg im Breisgau, 1912.

Heinzelmann (1979), M. Heinzelmann, *Translationsberichte und andere Quellen des Reliquienkultes* (Sources du M.A. 33: Reliquienkult), Turnhout, 1979.

Heitz (1963), C. Heitz, *Recherches sur les rapports entre Architecture et Liturgie à l'époque carolingienne*, Paris, 1963.

Heitz (1974), C. Heitz, "Architecture et liturgie processionelle à l'époque préromane", in: *Revue de l'Art* 24 (1974) 30-47.

Heitz (1987), C. Heitz, "Eucharistie, Synaxe et espace liturgique", in: *Segni e riti nella chiesa altomedievale occidentale*, 11-17 aprile 1985, vol. II, Spoleto, 1987, 609-638.

Heliot (1964-65), Pierre Heliot et Marie-Laure Chastang, "Quêtes et voyages de reliques au profit des églises Francaises du Moyen-Age", in: *Revue d'histoire ecclésiastique* LIX (1964) 789-822; LX (1965) 5-32.

Hermann (1953), A. Hermann, "Charon", in: *RAC* II (1953) 1040-1061.

Hermann-Mascard (1975), Nicole Hermann-Mascard, *Les reliques des saints. Formation coutumière d'un droit*, Paris, 1975.

Hermans (1983), J. Hermans, *Uw geheim ligt op de tafel des Heren. De eucharistie in oud-christelijke geschriften. Een bloemlezing*, Brugge, 1983.

Herwaarden v. (1978), J. v. Herwaarden, *Opgelegde bedevaarten*. Een studie over de praktijk van opleggen van bedevaarten (met name in de stedelijke rechtspraak) in de Nederlanden gedurende de late middeleeuwen (ca 1300- ca 1550), Assen-Amsterdam, 1978.

Herwaarden v. (1980), J. v. Herwaarden, R. de Keyser, "Het gelovige volk in de late middeleeuwen", in: *Algemene Geschiedenis der Nederlanden*, IV, Haarlem, 1980, 405-420.

Herwaarden v. (1982), J. v. Herwaarden, "Geloof en geloofsuitingen in de 14e en 15e eeuw. Eucharistie en lijden van Jezus", in: *Hoofsheid en devotie in de middeleeuwse maatschappij*, Handelingen van het wetenschappelijk colloquium te Brussel, 21-24, okt. 1981, ed. J.D. Janssens, Brussel, 1982, 176-207.

Hillgarth (1986), J.N. Hillgarth, *Christianity and Paganism, 350-750. The Conversion of Western Europe*, Philadelphia, 1986.

Hofmeister (1957), T.Ph. Hofmeister, *Die christlichen Eidesformen*, München, 1957.

Hofmeister (1963), T. Ph. Hofmeister, "Wo und wann wird die Ordensprofess abgelegt", in: W. Dürig, *Liturgie, Gestalt und Vollzug*, München, 1963, 114-137.

Honselmann (1962), K. Honselmann, "Reliquientranslationen nach Sachsen", in: *Das erste Jahrtausend. Kultur und Kunst im werdenden Abendland an Rhein und Ruhr*, I, Düsseldorf, 1962, 159-193.

Hubert (1961), Jean Hubert, "La basilique de Martin le confesseur", in: *Revue d'histoire de l'église de France* 47 (1961) 215-221.

Hubert (1977), Jean Hubert, *Arts et vie sociale de la fin du monde antique au Moyen Age*. Etudes d'archeologie et d'histoire. Recueil offert à l'auteur par ses élèves et ses amis, Genève, 1977.

Hubert (1977a), Jean Hubert, "Cryptae inferiores et cryptae superiores dans l'architecture religieuse de l'époque carolingienne", in: Hubert, *Arts et vie sociale*, 1477, 409-415 (first publication in Mélanges d'histoire dédiés à L. Halphen, Paris, 1951).

Hubert (1982), Jean Hubert et Marie-Clotilde Hubert, "Piété chrétienne ou paganisme? Les statues-reliquaires de l'Europe Carolingienne", in: *Christianizzione ed organizzazione delle campagne nell' alto medioevo: espansione e resistenze Settimane di studio* 28 (Spoleto, 1982) 234-275.

Huizinga (1921²), J. Huizinga, Herfsttij der Middeleeuwen, Haarlem, 1921² ; (1990), *The Waning of the Middle Ages*, Penguin Books, London, 1990.

Hyvernat (1888), H. Hyvernat, *Album de paléographie Copte pour servir à l'introduction paléographique des Actes des Martyrs de l'Egypte*, Paris, 1888.

Jone (1950-55), P. Heriberto Jone, *Commentarium in Codicem Iuris Canonici*, 3 vol., Paderborn, 1950-55.

Jong de (1982), Mayke de Jong, "Monniken, ridders en geweld in het elfde eeuwse Vlaanderen", in: *Sociologische Gids* 29 (1982) 279-296.

Jong de (1986), Mayke de Jong, " 'Volk' en geloof in vroegmiddeleeuwse teksten", in: G. Rooyakkers en T. v.d. Zee (ed.), *Religieuze volkscultuur*, Nijmegen, 1986, 16-35.

Jounel (1987), P. Jounel, "Le culte des reliques et son influence sur l'art chrétien", in: *LMD* 170 (1987) 29-57.

Jungmann (1941), J.A. Jungmann, *Gewordene Liturgie*, Innsbruck, 1941.

Jungmann (1943), J.A. Jungmann, "Accepit panem", in: *ZkTh* 67 (1943) 162-165 (also in: *Liturgisches Erbe und pastorale Gegenwart*, 1960, 366-372).

Jungmann (1952), J.A. Jungmann, "Die Andacht der vierzig Stunden und das Heilige Grab", in: *LJ* 2 (1952) 184-198.

Jungmann (1952a), J.A. Jungmann, "Ein Symbol Kirchlicher Einheit und sein Nachleben im Mittelalter", in: *Colligere fragmenta*. Festschrift Alban Dold, Texte und Arbeiten I,2, Beiheft, Beuren, 1952, 185-190 (also in: *Liturgisches Erbe und pastorale Gegenwart*, 1960, 379-389).

Jungmann (1962), J.A. Jungmann, *Missarum Sollemnia*, 2 vol., Wien, Freiburg, Basel, 1962.

Jungmann (1974), J.A. Jungmann, "Rezension zu Häussling", in: *ZkTh* 96 (1974) 303-306.

Keller (1951), H. Keller, "Zur Entstehung der sakralen Volkskulptur in der ottonischen Zeit", in: *Festschrift H. Jantzen*, Berlin, 1951, 71-91.

Keller (1956), H. Keller, "Zur Entstehung der Reliquienbüste aus Holtz", in: *Kunstgeschichtliche Studien für Hans Kaufmann*, Berlin, 1956, 71-80.

Keller (1965), H. Keller, "Der Flügelaltar als Reliquienschrein", in: *Studien zur Geschichte der Europäischen Plastik*, Festschrift für Theodor Müller am 9 April 1965, München, 1965, 125-144 (Neudruck in: Blicke vom Monte Caro, Kleine Schriften, Frankfurt, 1984, 61 sqq.).

Keller (1975), H. Keller, "Reliquien in Architecturteilen beigesetzt", in: *Beiträge zur Kunst des Mittelalters. Festschrift für Hans Wentzel*, Berlin, 1975, 105-114.

Kennedy (1944), L. Kennedy, "The moment of the Consecration and the Elevation of the Host", in: *Medieval Studies* 6 (1944) 121-150.

Kettel (1953), J. Kettel, "Zur Liturgie des Gründonnerstag", in: *LJ* 3 (1953) 60-74.

Khoury (1966), E. Khoury, "Les canons sur l'eucharistie in 'Kitâb al-Huda'", in: *Melto* 2 (1966) 251-171.

Kidd (1958), B.J. Kidd, *The later medieval doctrine of the Eucharistic Sacrifice*, London, 1958.

Kieckhefer (1984), R. Kieckhefer, *Unquiet Souls*, London, 1984.

King (1965), A.A. King, *Eucharistic Reservation in the Western Church*, London, 1965.

Klauser (1969), T. Klauser, *A short history of the western liturgy*, London, 1969.

Klauser (1974), T. Klauser, "Die liturgischen Austauschbe ziehungen zwischen der Römischen und fränkisch-deutschen Kirche vom achten bis zum elften Jahrhundert", in: *Gesammelte Arbeiten*, ed. E. Dassmann, Münster i. W., Aschendorff, 1974, 139- 154.

Klauser (1974a), T. Klauser, "Christliche Märtyrerkult,heidnischer Heroenkult und spätjüdische Heiligenverehrung", in: *Gesammelte Arbeiten*, ed. E. Dassmann, Münster i. W., Aschendorff, 1974, 221-229.

Knowles (1971), D. Knowles, *Thomas Becket*, California, 1971.

Koldeweij (1985), A.M. Koldewij, *Der gude Sente Servas*, Assen-Maastricht, 1985

Koldeweij (1985a), A.M. Koldewij en P.M.L. van Vlijmen, *Schatkamers uit het Zuiden*, Utrecht, 1985.

Köstler (1912), R. Köstler, "Der Anteil des Christentums an den Ordalien", in: *Zeitschrift der Savigny-Stiftung für Rechtsgeschichte* Kan. Abt. 2 (1912) 208-148.

Kötting (1950), B. Kötting, *Peregrinatio Religiosa*, Münster i. W., 1950.

Kötting (1965), B. Kötting, *Der frühchristliche Reliquienkult und die Bestattung im Kirchengebäude*, Köln und Opladen, 1965.

Kraus (1886), F.X. Kraus, *Real-Encyclopädie der christlichen Altertümer*, Freiburg, 1886.

Kraus (1972), A. Kraus, *Die Translatio S. Dionysii Areopagitae von St. Emmeram in Regensburg*, München, 1972.

Kroos (1985), R. Kroos, "Vom Umgang mit reliquien", in: *Ornamenta Ecclesiae*. Kunst und Künstler der Romanik. Katalog zur Ausstellung des Schnütgen-Museums in der Josef-Haubrick-Kunsthalle, III, Keulen, 1985, 25-49.

Kyriakakis (1947), J. Kyriakakis, "Byzantine burial customs: Care of the deceased from death to the prothesis", in: *Greek Orthodox Theological review* 19 (1974) 37-72.

Lane Fox (1986), R. Lane Fox, *Pagans and Christians*, Harmondsworth, 1986.

Lauwers (1987), M. Lauwers, "Religion populaire, culture folklorique, mentalités. Notes pour une antropologie culturelle du moyen âge", in: *Revue d'Histoire Ecclésiastique* 82 (1987) 221-258.

Lauwerijs (1952-1954), L. Lauwerys, *Het H. Bloed van Boxtel-Hoogstraten*, I-III, Brecht, 1952-1954.

Leclercq (1947), J. Leclercq, "Une prière des moines de Saint-Airy", in: *Revue Bénédictine* 62 t. 57 (1947) 224-226.

Leclerq (1962), J. Leclerq, F. Vandenbroucke et L. Bouyer, "La spiritualité du moyen âge", II, *Histoire de la spiritualité chrétienne*, Paris, 1962.

Lefeuvre (1932), P. Lefeuvre, *Courte Histoire des Reliques*, Paris, 1932.

Legner (1989), Anton Legner, *Reliquien: Verehrung und Verklärung*. Skizzen und Noten zur Thematik und Katalog zur Ausstellung der Kölner Sammlung Louis Peters im Schnütgen-Museum, Köln, 1989.

Le Goff (1977), J. Le Goff, *Pour un autre Moyen Age*. Temps, travail et culture en Occident: 18 essais, Paris, 1977.

Le Goff (1982), J. Le Goff, *La civilisation de l'Occident*, Paris, 1982.

Leitmaier (1953), Ch. Leitmaier, *Die Kirche und die Gottesurteile*. Eine rechtshistorische Studie Wiener rechtsgeschichtl. Arbeiten 2, Wien, 1953.

Lengeling (1966), E.J. Lengeling, "Die Bedeutung des Tabernakels im katholischen Kirchenraum", in: *LJ* 6 (1966) 156-187.

Lettinck (1983), N. Lettinck, *Geschiedbeschouwing en beleving van de eigen tijd in de eerste helft van de twaalfde eeuw*, Amsterdam, 1983.

Lexikon des Mittelalters, München und Zürich, 1977 sqq.

Little (1975), L. K. Little, "Formules monastiques de malédiction aux IXe et Xe siècles", in: *Revue Mabillon* LVIII (1975) 377-399.

Little (1979), L.K.Little, "La morphologie des malédictions monastiques", in: *Annales* (Economies, Sociétés, Civilisations), (1979) 43-60.

Little (1991), L.K. Little, "Spiritual Sanctions in Wales", in: Blumenfeld-Kosinki (1991), 67-80.

Loomis (1948), C. Grant Loomis, *White Magic*. An introduction to the Folklore of Christian Legend, Cambridge, Massachusetts, 1948.

Lotter (1988), F. Lotter, "Hostienfrevelvorwurf und Blutwunderfälschung bei den Judenverfolgungen von 1298 ('Rintfleisch') und 1336 ('Armleder')", in: *Fälschungen im Mittelalter*, Teil V, Fingierte Briefe, Frommigkeit und Fälschung, Realienfälschungen, Hannover, 1988, 533-581.

Lucius (1904), E. Lucius, *Die Anfänge des Heiligenkults in der christlichen Kirche*, Tübingen, 1904.

Lukken (1990), G. Lukken, "Les transformations du rôle liturgique du peuple: la contribution de la sémiotique à l'histoire de la liturgie", in: *Omnes circum adstantes*, contributions towards a history of the role of the people in the liturgy. Presented to Herman Wegman, ed. by Charles Caspers and Marc Schneiders, Kampen, 1990, 15-30.

Macquarrie (1972), J. Macquarrie, "Benediction of the blessed Sacrament", in: *Paths in spirituality*, New York, 1972, 94-162.

Maffei (1942), E. Maffei, *La Réservation eucharistique jusqu'à la Renaissance*, Bruxelles, 1942.

Margry (1988), P.J. Margry, *Amsterdam en het mirakel van het heilig sacrament. Van middeleeuwse devotie tot 20e-eeuwse stille omgang*, Amsterdam, 1988.

Marquès-Rivière (1950), J. Marquès-Rivière, *Amulettes, talismans et pentacles dans les traditions orientales et occidentales*, Paris, 1950.

Marrou (1964), H.I. Marrou, "Van de vervolging van Diocletianus tot de dood van Gregorius de Grote", dl. II of: *Geschiedenis van de kerk*, red. L.J. Rogier et al., Hilversum, 1963-74.

Martimort (1955), A.G. Martimort, "Les diverses formes de procession dans la liturgie", in: *LMD* 43 (1955) 43-73.

Martimort (1978), A.G. Martimort, *La documentation Liturgique de Dom Edmond Martène*, Studi e testi 279, Città del Vaticano, 1978.

Martimort (1983), A.G. Martimort, *L'Eglise en prière*, I-IV, 1983.

Martin (1987), J. Martin, *Atlas zur Kirchengeschichte*, herausgegeben von Hubert Jedin, Kenneth Scott Latourette, Jochen Martin, bearbeitet von Jochen Martin, Herder, Freiburg, Basel, Rom, Wien, 1987.

Matern (1962), G. Matern, *Zur Vorgeschichte und Geschichte der Fronleichnamsfeier, besonders in Spanien*, Münster, 1962.

Mayer (1926), A.L. Mayer, "Liturgie und Geist der Gotik", in: *JLw* 6 (1926) 68-97.

Mayer (1938), A.L. Mayer, "Die heilbringende Schau in Sitte und Kult", in: *Heilige Ueberlieferung. Festschrift Ildefons Herwegen*, hrsg. von Odo Casel, Münster, 1938, 234-262.

McCulloh (1980), J.M. McCulloh, "From antiquity to the middle ages: continuity and change in papal relic policy from the 6th. to the 8th. century", in: *Pietas. Festschrift für Bernhard Kötting*, herausgegeben von E. Dassmann und K. Suso Frank, Münster i. W., 1980, 313-324.

Meer v.d. (1947), F. van der Meer, *Augustinus de Zielzorger*, Utrecht, Brussel, 1947.

Meer v.d. (1962), F. van der Meer, *Keerpunt der Middeleeuwen*, Utrecht, 1962.

Meer v.d. (1979), F. van der Meer en G. Bartelink, *Gregorius de Grote: Het leven van Benedictus*, Nijmegen, 1979.

Mély de (1904), F. de Mély, *Exuviae sacrae constantinopolitanae. La croix des premières croises. La sainte lance - la sainte couronne*, Paris, 1904.

Mens (1946), A. Mens, "De verering van de h. eucharistie bij onze vroegste begijnen", in: *Studia Eucharistica*, 1946, Bussum, Antwerpen, 157-186.

Mens (1947), A. Mens, *Oorsprong en betekenis van de Nederlandse Begijnen- en Begardenbeweging*, Antwerpen, 1947.

Meyer (1950), E. Meyer, "Reliquie und Reliquiar im Mittelalter", in: *Eine Gabe der Freunde für Carl Georg Heise*, Berlin, 1950, 55-66.

Meyer (1963), H.B. Meyer, "Die Elevation im deutschen Mittelalter und bei Luther", in: *ZkTh* 85 (1963) 162-217.

Meyer (1965), H.B. Meyer, *Luther und die Messe*, Paderborn, 1965.

Michaud-Quantin (1971), P. Michaud-Quantin, "Textes pénitentiels languedociens au XIIIe siècle", in: *CF* 6 (1971) 151- 172.

Mitchell (1982), N. Mitchell, *Cult and Controversy: The Worship of the Eucharist Outside Mass*, New York, 1982.

Mitterwieser (1930), Al. Mitterwieser, *Geschichte der Fronleichnamprocessionen in Beieren*, Munich, 1930.

Montclos de (1971), J. de Montclos, *Lancfranc et Bérenger*, Leuven, 1971.

Moolenbroek v. (1989), J.J. van Moolenbroek, Omgang met de duivel, demonen en doden in dertiende-eeuws Nederland volgens exempels van Caesarius van Heisterbach. Over geleerde cultuur en volksgeloof, in: *Contextualiteit en christelijk geloof*, red. J. Tennekes en H.M. Vroom, Kampen, 1989, 130-150.

Mordek (1986), H. Mordek, *Überlieferung und Geltung normativer Texte des frühen und hohen Mittelalters*, Sigmaringen, 1986.

Morris (1972), C. Morris, "A critique of popular religion: Guibert of Nogent on The Relics of the Saints", in: G.J. Cumingand Derek Baker, *Popular Belief and Practice*, Cambridge, 1972.

Murcier (1855), A. Murcier, *La sépulture chrétienne en France d'après les monuments du XIe au XVIe siècle*, Paris, 1855.

Nagel (1956), A. Nagel, "Das heilige Blut Christi", in: *Festschrift zur 900 Jahr Feier des Klosters Weingarten 1056- 1956*, Weingarten, 188-229.

Neunheuser (1963), B. Neunheuser, *Eucharistie in Mittelalter und Neuzeit*. Handbuch der Dogmengeschichte, Bd. IV, 4b, Freiburg, Basel, 1963.

Nickl (1930), G. Nickel, *Der Anteil des Volkes an der Messliturgie im Frankenreich*, Innsbruck, 1930.

Niedermeier (1974-75), H. Niedermeier, "Über die Sakramentsprozessionen im Mittelalter. Ein Beitrag zur Geschichte der kirchlichen Umgänge", in: *Sacris erudiri* 22 (1974-75) 421-436.

Nottarp (1956), H. Nottarp, *Gottesurteilstudien*, München, 1956.

Nussbaum (1961), O. Nussbaum, *Kloster, Priestermönch und Privatmesse*, Bonn, 1961.

Nussbaum (1964), O. Nussbaum, *Das Brustkreuz des Bischofs*, Mainz, 1964.

Nussbaum (1965), O. Nussbaum, *Der Standort des Liturgen am christlichen Altar vor dem Jahr 1000*, 2 vol., Bonn, 1965.

Nussbaum (1969), O. Nussbaum, *Die Handkommunion*, Köln, 1969.

Nussbaum (1979), O. Nussbaum, *Die Aufbewahrung der Eucharistie*,Bonn, 1979.

Oakley (1979), F. Oakley, *The Western Church in the later middle ages*, London, 1979.

Oberman (1981), Heiko A. Oberman, *Wurzeln des Antisemitismus*, Berlin, 1981.

Pas v.d. (1984), W. van der Pas, "Reliekencultus, ritueel en regulatie in de volle middeleeuwen", in: *Skript* 6 (1984) 320-334.

Pascher (1968), J. Pascher, "Die Prozession", in: *LJ* 18 (1968) 113-120.

Pax (1959), W. Pax, "Bittprozessio"", in: *RAC* II, 421-429.

Pernoud (1984), Régine Pernoud, *Les saints au Moyen Age*, Paris, 1984.

Petrakakos (1905), Demetrios A. Petrakakos, *Die toten im Recht nach der Lehre und den Normen des orthodoxen morgenländischen Kirchenrechts und der Gesetzgebung Griechenlands*, Leipzig, 1905 (Nachdr. Aalen, 1971).

Philippeau (1948), H.R. Philippeau, "La maladie dans la tradition liturgique et pastorale", in: *LMD* 15 (1958) 53-81.

Pinsk (1924), J. Pinsk, "Die Missa Sicca", in: *JLw* 4 (1924) 90-118.

Pijper (1907), F. Pijper, *Middeleeuwsch Christendom. De verering der H. Hostie*, 's-Gravenhage, 1907.

Platelle (1962), H. Platelle, *Le temporel de l'abbaye de Saint-Amand des origines à 1340*, Paris, 1962.

Platelle (1965), H. Platelle, *La justice seigneuriale de l'abbay de Saint-Amand*, Paris-Louvain, 1965.

Platelle (1980), H. Platelle, "La religion populaire entre la Scarpe et la Lys d'après les Miracles de Sainte Rictrude de Marchiennes (XIIème siècle)", in: H. Roussel et F. Suard, *Alain de Lille, Gautier de Châtillon, Jakemart Giélée et leur temps* (Colloque 1978), Lille, 1980, 365-402.

Platelle (1980a), H. Platelle, "Crime et châtiment à Marchiennes. Etude sur la conception et le fonctionnement de la justice d'après les Miracles de sainte Rictrude" (XIIe s.), in: *Sacris erudiri* 24 (1980) 155-202.

Pognon (1947), E. Pognon, "Adémar de Chabannes, Moine de Saint-Cybard d'Angoulême, Chronique", in: *L'an mille*, Paris, 1947, 143-209.

Pol v.d. (1967), W.H. van de Pol, *Het einde van het conventionele Christendom*, Roermond, Maaseik, 1967

Post (1955), R. Post, "Het sacrament van mirakel te Amsterdam", in: *Studia Catholica* 30 jrg. 4 (1955) 241-261.

Prinz (1967), F. Prinz, "Stadrömisch-italische Martyrreliquien und fränkischer Reichsadel im Maas-Moselraum", in: *Historisches Jahrbuch* 87 (1967) 1-25.

Quirin (1952), K.L.Quirin, *Die Elevation zur hl. Wandlung in der Römischen Messe. Ihr Entstehung und Geschichte bis zum Ende des 16 Jahrhundert*, Mainz, 1952.

Rahn (1901), J.R. Rahn und H. Zeller-Werdmuller, "Das Fraumünster in Zürich. Die Baubeschreibung des Fraumünsters", in: *Mitteilungen der Antiquarischen Gesellschaft in Zürich* Bd.XXV, Heft 2, 39 -68.

Raible (1908), F. Raible, *Der Tabernakel einst und jetzt*, Freiburg im Breisgau, 1908.

Riché (1976), P. Riché, "Translations de reliques à l'époque carolingienne", in: *Le Moyen âge* 82 (1976) 201-218.

Riché (1991), P. Riché, "Les carolingiens en quête de sainteté", in: Tilliette (1991), 217-224.

Rode (1957), R. Rode, *Studien zu den mittelalterlichen Kind-Jesu-Visionen*, Frankfurt am Main, 1957.

Rordorf (1972), W. Rordorf, "Aux origines du culte des martyrs", in: *Irenikon* 45 (1972-no.3) 315-331.

Rossi de (1863), G. G. B. de Rossi, *Bullettino di Archeologia Christiana* (aprile), Roma, 1863.

Rothkrug (1977), L. Rothkrug, "Popular Religion and Holy Shrines", in: James Obelkevich, *Religion and the People*, Chapel Hill, 1979, 20-86.

Rothkrug (1980), L. Rothkrug, *Religion Practices and Collective Perceptions: Hidden Homologies in the Renaisanze and Reformation* (Historical Reflections/ Reflexions Historiques, vol. 7, no. 1), Waterloo, 1980.

Rubin (1991), M. Rubin, *Corpus Christi. The Eucharist in Late Medieval Culture*, Canbridge, New York, 1991.

Rupin (1890), E. Rupin, *L'oeuvre de Limoges*, Paris, 1890.

Rush (1941), A.C. Rush, *Death and Burial in christian Antiquity*, Washington, 1941.

Rush (1974), A.C. Rush, "The Eucharist, the Sacrament of the Dying in Christian Antiquity", in: *The Jurist* 34 (1974) 10-35.

Sartori (1899), P. Sartori, "Die Totenmünze", in: *Archiv für Religionswissenschaft*, 2, Freiburg in Breisgau, Leipzig, Tübingen, 1899, 205-225.

Saxer (1980), V. Saxer, *Morts, Martyrs, reliques en Afrique chrétienne aux premières siècles*, Paris, 1980.

Schefers (1990), H. Schefers, "Einhards römische Reliquien", in: *Archiv für hessische Geschichte und Altertumskunde* 48 (1990) 279-292.

Schillebeeckx (1967), E. Schillebeeckx, *Christus' tegenwoordigheid in de Eucharistie*, Bilthoven, 1967.

Schillebeeckx (1984), E. Schillebeeckx, *Pleidooi voor mensen in de kerk*, Baarn, 1984.

Schilling (1887), A. Schilling, "Die religiösen und kirchlichen Zustände der ehemaligen Reichstadt Biberach unmittelbar vor Einführung der Reformation", in: *Freiburger Diöcesan Archiv* 19 (1887) 3-191.

Schmidt (1845), B. Schmidt, "Über mehrere christliche Grabinschriften aus dem 4 Jh., welche sich in dem Museum zu Trier befinden", in: *Jb des Vereins vor Altertumsfreunden im Rheinland7* (1845) 80-85.

Schmitt (1988), Jean-Claude Scmitt, "Les superstitions", in: J. Le Goff en R. Remons (eds.), *Histoire de la France religieuse*, Paris, 1988, vol. I, 417-551.

Schmitt (1992), Jean-Claude Schmitt, "De historicus en het bijgeloof in de middeleeuwen", in: *Millennium* 6 (1992) 40-54.

Schneider (1927), F. Schneider, "Das Suffragium pro pace nach dem Pater noster", in: *Cistercienser-Chronik* (1927) 108-114.

Schnitzler (1973), Th. Schnitzler, "Die erste Fronleichnamprozession" (Datum und Charakter), in: *Münchener Theologische Zeitschrift* 24 (1973) 352-362.

Schramm (1962), P.E. Schramm, F. Mütherich, *Denkmale der deutschen Könige und Kaiser*, I (768-1250), München, 1962.

Schreiber (1959), Georg Schreiber, *Die Wochentage im Erlebnis der Ostkirche und der christlichen Abendlandes*, Köln-Ooladen, 1959.

Schreiner (1966), K, Schreiner, "Zum Wahrheitsverständnis im Heiligen- und Reliquienwesen des Mittelalters", in: *Saeculum* XVII (1966) 131-169.

Schreiner (1966a), K. Schreiner, "Discrimen veri ac falsi, Ansätze und Formen der Kritik in der Heiligen- und Reliquienverehrung des Mittelalters", in: *Archiv für Kulturgeschichte* XLVIII (1966) 1-53.

Schuster (1907), Ildefonse Schuster, "L'abbaye de Farfa et sa restauration au XIe siècle sous Hugues I", in: *Revue Bénénedictine* 24 (1907) 17-35, 374-402.

Schwerin (1933), Cl. Frh. v. Schwerin, *Rituale für Gottesurteile* (Sitzungsberichte der Heidelberger Akademie der Wisenschaften), Heidelberg, 1932-33 (3Abh.).

Scribner (1987), R.W. Scribner, *Popular Culture and Popular Movements in Reformation Germany*, London and Ronceverte, 1987.

Seidlmayer (1939), M. Seidlmayer, *Die Anfänge des grossen abendländischen Schismas*, Münster i. W., 1939.

Semmler (1980), J. Semmler, "Mönche und Kanoniker im Franken reiche Pippins III und Karls des Grossen", in: *Untersuchungen zu Kloster und Stift Veröffentlichungen des Max Plank-Instituts für Geschichte*, 68, *Studien zur Germania Sacra*, 14 (Göttingen, 1980).

Sengspiel (1977), Oskar Sengspiel, *Die Beteutung der Pozessionen für das geistliche Spiel des Mittelalters in Deutschland*, Breslau, 1932, Hildesheim-New York, 1977 (repr.) 78-111.

Siben (1949), A. Siben, "Geschichte des Fronleichnamsfestes und der Fronleichnamprozession im alten Fürstbistum Speyer", in: *Archiv für mittelrheinische Kirchengeschichte im Auftrag der Gesellschaft für mittelrheinische Kirchengeschichte*, Speyer am Rhein, 1949.

Sigal (1976), P. Sigal, "Un aspect du culte des saints au XIe et XIIe siècles d'après la littérature hagiographique du midi de la France", in: *CF* 11 (1976) 39-59.

Sigal (1985), P. Sigal, *L'homme et le miracle dans la France médiévale* (XIe-XIIe siècle), Paris, 1985.

Smith (1990), Julia M. Smith, "Oral and written: saints, miracles and relics in Brittany, c. 850-1250", in: *Speculum* 65 (1990) 309-343.

Smits (1965), L. Smits, *Actuele vragen rondom de transsubstantiatie en de tegenwoordigheid des Heren in de eucharistie*, Roermond-Maaseik, 1965.

Snoek (1995), G.J.C. Snoek, "Sacramentsdevotie en Sacramentsdag. Over de oorsprong en betekenis van een kerkelijk feest", in: *Madoc* 9 (1995, 1) - in press -

Southern (1975), R.W. Southern, *The making of the Middle Ages*,Essex, 1975 (original ed. 1953).

Stemmler (1970), T. Stemmler, *Liturgische Feiern und Geistliche Spiele*, Studien zu Erscheinungsformen des Dramatischen im Mittelalter, Tübingen, 1970.

Stevenson (1986), K. Stevenson, *Eucharist and Offering*, New York, 1986.

Stewart MacAlister (1907), A. Stewart MacAlister, "Fifteenth Quaterly Report on the Excavation of Gezer", in: *Palestine Exploration Fund Quaterly Statement*, 1907, 184-204, 254-268.

Stock (1983), Brian Stock, *The Implications of Litteracy*, Princeton, New Jersey, 1983.

Stoett (1953), F.A. Stoett, *Nederlandse spreekwoorden en gezegden*, Zutphen, 1953.

Stückelberg (1902), E.A. Stückelberg, *Geschichte der Reliquien in der Schweitz* (Schriften der Schweizerischen Gesellschaft für Volkskunde 1 und 5), 2 vol., Zürich, 1902.

Stückelberg (1904), E.A. Stückelberg, *Aus der christlichen Altertumskunde*, Zürich, 1904.

Sumption (1974), J. Sumption, *Pilgrimage, an image of medieval religion*, London, 1974.

Taylor (1993), John E. Taylor, *Christians and the Holy Places*, The Myth of Jewish-Christians Origin, Oxford, 1993.

Ter Reegen (1956), O.F. Ter Reegen, *De Sacramentsprocessie*, onderzoek naar de bronnen van het processie-ceremonieel in het Caeremoniale Episcoparum, Nijmegen, 1956.

Thiers (1677), J.B. Thiers, *Traité de l'exposition du s. Sacrament de l'Autel*, 2 vol., Avignon, 1677.

Thiers (1679), J.B. Thiers, *Traité des superstitions qui regardent les sacraments*, 4 vol., Paris, 1679.

Thurston (1901), H. Thurston, "Benediction of the Blessed Sacrament", in: *The Month* 98 (1901) 58-69, 186-193, 264-276.

Tilliette (1991), Jean-Yves Tilliette, *Les fonctions des saints dans le monde occidental* (IIIe-XIIIe siècle), Actes du colloque organisé par l'École française de Rome avec le concours de l'Université de Rome 'La Sapienza', 27-29 oct. 1988, Rome, 1991.

Trexler (1980), R.C. Trexler, *Public Life in Renaissance Florence*, New York, 1980.

Tschan (1942-52), F.J.T. Tschan, *Saint Bernward of Hildesheim*, Publications in medieval studies. The University of Notre Dame, 3 vol., n. 6, 12, 13, Indiana, 1942-52.

Urlichs (1844), L. Urlichs, "Vasa diatreta in Coeln", in: *Jb. des Vereins von Altertumsfreunden im Rheinland* 5 (1844) 377-381.

Vaggaggini (1959), C. Vaggaggini, *Initiation théologique à la liturgie*, Bruges, Paris, 1959.

Vauchez (1975), A. Vauchez, *La spiritualité du moyen âge occidental*, Paris, 1975.

Vauchez (1981), A. Vauchez, *La Sainteté en Occident aux derniers siècles du moyen âge*, Rome, 1981.

Vauchez (1987), A. Vauchez, *Les Laics au Moyen Age*, Paris, 1987.

Verheul (1974), A. Verheul, *Grondstructuren van de eucharistie*, Brugge, Boxtel, 1974.

Verdam (1902), J. Verdam, "Een Nederlandse aflaatbrief uit de 14e eeuw", in: *ANK* I, 117-122.

Vieillard-Troiekouroff (1976), M. Vieillard-Troiekouroff, *Les monuments religieux de la Gaulle d'après les oeuvres de Grégoire de Tours*, Champion, 1976.

Vincent (1908), H. Vincent, "An Eucharistic find at ancient Gezer, Palestine", in: *The Ecclesiastical Review* 39 (1908) 389-401.

Vliet v. (1994), K. van Vliet, "Relieken in lood". Interview met kanunnik J.N. van Ditmarsch, in: *Madoc* 8 (1994, 4) 220-227.

Vloberg (1946), M. Vloberg, *Eucharistie dans l'Art*, 2 vol., Grenoble, Paris, 1946.

Vogel (1980), C. Vogel, "Une mutation cultuelle inexpliquée: Le passage de l'eucharistie communautaire à la messe privée", in: *Revue des sciences religieuses* 54 (1980) 231-250.

Vogel (1986), C. Vogel, *Medieval Liturgy: an introduction to the sources.* Revised and translated by W.G. Storey and N.K. Rasmussen, Washington, 1986.

Vogelius (1713), J.C. Vogelius, *Literas sanguine Jesu Christi firmatas.* Die mit dem Blute Jesu Christi unterzeichnete Schriften, praeside Andrea Schmidio, Helmstadii, 1713.

Vovelle (1985), M. Vovelle, *Mentaliteitsgeschiedenis* (original title: *Idéologies et Mentalités*, 1982, 1984), essays over leef- en beeldwereld, Nijmegen, 1985

Vroom (1981), W.H. Vroom, *De financiering van de kathedralenbouw in de middeleeuwen, in het bijzonder van de dom van Utrecht*, Maarssen, 1981.

Vroom (1992), W.H. Vroom, *In Tumultu Gosico.* Over relieken en geuzen in woelige tijden, Inaugurele rede. Universiteit van Amsterdam, 1992.

Ward (1981), Benedicta Ward, "The Miracles of St. Benedict", in: *Benedictus*, Studies in Honor of St. Benedict of Nursia, ed. E. Rozanna Elder, Cistercian Publications Kalamazoo, Michigan, 1981, 1-15.

Ward (1982), Benedicta Ward, *Miracles and the Mediaval mind.* Theory, record and event, 1000-1215, London, 1982.

Ward (1992), Benedicta Ward, *Signs and Wonders.* Saints, Miracles and Prayers from the 4th Century to the 14th, published by Variorum, Hampshire, Brookfield, Vermont, 1992

Wegman (1986), H.A.J. Wegman, "Theologie en Piëteit", in: *De Gelovige Thomas.* Beschouwingen over de hymne 'Sacris sollemniis' van Thomas van Aquino, Annalen van het Thymgenootschap, v. 74, n. 2, red. A.G. Weiler and G.A.M. Berkelaar, Baarn, 1986, 36-49.

Wegman (1989), H.A.J. Wegman, "De witte hostie", in: R.E.V. Stuip and C. Vellekoop, *Licht en Donker in de Middeleeuwen*, Utrecht, 1989, 107-120.

Wegman (1991), H.A.J. Wegman, *Riten en Mythen*, Liturgie in de geschiedenis van het Christendom, Kampen, 1991.

Weissenberger (1942), P. Weissenberger, "Die ältesten Statuta Monastica der Silvestriner", in: *RQS* 47 (1939; 1942) 31-109.

Wieland (192), Fr. Wielamd, *Altar und Altargrab der christlichen Kirchen im 4 Jahrhundert*, Leipzig, 1912.

Wordsworth (1892), Chr. Wordsworth, *The Manner of the coronation of King Charles the first 1626*, London, 1892.

Young (1920), K, Young, *The dramatic associations of the easter sepulchre*, Madison, 1920.

Zeiger (1935), I. Zeiger, "Professio super altare", in: *Analecta Gregoriana* 8 (1935) 161-185.

Zeiger (1936), I. Zeiger, "Professio in manus", in: *Acta Congressus Iuridici Internationalis* III, Roma, 1936, 187-202.

Zeiger (1940), I. Zeiger, "Professio super hostiam", in: *Archivum historicum Societatis Jesu* IX (1940) 172-188.

Zika (1988), Charles Zika, "Hosts, processions and pilgrimages: controlling the sacred in fifteenth-century Germany", in: *Past and Present* Febr. (1988) 25-64.

INDEX

The words marked with an asterisk (*) occur in the list 'A brief explanation of some technical terms' (p. 387-394).
Saints are listed in alphabetical order of their names, followed by 'St.'. Monasteries and such dedicated to a particular saint (e.g. the monastery of St. Amandus in Elnone) are listed under 'St.', followed by the saints' names in alphabetical order, thus: 'St. Amandus (Elnone), monastery of'.
Notes are not included in the index.

Studies in the History
of Christian Thought

EDITED BY HEIKO A. OBERMAN

50. HOENEN, M. J. F. M. *Marsilius of Inghen*. Divine Knowledge in Late Medieval Thought. 1993
51. O'MALLEY, J. W., IZBICKI, T. M. and CHRISTIANSON, G. (eds.) *Humanity and Divinity in Renaissance and Reformation*. Essays in Honor of Charles Trinkaus. 1993
52. REEVE, A. (ed.) and SCREECH, M. A. (introd.) *Erasmus' Annotations on the New Testament*. Galatians to the Apocalypse. 1993
53. STUMP, Ph. H. *The Reforms of the Council of Constance (1414-1418)*. 1994
54. GIAKALIS, A. *Images of the Divine*. The Theology of Icons at the Seventh Ecumenical Council. With a Foreword by Henry Chadwick. 1994
55. NELLEN, H. J. M. and RABBIE, E. (eds.) *Hugo Grotius – Theologian*. Essays in Honour of G. H. M. Posthumus Meyjes. 1994
56. TRIGG, J. D. *Baptism in the Theology of Martin Luther*. 1994
57. JANSE, W. *Albert Hardenberg als Theologe*. Profil eines Bucer-Schülers. 1994
58. ASSELT, W.J. VAN. *The Covenant Theology of Johannes Cocceius (1603-1669)*. An Examination of its Structure. *In preparation*
59. SCHOOR, R.J.M. VAN DE. *The Irenical Theology of Théophile Brachet de La Milletière (1588-1665)*. 1995
60. STREHLE, S. *The Catholic Roots of the Protestant Gospel*. Encounter between the Middle Ages and the Reformation. 1995
61. BROWN, M.L. *Donne and the Politics of Conscience in Early Modern England*. 1995
62. SCREECH, M.A. (ed.). *Richard Mocket, Warden of All Souls College, Oxford, Doctrina et Politia Ecclesiae Anglicanae*. An Anglican Summa. Facsimile with Variants of the Text of 1617. Edited with an Introduction. 1995
63. SNOEK, G.J.C. *Medieval Piety from Relics to the Eucharist*. A Process of Mutual Interaction. 1995
64. PIXTON, P.B. *The German Episcopacy and the Implementation of the Decrees of the Fourth Lateran Council, 1216-1245*. Watchmen on the Tower. 1995
65. DOLNIKOWSKI, E.W. *Thomas Bradwardine: A View of Time and a Vision of Eternity in Fourteenth-Century Thought*. 1995

Prospectus available on request

E. J. BRILL — P.O.B. 9000 — 2300 PA LEIDEN — THE NETHERLANDS